Marvel Graphic Novels
and Related Publications

Marvel Graphic Novels and Related Publications

An Annotated Guide to Comics, Prose Novels, Children's Books, Articles, Criticism and Reference Works, 1965–2005

ROBERT G. WEINER

Foreword by JOHN RHETT THOMAS

McFarland & Company, Inc., Publishers
Jefferson, North Carolina, and London

LIBRARY OF CONGRESS CATALOGUING-IN-PUBLICATION DATA

Weiner, Robert G., 1966–
Marvel graphic novels and related publications : an annotated guide to
comics, prose novels, children's books, articles, criticism and reference
works, 1965–2005 / Robert G. Weiner ; foreword by John Rhett Thomas.
p. cm.
Includes bibliographical references and indexes.

ISBN 978-0-7864-2500-6
illustrated case binding : 50# alkaline paper ∞

1. Comic books, strips, etc.—United States—Bibliography.
2. Marvel Comics Group—Bibliography. I. Title.
PN6725.W44 2008 741.5'973—dc22 2007044504

British Library cataloguing data are available

Cover art: Woman and superhero ©2008 Digital Vision;
explosion and earth with moon ©2008 Shutterstock

Manufactured in the United States of America

*McFarland & Company, Inc., Publishers
Box 611, Jefferson, North Carolina 28640
www.mcfarlandpub.com*

To Joe Duke, who always listened;
Joe Ferrer, Tom Gonzales, and Joey Davila, who were always there;
my parents, who love, nurture, and put up with
this forty-year-old son who reads comics; and
the memory of Grandma Bunnie, Grandpa Gil,
Grandma Ann, Grandpa Jack, and Uncle Irwin.

Also to
Alex Ross, Jim Starlin, Jack Kirby, Stan Lee, Alex Schoenburg, Roy
Thomas, Garth Ennis, Brian Michael Bendis, Bill Everett, Pete
Townshend, Siegal and Schuster, Carl Burgos, Marv Wolfman, Jerry
Garcia, Lon Chaney, Sr., Frank Zappa, Joe Simon, Steve Ditko, Gerry
Conway, Kenneth Anger, Gil Kane, Steranko, Chris Claremont, Peter
David, Bob Kane, Bill Finger, John Buscema, and everyone who has
ever worked on a comic. You are the creators of worlds!

Finally, to everyone who has ever loved
a Timely/Atlas/Marvel comic book,
and to all Marvel Zombies.

What I knew of life on Earth—of all life outside the confines of our Zoo—I learned from two sources—my mother's starry sages of peace, of love and Ocean Parkway, and those blessed things called books.

Books ... were my salvation and protection: I firmly believed that if well attended our leather-bound friends will never abandon or betray us and will certainly never die.—*Moonshadow*

We concern ourselves with heroes because they are mirrors in which we see ourselves.—*Clark Kent*

Few people outside of the industry have any idea of the massive effort involved in producing a single issue of a comic book.... Producing a single issue of a regular comic book can be an incredible physical, and mental grind.—*Tom Defalco*

In Ancient Rome, the masses were fed Bread and Circuses—today it's Tabloids and Televisions.—*Doctor Zero*

There is nothing that cannot be learned from Science—there is nothing that science is not capable of—if you learn its secrets give yourself to it. I can assure you it will not disappoint you with what you receive from it in return. All science asks is that you have faith in it—like any religion.—*Professor Henry Clerk*

I think we might claim that the comic book with its superheroes and super-villains and its scope is often close to the epic and might be considered a kind of modernized epic.—*Arthur Asa Berger*

Behold the world of enchantment and mysticism, of an ancient rite and nameless ritual; the world beyond the realm of mortal science, beyond the ken of human experience; far far beyond the pale of what we know—bordered only by the boundaries of what we dare imagine.—*Stan Lee*

Imagine an Earth without any super-heroes! It seems incredible!—*The Atom*

Acknowledgments

This project required years of research. Without the help and support of my family and friends, as well as many representatives of different universities, libraries, and companies, it would never have been completed.

Each of the individuals, organizations, and institutions listed below has supported this project in one way or another. Some have helped directly, in the research or writing phase. Others have helped indirectly, through their friendship, moral support, and/or encouragement. All have contributed a great deal, and to all I offer my heartfelt thanks.

Universities and Libraries. I would not have been able to do the research for this project without the aid of the employees of these institutions. Their interest in the project and their willingness to help me find resources or answers to my questions was invaluable. I am sure there were many more, whose names I never knew or have forgotten to list, who deserve acknowledgment as well. Thank you to all of the libraries that loaned me material to read and review, and all the librarians who processed my requests; Michigan State University and Randall W. Scott (for the many photocopies and answers to my questions); Texas Tech University English Department: Sam Dragga, Scott Baugh, Mike Shoenecke, and Stephen Jones; Texas Tech University Library: Marina and Ruth Oliver, Sandy River, Jack Becker, Tom Rohrig, and Brian Quinn; Texas Tech University Library Access Services (ILL & Circulation): Donell Callender and Susan Hidalgo (for putting up with my hundreds of requests over the years); Texas Tech University Southwest Collection: Bruce Cammack, Tai Kriedler, Lynn Whitfield, David Marshall, and Monty Monroe; West Texas Library System Inter Library Loan: Nancy Hill, Stephanie Zurinski, Angela Becknell, Sally Qurioz, and Emily Smith; Mahon Library, City of Lubbock: Special thanks to my bosses and my colleagues in the Reference Department, for your patience, understanding, and support. Administrators: Jane Clausen, Beth Carlberg; Circulation Dept.: Helen Viser, Lena Burgess and the entire circulation staff; Reference Dept.: Marit Dubois, Angela Kernell, Nancy Cammack, Mark Tate, Lacey Petty, Julie Ross, Amanda Shaw and Michael, and Erica Handley; Technical Services Staff: Susan Durett, Velia V., Portia Walker, and Pat Andrews; Godeke, Groves, and Patterson Libraries, City of Lubbock: all staff members.

Research Helpers and Supportive Organizations. Andy and the Tales of Wonder staff (for their prompt answers to my questions); Star Books and Comics; John Rhett Thomas and the folks at the Ezboard Masterworks site (who answered many questions, helped track down ISBNs, and were very helpful); David Palmer and Angels with Knives/Wounded Infidel; Andrew Howard, Doug, Nick Stephen Phillips, and Pappa Ralph of Ralph's Records; the Grateful Dead Scholars Group at the SWPCA; Deadwood Society; Terry, Sharon, Judy, Gretchen and Ron with Friends of the Library; *Comic Zone* (the Metropolis comic talk show); Mile High Comics; the Flatland Film Festival Steering Committee; Eddie and the Buddy Holly Center; my co–host and friend, Camille; Rob Helmerichs and the Trade Paperback Internet page; Congregation Shaareth Israel; the Louise Hopkins Underwood Center for the Arts; the Southwest Popular Culture Association; Kurt Amacker and Mania; Joel Hahn (for his much-needed help in tracking down information); David Gans (for the CDs and the friendship); 289 Films and Amy Maner; Eric Levy and Nicholas Meriwether (for the CDs and movies—you rock); and Robert Mora and Star Books; Michael Rhodes and the Comic News Group.

Special People. An extra special thank you and much love to Harold and May W., for reading this volume with a keen eye, and helping to organize and edit it. This book would not have been done without them.

Special thanks and love to Larry and Vicki Weiner for their patience and understanding, and a special thanks to the lovely Sarah Dulin for being there, and for her patience while listening to all my rants.

Special thanks to my esteemed colleague, and sometimes coauthor, Freedonia Paschall, and to my friend and Grateful Dead coauthor, David Dodd.

Thank you to Vera Burgett, Joe Teague, Charles Clair (for all the dinners and change), Ed and Janet Veal, Terry Gilliam, Joe and Geraldine, Barbara Baker, Mark Todd, Kent Nelson, Al Pratt, Ray Palmer, Jim Hammond, Harry Grub, Tooter Pipkin, Jessica Biel, Carter Slade, Chuck Chandler, Tom Servo, Cory Gilly, Dan Watkins, David Boris Karloff, Raven Jackson, Heather Jackson, George Jackson, Leroy Bencke, Floyd Pirtle, Marissa Blanco, Jim Johnson, Chris Caddell, Julie Story, Jill and Bill Kerns, the graceful Kathryn Oler, Dawn Wolf-Taylor, Peter Rollins, Sally Sanchez, Linda Whitebread, Ron Cirillo, Shawn Irving, Gerald Strickland, Paulette "Bullion Woman" Haiser, Lee Weldon Stephenson, Mary Ann Higdon, Donna and Bill Mcdonald, Monkia A., JB, Gary Burnett, Barry Barnes, Rebecca Adams, Corky M., Will Parril, John Oyerbides, Russ Swim, Terry Bolger, Kraig and Sarah Willis, Mike Nelson, Kevin Murphy, Joel Hodgson, Damon Greer, Americus AL, Lamas, David White, Greg Carey, Steve Lindell, Kinsey and Gaye Croslin, Frank Plemmons, Camelle Scioli-McNamara, Jim and Chris (in the morning), Doug Nelson, Chris Taylor, Leon Shturman, Joe Gulick, Mike Blevins, Mike Pawuk, John McCloud, Andrew Hunter, Carl Buchanan, Kirk Graves, Don Troutman, Manuela Gandara, Bill Mallet, Doug Suplia, Robert Mora, Francis Jardine, and Erika Johnson.

Finally, I want to thank Citizens for Prairie Dogs, Lynda Watson, and Joann Haddock and all my furry little critters (LeRoy, my best buddy; Shelia; Princess; Zowie; Remy; Sunshine; and, most of all, Poncho), who help keep my spirits up, and are always there to welcome me home. In part, this work also is dedicated to the memory of Clowy, the prairie dog.

Table of Contents

Section III. Special Volumes and Series

Section IV. Selected Marvel Publications

Section V. Selected Marvel-Related Publications

Foreword
by John Rhett Thomas

I remember when I was a kid, not long after the mania for comic books had first taken hold of me, I had devoured the stack of comics that I had built up through piecemeal acquisitions from cousins and neighbors who had gotten "too old" for four-color fantasies printed on cheap newspaper stock. I remember finishing off that healthy stack of comics and saying to myself, "What next?" This was a question dictated, in part, by how many lawns I could mow and in how much time, as well as how many new comics would circulate through the nearby used book store. When I say "new comics," I mean a fresh new stock of used, typically battered, beaten, but well-read comics.

"What next?" is a familiar question to any comic book fan taken in by the vast expanse of comic book universes created by comic books. Marvel Comics, in particular, is not just to be taken as a measure of its single parts. As great as are, say, the discrete stories told in *Fantastic Four 48–50* or *Amazing Spider-Man 31–33* or *Giant-Size X-Men 1*, they are also part of a bigger plot, one decades in the making and as grand as your imagination will allow it to be.

There are so many stories that make up the mosaic that have been told since the first issue of Marvel Comics unknowingly gave birth to a new universe. When the Human Torch melted his way through a wall on his way to dispatching a couple of gangster thugs, he could hardly have known anyone would still care nearly seventy years later. Fortunately, through recent years, comic book storytelling has been doled out not just in cheap newsprint monthly issues, but in a new format typically called a "collected edition" which does exactly what it says it does: it's a comic book edition that collects other comic books. Reprints, if you will, and typically in a more deluxe, sturdy format that often lends itself to being a proud addition to one's bookshelf. (Yes, for all you mothers out there, a collected edition is the kind of thing that doesn't usually pile up in a mess on the floor next to the baseball cards and videogame cartridges.)

Comic book companies, Marvel included, have for many reasons had to be selective when choosing the material that will go into these collected editions. The likelihood of every Marvel comic book being reprinted in a collected edition is an undertaking that shouldn't reasonably be expected—there's so much out there. But figuring what is out there, what is available to help bring readers closer to the best that these fantastic superhero universes have to offer, is what websites like mine are all about. Cataloguing the characters, events, and other informational arcana for die-hard fans of the medium has been an obsession almost as much as reading the stories themselves.

And so when Robert came to visit my message board forums seeking information for this book he was compiling, I recognized right away that he shared the same feelings as I do about this wonderful new way of experiencing comic books. The collected edition is here to stay. Comic readers, particularly of an older demographic, have really taken to this new format, and Robert's book is a brave attempt to make sure that no stone in the Marvel experience remains unturned, that any collected edition that has seen the light of day doesn't get left behind by readers or the librarians who serve them.

Enjoy this book for its glimpse at what lies in store for you as a reader. The capsule notations are meant to whet the appetite and lead you to the best of the best of what the medium has to offer. Thanks to Robert for taking the time—an inordinate amount of time— to compile this information. It's an invaluable service to comic fans and in keeping with the best parts of comic book fandom.

John Rhett Thomas
MarvelMasterworks.com
Editor/writer, Marvel Spotlight

Preface

This volume is intended to be a handbook, not only for the Marvel Comics fan and collector, but also for academic, public, and school librarians, who want to include Marvel graphic novels in their collections. While many of the publications in this work are known to most Marvel collectors, it is my hope that even the most knowledgeable collectors will find something new in it. There are some entries in this volume, which, to my knowledge, describe material not documented anywhere else.

This project, which I started almost five years ago, began as a labor of love. I love the Marvel characters and stories, and admire the creative writers and artists who write those stories and draw those characters. Five years later, my love and admiration has not diminished, but the amount of time, money, and intense "labor" I have invested in the project has been far greater than I anticipated, and so I have had to call an end to it.

The Scope

When I began this project, I intended to find, read, and document every Marvel and Marvel-related graphic novel ever published, but by the end of the second year, I realized how unrealistic that goal was. That is when I began to narrow the scope of the project, and faced the very difficult task of choosing what categories of publications to leave out. In the end, I decided to limit the scope by including only works that were published prior to 2005, and to exclude the following types of publications:

- Some books related to electronic, board, or card games; calendars; coloring books; poster books; pin-up books; and collections of fan magazines.
- Individual comics, unless they form a book, or are in Prestige format.
- Books published in languages other than English.
- Comic price guides, (e.g., *Standard Catalog of Comics*, *Comic Buyer's Guide*, or the *Overstreet Guide*) unless they have specific Marvel content.

Even after eliminating works published after 2004, and works that fall in the categories listed above, it was obvious that I would not be able to find, read, and document every one of the thousands of publications that remain. I have carefully selected the publications which are included in this book, and hope that, like me, the readers will find them interesting and informative. Due to the volatile nature of graphic novel publishing, some of the publications listed in this volume may be out of print by the time it goes to press. Others may have been reissued.

Organization

Each entry begins with a bibliographic citation, which lists the writers/artists, the title of the publication, the publisher and publication date, ISBN (if available), and names of comic issues from which material is reprinted.

Entries for publications that feature more than one superhero, or which have been published in more than one format, may appear in more than one chapter or chapter subsection. Some of the chapters are divided into two or more titled subsections. This is particularly true of chapters which contain publications that feature many of Marvel's characters (e.g., chapters 3, 6, and 12). The entries in each chapter or subsection are arranged alphabetically by the last name of the first writer/artist listed in the citation. When there is more than one entry listed under the same name, the entries are listed chronologically by publication year.

Additional Notes

If you want to find the publications that are documented in this book, I recommend going to the Internet. You may be able to find a new or used copy of a specific publication at websites such as *www.milehightcomics.com*, *www.ebay.com*, *www.amazon.com*, *www.abebooks.com*, or *www.half.com*. There are other web sites that you may find helpful, including, *www.talesofwonder.com*, *www.marvelmasterworks.com/*, *www.math.ucla.edu/~alee/reprints.html*, *http://p206.ezboard.com/bmarvelmasterworksfansite*, and *http://e-lubbock.com/star/*. You also can use your local library's interlibrary loan department, a resource which I used extensively for this work.

I have tried hard to be as thorough as possible, but I realize that sometimes things do fall through the cracks. Hopefully, this volume doesn't have too many cracks, and will prove to be a comprehensive, easy-to-use source of information for a range of potential readers. I hope that anyone is interested in learning more about Marvel, Marvel characters, or both, regardless of their reasons or level of knowledge, will find this volume useful.

1

Graphic Novels and Literature, Then and Now

Definition

According to Merriam Webster's Online Dictionary, a novel is "an invented prose narrative that is usually long and complex and deals especially with human experience through a usually connected sequence of events." According to the same source, a graphic representation can be "a picture, map or graph used especially for illustration" or "the art or science of drawing a representation of an object on a two-dimensional surface." Wikipedia, the free-content Web-based encyclopedia, defines graphic novel as follows: "A graphic novel is a long-form work in the comics form, usually with lengthy and complex storylines, and often aimed at mature audiences. In contrast to the familiar comic magazines, a graphic novel is typically bound using materials of more durable qualities, using a light card stock for softcover bindings or a heavier card for the hardback editions, enclosed in a dust jacket." Each of these definitions appears to be straightforward, and it would seem to be a simple task to put them together to determine which publications are, or are not, graphic novels. However, there has been and still is quite a bit of controversy over applying the term "graphic novel" to "comics" publications.

To many people, the word "comics" conjures up "comic strips" from the funny pages of a newspaper, hack writing, and mindless, children's fare; but they are frozen in outdated stereotypes that do not match the graphic novels of today. It is true that not all comics are graphic novels, and not all graphic novels are comics, but there is an area in which the two meet, and many of the publications referenced in this volume are graphic novels, by any definition.

Then

Graphic literature has a long history, which probably started when some prehistoric being drew a picture in the soil, in order to record some event or thought, or possibly to communicate a thought or idea to another being. We do not have any evidence of such an event, but we do have evidence of graphic literature in the storytelling drawings of cave people, images which still exist in nearly every part of the world. There are many examples of graphic literature in more modern times, including the Japanese *Scrolls of Frolicking Animals*, from the tenth century; the first major graphic novel, *The Adventures of Obadiah Oldbuck*, by Rodolphe Toffler, which was published in the United States in 1842; and Lynn Ward's *God's Man: A Novel in Woodcuts*, which was done in 1929.

According to comics historian, writer, and artist Jim Steranko, the first mass-produced comic book was published in England, in the seventeenth century (p. 5). In the United States, the first comic strip was published in 1895, and one of the first full-length graphic novels, *A Contract with God, and Other Tenement Stories*, written by Will Eisner, was published by Baronet Books in 1978.

The Case for Graphic Novels

There are many who believe that the superheroes who appear in graphic novels published by Marvel and others have replaced traditional heroes, like Odysseus and Aeneas. They believe that these superheroes belong to a modern, legendary paradigm. Peter Sanderson says that "the stories of the Marvel Universe constitute a modern-day mythology, equally vast in scope, whose heroes' strivings, usually represented through physical conflict against their foes, serve as metaphors for our own struggles in life, on a grander scale" (p. 8).

Comic literature writer Danny Fingeroth states that heroic prose has been around as long as "there has been human communication and storytelling," and he points out that even the Bible has its own unique versions of the superheroes, in Moses, Samson, and Jesus (p. 37).[1] Fingeroth observes that even those who do not read comics, or go to superhero movies, "have no choice but to be exposed to the Superhero culture," and that the creators of Superman, and other famous comic heroes, "stumbled onto a metaphor system that everyone in modern society could understand at a glance" (p. 169). He also states that superheroes are "part of the DNA of our culture" (p. 171). As early as 1944, sociologist Harvey Zorbaugh argued that "comics deal with age-old themes familiar in the folklore, mythology, fairy tales, puppet shows, and even nursery rhymes of all people. Like folklore, the comics are an outgrowth of the social unconsciousness, and the problems of the relationship of the individual to his social world find expression through them.... Their hold on readers ... is deeply rooted in our emotional nature.... The potentialities [of comics], as a social force, are tremendous" (p. 203).

In the *Electric Kool-Aid Acid Test*, Tom Wolfe observed that author Ken Kesey believed that Batman, Captain Marvel (Shazam), Plastic Man, Human Torch, Captain America, Sub-Mariner, and other superheroes were "honest American myths." He believed they were replacing Hercules, Orpheus, Ulysses, and Aeneas, and could actually "touch you," myths who heralded a "glorious age," a "neon Renaissance" (pp. 35, 82). The superhero, who has become an allegory to our own lives, and provides a means of escape for both adults and children, is replacing the literary "classics" of bygone days. As early as 1966, *Esquire* magazine pointed out that college students named the Hulk and Spider-Man among the twenty-eight people who counted[2]; they regarded Stan Lee as their generation's Homer; and they viewed Marvel comics as twentieth-century mythology (this can apply equally to DC characters and other superheroes, as well as screen characters like those from *Star Trek*, *Star Wars*, etc.).

One can argue, with good reason, that keeping a character alive and interesting for such a long period takes incredibly talented creators and writers. The ability to write and draw a coherent story is no small feat. For this reason, one also can argue that graphic literature is one of the highest forms of literature. In his biography, Stan Lee tells an interesting story about *Godfather* author Mario Puzo, who worked for Martin Goodman on his male-targeted pulp magazines. Lee suggested to Puzo that he write a comic story, but Puzo found it easier to write full-length prose novels (pp. 137–138).

The reader may balk at the idea of comparing the literature of Shakespeare with graphic literature, but Stan Lee refers to Spider-Man as the "Superhero Hamlet" (p. 25). Alex Raymond, creator of Flash Gordon, takes this idea a step further when he points out that "a Comic artist ... begins with a white sheet of paper and dreams up the whole business.... [H]e is playwright, director, editor, and artist at once" (p. 13). Given the vast scopes of companies who work with thousands and thousands of editors, ideas, characters, plot twists, deaths, and births, molding these fictional universes into a coherent form is an extremely difficult process. Nevertheless, Marvel has accomplished this, and over the past sixty years, thousands of writers and artists have created Marvel's vast universe. Epic stories like *Earth X*, *Kree/Skrull War* and *Marvels* exhibit as much character development, and thought, as any work by Shakespeare,[3] Stephen King, F. Scott Fitzgerald, Charles Dickens, Leo Tolstoy, Margaret Mitchell, or Jack London. One group of statisticians has argued that Marvel's network of characters actually "mimics real-life networks" (Alberich).

A Philosophical Discussion

Are superheroes and their worlds real? Plato made a distinction between the real world and the shadow world. He viewed the real world as the world of ideas, and the world of experience, or sense knowledge, as the world of shadows. We achieve reality through perceptive contemplations, and phenomena are only copies of ideas. The fictional universe created by Marvel is from the world of ideas; therefore, to talk about Spider-Man, Captain America, or the Human Torch as actual persons would not be inappropriate. In his introduction to *Thor Masterworks Vol. 2*, 1993, Stan Lee states, "Even though we ourselves may write the stories, even though the characters are merely works of fiction—or are they?—we still think of them as real flesh-and-blood people, and we come to know them as well as we know our own friends and neighbors—or perhaps even better!"

Then Lee says that over the years Peter Parker has "become a true flesh-and-blood human to me and ... millions of others (Lee, *Untold*, 4). In his introduction to the *Silver Surfer Masterworks Vol. 2*, Lee says, "Even though he is a work of fiction ... a character ... of fantasy, I tend to think of him as a real living being.... So do many other readers throughout the world! They worry about him, agonize over his travails, share his frustrations, and cheer him with a dedication that borders on fanaticism."

Comic writer Mark Gruenwald tells about the infinite possibilities of parallel earths, worlds, and universes, which they call the Ominiverse. While Gruenwald deals with what he calls "fictional realities," his concepts are no less relevant in this context. He goes so far as to argue that "new parallel Earths are constantly being created whenever a divergent factor occurs" (p. 5) and therefore, conceptually, there could be "possible worlds," ad infinitum. According to philosopher Rod Girle, possible worlds can be "useful for helping people think about a wide range of things. Reality and actuality, possibility and necessity, action and process, knowledge and consciousness, obligation, and permission, identity and essence, have all been considered from the perspective of possible worlds" (pp. 3–4).

The Marvel Universe could be considered what Girle calls a "Worm World" or an Instant World; each possible world is understood in terms of a complete history of a possible world (pp. 42–43).[4] There are a whole series of predicate and modal logic theories which one could use to argue whether these worlds exist, or not. However, it is beyond the scope of this volume to get into a detailed discussion, using logical theory, or truth tables, of whether a world with Spider-Man actually exists. Suffice it to say that in some sense, because Spider-Man has been written about in movies, television, and film, there is, indeed, a world in which Spider-Man exists. You would be hard pressed to find a place in the United States, or Europe, where the concept of Spider-Man or Superman is alien. People know what Spider-Man is; therefore, in some sense, Spider-Man exists in a possible world.

One also can apply Professor Kenneth Laine Ketner's concept of "novel science" to the study of the Marvel Universe, and graphic novels in general. Ketner argues that "we could think of a novel as a tool for aiding readers to construct mental, or non-mental, diagrams." In other words, novels can be seen as constructs for reality. Ketner also says that within social science and science in general, "novels might be outstanding tools for analysis, the process of achieving deeper understanding" (pp. 279–280). Using the principles of social science, one can study the Marvel Universe in order to gain self-understanding, understanding of others, and understanding of one's surrounding communities (p. 282). The creators of the Marvel Universe have always injected a little reality, and some soap-opera type plots, into their stories, in order to make them relate to the human condition: reality within fantasy and fantasy within reality. Even the writers and artists who create these stories regard them as real. Artist Gene Ha says, "[Any] good piece of fiction is 'true.' It may tell of things that will never happen, but, within the story, the events do not lie or compromise." He also says that the characters he draws are alive to him (p. 3). An example of how the comic readers are made aware of real-life possibilities appears in the Spider-Man story in which his love, Gwen Stacy, is killed. According to Blumberg, "The death of Gwen Stacy touched everyone who read the tale; comic book fans learned more about the true nature of life and death in those forty some pages of four-color panels than at any other time" (p. 4).

Narrative fiction describes possible worlds. They usually have an internal logic or consistency, even when they are seemingly unrealistic. According to Girle, worlds can be part of one huge multiverse, in several dimensions (p. 2). When writing about the television show *Battlestar Galactica*, Tom Rogers comments, "Who is to say that the stories are not visions of the future, the past, or present? Perhaps the events that we see on the show are taking place in another cosmos, or in a parallel dimension, or during some other time period, or a combination of these possibilities" (p. 84).

Now

The old stereotypes and resistance to graphic literature have softened considerably in the past decade or two, and adult readers and libraries are now buying graphic literature in record numbers. The major companies have taken notice, and DC, Marvel, Image, Dark Horse, Devil's Due, Cross Gen (RIP), and many independent companies have started publishing large numbers of graphic novels. They are not only collecting and reprinting comic stories from the past, but they also are putting out new comic storylines. Capstone now has its own graphic novel imprints, called *Graphic Library*, for nonfiction and historical graphic novels. Now there are religious graphic novels, including the *Lion Graphic Bible* and the *Comic Book Bible*, and a graphic novel, *Keepers of the Faith*, by Jeffrey D. Jones, which is about Baptist leaders. While at one time this type of book was available only in comic bookshops and specialty stores, now major chains like Barnes and Noble, Borders, and Hastings have special areas and displays for them. The graphic novels area is now the fastest-growing section in many bookstores, and graphic novels, especially Japanese manga comics, are the fastest-growing marketing area in publishing.

Libraries are buying graphic novels and creating special displays to attract both new readers and current library patrons. The American Library Association's 2002 Annual Meeting had a preconference workshop on graphic novels, and library trade publications (including *Library Journal, Booklist, School Library Journal,* and *Publishers Weekly*) have stories and review columns on graphic literature. Many major organizations schedule conference sessions for academic discussions of graphic novels and comics, including the Southwestern Popular Culture Association, the American Culture Association, the American Library Association, and the Texas Library Association, among others. In recent years, Marvel Comics has upped the production of their trade paperback program. As a result, Marvel characters like Spider-Man, Captain America, Blade, Daredevil, and the Hulk are known throughout the world, and permeate all areas of mainstream culture.

There is a whole culture built around comics and graphic literature. The devotee is often referred to as a "fanboy," or, in less than flattering terms, a "genre geek" or "genre monkey." However, these terms are misleading. Graphic literature has even caught the eye of mainstream publications like *Entertainment Weekly,* which praised Marvel's *Ultimate Spider-Man* and *Black Panther* titles. Other graphic novels, including *Maus, Jimmy Corrigan: The Smartest Kid on Earth,* and *Batman: Mad Love* have won awards for their outstanding content. Superman, Batman, Human Torch, and Captain America have been with us for over fifty years, and stories and movies about such literary figures as Tarzan, Conan, Dracula, James Bond, and Sherlock Holmes continue to be told. All of these have become part of Western culture, and part of our mythology.

Another reason for the recent increase in the popularity of graphic novels, superhero feature films, and shows like *Smallville* and *Heroes* is that, since September 11, 2001, people want to see heroes to whom they can relate. They want to see "good guys" who have high moral standards and defeat the evildoers. Even anti-terrorist military figures like G.I. Joe have experienced a resurgence in popularity, and Marvel has reissued G.I. Joe comics in five volumes. Rhino Video put the *G.I. Joe* television show on DVD, and Image Comics is publishing new stories that feature the Joe team. Certainly, one can make parallels between the terrorist organization, Cobra, G.I. Joe's main nemesis, and the Taliban.

The popularity of superhero feature films shows that people want to see the struggle between right and wrong, and they want to see the hero or heroine ultimately do the right thing and defeat the forces of hate, destruction, and evil. They can associate these films with the struggle of humanity as a whole.

Superheroes are cool, and they appeal to men, women, children, and the elderly. I recently had a discussion about the X-Men with an eighty-year-old woman who is a patron of the library where I work.

Notes

1. Fingeroth also points out that comic book villains can also be closely tied to popular culture; for example, if there were no Dr. Doom, it's highly unlikely there would be *Star Wars* character Darth Vader.
2. This figure is taken from the back of the Lancer 1966 paperbacks of *Spider-Man* and the *Hulk.*
3. Bear in mind that Shakespeare wrote for the popular audience. Today he might actually write comics.
4. In addition to Girle's arguments, Mark Gruenwald argues that various vibrations, harmonics and "atomic instants" make up various parallel dimensions and universes. One can also factor in the use of whole and fractional numbers to determine dimensions. Time travel and entropy play a part in this as well. In his *Treatise and Primer,*

he puts together various diagrams and charts which outline both the DC and the Marvel universes and their relationships to various realities and worlds.

References

Alberich, R., J. Miro-Julia, F. Rossello. 2002. "Marvel Universe Looks Almost Like a Real Social Network." *http://xxx.lanl.gov/abs/cond-mat/0202174* (accessed November 11, 2006).

Blumberg, Arnold. 2003. "'The Night Gwen Stacy Died': The End of Innocence and the Birth of the Bronze Age" *Reconstruction: Studies in Contemporary Culture* 3. (Fall 2003). *http://reconstruction.eserver.org/034/blumberg.htm* (accessed November 11, 2006).

Fingeroth, Danny. 2004. *Superman On the Couch: What Superheroes Really Tell Us About Ourselves and Our Society.* New York: Continuum.

Girle, Rod. 2003. *Possible Worlds*: Cesham Bucks, UK: Acumem.

Gruenwald, Mark. 1976. *A Treatise on Reality in Comic Literature.* New York: Alternity.

Gruenwald, Mark, and Myron Gruenwald. 1977. *A Primer On Reality in Comic Books.* New York: Alternity.

Ha, Gene. 1997. "Foreword" in *Askani'Son*, by Scott Lobdell and Gene Ha. New York: Marvel.

Ketner, Kenneth Laine, Walker Percy, and Patrick H Samway. 1995. *A Thief of Pierce: The Letters of Kenneth Laine Ketner and Walker Percy.* Jackson: University Press of Mississippi.

Lee, Stan. 2003. "Introduction" in *Silver Surfer Masterworks Vol. 2*: New York: Marvel.

_____. 2003. "Introduction" in *Thor Masterworks Vol. 2.* New York: Marvel.

_____. 1997. "Introduction" in *Untold Tales of Spider-Man.* New York: Boulevard.

_____. 1986. "Spidey and Me" in *Best of Spider-Man.* New York: Ballantine.

Lee, Stan, and George Mair. 2002. *Excelsior: the Amazing Life of Stan Lee.* New York: Fireside.

Raymond, Alex. 1992. Quoted in *Illustrated History of Science Fiction Comics: The Taylor History of Comics 3*, by Mike Benton. Dallas: Taylor.

Rogers Tom. 1978. "Life in the Future," in *BattlestarGalactica.* New York: Ace.

Sanderson, Peter. *Marvel Universe.* New York: Abradale Press, 1996. ISBN: 0810981718: 8.

Steranko, Jim. 1970. *Steranko History of Comics.* Reading, PA: Supergraphics.

Wolfe, Tom. 1968. *Electric Kool-Aid Acid Test.* New York: Farrar, Straus and Giroux.

Zorbaugh, Harvey. 1944 "The Comics—There They Stand!" in *Journal of Educational Sociology* 18: 196–203.

2

Marvel Comics, Then and Now

One of the reasons Marvel had an edge over its main rival, DC,
was the way that its brand of super-heroics did not take place in a
fantasy vacuum, but in the turbulent here and now of American life.
—Geoff Dyer, "Comics in a Man's Life," in *Give Our Regards*

We know that some villain or other will do some bad deed or other and
our hero will have to defeat him in some way or other. That part of each
adventure is just the skeleton to me. The flesh and blood of each tale is the
human involvement, the dramatic choices that must be made, the complex
relationships that must be resolved. Basically the philosophical angle of each tale
is what really gives it life.—Stan Lee, "Spidey and Me," in *Best of Spider-Man*

It felt like a life, and Spidey felt like a person ... that I could identity with.
It was the history. A rich involving history, full of drama, and comedy,
and passion and romance and more: that's what hooked me into Spider-Man.
—Kurt Busiek, "Retroduction," in *Untold Tales*

Then

Marvel Comics, which was started by publisher Martin Goodman, had its origins in the "Pulp Era" of the 1930s. Goodman, who published western and detective pulps, also published a series of pulp magazines, including *Marvel Science Stories* and *Marvel Tales*. Marvel was originally called Timely Comics, and the very first comic book with the name Marvel in its title, *Marvel Comics #1*, was published by Timely in 1939. It featured the Human Torch on the cover.

Many of the earlier publishers of comics were Jewish, like many people who helped create Hollywood. Perhaps that is why, even before America entered World War II, Timely's stories featured several superheroes who battled the evils of Nazism; these comics foreshadowed what was to come. However, after World War II superhero titles were fading, and Timely changed its focus to crime, teens, and westerns, which at that time seemed to be popular. In the early 1950s, Timely became Atlas Comics, which in turn was the predecessor of Marvel Comics. Atlas tried to revive characters like Sub-Mariner, Human Torch, and Captain America, but they did not make an impact on the market, which is a shame because some of the 1950s stories are quite good. Western, horror, science fiction, and romance comics were, by far, the most popular comics in the 1950s. Atlas imploded and nearly went out of business toward the end of the decade. The company was in bad shape and nearly everyone was fired. Atlas only published a handful of titles during this period, most of which were weird tales of monsters and suspense, with a few westerns and romances thrown in.

Marvel Comics as we know it today did not have its crucial start until the first issue of the *Fantastic Four*, which was published in 1961. Both Stan Lee (born Stanley Martin Lieber) and Jack "The King" Kirby (born Jacob Kurtzberg), who created many of the characters in the current Marvel Universe, including the Fantastic Four, X-Men, and the Hulk, had worked for Timely. Other early Timely characters that transcended the gap and became part of the current Marvel Universe include Captain America, Human Torch, Ka-Zar, and the Sub-Mariner. The Black Widow, Marvel Boy, the Angel, the Destroyer, the Whizzer, the Falcon, Electro, Blazing Skull, Patriot, Hercules, Red Raven, the Terror, Young Allies, and the Vision also reappeared, but sometimes in different guises.

Nearly every Marvel comic published in the last forty years has the "Stan Lee Presents" banner printed on it. Stan Lee, the current chairman emeritus, singled out fans of Marvel books as special people, and was able to cultivate a rapport with Marvel readers, calling them "true believers." He encouraged readers to send in their opinions about the stories and characters, running some of these in the "Stan's Bullpen" section of comics. He was always respectful of readers, answering personal questions about the characters he created and the ideas he used to write his early stories. Lee even gave out "No-Prize" awards to those who could find mistakes in the comics. In this way, Marvel Comics was able to garner legions of fans that remain faithful to this day. Lee says, "I wanted Marvel to always be reader friendly ... [and] I wanted to be able to talk directly to the readers, just the way a fella would talk to a friend [which contributed to] ... a growing bond between our readers and us" (pp. 149–151).

Lee also came up with pet phrases, like "'nuff said," "hang loose" and "Excelsior!," which at times seem campy, but which struck a chord with Marvel's earliest readers, and are now part of the popular culture canon. He even gave the Marvel writers and artists "pet" names, which further personalized the public's perception of Marvel.

From the earliest "Age of Marvel" stories in the 1960s, the comics were unique in that they were not just aimed at children. Former Marvel editor Tom DeFalco clearly states, "Comics were originally not intended for kids" (p. 225). In support of this, in his essay "Spidey and Me," Lee says that the original Spider-Man comic was one of the first superhero comic books, "whose vocabulary [was] pitched to a college level readership." He argues that he never has "written down to our audience or tried to simplify the wordage because it is 'just a comic'" (Lee, "Spidey and Me," p. 6). Neither were the characters always teenagers. For example, in the second Spider-Man issue, Spider-Man's nemesis, the Vulture, is a senior citizen, and Reed Richards and Professor X are middle-aged. This mindset resulted in children, teenagers, college students and adults all enjoying comics. According to Harvey Zorbaugh, even during the early golden age of comics, in the mid 1940s, two sociologists pointed out in separate articles that many comic book readers were adults with relatively high cultural and intellectual backgrounds, and that readers' mean age was thirty (201, 208). Comic readers ranged from children to people in their seventies, despite the social criticisms comic books received. It actually takes more brain power to read a graphic novel or comic book than to read a novel or newspaper. Because graphic literature has a written and picture narrative, one uses both right and left sides of the brain to interpret the story. I am constantly amazed when people to whom I have recommended reading a particular graphic novel come back to me and say that they had difficulty reading and/or comprehending both the graphic and narrative texts. Apparently this is not easy for some people to do unless they are used to reading comics.

When Stan Lee created the Merry Marvel Marching Society (MMMS) as a lark in

1965, the response was overwhelming, and most of the responses came from college students. Branches of the fan club sprang up at colleges and universities, even at Oxford, Cambridge, and Harvard. Eventually, Martin Goodman had Lee disband the MMMS because it was too much of a financial drain on the company. In the 1970s, Marvel created Friends of Ol' Marvel (FOOM), in an attempt to reach its fans, but it also was disbanded because it was too costly. These official fan clubs were not profit-centered, despite the good will they garnered.

In 1966, Lancer Books published the Marvel Collector's Album, the first Marvel stories published in book form. These small paperbacks reprinted black and white stories of the Hulk, Fantastic Four, Spider-Man, Thor and Daredevil. Marvel got endorsements for these paperbacks from the *Village Voice, Esquire, New York Herald Tribune*, the *Michigan State News*, University of Massachusetts, Yale University, and the Missouri School of Mines, among others. While these endorsements were tongue in cheek, they illustrated Marvel's attempt, even then, to gain an image of respectability. In the early 1970s, Marvel started publishing more adult-oriented, black and white, oversize magazines, including *Savage Sword of Conan, Dracula Lives*, and *Tales of the Zombie*, which by-passed the Comics Code. In 1971, Marvel had problems with the original Code, when they published *Amazing Spider-Man 76*. It was not approved by the Code because one of the characters had a drug problem, and the issue dealt with the harsh realties of drug abuse. That issue was published without the Code's approval and did result in some changes in the Code's policies.

Marvel's first photo novels were *Origins of Marvel Comics* and its sequel, *Son of Origins of Marvel Comics*, which were published by Simon and Schuster in 1974 and 1975, respectively. Other books featuring Spider-Man, Captain America, Fantastic Four and others quickly followed. These are known by Marvel historians as the Fireside books.

In 1976, George Olshevsky started a massive program to publish a Marvel index. He published twelve books, in nine volumes, of what was projected to be a fifteen-book index. After finishing Index 9B, featuring Daredevil, he decided he had done enough, and unfortunately he discontinued the series. Marvel took up some of the slack by publishing indexes in comic book form. Marvel also published their own *Handbook to the Marvel Universe*, which told the history and described the powers of their various characters.

In the late 1970s and early 1980s, Marvel again started to publish small paperbacks, known as the Marvel Illustrated books, which were usually done in black and white. There were also published several volumes, known as the Pocket Paperbacks, featuring the more popular characters, including Conan, Spider-Man, and the Hulk, in color format. These books contain reprints of many of the original stories that Stan Lee created in the 1960s and were very successful. In the early 1980s, Marvel published reprints of the rare Spider-Man and Hulk newspaper strips. The Spider-Man strips are some of the best-written stories of Lee's entire career, and they, along with the Conan and Howard the Duck newspaper strips, need to be reprinted in their entirety.

Graphic Novels

The first prose novels that used Marvel characters the Avengers and Captain America were published in the late 1960s. Then in the late 1970s, eleven numbered novels that used Marvel characters were published. (They should be reprinted.) In the 1990s, there was a boon in Marvel character novels; there were novels for children, young adults, and adults, as well as volumes of short stories, some edited by Stan Lee. While most of these were not published by Marvel, they are documented in this book. The first Marvel large-format graphic novel was *The Death of Captain Marvel*, published in 1982. At that time, the term "graphic novel" (allegedly coined by the great Will Eisner) was new, but then other companies like DC also started to use the term.

In the 1980s, Marvel began publishing children's books, some of which are documented in this volume, but they certainly did not make use of their superhero characters the way they could have. Many of their children's books have absolutely no bearing on the Marvel Universe. Marvel also published several hardback imprints (e.g., Marvel Limited), which offer special stories and are limited to a few hundred copies. Books like the *X-Men: Famous Firsts*, *Best of the X-Men*, and the original printing of *Fantastic Firsts* are now sought after by collectors. There was a music imprint known as Marvel Music which published books about Bob Marley, the Rolling Stones, and Kiss, among others. In the late 1990s, Marvel started a new children's imprint known as Marvel Kids, but unfortunately they only published a few books. The four published under this imprint use Marvel characters (Fantastic Four, Hulk, Spider-Man, and X-Men) and are very well done. They are much better than those children's books Marvel published in the 1980s, which did not use Marvel characters. In spite of the fact that one might have to pay collectors' prices, the Marvel Kids books should give children endless hours of fun, and are well worth seeking out.

In the 1980s and '90s, Marvel did something unique in their publishing. They published religious comics and graphic novels, among which are *Life of St. Francis*, *Pope John Paul*, and *Mother Teresa*. They worked with Nelson Publishing to produce graphic novels about the life of Christ and Easter as well as Christian classics such as *The Screwtape Letters* and *Pilgrim's Progress*. They even devised a Christian-oriented superhero, the Illuminator. In the 1980s and early '90s, Marvel had a creator-owned imprint known as Epic. Epic published harder-edged material, designed for older readers. The Epic imprint was a creative flower, and by just glancing at the material documented in the Epic chapter in this volume, one can see its wide variety. During the 1990s, Marvel also had special imprints known as Marvel Select and Marvel Alterverse, some of which are documented in this volume.

Financial Crisis

By the mid–1990s, when Marvel was in a real financial slump, two billionaire tycoons, Ronald Perelman and Carl Icahn, were in a war to get Marvel. This was the worst period in Marvel's history. It got so bad that Marvel was dropped from the stock exchange and nearly went bankrupt. Throughout the years, the company had gone through numerous personnel and corporate changes. The books being produced were creatively dead; the stories and art were mediocre; and the sales were falling. By the mid–1990s, with bankruptcy looming and the fate of the company being decided by the courts, it looked as though Marvel was going to become defunct. This turmoil is well documented in Dan Ravi's *Comic Wars*.

With the help of people like Ike Perlmutter, Avid Arad, and Toy Biz, Marvel managed to overcome this slump. Arad, CEO of Marvel Studios, oversaw Marvel's commercial viability in the film industry. He was called one of the most powerful people in Hollywood by *Entertainment Weekly* and was compared to the likes of Steven Spielberg. Arad has since retired, and now Kevin Feige is head of the studio.

Marvel's former president, Bill Jemas, and editor in chief, Joe Quesada, were instrumental in turning Marvel around and making it once again the number one comic company in the world. Jemas and Quesada re-introduced Daredevil, Punisher, Ghost Rider, and others, as Marvel Knights. They also introduced the updated Ultimate line of comics, which is separate from the traditional continuity of Marvel, but true to the essence of its characters.

Spearheading a campaign to ignore the antiquated Comics Code, Jemas and Quesada started their own code for content and introduced the Max series, a new line of titles directly targeted to the mature adult. Jemas and Quesada's efforts and strategies, which helped turn Marvel around, are documented in *2000-2001 Year in Review: Fanboys and Badgirls Bill & Joe's Marvelous Adventure*, by Jim McLaughlin.

Movies, DVDs, and TV

When *Star Wars* came out in 1977, Marvel started doing movie adaptations and published them as small paperbacks or *Marvel Super Specials* (not documented in this volume unless republished in book form). Marvel has published *Star Trek*, *Hook*, *Blade Runner*, *Buck Rogers*, *James Bond*, and other movie adaptations.

With recent Marvel-based movies like *Blade 1–3*, *X-Men 1–3*, *Fantastic Four*, *Daredevil*, *Spider-Man 1 & 2*, and the *Hulk*, topping box office receipts, numerous studios are competing for the rights to produce films based on Marvel characters. All of these films grossed over $100 million worldwide on video and DVD. Today Marvel's icons are a hot commodity. In addition to having its own studio, Marvel has signed multipicture deals with major movie studios to produce full-length, animated movies for the small screen, video, and DVD. In 2006, Marvel Studios released its first direct-to-video animated features, *The Ultimates I* and *II*, to praise from both critics and fans; both volumes sold well. (Since the mid–1960s through today, there have been animated television programs featuring Marvel characters.)

While previous superhero movies and television shows had a certain charm, they were not always true to the characters, and often had bad scripts, acting, and effects. One only needs to compare the 1990 *Punisher* movie to the 2004 *Punisher* to see the improvement in quality. While the 2004 *Punisher* was not a blockbuster compared to *Spider-Man* or the *Hulk*, it still made over $50 million worldwide, and with its very strong DVD sales it became a viable franchise. According to a Reuters news story, Marvel's second-quarter profits in 2003 were seven times what they were the previous year, due in no small part to the licensing of blockbuster movie characters like Spider-Man and Hulk.

Television shows like *JLA*, *Heroes*, *Mutant X*, the *Animated Spider-Man*, *Teen Titans*, *X-Men Evolution*, *Smallville*, and others, have led independent ratings. Graphic literature characters are now at an all-time high. Superheroes, traditionally, but not always, the main characters in graphic literature (e.g., in *From Hell*), are now more popular than ever before, and no less than twenty films featuring superheroes either have been made or are in production. These films feature Iron Man, Gargoyle, Ghost Rider, Black Panther, Ant-Man, Luke Cage, Sub-Mariner, and Captain America, to name just a few. Marvel sequels *Spider-Man 3*, *Hulk 2*, *Punisher 2*, *Wolverine*, and *Fantastic Four 2*, are also forthcoming, and a few of these may be out by the time you read this.

Now

Early in this decade, Marvel reintroduced the Epic imprint (one book of which is documented in this volume), but, sadly, it did not last long. However, Marvel introduced a similar imprint called ICON for publishing and reprinting titles like Brian Michael Bendis's *Powers*. This imprint is much more specialized than Epic was.

In 2000, Marvel started to republish the Marvel Masterworks series. Like DC's Archive series (which DC keeps in perpetual print and expands every year by publishing new volumes), these books are treasures.

Marvel has made excellent strides in their graphic novel program. In 2002, they published close to a hundred full-length books and revived several of their past works. The program to republish out-of-print Masterworks volumes gathered steam, and all of the original Masterworks volumes have now been reprinted, along with versions that have variant reproductions of their original covers. In 2004, Marvel reprinted some of the Timely-era Golden Age stories with *Marvel Mystery Masterworks*. The earlier-published paperback volumes of the *Golden Age of Marvel 1–2* and *Captain America: The Classic Years* (which reprints the first ten issues of Simon and Kirby's masterpiece) have sold out. The *Golden Age Captain America, Sub-Mariner*, and *Human Torch Masterworks* have also done well. People have not forgotten and are still interested in these Golden Age stories. When Marvel published the *Essential Human Torch* book in 2003, many fans thought it was the original, android Human Torch, not the Fantastic Four's Johnny Storm. While this collection was a welcome addition to Marvel's publishing ventures, it also shows that people have not forgotten about those Golden Age heroes and desire to see more reprints of this material. Demand has also not been limited to the Timely-era Marvel. The Atlas-era material of the 1950s is now also being republished in the Masterworks program. Marvel's *Essential* series has been a godsend by reprinting many of the early Silver Age stories in a black-and-white, but highly readable and inexpensive format. As far as getting the most bang for your buck, this series is it. They have published unique items in this series, such as the *Essential Howard the Duck, Essential Tomb of Dracula*, and *Essential Dr. Strange*. These books have done well and Marvel should consider adding more than general superhero titles to the *Essentials* roster. In the early part of this decade, Marvel published western comics stories with an adult twist. The *Blaze of Glory, Apache Skies*, and *Rawhide Kid* have all done well. They should reprint many of those western stories from the 1950s, '60s and '70s. The time is right for those old stories featuring the original Ghost Rider (e.g., Phantom Rider/Night Rider), Rawhide Kid (Marvel did a *Rawhide Kid Masterworks* in 2006) and the Two-Gun Kid to be reprinted. Also in 2003, Marvel started a young-adult book series starring Mary Jane and published their first award-winning novel, *Mary Jane*. Titles like *Cage, Alias, Howard the Duck, War Machine, Rawhide Kid*, and *Fury*, all Max series books, have gotten rave reviews in such sources as *Rolling Stone* and *Ain't It Cool News*. Diamond Comic Distributors named Marvel the 2002 Publisher of the Year, and the *Knoxville News-Sentinel* gave accolades to Marvel for having the best comic, *New X-Men*; the best use of a character, Captain America; and the best writer, Geoff Johns.

In 2004, company officials decided to start a novel imprint using Marvel characters. Marvel movie novelizations based on Marvel characters like *Hulk, Spider-Man, X-Men, Daredevil, Punisher, Howard the Duck* (which was much better than the movie), and the first and third *Blade* movies provide a more in-depth look at the characters than the movies do. In 2005, Marvel published around two hundred fifty graphic novels, and in 2006 even more were being produced. In addition to the reboot of the Masterworks program, the early part of this decade saw Marvel producing beautiful hardcover books, including premier editions, omnibuses, and lovely oversize books.

In 2006, Marvel partnered with ABDO Publishing to form the Spotlight imprint. This imprint takes an issue of Marvel Comics that is aimed at a younger audience, such as Gus Beezer, and publishes it as a hardbound book for schools and libraries. Spotlight books, which are not documented in this volume, are made to hold up under the wear and tear of being handled by children. Despite the cost, more than $20 per copy, this is a wonderful idea. Marvel also partnered with Scholastic Books to bring comic-related materials into the schools to help children learn how to read.

On December 2, 2006, "Marvel Then and Now" was presented at UCLA. "Marvel Then and Now" featured Stan Lee, editor in chief Joe Quesada, and special guests who reminisced about Marvel past, and discussed its present and future. This event harkened back to the 1960s, when Lee did a series of lectures at universities and community centers.

The content of Marvel books has improved dramatically in the last few years, both in storytelling and art; individual Marvel comics show up in the top-ten sales list every month, and because of the success of Marvel characters in Marvel's books and movies, it seems as though Marvel is now unstoppable.

Stan Lee's design for the Marvel Universe was to set it in the real world, and most of the early stories were in New York City, where Lee and his family lived. Today the Superheroes roam the earth and beyond. Lee's vision was for Marvel Comics to become the next Disney. Although this has not happened yet, as long as Marvel characters continue to appear in blockbuster movies, action figures, graphic novels, and comics, and as long as their merchandising holds up, who knows what the possibilities might be.

Notes

1. Marvel's Ka-Zar character is based on the first Tarzan clone, Kazar, which had its beginnings in the pulp magazines in the 1930s and was one of the first characters to transcend from the pulps to comics. Marvel's Ka-Zar, which was resurrected in the 1960s, is not the same as Timely's Kazar. There is a reprint, in novel form, of the first Ka-Zar stories, described in this volume.

2. In addition to various Marvel-related cartoons, which started in the late 1960s and have continued, there were a few brief excursions into popular music. The British progressive rock band Icarus released *The Marvel World According to Icarus* in 1972 on the Sunrise label, and it has since been released as a limited-edition CD. Stan Lee also released *Spider-Man: Rock Reflections of a Superhero in 1976*, on the Lifesong label. It also has been released on CD.

References

Busiek, Kurt. 1997. "Retroduction" in *Untold Tales of Spider-Man*. New York: Boulevard Books.
Daniels, Les. 1992. *Marvel: Five Fabulous Decades of the Worlds Greatest Comics*. New York: Henry Abrams.
Dyer, Geoff. 2004. "Comics in a Man's Life" in Sean Howe ed., *Give Our Regards to the Atom Smashers: Writers On Comics*. New York: Pantheon Books.
Gruenberg, Sidonie Matsner. 1944. "The Comics as a Social Force." *Journal of Educational Sociology* 18: 4: 204–213.
Lee, Stan. "Introduction" in *Silver Surfer Masterworks Vol. 2*: New York: Marvel.
_____. 2003. "Introduction" in *Thor Masterworks Vol. 2*. New York: Marvel, 2003. ISBN: 0785111913: v.
_____. 1997. "Introduction" in *Untold Tales of Spider-Man*. New York: Boulevard Books.
_____. 1986. "Spidey and Me" in *Best of Spider-Man*. New York: Ballantine Books.
Lee, Stan, and George Mair. 2002. *Excelsior: the Amazing Life of Stan Lee*. New York: Fireside.
Zorbaugh, Harvey. 1944. "The Comics—There They Stand!" *Journal of Educational Sociology*, 18: 4: 196–203.

3

Major Characters, Teams, and Team-Ups

Avengers, Black Panther/Black Widow, Hawkeye, Hercules, Thunderbolts, and Ultimates

Perhaps I was never intended to be happy, but to defend
the happiness of ordinary people. —*Scarlet Witch*

Arcudi, John, Francisco Ruiz Velasco, Duncan Fegredo, et al. *Thunderbolts Vol. 1: How to Lose.* New York: Marvel, 2003. ISBN: 0785112480. Reprints *Thunderbolts 76–80.*

The Battler, Daniel Axum, who Spider-Man sent to jail, is out on parole and is trying to live a straight life. He comes in contact with an underworld boss who uses former super-villains as boxers. Daniel cannot resist the lure of big money, and beats up the Armadillo. Dillo gets kicked out of boxing and ends up homeless. The female super-villain, Man-Killer, is also recruited to box. The Scorpion and Spider-Man make appearances.

Austen, Chuck, Olivier Coipel, Sean Chen, et al. *Avengers Vol. 3: Lionheart of Avalon.* New York: Marvel, 2004. ISBN: 0785113 38X. Reprints *Avengers Vol. 3: 77–81.*

While in England, the Avengers come across the Wrecking Crew who are trying to rob a money truck. Thunderball breaks Captain America's jaw, and tries to smash Captain America with his ball, but a civilian woman—the mother of two children—steps in and uses Captain America's shield to protect herself. She is killed, and ends up in the mystical Avalon where the original Captain Britain gives her the mantle. With the Scarlet Witch beside her, she fights Morgan LeFay, who is about to kill the original Captain Britain, Brian Braddock. Just as the new Captain Britain is about to be killed for the second time, Captain America throws his shield and saves her. Captain Britain can never tell her children that she is

their mother. Hawkeye inadvertently helps the Wrecking Crew break out of their jail cell. Janet and Hank Pym get into a domestic argument over Hank's previous physical abuse. Janet Pym is learning to control her growing powers.

Austen, Chuck, Roy Thomas, Allan Jacobsen, et al. *Avengers Vol. 5: Once an Invader.* New York: Marvel, 2004. ISBN: 0785114815. Reprints *Avengers Vol. 3: 82–84*; *Invaders O*; *Avengers Vol. 1: 71*; *Invaders Annual 1.*

U.S. Agent John Walker puts together a new version of the Invaders, featuring the brilliant Blazing Skull, the Thin Man, Union Jack, Spitfire, and Tara, a new female Human Torch. The Invaders ask Namor for help in uprooting a dictator of Mazikhandar. Giant Man catches Hawkeye and the Wasp smooching, and the Avengers fight the Invaders, during their takeover of the country. The Avengers go up against the Hyena, Agent Axis (who has Captain America's original Shield), and the Shark. The Black Knight becomes an Avenger.

This book has a special reprint of an original Invaders story. It marks the triumphant return of a new version of the Invaders, featuring Golden Age characters, and artwork by the Golden Age cover artist Alex Schomburg. It also contains Roy Thomas's famous time-travel story in which Black Panther, Yellowjacket, and the Vision are sent back to France during World War II, and engage Captain America, Namor and the Human Torch in a cosmic game. Highly recommended.

Busiek, Kurt, Mark Bagley, Vince Russell, et al. *Thunderbolts: First Strikes*. New York: Marvel, 1997. ISBN: 0785105778. Reprints *Thunderbolts 1–2*.

In the wake of Onslaught, the Thunderbolts form to fill in for the missing Heroes. Everything is not what it seems however; the Thunderbolts are actually the Masters of Evil in disguise. Franklin Richards is kidnapped. Spider-Man, Black Widow, the New Warriors, and the Wrecking Crew all make appearances.

Busiek, Kurt, Mark Bagley, Vince Russell, et al. *Thunderbolts: Justice Like Lightning*. New York: Marvel, 2001. ISBN: 0785108173. Reprints *Thunderbolts Vol. 1: 1–4*; *Thunderbolts Annual 1997*; *Incredible Hulk 449*; *Tales of the Marvel Universe*; *Spider-Man Team Up Featuring ... 7*.

In the aftermath of the Onslaught tragedy in which most of Earth's heroes, including the Fantastic Four and the Avengers, were presumed dead, a new team called the Thunderbolts steps in. However, all is not what it appears to be, as the Thunderbolts are actually Baron Zemo's Masters of Evil in a different guise. The Thunderbolts gain the trust of the public, and become real heroes. They even allow a young girl, Jolt, to join their ranks. They go up against the Hulk and try to arrest Spider-Man for a murder he did not commit. Spider-Man ends up saving the life of Mach 1, who is actually his enemy the Beetle from the Enclave: The New Masters of Evil. The Black Widow and Arnim Zolo, the Bio-Fanatic, make appearances.

The book includes an origin story.

Busiek, Kurt, Alan Davis, Manuel Garcia, et al. *Avengers: The Kang Dynasty*. New York: Marvel, 2002. ISBN: 0785109587. Reprints *Avengers Vol. 3: 41–55*; *Avengers 2001 Annual*.

Kang comes to Earth with his son, the Scarlet Centurion, and demands immediate surrender. The Avengers, along with nearly everyone on the reserve roster, come together to defeat Kang, and Thor, who is a god, feels despair, knowing that he will outlive his friends. Several Avengers infiltrate the Triune Understanding, of which Triathlon was once a member. The leader of the Triune Understanding teams up with them temporarily, but tries to backstab them. Triathlon becomes one with the Triune's powerful force, which is eventually used against Kang. Kang's son ends up helping Warbird in the battle with the Master of the World. Warbird kills the Master of the World, so that the Avengers can use his technology to defeat Kang. Captain America engages in hand-to-hand combat with Kang on several occasions. Kang is defeated and put in prison, and Thor throws a giant party for his comrades. The Scarlet Centurion gets his father out of jail, but Kang kills his son for having betrayed him when he helped Warbird. Hank Pym

and his three alter egos go through a personality crisis. Warbird defeats the Deviant Glomm, and the 3-D Man's personalities are restored to their normal conditions.

This story is one of epic proportions. In addition to an all-too-brief appearance of the 3-D Man, one of Marvel's most interesting characters, there is a detailed history of his origin and his relation to Triathlon.

Busiek, Kurt, Fabian Nicieza, Barry Kitson, et al. *Avengers/Thunderbolts Vol. 2: Best Intentions*. New York: Marvel, 2004. ISBN: 078511422X. Reprints *Avengers/Thunderbolts 1–6*.

Under the leadership of Baron Zemo, the Thunderbolts, using satellite technology, devise a way to save the world. The Thunderbolts make the Avengers look bad by helping Cobalt Man before he melts down. Nobody except Hawkeye trusts the Thunderbolts, and in the Thunderbolts ranks everyone is watching everyone else. Tony Stark, disguised as Cobalt Man, infiltrates the Thunderbolts. Moonstone, who is power crazy, beats both the Avengers and the Thunderbolts. Zemo saves his enemy, Captain America. Then, after he steals the lunar gemstones, he disappears and Moonstone ends up brain dead. The Thunderbolts break up, and Songbird is offered an Avengers membership which she turns down. Abe Jenkins, the Beetle, is let out of prison and announces that he is going to reform the Thunderbolts. The Fantastic Four, Jolt, Nova, and Magneto make cameo appearances.

In this book, we also learn about Zemo's historical heritage.

Busiek, Kurt, George Perez, Scott Hama, et al. *Avengers: Supreme Justice*. New York: Marvel, 2001. ISBN: 0785107738. Reprints *Avengers Vol. 3: 5–7*; *Avenger/Squadron Supreme Annual 1998*; *Iron Man Vol. 3: 7*; *Captain America Vol. 3: 8*; *Quicksilver Vol. 1: 10*.

A Kree Invasion is thwarted by Captain America, Iron Man, and the Avengers. The Kree Supreme Intelligence is alive on the moon, and is not pleased with the Kree Lunatic Legion which seeks to turn all humans into Kree. The Legion captures Warbird in order to experiment on her and learn about her hybrid Kree/human physiology. Quicksilver comes back to the Avengers briefly, and uses the Inhumans' dog, Lockjaw, who gets hurt, to transport them. Warbird deals with a hidden demon, alcoholism, and gets fired from the team. The Avengers face off against the Squadron Supreme, and both the Squadron and the Avengers fight with Imus Champion. Captain America uses his first shield.

Busiek, Kurt, George Perez, Stuart Immonen, et al. *Avengers: Living Legends*. New York: Marvel, 2004. ISBN: 0785115617. Reprints *Avengers Vol. 3: 22–30*.

Wonder Man and the Vision fight, and Vision, who is jealous of Wonder Man, goes off by himself. Protesters gather outside of the Avengers' mansion; some protest because the Avengers have no black members, and others protest because they want the mutant members to be kicked out. The Avengers, with the help of Quicksilver, Spider-Man, Hercules, and Nova, save the Juggernaut from the Exemplars. Captain America, Thor, and others leave the team. Captain America, Warbird, and Silverclaw form a new team, and Triathlon is forced into the Avengers. Goliath, the Wasp, Warbird, and She-Hulk come back. The Avengers help Silverclaw and her mother, the god Peliali, fight against Kulan Gath. Silverclaw becomes an Avenger.

Busiek, Kurt, George Perez, Stuart Immonen, et al. *The Avengers Ultron Unlimited*. New York: Marvel, 2001. ISBN: 0785107746. Reprints *Avengers Vol. 3: 19–22*; *Avengers 0*.

The Avengers go up against the robot Ultron who has decimated the state of Slorenia and enslaved all of its inhabitants. Ultron kidnaps several Avengers, including Ant-Man, the Vision, and Wonder Man, but one of the newest Avengers, Justice, figures out a way to defeat Ultron. The Avengers also fight the female robot Alkhema.

According to *Wizard*, this series was one of "1999's Greatest Moments."

Busiek, Kurt, George Perez, Fibian Nicieza, et al. *Avengers/Thunderbolts Vol. 1: The Nefaria Protocols*. New York: Marvel, 2004. ISBN: 0785114459. Reprints *Avengers Vol. 3: 31–34*; *Thunderbolts 42–44*.

Wonder Man from the Avengers and Atlas from the Thunderbolts are kidnapped, then under Count Nefaria's guidance forced to do his biddings against their teammates. He manipulates ionic energy to control them. A crime boss, Madame Masque, who once had a romantic relationship with Tony Stark, is in trouble. Her father, Count Nefaria, has built an ionic-fuelled energy bomb. The Avengers and the Thunderbolts team up to stop him from using it. The Black Widow teams up with the Thunderbolts. Moonstone, who has gone AWOL, breaks into the Fantastic Four's headquarters. The Vision asks Warbird for a date, and Orge turns out to be Techno in disguise. Man Killer, Grim Reaper, Citizen V, and She-Hulk make appearances.

Busiek, Kurt, George Perez, Al Vey, et al. *Avengers: The Morgan Conquest*. New York: Marvel, 2000. ISBN: 0785107282. Reprints *Avengers Vol. 3: 1–4*.

The Avengers go back to medieval times to battle the spells of the villainess Morgan LeFay. She has commandeered the Twilight Sword, and attempts to remake reality in her image. The Avengers call together thirty-nine, all of whom were Avengers at one time or another, the largest gathering of Avengers in their history. Together, and with the help of the Scarlet Witch and Wonder Man, they fight and defeat LeFay. Vision is split in half. Some of the older Avengers include Sersi, Photon, Living Lighting, Rage, Moon Knight, and the very smelly Demolition Man.

Busiek, Kurt, Roger Stern, Carlos Pacheco, et al. *Avengers Legends Vol. 1: Avengers Forever*. New York: Marvel, 2003. ISBN: 07851075 68. Reprints *Avengers Forever 1–12*.

Seven time-displaced Avengers protect Rick Jones from death at the hands of Immortus. The Time Keepers believe that Rick Jones's use of the Destiny Force will bring an end to freedom in the universe, and that his ancestors, along with help of super-powered human militias, will enslave the universe. The Avengers ally themselves with their foe, Kang, to stop the death of Rick Jones. Kang muses over the details of his life and his various conquests. The Avengers also turn to the organic computer, the Supreme Intelligence of the Kree, for help. The Avengers go back and forth through time, and break up into various teams, as they try to track down Immortus. They end up in Immortus's limbo realm where Yellowjacket betrays them. Space Phantoms are Immortus's servants. After they kill him, the Time Keepers unsuccessfully try to transform Kang into Immortus. Marvel Boy, 3-D Man, Rawhide Kid, Two-Gun, Night Rider, Human Robot, Venus, and others make appearances.

Throughout the book, various points in the Avengers' and the Marvel Universe's history are brought out. Each event is annotated to refer back to the original issues, and nearly every Avenger, past, present, and future, makes an appearance. The history of the Vision/Human Torch debate is discussed in detail. Critically acclaimed as one of the best Avengers storylines, *Avengers Forever* is a loose sequel to the *Kree Skrull War*. The two books, read together, make a nice, continuous story.

Chichester, D.G., Larry Stroman and Mark Farmer. *Punisher/Black Widow: Spinning Doomsday's Web*. New York: Marvel, 1992. ISBN: 0871357364.

A group of terrorists free serial killer Dr. Peter Malum who once created a very destructive bomb, known as Project Pluto. The Black Widow, working for S.H.I.E.L.D., tries to bring Malum in, and nearly gets killed in the process. Nick Fury explains to her the seriousness of bringing him in, alive or dead, because there may be a newer version of the bomb. The Punisher is also tracking Malum, wanting to rid the world of another crazy serial killer. The Widow stops the Punisher from assassinating Malum so that she can learn where the "new" bomb is located and what Malum and the terrorists are up to. The Punisher and the Widow form a loose alliance, to track down Malum and his cronies. When she kills Malum in self defense, the Widow experiences firsthand what it is like to murder someone. (*Marvel Graphic Novel 74*)

Conway, Gerry, George Freeman, Ernie Colon, et al. *The Black Widow: The Coldest War*. New York: Marvel 1990. ISBN: 0871356430.

The Black Widow is asked to get some secret documents from the United Nations in order to be able to see her allegedly deceased husband, the Red Guardian. However, the Red Guardian is a robot, and she is being led into a trap. When the Widow is accused of being a double agent working for the Soviets, she has to prove her loyalty to America. Daredevil, Nick Fury, and the Avengers make appearances. (*Marvel Graphic Novel 62*)

Conway, Gerry, Jim Shooter, George Perez, et al. *Target Avengers: Earth's Mightiest Heroes*. New York: Marvel, 2004. ISBN: 0785115803. Reprints *Avengers Vol. 1: 161–162, 201. King Size Annual 6, 8*.

Ultron tries to create a mate by transforming the essence of Janet Pym, the Wasp, into his robot. Ultron causes Henry Pym to lose his memory, and become his ally against the Avengers. Doctor Spectrum also tries to steal Janet Pym's essence. The Avengers also go up against members from the Squadron Sinister, Thundra, and the Taskmaster. A Golden Age character, the Whizzer, makes a special appearance, helping the Avengers apprehend his son, Nuklo. The book also contains a special story about the Avengers' butler, Jarvis, who stands up to some hoods in his mother's neighborhood.

This Avengers book was published as part of the Marvel Age series, features art by George Perez, and went out of print shortly after it was published.

David, Peter, Ariel Olivetti, Jim Novak, et al. *The Last Avengers Story*. New York: Marvel, 1996. ISBN: 0781502183. Reprints *Last Avengers Story 1–2*.

This is a "what if" story that takes place far into the future when the original Avengers are aged, Hawkeye is blind, and Cannonball is a member of the Avengers. Ultron, who is fifty-nine years old, coaxes the old Avengers into battle with his team of villains, which includes Kang, Reaper, and Oddball. The Vision comes out of stasis and defeats Ultron after several Avengers die. The story is beautifully written and drawn.

David, Peter, Richard Starkings, Joe Kaufman, et al. *Tales to Astonish: Featuring the Hulk, Hank Pym, and the Wasp*. New York: Marvel, 1994. Reprints *Tales to Astonish Vol. 3: 1*.

Hank Pym and Janet Van Dyne visit Oslo, where they go up against a madman, Caine, who worships Loki. Loki gives Caine some of his powers, and Caine, disguised as Loki, tries to bring about an end to everything. The Hulk, Ant-Man, and the Wasp defeat him.

DeFalco, Tom, Roger Stern, Marc Silvestri, et al. *Avengers versus X-Men*. New York: Marvel, 1993. ISBN: 0871359677. Reprints *X-Men versus the Avengers 1–4*.

Several pieces of Magneto's former stronghold in outer space fall to earth as meteorites. Magneto goes to investigate, as do the Avengers and the Soviet Super Soldiers. Dr. Druid is a stowaway on their jet when the X-Men follow Magneto and end up in a fight with the Avengers and the Soviets. The Soviet Super Soldiers want Magneto to pay for his crimes against the Russian people, and the Avengers act as special deputies of the World Court to rein Magneto in. A group within the court wants Magneto to be found guilty of crimes against humanity, so that he can be held up as a martyr. This, in turn, would cause civil strife and possibly war. The World Court frees Magneto. In Singapore, the X-Men meet a group of mutants who seek their aid.

This story takes place after Magneto has reformed and is leading the X-Men.

Englehart, Steve, Bob Brown, Mike Esposito, et al. *The Avengers Defenders War*. New York: Marvel, 2002. ISBN: 0785108440. Reprints *Avengers Vol. 1: 115–118*.

The Avengers and the Defenders are deceived by Loki into fighting with each other. They eventually join forces to fight Dormammu, who is trying to swallow the earth into his evil dimension. The Defenders go back in time to the Middle Ages, to find and save the Black Knight.

Englehart, Steve, Sal Buscema, Dave Cockrum, et al. *The Avengers: Celestial Madonna*. New York: Marvel, 2001. ISBN: 0785108262. Reprints *Avengers 129–135*; *Giant Size Avengers 2–4*.

Kang seeks to harness the power of the Celestial Madonna, who is revealed to be Mantis, but Kang is thwarted by the Avengers and various future/past versions of himself, including Immortas and Rama-Tut. Kang brings Wonder Man, Frankenstein's Monster, the first Baron Zemo, the Ghost, and Midnight back from the dead to fight the Avengers. The Vision, who discovers that he is derived from the original Human Torch, delves into his past to learn the origin of the original Human Torch, and to learn how Professor Horton helped Ultron create the Vision. The Scarlet Witch learns a great deal about her magical powers, but ends up under the control of the dreaded Dormammu. The Scarlet Witch and the Vision get married. The Swordsman dies, but his form is resurrected by the sentient plants, the Cotati and Mantis. The Celestral Madonna marries the Cotati/Swordsman hybrid.

This landmark Avengers story includes a detailed study of the Kree origins and a history of how the Skrulls were involved in creating eons of hatred between the two races. It also includes origin tales for Mantis, Kree Supreme Intelligence, and Moondragon.

Fingeroth, Danny, Ron Lim, Jim Sanders, et al. *Avengers Deathtrap: The Vault.* New York: Marvel, 1991. ISBN: 0871358107.

Venom coordinates a prison break with several other super criminals, and the Avengers and Freedom Force team up to stop the escape. Armadillo, Rhino, and Scarecrow turn on Venom, because they want to serve out their sentences. The Rhino smashes himself into Venom's back, and Venom kills the warden of the Vault. There is a bomb threat, but Venom does not believe that there is a bomb set to go off. (*Marvel Graphic Novel 68*)

Gale, Bob, Phil Winslade, Tom Palmer, et al. *Ant-Man's Big Christmas.* New York: Marvel, 2000.

This is a Prestige mini-trade from the Marvel Knights series. The Avengers are celebrating Christmas, and Ant-Man and the Wasp don't want to go to either side of the family to celebrate. They receive a letter from a young boy, Larry, who asks for their help in brightening his Christmas. Larry's kin, who visit every Christmas, are not the nicest people. Ant-Man and the Wasp help the young man teach his Christmas guests the true meaning of the holiday in this hilarious tale. Larry's parents get to experience firsthand what the world is like to Ant-Man, by walking through a toy train landscape.

Grayson, Devlin, Greg Rucka, J. G. Jones, et al. *Black Widow.* New York: Marvel, 2001. ISBN: 0785107843. Reprints *Black Widow, Vol. 1: 1–3; Black Widow Vol. 2:1–3.*

A new Black Widow, Yelena Belova, seeks to destroy Natasha Romanov, whom she considers a traitor to Russia because she defected to the United States. Natasha is ordered to stop the operations of an Arabian warlord. Daredevil makes several appearances.

The book is a beautifully written and illustrated spy story, for Cold War junkies.

Gruenwald, Mark, Brett Breeding, Joe Rosen, et al. *Hawkeye.* New York: Marvel, 1988. ISBN: 0871353644. Reprints *Hawkeye 1–4.*

Hawkeye is fired from his job as security chief for Cross Technological Enterprises. He teams up with a new female hero, Mockingbird, to fight against Oddball and Bombshell. Ultimately, Hawkeye and his teammate foil plans by Crossfire to control the minds of the superhero world.

Gruenwald, Mark, Steven Grant, David Michelinie, et al. *The Avengers: The Yesterday Quest.* New York: Marvel, 1994. Reprints *Avengers 181–182, 185–187.*

Quicksilver and the Scarlet Witch's foster father put their essences into small, voodoo-like dolls. The Avengers help them break free. They both go to the land of Transia to find out the truth about their heritage. Quicksilver learns of his childhood from the

Bovine. The demon Chthon takes over the Scarlet Witch's body, and tries to destroy Quicksilver and the Avengers. Quicksilver and the Scarlet Witch do not find out who their true father is.

Harras, Bob, Steve Epting, Tom Palmer, et al. *Avengers/X-Men: Bloodties,* New York: Marvel, 1995. ISBN: 0785101039. Reprints *Avengers 368–369; Avengers West Coast 101; Uncanny X-Men 307; X-Men 26.*

An acolyte of Magneto, Exodus, seeks to purify Magneto's bloodline by killing his children and grandchild. When Quicksilver's baby girl Luna is kidnapped by the acolyte, Fabian Cortez, the X-Men team up with the Avengers, and go to the mutant island of Genosha. Genosha is in the midst of a civil war between the mutants and the humans. Nick Fury makes an appearance, and his S.H.I.E.L.D. forces take on the Avengers, who are warned by the UN not to intervene in the civil war. Cortez is killed.

This is one of the darkest, most true-to-life stories ever published by Marvel.

Johns, Geoff, Olivier Coipel, Andy Lanning, et al. *Avengers Vol. 2: Red Zone.* New York: Marvel, 2003. ISBN: 0785110992. Reprints *Avengers Vol. 3: 64–70.*

A flesh-eating disease hits Mount Rushmore, South Dakota. The Avengers are called in to help, and they discover that the disease was cultivated in a secret, government lab. The Avengers' liaison, Gyrich, has been feeding private and personal information about the Avengers to Secretary of Defense Rusk, and Rusk is responsible for the outbreak of the "Red Zone" disease. Rusk is actually the Red Skull, who wants to instill fear into the American public by starting a war with Wakanda, so that he can take hold of the government. She-Hulk is exposed to the virus and disappears. Iron Man and Black Panther make a pact to share scientific information. She-Hulk goes berserk and smashes the Vision and the Panther. Several of the Falcon's bird friends defeat the Red Skull, and his blood is used as the antidote to the flesh-eating virus. George W. Bush and Captain America exchange words, and Bush gives Carol Danvers a job as the Chief of Homeland Security.

Johns, Geoff, Keiron Dwyer, Rick Remender, et al. *Avengers Vol. 1: World Trust.* New York: Marvel, 2003. ISBN: 0785110801. Reprints *Avengers Vol. 3: 57–62; Marvel Double-Shot 2.*

Chaos and Order are separated, and various important cities throughout the world are transported to another dimension. A new Scorpio is using the Zodiac key to cause anarchy and war in the dimension of Chaos. The Avengers are called to figure out what the problem is, and to save the world. Black Panther, Falcon, and Sub-Mariner come back to the Avengers, and Yellow Jacket, Wasp, and Washington D.C. are transported to the Chaos dimension. Black Panther enlists the aid of Dr. Doom without the Avengers approval, and Iron Man nearly fights with the Panther. The Scarlet Witch is injured in a battle, and Vision takes care of her. Ant-Man saves the day by communicating with the Scorpions who turn on Scorpio. Henry Gyrich becomes the liaison for the Avengers as they are given a seat in the United Nations, much to the dismay of the U.S. government. Ant-Man, Scott Lange, loses custody of his child, and is offered permanent status as an Avenger. Captain America offers Sub-Mariner a chance to be an official Avenger again, but Mariner laughs it off.

The book also contains an Avengers comedy story drawn in the style of the Simpsons.

Johns, Geoff, Scott Kolins, Steve Sadowski, et al. *Avengers Vol. 3: The Search for She-Hulk*. New York: Marvel, 2004. ISBN: 07851120 22. Reprints *Avengers Vol. 3: 71–76*.

When She-Hulk has a run-in with Jack of Hearts, the balance of gamma radiation in her body is altered, and she turns back into a regular human. She goes in search of her cousin in Bone, Idaho, and the Avengers go in search of She-Hulk. When she does "Hulk-out," she becomes more like her destructive cousin, and begins destroying with little reason. When Hawkeye shoots her cousin Bruce Banner with an arrow, he turns into the Hulk, and both the Hulk and She-Hulk fight in a massive battle. Jack of Hearts restores her gamma radiation levels. Henry Pym again asks the Wasp, Janet Van Dyne, to marry him, but the Whirlwind ruins their little rendezvous. A murderous pedophile kidnaps Cassie, the daughter of Ant-Man, Scott Lang. Ant-Man and Jack of Hearts save Cassie, and then Ant-Man goes out into space with the pedophile. Hawkeye rejoins the Avengers.

Krueger, Jim, Matt Smith, Steve Mitchell, et al. *Timeslip: The Coming of the Avengers*. New York: Marvel, 1998. ISBN: 0785106723.

Odin forms the Avengers who do battle with several of the gods in Asgard. Xavier is killed during a battle with Hermod, and Jean Grey's anguish over his death causes Odin to cry. Loki tries to take over Asgard, but learns that there is no glory in ruling a kingdom of one.

This is a bizarre, alternate-universe story, in which Odin decides to destroy the Earth, and bring his son Thor back to Asgard. Thor tries to prove to Odin that some humans have honor, and are just as worthy of life as anyone in Asgard. This version of the formation of the Avengers features Murdock, the Blind; Thor; Connors, the One-Armed Warrior; Xavier, the Fallen; Jack Fireheart; and Smithers, the Green Knight.

Layton, Bob, Christie Scheele, Bob Sharen, et al. *Hercules: Prince of Power*. Marvel Comics: New York, 1997. ISBN: 0785105557. Reprints *Hercules* Vol. 1: 1–4; *Hercules* Vol. 2: 1–4.

Hercules takes on Galactus and teams up with the unlikeliest of allies, a Skrull. Galactus finds Hercules so funny that he actually decides not to destroy the world that Hercules wants to protect. Galactus takes his helmet off, and has a drink with Hercules. On Titan, Hercules and his allies encounter Shreck, who stole Captain Marvel's power bands from his grave. Hercules goes to Olympus and discovers that Zeus has gone mad; he has killed all the other gods, and plans to kill Hercules too.

This is a new take on a traditional Greek hero, within the confines of the Marvel Universe. It is one of the funniest and cleverest graphic novels. In 1988, the first four issues were published as *Hercules: Prince of Power*. ISBN: 0871353652

Layton, Bob, John Workman, George Roussos, et al. *Hercules: Full Circle*. New York: Marvel, 1988. ISBN: 0871353970.

Hercules and his companions are captured by Emperor Arimathes who has a passionate hatred of Hercules. He finds out that Arimathes is his son, and that the Emperor's mother has turned Arimathes against his father. Arimathes plans on invading the peace-loving Omacron star system. The Prince of Power escapes with the help of his friends, and tries to stop Arimathes from massacring the Omacron system. He challenges his son to a duel to the death, to teach him humility. (*Marvel Graphic Novel 37*)

Macchio, Ralph, George Perez, Brett Breeding, et al. *Black Widow: Web of Intrigue*. New York: Marvel, 1999. Reprints *Marvel Fanfare 10–13*.

Natasha's chauffeur and childhood guardian Ivan Petrovich is missing, and may have defected back to the Soviets. S.H.I.E.L.D. brings the Black Widow in to investigate, despite Nick Fury's misgivings about her personal stake in the mission. The Black Widow is captured and has to contend with numerous villains, including the Iron Maiden who has a personal score to settle. When she is captured, a "fake" Black Widow is sent back to S.H.I.E.L.D. Damon Dran, who has captured her, plans to use a brainwashed Ivan against her. Snap Dragon and Jimmy Woo make appearances.

McGregor, Don, Dwayne Turner, et al. *Black Panther: Panther's Prey 1–4*. New York: Marvel, 1991. ISBN: 0871357232 (vol. 1); 0871357240 (vol. 2); 0871357259 (vol. 3); 0871357267 (vol. 4).

Solomon Prey, a man who had wings surgically attached to his back, seeks the death of the Black Panther. He is trafficking crack and selling Vibranium illegally, from Wakanda. As a result, one of the Panther's young friends dies. Prey's men implant bombs in Wakanda's sacred Vibranium Mound. Despite protests from his advisors, T'Challa—whose ex-girlfriend has taken up with Prey, and also wants to destroy the Panther—goes to the United States to ask for the hand of singer Monica Lynn. Prey wounds T'Challa a number of times, and even buries him alive. When T'Challa removes a chip from one of Venom's snakes, he finds out that there is a spy in his organization.

Panther's Prey is a sequel, of sorts, to the 1988 *Panther's Quest* storyline.

Michelinie, David, John Byrne, Gene Day, et al. *BackPack Marvels: The Avengers: Nights of Wundagore*. New York: Marvel, 2001. ISBN: 0785107657. Reprints *Avengers Vol. 1: 181–189*.

The Scarlet Witch and Quicksilver are drawn to the remote Wundagore Mountains. An evil, that wants to twist nature to its will, lurks within the mountains. The Avengers battle with the demon Chthon. The Avengers are asked to comply with affirmative action.

This book includes a profile and history of Quicksilver and the Scarlet Witch.

Michelinie, David, Bob Hall, Ken Lopez, et al. *Emperor Doom: Starring the Mighty Avengers*. New York: Marvel, 1987. ISBN: 0871352567.

Doctor Doom kidnaps the Purple Man, and using a powerful crystal he is able to harness the Purple Man's mind-controlling powers. Doom takes over the earth and, as Emperor Doom, he builds his version of Utopia. He uses the Sub-Mariner to subdue the Avengers, and bring them under his control. However, Wonder Man, who was in a state of suspended animation when Doom took over, is not under his control, and is considered an outlaw. When Wonder Man wakes up, he convinces Captain America that the Avengers have been had, and they proceed to deprogram the other Avengers. The Sub-Mariner also rebels against Doom's brainwashing, and Doom loses his Utopia. Ronald Reagan and Margaret Thatcher make cameo appearances. (*Marvel Graphic Novel 27*)

Millar, Mark, Bryan Hitch, Andrew Currie, et al. *The Ultimates Vol. 1*. New York: Marvel, 2002. ISBN: 0785109609. Reprints *Ultimates 1–6*.

As the Ultimate Universe's answer to the Avengers, Tony Stark and Nick Fury put together a group of Supervillain fighters that includes Captain America, Giant Man, the Wasp, Iron Man, Nick Fury, Bruce Banner, and Thor. Captain America is revived after being frozen for more than fifty years, and he meets up with his old partner Bucky, who is now old and feeble. Thor is a socialist, and all the heroes do not have secret identities. Banner combines his Hulk serum with the Super Soldier formula, and becomes the Hulk. He goes rampaging through New York, and wants to fight Freddie Prinze Jr., who is having dinner with his wife, Betty Ross. Giant Man and the Wasp get into a fight, which escalates into physical violence.

Millar, Mark, Paul Neary, Andrew Currie, et al. *The Ultimates Vol. 2: Homeland Security*. New York: Marvel, 2004. ISBN: 078511078X. Reprints *Ultimates 7–13*.

In the wake of the Hulk's destruction, Captain America gives a eulogy for those who died. The Wasp, Janet Pym, is put in the hospital after she is beaten up by her husband Giant Man, and Captain America tracks him down and gives him a severe beating. Groups of shape-shifting aliens who were allies of Hitler have been influencing human affairs since World War II, and the Hulk is brought out to "smash" the aliens. Black Widow, Hawkeye, Quicksilver, and the Scarlet Witch are introduced to the team. Thor and Iron Man help save the world from the aliens' bomb. The Hulk tries to eat Hawkeye.

We learn a little more about Captain America's past during the 1940s and the war, when, because of the aliens, he almost died.

Milligan, Peter, Mike Allred, Nick Dragotta, et al. *X-Statix Vol. 4: X-Statix Vs. The Avengers*. New York: Marvel, 2004. ISBN: 0785115374. Reprints *X-Statix 19–26*.

Myles, Vivasector, is dating Brandon, a teen heart-throb. He participates in an experiment that will free him of his wolf-like, mutant powers. The scientist, who is working with Myles and who worked for Professor X in the past, is secretly draining Myles of his powers so that he can take them over. He leaves X-Statix. When Myles attends his father's sixtieth birthday party, the "fake" Vivasector crashes the party and takes Myles' father hostage. They duke it out with help of the rest of the X-Statix. Captain America tells the press that he thinks the X-Statix is irresponsible, that they are not serious crime fighters. When a group of terrorists kidnap Doop, and use him for a weapon, the X-Statix ask the Avengers for help in rescuing him. However, his brain blows up and parts of it scatter all over the world. Rather than working together, X-Statix and the Avengers are now at odds: Captain America fights the Anarchist; the Scarlet Witch fights against Dead Girl; Hawkeye fights Vivasector; and Venus Dee Milo fights the Ant-Man. Iron Man and Mr. Sensitive take each other on at the Church of the Naked Truth. They both get naked, fight each other, and then take on Surrender Monkey. The last piece of Doop's brain ends up in Asgard, where Doop swallows Mjolnir, Thor's hammer. Doop's back-up brain, which is in his butt, starts to burn out, and the Avengers and X-Statix put him back together. Doop is back in the care of X-Statix. Captain America relents, and agrees that X-Statix is responsible. They decide to break up, but take on one last mission, which goes horribly wrong.

In this book the reader learns a little bit about Doop's history, but not much.

Oeming, Michael, Avon, Andrea Divito, Daniel Berman, et al. *Avengers Disassembled: Thor*. New York: Marvel, 2004. ISBN: 0785115994. Reprints *Thor 80–85*.

The hour of Ragnarok is upon Asgard, and Thor and his colleagues struggle against the destruction of the Golden Realm. Loki wants Asgard for himself, and makes "unholy" alliances to get it. The Enchantress, Balder, Warriors Three, and Sif all come to an end. Beta Ray Bill lends his hand to help in Asgard's time of need, and Thor learns that he must undergo the same trials as Odin. His hammer Mjolnir is shattered. Thor must be Asgard's destroyer in order to be its savior, so he actually gives Surtur free reign to destroy. Thor chops off Loki's head.

Olshevsky, George, Tony Frutti, Neal Adams, et al. *The Marvel Comics Index: Avengers 3.* Ontario: G&T Enterprises, 1976. ISBN: 0943348501 (Marvel Index Set).

This is an index and history of the *Avengers, Avengers Annual,* and *Giant Size Avengers,* up to 1976. It also includes indexes to the original 1950s *Black Knight, Captain Marvel,* and *The Defenders,* with cross indexes to major characters. There are Avengers lineups and storylines, as well as a history of Marvel Superhero teams, from such as the All Winners Squad from Marvel's Timely years.

Olshevsky, George, Tony Frutti, Michael Higgins, et al. *The Official Marvel Index to the Avengers 1–7.* New York: Marvel, 1987–1988.

The Avengers Index was Volume 5 in the series, with the X-Men being the only other set done in Prestige format. All other issues in the index series were done as comic books. Each entry contains character cross-references, a synopsis of the issue, information about authors and artists, and date. The series covers *The Avengers Vol. 1: 1–145.* Other titles indexed include: *Giant Size Avengers; King Size Avengers; Marvel Superheroes; Ka-Zar;* and *Defenders.*

Perez, George, Gerry Conway, Joe Rosen, et al. *Avengers Legends Volume 3.* New York: Marvel 2003. ISBN: 0785109994; 0785107177 (1999, *Avengers Visionaries, George Perez*). Reprints *Avengers 161–162, 194–196, 201; Avengers Annual 6, 8.*

This volume, which showcases the art of George Perez, is Book 1 in the George Perez Series. The story is the same as *Target Avengers: Earth's Mightiest Heroes,* by Gerry Conway and George Perez (ISBN: 0785115 803).

Priest, Christopher, Joe Jusko, Mike Manley, et al. *Black Panther: Enemy of the State.* New York: Marvel, 2002. ISBN: 0785108297. Reprints *Black Panther Vol. 2: 6–12.*

The Black Panther, exiled from his home, Wakanda, tries to regain his throne from the insane Achebe. With Captain America's help, he successfully defeats Achebe. In a climactic ending, T'Challa fights against his brother Hunter, "the White Wolf." The Avengers make appearances.

Priest, Christopher, Mark Texeira, Vince Evans, et al. *Black Panther: The Client.* New York: Marvel, 2001. ISBN: 0785107894. Reprints *Black Panther, Vol. 2: 1–6.*

This series was critically acclaimed by *Entertainment Weekly* as a "swashbuckling, political thriller." The narrative, which begins with the Black Panther investigating a young girl's murder in New York, is told through the eyes of Everett P. Ross. In the story, the Black Panther outsmarts Mephisto for the souls of his kingdom, in Wakanda.

Ricketts, Mark, John Jackson Miller, Tony Harris, et al. *Avengers Disassembled: Iron Man.* New York: Marvel, 2004. ISBN: 07851165 32. Reprints *Iron Man 84–89.*

As secretary of state, Tony Stark is asked to find out about and disable a secret weapons project on which his father had worked. The problem is that it is below the Avengers' mansion. He is ordered not to tell the Avengers about this project, which the Government had authorized against its citizens. Stark is fired from his position as secretary of state, and says some very nasty things in public to the ambassador from Latveria. Iron Man breaks into a meeting at Star Enterprises and kills the attendees. He proceeds to kill Stark's girlfriend, and break into Stark's home. This evil Iron Man, who is actually a former industrialist, has it in for Stark, and as Iron Man wants to bring him down. Stark puts on his real Iron Man uniform, and stops this doppelganger. Then he publicly resigns as Iron Man.

The book includes cover sketches/inks.

Ridout, Cefn, et al. *Fury: Black Widow: Death Duty.* New York: Marvel, 1995. ISBN: 07 8510156X.

The Black Widow returns to Russia to investigate the death of a diplomat which takes place on the grounds of the U.S. Embassy. Black Widow teams up with Night Raven against the Russian Mafioso. Night Raven engages in his one-man war against crime, and reveals his secrets to the Black Widow. He wants to kill the woman, Yi Yang, who made him immortal.

In this book, the Marvel U.K. pulp hero Night Raven makes his first appearance in the more traditional Marvel Universe. The story ties up many of the loose ends in the Night Raven saga. Even though Nick Fury's name is in the title, he appears very briefly in the story.

Shooter, Jim, David Michelinie, Bill Mantlo, et al. *Avengers Legends Vol. 2: The Korvac Saga.* New York: Marvel, 2003. ISBN: 07851091 96; 0871357607 (1991). Reprints *Avengers Vol. 1: 167–168; 170–177.*

The Guardians of the Galaxy follow Korvac, the Machine Man, from the thirty-first century to the Avengers' time. Korvac assumes the identity of a human named Michael, and wants to bring a new age to the universe. The Collector's daughter, who is sent to spy on Michael, falls in love with him. The Collector kidnaps the Avengers in order to save their lives from Korvac, but Korvac ends up killing him. Ultron's wife Jacosta aids the Avengers, and Ms. Marvel lends a helping hand when they try to destroy Ultron. The Avengers also do battle with Tyrak; their security clearance is revoked.

Stern, Roger, John Buscema, Tom Palmer, et al. *The Avengers: Under Siege.* New York: Marvel, 1998. ISBN: 0785107029. Reprints *Avengers, 270–271, 273–277.*

Sub-Mariner is inducted into the Avengers. When the Avengers' mansion is attacked by Baron Zemo and the Masters of Evil, Jarvis and the Black Knight, who are taken off guard, are captured and horribly beaten. Captain Marvel is sent to another dimension. Hercules gets drunk and is subsequently defeated. Zemo taunts Captain America, and tears up pictures of him with Bucky, which causes Captain America to feel isolated. Ant-Man, Scott Lang, helps the Wasp, and Thor defeats the Masters of Evil. Namor is sued.

This story contains some very human elements. The introduction is by Roger Stern.

Thomas, Roy, Neal Adams, Sal Buscema, et al. *The Avengers: Kree-Skrull War.* New York: Marvel, 2000. ISBN: 0785107452. Reprints *Avengers 89–97.*

Earth becomes a battleground for a pointless war between the Skrull and the Kree. Ant-Man goes inside the Vision to correct a possible error in his programming, brought about by an encounter with Skrulls. Captain America, Thor, and Iron Man dis-

band the Avengers. Anti-alien hysteria is directed toward the Avengers for aiding Captain Marvel. The Avengers go to trial, where they are portrayed as anti–American, and the Avengers' mansion is ransacked by an angry public which views them as traitors. Captain Marvel is captured by the Skrull, and is forced to design the Omni-Wave weapon. Rick Jones, at the urging of the Kree Supreme Intelligence, lets loose the Destiny Force and stops the war. The Vision begins to show his feelings for the Scarlet Witch. Nick Fury and Annihilus appear briefly.

The Skrulls, originally from *Fantastic Four 2,* are central to the story. Rich Jones plays a prominent role, and there are cameo appearances by the original Vision, Human Torch, Angel, Patriot, Blazing Skull, and others from the Golden Age. Some view this Avengers storyline as the best ever written.

Thomas, Roy, Tony Isabella, Sal Buscema, et al. *Thunderbolts: Marvel's Most Wanted.* New York: Marvel, 1998. ISBN: 0785106553. Reprints *Captain America 168; Incredible Hulk 228–229; Strange Tales 123, 141–143; Marvel Two-in-One 56, 54; Avengers 21–22.*

The Thunderbolts are a team of supervillains, posing as heroes. This collection includes some of the first stories that featured Meteorite, the Beetle, Techno, Atlas, Songbird, and the second Baron Zemo, who made up the original team of Thunderbolts. It contains an appearance by the first Power Man, and includes stories with Captain America, Falcon, Avengers, Thing, Hulk, Thundra, Human Torch, Nick Fury, and Quasar.

Captain America, Fury, Human Torch, Namor, and Golden-Age Characters

I believe that everyone should be free to achieve their full potential
to become the best person they can ... fulfill their American Dream....
My American Dream is to help make this country the kind of place
where that's possible ... to inspire by example. — *Captain America*

I believe America to be a weak morally bankrupt country
whose societal underpinnings are being eaten away. It is
my goal to speed up that process. — *The Red Skull*

Austin, Chuck, John Ney Rieber, Jae Lee, et al. *Captain America Vol. 3: Ice.* New York: Marvel, 2003. ISBN: 0785111034. Reprints *Captain America Vol. 4: 12–16.*

Steve Rogers receives a strange package which shows pictures of the U.S. government putting him into a frozen state of suspended animation. The government believes that Captain America might be against using the atomic bomb, and wants to safeguard

that decision by freezing him in ice. The Interrogator, who is from the undersea Kingdom of Lemuria, succeeds in getting Captain America to kill. Namor, the Avengers, and Baron Blood make appearances.

Burgos, Carl, Bill Everett, Tom Brevoort, et al. *Marvel Mystery Comics 65th Anniversary Commemorative Edition.* New York: Marvel, 2004. Reprints *Marvel Mystery Comics 8–10.*

The Torch is brought in to rein in Namor's war against humanity, and a titanic battle ensues. Namor and the Torch are pretty evenly matched, but eventually Namor captures the Torch and puts him in a glass prison. Namor promises to leave humanity alone if the Torch will leave him alone.

This amazing tale is a perpetual favorite among fans of the Golden Age stories. This book is a 48-page, cardstock-cover commemorative comic.

Burgos, Carl, Bill Everett, Jack Kirby, et al. *Marvel Mystery Comics 1*. New York: Marvel, 1999. Reprints *Marvel Mystery Comics 23, 26, 74; Comedy Classics 9; Captain America Comics 2, 9*.

The original Human Torch is pitted against criminal mastermind Parrot. Vision goes up against Khor, the Black Sorcerer, and Namor. Namor is captured by an evil scientist who wants to create a race of sub-humans. Thor's son, Hurricane, goes to a Brazilian jungle where the green plague is menacing the inhabitants, and the Angel goes up against the bizarre, armless Tiger Man. The Silver Scorpion solves a case in which an evil doctor is a "beauty butcher" who robs young women of their youth. Captain America and Bucky fight the White Death.

This combo, a book-shelf comic, celebrates the Golden Age of Marvel.

Burgos, Carl, Bill Everett, Alex Schomburg, et al. *Timely Presents The Human Torch*. New York: Marvel, 1999. ISBN: 0785105913. Reprints *Human Torch 5*.

The Sub-Mariner, who has delusions of grandeur, thinks he can take over the Earth and be the next Napoleon. With a lady friend egging him on to take over the planet, the Mariner fights the Germans, Italians and the British. He takes Toro captive, but Toro escapes. The Human Torch is put under a mind spell. When the Torch sees the American flag, he realizes that he has been fighting for the wrong side, and fights Namor to stop his attempt to conquer the world. Eventually, Namor and the Torch team up against the Nazis. Stalin, Churchill, Hitler, and Mars, the God of War, make cameo appearances.

The book includes an essay by Roy Thomas in which he details how the various battles between the Human Torch and the Sub-Mariner came about. The entire 1941 issue, *Human Torch 5*, is reprinted.

Chaykin, Howard, Ben Schwartz, Andrew Currie, et al. *Captain America: Nick Fury: Blood Truce*. New York: Marvel, 1995. ISBN: 9000019680.

S.H.I.E.L.D. wants to hire Colonel Panshin, a former KGB agent and torturer. Several rogue S.H.I.E.L.D. agents, who believe it is wrong for the United States to hire former agents from the Soviet Union, try to stop this plan. They hire Agent Orange to kidnap Panshin's child. Nick Fury, Captain America, and the Titanium Man team up to protect Panshin and rescue his child. S.H.I.E.L.D. forms an uneasy alliance with A.I.M.

This story takes place right after the Berlin Wall fell.

Chichester, D. G., Klaus Janson, Margaret Clark, et al. *The Punisher & Captain America: Blood and Glory 1–3*. New York: Marvel, 1993. ISBN: 0871358867 (Vol. 1); 087135 8875 (Vol. 2); 0871358883 (Vol. 3).

The Punisher is used as a pawn to assassinate Captain America who he mistakenly thinks is running drugs. Captain America survives a gun wound, but stages his own death. He ends up working with the Punisher to stop drug- and gunrunning by high officials in the government. Through their combined efforts, they expose the conspiracy and become uneasy friends.

DeMatteis, J. M., Mike Zech, John Beatty, et al. *Captain America: Deathlok Lives*. New York: Marvel, 1993. ISBN: 0785100199. Reprints *Captain America 286–288*.

Luther Manning's clone goes back in time to find his counterpart, Deathlok. He and Captain America find a programmed Deathlok at the Brand Corporation. The clone merges with Deathlok, and goes into the future with Captain America to stop the cybernetic Hellinger from destroying all human life.

Ennis, Garth, Derick Robertson, Jimmy Palmiotti, et al. *Fury*. New York: Marvel, 2002. ISBN: 0785108785. Reprints *Fury Vol. 3: 1–6*.

Nick Fury finds that now, in an era of political correctness, bureaucrats run S.H.I.E.L.D. When a political coup occurs on Napoleon Island, Fury and his team of soldiers try to stop it.

This series, which has been critically acclaimed by *Rolling Stone* as a "cool comic," is intended for adult audiences. It contains a lot of violence and "adult" language.

Gibbons Dave, Lee Weeks, Tom Palmer, et al. *Captain America Vol. 4: Cap Lives*. New York: Marvel, 2004. ISBN: 0785113185. Reprints *Captain America Vol. 4: 17–20; Tales of Suspense 66*.

The Red Skull takes over from Hitler to become the Fuehrer of the World. New York is now New Berlin. The Skull asks Captain America to be his partner, and offers to give him the state of California. However, Captain America refuses to help the Skull, and—along with Reed Richards, Stephen Strange, Frank Castle, Nick Fury and other Marvel heroes—becomes part of the underground resistance to the Nazis. It turns out that Bucky was not killed in World War II, and is the leader of the resistance. Victor Von Doom creates a time machine for the Skull, and the

Red Skull also plans to become the absolute ruler of time.

This is a "what if" story that has Captain America revived, in 1964, not by the Avengers, but by the Nazis. It is a well-written and beautifully illustrated alternative-universe story. The book also includes the origin of the Red Skull, written by Lee/Kirby, and is recommended as one of the best Captain America stories ever published.

Gruenwald, Mark, Kieron Dwyer, Danny Bulanadi, et al. *Captain America: The Bloodstone Hunt.* New York: Marvel, 1993. ISBN: 0871359723. Reprints *Captain America 357–364.*

Baron Zemo's son and several hired supervillains search the earth for fragments of the Bloodstone, so that Zemo can revive his dead father. Captain America, and his former foe Diamondback also search for the fragments, to stop Zemo. Cross Bones, an employee of the Red Skull, trails both parties. Captain America and Diamondback encounter the Living Mummy, and Zemo falls into a volcano. Diamondback is almost killed, and Captain America comes to her aid, only to find that he is in a trap.

Gruenwald, Mark, Ron Lim, Danny Bulanadi, et al. *Captain America: Streets of Poison.* New York: Marvel, 1994. ISBN: 07851005 71. Reprints *Captain America 372–378.*

A blast in a warehouse full of the drug called "ICE" causes Captain America's blood to be over filled with the Super Soldier serum and ICE. He starts a one-person crusade against the drug pushers, and alienates all his friends in the process. He even goes so far as to expel Black Widow from the Avengers. His friends have to intervene to get Captain America to realize that he has a problem. He has a blood transfusion, which takes the Super Soldier serum out of his blood. When the Red Skull and Kingpin vie for control of the drug trade in New York City, there are casualties on both sides, and Kingpin and the Skull have a fistfight to decide who controls. Wilson Fisk beats the Red Skull with his bare hands. Captain America and Bullseye fight. Captain America beats Dardevil, nearly killing him. Crossbones discovers who Daredevil is, but doesn't really care, and Diamondback is shot.

This book has an introduction by Mark Gruenwald and an afterword by Ralph Macchio. It is one of the best Captain America stories published in book form.

Harras, Bob, Paul Neary, Kim DeMulder, et al. *Nick Fury vs. S.H.I.E.L.D.* New York: Marvel, 1989. ISBN: 087135554X. Reprints *Nick Fury vs. S.H.I.E.L.D., 1–6.*

When he learns about a special project called Delta, Nick Fury is convinced that a menacing force has infiltrated S.H.I.E.L.D. Fury is declared a traitor by the ruling council, and tries to escape. S.H.I.E.L.D.

is controlled by a group of androids who belong to a bizarre religious cult. When Clay Quaterman dies, he is resurrected as an android, and he turns on S.H.I.E.L.D. whose old enemies, Hydra and A.I.M., also are controlled by the ruling council.

This is an excellent spy thriller.

Hogan, Peter, Leonardo Manco, et al. *Captain America/Nick Fury: The Otherworld War.* New York: Marvel, 2001.

This direct edition is in graphic novel format. It is set during World War II, and presents a tale in which Captain America, Bucky, and Sgt. Fury, along with his Howling Commandos, must do battle in the heart of Nazi territory. It includes encounters with the Ancient One, Dormammu, and the Red Skull.

Kirby, Jack, Frank Giacoia, John Romita, et al. *Captain America and the Falcon: Madbomb.* New York: Marvel, 2004. ISBN: 07851155 79. Reprints *Captain America Vol. 1: 193–200.*

A group of separatists, who want America to be ruled by the rich elite, develop a mind-controlling bomb to be set off during the bicentennial. Captain America and the Falcon infiltrate the underground world set up by elite ruler William Taurey. Captain America and Falcon participate in a barbaric sport, in which teams fight to the death to win a pot of gold. Captain America reveals his identity as Steve Rogers to the daughter of the scientist who created the madbomb. One of Captain America's ancestors, also named Steve Rogers, fought during the Revolutionary War and killed a Tory, one of Taurey's relatives.

In this book, Kirby presents his vision of the world of 1984. Highly recommended.

Kirby, Jack, Joe Simon, et al. *Captain America: The Classic Years Vol. 1.* New York: Marvel, 1998. ISBN: 078510660X. Reprints *Captain America Comics 1–5.*

This volume presents Captain America and his pal Bucky Barnes in their original adventures against the Nazis, from comics' the Golden Age. In addition to Captain America's origin story, this collection contains tales of fights with Nazi spies and saboteurs, including Sando, the Oriental Giants, the Unholy Legion, and the Hunchback of Hollywood. Of course, Captain America and Bucky foil all of their evil plans. A meeting with Hitler, and the first appearance of the Red Skull, who is revealed to be the industrialist George Maxon, and who is seemingly killed, are also included. Naturally, the Red Skull comes back to continue his reign of death and terror. One interesting episode takes place when Steve Rogers and Bucky are working as extras in a movie, in which a deformed Hunchback is killing folks. This movie features the Hollywood star Goris Barloff, and when Bucky is hurt, he is taken to a hospital where all is not what it seems to be, where horrible experiments are being performed.

Kirby, Jack, Joe Simon, et al. *Captain America: The Classic Years Vol. 2.* New York: Marvel, 2000. ISBN: 0785107436. Reprints *Captain America Comics 6–10.*

In Volume 2, Captain America and Bucky still fight Nazis and spies, but more emphasis is on their solving seemingly supernatural murders. In this book they also continue to assist FBI agent Betty Ross who begins to suspect the connection between Captain America and Steve Rogers. Some of the ghouls they expose include the Camera Fiend; Fang; the Black Talon Man, who could not die; Black Witch; and the White Death. There is an Agatha Christie–like murder mystery, "The Strange Case of Who Killed Doctor Vardoff," and the Sherlock Holmes–like mystery, "The Phantom Hound of Cardiff Moor." Captain America exposes a female German spy who he sends back to Germany, saying, "Your kind don't deserve to be in a free land." The Red Skull appears in an episode in which impostors of Captain America and Bucky are at a carnival, swindling people out of their money; the Red Skull believes them to be the real thing.

Kraft, David Anthony, Stan Lee, Jack Kirby, et al. *Captain America: The Secret Story of Marvel's Star-Spangled Super Hero.* Chicago: Children's Press, 1981. ISBN: 0516024116 (trd); 0824980123 (pbk). Reprints *Avengers 4, Tales of Suspense 81, Captain America 250.*

This book combines narrative and graphic text to explain the origin and life of Captain America, retold in a modern context. In it, Captain America outwits the Red Skull who has the Cosmic Cube, and joins the Avengers. President Franklin D. Roosevelt gives Cap a new shield. There also is a picture of Captain America in front of the Declaration of Independence.

Lee, Stan, Jack Kirby, Jim Steranko, et al. *Captain America: Sentinel of Liberty.* New York: Simon and Schuster, 1979. ISBN: 0671252 313 (trd); 0671252321 (pbk). Reprints *Captain America Comics 3; Avengers 4; Tales of Suspense 59, 63, 79–81; Captain America 110, 122.*

This collection of narrative essays and graphic text features the origin story of Captain America, and a reprint of Stan Lee's "Captain America Foils the Traitor's Revenge," the first short story he ever wrote for Marvel. It also contains essays in which Captain America is revived after being suspended in ice; he joins the Avengers; the Red Skull returns and has the Cosmic Cube; Captain America meets the Hulk for the first time; he allows Rick Jones to wear Bucky's old costume and fight against Madame Hydra; and battles with the Scorpion.

Lee, Stan, Alex Ross, Jim Steranko, et al. *Captain America: Red White and Blue.* New York: Marvel, 2002. ISBN: 078511033X.

Reprints *Marvel Fanfare 18; Captain America Vol. 1: 111, Tales of Suspense 66; Captain America Marvel Knights 1.*

This is a special volume commemorating Captain America's sixtieth anniversary. Most of the twenty stories in it were composed just for this volume. The credits read like a who's who of modern comics, and the stories range from Captain America's adventures in World War II, to the attacks on September 11, 2001. One story sets Captain America in the fifties, fighting Communism. The only thing missing from this volume is an original Jack Kirby/Joe Simon story from the 1940s. This is a deluxe hardcover book.

Mackie, Howard, Lee Weeks, Al Williamson, et al. *Captain America Ghost Rider: Fear.* New York: Marvel, 1992. ISBN: 0871359472.

Captain America and Ghost Rider go up against a savage killer known as the Scarecrow who makes his victims deal with the fears lurking inside of them. Scarecrow kidnaps Stacy, thinking she is his mother, and stuffs her with straw. Ghost Rider is still considered a villain by the police, but Captain America knows that he is not a villain.

Mills, Tarpe, Tom Fagan, Robert K. Wiener. *Miss Fury.* Cambridge, MA: Archival Press, 1979. ISBN: 0915822318. Reprints Marvel/ Timely's *Miss Fury 1.*

At first, Marla Drake, a wealthy singer-socialite, who starts fighting crime because she is bored, is considered a villain. She ends up foiling a conspiracy between Baroness Erica Von Kampf and General Bruno who want to obtain vital information that will help the Third Reich. Marla confides in her maid Francine and her doorman Cappy, who know that she is Miss Fury. She helps stop the spread of Acrothorium, a chemical that denigrates any metal with which it comes in contact, and which the Third Reich wants. Miss Fury fights a doppelganger who sports her costume with a cape.

This collection reprints what were originally newspaper comic strips, but were later reprinted by Timely in an eight-issue series. Miss Fury, who was originally called the Black Fury, was created by Tarpe Mills, one of the first female comic writers and artists. The book has plenty of action and character development, and a plot that is a step above most of the Golden Age comic material. It is well worth seeking out.

Morales, Robert, Chris Bachalo, Time Townsend, et al. *Captain America Vol. 5: Homeland.* New York: Marvel, 2004. ISBN: 0785113967. Reprints *Captain America Vol. 4: 21–28.*

Captain America is brought in to be an impartial judge for the trial of an antiwar, Muslim activist, who is accused of terrorist activities against the United States. A group of real terrorists kidnap the accused terrorists, and go to Cuba, where numerous biological weapons are stored. Captain America, Nick Fury, and the Cuban military are brought in to find the terrorists. Captain America meets Fidel Castro. He is asked to run for vice president, and declines. Along with Iron Man, Captain America finds a toy from the future. This toy can bend realities, and is highly destructive. The daughter of Isaiah Bradley, Becky Barnes, who is from another reality, fights Steve Rogers's new girlfriend, and his new gal dumps him. The origin of Bucky is retold in this book.

Morales, Robert, Kyle Baker, Wes Abbot, et al. *Truth: Red White and Black Vol. 1.* New York: Marvel, 2004. ISBN: 0785110720. Reprints *Truth: Red White and Black 1–7.*

Before Steve Rogers became Captain America, black soldiers were injected with the Super Soldier serum, in order to test it before it was tested on white soldiers. Many of the soldiers died from the side effects. One young black man, Isaiah, who manages to tolerate the serum, dons a prototype Captain America costume. When Isaiah is shipped over to Germany to fight the Nazis, he comes across a concentration camp in Scharzebittle, Germany, in October 1942. After he survives a gassing of the Jews, the Nazis take him to Hitler. Even though Hitler intends to stab Isaiah in the back because he is of "an inferior race," Hitler tries to get Isaiah to join the Nazi cause. However, Isaiah escapes, and his wife tells the story of the black Super Soldier program to Captain America, who seeks to find the whole truth behind this conspiracy. As a result of the serum, Isaiah has the mental ability of a child, and Captain America gives Isaiah's Captain America costume back to him.

This volume puts a new spin on the story of Captain America's origins. According to Robert Morales, one of the inspirations for *Truth* was the Tuskegee Project, which was under the control of the U.S. Public Health Service, from 1932 through 1972. This program, which turned out to be a tragedy, dealt with black men who had syphilis. In this book, Morales creates his own version of events that took place in that project, and provides a one-sided, fictionalized look at what life was like when the American society was "colored" and "white." The book also has an "historical" appendix, written by Morales, in which he documents selected parts of his story in order to support his version. Paired with a volume that presents a factual picture of life during those years, this might be useful in a classroom. In any event, *The Truth* deserves a place in academic and public libraries.

Nicieza, Fabian, Kevin Maguire, Steve Carr, et al. *The Adventures of Captain America: Sentinel of Liberty 1–4.* New York: Marvel, 1991–1992. ISBN: 0871358115 (Vol. 1): 0871358123 (Vol. 2): 0871358131 (Vol. 3): 087135814X (Vol. 4).

Steve Rogers and a group of four candidates, including one African American, are tested for their ability to participate in Project Rebirth. Rogers is injected with the serum, and becomes Super Soldier Captain America. Adolph Hitler wants the formula for the serum in order to create his own army, and he uses the Red Skull to capture Captain America. The Skull and Captain America fight in a stadium, in front of Hitler. The woman with whom Rogers falls in love is actually a Nazi spy known as Agent X. Captain America adopts the Army mascot, Bucky Barnes, as his partner.

This is another retelling of Captain America's origin story, which takes place at the start of World War II.

Olshevsky, George, Tony Frutti, Jim Steranko, et al. *Marvel Comics Index 8A: Heroes from Tales of Suspense Book 1: Captain America.* Ontario: G&T Enterprises 1979. ISBN: 0943348501 (Marvel Index Set).

This volume contains the history and synopsis of Captain America up to 1979, including his origins in the nineteen forties. Titles that are indexed include *Yellow Claw, Tales of Suspense, Captain America, Captain America Annuals, Giant Size Captain America,* and *Marvel Treasury Edition Captain America.* There is a personnel cross-index included.

Priest, Christopher, Joe Bennett, Robert Kirkman, et al. *Avengers Disassembled: Captain America.* New York: Marvel, 2004. ISBN: 0785116486. Reprints *Captain America and the Falcon 5–7; Captain America 29–32.*

The Falcon is arrested for violating national security. Captain America and the Falcon get a blood sample from Luke Cage. They want to synthesize a "super serum" patch for the captured new Super Soldier who looks an awful lot like Bucky. Captain America and the Scarlet Witch start to have an affair, but it could all be in Captain America's mind. Captain America takes down Mr. Hyde and rescues a prominent senator and presidential hopeful from the clutches of Hydra. He meets his former lover Diamondback who helps him on these missions. They are captured by the Cobra and the serpent society. Diamondback is actually working with the Red Skull, but when she refuses to kill Captain America, the Skull breaks her neck. When Captain America and the Skull fight, Captain America is beaten, almost to a pulp. Batroc threatens to blow up a football stadium, and Nick Fury, Modok, Yellowjacket, Jonah Jameson, and Iron Man make appearances.

Nothing is what it appears to be in this book. The book includes cover sketches by Dave Johnson.

Priest, Christopher, Bart Sears, Rob Hunter, et al. *Captain America and the Falcon Vol. 1: Two Americas.* New York: Marvel, 2004. ISBN: 0785114246. Reprints *Captain America and the Falcon 1–4.*

The Falcon goes to Cuba to save reporter-activist Leila Tylor who was about to expose the dealings of a drug cartel to the U.S. government. She has also found a special type of virus that Uncle Sam wants back. A "new" Captain America—bred in a lab with a new version of serum,—is also in Cuba. He was approached by "Spooks," shortly after the Oklahoma City bombings. This version of Cap is extremely right-wing, and has no problem killing for God and country. The two Captain Americas go head to head in a titanic battle. The Falcon's Redwing is hurt. Scarlet Witch, Nick Fury, Yellowjacket, and Iron Man make cameo appearances.

The volume contains a cover gallery.

Raab, Ben, John Cassaday, Dave Stewart et al. *Union Jack.* New York: Marvel, 2002. ISBN: 078510934X. Reprints *Union Jack 1–3.*

The third Union Jack, Joey Chapman, fights against a vampire group that is in search of the Holy Grail in order to extend their powers. Chapman's best friend, Kenneth Crichton, is turned into a vampire, and is forced to fight. The late Baron Blood's baroness is a master vampire who shatters the Holy Grail and kills her clan in the process. Crichton dons the costume of his great uncle Baron Blood.

This is an excellent story, starring a little-known Marvel character.

Rieber, John Ney, Chuck Austen, Trevor Hairsine, et al. *Captain America Vol. 2: The Extremists.* New York: Marvel, 2003. ISBN: 0785111026. Reprints *Captain America Vol. 4: 7–11.*

After he reveals his identity, Steve Rogers settles into a regular neighborhood. He finds himself at odds with Nick Fury and S.H.I.E.L.D. when several agents, including Barricade, try to capture him. However, Captain America is deceived because none of the agents who try to capture him are in good standing with the agency. He ends up working with Fury to rein in a former ally, Redpath. Redpath, a Native American, wants the United States to pay for the past genocide of his people. Since Redpath can make hurricanes and tornados, Captain America calls on Thor to help defeat him. Clones of Captain America and Bucky were being made, right under Captain America's nose, without the sanction of S.H.I.E.L.D.

This volume is recommended.

Rieber, John Ney, John Cassaday, Dave Stewart, et al. *Captain America Vol. 1: The New Deal.* New York: Marvel, 2003. ISBN: 07851 09781. (trd); 0785111018 (pbk). Reprints *Captain America Vol. 4: 1–6.*

Captain America tries to help survivors after the 9/11 attack, and vows to fight terrorists. Fury tries to get Captain America to stop helping the survivors of 9/11, and join him on a mission. Captain America tells him to go by himself. When the tiny town of Centerville is held hostage by terrorists, Captain America goes to rescue the hostages and fight the terrorists. He appears on live television, talking about killing the terrorists, and tells the world that he's Steve Rogers. He goes to Dresden to fight another terrorist group. Whenever Captain America appears, mysterious tags with strange technology, seem to show up on the terrorists.

This volume has an introduction written by Max Allan Collins, an original script, and a character study of Captain America, by John Cassaday. It contains reprints of various *Wizard* Captain America covers.

Robinson, James, Colin MacNiel, Richard Starkings, et al. *Tales of Suspense featuring Iron Man and Captain America: Men and Machines.* New York: Marvel, 1995. Reprints *Tales of Suspense Vol. 2: 1.*

Iron Man and Captain America are brought in by Nick Fury to help take down a terrorist organization known as D.A.N.T.E., whose members are former East German secret police. The terrorists have their own army of "iron men" who threaten the security of the world. D.A.N.T.E. captures Captain America; Captain America and Iron Man put aside their differences, and work and fight together.

This is from the Marvel Select imprint, with a glossy cover.

Spillane, Mickey, Jack Kirby, Carl Burgos, Joe Simon, et al. *The Golden Age of Marvel Comics Vol. 2.* New York: Marvel, 1999. ISBN: 0785107134. Reprints *Marvel Mystery Comics 1, 13, 23, 26, 27; Daring Mystery Comics 1; Captain America Comics 1; Red Raven Comics 1; U.S.A Comics 1; All Winners Comics 1; Comedy Comics 9.*

This wonderful collection of Timely/Marvel superhero stories from the Golden Age of the 1940s includes stories of the origins of the original Human Torch, Fiery Mask, Red Raven, the original Vision, the Whizzer, Captain America and Bucky. Other characters included in this volume are Hurricane, Tusk, Citizen V, Black Marvel, the Fin, and the Sub-Mariner. In most of the stories, the heroes are fighting Nazis, and in one Captain America fights zombies who are in service of the Nazis. Other stories have a *noir,* hardboiled—crime aspect. The weirdest story is one about Citizen V who works for the British against the Nazis, and gets captured. The introduction is by novelist Mickey Spillane. This volume is well worth seeking.

Steranko, Jim, Joe Sinnott, Frank Giacoia, et al. *Nick Fury: Who Is Scorpio?* New York: Marvel, 2000. ISBN: 0785107665. Reprints *Nick Fury: Agent of S.H.I.E.L.D. 1–6.*

In this book Nick Fury faces an operative known as Scorpio in a tale that can only be described as a psychedelic spy thriller. Scorpio infiltrates the Las Vegas S.H.I.E.L.D. complex; Jimmy Woo becomes a S.H.I.E.L.D. agent; the Centurius plans to build his own Garden of Eden, and to destroy all of humanity, in order to start over; Nick Fury enlists the aid of the Monster movie crew, to help him defeat the Centurius; Fury uncovers a modern Nazi underground base, in a tale that is similar to Arthur Conan Doyle's *Hound of the Baskervilles*, featuring Sherlock Holmes; and Scorpio, posing as Nick Fury, engages in a game to the death with a Life Model Decoy that actually *is* Fury. This is Steranko's masterwork.

Steranko, Jim, Joe Sinnott, Sam Rosen, et al. *Marvel Presents Captain America: Collector's Edition.* London: Marvel Comics International, 1981. ISBN: 0862270391.

In a fit of anger, the Hulk throws Rick Jones. Jones dons Bucky's old costume in order to help Captain America do battle with Hydra. Captain America's identity as Steve Rogers becomes known, but Captain America fakes his own death, so his secret identity remains.

Steranko, Jim, Roy Thomas, Stan Lee, et al. *Nick Fury: Agent of Shield.* Marvel Comics: New York, 2000. ISBN: 0785107479. Reprints *Strange Tales 150–168.*

The Supreme Hydra infiltrates S.H.I.E.L.D. and poses as a trusted agent. His various attempts to kill Nick Fury fail, and Fury ends up following him to the Hydra base for an action-packed showdown. The Supreme Hydra is revealed to be Fury's old Nazi nemesis Baron Strucker who nearly kills Fury with his Satan Claw. Captain America and Fury help FBI agent Jimmy Woo against Golden-Age villain Yellow Claw. Woo is in love with the Claw's niece, Suwan, who nobly sacrifices herself to save others. Fury has a terrible dream about aliens who plan to destroy earth. Dr. Doom, Mr. Fantastic, the Thing and the Prime Mover make cameos.

This volume—in which a super spy fights the evil Hydra hordes—is Marvel's answer to James Bond. It features groundbreaking work from artist/writer Jim Steranko, who gave comic art its psychedelic and pop-art feel. The book includes a detailed schematic of the Helicarrier, a cover gallery, and Steranko's original try out pages from *Strange Tales.* It is highly recommended.

Stern, Roger, John Byrne, Joe Rubinstein, et al. *Captain America: War and Remembrance.* New York: Marvel, 1990. ISBN: 0871356570. Reprints *Captain America 247–255.*

Captain America faces some of his most infamous villains including Dragon Man, Batroc, and Mr. Hyde, who all team up together, and he faces a difficult decision about whether he should run for president. Baron Blood returns, and it is up to Captain America to stop him. Nick Fury, FDR, the Beast, the original Union Jack, and the Invaders all make appearances.

This book also contains a Captain America origin story and detailed introductions by Roger Stern and Jim Salicrup.

Thomas, Roy, Bill Everett, Jack Kirby, et al. *The Golden Age of Marvel Comics Vol. 1.* New York: Marvel, 1997. ISBN: 0785105646. Reprints *Motion Pictures Funnies Weekly 1; Marvel Comics 1; Marvel Mystery Comics 8, 17, 25, 42; Captain America Comics 7, 22; All-Winners Comics 12; Astonishing 5; Venus 18; Young Men Comics 24, 26; Black Knight 2; Yellow Claw 3.*

This is a wonderful collection of reprints from the 1940s and 50s, the Golden Age of Comics, when Marvel was Timely/Atlas Comics. It includes the infamous team of Sub-Mariner and the original Human Torch against the Nazis, as well as the very first Sub-Mariner story. It also contains episodes in which the Red Skull returns from the dead; Bucky poses as a Nazi Youth, is found out, and Captain America frees him; Namor discovers an underwater Nazi base; the original Black Knight fights some Vikings; the Yellow Claw perfects a way to shrink men in order to get vital secrets, but agent Jimmy Woo stops him; and Captain America is accused of becoming a traitor and joining the reds. This volume includes the complete reprint of *Young Men 24*, which relaunched Captain America, the Human Torch, Namor, and Captain America's main nemesis, the Red Skull. Other stories feature the original Vision, the original Angel, Venus, and Marvel Boy.

Thomas, Roy, Bill Finger, et al. *Timely Comics Presents: All Winners Comics.* New York: Marvel, December 1999. Reprints *All Winners 19.*

In this edition, Captain America, Bucky, Toro, Human Torch, the Whizzer, and Ms. America all band together to fight the evil villain Isba who is threatening the world with an atomic bomb. Roy Thomas provides a history of the All Winners Squad, the very first Marvel team, along with some Golden Age historical information about Timely Comics. This is a very nice edition.

Waid, Mark, Ron Garney, Dale Eaglesham, et al. *Captain America: To Serve and Protect.* New York: Marvel, 2002. ISBN: 0785108386. Reprints *Captain America Vol. 3: 1–7.*

Captain America returns from an alternate universe to discover that in Japan, during a showing of the Captain America movie, a secret group of terrorists plan to kill innocents. Lady Deathstrike and Captain America duke it out. Cap-mania has spread throughout the world, and Captain America does not know how to react to such hero worship. He loses his shield in the ocean, and when he finds a replica of his original shield at the Smithsonian, he starts to use it. The Supreme Hydra is actually a Skrull. The Skrulls capture Captain America and pose as him, giving a press conference and telling people to watch out for America's enemies. This causes a witch hunt in which many innocent lives are ruined. Captain America and Thor share a milk shake. The Fantastic Four, the Avengers, Bill Clinton, and Namor make appearances.

Waid, Mark, Ron Garney, Scott Koblis, et al. *Captain America: A Man Without a Country*. New York: Marvel, 1998. ISBN: 0785 105948. Reprints *Captain America 450–453*.

Captain America is framed for a crime he did not commit. His American citizenship is revoked and his costume is taken away. Captain America asks for the aid of Dr. Doom to help stop a war between Moldavia and the United States.

Waid, Mark, Ron Garney, Scott Koblish, et al. *Captain America: Operation Rebirth*. New York: Marvel, 1999. ISBN: 0785102191. Reprints *Captain America Vol. 1: 445–448*.

The Super Soldier serum which made Steve Rogers into Captain America is also killing him. His greatest enemy, the Red Skull, revives him using an injection of new serum from his blood. Captain America teams up with the Skull to stop an evil group from using the Cosmic Cube to build a new Reich. Captain America's old flame Sharon Carter goes along for the ride. When they raid a complex, Captain America saves the Skull from being shot. Using the Cube, the Skull puts Captain America in a bizarre world in which Bucky and he are still fighting Nazis. In this world, Captain America's mother is still alive, and the original Human Torch, Namor, Bill Clinton, the Thing, and Quicksilver make cameos. Captain America figures out that everything is false, and breaks out of the loop; he takes the Cube from the Skull, and the Red Skull is absorbed into the Cube.

Mark Waid, Ron Garney and Ralph Macchio each give a brief introduction.

Conan/Kull

I have nothing against a few lusty nights, woman.—*Conan*

Kraar, Don, Gary Kwapisz, Art Nichols, et al. *Conan the Barbarian: The Witch Queen of Acheron*. New York: Marvel, 1985. ISBN: 0871350858.

A prostitute sells out Conan to the military, and he proceeds to makes a total mess of the town he is visiting. Eventually they capture him and are about to put him to death, but the prince finds a gold coin on Conan, and wants more of the treasure. Conan agrees to take them to the lost mines of Acheron. Conan helps the prince against a warring tribe that is also after the treasure. They encounter a dead witch who oversees the mine, and pull the sword from her heart. The witch's spirit enters the prince's concubine. They encounter the reptilian scorpions' creatures that are the protectors of the mines. (*Marvel Graphic Novel 19*)

Kraar, Don, John Severin, Marie Severin, et al. *Conan the Reaver*. New York: Marvel, 1987. ISBN: 0871352893.

Conan becomes a guardsman for a king from whom he wants to steal treasure. The city is besieged by the Cult of the Red Mist which sacrifices innocent people to an octopus-like monster known as the Mother of Darkness. While attempting to steal the keys to the treasure room, Conan is caught by the king. In exchange for his life, he promises to make sure that the king's wife and illegitimate, adopted son are safe from those who would usurp the king. Conan saves the queen and defeats the Mother of Darkness. (*Marvel Graphic Novel 28*)

Moench, Doug, Paul Gulacy, Gary Martin, et al. *Conan The Barbarian: The Skull of Set*. New York: Marvel, 1989. ISBN: 0871355795.

Conan is hired to transfer a prince's precious jewels and money. He is caught right in the middle of a group of warring tribes and is pursued by Hillman on one side and soldiers on the other. He rescues a group of travelers which includes a fat merchant, an aristocrat and his wife, and the priestess of Mitra. They end up stranded on a sacred ground of Set. The Mitra priestess tries to stop a priest of Set from unleashing the demon Khorus upon the world. Statues rise, and Khorus is resurrected using the Skull of Set. Much to his displeasure, Conan also has to use the Skull to destroy Khorus. (*Marvel Graphic Novel 53*)

Olshevsky, George, Tony Frutti, Tim Conrad, et al. *The Marvel Comics Index 2: Conan*. Ontario: G&T Enterprises, 1976. ISBN: 0943 348501 (Marvel Index Set).

This volume includes histories of Conan, Ka-Zar, and Kull. The publications indexed include *Conan the Barbarian; King Size Conan, Savage Sword of Conan, Savage Sword of Conan Annua, Ka-Zar Lord of the Jungle, Kull the Conqueror, Kull the Destroyer, Kull and the Barbarians, Savage Tales, Chamber of Chills, Chamber of Darkness, Monsters on the Prowl, Tower of Shadows, Creatures on the Loose*, and *Worlds Unknown*. The volume has cross indexes by personnel and characters, and cover galleries.

Thomas, Roy, John Buscema, Neal Adams, et al. Chronicles of Conan Vol. 6. Milwaukie,

OR: Dark Horse, 2004. ISBN: 15930727 40 Reprints Marvel's *Conan the Barbarian 35–42*.

Conan's sidekick Monkey Face is killed because of his greed for a gem, the Azure Eye of Kara-Sher. Conan saves the life of King Yildiz from a golem-like stone creature, and has an affair with Amytis, wife of Narium Bey, the king's commander of the guard. The commander is exceedingly jealous, and puts the spell of Lilitu, the Were-woman, and her husband on the barbarian. Through the intervention of an old sorcerer, Gimil-Ishbi, Conan learns how to keep the Lilitu away, but he ends up killing the old magician. Conan and the giant Juma have an adventure with the Golden Skull, in which the spirit of an old sorcerer, originally killed by King Kull, is reborn in gold through the death of another. Conan and Juma are put into slavery. When Conan and Juma take some gold, a giant slug-like creature takes after them, and, eventually absorbs the golden sorcerer. Conan fights a giant alligator monster, and meets the goddess Ishtar. He becomes enchanted by Zhadoor, and fights a gargoyle.

Roy Thomas provides an issue-by-issue commentary. He describes how, by the time he got to these issues, he finally felt comfortable writing Conan stories. He also tells how Hallmark Minting offered an official, bronze medallion of Conan, the Hulk, and Spider-Man.

Thomas, Roy, John Buscema, Ken Bruzenak, et al. *Conan the Rogue*. New York: Marvel, 1991. ISBN: 0871358425.

A dwarf—the brother of the leader, Skhamgar Shah, at Fort Ghori—conspires with the vizier of a rival kingdom, Tarsu Khan, which is ruled by King Vezdigerd, to take over leadership and form an alliance. Conan foils an assassination attempt that is arranged by the vizier. When the two kings meet, it goes horribly wrong, and the nephew of the dwarf is killed by a cobra bite. War is declared, and Conan is put into the arena where he beats all of his opponents. Conan takes the Shah's daughter hostage, and manages to escape. They go to the forbidden Nightmare Swamp where they meet dinosaur- and zombie-like creatures who are under the spell of the demon Aksha Thushtra who feeds on the life of human souls. Conan's hostage becomes horribly disfigured as her soul is squeezed out of her. Conan defeats the leader of the zombies, and refuses to give his soul to the demon. (*Marvel Graphic Novel 69*)

Thomas, Roy, John Buscema, Ernie Chua, et al. *Chronicles of Conan Vol. 5: The Shadow in the Tomb and Other Stories*. Milwaukie, OR: Dark Horse, 2004. ISBN: 1593071752. Reprints Marvel's *Conan the Barbarian 27–34*.

Conan rescues a slave girl, and goes to the Gates of the Devil castle where the magical stone Blood of Bel-Hissar resides. The slave girl betrays Conan.

Conan fights with the ape god of Zembabwei, and saves another slave girl. He speaks out against the Tarim god, and almost is taken captive. He stops the sorcerer Ormraxes from performing his sinister magic, and reminisces about the time he fought his mystical shadow in a tomb after touching a cursed sword. He fights with a huge ogre, one of the Vanir, and defeats him. In the city of Wan Tengri, which is surrounded by mystical flames, Conan helps free a princess who had been taken captive by seven sorcerers. He is taken prisoner, and fights in the arena against a tiger, the gauntlet of the seven Deaths and death, disguised as woman. Death tells him how to free the princess and the city from the seven warlocks. He becomes an honorary member of Wan Tengri's Brotherhood of Thieves, gaining a sidekick in the process.

In the afterword, Roy Thomas describes the process of writing these stories, issue by issue. Most of the stories in this volume were adapted directly from Robert Howard's original stories. Thomas also adapted Norvell Page's John Prester stories, *Flame Winds* and *Sons of the Bear God*, into Conan tales.

Thomas, Roy, John Buscema, Robert Ervin Howard, et al. *Conan of the Isles*. New York: Marvel, 1988. ISBN: 0871354837.

The prophet Epemitreus visits an aging Conan in a dream. He gives up the throne of Aquilonia, and leads one last expedition to the Western Sea. People are disappearing, and Conan goes to investigate the "Red Terror." He makes an ally of the king of thieves in Ptahuacan. The people, who are the last remaining souls from Atlantis, still practice human sacrifice.

Conan is called "Amra" throughout most of the story, which is based on an original novel by L. Sprague DeCamp and Lin Carter. Chronologically, this story is Conan's last. (*Marvel Graphic Novel 42*)

Thomas, Roy, Gerry Conway, Mike Docherty, et al. *Conan The Barbarian: The Horn of Azoth*. New York: Marvel, 1990. ISBN: 0871356392.

This story is based on Roy Thomas's original screenplay for the second Conan movie, *Conan the Destroyer*. In the preface, Thomas and Conway write a very detailed explanation of how the screenplay "got lost in the shuffle." In the story, Conan has to stop the high priest Karanthes, who wants to "ravage the Hyborian Age of Man," from releasing the evil god Azoth. Conan rips the horn off of the lumbering, wicked deity to exterminate it. It is too bad this story was not used; it would have made a great movie. (*Marvel Graphic Novel 59*)

Thomas, Roy, Michael Docherty, Alfredo Alcala, et al. *Conan: The Ravagers Out of Time*. New York: Marvel, 1992. ISBN: 08713591 11.

The ancient sorcerer Rotath transports Conan and Red Sonja back into the time of King Kull. Kull had originally killed Rotath, but Rotath's essence was imbued into a gold-eating giant slug. When Conan and Kull fight, they end up with a stand-off. Kull is trying to defend his kingdom against the Ape Lords, who are under the spell of Rotath. Kull finds the day-to-day bureaucratic aspects of ruling boring, and desires some action. Both Conan and Kull have ties to the Pict sorcerer Gonar. Rotath wants to transfer his essence into both Conan and Kull. Although Conan and Kull start out as adversaries, they end up as colleagues, fighting a greater enemy. Red Sonja has the hots for Kull, even though they are transferred back to their time in the future.) (*Marvel Graphic Novel 73*)

Thomas, Roy, Barry Windsor-Smith, John Buscema, et al. *Chronicles of Conan Vol. 4: The Song of Red Sonja and Other Stories*. Milwaukie, OR: Dark Horse, 2004. ISBN: 159307025X. Reprints Marvel's *Conan the Barbarian 23–26*; *Savage Tales 2–3*.

Conan fights the slayer known as the Vulture, and meets Red Sonja for the first time. Conan and Sonja seek to steal some jewels, but one of the jewels is enchanted with a monster serpent. The Wizard, Kharam Akkad, tries to kill Conan because he saw a vision of Conan killing him, in a magic mirror that King Kull once encountered. The True Tarum, a holy man, turns out to be nothing more than a bumbling idiot, and he is killed. Conan and his female companion Valeria end up in a mystical city where two groups of inhabitants are fighting.

In the afterword, Roy Thomas gives a description of his work on the issues, and tells the story behind *Conan 22*.

Thomas, Roy, Barry Windsor-Smith, Robert Ervin Howard, et al. *Chronicles of Conan Vol. 1: The Tower of the Elephant and Other Stories*. Milwaukee, OR: Dark Horse, 2003. ISBN: 1593070160. Reprints Marvel's *Conan the Barbarian 1–8*.

Conan is enslaved by the Beast Men, and starts a rebellion to free the human slaves. He meets the Grim Grey War God, Borri, and frees the alien Elephant god from the sorcerer who is holding him captive. The daughter of the wizard Zukala, who terrorizes a village in the form of a tiger, is in love with Conan, and refuses to hurt him, even on the command of her father. Conan kills several supernatural gods, including the bat-like Night-God; the Medusa-like Lurker Within, who is servant of Thoth-Amon; and the Serpent God, who uses zombies to protect its treasures.

In this volume, the first Conan comics are reprinted in new, re-mastered color. Roy Thomas writes a personal remembrance of issues 1–8, and about how Marvel first started publishing Conan books.

Thomas, Roy, Barry Windsor-Smith, Gil Kane, et al. *Chronicles of Conan Vol. 3: The Monster of the Monoliths and Other Stories*. Milwaukee, OR: Dark Horse, 2003. ISBN: 1593070241. Reprints Marvel's *Conan the Barbarian 14–15*; *17–22*.

Conan meets Michael Moorcock's Elric of Melnibone during an inter-dimensional war against the Green Empress. Conan befriends the redheaded Fafnir, and they help to dethrone Gothan, the Priest of the Dark God, at the bequest of a scheming princess who betrays them to the bat-like Dark God. Conan and Fafnir go to war for the Turans against the city of Makkalet. Fafnir has his arm cut off, and is left for dead. Conan fights the Black Hound of Makkalet's high priest, and goes up against the froglike Monster of the Monolith.

Roy Thomas writes his personal remembrances of these issues, including the enlistment of Gil Kane.

Thomas, Roy, Barry Windsor-Smith, Sam Rosen, et al. *Chronicles of Conan Vol. 2: Rogues in the House and Other Stories*. Milwaukee, OR: Dark Horse, 2003. ISBN: 1593070233. Reprints Marvel's *Conan The Barbarian 9–13*; *16*.

Conan's concubine Jenna betrays him while in a Corinthian city state. Conan breaks out of prison and throws Jenna into a pile of feces. He fights against the Man Beast, Thank, and kills the Red Priest, Nabonidus. Conan's friend Burgun is hanged, and Conan goes to the priest who betrayed his friend, and the bull-god Anu is summoned. He fights the Lovecraftian Octopus, Dweller in the Dark, and the Spider God. The Frost Giant's daughter tries to lure Conan to his death, but he ends up killing her brothers instead.

Roy Thomas's personal remembrances of these issues appear in this volume.

Zelenetz, Alan, Com Vincent, Michael Heisler, et al. *Kull: The Vale of Shadow*. New York: Marvel, 1989. ISBN: 0871355582.

King Kull is near death after being wounded in a war against the Kingdom of Commoria. His loyal kinsmen tell one another about various adventures they have had with the king, including some of their first meetings. Kull fights in a gladiatorial arena, against both a bull and a fighter. Death appears to Kull as a beautiful, green woman, who is trying to get him to join her. Kull makes love to her, but his will to live is too strong for death to take away. (*Marvel Graphic Novel 47*)

Cosmic Heroes and Supernaturals/Blade, Captain Marvel, Dr. Strange, Dracula, Ghost Rider, Silver Surfer, Thanos, et al.

No power is mindless, power is cruel! There must be reason beyond the madness.—*The Silver Surfer*

The military fears what it does not understand.—*The Silver Surfer*

knowledge is the mightiest power of all—*Dr. Strange*

Andreyko, Marc, P. Craig Russell, Lovern Kindercrski, et al. *Dr. Strange: What Is It That Disturbs You Stephen?* New York: Marvel, 1997. ISBN: 0785105883.

Dr. Strange goes to the mystical realm of Ditkopolis where his servant Wong has been taken captive. He meets two sisters, Celeste and Electra, both of whom are sorceresses. Electra tries to get Strange to become her King, and when Strange refuses, she tries to overpower him with evil magic. Strange defeats her and frees Wong.

Andreyko, Marc, Bart Sears, Mark Pennington, et al. *Blade: Sins of the Father.* New York: Marvel, 1998. ISBN: 078510707X.

Blade helps a vampire woman destroy her father who is a master vampire. She betrays Blade and seeks power for herself. Blade ends up on a cross-like stake. He kills the lady vampire, and her lover Deacon Frost makes an appearance.

These events take place just before the first *Blade* movie.

Byrne, John, Rick Taylor, Electric Pickle, et al. *Darkseid vs. Galactus: The Hunger.* New York: Marvel/DC, 1995. ISBN: 1563891824

The Silver Surfer is still the herald of Galactus who came to Apokolips to feed. Darkseid defends his world. Orion battles with the Surfer. Galactus finds Darkseid's world devoid of life force.

Chariton, Dan, Stacy Weiss, L. Medina, et al. *Silver Surfer Vol. 1: Communion.* New York: Marvel, 2004. ISBN: 0785113193. Reprints *Silver Surfer Vol. 4: 1–6.*

The Silver Surfer is abducting children all over the world to make them part of some alien experiment. One mother whose autistic child was abducted by the Surfer seeks to cosmically communicate with her child, and befriends a wealthy engineer whose son also was taken. The children learn of their cosmic powers, and are being taught how to use them by the "Greys," with the Surfer overseeing everything. This is a cosmic tale in which the Surfer goes to meet with the Singularity, or God of the Universe. Vice President Richard Cheney makes a cameo. The young autistic girl is returned to earth by the Silver Surfer.

David, Peter, Chris Cross, Ron Lim, et al. *Captain Marvel: First Contact.* New York: Marvel, 2001. ISBN: 0785107916. Reprints *Captain Marvel Vol. 3: 0–6.*

Rick Jones is bonded with Captain Mar-Vell's son Genis, and he does not want to tell his ex-wife. The "new" Captain Marvel is arrested for causing mayhem, and saving the city from threats only he can see. Jones' ex-wife Marlo is acting for a Blair-Witch–type reality show called the "Monster Tapes." The producer wants the power of the Wendigo, and wants to be a monster himself. They also encounter the Hulk, who is not very thrilled about having to fight the Wendigo. Moondragon and her father, Drax the Destroyer, both bust into Rick's apartment. Genis and Drax end up in a huge battle which takes them to the Microverse. Jarella's sister, who is actually an imposter, believes Drax is the Hulk and tricks him into fighting for her.

This volume is well-written, fun to read, and, most importantly, it is downright hilarious in parts. It contains a several-page history of Rick Jones in the Marvel Universe.

David, Peter, Chris Cross, Ivan Reis, et al. *Captain Marvel Vol. 1: Nothing to Loose.* New York: Marvel, 2003. ISBN: 0785111042. Reprints *Captain Marvel Vol. 4: 1–6.*

Genis, Captain Marvel, becomes overwhelmed with his cosmic power to see the future. He decides that he wants to go insane, and he leaves Rick Jones in the Microverse for several months. Marvel asks the Punisher to teach him, and Castle learns about when he is supposed to die. Jones becomes romantically involved with Epiphany. Genis becomes a soldier with the Kree, and dons the green costume. He appears to commit suicide just after he kills some high-ranking Krees. He visits the realm of death, and meets with his father, the original Captain Marvel, whom he brutalizes. When Eternity's son Entropy destroys the Universe and then becomes Eternity, the Universe is reshaped.

David, Peter, Kyle Hotz, Ivan Reis, et al. *Captain Marvel Vol. 2: Coven.* New York: Marvel, 2003. ISBN: 0785113061. Reprints *Captain Marvel Vol. 4: 7–12.*

While Rick Jones is trying to keep the reins on Marvel, he develops a god complex due to his cosmic awareness. Marvel goes to Asgard and is very arrogant in his approach to Norse gods. He battles with Thor and Balder. He reveals to Thor the true story of the atrocities that Odin and the Asgardians played on the Storm Giants, Sturm and Drang. After Marvel gives some cosmic powers to Coven, a convicted serial killer, Coven tries to assassinate Rick Jones. Captain Marvel sets up his own kangaroo court of justice, and in the process teaches Jones a valuable lesson. Spider-Man makes a cameo appearance.

David, Peter, Aaron Lopresti, Pat Quinn, et al. *Captain Marvel Vol. 4: Odyssey*. New York: Marvel, 2004. ISBN: 0785115307. Reprints *Captain Marvel Vol. 4: 19–25*.

Rick Jones's wife Marlo comes from the future to tell Rick that he was the reason she died, and she turns to dust in Marvel's arms. Jones sings a song about his wife, which is broadcast on television and the Internet, all over the world. In an attempt to save Marlo from dying in the future, Captain Marvel goes into the future where the Skrulls, the Kree, and the Shi'ar have taken over the Earth and are killing humans. He meets older versions of himself and his son. He frees humanity from the aliens. He keeps going into the future and meeting his son. Eventually Marvel's son takes the wristbands away from Rick Jones. In a future version of Earth in which aliens rule, Rick learns that all human knowledge came from a holographic history from Dr. Doom. Moondragon becomes indebted to Magnus. Eventually Genis realizes that he can think his son out of existence; thus all these horrible events never come to pass.

Rick Jones's comics awareness makes him realize that this run of Captain Marvel is coming to an end. This is a hilarious postmodern take that pokes fun at the comics themselves. There are many other plot twists, too numerous to mention here, but this series is highly recommended.

David, Peter, Michael Ryan, Paul Azaceta, et al. *Captain Marvel Vol. 3: Crazy Like a Fox*. New York: Marvel, 2004. ISBN: 07851134 01. Reprints *Captain Marvel Vol. 4: 13–18*.

Genis is totally insane, and threatens to destroy numerous races, including the Kree, the Skrulls, and the Shi'Ar, who he believes will be a threat to galatic peace. His mother comes back from the grave, and he battles his sister, who becomes the new Captain Marvel. Rick Jones meets several earlier versions of himself, and Genis gets him to kill himself. Marvel also meets other versions of himself.

This is a study in psychoanalysis.

DeMatteis, J.M., Dan Green, Ken Bruzenak, et al. *Doctor Strange: Into Shamballa*. New York: Marvel, 1986. ISBN: 0871351668.

The attendant at the old temple in the Himalayas gives Doctor Strange a gift, a puzzle box that was left by the Ancient One. Strange tries to solve the riddle of the box, and is transported to the mythical place, Shamballa. He is asked by the Lords of Shamballa to perform a three-part spell.

This book provides a nice insight into Strange's inner self, and includes a "trial by fire" for Strange. This is a very reflective and mystical tale. (*Marvel Graphic Novel 23*.)

Englehart, Steve, Frank Brunner, and Dick Giordano. *Dr. Strange: A Separate Reality* New York: Marvel, 2002. ISBN: 0785108 36X. Reprints *Marvel Premiere 9–10, 12–14; Dr. Strange Vol. 2: 1–2, 4–5*.

The Ancient One passes the mantle as master of the mystic arts to Dr. Strange, and then dies. Strange takes on the Living Buddha, KAA-U, and the Living Gargoyle. He accepts Clea as his disciple. Strange and his enemy Baron Mordo go to the past to seek out a powerful magician, Cagliostro, only to be deceived by Siseneg. Siseneg desires to become the overseer of the whole universe. In doing so he re-creates the universe. A fundamentalist Christian magician kidnaps Clea in an attempt to break away from Dr. Strange whom he views as evil. Strange frees the souls who have been eaten by the Soul Eater. The Eater is in the Eye of Agamotto's realm of unreality, where bizarre versions of the Defenders dwell, and reality and unreality intertwine.

Gerber, Steve, Marv Wolfman, Gene Colon, et al. *Blade II: The Official Comic Adaptation*. Marvel Comics, 2002. ISBN: 0785108971. Reprints *Blade II; Tomb of Dracula 45–53*.

Blade and Hannibal King are searching for Deacon Frost to settle vendettas with him. Frost creates a vampire clone of Blade, and they merge together in the heat of battle. Dracula wants to use a Satanist religious group to help sway the world for his objectives. He marries a woman who is pregnant with his child. Dracula actually feels love for this woman. A painting of Jesus Christ cries. Dracula fights an angel from God almighty, and wins the first round. The Silver Surfer and Dracula battle; the Surfer feebly tries to destroy Dracula. Daimon Hellstrom, the Son of Satan, makes an appearance.

This is the comic adaptation of the film *Blade II*, featuring a group of vampire-hunting vampires known as Reapers. This volume includes reprints of early Blade stories.

Giffen, Keith, Ron Lim, Al Milgrom, et al. *Thanos Vol. 5: Samaritan*. New York: Marvel, 2004. ISBN: 0785115404. Reprints *Thanos 7–12*.

Thanos turns himself into a prison where galactic prisoners are held. Here he encounters Lady Death. She tries to get him to "learn how to love" her, but Thanos more or less spurns her advances. He also encounters the Gladiator and Starlord who seek Thanos's aid. The Beyonder, the Maker, is also imprisoned. The Beyonder tries to get Thanos to remember their romantic time together, but Thanos also spurns this idea. The Beyonder, who apparently is insane, gets angry and blows up a part of the prison. Thanos and the Beyonder have another encounter in which he beats her, and she is reduced to a crying rubble. The winged and very annoying Skreet follows Thanos, and the Gladiator leaves the prison with an unwilling Starlord. A former herald of Galactus, the "Fallen One," also seeks to destroy Galactus. After an intense battle with both Thanos and Galactus, the Fallen One ends up being Thanos's herald.

Grayson, Devin, Trent Kaniuga, Danny Miki, et al. *Ghost Rider: The Hammer Lane.* New York: Marvel, 2002. ISBN: 0785109102. Reprints *Ghost Rider Vol. 3: 1–6.*

The Spirit of Vengeance once again inhabits Johnny Blaze. This time the Spirit is darker and more deadly. Sometimes Ghost Rider actually kills those the Spirit seeks. Johnny Blaze hires a hit man to kill the Ghost Rider. Of course, Ghost Rider knows what Blaze is up to, and refuses to bend. Blaze finally comes to terms with his alter ego, thinking that it is a pretty cool thing to be Ghost Rider, after all. Blaze meets a new biker chick, and off they go.

Herdling, Glen, John Buscema, Chris Ulm, et al. *Silver Surfer/Rune.* Marvel/Malibu 1995.

After a battle with Thor, Rune goes to Earth where he tracks down and steals infinity gems from their various owners. He defeats Adam Warlock and takes his gem. The Living Tribunal implores the Silver Surfer to defeat Rune and get the gems away from him, or the cosmic balance will become unbalanced. The Surfer has to contend with Deathurge before defeating Rune.

The story is continued in the comic book *Curse of Rune.* This book, which contains tales from the Ultraverse, is done in Prestige format.

Lee, Stan, John Buscema, Max Scheele, et al. *The Silver Surfer: Judgment Day.* New York: Marvel, 1988. ISBN: 0871354276 (trd) 0871356635 (pbk).

Mephisto tricks Nova into bringing Galactus to feed on worlds in which life abounds. The Silver Surfer intervenes and fights Nova. Galactus banishes the Surfer and Nova from space. Mephisto tries to trick the Surfer into giving him his soul, but the Silver Surfer suggests to Galactus that he feed on Mephisto's dark domain.

This book reunites the classic team of Stan Lee and John Buscema. (*Marvel Graphic Novel 38*)

Lee, Stan, Steve Ditko, Barry Smith, et al. *Dr. Strange: Master of the Mystic Arts.* New York: Simon and Schuster, 1979. ISBN: 0671252062 (trd); 0671248146 (pbk). Reprints *Strange Tales 111, 116, 119–120, 123,* *131–133; Amazing Spider-Man Annual 2; Marvel Premiere 3.*

Doctor Strange comes face to face with Baron Mordo. He returns to fight Nightmare and goes to the worlds "Beyond the Purple Veils." Loki tries to deceive Dr. Strange to foil Thor. Strange has to help Clea against her evil sister Shazana. Spider-Man and Dr. Strange meet for the first time, and Spider-Man is caught up in the mystical worlds. Something is disturbing the world of Dr. Strange, and not even Nightmare is willing to discuss who the culprit is. This latter story was the last story that Stan Lee wrote about Doctor Strange. The book is divided into various sections, with Stan Lee writing an introductory essay for each section. This is part of the Fireside series of Marvel reprints.

Lee, Stan, Jack Kirby, Joe Sinnott, et al. *The Silver Surfer.* New York: Simon and Schuster, 1978. ISBN: 0671228218 (trd); 06712422 53 (pbk).

Galactus tries to get the Surfer to bend to his will, and can't understand why the Surfer does not conform to his wishes. He even sends the Surfer a female love interest, Ardina, to show the him the error of his betrayal. Despite the violence shown by earthlings toward the Surfer, he affirms the right of humanity to exist.

This volume is a wonderful retelling of the Silver Surfer's battle with his creator Galactus in an effort to save Earth from destruction. It is one of the most beautifully illustrated and best-written Silver Surfer stories ever published.

Lee, Stan, Jack Kirby, Joe Sinnott, et al. *The Silver Surfer.* New York: Marvel, 1997. ISBN: 0785106529. Reprints *Silver Surfer Marvel Limited.*

This is a reprint of the 1978 Simon and Schuster Fireside book *The Silver Surfer*, annotated above, with a new introduction by Stan Lee.

Lee, Stan, Jack Kirby, Joe Sinnott, et al. *Silver Surfer: The Coming of Galactus.* New York: Marvel, 1992. ISBN: 087135957X. Reprints *Fantastic Four 48–50.*

The Watcher breaks his vow of non-interference to warn the Fantastic Four about the coming of the planet devourer, Galactus. His herald, the Silver Surfer, finds that the human race is worthy of saving, and rebels against his master. Reed Richards threatens Galactus with the Ultimate Nullifier. The Surfer is banished to Earth.

This book introduces the very first character named the Punisher, one of Galactus's minions, who almost defeats the Fantastic Four. Of all the Marvel stories I have read, this one still stands out as the favorite and most memorable from when I was a child.

Lee, Stan, Moebius, Dan Hosek, et al. *Silver Surfer: Parable.* Marvel Comics: New York,

1998. ISBN: 0871354918 (trd, Epic Comics, 1988); 0785106561. Reprints *Silver Surfer: Parable 1–2*.

In this spiritual tale the Surfer again encounters his maker Galactus, and tries to save the Earth. Galactus is made out to be a god for humanity, and even has his own priests.

Lee, Stan, Keith Pollard, Jose Rubinstein, et al. *The Silver Surfer: The Enslavers*. New York: Marvel, 1990. ISBN: 0871356171.

The Silver Surfer has to defend earth against an alien, Mrrungo-Mu, who is bent on enslaving the populace. Even Earth's most powerful super-beings cannot beat him. The Surfer uses cunning instead of brute force to defeat the alien threat. He is reunited with his love Shalla-Bal after many years of separation. (*Marvel Graphic Novel 58*)

Mackie, Howard, Andy Kubert, Joe Kubert, et al. *The Rise of the Midnight Sons*. New York: Marvel, 1992. ISBN: 0871359693. Reprints *Ghost Rider Vol. 2: 28, 31; Spirits of Vengeance 1; Morbius 1; Darkhold 1; Nightstalkers 1*.

Johnny Blaze and Ghost Rider team up with various monsters to fight against the age-old evil queen Lilith. Lilith calls forth her children to fight against the Spirits of Vengeance. Morbius's girlfriend, Martine Bancroft, tries to help him find a cure for his vampirism, but ends up getting killed. Blade and his group of monster hunters, the Nightstalkers, fight against Ghost Rider at first, but end up in an uneasy alliance with him. Dr. Strange makes several appearances.

This book is a massive crossover featuring the darker side of the Marvel Universe. It contains an interview with Howard Mackie and Tom DeFalco.

Mackie, Howard, Javier Saltares, Mark Texeira, et al. *Ghost Rider: Resurrected*. Marvel Comics: New York, 1991. ISBN: 0871358034. Reprints *Ghost Rider Vol. 2: 1–7*.

This is the story of the second Ghost Rider, Danny Ketch, who is possessed by the Spirit of Vengeance. It includes appearances by the Kingpin, the Punisher, Deathwatch and the Scarecrow.

Mackie, Howard, Ivan Velez, Cary Nord, et al. *Ghost Rider: Crossroads*. New York: Marvel, 1995.

Blackheart, with the Scarecrow, tries to capture both Johnny Blaze and Dan Ketch in a hellish dimension. Blackheart forces the spirit of Zarathos back on Johnny Blaze, while Ketch receives the Spirit of Vengeance, once again, to leave the netherworld. Both Blaze and Ketch see long-lost loved ones.

This special-cardstock book with a cut-out cover is part of the Marvel Edge imprint.

Mackie, Howard, Lee Weeks, Al Williamson, et al. *Ghost Rider/Captain America: Fear*. New York: Marvel, 1992. ISBN: 0871359472.

Both Captain America and Ghost Rider go up against a savage killer, the Scarecrow, who makes his victims deal with the fears that are lurking inside of them. He kidnaps Stacy, thinking that she is his mother, and stuffs her with straw. Ghost Rider is still considered a villain by the police, but Captain America sees that Ghost Rider is not a villain.

Mackie, Howard, Guang Yap, Bud LaRosa, et al. *Ghost Rider and Cable: Servants of the Dead*. New York: Marvel, 1992. Reprints *Marvel Presents 90–97*.

Cable and Ghost Rider try to save a young girl from being a sacrificed to the Grateful Undead's Warriors of the Dead. It turns out that this girl is already one of the Grateful Undead, and can't be killed. This reality horrifies her, as she is to be the bride of a dead master. She chooses true death, and the master learns the truth about how his servants have become assassins.

Marz, Ron, Darryl Banks, Terry Austin et al. *Green Lantern/Silver Surfer Unholy Alliances*. New York: Marvel/DC, 1995. ISBN: 1563892588.

The Silver Surfer comes up against the Cyborg Superman who just tore a planet apart. Parallax, Hal Jordan, who is a former Green Lantern, tries to get the Surfer to agree to go back in time to right certain wrongs. Thanos deceives the Green Lantern, Kyle Rayner, into aiding him. The Green Lantern and the Surfer fight against one another, while Hal Jordan and Thanos duke it out. Hal Jordan siphons some of the Surfer's power, but it is still too strong, even for Parallax.

Marz, Ron, Claudio Castellini, Chris Eliopoulos, et al. *Silver Surfer: Dangerous Artifacts*. New York: Marvel, 1996.

Thanos, who wants a comet's great power for himself, hires the White Raven to find it. An advanced alien race has made a city within the comet by subjugating an evil alien for its power source.

This is a one-shot Prestige story in which the Silver Surfer agrees to help Galactus find a power source within a comet.

Moench, Doug, Paul Gulacy, Jimmy Palmiotti, et al. *Shang Chi: Master of Kung Fu: Hellfire Apocalypse*. New York: Marvel, 2003. ISBN: 0785111247. Reprints *Shang Chi: Master of Kung Fu 1–6*.

A friend of Shang's who is in the British MI6 seeks Shang's aid in rescuing his wife, who was once Shang's girlfriend, and who has been captured by the immortal Saint German. German wants to reshape the world in his image, and to put together a weapon of mass destruction, based on the scalar-technology ideas of inventor Nikola Tesla. Believing his father to be dead, Shang confronts German and finds out that German is actually his father in a different guise. He learns that he has a brother, Moving Shadow, who stands behind German's evil plans. Shang and Shadow fight, and Shang defeats his brother, but does not kill him. German throws a knife into Moving Shadow's chest. MI6 infiltrates German's headquarters and stops the "scalar" weapon from destroying London. MI6 sets it to destroy the island, and Shang's father is buried under rubble from his island.

This story is part of Marvel's adult line of MAX books.

Muth, Jon, *Dracula: A Symphony in Moonlight and Nightmare.* New York: Marvel, 1986. ISBN: 0871351714.

This is the story of Dracula, told mainly from Lucy Seward's point of view. The book is a beautiful combination of text and watercolor painting, and was reprinted in 1992 by NBM (ISBN: 1561630608). (*Marvel Graphic Novel 25*)

Olshevsky, George, Tony Frutti, Jim Steranko, et al. *The Marvel Comics Index: Fantastic Four 4.* Ontario: G&T Enterprises, 1977. ISBN: 0943348501 (Marvel Index Set).

This is an index and history of the Fantastic Four and the Silver Surfer. It includes a cross index of personnel and major characters. Magazines indexed include *Fantastic Four, Fantastic Four Annual, Giant Size Super Stars, Giant Size Fantastic Four, The Human Torch,* and *The Silver Surfer,* up to 1977. It also includes an index and history of Marvel Boy, from the 1950s.

Perez, George, J.M. DeMatteis, Ron Garney, et al. *The Silver Surfer: Inner Demons.* New York: Marvel, 1998. Reprints *Silver Surfer Vol. 2: 123, 125–126.*

In the aftermath of Onslaught, the Surfer is trying to find his soul again. He seeks the aid of Alicia Masters, and runs afoul of the Hulk who also has lost his counterpart, Bruce Banner, and is dying. The Surfer's healing powers are diminished, but briefly he gives sight to Alicia. He seeks the aid of Dr. Strange, and together they travel through the Surfer's inner mind, which leads to more questions than answers.

Perez, George, Roy Lim, Terry Austin, et al. *Silver Surfer Superman.* New York: Marvel/DC, 1996. ISBN: 0785102930.

The Impossible Man and MXYZPTLK play a game with Superman and the Silver Surfer, and are sent to their respective universes where their worlds collide. Neither Superman nor the Surfer is amused. Metropolis ends up in a glass case, and the people blame the Surfer. Impossible Man becomes Galactus, and tries to chew MXYZPTLK like a piece of chewing gum.

Starlin, Jim, Mike Friedrich, Steve Englehart, et al. *Life and Death of Captain Marvel.* New York: Marvel, 2002. ISBN: 0785108378. Reprints *Captain Marvel 25–34; Iron Man 55; Marvel Feature 12; Death of Captain Marvel.*

The Super Skrull cons Mar-Vell into fighting him by posing as the Hulk and the Sub-Mariner, among others. Iron Man and the Thing take on the Blood Brothers. Eon grants Marvel his "cosmic awareness," and Thanos finds the Cosmic Cube with which he seeks to the rule the universe. He sets himself as a god, but Mar-Vell uses Thanos's arrogance against him. Rick Jones gets a singing gig, but it is cut short by Nitro. Mar-Vell, an alien warrior from Kree Empire, eventually succumbs to death from an earthly illness, cancer. When Mar-Vell fought Nitro, he was exposed to a poisonous gas which resulted in his cancer. Many of the heroes from the Marvel universe, and even the Kree's enemies, the Skrulls, pay their respects to Mar-Vell on his death bed. Destroyer learns that Moondragon is actually his daughter.

This volume includes some of the most important Captain Marvel stories, including his run-ins with Thanos and the Controller. It is a beautifully written and illustrated book, and it is highly recommended for all libraries.

Starlin, Jim, Mike Friedrich; Steve Englehart, et al. *Life of Captain Marvel.* New York: Marvel, 1990. ISBN: 087135635X. Reprints *Captain Marvel 25–34; Iron Man 55; Marvel Feature 12.*

Captain Marvel, a Kree agent, is sent to spy on Earth. He grows to the love the planet, and ultimately becomes the protector of Earth and the entire universe. Thanos takes over Titan and seeks to rule the Universe, in the hopes of winning favor with Lady Death, whom he loves. The Thing and Iron Man duke it out with the Blood Brothers.

This *Marvel Graphic Novel* series book covers the origin of Drax and the Destroyer, and includes an introduction by Al Milgrom. It also has a cover gallery.

Starlin, Jim, Ron Lim, John Beaty, et al. *The Thanos Quest: Schemes and Dreams Vol. 1; Games and Prizes Vol. 2.* New York: Marvel, 1990–1991. ISBN: 0871356813 (1); 0871356821 (2).

Thanos requests that Lady Death be able to see the infinity gems. He argues that this would allow him to serve her better in his quest to slaughter half the universe. Through the power of the Infinity Well, Thanos learns the massive powers of each gem, and which Elders of the Universe are currently in possession of the six gems. He outwits nearly all the Elders, including the In-Betweener, the Gardner, the Collector, Grant Master, Runner, and the Champion, none of whom really knew the power they possessed in the gems. Thanos succeeds in becoming the god he always wanted to be, and tells Lady Death that they are now equals. Death is not amused. She argues that Thanos is now above her, and she is his servant. Thanos is not amused, and finds that his victory is hollow.

This storyline leads into the *Infinity Gauntlet* series. Both volumes were reprinted as a large, bookshelf comic in 2000. This collection takes place right after the "Rebirth of Thanos" storyline in the pages of the *Silver Surfer*. This was reprinted as the *Rebirth of Thanos* in 2006 (ISBN: 0785120467).

Starlin, Jim, Ron Lim, Tom Christopher, et al. *Silver Surfer: Rebirth of Thanos*. New York: Marvel, 1993. ISBN: 0871359685. Reprints *Silver Surfer Vol. 2: 34–38*.

Thanos comes back from the grave as the servant of Lady Death. She asks him to slaughter half the beings in the universe, because there is a cosmic imbalance; there are more beings being born and living than there are dying. The Silver Surfer sees all this in a dream, and Thanos is told that the Surfer is the only being who can stop him. The Surfer figures out how to track Thanos, and tries various methods to destroy him. Surfer destroys someone who was cloned to look like Thanos; Thanos tricked the Surfer. While chasing Thanos, the Surfer meets She-Hulk, the Destroyer, and the Impossible Man who tells the Surfer to lighten up and learn to joke. Thanos meets his supposed granddaughter, Nebula.

This book, which is one of the most difficult Marvel graphic novels to find, includes Gamora's origin story, and an introduction by Ralph Macchio. This was reprinted as the *Rebirth of Thanos* in 2006 (ISBN: 0785120467).

Starlin, Jim, Al Milgrom, Christie Scheele, et al. *Thanos Vol. 2: Infinity Abyss*. New York: Marvel, 2003. ISBN: 0785109854. Reprints *Thanos: Infinity Abyss 1–6*.

Thanos created several doppelgangers of himself, and they want to destroy the Universe for their cult, Nihilism. They believe that this will bring some kind of true enlightenment. The real Thanos is the only one who can stop the doppelgangers. Adam Warlock is revived from his cocoon. Dr. Strange, Spider-Man, Pip the Troll, Gamora, Captain Marvel and Moondragon are featured. Eternity and Inifinity seem to have merged, and find Warlock's presence to be an annoyance. Thanos teams up with the heroes to defeat the doubles and a Galactus version, Omega. Warlock and Gamora finally get to be together.

This is another cosmic storyline that features a more subdued Thanos, and is told through Warlock's eyes. It is excellently written and wonderfully drawn.

Starlin, Jim, Al Milgrom, Christie Scheele, et al. *Thanos Vol. 3: Marvel Universe: The End*. New York: Marvel, 2003. ISBN: 078511

1166, Reprints *Marvel Universe: The End 1–6*.

A great threat from Earth's past, Ancient Egypt, comes to present day Earth and declares that he is the world ruler. Apparently, in the eighteenth dynasty, Pharaoh Akenaten was taken by a representative of the Celestial Order and given omnipotence. Because all other super beings are either dead or indisposed, Thanos, who is searching for the power in the Heart of the Universe, makes a "loose" alliance with the Defenders. They find the Heart of the Universe, and fight with other aliens in the Celestial Order. Thanos sees his opportunity, and takes the power for himself. All of the super beings, including the keepers of the universe, like the Living Tribunal, Eternity, Lord Chaos and Order, are insects compared to the might of Thanos. Even the mythological deities, like Zeus, Vishnu, Shou-Hsing, and Horus are no match for him. Thanos realizes that such power is nothing more than cancer, and ultimately he finds it unfulfilling. Warlock helps him see the error, and Lady Death finally speaks to Thanos and gives him a kiss. Thanos sacrifices himself, as a healer of the Universe, to make things right within it. George W. Bush, Colin Powell, Richard Cheney, and Saddam Hussan are among contemporary political figures who make appearances.

The book is one of Starlin's masterpieces.

Starlin, Jim, Al Milgrom, Christie Scheele, et al. *Thanos Vol. 4: Epiphany*. New York: Marvel, 2004. ISBN: 078511355X. Reprints *Thanos 1–6*.

After becoming an all-powerful god, Thanos ponders where to go next. Warlock comes to Thanos and aids him in his quest. Thanos desires redemption for the pain he caused to the Rigellians who attempt to take Thanos and Warlock captive, but to no avail. Thanos helps them against Galactus. Galactus has been a dupe for a dimension eating creature, the Hunger. Thanos and Galactus team up to try and destroy Hunger. Thanos's mind melds with Galactus's, and he realizes Galactus's purpose in the grand scheme of the universe. The Hunger seeks the soul gems for his own conquest, Warlock briefly looses his gem to Galactus's Punishers, and the Recorder gets blown up. Thanos also has Pip the Troll and Moondragon aid him. Galactus and Thanos have a very interesting, philosophical, cosmic discussion after they defeat Hunger. Pip gets drunk, and Thanos puts him into the garbage disposal.

This book recaps much of Thanos's history, from childhood through his relationship with Lady Death, and on to his subsequent schemes.

Starlin, Jim, Steve Oliff, James Novak, et al. *The Death of Captain Marvel*. New York: Marvel, 1982. ISBN: 0939766116.

Captain Marvel dictates his memoirs into a tape machine. He dies of cancer, meets with Thanos and

Lady Death, and is taken to a place of eternal sleep. Nearly the whole Marvel universe shows up on Titan to pay their respects to Mar-Vell. Even some Skrulls come to pay tribute to their "greatest enemy" by giving him the Royal Skrull Medal of Valor. (*Marvel Graphic Novel 1*)

Starlin, Jim, George Perez, Ron Lim, et al. *Thanos Vol. 1: The Infinity Gauntlet*. New York: Marvel, 2003. ISBN: 0871359448. Reprints *Infinity Gauntlet 1–6*.

Thanos has acquired all six soul gems, which makes him the most powerful being in the universe. He tries to win Mistress Death's favor by destroying half the universe and sending them into Death's domain, but Mistress Death continues to spurn his attempts to garner her affection. Warlock comes back from the Soul Gem Universe in an attempt to stop Thanos. He gathers together earth's mightiest heroes, including Eternity, Master Choas, Lord Order, two Celestials, and several other of the most powerful beings. However, nothing seems to work, and Thanos defeats them all. When he is not looking, Thanos's granddaughter Nebula steals the gems from Thanos's hand. Then Thanos has to team up with the heroes to stop her. Adam Warlock ends up taking the gems to his portion of the universe, with the aid of the Silver Surfer. Thanos blows up, and goes to the Soul Gem Universe.

One of Marvel's crowning achievements in epic storytelling, this was reprinted in 2006 (ISBN: 07851 23490).

Starlin, Jim, Bill Reinhold, Linda Lessman, et al. *Silver Surfer: Homecoming*. New York: Marvel, 1991. ISBN: 0871358557.

The planet Zenn La is captured by a benevolent being and stored with a private collection of planets. The Surfer, with the help of Moondragon, invades the being and rescues Zenn-La. The alien being sees the Surfer as an intruder, fights him, and is defeated in battle. Moondragon and the Surfer save Zenn-La, but at the cost of the Surfer's one true love, Shalla-Bal. (*Marvel Graphic Novel 71*)

Walsh, Brian Patrick, Mike Deodato Jr., Will Conrad, et al. *Witches Vol. 1: The Gathering*. New York: Marvel, 2004. ISBN: 07851150 80. Reprints *Witches 1–4*.

Dr. Strange brings together three sorceresses: his student, Topaz; Jennifer Kale; and Satan's daughter, Satana. The Tome of Zhered-Na is opened, and a creature known has Hellphyr is released. The Hell-phyr eats mystical energy, and even has the potential to destroy Dr. Strange. At first the girls don't like each other, but in the end they form a team. They find Dr. Strange to be sexist and condescending toward them, and Strange and the vampire sorceress do battle. Kale's brother is taken over by Hellphyr, and the Devil watches the team, which includes his daughter, try to stop the creature and save Jennifer's brother. Even though Jennifer Kale is the rightful owner, Strange demands that the Tome be given to him. He dismisses his student Topaz for betraying him.

Wolfman, Marv, Chris Claremont, Christopher Golden, et al. *Blade: The Vampire Slayer: Black and White*. New York: Marvel, 2004. ISBN: 0785114696. Reprints *Vampire Tales 8–9*; *Marvel Preview 3, 6*; *Marvel Shadows and Light 1*; *Blade: Crescent City Blues 1*.

The Vampire Legion is trying to take over London, and ends up killing Blade's foster mother. They frame Blade for the murder of a young child. His girlfriend Safron gets kidnapped by the Vampires, and is almost turned into a vampire. Blade gets bitten by a vampire. Blade goes to a house filled with children vampires. He hesitates killing them, until they attack him. Blade goes to New Orleans where Deacon Frost is trying to take over the underworld. Brother Voodoo, Hannibal King, and Safron help him take down Frost's vampire empire. Blade has to battle his mother who is also a vampire. Dracula makes an appearance.

This book includes a "Short Picto-History of Blade." It is a black-and-white collection of various Blade stories taken from some Marvel magazines of the 1970s, and it includes his origin story.

Wolfman, Marv, and Gene Colan, *Tomb of Dracula Megazine*. New York: Marvel, 1996. Reprints *Tomb of Dracula 12–16*.

Edith Harker is taken by Dracula and turned into a vampire. Blade finally kills Dracula, but before they can chop off his head, the villagers take Dracula's body. Dracula lies there dead until a Christian priest with delusions of grandeur believes that his power through Christ can raise the dead. At a public revival, Dracula is raised, but he tells the minister that it is not God's power that flows through him, but a power of much evil. The congregation tries to exorcise the "demon" from Dracula. The dead, unearthed body keeps terrorizing the countryside, and even beats Dracula in a fight. Dracula reminisces about his return to Transylvania in 1969, when the Scotsman briefly succeeded in killing him.

There is an afterword by editor Glen Greenberg.

Daredevil and Elektra

Va-Voom, I feel as Giddy as a Guppy in a Goblet.—*Daredevil*

Only a madman would be a costumed clown in the first place.—*Matt Murdock*

Bendis, Brian Michael, Chuck Austen, Nathan Eyring, et al. *Elektra: Scorpion Key*. New York: Marvel, 2001. ISBN: 0785108432. Reprints *Elektra Vol. II. 1–6*.

Nick Fury asks Elektra to assassinate Saddam Abed Dasam, the ruler of Iraq, and to steal an ornate box that is adorned with two black scorpions. Electra takes the assignment, but she does it her own way, without any protocols.

This has beautifully done artwork and excellent dialogue.

Bendis, Brian Michael, Rob Hayes, David Self, et al. *Daredevil: Ninja*. Marvel Comics: New York, 2001. ISBN: 0785107800. Reprints *Daredevil Ninja: 1–3*.

Matt Murdock is kidnapped and taken to Japan by several ninjas from Stick's old order. The Hand has decimated their ranks to only a few and Daredevil is brought in to stop the Hand from getting a mystical artifact.

This book includes a gallery of covers, pin-ups, and sketches, and an Afterword by artist Rob Hayes. This collection is put together as though it is a movie.

Bendis, Brian Michael, David Mack, Comicraft, et al. *Daredevil Vol. 3: Wake Up*. New York: Marvel 2002. ISBN: 078510948X. Reprints *Daredevil Vol. 2: 16–19*.

Reporter Ben Ulrich is searching for the story behind Leapfrog's son who is in a catatonic state. The son keeps repeating the name "Daredevil," and Ulrich seeks out Daredevil for an explanation. The child was abused badly, and Ulrich ends up taking the child to his house for an extended stay. Ulrich wants to write the boy's story for the *Daily Bugle*, but Jonah Jameson wants him to write about the Kingpin.

This volume is wonderfully written and drawn.

Bendis, Brian Michael, Alex Maleev, Manuel Gutierrez, et al. *Daredevil Vol. 5: Out*. New York: Marvel, 2003. ISBN: 0785110747. Reprints *Daredevil Vol. 2: 32–40*.

There is a leak to the press that Matt Murdock is Daredevil, the *Daily Globe* breaks the story, and Murdock's life becomes nothing short of a circus. Murdock decides to sue the *Globe* for libel. Foggy tries to get him to give up his career as a crime fighter. Murdock has dinner with Kingpin's wife Vanessa, who reveals who is responsible for the leak. Donald Trump buys Fisk Towers. Murdock defends the White Tiger who is blamed for the death of a policeman, and when the Tiger is found guilty, he goes berserk. Luck Cage and Iron Fist make cameos.

Bendis, Brain Michael, Alex Maleev, Mat Hollingsworth, et al. *Daredevil Vol. 4: Underboss*. New York: Marvel, 2002. ISBN: 0785110 240. Reprints *Daredevil Vol. 2: 26–31*.

A new gangster infiltrates Kingpin's outfit and wants Matt Murdock killed. Kingpin decides against this, but his son reveals to the henchmen that Murdock is in reality Daredevil. Wilson Fisk is blind and considered weak, so, with the help of his son, a group of his henchmen plan a coup. An attempt is made on Wilson Fisk's life and he gets cut up. His wife Vanessa puts hits on the men who participated in the coup, including her son. Then she takes the Kingpin's money and disappears.

This book includes Alex Maleev's sketchbook for issue 30.

Bendis, Brian Michael, Alex Maleev, Matt Hollingsworth, et al. *Daredevil Vol. 6: Lowlife*. New York: Marvel, 2003. ISBN: 078511 1050. Reprints *Daredevil Vol. 2: 41–45*.

Kingpin's absence, because he is near death, brings out all kinds of low-ranked hoods waiting to fill his shoes. The Owl and a band of the Kingpin's former employees want to take Daredevil down. When Daredevil saves a young, blind girl from being run over, she hears that Matt Murdock is being accused of being Daredevil, and she visits him. She recognizes him as Daredevil by listening to his voice. Murdock becomes a suspect in the brutal slaying of publisher, Mr. Rosenthal, and Luke Cage snubs Murdock when he visits.

Bendis, Brian Michael. Alex Maleev, Matt Hollingsworth, et al. *Daredevil Vol. 7: Hardcore*. New York: Marvel, 2003. ISBN: 078511 1689. Reprints *Daredevil Vol. 2: 46–50*.

The Kingpin returns to New York and wants to set his empire up again. He employs Typhoid Mary to weed out anyone who would oppose him, including Matt Murdock. Mary takes on Jessica Jones and Luke Cage, and sets Matt's face on fire. While at Matt's apartment, Bullseye attempts to assassinate Matt's new girlfriend. Daredevil catches him, and uses a knife to carve scars into Bullseye's head in retribution for the death of two of his former girlfriends. When the Kingpin falls from power, he attempts to take back Hell's Kitchen, and kills anyone who opposed him when he fell. Daredevil engages in hand-to-hand combat with the Kingpin, and beats him badly. Daredevil then declares that he is now running Hell's Kitchen, and Boomerang sues Matt Murdock.

This is pulp fiction/*noir* at its finest.

Bendis, Brian Michael, Alex Maleev, Matt Hollingsworth, et al. *Daredevil Vol. 9: King of Hell's Kitchen*. New York: Marvel, 2004. ISBN: 0785113371. Reprints *Daredevil Vol. 2: 56–60*.

Matt Murdock declares himself the new kingpin of Hell's Kitchen, and wipes out crime in the whole area. He also gets married and does not don the Daredevil costume for a year. The Japanese gangsters, the Yakuza, believe that Hell's Kitchen is ripe for new drug traffic and vice, and they take on Murdock. Reed Richards, Peter Parker, Stephen Strange, and Luke Cage all try to tell Matt to "cool it," as crime is seeping into their neighborhoods at an alarming rate. The Yakuza beat up Murdock pretty badly. Then, when reporter Ben Ulrich asks him if he's having a nervous breakdown because of the death of Karen Page, Matt questions his motives, and his marriage, and dons the Daredevil costume again. Iron Fist also makes an appearance.

Bendis, Brian Michael, Alex Maleev, Matt Hollingsworth, et al. *Daredevil Vol. 10: The Widow*. New York: Marvel, 2004. ISBN: 0785113940. Reprints *Daredevil Vol. 1: 81*; *Daredevil Vol. 2: 61–65*.

Matt Murdock's wife files for divorce. The Avengers capture Madame Hydra in Bulgaria, and the Bulgarian government wants to trade Madame Hydra for the Black Widow. After Nick Fury alerts the Widow that she is going to be used a pawn, she shows up at Murdock's doorstep, and tries to rekindle their romance. Throughout her stay with Murdock they are trailed by an assassin. Murdock refuses to accept Jigsaw's bribe to leave him alone to pursue his criminal activities, and when Jigsaw breaks into Murdock's house, the Black Widow stops him. The Black Widow saves Daredevil's life. After Nick Fury offers Murdock a job in S.H.I.E.L.D., Murdock seeks Dr. Strange's advice. When Murdock declares himself the kingpin of Hell's Kitchen, the Punisher sees him as an enemy. Captain America, Luke Cage, the Hulk, and others make appearances.

In this book there is also a reprint of the Black Widow's first appearance in the pages of *Daredevil*. *Daredevil 65* is the fortieth-anniversary special in which different artists took turns drawing Daredevil.

Chichester, Dan, Scott McDaniel, Hector Collazo, et al. *Elektra: Root of All Evil 1–4*. New York: Marvel, 1995.

This cardstock series was part of the Marvel Select line, and features Elektra against a very evil group of ninjas known as the Snakeroot. In this volume, the Snakeroot's magic sword Sakki requires the special blood of innocent people. Elektra, with the help of Nick Fury, forms her own ninja group to stop the Snakeroot, but Snakeroot is more than a match for Elektra's group, and most of them are killed. We also learn that Elektra's brother killed their mother, and that her father hated his wife's promiscuous ways. Stick's bizarre relationship with Elektra is explored.

Chichester, Dan, Scott McDaniel, Ralph Macchio, et al. *Daredevil: Fall from Grace*. New York: Marvel, 1993. ISBN: 0785100245. Reprints *Daredevil 319–325*.

Daredevil, in his black-and-red costume, tries to find remnants of a secret government virus, About Face, that molds the user into whatever he/she wants to be. Many forces, including S.H.I.E.L.D., Hellspawn the Hand, Snakeroot, and Morbius, also are trying to find the virus to use for their own purposes. Elektra and a clone that has her evil essence are brought back to life. Matt Murdock is exposed in a newspaper as Daredevil and Murdock's doppelganger dies. Nick Fury also makes an appearance.

Chichester, Dan, Lee Weeks, Al Williamson, et al. *Daredevil: Fall of the Kingpin*. New York: Marvel, 1993. ISBN: 0871359650. Reprints *Daredevil 397–400*.

Daredevil exposes the Kingpin and his dealings with the terrorist group HYDRA. Matt Murdock, who had been disbarred after being framed for a crime by the Kingpin, tries to get his law practice back, and HYDRA destroys most of Kingpin's empire.

This is an intense story with appearances by Typhoid Mary and Nick Fury.

Cohn, Mitch, John Byrnem, Fred Hembeck, et al. *The Daredevil Chronicles*. Albany: Fanta-Co Enterprises, 1982.

This is a magazine-style book that covers all aspects of the *Daredevil* series. Topics that are covered include Daredevil facts, Daredevil and artist Wally Wood, and Daredevil's villains. "The Birth of a Soap Opera," by Steve Webb, includes interviews with Frank Miller, Klaus Janson, and Denny O'Neil. In the book, Marvel's Daredevil finally meets the Daredevil of the Golden Age. The book also includes a Daredevil checklist. It is well worth seeking out.

Jenkins, Paul, Phil Winslade, Tom Palmer, et al. *Daredevil/Spider Man*. New York: Marvel, 2001. ISBN: 0785107924. Reprints *Daredevil/Spider Man 1–4*.

Someone takes a jab at all the Kingpin's takes, and dares Fisk to come out in the open. A group that includes the Owl, Gladiator, and the Stilt Man, led by the mysterious Copperhead, is trying to topple the Kingpin. Fisk, who is hospitalized, hires Matt Murdock to represent him, and Daredevil and Spider-Man team up to figure out what is going on. When the two criminal groups end up in violent gang warfare, the Copperhead tries to bring out an army of the living dead. When Spider-Man makes a joke, Daredevil gripes him out.

Jones, Bruce, Manuel Garcia, Scott Hanna, et al. *Daredevil: The Movie*. New York: Marvel, 2002. ISBN: 0785109595. Reprints *Daredevil: Movie Adaptation; Daredevil Vol. 2: 32; Ultimate Daredevil and Elektra 1; Spiderman's Tangled Web 4*.

Daredevil is born after the death of his father who died at the hands of the Kingpin. By day, Matt Murdock is a blind lawyer from Hell's Kitchen who meets and falls in love with Elektra. The Kingpin hires Bullseye to kill Elektra's father. Elektra meets Matt Murdock when she goes to college. Daredevil's identity is sold to a newspaper, and the Kingpin kills one of his people who fails at an assignment.

This is the official comic adaptation of the hit movie *Daredevil*.

Lee, Stan, Bill Mantlo, Gary Friedrich, et al. *The Greatest Spider Man & Daredevil Team Ups*. New York: Marvel, 1996. ISBN: 0785 10223X. Reprints *Amazing Spider Man 16, 396; Marvel Team Up 56, 73; Daredevil 270; Spectacular Spider Man 26–28, 219*.

Daredevil and Spider-Man go against the Ringmaster and his Circus of Crime which includes the Masked Marauder, Blizzard, Owl and the Vulture. They also go up against, and nearly lose to, Blackheart, Mephisto's son.

This book gathers together some of the best stories in which Daredevil and Spider-Man team up, and it contains stories in which Daredevil wears all three of his costumes: yellow, red, and gray/black. The introduction is by Ralph Macchio.

Loeb, Jeph, Tim Sale, Richard Starkings, et al. *Daredevil: Yellow*. New York: Marvel, 2002. ISBN: 0785108408. Paperback version: *Daredevil Legends Vol. 1*. ISBN: 07851096 92. Reprints *Daredevil Yellow 1–6*.

Foggy Nelson wants to propose to the secretary, Karen, but Matt Murdock loves her as well. Daredevil saves Karen from the Owl, and she suggests that he change his costume from yellow to red.

This book chronicles Daredevil's early crime-fighting career when he wore a yellow costume. This is one of the best written/drawn books of 2002.

Mack, David, Cory Petit, Joe Quesada, et al. *Daredevil Vol. 8: Echo-The Vision Quest*. New York: Marvel, 2004. ISBN: 07851123 24. Reprints *Daredevil Vol. 2: 51–55*.

Maya Lopez, a Native American, visits the Kingpin in jail, and visits Daredevil. She meets with an Indian elder she has known since childhood, and embarks on a vision quest to gain understanding. During her quest, she meets Wolverine for the first time.

This book is beautifully written and drawn by David Mack, and focuses on Daredevil's former lover/enemy, Echo, aka Maya Lopez. The story is told through the eyes of Maya. It tells about her life growing up deaf, losing her father, living with the Kingpin, and going to a special school. The book should be nominated for an award. It is highly recommended for all libraries, and for readers of any age, for its portrayal of Echo.

Mack, David, Joe Quesada, David Ross, et al. *Daredevil Vol. 2: Parts of a Hole*. New York: Marvel, 2002. ISBN: 0785108084. Reprints *Daredevil Vol. 2: 9–15*.

Daredevil fights Echo, a deaf master of the martial arts, who believes that Daredevil is responsible for her father's death. When she finds out that the Kingpin is actually responsible, she shoots him, and Matt Murdock develops a romance with her.

In this book, Kingpin's origin is revealed. This volume is beautifully written and drawn.

McKenzie, Roger, Frank Miller, Klaus Janson, et al. *Daredevil: Marked for Death*. New York: Marvel, 1990. ISBN: 0871356341. Reprints *Daredevil 159–164*.

This is a retelling of the Daredevil origin story, as told to a reporter who knows Daredevil's real identity. In the book, Bullseye kidnaps the Black Widow, and Daredevil, who fights the Hulk, ends up in the hospital.

Miller, Frank, Steve Buccellato, Clarissa Marrero, et al. *Daredevil Visionaries Frank Miller Vol. 2*. New York: Marvel, 2001. ISBN: 0785107711. Reprints *Daredevil Vol. 2: 168–182*.

Daredevil saves Bullseye from an oncoming train. Gladiator and Elektra team up briefly to save Matt Murdock from an assassination plot. The love saga between Daredevil and Elektra comes to a full boil when he encounters her as a deadly assassin. Elektra takes on the Hand. After she ends up homeless, staying with the sewer people, Daredevil rescues Vanessa, the Kingpin's wife. Murdock infiltrates the Kingpin's organization. Kingpin hires Elektra to assassinate Foggy Nelson. However, Elektra dies at the hand of Bullseye, and the Kingpin becomes the crime lord of New York again. Matt loses his radar when a bomb goes off next to him, and he goes back to study with his old sensei Stick, to hone his radar. Luke Cage and Iron Fist make appearances.

Miller, Frank, Klaus Janson, Ralph Macchio, et al. *Elektra Saga*. New York: Marvel, 1989. ISBN: 0871355760. Reprints *Elektra Saga 1–4; Parts of Daredevil 168, 174–180, 187–190; Bizarre Adventures 28*.

Elektra and Matt Murdock meet and become romantically entangled. When her father is murdered, she leaves Murdock and goes to study the ninja arts. She is rejected by Stick, the man who taught Murdock, for having too many past demons. She goes to the Hand, learns the art of assassination, and ultimately rejects the Hand's leader. The Hand puts a hit on Murdock, and Elektra saves his life. The Kingpin employs her to kill Foggy Nelson, but she takes pity on him and lets him go. Bullseye breaks out of prison and kills Elektra. Murdock, not believing she is dead, goes into a crazed depression, and the Hand robs Elektra's grave in order to bring her back to life. The Gladiator and the Black Widow make appearances.

This is a collection of reprinted material from various *Daredevil* issues, highlighting the Elektra material. However, it also contains material that makes the story coherent. This was also reprinted in the *Elektra Megazine 1–2*. The *Elektra Saga* deserves to be reprinted.

Miller, Frank, Klaus Janson, Denny O'Neil, et al. *Daredevil Visionaries: Frank Miller Vol. 3*. New York: Marvel, 2001. ISBN: 078510 8025. Reprints *Daredevil Vol. 1: 183–191*; *What If Vol. 1: 28, 35*; *Bizarre Adventures 28*.

Daredevil and the Punisher meet for the first time. The Punisher shoots Daredevil with a tranquilizer. Both the Punisher and Daredevil are trying to stop drug dealers who are selling their dope to kids. Murdock inadvertently ends up representing a murderer, and, as Daredevil, he stops a kid from killing someone. After he has nearly ruined her life, Matt Murdock asks Heather to marry him. Heather finds out that her business is building bombs, and that the Kingpin is involved. When Foggy goes undercover as hit-man Guts Nelson, he even intimidates the Kingpin. Turk steals the Stiltman's costume. When Daredevil's hearing is injured, all sounds become too loud, and he seeks out his old sensei Stick who is in the middle of a war with the Hand. The Hand resurrects the warrior Kirigi, but he is defeated by Stick and his disciples. Stick helps Daredevil heal. The Hand poisons the Black Widow, who aides in the battle, and Stick ends up combusting after their battle. Foggy and the Widow help split up Matt and Heather. We learn about Elektra's training under Stick, and her subsequent banishment. The Hand resurrects Elektra. Daredevil spends some time with Bullseye, playing Russian roulette in the hospital. We also learn what would happen if Daredevil was a S.H.I.E.L.D. agent; Bullseye would not have killed her.

This is the third and final volume in Marvel's tribute to artist/writer Frank Miller's classic run on *Daredevil*. The classic storyline, "Child's Play," featuring Daredevil and the Punisher, is reprinted. The book includes a black-and-white Elektra story, an art gallery from the *Elektra Saga* trade paperback, and an introduction by Klaus Janson. One story is told from the perspective of Foggy Nelson.

Miller, Frank, Klaus Janson, Joe Rosen, et al. *Daredevil: Punisher: Child's Play*. New York: Marvel, 1988. ISBN: 0871353512. Reprints *Daredevil 183–184*.

The Punisher breaks out of jail to fight the drug dealers who are spreading angel dust to the youth. Daredevil and the Punisher meet, and Daredevil tries to take the Punisher down. Matt Murdock defends a murderous drug lord who he believes is innocent but is actually guilty of murder. Daredevil disagrees with the Punisher's methods of controlling crime.

Miller, Frank, Klaus Janson, Glynis Wein, et al. *Dardevil: Gang War*. New York: Marvel, 1999. ISBN: 0871358808. Reprints *Daredevil 169–172*; *180*.

Wilson Fisk's wife Vanessa is kidnapped, and when Bullseye tries to assassinate Fisk, Daredevil is caught in the middle of a gang war.

This story contains Daredevil's first encounter with the Kingpin.

Miller, Frank, David Mazzucchelli, Joe Rosen, et al. *Daredevil Legends Vol. 2: Born Again*. New York: Marvel, 2003. ISBN: 08713529 74. Reprints *Daredevil Vol. 1: 227–233*.

In return for some money, Karen Page identifies Matt Murdock as Daredevil. The Kingpin pays for this information, and kills everyone who has come in contact with it. He tries to break the will of Murdock by having his law license, home, and privacy taken away, and by framing him for various crimes. Foggy Nelson tries to help, but Murdock goes into hiding. Kingpin hires the ultrapatriotic and mentally ill Nuke to cause chaos in New York, and in the process kills innocent people. Both Daredevil and Captain America have to rein him in. Matt Murdock meets his mother for the first time, in a church where she is a nun. Reporter Ben Ulrich tries to find out the truth behind the story, but the Kingpin blocks him at every turn, almost killing Ulrich in the process. Karen Page comes back to get help from Matt Murdock and confesses her betrayal.

Miller, Frank, Roger McKenzie, Klaus Janson, et al. *Daredevil Visionaries: Frank Miller Vol. 1*. New York: Marvel, 2000. ISBN: 0785 107576. Reprints *Daredevil Vol. 1: 158 161*; *163–167*.

After watching a film of him in action, Bullseye hires Slaughter to kill Daredevil. The Black Widow is captured by Bullseye to lure Daredevil. Bullseye ends up going mad. Daredevil fights with the Hulk, and ends up in the hospital. *Daily Bugle* reporter Ben Ulrich figures out that Matt Murdock is Daredevil, and while visiting Daredevil in the hospital, he learns the true origin of Murdock's transformation into Daredevil. In order to save Daredevil's career, Ulrich destroys his prize-winning expose on Murdock/Daredevil. Daredevil fights with Doc Ock, and when the Black Widow learns of Murdock's love for Heather Glen, she leaves New York to go back to Russia.

This is Frank Miller's first work on *Daredevil* as an artist.

Miller, Frank, John Romita Jr., Al Williamsom, et al. *Daredevil Legends Vol. 3: Man Without Fear.* New York: Marvel, 2003. ISBN: 0785100466. Reprints *Daredevil: Man Without Fear 1–5.*

This is a retelling of the Daredevil's origin. It relates how young Matt Murdock lost his father, and how he took revenge on those who killed his father. The story goes into detail about Murdock's early martial arts training, and his relationships with Elektra and Foggy Nelson.

Miller, Frank, Bill Sienkiewicz, Jim Novak, et al. *Daredevil: Love and War.* New York: Marvel, 1986. ISBN: 0871351722.

Because his wife is sick, Kingpin kidnaps a specialist doctor and the doctor's blind wife. Daredevil rescues the doctor's wife, but the doctor takes Kingpin's wife Vanessa away from him.

This is a very intense psychological drama which is beautifully illustrated with mixed media. (*Marvel Graphic Novel 24*)

Miller, Frank, Bill Sienkiewicz, Jim Novak, et al. *Elektra Assassin.* Marvel Comics: New York, 2000. ISBN: 0871353091. Reprints *Elektra* vol. 1: 1–8.

Elektra kills the president of San Concepcion, South America. She also kills a number of S.H.I.E.L.D. agents, and brainwashes a cyborg agent into following her. S.H.I.E.L.D has been making cyborg soldiers out of killers and molesters, in their Ex-Tech Op Division. Elektra and her cronies seek to kill presidential hopeful Ken Wind who they believe will start World War III with the Soviets by pushing the button for a nuclear missile attack.

This is a surrealist tale about various aspects of Elektra's past and present. Many details about Elektra not covered in previous comics are given here. The writing is thought provoking, and the artwork is quite beautiful. Miller writes in a non-narrative syle for this volume. Also see the Epic and Hardcover chapters in this book.

Nocenti, Ann, John Romita Jr., Al Williamson et al. *Daredevil Legends Vol. 4: Typhoid Mary.* New York: Marvel, 2003. ISBN: 0785110410. Reprints *Daredevil Vol. 1: 254–257; 259–263.*

Matt Murdock helps a young boy who was blinded by swimming in a lake full of chemicals. He takes to court the company responsible for the boy's blindness. Typhoid Mary, who in addition to having a multiple personality disorder is schizophrenic, comes to New York where she starts robbing and killing criminals. The Kingpin hires her to break Matt Murdock's heart. Typhoid fights Daredevil, and hires a group of thugs to beat him up, to the point of death. Then Typhoid drops him from a ledge, to his supposed death. The Punisher and Daredevil have a spectacular fight.

When children begin disappearing, Daredevil exposes a child pornography ring. The Human Torch tries to find Daredevil, but makes himself look like a fool in a Hell's Kitchen bar. Daredevil fights a demon that has taken over New York. Karen Page goes back to using drugs. The Black Widow makes an appearance.

Olshevsky, George, and Tony Frutti. *The Marvel Comics Index 9B: Daredevil.* San Diego: Pacific Comics Distributors, 1982. ISBN: 0943348536.

This is an annotated index for *Daredevil 1–181* that includes various specials and annuals. Each entry has artist's name, writing credits, and a brief statement about the content. Other comics that are indexed include *Jungle Action,* featuring the Black Panther; *Shanna the She Devil; Black Goliath; The Human Fly;* and *Dazzler.* There is a personnel cross-index and a major characters cross-index. For each character, there is a historical synopsis, along with some interesting facts (e.g., the Human Fly was based on an actual person).

Rodi, Robert, Sean Chen, Tom Palmer, et al. *Elektra Vol. 3: Relentless.* New York: Marvel, 2004. ISBN: 0785112227. Reprints *Elektra Vol. 2: 23–28.*

One of Elektra's victims tries to elude her by hiring bodyguards and trying to hide where she can't find him. However, he is not successful, and he finally meets his fate at her hands. Elektra is hired by an opposing, minority tribe leader, to assassinate the tyrannical female dictator of the African country Djanda. She manages to worm her way into the palace by seducing the dictator's son. She kills the son, but the ruler's bodyguard is waiting, and captures her. She escapes, and kills the dictator, but then she finds out that she was double-crossed by the man who hired her. She also kills three corporate bosses, who tried to double-cross her.

In this book, Elektra's victim's attempts to evade her are shown through his eyes.

Rodi, Robert, Will Conrad, Jon Proctor, et al. *Elektra Vol. 4: Frenzy.* New York: Marvel, 2004. ISBN: 0785113983. Reprints *Elektra Vol. 2: 29–35.*

Elektra is hired to kill the leader of an insurrection in the Asian island of Naou. The leader claims to be the prophet Piaka Loio, the incarnation of Bara, the god of war. The prophet is just a child, and Elektra destroys him by killing his army, thus leaving the boy homeless and without a cause. The son of a mob boss hires her to kill his father, but, because she catches a very bad cold, for the first time in her life she is not able to do the job.

In this book, Elektra's life, death, and resurrection are told from the perspective of Elektra's mind.

Rucka, Greg, Joe Bennett, Danny Miki, et al. *Elektra Vol. 2: Everything Old Is New Again.*

New York: Marvel, 2003. ISBN: 0785111
085. Reprints *Elektra Vol. 2: 16–22.*

Elektra is introduced to the old martial arts master
Drake. Elektra asks Drake to become her sensei, but
Drake refuses because she believes that there is no
goodness left in Elektra's heart. Elektra continues to
hound Drake until she finally agrees to help her.
Drake teaches Elektra many different things, not all
of which have to do with martial arts fighting. She
gets Elektra to clean a sandbox, and work in a soup
kitchen. The Hand is searching for Elektra, and kills
anyone in their path to finding her. Drake and Elektra fight off the Hand. Drake is poisoned, and Elektra defeats the Hand, killing them all.

Rucka, Greg, Salvador Larroca, Danny Miki, et
    al. *Ultimate Daredevil and Elektra Vol. 1.*
    New York: Marvel, 2003. ISBN: 07851107
    63. Reprints *Ultimate Daredevil and Elek-
    tra 1–4; Daredevil Vol. 2: 9.*

Elektra goes to college and meets Matt Murdock.
They form a romantic relationship which is spoiled
when he stops Elektra from killing the son of a
wealthy businessman. This rich kid had raped one of
Elektra's best friends, and blew up the dry cleaning
business her father owns, almost killing him in the
process. The rich kid puts a hit on Elektra.

A sketchbook and the first part of the "Parts of the
Hole" storyline are included.

Rucka, Greg, Carlo Pagulayan, Danny Miki, et
    al. *Elektra Vol. 1: Introspect.* New York: Mar-
    vel 2002. ISBN: 0785109730. Reprints
    *Elektra Vol. 2: 10–15. Marvel Knights Dou-
    ble Shot 3.*

Elektra desperately seeks work as an assassin, but
her former employers see her as a liability, and nobody will hire her. A group of people whose lives she
has ruined because of her profession kidnap Elektra,
drug her, and put her out in the desert to die. They
want her to die, and to see herself as the monster she
is. When a combat unit is dispensed to track her down
in the desert, she kills them all.

This volume also contains the short story "Elektra
Trust."

Smith, Kevin, Joe Quesada, Jimmy Palmiotti,
    et al. *Daredevil: Marvel's Finest.* New York:
    Marvel, 1999. ISBN: 0785107150. Reprints
    Daredevil Vol. 2: 1–3.

Daredevil saves a baby who is then given to Matt
Murdock. Karen Page has AIDS, and Daredevil goes
up against Baal. Black Widow also makes an appearance.

There is a sketchbook with this volume.

Smith, Kevin, Joe Quesada, Jimmy Palmiotti,
    et al. *Daredevil Vol. 1: Guardian Devil.* New
    York: Marvel, 2003. ISBN: 0785107371,

0785107355 (2001 ed). Reprints *Daredevil
Vol. 2: 1–8.*

Mysterio sets into motion a conspiracy to bring
down Daredevil and his alter ego Matt Murdock.
Murdock's mother is beaten up by Bullseye. Karen
Page admits to having AIDS, and is killed by Bullseye while trying to protect Daredevil. Daredevil con-
sults with Dr. Strange and Mephisto, believing that
supernatural forces are at work in his life. Mysterio
drugs Daredevil with a hallucinogen. Foggy Nelson
is also drugged, and he is blamed for the murder of a
woman with whom he is having an affair. Daredevil
strikes the Black Widow, and figures out Mysterio's
plan, which does not break his spirit. Spider-Man
tries to console Daredevil who is grieving over the
death of his former lover, Karen Page. Karen leaves
her estate to Murdock. Mysterio kills himself, and
Daredevil saves the baby Mysterio kidnapped. Liz
Osborn leaves Foggy because of an affair.

The introduction is by movie star Ben Affleck, who
played Daredevil in the feature film.

Starlin, Jim, Joe Chiodo, Janice Chiang, et al.
    Daredevil/Black Widow: Abattoir. New
    York: Marvel, 1993. ISBN: 0871359944.

Two serial killers have been stalking S.H.I.E.L.D.
agents and New York citizens who have telepathic
ability. Black Widow is caught by the killers while
shadowing a mark. She is taken to a bizarre charnel
house where she is tortured and learns the horrible
past of Rose and her childhood. The Widow realizes
that a bad childhood is no excuse for mindless slaughter of human beings. Daredevil is trailing behind, and
ends up driving a taxicab. The Widow gets beaten up
pretty badly, as does Daredevil. In the last moment
of Rose's life, she forces a kiss on the Widow. Rose
believed that by torturing and draining her telepathic
victims of blood, she becomes special and eliminates
what she sees as the competition.

This is the darkest Daredevil this side of the work
of Frank Miller and Brian Bendis. It reads like a
twisted, comic-*noir* slasher film, and is quite good.
This was the last oversize *Marvel Graphic Novel* published in that particular series. (*Marvel Graphic Novel
75*)

Wolfman, Marv, Jim Shooter, Frank Miller, et
    al. *Daredevil Vs. Bullseye Vol. 1.* New York:
    Marvel, 2004. ISBN: 0785115625. Reprints
    Daredevil Vol. 1: 131–132, 146, 169, 181, 191.

Bullseye lures Daredevil into a fight in front of a
large crowd at the circus. He also lures him into a fight
in front of television cameras. When Daredevil, as
Matt Murdock, stops Bullseye from stealing a gun,
Bullseye hits Murdock in the temple with a golf ball.
Bullseye breaks out of a mental institution, and sees
Daredevils everywhere. Daredevil saves Bullseye from
being run over by a train, and Elektra ends up being
killed by Bullseye. When Daredevil drops him from a
window, Bullseye is crippled. Daredevil visits Bullseye
in the hospital, and, while playing Russian Roulette,

tells him the story of what made Matt Murdock don the Daredevil costume.

This collection includes Bullseye's very first appear-

ance, and brings together some of Daredevil's and Bullseye's historic battles.

Fantastic Four/Dr. Doom and Inhumans

Victor Von Doom is not without compassion. —*Dr. Doom*

The only thing that grabs me is IT'S CLOBBERIN' TIME.... Look buster—
when I belt a guy, I expect 'im to stay belted! —*The Thing*

Aguirre-Sacasa, Roberto, Steve McNiven, Mark Morales, et al. *Marvel Knights 4: Vol. 1: Wolf at the Door*. New York: Marvel, 2004. ISBN: 0785114718. Reprints *Marvel Knights 4: 1–7*.

The Fantastic Four learn that they are completely broke, and that their trusted advisor has embezzled thousands of dollars from them. They have to close the Baxter Building, lay off 24,213 people, get jobs, and move to a small apartment. Sue, the Invisible Girl, goes to work as a teacher, and her brother Johnny, the Human Torch, wants to be a fireman. The Thing goes to work for a construction company, and Reed, Mr. Fantastic, starts to work for a law firm. Hammerhead tries to get Mr. Fantastic to team up with him to find the former associate who embezzled from them both. The Fantastic Four go on a camping trip and discover the Jersey Devil and its origin.

Bendis, Brian Michael, Mark Millar, Adam Kubert, et al. *Ultimate Fantastic Four Vol. 1: The Fantastic*. New York: Marvel, 2004. ISBN: 0785113932. Reprints *Ultimate Fantastic Four 1–6*.

Reed Richards is taken to a government think tank for young geniuses. His teacher, Dr. Storm, is the father of Sue and Johnny, and they develop a strong bond with Reed. He befriends Victor Von Damm who alters an experiment to transfer matter through the N-Zone. Reed's friend Ben Grimm is also there during the experiment, and the four of them are transformed. They end up in different parts of the world. Dr. Molekevic, a fired teacher who is obsessed with Sue Storm, kidnaps her. He sends a monster to the surface, and Reed, Ben, and Johnny work as a team to defeat it. They go to the bowels of the Earth to save Sue, and defeat the Mole Man and his artificially created life.

This story of the Fantastic Four's origin includes a cover gallery and sketchbook.

Busiek, Kurt, Ricardo Villagran, Richard Starkings, et al. *Strange Tales Featuring Dr. Strange, The Thing and the Human Torch*. New York: Marvel 1994. Reprints *Strange Tales Vol. 3:1*.

The Thing, Human Torch, and Nick Fury swap stories over a card game. They talk about the power of storytelling, and the belief that some creature, created out of one's imagination, can become real. Wyatt Wingfoot, Dr. Strange, the Thing, and the Human Torch confront a menace from their imagination who is able to defeat them all.

This book is a deluxe graphic novel from the Marvel Select imprint. It is a nice tribute to the early monster stories of Stan Lee and Jack Kirby.

Byrne, John, Jim Novak, Bjorn Heyn et al. *Fantastic Four Visionaries Vol. 1: John Byrne Book 1*. New York: Marvel, 2001. ISBN: 078510 7797. Reprints *Fantastic Four 232–240*.

Diablo tries to best the Fantastic Four using elemental creations. The Human Torch becomes a detective, and clears the name of an old classmate who was framed for a murder he did not commit. The trail leads him to Hammerhead. The Thing has to go through the Living Planet Ego's ear, in order to put a bomb in his brain matter. The Fantastic Four are put into tiny robotic bodies by Dr. Doom and the Puppet Master. Johnny Storm's girlfriend Frankie Raye, who is actually the daughter of Phineas Horton, the creator of the original Human Torch, also has flaming powers. Ben Grimm's famous Aunt Petunia is finally revealed, after 239 issues. The Fantastic Four help the Inhumans move their city of Attilan to the moon, and Quicksilver and Crystal's baby is born. Dr. Strange, Nick Fury, and the Watcher all make appearaces.

This is the first collection of Byrne's historic run of Fantastic Four comics.

Byrne, John, Jim Novak, Rick Parker et al. *Fantastic Four Visionaries Vol. 2: John Byrne Book. 2*. New York: Marvel, 2004. ISBN: 0785114645. Reprints *Fantastic Four 241–250*.

The Fantastic Four and the Black Panther investigate a power source in Africa, near Wakanda. They find an alien world based on Ancient Rome that is led by a former scout of Emperor Caligula Gaius Tiberius Augustus Agrippa. Terrax wants the Fantastic Four to help him destroy Galactus. Galactus is nearly destroyed, but Reed Richards saves him. Franklin

Richards discovers his all-powerful mutant power. In Latveria, the Fantastic Four fight a bunch of Dr. Doom's robots, and help Doom get his throne back. The Inhumans and the Fantastic Four end up exploring a space ship that is the size of many galaxies, and an alien that is the size of the Earth. Gladiator thinks the Fantastic Four are posing as Skrulls, and fights them. The X-Men, Captain America, Spider-Man, the Avengers, and Dr. Strange all make appearances.

Byrne, John, Jim Novak, Glynis Wein et al. *Fantastic Four: The Trial of Galactus.* New York: Marvel, 1989. ISBN: 0871355752. Reprints *Fantastic Four 242–244; 257–262; What the—? 2.*

Reed Richards saves Galactus from certain death. Galactus turns Frankie Raye into his herald Nova, and destroys a Skrull world. Doctor Doom and Tyros try to destroy the Fantastic Four, but the Silver Surfer intervenes and destroys Doom. Reed Richards is put on trial for saving Galactus, which many other alien races considered a crime. The Watcher, Odin, Galactus, and even Eternity get involved in the trial to save Richards's life.

John Byrne writes himself in as a character chronicling the trial. The story includes a short segment from Marvel's humor magazine *What The—?*

Claremont, Chris, Jon Bogdanove, Terry Austin, et al. *Fantastic Four vs. the X-Men.* New York: Marvel. 1994. ISBN: 0871356503. Reprints *Fantastic Four vs. The X-Men 1–4.*

Franklin Richards dreams that his father, Mr. Fantastic, and Dr. Doom are the same, and that Richards's diary reveals that he intended to have his ship go through the cosmic rays, and mutate Sue, Johnny and Ben. Sue finds the diary and learns that Reed apparently did know about the dangers of cosmic rays before they made their journey. This leads Reed to doubt everything on which his life is based. Ben Grimm takes this news very hard, and feels betrayed by Richards. Therefore, when he is asked by the X-Men to help save Kitty Pryde's life, his insecurities stop him from helping her. The Fantastic Four and She-Hulk fight with the X-Men, and Johnny Storm singes Sue Storm's arm, burning her badly. Magneto tries to gain the Fantastic Four's trust. When Dr. Doom offers to help the X-Men save Kitty from phasing into infinity, the X-Men go to Latveria and take Doom up on his offer to help, despite their misgivings about his motives. During his dream state, Franklin visits Kitty, using his astral projection. Reed must get over his insecurities and help Kitty, because Doom may actually do more damage.

This story is beautifully written. It has intense drama, human frailty, and good battle sequences.

Claremont, Chris, Pascual Ferry, Scott Hanna, et al. *The Fantastic 4th Voyage of Sinbad.* New York: Marvel, 2001.

The Fantastic Four take four voyages and meet up with the legendary sailor Sinbad. They join forces with him to fight the Jihad, who drains the life forces from his victims.

DeFalco, Tom, Paul Ryan, Mike Lackey, et al. *Fantastic Four: Nobody Gets Out Alive.* New York: Marvel, 1994. ISBN: 0785100636. Reprints *Fantastic Four 387–392.*

Reed Richards, who is from an alternative universe and time stream, is traveling in various alternate realities, calling himself Dark Raider, and killing all of his counterparts. He is trying to redeem himself for allowing Galactus to destroy Earth and kill the Fantastic Four. Johnny Storm's Skrull lover, who gives birth to a weapon while saying it's their child, deceives the Human Torch. In this adventure, Scott Lang, using Henry Pym's old costume, is Ant-Man, and the Sub-Mariner is a guest member of the Fantastic Four. The Watcher interferes, and kills the alternative Reed Richards. Franklin Richards, the Avengers, and Black Panther make appearances.

Dixon, Chuck, Leonardo Manco, Klaus Janson, et al. *Doom.* New York: Marvel, 2002. ISBN: 0785108351. Reprints *Doom 1–3; Doom the Emperor Returns 1–3.*

Dr. Doom is stranded on an alternative Earth called Planet Doom. He is captured and sent to the slave pits of the tyrant Al-Khalad. He finds some interesting secrets about the planet, and is able to turn the tables in his favor. Franklin Richards puts Doom in these various scenarios to test him, and prove that Mister Doom is not a "bad man." Doom tries to outwit Franklin, but to no avail. Doom fights a monster straight out of a Lovecraft story.

This "what if" story has the feel of a Mad Max movie.

Ellis, Warren, Stuart Immonen, Dave Stewart, et al. *Ultimate Fantastic Four Vol. 2: Doom.* New York: Marvel, 2004. ISBN: 0785114572. Reprints *Ultimate Fantastic Four 7–12.*

Victor Von Damme, who sabotaged Reed's experiment with the N-dimension, did not escape unscarred. Damme sends lethal robotic insects from Denmark to kill Reed and his friends at the Baxter Building. Reed and the rest of the Fantastic Four try to find Von Damme before the army finds him. Von Damme's colony of squatters, who are given free food and lodging in exchange for loyalty to him, become mind-controlled zombies who attack the Fantastic Four and are freed by them. Victor Von Damme, who is a descendant of the Vlad Tepees, the original Dracula, is left alone in his iron mask with no followers.

Ellis does an excellent reimagining of the Doom mythos.

Gruenwald, Mark, Ralph Macchio, John Byrne, et al. *The Thing: Project Pegasus Saga.* New

York: Marvel, 1988. ISBN: 0871353504. Reprints *Marvel Two-in-One 53–58, 60*.

The Thing joins the security team at the energy research center's Project Pegasus. Deathlok breaks into the center, and Quaser and the Thing fight him. Several inmates attempt to break out. Wundarr becomes the Aquarian, Black Goliath becomes Giant Man, and they all battle Nth Man.

A short tale, featuring the Impossible Man, is included as a bonus.

Jenkins, Paul, Jae Lee, Richard Starkings, et al. *The Inhumans*. New York: Marvel, 2000. ISBN: 0785107533. Reprints *Inhumans Vol. 2: 1–12*.

This is an epic tale featuring the artificially created Inhumans in their struggle to lead a peaceful life. The Inhumans are on the brink of war with the rest of humanity, and the Sub-Mariner is asked to intervene and save them from their own destruction. This is a fantastic blending of superhero mythos, science fiction, and fantasy art.

Jurgens, Dan, Art Thiebert, Greg Wright, et al. *Superman/Fantastic Four: Infinite Destruction*. New York: DC/Marvel, 1999. ISBN: 1563894432.

Superman finds out that Galactus had a hand in devouring Krypton. He goes to the Marvel Earth to seek the aid of the Fantastic Four in dealing with Galactus. Against his will, Superman is turned into the Herald of Galactus. Uneasily, the Fantastic Four team-up with the Superman Cyborg to find and deal with the devourer of worlds. The real Superman breaks free with the help of the Fantastic Four, and Galactus destroys the Cyborg.

This is an oversized graphic novel.

Kraft, David Anthony, Jack Kirby, Stan Lee, et al. *The Fantastic Four: The Secret Story of Marvel's Cosmic Quartet*. Chicago: Children's Press, 1981. ISBN: 0516024124 (trd); 082498014X. Reprints *Fantastic Four 1, 83, 203*.

Maximus has taken over the Inhumans' kingdom, and plans to take over the world. Blackbolt and the Inhumans, with the help of the Fantastic Four, defeat him. A young mutant child is able to produce evil, radioactive versions of the Fantastic Four with his subconscious.

This book, a combination of graphic and narrative text, tells the origin story of the Fantastic Four and its villains.

Lee, Jim, Scott Williams, Brandon Choi, et al. *Fantastic Four: Heroes Reborn*. New York: Marvel, 2000. ISBN: 0785107444. Reprints *Fantastic Four Vol. 2: 1–6*.

A Skrull is posing as S.H.I.E.L.D. agent Wyatt Wingfoot, and becomes Dr. Doom's lackey. Through the power of the Silver Surfer, he becomes the Super Skrull. Reed Richards saves Namor's life, and the Thing beats Giganto.

This is an updated retelling of the Fantastic Four's origin, and the story of their first encounters with the Mole Man, Dr. Doom, Sub-Mariner, Silver Surfer, Super Skrull, and the Black Panther. For example, Ben Grimm served in the Gulf War, instead of World War II. It is an outstanding tribute to Stan Lee and Jack Kirby's original series.

Lee, Stan, Jack Kirby, John Buscema, et al. *It's Clobberin' Time: Hulk vs. Thing: Four Stories Featuring the Green Goliath Going Toe-to-Toe with the Ever Lovin' Blue Eyed Thing*. New York: Marvel, 1999. Reprints *Fantastic Four Volume 1: 25–26, 112, Marvel Features 11*.

The Hulk gets angry when he hears that Captain America has replaced him in the Avengers. He goes on a rampage, and the Fantastic Four try to stop him. Reed Richards gets extremely sick and is bedridden. The Thing and the Hulk fight, and as usual the Hulk wins. When the Fantastic Four meet the Avengers for the first time, they seem to get in each other's way; in their third meeting, the Hulk almost kills the Thing. The Hulk and the Thing fight for the amusement of Kurgo, Master of Planet X, and the Leader, who make bets as to who will win.

Lee, Stan, Jack Kirby, John Byrne, et al. *Greatest Villains of the Fantastic Four*. New York: Marvel, 1995. ISBN: 0785100792. Reprints *Fantastic Four Annual 5; Fantastic Four 100, 259–260, 289–290*.

The Fantastic Four meet Psycho Man, who is from the Sub Atomic Universe and who wants to control the Earth. Along with She-Hulk and Nick Fury, the Fantastic Four battle Blastaar and Annihilus. Reed Richards sacrifices himself in his battle with Annihilus, and the Silver Surfer and Doc Doom fight Galactus's herald, Tyros. Doom is believed killed. The Black Panther and the Inhumans make appearances, as do villains Puppet Master, the Thinker, and android versions of Kang, Dragon Man, Doctor Doom, and the Hulk.

Lee, Stan, Jack Kirby, John Byrne, et al. *The Villainy of Doctor Doom*. New York: Marvel, 1999. ISBN: 0785107320. Reprints *Fantastic Four Annual 2; Fantastic Four Vol. 1 39, 40, 239, 240; selections from Fantastic Four Vol. 1 84–87*.

This book contains a number of stories in which the Fantastic Four fight Dr. Doom. It also contains Dr. Doom's origin story. Other stories include one in which Doom overtakes the Baxter Building, and the Fantastic Four team up with Daredevil to take it back, and another in which the Fantastic Four help Doom retake his throne as lord of Latveria.

Lee, Stan, Jack Kirby, Joe Sinnott, et al. *The Fantastic Four*. New York: Fireside: Simon and Schuster, 1979. ISBN: 067124955X (trd); 067124812X (pbk). Reprints *Fantastic Four 4, 49–51, 86.*

This issue contains the Fantastic Four's first encounter with the Sub-Mariner and the famous "Galactus Trilogy," in which the Silver Surfer and the Watcher help the Fantastic Four stop Galactus from draining the Earth of its life-force. This is the first appearance of the Silver Surfer and the original Punisher. Stan Lee prefaces each story.

McKeever, Sean, Makoto Nakatsuka Gurihiru, Joe Dodd, et al. *Marvel Age Fantastic Four Vol. 1: All for One*. New York: Marvel, 2004. ISBN: 0785114688. Reprints *Marvel Age Fantastic Four 1–4.*

The Fantastic Four are created when Reed Richards, Sue and Johnny Storm and Ben Grimm pass through a series of cosmic radiation during a space flight. They have to stop the Mole Man from using his monsters to destroy humanity. A group of alien Skrulls impersonate the Fantastic Four, making it look like they are criminals. The Miracle Man tries to best the Fantastic Four through his hypnotic techniques. Johnny Storm finds the amnesiac Sub-Mariner in a homeless shelter. He regains his memory, and goes ballistic towards humanity.

This is a modern retelling, done in manga style, of the original Fantastic Four stories by Stan Lee and Jack Kirby.

Morrison, Grant, Jae Lee, Jose Villarrubia, et al. *Fantastic Four 1234*. New York: Marvel, 2002. ISBN: 0785110402. Reprints *Fantastic Four 1234: 1–4.*

Dr. Doom bends reality to destroy the Fantastic Four. He turns the Thing into Ben Grimm, who nearly gets hit by a car, and almost dies. He tries to get the Sub-Mariner to turn against the Fantastic Four and Reed Richards, by wooing Sue Richards, and he makes an offer to the Mole Man for dominion under the Earth. Reed Richards's mind is more powerful, and turns Doom's reality-bending machine against him. The Sub-Mariner kisses Sue Richards. This book is beautifully drawn and written.

Nocenti, Ann, Bret Blevins, Al Willamson, et al. *The Inhumans*. New York: Marvel, 1988. ISBN: 0871354357.

Medusa is pregnant with Black Bolt's child. The ruling council forbids her to have the child, and she runs away to Earth, to give birth. A band of Inhumans follow her, including Bolt's insane brother "Mad Max" who tries unsuccessfully to woo Medusa. (*Marvel Graphic Novel 39*)

Olshevsky, George, Tony Frutti, Jim Steranko, et al. *The Marvel Comics Index 4: Fantastic Four*. Ontario: G&T Enterprises, 1977. ISBN: 0943348501 (Marvel Index Set).

This collection is an index and history of the Fantastic Four and the Silver Surfer. It includes a cross index of personnel and major characters. Magazines indexed include *Fantastic Four, Fantastic Four Annual, Giant Size Super Stars, Giant Size Fantastic Four, The Human Torch*, and *The Silver Surfer*, up to 1977. It also includes an index and history of Marvel Boy from the 1950s.

Pacheco, Carlos, Jeph Loeb, Rafael Marin, et al. *Fantastic Four: Flesh and Stone*. New York: Marvel, 2001. ISBN: 0785107932. Reprints *Fantastic Four Vol. 3: 35–39.*

The Fantastic Four are bankrupt, and have to deal with some of their older foes, including Diablo and the Super Skrull. Ben Grimm acquires the ability to turn back and forth into the Thing. Johnny Storm becomes a movie star, and the Fantastic Four get a new Baxter Building from space. The Grey Gargoyle and the Avengers make appearances.

Pacheco, Carlos, Rafael Marin, Jeph Loeb, et al. *Fantastic Four: Into the Breach*. New York: Marvel, 2002. ISBN: 0785108653. Reprints *Fantastic Four Vol. 2 40–45.*

The Gideon Corporation thinks it owns the negative zone in which Mr. Fantastic, Sue, and the Thing are stranded, and the Human Torch creates a new Fantastic Four to fight the corporation. The Sub-Mariner fights the Torch, but eventually joins him, as do Namorita, Ant-Man, and the She-Hulk. Annihilus, the Hellscout, and Maximus make appearances.

Simonson, Walt, Arthur Adams. Art Thiebert, et al. *The New Fantastic Four: Monsters Unleashed*. New York: Marvel, 1992. ISBN: 0871356570. Reprints *Fantastic Four, 347–349.*

The Fantastic Four is immobilized by a rogue, female Skrull, who wants to overthrow the Skrull Empire. Spider-Man, Ghost Rider, the Hulk and Wolverine are unknowingly teamed up to assist her. They all end up on Monster Island with the Mole Man, and Ghost Rider gives the female Skrull his penance stare.

Starlin, Jim, Berni Wrightson, Jim Novak, et al. *The Incredible Hulk and the Thing in the Big Change*. New York: Marvel, 1987. ISBN: 0871352990.

The Thing and the Hulk get transported to an alien world, Maltriculon, which is based on commercial enterprise. The plans for a new food-enhancer sauce have been stolen, and they are employed to retrieve it for its rightful owner. An alien, Stamben Malelet, promises them any two wishes if they get the food-enhancer plans back. They fight a being who is a combination of the Hulk and the Thing. After they achieve their goal, the Hulk wants to go back home and get something to eat. The Thing, needless to say, is not amused. The Watcher makes an appearance.

This is one of the funniest, cleverest Marvel books ever written. (*Marvel Graphic Novel 29*)

Stern, Roger, Michael Mignola, Mark Badger, et al. *Doctor Strange and Doctor Doom: Triumph and Torment.* New York: Marvel, 1989. ISBN: 0871356600.

The demonic Mephisto has captured the soul of Doom's mother. Doom must align himself with Dr. Strange, and go to the evil domain to rescue her. Oshtur, Hoggoth, Agamotto, and the Vishanti make appearances. (*Marvel Graphic Novel 49*)

Sturm, James, Guy Davis, Michel Vrana, et al. *Fantastic Four Legends Vol. 1: Unstable Molecules,* New York: Marvel, 2003. ISBN: 078 5111123. Reprints *Fantastic Four 1; Fantastic Four Unstable Molecules 1–4.*

This postmodernist take on the Fantastic Four purports to tell the true story behind the characters in the Fantastic Four comic book. Lee/Kirby used actual people to tell the stories of the Fantastic Four's adventures. Sturm relies on several primary source documents, including the journal of Susan Sturm; Professor Harvey Beyers's *The Fantastic Four: The World They Lived in and the World They Created*; *Hot Time*; and *Hot Rods, My High School Years with the Human Torch,* by Johnny Sturm's boyhood pal. The collection gives an excellent survey of life during the 1950s, including a look at Cold War science, the Beatniks, and the boxing industry. It is highly recommended for anyone wanting to know the real people behind the comics.

Sumerak, Mark, John Layman, Stan Lee, et al. *Marvel Age Fantastic Four Volume 2: Doom.* New York: Marvel, 2004. ISBN: 0785115 501. Reprints *Marvel Age: Fantastic Four 5–8.*

The Fantastic Four meets Dr. Doom who sends them back in time for Blackbeard's treasure, and the pirates think that the Thing is Blackbeard. Dr. Doom tricks the Sub-Mariner into betraying the Fantastic Four, only to be betrayed himself. Doom is drifting into space. The Fantastic Four deal with Kurgo and the aliens from Planet X, and the Puppet Master tries to control the Fantastic Four. Sue Storm finds Prince Namor attractive, and the Thing meets Alicia Masters for the first time.

This book is a modernization of the Fantastic Four, for all ages. It is based on Stan Lee's and Jack Kirby's original plots.

Waid, Mark, Karl Kesel, Mike Wieringo, et al. *Fantastic Four Vol. 5: Disassembled.* New

York: Marvel, 2004. ISBN: 0785115366. Reprints *Fantastic Four, 514–519.*

The Fantastic Four have lost public favor, and the Wizard assembles a new Frightful Four, featuring Hydro-Man, Fire Maiden, and the Trapster. Johnny Storm has been emailing the Wizard's/Fire Maiden's daughter Cole, who inadvertently helps the Frightful Four gain access to the Fantastic Four's headquarters, where they are defeated. This defeat is shown on television as the Wizard tries to break and humiliate the Fantastic Four, but the Fantastic Four infiltrate the Wizard's stronghold for a rematch. Cole wants to be free from her superpowers, and asks Reed to cure her. Manhattan is taken from the rest of the world by a fleet of miles-high, alien spacecraft that seeks to save planets from Galactus's hunger. The aliens want to kill the Invisible Girl, who has the power to help Galactus, but things are not always what they seem to be, and Johnny Storm gets his sister's powers.

Waid, Mark, Howard Porter, Norm Rapmund, et al. *Fantastic Four Vol. 3: Authoritative Action.* New York: Marvel, 2004. ISBN: 0785 111980. Reprints *Fantastic Four 503–508.*

With Dr. Doom out of Latveria, Reed Richards sets the Fantastic Four up as the rulers of the country. He attempts to show the citizens that they are free from Doom, but he almost acts like a dictator. He roots out any dissidents, and even uses Doom robots against the Thing and the Human Torch. Hungary wants to take over Latveria, and the United Nations does not recognize the Fantastic Four as Latveria's rightful leaders. A full-scale war is about to break out, and Nick Fury is called in to moderate. Reed goes to Hell, and brings Doom back to the Mobius dimension, where they spend the rest of eternity. The Fantastic Four rescue Reed, and Doom takes over the various bodies of the foursome. Ben Grimm, the Thing, is killed by a S.H.I.E.L.D. gun, and the Fantastic Four are bankrupt. Half of Reed's face is blown off.

Waid, Mark, Mike Wieringo, Casey Jones, et al. *Fantastic Four Vol. 2: Unthinkable.* New York: Marvel, 2003. ISBN: 0785111115. Reprints *Fantastic Four Vol. 3: 67–70; Fantastic Four 500–502.*

Victor Von Doom tracks down an old lover, and destroys her soul in return for the powers of a sorcerer. He has a bond with Reed and Susan's daughter, Val, and kidnaps her to lure the Fantastic Four to his home. He sends Franklin Richards to a place inhabited by demons, Hell. The Fantastic Four unsuccessfully try to rescue him, and Doom uses his magical powers to torture them. He even has the Thing fight the Mindless Ones, and humbles Reed Richards by locking him up in a room, and forcing him to study magic. Reed, a scientist who does not believe in magic, finds this most difficult. Dr. Strange, in his astral form, tries to teach Reed some basic lessons in sorcery, and Reed is finally able to use magic against Doom. However, Doom manages to scar Richards's face. Franklin is saved, but has a very hard time adjusting to normalcy; he sees demons everywhere he goes.

The book has a special section that contains deleted scenes and outtakes; commentary by Waid; scripts; the original synopsis of *Fantastic Four 1*, by Stan Lee; Hembeck's 500th issue tribute; and a "printography" which includes the covers of every *Fantastic Four* issue up to Issue 500.

Waid, Mark, Mike Wiergino, Karl Kesel, et al. *Fantastic Four Vol. 1: Imaginauts.* New York: Marvel, 2003. ISBN: 0785110631. Reprints *Fantastic Four Vol. 3: 56; 60–66.*

Johnny Storm admits to his sister Sue Richards that all the gags mailed to Ben Grimm from the Yancy Street Gang were actually from him. Grimm goes on a rampage to track down the source of the pranks. Sue, who wants Johnny to act more mature, gives him the job of handling the finances within the Fantastic Four's corporation. Mr. Fantastic's mathematical computer counterpart comes to life, and, driven mad with jealousy, threatens the Fantastic Four. Insects from another dimension find their way into the Baxter Building. Franklin is jealous of his sister, and Reed has tests run on her to make sure she is normal. Ben Grimm, the Thing, goes back to Yancy Street, and, while battling Powderkeg, rediscovers his Jewish roots.

Leonard Pitts of the *Miami Herald* discusses how the Fantastic Four's creators, Lee and Kirby, always envisioned the Thing as being Jewish. Mark Waid has included his brilliant *Fantastic Four Manifesto*.

Waid, Mark, Mike Wieringo, Karl Kesel, et al. *Fantastic Four Vol. 4: Hereafter.* New York: Marvel, 2004. ISBN: 0785115269. Reprints *Fantastic Four 509–513.*

The Fantastic Four have fallen out of public favor, and have to liquidate their assets. Reed Richards, who is totally torn up over the death of the Thing, steals Grimm's body, and develops a machine to take them to heaven and retrieve Ben Grimm. In heaven they meet Grimm's brother Danny and the Almighty himself, who looks an awful lot like artist Jack Kirby. In fact, God is drawing Galactus while talking to the Fantastic Four. He erases Reed's facial scar, working from numerous sculptures that Grimm's ex-girlfriend Alicia had made of the Thing. The Human Torch has a hard time dealing with the fall from favor with the public, and asks Spider-Man for advice on how to deal with it. They end up having a fight with Hydro-Man at a water park. Sue uses Namor as a way to get Reed to pay attention to her, and she meets one of Reed's old flames.

Hulk and She-Hulk

Do you have any idea what you've done?—*Joe Fixit, the Grey Hulk*

UMMMM—Hulk likes beans.—*Incredible Hulk*

Azzarello, Brian, Richard Corban, Studio F, et al. *Banner: Startling Stories.* New York: Marvel Comics, 2001. ISBN: 078510853X. Reprints *Startling Stories: 1–4.*

The Hulk goes on a tremendous rampage, destroying cities and killing people. Doc Samson is brought in to rein him in.

Byrne, John, Kim DeMulder, Petra Scotese, et al. *The Sensational She-Hulk.* New York: Marvel, 1985. ISBN: 087135084X.

She-Hulk and her boyfriend are kidnapped by S.H.I.E.L.D. agents. She is forced to go under a number of uncomfortable medical tests on the S.H.I.E.L.D. ship. She ends up fighting a group of intelligent cockroaches bent on stealing her individuality. (*Marvel Graphic Novel 18*)

Byrne, John, Bob Wiacek, Glynis Oliver, et al. *Sensational She-Hulk.* New York: Marvel, 1992. ISBN: 0871358921. Reprints *Sensational She-Hulk 1–8.*

She-Hulk interacts with the writer and the read-ers. The Headmen employ the Ringmaster and Circus to test She-Hulk. In homage to *Hulk 2*, the Headmen also employ Toadmen to give She-Hulk the illusion of an alien invasion. The Toadmen turn out to be just men in suits. Spider-Man helps She-Hulk get free from the Headmen. The old Timely character Blonde Phantom is employed by a law firm who wants to hire She-Hulk. There also are appearances by the Stilt Man, Reed Richards, Robocop Xemu, and Santa Claus.

John Byrne's famous run on *Sensational She-Hulk* is considered to be a postmodern take on Superhero comics. It is highly recommended that Marvel should reprint this humorous, fun trade.

David, Peter, Dale Keown, Jan Duursema, et al. *Incredible Hulk: Ghost of the Past.* New York: Marvel, 1996. ISBN: 0785102612. Reprints *Incredible Hulk 397–400.*

The Leader is using gamma radiation to seemingly benefit mankind. The Hulk is able to spoil his evil plan. Ironclad, Vapor, X-Ray, Rick Jones, Hydra, and the Scarlet Witch make appearances.

David, Peter, Dale Keown, Dan Panosian, et al. *The Hulk: Pitt*. New York: Marvel, 1997. ISBN: 0785102973.

A young orphan, Timmy, has inter-dimensional powers to bend reality. He wants to see his mom, but the being Pitt comes to Earth looking for him. Rick Jones tries to console the boy. The Hulk and Pitt get into a massive fight. The Hulk believes he is protecting Timmy from Pitt.

David, Peter, Dale Keown, Joe Weems, *The End: Hulk*. New York: Marvel, 2002.

Bruce Banner, the Hulk, is the last survivor on Earth after a nuclear holocaust. The robotic Reader leaves a flying camera to observe the actions of the Hulk. Hulk tries to destroy the camera but Banner watches the action and, during one scene, sees how the Hulk regenerates after being eaten by bugs (a particularly gruesome scene). Banner has a heart attack and only the Hulk remains, along with the bugs.

An earlier version was published as "The Last Titan" in the anthology *The Ultimate Hulk*.

David, Peter, Stan Lee, Jack Kirby, et al. *Incredible Hulk: Beauty and the Behemoth*. New York: Marvel, 1998. ISBN: 0785106596. Reprints *Incredible Hulk 1, 169, 319, 344, 372, 377, 466*.

This is a collection of stories mostly dealing with Bruce Banner/Hulk's relationship with his love Betty Ross. It includes her transformation into Harpy, and Banner and Betty's marriage. The Grey Hulk and Green Hulk, along with Banner, end up fighting a battle within their minds. Doc Samson acts as the therapist. There are appearances by Modok, Bi-Beast, and the Leader.

David, Peter, Stan Lee, Roy Thomas, et al. *Hulk Megazine 1*. New York: Marvel, 1996. Reprints *Hulk 3; Incredible Hulk 147, 222, 226, 331, 333; Tales to Astonish 90–91; Marvel Fanfare 29; Incredible Hulk Annual 1*.

While in the desert, the Hulk believes he is in a paradise. The Grey Hulk goes up against a wife-beating sheriff, and Betty meets up with an old flame. The Abomination kidnaps Betty. The Hulk deals with a cannibalistic child who has been turned into a greater monster than himself. After saving Bruce Banner, a bizarre "white glass-skinned woman" tries to turn Banner/Hulk into a glass sculpture.

This is a nice collection of historic Hulk stories and covers that includes material on the Hulk's origin and the origin of the Abomination. There is an afterword by editor Gary Greenberg.

David, Peter, Todd McFarlane, Erik Larson, et al. *The Incredible Hulk: Ground Zero*. New York: Marvel, 2001. ISBN: 0871357925. Reprints *Incredible Hulk, Vol. 1: 340–346*.

The Grey Hulk, Rick Jones, and Clay Quaterman try to find out where the government has stored several gamma bombs, in order to destroy them. The Leader finds these bombs and uses them to blow up the city of Middletown and the Hulk in the process. The X-Men make a guest appearance, with the Hulk fighting Wolverine.

A sequel, "The Beast with Nine Bands," was published in the anthology *The Ultimate Hulk*.

David, Peter, George Perez, Tom Smith, et al. *Hulk: Future Imperfect*. New York. 1994. ISBN: 0785100296. Reprints *Hulk: Future Imperfect 1–2*. ISBN: 0871359618 (1); 08713 59626 (2).

This is the groundbreaking collaboration between writer Peter David and George Perez, in which the Hulk meets an alternate version of himself in the distant future. The Maestro is a brilliantly evil and power hungry version of Banner, who rules over Dystopia. Rick Jones is an old, tired man, but still has the rebellious spirit, and wants to rise up against the Maestro. He explains to the Hulk just what has happened in this "future" world. Jones has a trophy room full of superbeing memorabilia, including the helmets for Magneto, Ant-Man, Black Knight, Nova, and Thor. There also are costumes for Captain America, Spider-Man, Dr. Strange, and an old Sentinel Head, among much material preserved in a museum-like atmosphere. This is one of Peter David's masterworks, and should be reprinted.

David, Peter, Richard Starkings, Joe Kaufman, et al. *Tales to Astonish: Featuring the Hulk, Hank Pym and the Wasp*. New York: Marvel, 1994. Reprints *Tales to Astonish Vol. 3: 1*.

Hank Pym and Janet Van Dyne visit Oslo where they have to go up against a madman, Caine, who worships Loki. Loki gives Caine some of his powers, and Caine, disguised as Loki, tries to bring about the end of everything, Ragnarok, the Twilight of the Gods. Pym, the Hulk, Ant-Man and the Wasp defeat Caine.

Jenkins, Paul, Ron Garney, Mike McKone, et al. *Incredible Hulk: Dogs of War*. New York: Marvel, 2001. ISBN: 0785107908. Reprints *Hulk Vol. 1: 12–20*.

Bruce Banner remembers incidents of child abuse, discovers that he has multiple personalities that he finds within in his mind, and seeks help from an old girlfriend, Angela, who is a psychiatrist. General Ryker, who experimented with gamma radiation on various people, including his wife, tries to take down the Hulk. Throughout the book, the Hulk goes from being Banner to the Grey Hulk and the Green Hulk. Angela argues with Doc Samson about whether the intelligent Green Hulk is actually Bruce Banner. Everybody is afraid of Ryker, including Nick Fury. Thunderbolt, Ross, betrays Banner, Doc Samson, and the ex-girlfriend to Ryker. It is learned that Ryker actually killed Kennedy, and is engaged in other covert activities.

There is an afterword by Paul Jenkins.

Johns, Geoff, Scott Kolins, Steve Sadowski, et al. *Avengers Vol. 3: The Search for She-Hulk.* New York: Marvel, 2004. ISBN: 07851120 22. Reprints *Avengers Vol. 3: 71–76.*

When She-Hulk has a run-in with Jack of Hearts, the balance of gamma radiation in her body is altered, and she turns back into a regular human. She goes in search of her cousin in Bone, Idaho, and the Avengers go in search of She-Hulk. When she does "Hulk-out," she becomes more like her destructive cousin, and begins destroying with little reason. When Hawkeye shoots her cousin Bruce Banner with an arrow, he turns into the Hulk, and both the Hulk and She-Hulk fight in a massive battle. Jack of Hearts restores her gamma radiation levels. Henry Pym again asks the Wasp, Janet Van Dyne, to marry him, but the Whirlwind ruins their little rendezvous. A murderous pedophile kidnaps Cassie, the daughter of Ant-Man, Scott Lang. Ant-Man and Jack of Hearts save Cassie, and then Ant-Man goes out into space with the pedophile. Hawkeye rejoins the Avengers

Jones, Bruce, Mark Bagley, James Shamus, et al. *Hulk: Official Movie Adaptation.* New York: Marvel, 2003. ISBN: 0785111557. Reprints *Hulk: The Movie Adaptation*; *Ultimates 5*; *Incredible Hulk 34*; *Ultimate Marvel Team-Up 2–3.*

David Banner experiments on himself, and fathers a son with unique abilities. When Bruce Banner saves one of his coworkers, he is caught in a blast of gamma radiation which unleashes the monster inside of him. The military tries to capture the Banner/Hulk, but he ends up escaping. Banner's father becomes the Absorbing Man, and, while battling his son, he absorbs too much of the Hulk's rage.

This is the Marvel Comics adaptation of the hit movie *Hulk*, written by James Shamus. It includes recent *Hulk* comics which have become classics, among which are stories from the Marvel's Ultimate Universe.

Jones, Bruce, Mike Deodato Jr., Wes Abbott, et al. *Incredible Hulk Vol. 4: Abominable.* New York: Marvel, 2003. ISBN: 0785111131. Reprints *Incredible Hulk Vol. 2: 50–54.*

The covert group that has been hounding the Hulk for his blood, frees the Abomination from his military prison on the condition that he is willing to defeat the Hulk. Emil Blonsky's wife makes friends with Bruce Banner, and seduces him. The covert group videotapes her affair with Banner, and shows it to the Abomination who is not happy about it. The Hulk and the Abomination finally come to blows. The Hulk defeats him, and. Bruce Banner retains his strength as the Hulk.

This book contains great fight sequences between the Hulk and the Abomination. This is the best written of the Jones series so far.

Jones, Bruce, Mike Deodato Jr., Randy Gentile, et al. *Incredible Hulk Vol. 6: Split Decisions.* New York: Marvel, 2004. ISBN: 078511 2383. Reprints *Incredible Hulk Vol. 2: 60–65.*

A clandestine organization wants the Hulk's blood to produce their version of a Super Soldier. It has created an android/animal hybrid, the Krills, who eat humans and are programmed to get the Hulk's blood. When they attack Nadia Blonsky's place, Doc Samson and Sandra Verdugo attempt to aid Nadia and Bruce Banner. Samson finds out he has a child, Ricky, who is being held prisoner by this mysterious clandestine organization, and that Sandra is Ricky's mother. Sandra and Ricky are seemingly blown up. The Hulk/Banner has been cloned. Betty Ross reveals herself to be alive, but with a new face. Banner tells Nadia he loves her.

In this volume, the *X-Files*–like conspiracy continues, and Mr. Blue is revealed.

Jones, Bruce, Mike Deodato, Jr., Darick Robertson, et al. *Incredible Hulk Vol. 8: Big Things.* New York: Marvel, 2004. ISBN: 0785115331. Reprints *Incredible Hulk 70–76.*

Bruce Banner is caught by the Feds, but is then let go by one of them who has cancer. The brother of one of Tony Stark's associates, who had killed herself, is hunting for Stark. The brother infiltrates Stark's home and is taken prisoner. Banner finds Stark and together they work on an Iron Man suit that can withstand gamma radiation. Banner even dons the Iron Man suit. The Hulk and Iron Man fight each other in several battles that harken back to the Silver Age, and Banner wakes up in a post-apocalyptic future world. The Leader gets the Hulk to do his bidding by controlling Banner's mind. When Doc Samson, Betty, and Nadia try to help free Banner from the Leader's control, they find the Leader is just a brain without a body, existing in a liquid vat. The Leader wants to transfer his mind into the Hulk's body, but when the vat is broken, the Leader's brain falls apart. Flying glass kills Nadia. The Hulk beats Doc Samson to a pulp, and Betty calls Banner a freak.

Jones, Bruce, Garth Ennis, Dougie Braithwaite, et al. *Incredible Hulk Vol. 7: Dead Like Me.* New York: Marvel, 2004. ISBN: 07851139 91. Reprints *Incredible Hulk Vol. 2: 66–69*; *Hulk Smash 1–2.*

Doc Samson takes Betty Ross to his place in the forest where Betty tells him she has cancer. Samson wants to use the Hulk's blood to save her. Banner decides to leave Nadia, but his clone comes back to life. The Hulk and the Hulk's clone fight, until the Hulk dismembers his clone. While the army is ineffectually trying to contain the Hulk, the Hulk learns a lesson in selflessness from a lieutenant who is willing to sacrifice himself for his men.

Jones, Bruce, Leandro Fernandez, Dave Sharpe, et al. *Incredible Hulk Vol. 5: Hide in Plain Sight*. New York: Marvel, 2003. ISBN: 0785111514. Reprints *Incredible Hulk 55–59*.

Even though Crusher Creel, the Absorbing Man, is locked up, he is able to enter people's minds through telepathy. He forces a young woman to commit suicide by jumping in front of a train. The young lady's best friend runs into Bruce Banner, and they strike up a friendship. Creel seeks to possess the Hulk in order to help him break out of his prison. He threatens to kill a young child if Banner/Hulk does not help him. The Hulk does Creel's bidding, only to be outwitted by Creel, who enters the mind of a dead person.

Jones, Bruce, Stuart Immonen, Scott Koblish, et al. *Incredible Hulk Vol. 3: Transfer of Power*. New York: Marvel, 2003. ISBN: 0785110658. Reprints *Incredible Hulk Vol. 2: 44–49*.

Bruce Banner is still on the run from agent Pratt who keeps dying and coming back to life. Banner is hit by a car, and nursed back to life by Sandra. Sandra and Banner are on the run from Pratt. Pratt, who has some of Banner's radiated blood, becomes a mini-Hulk and beats Banner to a pulp. He tempts Sandra with her kidnapped son Ricky, but it turns out that Ricky is nothing but a robot.

The Hulk finally makes an appearance in issue 49, and smashes Pratt into little pieces. Most of this book centers on Bruce Banner, with the Hulk only appearing once. It is a very dark and twisted tale.

Jones, Bruce, Scott Kolins, Lee Loughridge, et al. *Hulk Legends Vol. 1: Hulk/Wolverine Six Hours*. New York: Marvel, 2003. ISBN: 0785111573. Reprints *Hulk/Wolverine Six Hours 1–4*; *Incredible Hulk 181*.

Bruce Banner and Wolverine get involved with saving the life of a teenager who was bitten by a coral snake and is on the verge of death. The Hulk/Banner's blood is used to save the teenager. They also inadvertently get involved in a drug deal gone bad, in which the Shredder is killing practically anyone with whom he comes in contact. Wolverine battles the Shredder, who has beaten him before, and finally triumphs over him. The Shredder is killed by a wildcat.

This book includes an extra reprint of the very first Wolverine appearance, in which he battled the Hulk and the Wendigo.

Jones, Bruce, John Romita Jr., Tom Palmer, et al. *Incredible Hulk Vol. 1: Return of the Monster*. New York: Marvel, 2002. ISBN: 07851

09439. Reprints *Incredible Hulk Vol. 2: 34–39*.

Bruce Banner is on the run because the Hulk is accused of killing a young boy. The boy was not killed, but is being held hostage by a group trying to frame the Hulk. Several well-trained assassins are working to track down Banner and the Hulk. One of the assassins is the mother of the boy who was kidnapped. Doc Samson helps Banner escape. Banner has a mysterious email pal, Mr. Blue, who is helping him.

Jones, Bruce, Lee Weeks, Kaare Andrews, et al. *Incredible Hulk Vol. 2: Boiling Point*. New York: Marvel, 2002. ISBN: 0785109056. Reprints *Incredible Hulk Vol. 2: 40–43*.

Bruce Banner is minding his own business when a thief tries to rob a convenience store, and takes the customers hostage. A police team surrounds the store, and tries to reason with the thief. A group posing as the FBI kidnaps Banner and Hulk. The Hulk catches a bullet with his teeth.

Kieth, Sam, Richard Isanovf, Richard Starkings, et al. *Wolverine Legends Vol. 1: Wolverine/Hulk*. New York: Marvel, 2003. ISBN: 0785111387. Reprints *Wolverine/Hulk 1–4*.

Wolverine comes across the spirit of little girl Po, who needs help from him and her uncle Bruce Banner to get out of a plane that her father had crashed twenty years earlier. Po's spirit is forced to wander in limbo until she and her father can be found and freed from the plane's safety belts. Wolverine and Hulk dig up the crashed plane and free Po's spirit. The Hulk cries at the end.

Kraft, David Anthony, Stan Lee, Jack Kirby, et al. *The Incredible Hulk: The Secret Story of Marvel's Gamma-Powered Goliath*. Chicago: Children's Press, 1981. ISBN: 051602 4132, 0824980131. Reprints *Hulk 1*; *Incredible Hulk 125, 227*.

The original story of the Hulk is recounted in this book, using a combination of narrative and graphics.

Lee, Stan, Peter David, Al Milgrom, et al. *Hulk Transformations*. New York: Marvel, 1996. ISBN: 0785108620; 0785102620 (2002). Reprints *Incredible Hulk 3, 6, 272, 315, 324, 347, 377*.

This is a collection of Hulk stories related to his transformations. It includes his second transformation into the Grey Hulk, and his fights against the Ringmaster, Wendigo, and Sasquatch. In one story, Doc Samson hypnotizes Bruce Banner. The Green Hulk, Grey Hulk, and Banner fight against an even greater demon in his subconscious.

Lee, Stan, Steve Ditko, Jack Kirby, et al. *Incredible Hulk*. New York: Simon and Schuster, 1978. ISBN: 0671242695 (trd); 0671242 245 (pbk). Reprints *Tales to Astonish 60–74, 88; Avengers 3; Incredible Hulk 3; Fantastic Four 12*.

The Fantastic Four battle the Hulk, and there is a great fight between the Thing and Hulk. The Avengers fight both the Hulk and the Sub-Mariner. Major Talbot follows Bruce Banner, believing that he has some connection to the Hulk, and is also a communist spy. The communists take Bruce Banner prisoner. The Chameleon, the Ringmaster, Boomerang, Rick Jones, and the Humanoid make appearances.

In this volume there are stories about the origin of the Hulk and the origin of the Leader, and there are several stories in which the Leader tries to align himself with the Hulk, and even saves his life. This is a special collection that came out in conjunction with the *Hulk* television show, and the cover advertises the Hulk as a national TV star.

Lee, Stan, Jack Kirby, John Buscema, et al. *It's Clobberin' Time: Hulk vs. Thing: Four Stories Featuring the Green Goliath Going Toe-to-toe with the Ever Lovin' Blue Eyed Thing*. New York: Marvel, 1999. Reprints *Fantastic Four Vol. 1: 25–26, 112, Marvel Features 11*.

The Hulk gets angry when he hears that Captain America has replaced him in the Avengers. He goes on a rampage, and the Fantastic Four try to stop him. Reed Richards gets extremely sick and is bedridden. The Thing and the Hulk fight, and as usual the Hulk wins. When the Fantastic Four meet the Avengers for the first time, they seem to get in each other's way, and in their third meeting, the Hulk almost kills the Thing. The Hulk and the Thing fight for the amusement of Kurgo, Master of Planet X, and the Leader, who make bets as to who will win.

McDuffie, Dwayne, Robin D. Chaplik, June Brigman, et al. *She-Hulk: Ceremony*. New York: Marvel, 1989. ISBN: 0871356325 (1); 0871356333 (2).

She-Hulk has thoughts about marriage and having children, and realizes that she loves Wyatt Wingfoot. They team up together against an evil shaman, a very wealthy industrialist who seeks to drain the world of all its human energy. Wingfoot and She-Hulk go to Oklahoma, to the reservation where the shaman has decimated and relocated the tribe. Wingfoot realizes that his true destiny is to be chief of the tribe and a shaman in his own right.

Olshevsky, George, Tony Frutti, Ken Steacy, et al. *The Marvel Comics Index: Tales to Astonish 7A: Book One The Incredible Hulk*. Ontario: G&T Enterprises, 1978. ISBN: 0943348501 (Marvel Index Set).

This volume gives a synopsis and history of the Hulk, Wasp, and Henry Pym. It indexes *Tales to Astonish, Incredible Hulk 2nd series, Hulk Annuals, Giant Size Hulk, Rampaging Hulk*, and the *Hulk Magazine* up to 1978. It also contains a major character and personnel cross-index.

Slott, San, Juan Bobillo, Paul Pelletier, et al. *She-Hulk Vol. 1: Single Green Female*. New York: Marvel, 2004. ISBN: 0785114432. Reprints *She-Hulk 1–6*.

She-Hulk gets booted out of the Avengers mansion for bringing home different guests every night and abusing her Avengers privileges. She gets fired from her job, and gets dumped by her model boyfriend. A law firm that specializes in superhuman law hires her, and the director requests that Jennifer not transform to She-Hulk while on the job. Spider-Man sues J.J. Jameson and the *Daily Bugle* for printing falsehoods about Spider-Man, and Jennifer goes out on a date with Jameson's son, John/Man Wolf. As She-Hulk she helps recapture numerous supervillains who break out of prison. Modok, Blizzard, Nova, Mad Thinker, Scorpion, the Thing, Yellowjacket, the Wasp, and the Scarlet Witch make appearances.

This book is a terrific relaunch of the *She-Hulk* series.

Starlin, Jim, Bernie Wrightson, Jim Novak, et al. *The Incredible Hulk and the Thing in the Big Change*. New York: Marvel, 1987. ISBN: 0871352990.

The Thing and the Hulk are transported to an alien world, Maltriculon, based on a commercial enterprise. The plans for a new food enhancer sauce have been stolen, and they are employed to retrieve and return them to their rightful owner. An alien, Stamben Malelet, promises them any two wishes if they will get the food enhancer plans back. They fight a being who is a combination of the Hulk and the Thing. The Hulk wishes to go back home and get something to eat after they achieve their goal. The Thing, needless to say, is not amused. The Watcher makes a cameo appearance.

This is one of the funniest, cleverest Marvel books ever written. (*Marvel Graphic Novel 29*)

Stern, Roger, Steve Rude, Al Milgrom, et al. *The Incredible Hulk vs. Superman: Double Lives*. New York: Marvel: DC, 1999. ISBN: 0785107363.

In this volume, Lex Luthor tries to use the Hulk to defeat Superman, and Clark Kent interviews Bruce Banner.

Thomas, Roy, Herb Trimpe, Sam Rosen, et al. *Hulk Annual*. London: Marvel Ltd., 1981. ISBN: 0862270359. Reprints *Incredible Hulk 127, 129, 184*.

The Hulk befriends Mogal to help carry out Tyrannus's battle against the Mole Man. When he finds out that Mogal is just a robot, the Hulk destroys him. The Leader uses the Glob to fight the Hulk, but the Glob is smashed into many pieces. The Hulk also battles the Shadow, an alien entity who is killed by light. Some carnival promoters try to keep the Hulk on display in a cage.

This hardback annual contains five separate Hulk stories, and includes the prose stories, "A hostage of Hulk" and "Caged."

Wein, Len, Herb Trimpe, Jack Abel, et al. *Wolverine Battles the Incredible Hulk*. New York: Marvel, 1986. ISBN: 0871356120. Reprints *Incredible Hulk 180–181; Marvel Treasury Edition 26*.

This volume contains the first appearance of Wolverine as Weapon X in the pages of the *Hulk* comics. He tries to get rid of the Hulk, but comes across the green behemoth battling Wendigo. Wolverine teams up with the Hulk to battle Wendigo, and then turns on him. It also contains a bar battle story (in which Wolverine fights Hercules) and a narrative history of the Wolverine character.

Iron Man and War Machine

The human race is primitive, atavistic, and obsolete. You inferior species
must give way to a new and better society of artificial life forms.
—*Mental Organism Designed for Killer (MODOK)*

As long as we define humanity as being humane, regardless of biology,
then the Age of Humanity can never truly be snuffed out, no matter
how much technology changes our future.—*Iron Man*

Austen, Chuck, Victor Lopez, Wild and Woolly Press, et al. *U.S. War Machine*. New York: Marvel, 2001. ISBN: 0785108548. Reprints *War Machine 1–12*.

Tony Stark fires Jim Rhodes and starts drinking again. S.H.I.E.L.D. hires Rhodes to train an army using the War Machine armor. They want to stop a group of terrorists, which eventually leads to Dr. Doom. Dum Dum Dugan plays a prominent role in the story. The A.I.M. group plans to kill all non–white people.

This story is part of Marvel's adult Max line and is in black and white.

Busiek, Kurt, Richard Howell, Bob McLeod, et al. *Iron Man: The Iron Age 1–2*. New York: Marvel, 1998. ISBN: 0785106774 (Vol. 1); 0785106693 (Vol. 2).

After he inherits Stark Industries, Tony Stark hires Pepper Potts as his secretary. A covert group of businessmen try their hardest to put Tony Stark out of business so that they can buy Stark Industries for themselves. Iron Man fights the Saboteur who is trying to destroy Stark Industries from within. Tony hires Happy Hogan as his driver, but Hogan wants to be Stark's protector. The world learns that Iron Man is Stark's bodyguard. Someone impersonating Stark takes Happy and others hostage on a huge helicarrier in the sky. Iron Man exposes the impersonator when he attempts to take over Stark Industries. Stark eventually understands the great responsibility he has to run Stark Industries, and becomes less of a playboy.

This is a modern retelling of the Iron Man saga, from his beginnings to the present day. It includes an appearance by the original Avengers, and an Iron Man source chart.

Michelinie, David, Mark Bright, Barry Windsor-Smith, et al. *Iron Man: Armor Wars*. New York: Marvel, 1990. ISBN: 0871356279. Reprints *Iron Man 225–232*.

Justine Hammer steals some of Tony Stark's Iron Man technology. Iron Man rages a one-man war on all those who have it. He fights S.H.I.E.L.D., Captain America, Crimson Dynamo, Stilt Man, and the Beetle, among others. Stark fires his alter ego, Iron Man, and is booted out of the Avengers. The Gremlin is killed. Stark develops a new armor which is better and makes him more equipped to fight.

This volume is scheduled to be reprinted in 2007 (ISBN: 078512506X).

Michelinie, David, Bob Layton, John Romita Jr., et al. *Iron Man Vs. Doctor Doom*. New York: Marvel, 1994. ISBN: 0785100628. Reprints *Iron Man 149–150, 249–250*.

Both Doom and Stark go into the past. Iron Man helps King Arthur destroy Morgan LeFay; her new partner, Doom; and her legion of zombies. Iron Man and Doom are also sent to the future to help Merlin and Arthur. They both meet their descendants, the evil Iron Man and Doctor Doom of the future, and their twentieth-century counterparts destroy them both.

This book contains two separate stories involving Iron Man's conflict with Dr. Doom.

Michelinie, David, John Romita Jr., Bob Layton, et al. *Power of Iron Man*. New York: Marvel, 1989. ISBN: 087135599X. Reprints *Iron Man 120–128.*

Tony Stark fights alcoholism. Justin Hammer causes Iron Man's armor to malfunction, which results in Iron Man inadvertently murdering someone in front of the media. Tony Stark is taken captive on Hammer's island. Stark Enterprises stock is bought right under Stark's nose by S.H.I.E.L.D., which furthers his descent into alcoholism.

This is considered to be the pinnacle of Iron Man stories. It includes a retelling of the original Iron Man story in which he first dons his gray armor. It has appearances by Sub-Mariner, Nick Fury, Blizzard, Melter, and Ant-Man, among others. Stan Lee writes the introduction. The Institute for Scientific Analysis, a center for the study of alcoholism, praised the series. This was reprinted as the *Demon in the Bottle* in 2006. ISBN: 0785120438.

Olshevsky, George, Tony Frutti, Ken Steacy, et al. *Marvel Comics Index 8B: Heroes from Tales of Suspense Book 2: Iron Man.* Ontario: G&T Enterprises, 1978. ISBN: 09433485 01 (Marvel Index Set).

This is a synopsis and history of Iron Man through 1978. Titles indexed include *Invincible Iron Man, Iron Man and Submariner, Iron Man Annual,* and *Giant Size Iron Man.* Other indexed titles are *The Cat, Nova, Omega: The Unknown, Ms. Marvel, Skull: The Slayer, Inhumans,* and *Amazing Adventures.* There also is a personnel cross-index and a major characters index.

Quesada, Joe, Sean Chen, Alitha Martinez, et al. *Iron Man: Mask in the Iron Man.* New York: Marvel, 2001. ISBN: 0785107762. Reprints *Iron Man Vol. 3: 1–2, 26–30.*

Tony Stark is exposed as Iron Man. Everyone he loves is killed, and he is booted out of the Avengers. He starts drinking again, and fights the Mandarin. His armor becomes sentient and kills Whiplash. Stark rejects his partnership with the Iron Man armor, which almost kills him.

This is all a hallucination. It is an excellent, exciting, philosophical tale that includes original sketches.

Ricketts, Mark, John Jackson Miller, Tony Harris, et al. *Avengers Disassembled: Iron Man.* New York: Marvel, 2004. ISBN: 07851165 32. Reprints *Iron Man 84–89.*

As secretary of state, Tony Stark is asked to find out about and disable a secret weapons project on which his father had worked. The problem is that it is below Avengers' Mansion, and he is ordered not to tell the Avengers about the project which the government had authorized against its citizens. Stark is fired from his position as secretary of state, and says some very nasty things in public to the ambassador from Latveria. Iron Man breaks into a meeting at Star Enterprises and kills the attendees. He proceeds to kill Stark's girlfriend and break into Stark's home. This evil Iron Man, who is actually a former industrialist, has it in for Stark, and as Iron Man wants to bring him down. Stark puts on his real Iron Man uniform, and stops this doppelganger. Then he publicly resigns as Iron Man.

The book includes cover sketches/inks.

Robinson, James, Colin MacNiel, Richard Starkings, et al. *Tales of Suspense Featuring Iron Man and Captain America: Men and Machines.* New York: Marvel, 1995. Reprints *Tales of Suspense Vol. 2: 1.*

Iron Man and Captain America are brought in by Nick Fury to take down a terrorist organization known as D.A.N.T.E. (former East German secret police). The terrorists have their own army of "iron men" which threatens the security of the world. They capture Captain America. Iron Man and Captain America put aside their differences to work and fight together.

This glossy-covered book is from the Marvel Select imprint.

Saenz, Mike, William Bates, Archie Goodwin, et al. *Iron Man: Crash.* New York: Epic, 1988. ISBN: 0871352915.

Iron Man is in his seventies, and he sells his Iron Man weapon schematics to a firm in Japan which outbid S.H.I.E.L.D. for the information. An industrial spy group, the Digital Dreadnoughts, intercepts the information, and Iron Man goes to clean up the damage. Nick Fury makes a cameo.

This is a surreal look at the future, in which power is based on information, not on military might. It is the first cyberpunk graphic novel and the first completely computer-generated graphic novel. There is a section on the "Making of *Crash,*" by the author. (*Marvel Graphic Novel 33*)

Simonson, Walt, Bob Wiacek, William Rosado, et al. *Iron Man 2020.* New York: Marvel, 1994.

The Iron Man for the future, Arno Stark, is the heir to Tony Stark's empire, including Tony's Iron Man armor. Stark places his life in jeopardy in order to save his company from going under. A ruthless company asks Stark to perform a rescue operation as Iron Man. Unlike the original Iron Man, Arno's Iron Man is self-serving and manipulative.

Thomas, Roy, Barry Smith, Jim Mooney, et al. *The Many Armors of Iron Man.* New York: Marvel, 1992. ISBN: 087135926X. Reprints *Iron Man 47, 142–144, 152–153, 200, 218.*

This is a collection of stories that showcase the different types of Iron Man armor Tony Stark has used throughout his years as the Golden Avenger. It includes Space Armor, Stealth Armor, Deep Sea Armor, and the unseen design for the War Machine. The original Grey Armor is used in a story about the first meeting between between Iron Man and his lifelong friend Jim Rhodes while they were in Vietnam.

Punisher, Shadowmasters, and the 'Nam

People I get close to don't last long. — *Frank Castle*

If there is any killing to be done here, scum ... I'll decide it. — *The Punisher*

Baron, Mike, Hugh Haynes, Jimmy Palmiotti, et al. *Punisher/G-Force*. New York: Marvel, 1992. ISBN: 0871358948.

The Punisher goes after drug lords, who are using Star Wars technology to further their aims. He inadvertently shoots up and becomes sick.

Baron, Mike, Bill Reinhold, Mark Badger, et al. *Punisher: Empty Quarter*. New York: Marvel, 1994.

The Punisher infiltrates a Middle Eastern terrorist group in order to stop their plans to terrorize the West, and meets a former lover who is with Israeli Intelligence. The Punisher impersonates Saracen until the real one shows up. The Jackal, who controls the terrorist group, and Saracen, who killed Castle's aunt and uncle, are the Punisher's targets.

Baron, Mike, Bill Reinhold, Willie Schubert, et al. *Punisher: Intruder*. New York: Marvel, 1989. ISBN: 0871355442 (trd); 08713574 7X (pbk).

Frank Castle witnesses an attack by government agents on the wrong family. A young girl who witnesses the attack and survives is taken to a nunnery, while the agents look for her in order to kill her. Castle finds out that a rogue government agent is killing people, and running drugs under the guise of an anti-drug, law enforcement agent. The Punisher infiltrates the operation and destroys it. Before Castle became the Punisher, he considered becoming a priest. (*Marvel Graphic Novel 51*)

Chichester, D.G., Klaus Janson, Margaret Clark, et al. *The Punisher & Captain America: Blood and Glory 1–3*. New York: Marvel, 1993. ISBN: 0871358867 (Vol. 1); 08713 58875 (Vol. 2); 0871358883 (Vol. 3).

The Punisher is used as a pawn to assassinate Captain America whom he mistakenly thinks is running drugs. Captain America survives a gun wound, but stages his own death. He ends up working with the Punisher to stop drug- and gunrunning by high officials in the government. Through their combined efforts, they expose the conspiracy and become uneasy friends.

Chichester D.G., Larry Stroman, and Mark Farmer. *Punisher/Black Widow: Spinning Doomsday's Web*. New York: Marvel, 1992. ISBN: 0871357364.

A group of terrorists free serial killer Dr. Peter Malum who once created a very destructive bomb known as Project Pluto. The Black Widow, working for S.H.I.E.L.D., tries to bring Malum in, and nearly gets killed in the process. Nick Fury explains to her the seriousness of bringing him in, alive or dead, because there may be a newer version of the bomb. The Punisher is also tracking Malum, another crazy serial killer who needs to be eliminated. The Widow stops the Punisher from assassinating Malum, so that she can learn where the "new" bomb is located, and what Malum and the terrorists are up to. The Punisher and the Widow form a loose alliance to track down Malum and his cronies. When she kills Malum in self defense, the Widow experiences firsthand what is like to murder someone. (*Marvel Graphic Novel 74*)

Conway, Gerry, Dave Cockrum, Jeff Albrecht, et al. *The Punisher: Bloodlines*. New York: Marvel, 1991. ISBN: 0871358751.

The Punisher goes to San Domingo, in Central America, to stop a drug cartel. He comes into contact with an old war buddy from Vietnam, who is married to one of Castle's old flames. The Punisher's buddy and his wife are both ruthlessly murdered. Their young daughter and the drug lord's estranged son, who the couple had adopted, live, but are kidnapped by the drug lord The Punisher rescues them, and kills the head honcho. Castle has a run in with a blood thirsty tiger.

Conway, Gerry, Tony DeZuniga, Archie Goodwin, et al. *Classic Punisher*. New York: Marvel, 1989. ISBN: 0871355833. Reprints *Marvel Preview Presents 2*; *Marvel Super Action 1*.

This book contains black-and-white reprints, along with a new eight-page story in which the Punisher tracks down a group of assassins who are funded by a wealthy businessman who wants to take over the country. The story of how Frank Castle became the Punisher as the result of seeing his family gunned down by some mobsters also is included.

Dixon, Chuck, John Buscema, Jim Novak, et al. *The Punisher: A Man Named Frank*. New York: Marvel, 1994. ISBN: 0785100555.

Frank Castle is left for dead after his family is robbed and killed by four desperados. The desperados' faces are hidden, but their leader is wearing a crucifix that was a gift from Frank to his wife. Castle tries to walk away, but he passes out. He is eventually nursed back to health by some kind nuns. Castle spends the next several years on a personal vendetta to find the men who killed his family.

This is an amazing re-envisioning of the Punisher's

origins and quest. It is a shame that this Punisher storyline was not taken further. It is a "What if," *Elseworlds* type of story that features Frank Castle at the end of the old West, 1910–1915.

Dixon, Chuck, John Romita Jr., Klaus Janson, et al. *Punisher: War Zone.* New York: Marvel, 2002. ISBN: 0785109234. Reprints *Punisher War Zone 1–6.*

The Punisher infiltrates the New York mob using the alias "Johnny Tower." He kills the main mob bosses and their henchmen. When he teams up with special agent Walker, the guns start blazing. The mob boss's brother almost gets killed, and takes revenge.

Dixon, Chuck, Jorge Zaffino, Ken Lopez, et al. *The Punisher: Kingdom Gone.* New York: Marvel, 1990. ISBN: 087135652X.

The Punisher goes to a tropical island where he is caught between two opposing armies. He is trying to track down a very powerful drug lord. (*Marvel Graphic Novel 64*)

Duffy, Jo, Jim Novak, Jorge Zaffino, et al. *The Punisher in Assassin's Guild.* New York: Marvel, 1988. ISBN: 0871354608.

The Punisher investigates the workings of an assassins' guild in New York City. A Chinese restaurant is the front for the guild. A corrupt lawyer, who was friends with someone in the guild, was able to get a young girl's killer exonerated. The Punisher, who sleeps with a member of the guild, makes a loose alliance with the guild. Working together, the guild members and the Punisher take out the boss, who is behind the lawyer who has been making problems and causing police records to disappear. A teenage guild apprentice is killed in the fallout.

This book is highly recommended. (*Marvel Graphic Novel 40*)

Ennis, Garth, Steve Dillon, Tom Mandrake, et al. *The Punisher Vol. 4: Full Auto.* New York: Marvel, 2003. ISBN: 0785111492. Reprints *Punisher Vol. 4: 19–26.*

Frank Castle does surveillance on two crooked police officers. One of them beats his wife, and the other is involved in cocaine dealing in order to pay off his mob debts. The Punisher finds the cocaine and blows up the warehouse. Ghosts are haunting a hood, trying to get him to kill the Punisher, but the hood ends up being eaten by a giant squid. Frank teams up with a social worker to find and destroy a cannibal who is recruiting homeless people to find him more homeless people to eat. The underground of New York is turned into a charnel house.

Ennis, Garth, Steve Dillon, Jimmy Palmiotti, et al. *Punisher Vol. 1: Welcome Back Frank.* New York: Marvel, 2001. ISBN: 07851078 35. Reprints *Punisher Vol. 3 1–12.*

The Punisher goes back to the streets of Manhattan to bring down a powerful Gnucci crime family. He also has to deal with several copycat vigilantes, known as the Holy, Elite, and Mr. Payback. The Punisher fights a gargantuan killer known as the Russian, who is finally brought down when a hot pizza is thrown on his face.

This groundbreaking series brought the Punisher back into the limelight among comic fans.

Ennis, Garth, Steve Dillon, Jimmy Palmiotti, et al. *Punisher Vol. 2: Army of One.* New York: Marvel, 2002. ISBN: 0785108394. Reprints *Punisher Vol. 4 1–7.*

Again Frank Castle goes up against the Russian, who this time is wearing the body of a woman, and fights General Kreigkopf on Grand Nixon Island. Spider-Man also makes an appearance, teaming up with the Punisher.

The last story in this collection is wordless.

Ennis, Garth, Steve Dillon, Darick Robertston, et al. *Punisher Vol. 3: Business as Usual.* New York: Marvel, 2003. ISBN: 0785110143. Reprints *Punisher Vol. 4: 13–18.*

The Punisher goes to South America to rescue a Mafia don from terrorists. He rescues the Mafia boss, then, when the bosses have a meeting back in the States, the Punisher kills them all. He gets into a fight with Wolverine while they are both on the trail of a leg-chopping maniac. It turns out that a group of Mafia-style midgets and dwarves are trying to take over New York crime, and are cutting people down to size. The Punisher blows Wolverine's face off, and drives a steam roller over him. Frank also goes to Ireland.

Ennis, Garth, Leandro Fernandez, Tim Bradstreet, et al. *Punisher, Max, Volume 2: Kitchen Irish.* New York: Marvel, 2004. ISBN: 0785115390. Reprints *Punisher 7–12.*

While Frank Castle is eating in a diner the place is bombed. Several Irish groups in Hell's Kitchen, have declared war on one another, and are competing for a twenty-million-dollar prize. Castle and an MI-6 agent declare war on the Irish gangs.

The story is filled with torture, decapitation, and hate. It is one of the most extreme Punisher stories in the history of the comic. Finn Cooley, who has half of his face blown off, is one of the "great" adversaries in this book. The twenty-million-dollar prize is not what it seems, and everybody dies. The book includes a Punisher sketch and a page layout by the artist. This book is not for the squeamish.

Ennis, Garth, Cam Kennedy, Tim Bradstreet, et al. *The Punisher Vol. 5: Streets of Laredo.* New York: Marvel, 2003. ISBN: 07851109 68. Reprints *The Punisher Vol. 4, 27–32.*

Elektra gets to the Punisher's targets before he does, and gets them more efficiently. The Punisher ends up asking Elektra out for a date. Frank Castle goes to the small Texas town of Branding where he investigates an arms dealer. The sheriff of the town is involved with the arms dealer's son, but the bigoted minister of the town, who hates gay people, kills the arms dealer's son. This event makes the arms dealer and her posse go berserk and attack the town. The Punisher blows up the compound, and the sheriff is shot. The Punisher has a showdown with the arms dealer, and she gets a spike through the neck.

This book also contains the sad story of the police officer, Soap, who runs the Punisher Task Force.

Ennis, Garth, Lewis Larosa, Tom Palmer, et al. *Punisher, Max, Vol. 1: In the Beginning*. New York: Marvel, 2004. ISBN: 0785113916. Reprints *Punisher Vol. 5: 1–6.*

Frank Castle relives the death of his family. Among the mobsters he kills, is a hundred-year-old mob boss; after his death, the mob puts a hit out on the Punisher. The CIA, which also wants the Punisher, enlists the help of the Punisher's old friend, Micro. Micro leads the agents to Castle, and they capture him. The mob finds out where the CIA is holding Castle prisoner, and a bloodbath ensues. The CIA wants to hire the Punisher to take out dictators, and other anti–American politicos abroad, but Castle declines. He blows Micro's head off for betraying him.

This new Punisher is part of the adult Max line, which contains adult language and adult situations.

Ennis, Garth, John McCrea, Tim Bradstreet, et al. *The Punisher Vol. 6: Confederacy of Dunces*. New York: Marvel, 2004. ISBN: 0785113444. Reprints *Punisher Vol. 4: 33–37.*

Wolverine, Daredevil, and Spider-Man team up to bring the Punisher down, once and for all. Frank Castle outwits them at every turn, and makes these superheroes look like idiots. He provokes Wolverine into a feral rage, and while the Punisher gets away, Spider-Man and Daredevil have to calm Wolverine down. Castle finds amnesiac Bruce Banner, and, by feeding him a special stew, nurtures him back to health. The Punisher knows who Banner is, and intends to bring out the Hulk. During an attempt to capture the Punisher, the Hulk is let loose, and the Punisher gets away a second time. Again, the Heroes just look stupid. Police officer Soap leaves the Punisher Task force to become a porn star.

This book is witty and highly recommended.

Ennis, Garth, Darick Robertson, Tom Palmer, et al. *The Punisher: Born*. New York: Marvel, 2004. ISBN: 0785112316 (trd); 078511 0259 (pbk) Reprints *Born 1–4.*

In 1971, during his third tour of duty, Frank Castle is in Vietnam/Cambodia. He is a fearless Army captain who will kill anything that moves, including his own men if they get out line. He is already starting to punish those who he feels deserve punishment.

This story is brutal, but it gives an inside look at what life was like for soldiers toward the end of the war. The true story behind the birth of the Punisher includes sketches, character designs, layouts, a Vietnam photo reference, and Ennis's original proposal for the series. It is part of Marvel's Max adult line.

Grant, Alan, John Wagner, Cam Kennedy, et al. *The Punisher: Blood on the Moors*. New York: Marvel, 1991. ISBN: 0871358549.

The Punisher goes to Scotland to track down a huge cocaine deal. Many high-powered crime lords are meeting there to discuss sending cocaine throughout the world, melted down in whisky bottles. When the crime lords' goons get the Punisher drunk and leave him for dead in the snow, an ancient Scottish ghost, The Clansman, comes to his aid. The Clansman and the Punisher team up against the cocaine dealers, and destroy them and their operation. After he is shot to death, the Clansman turns out to be a mortal police inspector. (*Marvel Graphic Novel 70*)

Grant, Steve, Jo Duffy, Mike Zeck, et al. *The Punisher: Circle of Blood*. New York: Marvel, 2001. ISBN: 0871353946. Reprints *Punisher Vol. 1: 1–5.*

A group known as the Trust breaks the Punisher out of jail to work for them. The Trust's goal is the illumination of all organized crime. As the Punisher begins his war, the Trust allows innocent people to be caught in the crossfire. The Punisher turns against the Trust because of their sloppy methods. The Trust brainwashes criminals and turns them into Punisher clones. Jigsaw tries to destroy the Punisher.

The book contains a cover gallery and a synopsis of those *Spider-Man* comics in which the Punisher first appeared. This was originally published in 1988.

Grant, Steven, Mike Zeck, John Beatty, et al. *The Punisher: Return to Big Nothing*. New York: Marvel/Epic, 1989. ISBN: 08713555 31 (trd); 0871356619 (pbk).

The Punisher stops an illegal arms deal from taking place. It turns out that Gorman, who was a sergeant under Frank Castle during 'Nam, is the mastermind behind the arms dealings. Gorman often referred to Castle as a big nothing, and was quite abusive during their tour of duty. The Punisher tracks down the sergeant, and kills him and his underlings.

Havanagh, Terry, Scott McDaniel, Keith Williams, et al. *Spider-Man/Punisher/Sabretooth: Designer Genes*. New York: Marvel, 1993. ISBN: 0871359898.

Several lab animals and homeless people are found dead and disemboweled. Apparently the Roxxon Corporation is trying to combine human and animal DNA as "designer genes" to create hybrid beings. Both the little brother of the doctor/scientist doing the experiments and the head of the department are hybrid beings. Apparently the scientist did experiments on Sabertooth and Wolverine in Canada, under Department H, and Sabertooth is seeking revenge against the doctor. Spider-Man and the Punisher want to bring Sabertooth in for murders they believe he has committed.

One of the funniest parts of the book is when Spider-Man is trying to stop the Punisher from killing Sabertooth. Spider-Man and the Punisher form an uneasy alliance, but all the while Spider-Man wants to turn the Punisher in to the police.

Henderson, Chris, Mike Harris, Janice Chiang, et al. *The Punisher: The Prize.* New York: Marvel, 1990. ISBN: 0871357356.

The Punisher goes undercover in the international espionage community to find a stolen, secret weapon that was taken to Mexico. The secret weapon turns out to be Iron Man's original Grey Armor. This "new" Iron Man almost defeats the Punisher.

Lomax, Don, Alberto Saichann, Steve Dutro, et al. *The Punisher Invades the 'Nam.* New York: Marvel, 1994. ISBN: 0785100083 Reprints *The 'Nam 52–53; 67–68.*

Castle, who must rescue a group of American airmen who have landed in Laos, catches a U.S. general who is in the opium trade. The American airmen are prisoners in a camp known only as the Death Hole, where an insane Doctor performs vivisection experiments on live human victims.

This is a tale about Frank Castle's pre–Punisher days as a soldier in Vietnam.

Mackie, Howard, Ron Garney, Al Milgrom, et al. *Ghost Rider, Wolverine, Punisher: The Dark Design.* New York: Marvel, 1994. ISBN: 0752206915.

Once again, Ghost Rider, the Punisher, and Wolverine are brought in to defeat Blackheart, and stop his reign of terror. Blackheart wants to assassinate his father Mephisto, and bring a new order into Hell. Ghost Rider is possessed by the spirits, and is almost lost, but the desire to help the innocents saves him. Just as Ghost Rider is about to demolish Blackheart, Lucy comes and forgives him for his evil. Mephisto makes an offer to let his son rule Hell with him, but Blackheart stabs him with a knife dipped in the blood of innocents.

This is a direct sequel to *Hearts of Darkness*, in which Blackheart has built up an army of possessed souls, and seeks Lucy's soul.

Mackie, Howard, John Romita Jr., Klaus Janson. *Ghost Rider: Wolverine, Punisher: Hearts of Darkness.* New York: Marvel, 1991. ISBN: 0871358735.

The Punisher, Wolverine and Ghost Rider go to the city of Christ's Crown. They team up against Mephisto's son, Blackheart, who is angry at his father

for his diminished status as a petty deity. He tries to steal the souls of the innocents, including that of a young girl. Ghost Rider learns a little bit about his past and the spirit that possesses him. He goes into the dark abyss to keep Blackheart from getting more innocent souls. After the Punisher blows Blackheart into little pieces, Mephisto comes to pick him up.

Miller, Frank, Klaus Janson, Joe Rosen, et al. *Daredevil: Punisher: Child's Play.* New York: Marvel, 1988. ISBN: 0871353512. Reprints *Daredevil 183–184.*

The Punisher breaks out of jail to fight the drug dealers who are spreading angel dust to the youth. Daredevil and the Punisher meet, and Daredevil tries to take the Punisher down. Matt Murdock defends a murderous drug lord who he believes is innocent, but is actually guilty of murder. Daredevil disagrees with the Punisher's methods of controlling crime.

Milligan, Peter, Gerry Conway, Garth Ennis, et al. *The Punisher: Official Movie Adaptation.* New York: Marvel, 2004. ISBN: 0785114106. Reprints *Punisher The Movie 1–3; Amazing Spider-Man Vol. 1: 129; Punisher Vol. 3: 1.*

This book is an adaptation of the blockbuster movie *The Punisher.* It is Marvel's second adaptation of the original movie, also named *The Punisher.* The first was a 1990 movie starring Dolph Lungren as the Punisher. It went straight to video, and then to obscurity. It was awful, but this time they got it right. This adaptation tells the story of FBI agent Frank Castle who is betrayed by a fellow agent to a mobster boss whose son was killed in a sting operation. In this adaptation, Castle's wife, children, mother, and father, are killed by a mobster. Castle is left for dead, but survives and vows revenge. As the Punisher, his goal is to make the streets safe from killers, rapists, child pornographers, and, basically, all low-life, criminal scum. Castle takes revenge on the mobster by killing his family and his organization. This adaptation is well written, and well put together. It also contains the Punisher's first appearance, in which he fights Spider-Man as an unknowing pawn of the Jackal. It is Garth Ennis's first issue in the newest Punisher series, and is recommended for Punisher fans.

Milligan, Peter, Lee Weeks. Tom Palmer, et al. *Wolverine/Punisher Vol. 1.* New York: Marvel, 2004. ISBN: 0785114327. Reprints *Wolverine/Punisher 1–6.*

Criminals who are on the run from the Punisher find their "paradise" in the mythical Erewhon. This town is supposed to be a place where criminals can be safe from the law and the Punisher. When Wolverine and the Punisher follow the trail of a murderer to Erewhon, they find that they have fallen into a trap set by the syndicate of the town. Both Logan and Castle are taken prisoner, and Wolverine gets an arrow shot through his head. The townspeople revolt against the elite of Erewhon who are actually modern-day Nazis, and who have kept the body of Hitler preserved for inspiration.

Murray, Doug, Michael Golden, John Beatty, et al. *The 'Nam Vol. 2*. New York: Marvel, 1988. ISBN: 0871353520. Reprints *The 'Nam, 5–8*.

After Marks is in 'Nam for several months, he starts to drink heavily, and he almost becomes a liability for ·his platoon. One issue in this series is composed of three different stories, about several soldiers who switch sides from the Viet Cong. It also tells about a sergeant who gets into trouble with the Army's Criminal Intelligence Division for taking bribes. This volume contains a glossary of terms, a map, and a brief introduction by Doug Murray. It also contains an extra tale, "The Tunnel Rat."

Murray, Doug, Michael Golden, John Beatty, et al. *The 'Nam Vol. 3*. New York: Marvel, 1989. ISBN: 0871355434. Reprints *The 'Nam, 9–12*.

Ed Marks sees one of his soldier buddies killed, someone whose term of duty was about to be finished. He learns all the tricks of trading with the Vietnamese. The platoon serves Christmas dinners to children, one of whom has a grenade strapped to his body, and blows up.

The text of issue 12 is written as a letter to Marks's mother, describing his life in 'Nam. The volume contains a glossary of terms and a brief introduction by Doug Murray. It is a shame that these books are out of print because they are excellent. Marvel should republish the whole series in trade paperback form.

Murray, Doug, Michael Golden, Armando Gil, et al. *The 'Nam Vol. 1*. New York: Marvel, 1987. ISBN: 08713528422 (1987); 0785107 185 (1999). Reprints *The 'Nam, 1–4*.

Originally published in 1987, this series tells about life in the Vietnam conflict. Each issue covers roughly a month in the war. The main protagonist is Edward Marks whose tour of duty is told over three volumes and twelve issues. Marks learns the ropes and quickly adapts to life as a soldier. The 1987 edition includes a map, a short historical survey, and a 'Nam glossary of terms; the 1999 edition has an introduction by Larry Hama. This series was praised by a veterans' group, the Bravo Organization, as the best popular-culture depiction of the conflict. It was chosen over the movie *Platoon*.

Potts, Carl, Brent Anderson, Janice Chiang, et al. *The Punisher Movie Special*. New York: Marvel, 1990. ISBN: 0871356724.

Frank Castle is a police officer whose family is killed by a mob boss, Franco, whom he is trying to convict. He starts his one-man war on crime, killing anyone associated with the mob. When Franco's children are kidnapped by the Japanese mob, he hires the Punisher to rescue them. Castle saves the children, but when Franco tries to kill him, he kills Franco.

This book is based on the 1990 *Punisher* movie starring Dolph Lundgren. This book is much better than that movie.

Potts, Carl, Dan Lawlis, Tod Smith, et al. *Shadowmasters 1–4*. New York: Marvel, 1989–1990. ISBN: 0871355469 (1); 0871355477 (2); 0871355485 (3); 087135493 (4).

An American soldier befriends Shigeru Ezaki the mayor of a small town in Japan. The mayor is also the last of the Shadowmaster Ninja's. The ninja helps stop renegade soliders who seek to go back to the old Japanese regime, and who terrorize anyone who gets in their way, including innocent citizens. The renegades form the Sunrise Society, and also infiltrate Japanese businesses. Seeking revenge, the head of the Sunrise Society kidnaps Ezaki and kills his American friend. Ezaki had been training his children and the son of his friend in the ninja arts, and they become the new band of Shadowmasters who seek to put down the Sunrise Society and avenge their families. The Society uses Ezaki for their cloning experiments.

In the Punisher comics, the Shadowmasters sometimes aid him in his war on crime. The origin of the shadowmaster ninja clancoincided with the U.S. surveillance of the Japanese shortly after Hiroshima and Nagasaki were bombed.

Potts, Carl, Jim Lee, Jim Novak, et al. *The Punisher: Eye for an Eye*. New York: Marvel, 1991. ISBN: 0871357771. Reprints *Punisher War Journal 1–3*.

The Punisher helps a kidnapped mother and child who are trying to get away from her underworld boyfriend. At the spot where his family was killed, Frank meets a young boy whose father was the mobster who killed the Punisher's family. The youth learns that a former Rikers inmate, Hector Montoya, was responsible for his family's death. When Montoya is released, the youth, seeking revenge for his father's death, stalks Montoya, with the Punisher trailing him. After it is too late, the Punisher and the youth learn that it was actually the youth's father's betrayal that was at fault. Daredevil helps save the Punisher's life, and returns his gun to him.

Daredevil provides some comic relief to the narrative by always getting in the Punisher's way.

Potts, Carl, Jim Lee, Jim Novak, et al. *The Punisher: Wolverine: The African Saga*. New York: Marvel, 1989. ISBN: 0871356112. Reprints *Punisher War Journal 6–7*.

The Punisher goes to Africa for some rest and relaxation, but winds up in the middle of a poaching trade. The Punisher goes as a bodyguard to help Professor Wyeth who is searching for rare animals and dinosaurs. He meets Wolverine for the first time, and, because each thinks the other is fighting on the side of the poachers, they have several intense battles between them. They almost destroy each other, but finally make a truce. They discover that there are dinosaurs in Africa. A wealthy Texas man, who wants to make wall trophies of rare animals, hires Norma to become the professor's wife so that she can poach the animals for him.

Sniegoski, Tom, Christopher Golden, Pat Lee, et al. *Wolverine/Punisher: Revelation.* New York: Marvel, 2000. ISBN: 0785107290. Reprints *Wolverine/Punisher Revelation 1–4.*

Wolverine teams up with the Punisher to help track and contain a mutant Morlock, Revelation, who unwittingly kills people who happen to come near her. The mutant was in stasis for many years before being awakened in the tunnels of New York. Wolverine and Punisher have to contend with robots searching to destroy Revelation. Wolverine's current girlfriend gets killed, and the Punisher is being observed by a band of Angels known as the Council of Thrones.

Daredevil and Storm make cameo appearances. The illustrations in this book are drawn in a manga style.

Starlin, Jim, Tom Grindberg, Phil Felix, et al. *Punisher: Ghosts of the Innocent.* New York: Marvel, 1993. ISBN: 0871359588 (1); 087 1359596 (2).

The Punisher goes after one of the Kingpin's drug cronies. One of Kingpin's men hijacks a bus full of school children, but gets away. The bus crashes and the Punisher is the only one left alive. While in the hospital, an attempt is made on his life, and the ghosts of the dead children haunt Frank, as does the ghost of his wife. The Kingpin plays a game with the Punisher, and hides the man responsible for the bus crash. Kingpin eventually strikes a deal with the Punisher, and, after Castle makes an attempt on his life and costs his operation millions of dollars, Kingpin turns the hijacker over to Castle.

Starlin, Jim, Bernie Wrightson, Bill Wray, et al. *Punisher P.O.V. 1–4.* New York: Marvel, 1991. ISBN: 087135778X (1); 0871357798 (2); 0871357801 (3); 087135781X (4).

Deke, a social anarchist, is released from prison and immediately resumes his radical ways by bombing a bank. Another bomb blows up while Deke and his partner are working on it; his partner is killed and Deke is burned. While taking refuge in the sewers, under his father's laboratory, Deke is exposed to a variant form of the Super Soldier serum, which makes him an almost indestructible mutant. The Punisher is after him, because of all the innocents he has killed. Deke's father hires the Kingpin and the Punisher form a truce, each looking out for the other. Nick Fury and S.H.I.E.L.D. are looking for Deke, for government purposes, and eventually they take him away. Local law-enforcement people arrest the Punisher. The Punisher has a showdown with a fat, crazy monster-hunter who is hallucinating and killing people he thinks are monsters.

These books are also known as *Punisher Point of View.*

Wagner, John, Phil Gascoine, Steve Buccellato, et al. *The Punisher: Die Hard in the Big Easy.* New York: Marvel, 1992. ISBN: 0871359545.

The Punisher goes to New Orleans to stop some drug smugglers. While he is there, he encounters an evil voodoo priest known as the Mortician. The Punisher has been stepping on too many toes, and the Mortician is brought in to stop him. He injects Frank with a "living death" serum, to turn the Punisher into a zombie who will serve the voodoo priest. The Mortician even makes a Punisher doll. However, despite being buried alive, the Punisher's will is so strong that he survives, and the effects of the drug wear off. Eventually the tables are turned, and it is the Mortician who is buried alive.

Wright, Gregory, Todd Smith, Danny Bulanadi, et al. *The Punisher: No Escape.* New York: Marvel, 1990. ISBN: 0871356465.

A mob boss hires Paladin to do away with the Punisher, who is causing him all kinds of problems. The Washington-based Commission for Superhuman Activities asks the U.S. Agent to capture the Punisher, and put him in jail. The mob boss kidnaps Microchip, and Paladin and the U.S. Agent end up fighting on the same side as the Punisher in order to defeat the mob. The U.S. Agent, who understands the Punisher's mission, ends up being reprimanded.

Spider-Man, Spider-Woman, Spider-Girl, Venom, and Carnage

I just said to myself, "Hey, what would ol' spider-Man do? The Webslinger's been my main man for years.—*A young child who admires Spider-Man*

Three two-Bit car thieves attacking your friendly neighborhood wall crawler.... Come on now, you just gotta be kidding me.—*Spider-Man*

All of a sudden I'm as in as Tiny Tim.—Spider-Man

The Bugle wants to know if those young anarchists
will be punished, Stacy.—*J.J. Jameson*

Aguirre-Sacasa, Roberto, Stan Lee, John Romita, et al. *Spider-Man 2: The Movie.* New York: Marvel, 2004. ISBN: 0785114114. Reprints *Spider-Man 2: The Movie 1; Amazing Spider-Man 50; Ultimate Spider-Man 14–15.*

Peter Parker gives up being Spider-Man to try to have more of a personal life. He confesses his love to Mary Jane who is about to be married. The scientist Otto Octavius, about whom Parker is writing a term paper, becomes Doctor Octopus, in an experiment gone horribly wrong. Doctor Octopus terrorizes New York and brings Spider-Man to Harry Osborn. Spider-Man's alter ego Peter Parker is revealed to Harry Osborn, Doc Ock, and Mary Jane. The book also contains the classic reprint of Parker giving up Spider-Man; a storyline with Doc Ock from the "Ultimate Universe," written by Brian Michael Bendis; and a Spider-Man encyclopedia entry on Doctor Octopus.

This is a comic adaptation based on the hit movie *Spider-Man 2*, screenplay by Alvin Sargent.

Andrews, Kaare, Skottie Young, Pat Duke, et al. *Marvel Mangaverse Vol. 3: Spider-Man: Legend of the Spider-Clan.* New York: Marvel, 2003. ISBN: 078511114X. Reprints *Spider-Man: Legend of the Spider-Clan 1–5.*

Peter Parker comes from a long line of Spider-Clan ninjas. His sensei and trainer was his Uncle Benjamin, who was murdered by Venom. He inadvertently becomes one with an evil amulet controlled by the forces of darkness. The Shadow Clan takes Parker under its wing. There are appearances by manga versions of the Green Goblin, the Black Cat, Daredevil, Venom and the Kingpin. Dr. Octopus is actually Peter's high school teacher.

Bendis, Brian, Mark Bagley, Scott Hanna, et al. *The Pulse Vol. 1: Thin Air.* New York: Marvel, 2004. ISBN: 0785113320. Reprints *The Pulse 1–5.*

Jonah Jameson hires Jessica Jones to work on the costumed vigilante beat for the *Daily Bugle.* Star reporter Ben Ulrich is to work on the section named "The Pulse." Apparently, the *Bugle* has been losing readership, and Jameson's anti-hero editorials are part of the problem, so he relents and hires a super-powered person. Jessica Jones is pregnant with Luke Cage's baby, and feels she needs the insurance, so she accepts his offer. When another *Bugle* reporter, working on a story covering the ten most powerful people in New York, finds out that Oscorp employees have been disappearing, she confronts Osborn. He strangles her, and drops her from his glider into a lake. Then—when

Jones, Spider-Man, Ulrich, and the police go after Osborn—he nearly kills Jones's baby, and a crazed Luke Cage destroys the limo in which Norman is riding. This brings out the Goblin, and the *Daily Bugle* outs Osborn as the Green Goblin. Spider-Man tries to calm things down, but only gets in the way. Ben Ulrich figures out that Peter Parker is Spider-Man, and his pulp book about Osborn, *Legacy of Evil,* is going to get reprinted. The Vulture makes a cameo appearance.

This critically acclaimed series features the same team that worked on *Ultimate Spider-Man.* A cover sketchbook is included.

Bendis, Brian Michael, Mark Bagley, Scott Hanna, et al. *Ultimate Spider-Man Vol. 11: Carnage.* New York: Marvel, 2004. ISBN: 0785114033. Reprints *Ultimate Spider-Man 60–65.*

Spider-Man gets hurt during a battle and goes to Dr. Curt Connors for medical help. Dr. Connors asks Parker if he can use a blood sample in some experiments. He builds upon Parker's father's work and creates a bizarre creature that absorbs the life essences of human beings. The Carnage creature is trying to complete itself by taking the image of Parker's father. He goes to Parker's house and kills Gwen Stacy, and Parker throws the creature into a boiling vat. When the lab gets shut down, Connor's assistant Ben Riley steals one of the chemical samples. Mary Jane is the last person to speak to Gwen before her death. Mary Jane slugs Flash Thompson with a book, and Parker decides to give up being Spider-Man.

Bendis, Brian Michael, Mark Bagley, Jim Mahfood, et al. *Ultimate Spider-Man Scriptbook.* New York: Marvel, 2004. ISBN: 0785115293. Reprints scripts from *Ultimate Spider-Man 1/2: 13, 28, 45; Ultimate Spider-Man Super Special; Marvel Team Up 9, 11.*

Bendis personally picked the scripts included in this nice collection. Each script has commentary stating why Bendis chose to include the script in the volume. He wrote a detailed introduction explaining his personal trials when he was trying to get published in the comics industry, describing how Marvel rejected many of his early, unsolicited manuscripts. This is a cool book.

Bendis, Brian Michael, Mark Bagley, Art Thiebert, et al. *Ultimate Spider-Man Vol. 2: Learning Curve.* New York: Marvel, 2001. ISBN: 0785108203. Reprints *Ultimate Spider-Man 8–13.*

In this volume Peter Parker reveals his identity to Mary Jane, gets a job at the *Daily Bugle*, and battles with the Kingpin.

Bendis, Brian Michael, Mark Bagley, Art Thiebert, et al. *Ultimate Spider-Man Vol. 3: Double Trouble.* New York: Marvel, 2002. ISBN: 0785108793. Reprints *Ultimate Spider-Man 14–21.*

In this volume Spider-Man fights both Doc Ock and Kraven on live television, Aunt May is upset at Peter for coming in late and for lying, and Gwen Stacy gets in trouble at school.

Bendis, Brian Michael, Mark Bagley, Art Thiebert, et al. *Ultimate Spider-Man Vol. 4: Legacy.* New York: Marvel, 2002. ISBN: 0785 109684. Reprints *Ultimate Spider-Man 22–27.*

Norman Osborn tries to get Peter Parker/Spider-Man to work for him by threatening his family. As the Green Goblin, he kidnaps Mary Jane and almost kills her by throwing her off of a roof. Nick Fury tells Parker he is watching him and his dealings with Osborn. Osborn's son Harry ends up stabbing his father with a wooden board. Nick Fury tells Parker that when he turns eighteen, he's going to belong to S.H.I.E.L.D.

Bendis, Brian Michael, Mark Bagley, Art Thiebert, et al. *Ultimate Spider-Man Vol. 5: Public Scrutiny.* New York: Marvel, 2003. ISBN: 0785110879. Reprints *Ultimate Spider-Man 28–32.*

A fake Spider-Man has been committing robberies and crimes, trying to frame the real Spider-Man. The public turns against Spider-Man, and Mary Jane breaks up with Peter Parker. Gwen Stacy stays with the Parkers. Captain Stacy gets killed in the line of duty. This includes an appearance by Iron Man and the Rhino.

Bendis, Brian Michael, Mark Bagley, Art Thiebert, et al. *Ultimate Spider-Man Vol. 6: Venom.* New York: Marvel, 2003. ISBN: 0785110941. Reprints *Ultimate Spider-Man 33–39.*

Spider-Man's most popular foe gets the Ultimate Universe treatment. Peter Parker learns that his father and Eddie Brock's father were working on a cure for cancer before they died. They created a symbiotic life form that was supposed to bond with the host and destroy the disease. Eddie Brock was one of Peter's childhood buddies, and he makes contact with him again. Parker learns that Brock has been trying to keep their fathers' experiments alive. When Peter tries to get a sample of the symbiotic form, he spills some on himself. This transforms him into another version of Spider-Man who almost kills someone. Parker rids himself of the symbiotic invader, but Eddie Brock joins with it and becomes Venom. Curt Connors discovers that Parker is Spider-Man.

Bendis, Brian Michael, Mark Bagley, Art Thiebert, et al. *Ultimate Spider-Man Vol. 7: Irresponsible.* New York: Marvel, 2003. ISBN: 0785110925. Reprints *Ultimate Spider-Man 40–45.*

Peter and Mary Jane get back together, and admit that they love another. He is without a Spider-Man costume, and has to use a homemade costume sewn by Mary Jane. A mutant from a sister high school, Geldoff, is causing havoc by blowing up cars. Peter tries to reason with him, to no avail. The X-Men show up and take both Spider-Man and Geldoff to the X-Mansion. The X-Men find out Spider-Man's secret and identity. Geldoff was experimented on while he was in the womb. X-Man member Kitty has a crush on Spider-Man. Aunt May, who sees a therapist, has very strange notions about Spider-Man and her nephew, Peter. May and Peter go to see a movie.

Bendis, Brian Michael, Mark Bagley, Art Thiebert, et al. *Ultimate Spider-Man Vol. 8: Cats and Kings.* New York: Marvel, 2004. ISBN: 0785112502. Reprints *Ultimate Spider-Man 47–53.*

Peter Parker loses his job when he asks Jonah why they let Kingpin out of jail after he murdered someone, and he gets kicked out of his classes when he questions the teacher about a justice system that would let a murderer free. Sam Bullit runs for DA and Jonah Jameson almost gets beaten up by thugs after the *Daily Bugle* questions his ties to the Kingpin and organized crime. Spider-Man saves him. When the Black Cat steals a precious historical tablet, Spider-Man tries to stop her. She puts a personal ad in the *Bugle* asking Spider-Man for a date. Elektra is hired by Wilson Fisk to take down both Spider-Man and the Black Cat. The Cat is captured and beaten senseless, but escapes with Spider-Man's help. Jonah apologizes to Parker and gives him his job back. He tells him the story of his missing son. Mary Jane runs away from home when her father forbids her to date Peter Parker.

Bendis, Brian Michael, Mark Bagley, Art Thiebert, et al. *Ultimate Spider-Man Vol. 9: Ultimate Six.* New York: Marvel, 2004. ISBN: 0785113126. Reprints *Ultimate Spider-Man 46; Ultimate Six 1–7.*

The Green Goblin, Doc Ock, the Sandman, Electro and Kraven are put into a special S.H.I.E.L.D. prison for illegally experimenting on themselves and being a danger to society. Nick Fury updates the Ultimates on the situation, and Hank Pym is the special liaison psychologist to the super villains. With the help of Doc Ock they all break out and form a team to destroy Fury. Norman Osborn, the Green Goblin, wants Spider-Man, whom he refers to as his son, to join in evil pursuits. Spider-Man's identity is revealed to the Ultimates. The super villains trash the White House. With Spider-Man's help, the Ultimates recapture the villains. Captain America has some misgivings about the role the government takes in creating "enhanced" beings.

Bendis, Brian Michael, Mark Bagley, Art Thiebert, et al. *Ultimate Spider-Man Vol. 10: Hollywood*. New York: Marvel, 2004. ISBN: 0785114025. Reprints *Ultimate Spider-Man 54–59*.

A film company is in New York to film a fictional account of Spider-Man and his adventures. Peter Parker is not very happy about this and visits the set. Doc Ock, whose ex-wife is being used as a consultant for the movie, breaks out of prison using his mental telepathy to control his mechanical arms. He kidnaps Spider-Man from the movie set and takes him to Brazil. Gwen Stacy figures out that Peter Parker is also Spider-Man, and comes to grips with it. Director; Sam Rami producer and CEO of Marvel Studios, Avi Arad; and star Tobey Maguire make special appearances. High school classmate Kong gets a bit part in the movie.

Bendis, Brian Michael, Michael Gaydos, Cory Petit, et al. *Alias Vol. 3: The Underneath*. New York: Marvel, 2003. ISBN: 0785111654. Reprints *Alias 10, 16–21*.

Jessica Jones is hired by Jonah Jameson to find out the identity of Spider-Man. Teenager Mattie Franklin, the third Spider-Woman, who has been adopted by Jameson and has been missing, shows up at Jones's apartment stoned out of her mind. When Jones confronts Jameson, he accuses her of kidnapping Mattie. Jones searches for Mattie, whose boyfriend has her hooked on some kind of drug, and who is being used as a drug source. The original Spider-Woman, Jessica Drew, also thinks that Jones has kidnapped Mattie, and a fight ensues. They eventually work together to save Mattie from the drug pushers. The New Warrior, Speedball, makes a cameo appearance. Scott Lang and Jessica get into a fight, but Lang eventually admits his love for her.

Bendis, Brian Michael, Bill Jemas, Mark Bagley, et al. *Ultimate Spider-Man Vol. 1. Power and Responsibility*. Marvel Comics: New York, 2001: ISBN: 078510786x. Reprints *Ultimate Spider-Man: 1–7*.

In this volume Peter Parker is bitten by a radioactive spider, and after his Uncle Ben is murdered, he dons the Spider-Man costume. The book also contains the story of the origin of the Green Goblin, Norman Osborn. The *Ultimates* line, which retells the original stories of many of Marvel's most famous characters in a modern setting, is outside the regular continuity of the Marvel Universe. This series was highly praised by *Entertainment Weekly* as having "a hero for

the millennium." This is one of the best written and most successful graphic novels of all time.

Bendis, Brian Michael, Ted McKeever, Jim Mahfood, et al. *Ultimate Marvel Team Up Vol. 2*. New York: Marvel, 2003. ISBN: 0785112995. Reprints *Ultimate Marvel Team Up 9–13*.

In this Ultimate, Spider-Man meets Man-Thing, Dr. Strange, the Fantastic Four, and the alien Skrulls. Peter Parker meets up with the X-Men in the mall, and Wolverine introduces himself as Peter's cousin.

Bendis, Brian Michael, Terry Moore, Rick Mays, et al,, *Ultimate Marvel Team Up Vol. 3*. New York: Marvel, 2003. ISBN: 0785113002. Reprints *Ultimate Marvel Team Up 14–16*; *Ultimate Spider-Man Super Special*.

In this volume, Spider-Man teams up with the Black Widow and Master of Kung Fu, Shang-Chi. He also meets Blade and Elektra, and tries to join the Fantastic Four. Daredevil tries to talk him out of being Spider-Man.

Bendis, Brian Michael, Matt Wagner, J.C., et al. *Ultimate Marvel Team Up*. New York: Marvel, 2001. ISBN: 0785108076. Reprints *Ultimate Marvel Team Up 1–5*.

In this volume Spider-Man teams up with Wolverine, the Hulk, and Iron Man from the Ultimate Universe. Nick Fury also makes an appearance.

Bernardo, Mark, Peter Sanderson, Bob Budiansky, et al. *Spiderman Unmasked*. New York: Marvel 1996. ISBN: 0785102752.

This is an encyclopedic look at Spider-Man and his career. It includes a retelling of his origin, based on *Amazing Fantasy 15*, and chapters on Spider-Man's friends, villains, and allies. There is a "Web of Like" chart; there are sections on the *Daily Bugle*, Empire State University, and Midtown High School; and there is a rating of Spider-Man's opponents.

Busiek, Kurt, Pat Olliffe, Al Vey, et al. *The Untold Tales of Spider-Man*. New York: Marvel, 1996. ISBN: 0785102639. Reprints *Untold Tales of Spider-Man 1–8*.

Spider-Man meets Captain Stacy and offers his services as an "unofficial" police officer. He helps a young boy who has mutated into a bat creature known as Batwing. The *Daily Bugle* argues that Spider-Man is Sandman's cohort. He has a less-than-positive encounter with Thunderbolt Ross, which involves the Vulture. The Human Torch and Spider-Man reluctantly team up against the Wizard. John Jameson ponders whether Spider-Man would be a good candidate to be an astronaut. Several of Peter Parker's schoolmates help Spider-Man defeat Electro. Norman Osborn contemplates becoming the Green Goblin, when his guise as the Headsman doesn't work.

This is a collection of stories which take place at various points in Spider-Man's early life while he is still a high school student.

Busiek, Kurt, Roger Stern, Neil Vokes, et al. *Untold Tales of Spider-Man: Strange Encounter*. New York: Marvel, 1998. ISBN: 0785107096.

Peter Parker is still in high school in this tale of the early years of Spider-Man. The mystical Lantern of Lantarr is stolen by some petty crooks who come under the control of Baron Mordo. Dr. Strange seeks the help of Spider-Man to stop Mordo's plans. Betty Brant, Flash, J. J. Jameson, Peter Parker and Liz Allen are transported to another dimension where they encounter Mordo, and Dr. Strange helps Spider-Man battle Mordo. Mordo ends up being transported to Dormammu, much to his displeasure. Jameson admits Spider-Man is a hero, but Strange erases the visit to the dimension from their minds. The Ancient One also makes an appearance.

Claremont, Chris, Michael Golden, Dave Cockrum, et al. *X-Men & Spider-Man: Savage Land*. New York: Marvel, 2002. ISBN: 0785108912. Original ed., *The Savage Land*, 1987 (ISBN: 0871353385). Reprints *Marvel Fanfare 1–4*.

Spider-Man and the Angel go to the Savage Land to help find Kurt Lykos. They are captured and turned into mutant beasts by Brainchild's machine. Ka-Zar helps free them, and Lykos uses his energy-siphoning power to turn them back into their respective selves. As a result, Sauron is reborn, and the Angel requests help from the X-Men to stop Sauron. The X-Men are quickly taken hostage and transformed into beasts, and Ka-Zar and the Angel have to rescue the X-Men from Sauron's clutches. Professor X finds a cure for the Pteranodons virus which resulted in Lykos turning into Sauron.

Claremont, Chris, Michael Golden, Jim Novak, et al. *Spider-Man Strange Adventures*. New York: Marvel, 1996. ISBN: 0785102213. Reprints *Marvel Fanfare 1–2*; *Amazing Spider-Man 100–102*; *Howard the Duck 1*; *Amazing Spider-Man Annual 14*.

Angel and Spider-Man are mutated into monsters in the Savage Land. Ka-Zar is a guest, and Sauron is reborn. Peter Parker grows six arms and battles Morbius and the Lizard. Spider-Man helps Howard the Duck against a cosmic accountant, and he also teams up with Dr. Strange.

This is a collection of weird stories involving Spider-Man. It also contains the first appearance of Morbius.

Conway, Gerry, Stan Lee, Ross Andru, et al. *Spider-Man in Fear Itself*. New York: Marvel, 1992. ISBN: 0871357526.

A wealthy terrorist known as the Baroness has the White Ninja steal the Cassidy Crystals from Osborn Chemicals. The Cassidy Crystals can be used to form a "fear gas" that puts one into a panic, in which one's deepest fears come forth from the psyche. The Baroness plans to launch a bomb over the Earth, and expose the populace to the gas. Spider-Man and Silver Sable go to Bavaria to find the Baroness, and see what she is up to. The White Ninja exposes Spider-Man to the gas, causing him to wrestle with his demons and go mad, until the effect of the gas wears off. The Baroness is not who she appears to be. Mary Jane is saved from a group about to gang rape her, and Spider-Man goes after them. Mary Jane stops him from nearly killing the hoodlums.

This book includes appearances by Adolph Hitler, Baron Zemo, and Arnin Zola. (*Marvel Graphic Novel 72*)

Conway, Gerry, David Michelinie, Todd McFarlane, et al. *Spider-Man: Cosmic Adventures*. New York: Marvel, 1993. ISBN: 0871359634. Reprints *Spectacular Spider-Man 158–160*; *Web of Spider-Man 59–61*; *Amazing Spider-Man 327–329*.

Spider-Man inherits "cosmic powers" through an electrical accident. He becomes so powerful that even the Hulk can't fight against him. Spider-Man almost kills the Hulk, and fights several of his traditional foes, including Goliath, Titania, Brothers Grimm and others. Dr. Doom, Kingpin, Wizard, Red Skull, and Magneto all conspire against Spider-Man, and for a brief moment Spider-Man's cosmic powers turn him into Captain Universe.

Conway, Gerry, David Michelinie, Todd McFarlane, et al. *Spider-Man: Son of the Goblin*. New York: Marvel, 2004. ISBN: 07851 15633. *Amazing Spider-Man Vol. 1: 136–137*; *312*; *Spectacular Spider-Man Vol. 2: 189, 200*.

Harry is hiding in the shadows, watching, when his father, the Green Goblin, dies at the hands of Spider-Man. He tries to kill Peter Parker by planting a bomb in his apartment. As a result, Mary Jane is taken to the hospital, and after Spider-Man defeats him, Harry is taken to a mental hospital, raving that Peter Parker is Spider-Man. The Green Goblin goes up against the Hobgoblin, and the Goblin plants a bomb in the new Norman Osborn Foundation, hoping to trap Spider-Man. In the end, he saves Mary Jane, Norm Jr., and Spider-Man from the bomb, but the toll from chemicals and insanity is too great, and Harry Osborn dies.

This is a nice collection of stories featuring Harry Osborn as he takes the mantel of the Green Goblin from his father, Norman Osborn. It is recommended.

Conway, Gerry, Alex Saviuk, Andy Mushynsky, et al. *The Amazing Spider-Man: Parallel Lives*. New York: Marvel, 1989. ISBN: 0871355736.

This book reviews the history of Peter Parker/Spider-Man and Mary Jane, in parallel. Many of the important events of Spider-Man's life are retold, including the initial spider bite; his appearance against Crusher Hogan; letting the burglar go; Uncle Ben's death; Aunt May's brush with death by radiation; Doc Ock moving in with Aunt May; the wedding of Peter Parker and Mary Jane; and Ock's subsequent terrorization of the Parker household. Part of the story is also told through Mary Jane's eyes. Mary Jane puts on the facade of a happy-go-lucky party girl, but deep inside she bears the anguish of seeing her family fall apart. In the book, Mary Jane meets Peter Parker, and tells him he has hit the jackpot. This is an excellent tribute to the history of Spider-Man and Mary Jane, complete with all the trials and tribulations in their lives. (*Marvel Graphic Novel 46*)

Conway, Gerry, Len Wein, Archie Goodwin, et al. *Spider-Man: Clone Genesis*. New York: Marvel, 1995. ISBN: 0785101586. Reprints *Amazing Spider-Man 141–151*; *Giant Size Spider-Man 5*.

The Jackal, the mastermind behind Clone Sage, has cloned Gwen Stacy, and she comes back two years after her "death" with no memory. Peter Parker thinks he is going insane, and Aunt May has a heart attack after seeing the Gwen clone. The Scorpion attacks Aunt May at the hospital, and after defeating him, Spider-Man makes him apologize to her. Mary Jane and Peter kiss for the first time. The Jackal turns out to be one of Peter's professors who knows his secret identity. He is seemingly killed, as is the Peter Parker clone. The police almost capture Spider-Man. The Jackal forces Peter to relive the Gwen Stacy incident on the bridge. Spider-Man disposes of his clone in a fiery chimney. There are appearances by Mysterio, Cyclone (who captures Jonah Jameson and Robbie), Tarantula, Kingpin, Spider Slayer, Vulture, and the Spider Clone.

There is an introduction by Gerry Conway. This is the beginning of the controversial Clone Sage storyline.

David, Peter, Rich Buckler, Robbin Brosterman, et al. *The Death of Jean DeWolff*. New York: Marvel, 1990. ISBN: 0871357046. Reprints *Peter Parker: Spectacular Spider-Man 107–110*.

A prominent police officer, Jean DeWolff, who befriended Spider-Man, is brutally murdered by the Sin Eater. He starts terrorizing New York, believing he is doing God's work by killing anyone he feels has sinned against the Lord. He even kills a priest during confession. Both Spider-Man and Daredevil are trying to solve the case, and both go to the Kingpin for help. Daredevil stops Spider-Man from killing the Sin Eater, and reveals his alter identity, Matt Murdock, to Spider-Man, as an act of friendship. It turns out that the Sin Eater is the detective assigned to the DeWolff case.

The Sin Eater concept is based on an old folktale.

David, Peter, Stuart Immonen, Joe Rosas, et al. *Spider-Man/Gen 13*. New York: Marvel/DC, 1996. ISBN: 0785102914.

In this book, Spider-Man and Gen 13 team up to defeat Glider and her band of goons.

David, Peter, Rick Leonardi, Al Williamson, et al. *Spider-Man 2099 Meets Spider-Man*. New York: Marvel, 1995. ISBN: 0785101 90X.

Spider-Man and Miguel O'Hara end up in each other's time. Miguel, Spider-Man 2099, goes to the *Daily Bugle* to find some important information, and ends up pushing Jonah Jameson. Spider-Man ends up fighting the 2099 version of the Vulture, while his counterpart fights Venom. They end up meeting in a time warp to fight the Hobgoblin of 2211, and then they team up with Spider-Man from 2500.

These events take place before *Spectacular Spider-Man 226*.

DeFalco, Tom, J. M. DeMatteis, Terry Kavanagh, et al. *Spider-Man: Maximum Carnage*. New York: Marvel, 2004 ISBN: 078 5109870; 0785100385 (1994). Reprints *Amazing Spider-Man 378–380*; *Spectacular Spider-Man 201–203*; *Spider-Man 35–37*; *Spider-Man Unlimited 1–2*; *Web of Spider-Man 101–103*.

Carnage escapes from prison and builds an army of lunatics, including Shriek, Spider-Man Doppelganger, Demigoblin, and Carrion. They rampage New York, murdering at will and causing people to riot. Spider-Man teams up with his nemesis Venom, along with Firestar, Deathlok, Cloak and Dagger, the vampire Morbius, Iron Fist, Black Cat, and Captain America, to help stop Carnage. Dagger, Venom, and Carnage almost die.

This is one of the biggest Spider-Man crossovers ever published.

DeFalco, Tom, Pat Olliffe, Ron Frenz, et al. *Marvel Age Spider-Girl Vol. 1: Legacy*. New York: Marvel, 2004. ISBN: 0785114416. Reprints *Spider-Girl 0–5*.

May Day, Peter and Mary Jane Parker's daughter, discovers she has inherited her father's powers. Her father, the original Spider-Man, now works in a police lab. In spite of his outcry, May Day decides to adopt his mantel as Spider-Girl, and struggles to come to grips with her powers and the responsibility she bears to help others. When Norman Osborn's grandson Normie dons his grandfather's Green Goblin costume and tries to destroy Peter Parker, Spider-Girl puts on her father's old costume and saves her father's life. Then she and her father burn his old costume, and she puts on an acrobat uniform. Some of the other characters she meets include Crazy Eight, Dark Devil, Dragon King, Kingpin, Mr. Nobody, and Venom.

Spider-Girl also meets the Fantastic Five, and helps them stop a dimension/time travel criminal.

This digest-size paperback is part of the Marvel Age series, a new line of graphic novels, modestly priced and designed to appeal to first-time comics readers and younger children. It reprints the brilliant series that was put out in trade paperback a few years ago. This volume should be enjoyed by young and old alike; it is highly recommended to anyone who loves the Spider-Man character, and should be in every library. It has good writing, art, and value. I hope that more Spider-Girl volumes will follow.

DeFalco, Tom, Pat Olliffe, Al Williamson, et al. *Spider-Girl: A Fresh Start*. New York: Marvel, 1999. ISBN: 0785107207. Reprints *Spider-Girl 1–2*.

Peter Parker's teen-age daughter, May Day, inherits amazing powers from her father. She becomes Spider-Girl, much to her father's dismay. She defeats Crazy Eight and encounters Dark Devil.

DeFalco, Tom, Roger Stern, Ron Frenz, et al. *Spider-Man: The Saga of the Alien Costume*. New York: Marvel, 1991. ISBN: 08713539 62. Reprints *Amazing Spider-Man 252–260*.

Spider-Man, with help of Reed Richards, finds out that his black costume is actually alive. It's an alien symbiotic being that lives off of its human hosts and controls them. Spider-Man becomes more aggressive as a result, and takes Peter Parker out on adventures while Parker is trying to sleep, thus zapping his energy. With Reed Richards's help, the symbiotic costume is removed. Appearances are made by Black Cat, Jack O'Lantern, Red Ghost and Super Apes, Hobgoblin, Mr. Fantastic, and Human Torch, among others.

DeFalco, Tom, Al Williamson, Pat Olliffe, et al. *Spider-Girl*. Marvel Comics: New York, 2001. ISBN: 0785108157. Reprints *Spider-Girl 1: 0–5*.

Peter Parker's teenage daughter May Day inherits his spider powers. Her father fights against her continuing his legacy. She encounters Green Goblin's grandson Dark Devil and Crazy Eight, among others.

This is one of the best-written graphic novels ever published. It is reprinted in the *Marvel Age Spider-Girl* series.

DeFalco, Tom, All Williamson, Pat Olliffe, et al. *Spider-Girl Vol. 2: Like Father Like Daughter*. New York: Marvel, 2004. ISBN: 07851 16575. Reprints *Spider-Girl 6–11*.

May learns that her Uncle Phil is also training two sisters jointly known as Ladyhawk. Spider-Girl knocks out Dark Devil and battles with Nova. She learns why her father finally gave up being Spider-Man. Peter Parker helps his daughter May Day/Spider-Girl defeat Mr. Nobody and Crazy Eight. He finally accepts the fact that his daughter is going to play superhero, and decides to help train her himself. Dark Devil is also training her in his own way, and saves her from being unmasked and possibly killed. She goes back in time to find Spyral, and ends up fighting the Human Torch and her younger father, when he was Spider-Man. She also has to battle Jonah Jameson, Spider Slayer, in a tribute to the early Ditko/Lee issues of *SpiderMan*. She meets her mom as well.

This is the second volume in the Marvel Age reprints of *Spider-Girl*, and it too is highly recommended.

DeMatteis, J.M., Mark Bagley, Scott Hanna, et al. *Spider-Man and Batman: Disordered Minds*. New York: DC/Marvel, 1995. ISBN: 0785101926.

In this book, Spider-Man and Batman team up to fight Carnage who is loose in Gotham. Carnage tries to team up with the Joker, but is rejected.

DeMatteis, J. M., Graham Nolan, Karl Kesel, et al. *Batman & Spider-Man: New Age Dawning*. New York: DC/Marvel, 1997. ISBN: 1563893088.

In this volume, Batman and Spider-Man go head to head with the Kingpin and the Demon.

DeMatteis, J.M., John Romita Jr., Klaus Janson, et al. *Spider-Man: The Lost Years*. New York: Marvel, 1996. ISBN: 0785102027. Reprints *Spider-Man: the Lost Years 1–3*.

In this book, alleged clones, Ben Riley and Kaine, go to Salt Lake City and become part of police investigations involving a mob boss. Both characters also have failed romances. This is part of the convoluted clone saga which shook up Spider-Man's world.

DeMatteis, J.M., Mike Zeck, Bob McLeod, et al. *The Amazing Spider-Man: Fearful Symmetry Kraven's Last Hunt*. New York: Marvel, 1997. ISBN: 0871356910. Reprints *Web of Spider-Man 32–33*; *Amazing Spider-Man 293–294*; *Spectacular Spider-Man 131–132*.

Kraven drugs Spider-Man and buries him. He is obsessed with defeating Spider-Man, and sees himself engulfed in spiders as he descends into madness. Kraven goes out in a Spider-Man costume to fight crime for two weeks, and, as Spider-Man, he brutally murders hoods. He catches Vermin and tortures him. When Spider-Man finally confronts Kraven, he ends up in a battle with Vermin, and Kraven commits suicide.

This series shook up the comics world for its seriousness and dark tone. Most of the story is narrated from Kraven's perspective, and we learn a great deal about his family and his history. This book includes a detailed introduction from Stan Lee and an afterword by Glen Herdling and Jim Salicrup. It was reprinted as a hardback in 2006, and is highly recommended. ISBN: 0785124004 (ltd); 078512330X.

Dematteis, J.M., Mike Zeck, Bob McLeod, et al. *Amazing Spider-Man: Soul of the Hunter.* New York: Marvel, 1992. IBSN: 07851359 421.

In this book, Spider-Man wrestles with Kraven's zombie-like ghost, in order to set his soul free. This is a good story about the futility of committing suicide.

Dezago, Todd, Tom DeFalco, and Howard Mackie. *Spider-Man: Identity Crisis.* New York: Marvel, 1998. ISBN: 0785106634. Reprints *Spider-Man 91–92; Spectacular Spider-Man 257–258; Sensational Spider-Man 27–28; Amazing Spider-Man 434–435.*

Norman Osborn frames Spider-Man for a murder that was committed by the Trapster. In order to clear his name, Spider-Man dons four different superhero identities: Prodigy, Dusk, Riocchet, and Hornet. Peter Parker, as Dusk, teams up with the Trapster, hoping to eventually get a confession out of him. Eventually his name is cleared, and he gets rid of these other superhero identities.

This story includes appearances by Vulture, Fantastic Four, Conundrum, and Jack O' Lantern, among others. The volume also contains a sketchbook that details the designs of the four alter–Spider-Man personae.

Dezago, Todd, J.M. DeMatteis, Luke Ross, et al. *Spider-Man: Revelations.* New York: Marvel, 1997. ISBN: 0785105603. Reprints *Spectacular Spider-Man 240; Sensational Spider-Man 11; Amazing Spider-Man 418; Peter Parker: Spider-Man 75.*

Peter Parker finds out that he is the real Spider-Man, and Ben Riley is the clone. Norman Osborn returns from his alleged death as the Green Goblin, and kills Riley. Mary Jane, Parker's wife, loses their baby. This is the end of the infamous clone saga.

Dezago, Todd, Mike Raicht, Shane Davis, et al. *Marvel Age Spider-Man Vol. 4: The Goblin Strikes.* New York: Marvel, 2004. ISBN: 0785115498. Reprints *Marvel Age Spider-Man 13–16.*

The Green Goblin becomes the leader of the Enforcers, and lures Spider-Man to Califorinia to film a movie. Spider-Man realizes, after it's too late, that they are fighting for real. Spider-Man, the Enforcers, and the Goblin disturb the Hulk in a cave. Television hunter Kraven comes to America and declares that he is hunting Spider-Man with his pal the Chameleon. Daredevil meets Spider-Man for the first time when they team up against the Ringmaster, who has hypno-

tized Spider-Man to do his bidding. At a party in honor of Spider-Man, the Human Torch saves a guest from the Green Goblin. Everyone thinks Spider-Man is a coward, and he leaves when he finds out Aunt May has been taken to the hospital.

This issue is based upon the original stories of Stan Lee, Steve Ditko, and Jack Kirby, and is updated for modern readers. Volumes 1 and 2 of this series appear in this subsecton, under writer "Quantz, Dan."

Dezago, Todd, Mike Raicht, Steve Ditko, et al. *Marvel Age Spider-Man Vol. 3: Swingtime Digest.* New York: Marvel, 2004. ISBN: 078511548X. Reprints *Marvel Age Spider-Man 9–12.*

Spider-Man encounters the Enforcers and Mysterio for the first time. The Big Man of the Enforcers is actually a reporter, Fredrick Foswell, who works for the *Daily Bugle.* Betty Brant's brother Ben gets involved with some crooks, and Spider-Man tries to set him straight. Betty is kidnapped by Doc Ock, in an attempt to lure Spider-Man out into the open, and Peter Parker is unmasked as Spider-Man when he attempts to save her. Because he has a terrible cold, he is not at his full Spider-Man power, and no one believes that Parker actually is Spider-Man. Mysterio poses as Spider-Man, and commits several crimes.

This book is based on the original plots of Stan Lee and Steve Ditko. Volumes 1 and 2 of this series appear in this subsecton, under "Quantz, Dan."

Dezago, Todd, Mike Wieringo, Richard Case, et al. *Spider-Man: The Savage Land Saga.* New York: Marvel, 1997. ISBN: 07851056 38. Reprints *Sensation Spider-Man 13–15.*

In this book, Spider-Man, Ka-Zar, and Shanna team up against Roxxon Oil Company which wants to exploit the Savage Land's resources for petroleum and profit. Roxxon's presence would turn the Savage Land into a lifeless terrain. Hulk makes a cameo.

Ennis, Garth, John McCrea, John Milligan, et al. *Spider-Man's Tangled Web Vol. 1.* New York: Marvel, 2001. ISBN: 0785108033. Reprints *Spider-Man: Tangled Web 1–6.*

This volume contains three stories that deal with day-to-day issues in Spider-Man's world. In "The Thousand," an old enemy figures out how Spider-Man got his powers and tries the experiment; in "Severance Package," a high ranking mobster works for the Kingpin, but fails in his mission; and in "Flowers for Rhino," the Rhino does some soul searching, gains intelligence, and falls in love.

Fingeroth, Danny, Kerry Gammill, Stan Lee, et al. *Deadly Foes of Spider-Man.* New York: Marvel, 1993. ISBN: 0871359863. Reprints *Deadly Foes of Spider-Man 1–4.*

This volume features the Rhino, Speed Demon, Boomerang, Hydro Man, and their leader, the Beetle, as a new force of evil for Spider-Man to contend with. They go around robbing vaults, but are actually pawns in the hands of the Kingpin; Speed Demon attempts to move in on Boomerang's girlfriend, who is also Ringer's widow, but she has an agenda of her own; Boomerang ends up in jail; the Rhino, who wants to remove his Rhino costume and go straight, saves Spider-Man's life, but the Kingpin betrays the Rhino and kills the doctor who was working with him; the Shocker is portrayed as a scared little child; and the Punisher and the Tinkerer make cameo appearances. This is a story of using and betraying. The volume includes a pin-up gallery. Wilson Fisk wrote the introduction.

Fingeroth, Danny, Ron Lim, Jim Sanders, et al. *Venom: Deathtrap: The Vault.* New York: Marvel, 1993. ISBN: 0871359758. Reprints *Avengers: Deathtrap: The Vault: Marvel Graphic Novel 68.*

Venom, with several other supercriminals, coordinates a prison break, and the Avengers and Freedom Force team up to stop the escape. Armadillo, Rhino, and Scarecrow turn on Venom, because they want to serve out their sentences. The Rhino smashes himself into Venom's back, and Venom kills the warden of the Vault. There is a bomb threat, but Venom does not believe that there is a bomb set to go off.

This features a cover that is smaller in size and different than the one on the original graphic novel.

Hama, Larry, Andrew Wildman, Art Nichols, et al. *Venom: Carnage Unleashed.* New York: Marvel, 1996. ISBN: 0785101993. Reprints *Venom: Carnage Unleashed 1–4.*

While in prison, Cletus Kasady signs away the rights to an online computer game that is based on his exploits as Carnage. When he discovers that he can send himself over the Internet, he kills the person designing the game, and takes control of the prison. Venom tries to stop the rampage, and he and Carnage end up fighting in cyberspace. Venom accidentally kills an innocent, whom he mistakenly thinks is a junkie.

Havanagh, Terry, Scott McDaniel, Keith Williams, et al. *Spider-Man/Punisher/Sabretooth: Designer Genes.* New York: Marvel, 1993. ISBN: 0871359898.

Several lab animals and homeless people are found dead and disemboweled. Apparently the Roxxon Corporation is trying to combine human and animal DNA as "designer genes" to create hybrid beings. Both the little brother of the doctor/scientist doing the experiments and the head of the department are hybrid beings. Apparently the scientist did experiments on Sabretooth and Wolverine in Canada, under Department H, and Sabretooth is seeking revenge against the doctor. Spider-Man and the Punisher want to bring Sabretooth in for murders they believe he has committed.

One of the funniest parts of the book is when Spider-Man is trying to stop the Punisher from killing Sabretooth. Spider-Man and the Punisher form an uneasy alliance, but all the while Spider-Man wants to turn the Punisher in to the police.

Jenkins, Paul, Mark Buckingham, Wayne Faucher, et al. *Peter Parker: Spider-Man Vol. 4: Trials and Tribulations.* New York: Marvel, 2003. ISBN: 0785111506. Reprints *Peter Parker: Spider-Man Vol. 2: 35, 37, 48–50.*

A young African American who lives in the slums and whose mother dies, imagines Spider-Man befriending him. Afterward, Spider-Man and the Human Torch battle the Vulture during a horrible snowstorm, and Spider-Man faces a young Indian goddess whom he helps contain a deadly virus. Flash Thompson is still in critical condition, and Spider-Man inadvertently helps Hammer Head. Peter has a heart-to-heart talk with Aunt May about his Spider-Man adventures.

Jenkins, Paul, Mark Buckingham, Dan Green, et al. *Peter Parker: Spider-Man Vol. 2 One Small Break.* New York: Marvel, 2002. ISBN: 0785108246. Reprints *Peter Parker: Spider-Man Vol. 2: 27–28, 30–34.*

In this volume Spider-Man deals with the Robot Master; a new villain, Fusion, who can take the powers of other super beings; and a benign superbeing, named William. Parker reminisces about going to Mets games with Uncle Ben. This book picks up where *Revenge of the Green Goblin* leaves off.

Jenkins, Paul, Mark Buckingham, Sean Phillips, et al. *Peter Parker: Spider-Man Vol. 1 A Day in the Life.* New York: Marvel, 2000. ISBN: 0785107770. Reprints *Webspinners: Tales of Spider-Man 10–12*; *Peter Parker: Spider-Man Vol. 2: 20–22, 26.*

Peter examines his life and the tragedy of it, including the deaths of Uncle Ben, Captain Stacy, the Chameleon, and Gwen Stacy. The Human Torch, Doc Ock, Sandman, and the Green Goblin all make appearances.

This book presents the human, soul-searching side of Peter Parker, and collects some of Paul Jenkins's first Spider-Man writings. This is one of the darkest, most depressing Spider-Man books ever published.

Jenkins, Paul, Humberto Ramos, Wayne Faucher, et al. *Peter Parker: Spider-Man Vol. 3: Return of the Goblin.* New York: Marvel, 2002. ISBN: 0785110194. Reprints *Peter Parker: Spider-Man Vol. 2: 44–47.*

Norman Osborn returns to haunt Peter Parker, and essentially wants a fight to the death. Osborn, who has video footage of the incident, implicates Spider-

Man in the death of Gwen Stacy. The Goblin kidnaps Flash Thompson who is a member of Alcoholics Anonymous. After forcing him to drink hard liquor, the Goblin puts Thompson into a car that he crashes into the school where Parker teaches. In response to this, Parker breaks into an important business meeting that Osborn is conducting with the Japanese.

Jenkins, Paul, Humberto Ramos, Wayne Faucher, et al. *Spectacular Spider-Man Vol. 1: The Hunger*. New York: Marvel, 2004. ISBN: 0785111697. Reprints *Spectacular Spider-Man 1–5*.

Venom, who tries to survive without Eddie Brock, is sucking the adrenaline out of people's bodies. Eddie Brock has cancer and is dying, and cannot survive without his symbiote. However, the symbiote only wants to bond with Peter Parker/Spider-Man, and is rejecting Eddie Brock. Brock goes to confession. The Fantastic Four help Spider-Man try to contain the symbiote, but to no avail. Flash Thompson comes home from the hospital, but is a vegetable. Spider-Man saves both Brock's and the symbiote's life, and Venom is reborn.

Jenkins, Paul, Humberto Ramos, Wayne Faucher, et al. *Spectacular Spider-Man Vol. 2: Countdown*. New York: Marvel, 2004. ISBN: 0785113134. Reprints *Spectacular Spider-Man 6–10*.

Doc Ock kidnaps a high-ranking Palestinian official, and threatens to kill him and start World War III if Spider-Man does not take off his mask and reveal his identity to the world. We learn a great deal about Doc Ock's early life, including the death of his father. Spider-Man gets some help from his New Zealander neighbor, the Kiwi Kid.

Jenkins, Paul, Michael Ryan, Humberto Ramos, et al. *Spectacular Spider-Man Vol. 4: Disassembled*. New York: Marvel, 2004. ISBN: 0785116265. Reprints *Spectacular Spider-Man 15–20*.

The Queen Ana, who is an experiment gone awry from World War II, has the ability to use as a drone any human who has an insect-oriented gene. She also has the ability to detonate a bomb that can kill all life within a 600 mile radius. Captain America knows about this bomb, but Nick Fury does not. After the Queen captures Spider-Man, and gives him a kiss, Spider-Man begins to change into a *real* spider, with whom the Queen wants to mate. Captain America believes the Queen is more dangerous than the Hulk. Iron Man and the X-Men make appearances.

As in the Spider-Man movie, Spider-Man gets organic web-shooters in this volume.

Jenkins, Paul, Damion Scott, Paolo Rivera, et al. *Spectacular Spider-Man. Vol. 3: Here*

There Be Monsters. New York: Marvel, 2004. ISBN: 0785113339. Reprints *Spectacular Spider-Man 11–14*.

Curt Connors, distraught over the death of his wife, and refusing to take his mental health medications, goes slightly crazy. He becomes the Lizard and kidnaps his son. Spider-Man finds out that Connors has control over the Lizard, and eventually Connors turns himself in to the police. A young boy, Joey, who has cerebral palsy, witnesses Spider-Man fighting Morbius, the vampire, and just as Morbius is going to bite Joey and transform him, Spider-Man steps in and stops him.

This story is beautifully painted by newcomer Paolo Rivera.

Jenkins, Paul, Phil Winslade, Tom Palmer, et al. *Daredevil/Spider-Man*. New York: Marvel, 2001. ISBN: 0785107924. Reprints *Daredevil/Spider-Man 1–4*.

Someone who has been taking jabs at all the Kingpin's takes dares Fisk to come out in the open. A group consisting of the Owl, Gladiator, the Stilt Man, and the mysterious Copperhead, its leader, has been trying to topple the Kingpin. Fisk is put into the hospital, and hires Matt Murdock to represent him, and Daredevil and Spider-Man team up to figure out what is going on. The two criminal gangs end up in a violent war, and the Copperhead tries to bring out an army of the living dead. While Spider-Man makes a joke, Daredevil gripes him out.

Jones, Bruce, Lee Weeks, Kaare Andrews, et al. *Spider-Man's Tangled Web Vol. 2*. New York: Marvel, 2002. ISBN: 0785108742. Reprints *Spider-Man's Tangled Web 7–11*.

Spider-Man has a unique relationship with a cab driver who knows his secret identity. Spider-Man encounters Electro close to the home of two boys, one of whom idolizes a comic character, Insect Man. Spider-Man has to fight Vulture on Valentine's Day, causing Peter Parker, because of injuries, to stand up two women with whom he has a dates. The Vulture steals a diamond for his girlfriend.

Larsen, Erik, Gregory Wright, Chris Eliopoulos, et al. *Spider-Man: The Revenge of the Sinister Six*. New York: Marvel, 1994. ISBN: 0785100474. Reprints *Spider-Man 18–22*.

Doc Ock gets new adamantium arms and re-forms the Sinister Six. At first, Ock has a hard time convincing the others to rejoin, because he betrayed them the first time. In an attempt to kill Ock, Sandman is turned into glass. Spider-Man teams up with Ghost Rider, Fantastic Four, Deathlok, Solo, Hulk, and Nova to fight against the Sinister Six, ultimately defeating them. Peter Parker is upset that Mary Jane has a nude acting role. Mary Jane throws a surprise birthday party for Peter Parker.

Lee, Stan, Alan Davis, Mark Farmer, et al. *Spider-Man Official Comic Adaptation*. New York: Marvel, 2002. ISBN: 078510903X. Reprints *Spider-Man: The Movie*; *Ultimate Spider-Man 8*; *Peter Parker Spider-Man 35*; *Spider-Man's Tangled Web 10*.

Spider-Man goes up against the Green Goblin. Two brothers get to witness a battle between Spider-Man and Electro, right on their doorstep, and the older brother tries to stand up to Electro. Peter Parker goes to work for the *Daily Bugle* as a photographer and webmaster. A young African-American child is a secret sidekick to Spider-Man in a heart-warming tale.

This is the adaptation of the first *Spider-Man* movie written by creator Stan Lee. It contains some background material that was not in the movie.

Lee, Stan, Steve Ditko, Sean Chen, et al. *Spider-Man vs. Doctor Octopus*. New York: Marvel, 2000. ISBN: 0785107428. Reprints *Amazing Spider-Man 3, 130–131*; *Amazing Spider-Man Annual 15*; *Marvel Tales 38–41*.

This collection covers the origin of Doctor Octopus and Spider-Man's most famous battles with him. It includes the storyline in which Doc Ock almost marries Aunt May, and a battle between Spider-Man and the Punisher, in which Spider-Man ends up saving the Punisher from Doc Ock.

Lee, Stan, Steve Ditko, Danny Fingeroth, et al. *The Very Best of Spider-Man*. New York: Marvel, 1994. ISBN: 0785100458. Reprints *Amazing Fantasy 15*; *Amazing Spider-Man 33, 50, 248; 271, 317, 365*; *Spectacular Spider-Man 189*.

This is a collection of famous stories from Spider-Man's thirty-year career, including "What Ever Happened to Crusher Hogan"; "The Osborn Legacy," in which Harry Osborn dons the identity of the Green Goblin; and "The Kid Who Collects Spider-Man," in which Peter Parker reveals his identity to a terminally-ill child.

Lee, Stan, Steve Ditko, Sam Rosen, et al. *Spider-Man vs. The Green Goblin*. New York: Marvel, 1995. ISBN: 05810139X. Reprints *Amazing Spider-Man 17, 96–98, 121–122*: *Spectacular Spider-Man 200*.

This book contains the most famous battles between Spider-Man and the Green Goblin. This book follows the death of Gwen Stacy storyline. It includes Harry Osborn's freak-out on acid, his becoming the second Green Goblin, and his subsequent death after saving Spider-Man.

Lee, Stan, Steve Ditko, Sam Rosen, et al. *Spider-Man's Greatest Team-Ups*. New York: Marvel, 1996. ISBN: 0785102035. Reprints *Spider-Man Annual 2–5, 15*; *Daredevil 16–17*; *Marvel Team-Up 100*; *Spider-Man 15*.

Spider-Man teams up with Daredevil, Dr. Strange, Fantastic Four, the Beast, Punisher, and the Avengers. Spider-Man fights Daredevil, thinking he's a criminal. He is offered membership in the Avengers if he can bring in the Hulk, but fails their test when he refuses to turn Hulk over to them. The Beast and Spider-Man team up against a powerful baby mutant. The mutant, Karma, makes her first appearance, and Spider-Man teams up with her and the Fantastic Four. He also teams with the Punisher against Doc Ock, who wants to poison the water supply.

There are other stories in this volume.

Lee, Stan, Steve Ditko, Art Simek, et al. *Spider-Man's Greatest Villains*. New York: Marvel, 1995. ISBN: 0785101365. Reprints *Amazing Spider-Man 12, 13, 69, 82, 224, 316*; *Amazing Spider-Man Annual 28*; *Web of Spider-Man 38*.

This issue contains Spider-Man's most intense battles with some of his most famous villains, including the Vulture, Mysterio, Electro, Kingpin, Venom, Hobgoblin, Carnage, and Doctor Octopus.

Lee, Stan, Gil Kane, John Romita, et al. *Amazing Spider-Man: Death of Gwen Stacy*. New York: Marvel, 2002. ISBN: 0785110267; 0785107169 (1999). Reprints *Amazing Spider-Man 96–98, 121–122*.

In this book, Harry Osborn overdoses on pills. He also has a bad trip on LSD, and the Goblin is supposedly killed. This is the original story of the death of Peter Parker's girlfriend Gwen Stacy, at the hands of the original Green Goblin. It was a groundbreaking series because of its drug content. Stan Lee published it without the approval of the Comics Code. It is highly recommended.

Lee, Stan, Bill Mantlo, Gary Friedrich, et al. *Greatest Spider-Man & Daredevil Team Ups*. New York: Marvel, 1996. ISBN: 0785 10223X. Reprints *Amazing Spider-Man 16, 396*; *Marvel Team Up 56, 73*; *Daredevil 270*; *Spectacular Spider-Man 26–28, 219*.

This volume is a collection of some of the best stories in which Daredevil and Spider-Man team up. In it, they go to battle with the Ringmaster and his Circus of Crime, Masked Marauder, Blizzard, Owl, and the Vulture. They also go up against, and nearly lose to, Blackheart, Mephisto's son. It includes stories in which Daredevil wears all three of his costumes, yellow, red, and gray/black. The introduction is by Ralph Macchio.

Lee, Stan, John Romita, Tom DeFalco, et al. *Spider-Man: Kingpin to the Death*. New York: Marvel, 1997. ISBN: 0785106537.

Spider-Man is going around killing folks, mostly criminals, in New York. The Kingpin has been hiring people to dress up as Spider-Man, and has been injecting them with a deadly drug called the Death's Arrow. The Kingpin sells the drug to a world-renowned assassin, Zoltaro, who ends up being betrayed by the Kingpin and is killed. Daredevil believes in Spider-Man's innocence, and they team up against the Kingpin. Daredevil almost dies when he is injected with the deadly drug, and it is up to Spider-Man to find the antidote.

Stan Lee and John Romita Sr. were reunited for this 1997 graphic novel. Romita includes a detailed sketchbook of characters who are in the story, with commentary. The afterword is by both Stan Lee and Romita, who admits that Daredevil is his favorite character to draw. This classic Marvel story was also known simply as *Kingpin*.

Lee, Stan, John Romita, Floro Dery, et al. *The Best of Spider-Man*. New York: Ballantine Books, 1986. ISBN: 0345325931.

Aunt May is used by Doc Ock in his attempt to steal a rare museum artifact. Ock's snowing of Aunt May is a contant frustration for Peter Parker. Spider-Man backs the Kingpin for mayor until he realizes that Wilson Fisk intends violence against any competition, and the Kingpin's wife Vanessa is shot. The Prowler wants to join Spider-Man, and Parker briefly gives up being Spider-Man. Peter Parker decides to turn criminal and steals a diamond, but he decides that he is a dismal failure at being a crook. Spider-Man is a guest on the television show *That's Incredible*. There is a color section from the Sunday papers that has someone claim he is Spider-Man to get some money, and Jonah Jameson pretends to be Spider-Man to win the love of the richest woman in the world.

These eight Spider-Man stories, taken from the newspaper strip, received more fan mail than any other Spider-Man stories. In the lengthy, detailed essay, "Spider-Man and Me," Lee writes about his relationship to Spider-Man through the years.

Lee, Stan, John Romita, Larry Lieber, et al. *The Spectacular Spider-Man: Lo This Monster*. New York: Marvel, 2002. ISBN: 07851083 27. Reprints *Spectacular Spider-Man Magazine 1*.

In this book, Spider-Man investigates a corrupt politician's bid to become mayor of New York, and ends up fighting a giant strong man. This is a reprint of the original 1968 *Spider-Man* magazine. It includes an updated retelling of the story of Spider-Man's origin.

Lee, Stan, John Romita, Jim Mooney, et al. *Spider-Man: The Death of Captain Stacy*. New York: Marvel, 2004. ISBN: 0785114556. Reprints *Amazing Spider-Man Vol. 1: 88–92*.

Doc Ock gains control of his arms from prison, through mental telepathy. He takes a military plane hostage, and after Spider-Man shows up, they duel and the plane explodes. While fighting on a rooftop, the falling rubble is about to smash a child, and Captain Stacy rescues the boy. With his dying breath, Stacy asks Spider-Man to take care of his daughter, Gwen. Spider-Man is blamed for the death of Captain Stacy. Iceman also appears in this story.

In 2000, the *Death of Captain Stacy* was reprinted in regular comic form. In this issue, there are reproductions of covers from the *Marvel Tales* reprints and a piece by Alex Ross from *Marvels*.

Lee, Stan, John Romita, Sammy Rosen, et al. *The Amazing Spider-Man*: New York: Simon and Schuster, 1979. ISBN: 0671248 847 (trd); 0671248168 (pbk). Reprints *Amazing Spider-Man 42–43, 82, 96–98*.

Spider-Man fights John Jameson who believes that Spider-Man is a villain. Peter Parker meets Mary Jane for the first time. Harry Osborn is hospitalized due to an overdose of drugs, and Spider-Man shows the Green Goblin his ailing son in order to snap him back to sanity. Peter Parker goes to work for Norman Osborn.

This volume reprints the famous Spider-Man anti-drug storyline.

Liefeld, Rob, Fabian Nicieza, Todd McFarlane, et al. *X-Force and Spider-Man: Sabotage*. New York: Marvel, 1992. ISBN: 08713595 37. Reprints *Spider-Man 16*; *X-Force 3–4*.

After Black Tom takes a number of prisoners at the World Trade Center, Siryn teams up with X-Force, and Tom has the Juggernaut fight to keep X-Force and Spider-Man from rescuing the hostages. Black Tom defeats Sunspot, but Cable defeats Tom, and leaves him for dead. However, unknown to Cable, Deadpool rescues Tom. Juggernaut fights Warpath, Spider-Man, Shatterstar, Cannonball, and others, but none of them are able to defeat him. Shatterstar stabs Juggernaut in the eye. Most of the book revolves around the battle with Juggernaut, but Cable manages to tick off some folks, as well.

Loeb, Jeph, Tim Sale, Richard Starkings, et al. *Spider-Man: Blue*. New York: Marvel, 2004. ISBN: 0785110712 (pbk); 07851106 23 2003 (trd). Reprints *Spider-Man Blue 1–6*.

Peter Parker relates his feelings about his first meetings with both Gwen and Mary Jane, documented on audio tape, and moves from Aunt May's house into Harry Osborn's apartment for the first time. Parker's insecurities about Gwen and Mary Jane are defining points in the story. Villains include The Vulture, Green Goblin, Rhino, the Lizard, and Kraven.

In this book, Tim Sale drew Spider-Man, as a tribute to John Romita. Romita wrote the introduction, which discusses how much he liked this previously untold story about Parker and Gwen. It also has a tribute to the original issue in which Mary Jane utters the line, "You just hit the jackpot." This is a wonderful story, with great artwork. It is a moving tribute to the original comics.

Mackie, Howard, Norman Felchle, Richard Starkings, et al. *Spider-Man: Made Men.* New York: Marvel, 1998. ISBN: 07851058 16.

Daily Bugle reporter Ben Ulrich tells the tale of two childhood friends who took different paths into the world of the Marvel mob criminals. One of them was an agent for the Secret Service and the other worked for the Kingpin. Included are parts of Ulrich's unpublished book, *Made Men*, about New York's crime bosses, including Hammerhead, Kingpin, the Rose, Norman Osborn, Silvermane, and Fortunato. There are cameo appearances by the Punisher, Spider-Man, Captain America, and Daredevil.

Mackie, Howard, Ron Randell, Sam Delarosa, et al. *Venom: Separation Anxiety.* New York: Marvel, 1995. ISBN: 078510188. Reprints *Venom Separation Anxiety 1–4*

Eddie Brock and the alien symbiote are separated and held prisoner. Several other symbiotes break Brock out of prison. They broke out of a government lab, and want Brock to teach them how to live with their alien symbiotes. The Venom alien also breaks out, and searches for Brock. One of the other symbiotes is systematically killing her comrades, and has a showdown fight with Venom. Meanwhile the government is looking for Brock/Venom, and a reporter wants to interview Brock.

This book deserves to be reprinted.

Mackie, Howard, Alex Saviuk, Joe Rubinstein, et al. *Spirits of Venom.* New York: Marvel, 1993. ISBN: 0785100091. Reprints *Web of Spider-Man 95–96*; *Spirits of Vengeance 5–6*.

In this book, Spider-Man saves Hobgoblin from the Hob-Demon and the Spider-Man doppleganger. He runs into Blaze, Venom, and Ghost Rider on the trail of Deathspawn. This is one of Spider-Man's darker adventures.

Matthews, Brett, Vatche Mavlian, Paul Morris, et al. *Spider-Man Legends Vol. 4: Spider-Man & Wolverine.* New York: Marvel 2003. ISBN: 0785112979. Reprints *Spider-Man & Wolverine 1–4*; *Spider-Man/Daredevil 1.*

Peter Parker is taken away from his teaching duties by Nick Fury, who wants him to rescue a "special" person, who turns out to be Wolverine. They uncover a rogue government plot called "Stuff of Legends" in which a mutant-hating scientist has created a drug that makes superhumans powerless. Because of the political nature of the job, Nick Fury's and

S.H.I.E.L.D.'s hands are tied, and they can't do anything to stop the program. Spider-Man and Wolverine manage to shut the program down, but have to face the wrath of Aunt May who was expecting Peter for dinner. Naturally, he missed his appointment with her. Wolverine stays to have supper with Aunt May and Peter Parker, and ends up carving the roast.

There also is a short story in which Spider-Man, Daredevil, and reporter Ben Ulrich help rescue a young girl who is kidnapped. The writing in this volume is very clever and well worth reading.

McFarlane, Todd, David Michelinie, Bob McLeod, et al. *Spider-Man Legends Vol. 1: Todd McFarlane.* New York: Marvel, 2001. ISBN: 0785108009. Reprints *Amazing Spider-Man 298–305.*

This volume contains the Spider-Man issues in which Todd McFarlane did the artwork. It includes the infamous battles between Spider-Man and Venom, and appearances by Silver Sable, Sandman, the Prowler and the Fox. Many fans feel this is some of the best artwork ever done in the pages of *Spider-Man.*

McFarlane, Todd, David Michelinie, Rick Parker, et al. *Spider-Man Legends Vol. 2: Todd McFarlane.* New York: Marvel, 2003. ISBN: 0785110372. Reprints *Amazing Spider-Man Vol. 1: 306–314*; *Amazing Spider-Man Annual 10.*

Spider-Man goes up against the Chameleon, the Lizard, and Mysterio. Their rich landlord Jonathon Caesar kidnaps Mary Jane, with whom he is obsessed. Although Ceasar is caught and Mary Jane is rescued, Caesar has Peter and Mary Jane evicted from their condo, leaving them homeless, until they move back in with Aunt May. The Hobgoblin and the Green Goblin go up against one another, and the Hobgoblin threatens Harry Osborn's family.

This is the second volume showcasing the art of Todd McFarlane. It also contains a short story featuring the Prowler.

McFarlane, Todd, David Michelinie, Rick Parker et al. *Spider-Man vs. Venom.* New York: Marvel, 1990. ISBN: 0871356163. Reprints *Amazing Spider-Man 298–300, 315–317.*

In this book, Venom, who was Spider-Man's first black costume, feels betrayed by Spider-Man, because he got rid of the costume, and the parasitic costume completely possesses *Daily Globe* reporter Eddie Brock. This is a collection of the famous series drawn by Todd McFarlane, and it includes Venom's first appearance.

McFarlane, Todd, David Michelinie, Bob Sharen, et al. *Spider-Man Legends Vol. 3: Todd McFarlane.* New York: Marvel, 2004.

ISBN: 0785110399. Reprints *Amazing Spider-Man 315–323; 325; 328.*

Venom breaks out of prison and he fights Spider-Man. Vemon beats Spider-Man, and Parker finally gives in to him, which proves to be Venom's undoing. Eddie Brock shows up at Aunt May's house in order to make Peter Parker uncomfortable. Justin Hammer hires the Scorpion to kidnap an important general. Scorpion betrays Hammer, who then hires the Sandman and Whiplash to beat up on the Scorpion. Sebastian Shaw hires the Grey Hulk to kill Spider-Man. Harry Osborn finds his father's Green Goblin costume, and Mary Jane learns why no one will hire her for a modeling job.

This is the third Spider-Man collection to highlight the work of artist Todd McFarlane. It includes the complete *Assassination Plot* storyline, featuring Silver Sable, Captain America, Sabretooth, and Paladin.

McKeever, Sean, Steve Buccellato, Robbie Morrison, et al. *Spider-Man's Tangled Web Vol. 4.* New York: Marvel, 2003. ISBN: 078511 064X. Reprints *Spider-Man's Tangled Web 18–22; Peter Parker Spider-Man Vol. 2: 42–43.*

Two word-loving psychos, Typeface and Spellcheck, meet, and Typeface keeps trying ditch Spellcheck. Spider-Man takes care of Typeface. Grizzly, who is let out of jail, tries to find an online mate. At the face to face meeting, Grizzly finds out his prospective mate is the Rhino, his neighbor. They both decide to go back to crime because it is easier than going straight. Jonah Jameson has a heart attack, and goes to see a shrink to find out why he hates Spider-Man. The Sandman is eating pop stars on a beach television show, and when Spider-Man comes to help, he ends up being a guest on the mindless show. There also are appearances by the Fantastic Four, Puppet Master, Medusa and the Wasp.

McKeever, Sean, Takeshi Miyazawa, Norman Lee, et al. *Mary Jane Vol. 1: Circle of Friends.* New York: Marvel, 2004. ISBN: 078511 467X. Reprints *Mary Jane 1–4.*

While Mary Jane and Peter are still in high school, and before she knows that Peter Parker is Spider-Man, Liz Allen tries to get Mary Jane to take Harry Osborn to the prom. Spider-Man saves Mary Jane on the subway after the fight with Electro destroys it and nearly kills her. She goes through a series of jobs, including one working for Hippo Burgers, but never finds one that quite suits her. Liz is jealous of a "tramp" whom she believes Flash is interested in, and, after accidentally glancing at his notebook, Mary Jane realizes that Flash likes her. Liz catches Flash and Mary Jane hugging, and she wants Spider-Man to take her to the prom.

This is a fun book looking into the early, personal lives of some of the characters surrounding Spider-Man. It is part of the Marvel Age series.

Michelinie, David, Mark Bagley, Randy Emberlin, et al. *Spider-Man: Carnage.* New York: Marvel, 1993. ISBN: 0871359715. Reprints *Amazing Spider-Man 344–345, 359–363.*

In this issue, Spider-Man cannot stop Carnage alone, so he asks his foe Venom to help rein Carnage in. Carnage tries to kill Jonah Jameson. This issue covers the genesis of Carnage, Venom's spawn. It is one of the most popular Spider-Man stories.

Michelinie, David, Mark Bagley, Randy Emberlin, et al. *Spider-Man: Invasion of the Spider Slayers.* New York: Marvel, 1995. ISBN: 0785101004. Reprints *Amazing Spider-Man 368–373.*

Spencer Smythe's son Alistaire creates a number of Spider Slayer robots to terrorize and destroy Spider-Man, and ends up using inmates from a mental institution to help his Spider Slayers. Peter Parker's parents come back after a twenty-year stint in a Soviet prison, and are almost killed by the Mole. Mary Jane becomes addicted to cigarettes, and Felicia Hardy dons the Black Cat uniform again.

Michelinie, David, Erik Larsen, Terry Austin, et al. *Spider-Man: Return of the Sinister Six.* New York: Marvel, 1994. ISBN: 07851004 31. Reprints *Amazing Spider-Man 334–339.*

Dr. Octopus re-forms the Sinister Six, with Electro, Sandman, Hobgoblin, Mysterio, and the Vulture. He wants to take over the Earth by releasing a deadly chemical into the air. Aunt May's fiancée Nathan dies, and two obsessed fans stalk Mary Jane. The Sandman, one of the Sinister Six, ends up saving Spider-Man's life, and Spider-Man foils Octopus's plan. The chemical that he releases frees everyone from cocaine addiction, but will destroy the ozone layer.

Michelinie, David, Eric Larsen, Paris Cullins, et al. *Spider-Man: Venom Returns.* New York: Marvel, 1993. ISBN: 0871359669. Reprints *Amazing Spider-Man 330–347; Spider-Man Annual 25.*

In this book, Venom, who returns and goes to Peter Parker's house, follows Spider-Man in his never-ending quest for revenge. Carnage makes his first appearance as the killer Cletus Kasady.

Michelinie, David, Eric Larsen, Randy Emberlin, et al. *Spider-Man vs. Doctor Doom.* New York: Marvel, 1995. ISBN: 0785101101. Reprints *Amazing Spider-Man 349–350.*

The thief Black Fox steals an emerald from a museum, and Spider-Man attempts to solve the crime. The owner of the gem is Doctor Doom, whom Spider-Man battles.

Michelinie, David, Stan Lee, Jim Shooter, et al. *The Amazing Spider-Man: The Wedding.* New York: Marvel, 1992. ISBN: 08713577 04. Reprints *Not Brand Ecch 6*; *Amazing Spider-Man 290–292*; *Amazing Spider-Man Annual 21*; *Amazing Spider-Man Newspaper Strip.*

This is an amazing collection of Spider-Man stories about Peter Parker's engagement and marriage to Mary Jane. It includes a detailed report by Barry Dutter on the wedding of Spider-Man and Mary Jane at Shea Stadium in New York, on June 5, 1987. The Hulk, Iceman, Green Goblin, Firestar, and the New York Mets were in attendance, along with 80,000 fans. The ceremony script was written by Peter David and delivered by Stan Lee. The volume also contains photographs from the wedding, and a copy of Stan Lee's newspaper strip, in color and black and white, chronicling the courtship.

Michelinie, David, Ron Lim, Al Milgrom, et al. *Venom: Lethal Protector.* New York: Marvel, 1995. ISBN: 0785101071. Reprints *Venom Lethal Protector 1–6.*

Venom goes to San Francisco to find a new life. He made an uneasy alliance with Spider-Man, but when Spider-Man finds out that Venom is causing havoc, he goes in search of him. Venom ends up asking for Spider-Man's help to stop a greedy businessman from destroying the homes of a community living underground.

Michelinie, David, Todd McFarlane, Rick Parker, et al. *Spider-Man: The Assassin Nation Plot.* New York: Marvel, 1992. ISBN: 0871358891. Reprints *Amazing Spider-Man 320–325.*

Spider-Man comes across a plot to assassinate the King of Symkaria. He teams up with Paladin, Silver Sable, Solo, and Captain America to save the king, but Sabretooth, who was hired by the Red Skull, kills the Prime Minster, and assassins kill the King's wife. Captain America tries to get security clearance for Spider-Man, to no avail.

Milgrom, Al, Mark Bagley, Randy Emberlin, et al. *Spider-Man: Round Robin: The Sidekick's Revenge.* New York: Marvel, 1994. ISBN: 078510027X. Reprints *Amazing Spider-Man 353–358.*

Spider-Man teams up with Moon Knight, the Punisher, Darkhawk, and Nova to fight the Secret Empire. Moon Knight's ex-sidekick Midnight has become a cyborg bent on controlling the Secret Empire.

Millar, Mark, Terry Dodson, Rachel Dodson, et al. *Marvel Knights Spider-Man Vol. 1: Down Among the Dead Men.* New York: Marvel, 2004. ISBN: 0785114378. Reprints *Marvel Knights Spider-Man 1–4.*

While in prison, the Green Goblin, Norman Osborn, allegedly reveals Spider-Man's identity to another villain, who then desecrates Ben Parker's grave and kidnaps Aunt May. The Owl tricks Spider-Man into going after Electro and the Vulture who stole $20 million from the Owl. Spider-Man fights both, and the money is lost. The Black Cat helps capture the Vulture who wants the money to save his grandson who has cancer, and the Vulture is taken to the Owl who tortures him mercilessly. Jonah Jameson sees a photo of Spider-Man without his mask, a picture that was taken at the hospital.

This first Marvel Knights Spider-Man tale is a dark one indeed. Throughout the book Spider-Man is beaten, and he ends up in the hospital.

Miller, Frank, Stan Lee, Jack Kirby, et al. *Sensational Spider-Man.* New York: Marvel, 1988. ISBN: 0871355140. Reprints *King Size Annual: Amazing Spider-Man 6: 14–15*; *Amazing Spider-Man 8.*

Spider-Man teams with the Punisher against Dr. Octopus. Ock drugs the Punisher who gets caught by the police, and, while being arrested, argues that they are on the same side. Spider-Man helps Dr. Strange against Dormammu, who has teamed up with Dr. Doom, and Spider-Man tries to show off in front of the Human Torch's girlfriend, by challenging the Torch to a duel.

This is the last of the Lee/Kirby/Ditko collaboration.

Milligan, Peter, Clayton Crain, Cory Petit, et al. *Venom vs. Carnage.* New York: Marvel, 2004. ISBN: 0785115242. Reprints *Venom vs. Carnage 1–4.*

Carnage has a baby whom he attaches to a policeman. Venom tries to protect the policeman from Carnage who has a death wish for his own offspring. Venom wants the offspring, named Toxin, to be his partner in trying to destroy Spider-Man, but when Toxin decides to team with Spider-Man and be one of the good guys, Venom and Carnage team up to destroy him. The policeman leaves his wife to go out on his own, and try to figure out how to use Toxin as a force for good. The Black Cat is caught in the middle of this war.

This book contains beautiful, vivid illustrations by newcomer Clayton Crain.

Mitchell, Colin, Derec Aucoin, Keron Grant, et al. *Marvel Age: Spider-Man Doctor Octopus Vol. 1: Out of Reach.* New York: Marvel, 2004. ISBN: 0785113606. Reprints *Spider-Man/Doctor Octopus Out of Reach 1–5.*

Doc Ock reluctantly take a young science genius, Brigham Fontaine, under his wing. It turns out that Fontaine was once one of Peter Parker's students. He finds out that working for Doc Ock is not always what it is cut out to be. Fontaine idolizes Ock, but Ock cares little about having a young apprentice. They both try to destroy Spider-Man, but in the end Spider-Man has to rescue them.

This is a digest-sized book which is appropriate for all ages.

Olshevsky, George, Tony Frutti, Ronn Sutton, et al. *The Marvel Comics Index: Spider-Man 1*. Ontario: G&T Enterprises, 1976. ISBN: 0943348501 (Marvel Index Set).

This volume contains a history and index to Spider-Man comics. Magazines indexed include *Amazing Fantasy*, *Amazing Spider-Man*, *Amazing Spider-Man Annual*, *Spectacular Spider-Man*, *Amazing Spider-Man Mini-Comic*, *Giant-Size Superheroes*, *Giant Size Spider-Man*, and *Spider-Man Super Stories*. It also includes indexing for the pre–Spider-Man comic *Amazing Adult Fantasy*, and cross-indexing for personnel and major characters.

Owlsley, James, Mark Bright, Al Williamson, et al. *Spider-Man vs. Wolverine*. New York: Marvel, 1990. ISBN: 0871356457. Reprints *Spider-Man vs. Wolverine Vol. 2: 1*.

A group of former KGB agents end up dead in New York. When Peter Parker is sent to Germany with Ned Leeds, to investigate, Leeds is murdered. Charlemagne, a former lover and best friend of Wolverine, is also a former "free agent assassin/spy" who has a bounty on her head. Wolverine discovers that Peter Parker is Spider-Man, and when he and Spider-Man fight over Charlemagne, she asks Wolverine to kill her.

This is one of the few stories that featured Spider-Man in both his black-and-blue and red costumes.

Putney, Susan K.. Berni Wrightson, Jim Novak, et al. *The Amazing Spider-Man: Hooky* New York: Marvel, 1986. ISBN: 0871351544.

Spider-Man helps a young mystic, Mandi, who knows Spider-Man's identity, to go through a trial-by-fire initiation in her dimension. They have to battle a giant cockroach that keeps mutating into larger and more threatening creatures. (*Marvel Graphic Novel 22*)

Quantz, Daniel, Mark Brooks, Jonboy Meyers, et al. *Marvel Age Spider-Man Vol. 1: Fearsome Foes*. New York: Marvel, 2004. ISBN: 0785114394. Reprints *Marvel Age Spider-Man 1–4*.

In this volume, Dr. Doom tries to get Spider-Man to team up with him; the Human Torch inspires Peter Parker to continue as Spider-Man; Aunt May thinks Peter is doing something illegal; and Spider-Man fights the Vulture. The volume also covers the origins of Dr. Octopus and the Sandman. This is a smaller, budget-priced, digest-sized volume, which was published to appeal to younger kids and new readers. Each

story is based on an *Amazing Spider-Man* issue originally done by Stan Lee and Steve Ditko. The stories are updated to modern times, but the overall plots are the same as they were in the early issues. Volumes 3 and 4 of this series appear in this chapter subsection under "Dezago."

Quantz, Dan, Todd Dezago, Mark Brooks, et al. *Marvel Age Spider-Man Vol. 2: Everyday Hero*. New York: Marvel, 2004. ISBN: 0785114513. Reprints *Marvel Age Spider-Man 5–8*.

In this volume, Spider-Man goes to Florida to meet the Lizard and help Curt Connors's wife get her husband back; the Vulture breaks out of prison; and Roxxon creates a liquid-style android that is a living brain and a dangerous weapon. The volume covers the origin of Electro. This is a modern retelling of the early Spider-Man stories that were written by Stan Lee and Steve Ditko in the early 1960s. It contains a Marvel Age sketchbook. Volumes 3 and 4 of this series appear in this chapter subsection under "Dezago."

Romita, John Sr., Stan Lee, Mickey Demo, et al. *Spider-Man Visionaries: John Romita, Sr.* New York: Marvel, 2002. ISBN: 07851079 40. Reprints *Amazing Spider-Man 39–42, 50, 68–69, 108–109*.

The Green Goblin and Spider-Man discover each other's identities for the first time. Kingpin makes his first appearance. Peter Parker meets Mary Jane, and Spider-Man's first love is abducted on the day Peter Parker decides to stop being Spider-Man. Spider-Man teams up with Dr. Strange in a Vietnam-themed adventure. J. J. Jameson's son becomes a superhero who hates Spider-Man. The Rhino makes his first appearance.

This book is a tribute to the work of John Romita Sr. Issue 50 was the inspiration behind the movie *Spider-Man 2*.

Rucka, Greg, Scott Christian Sava, Richard Starkings, et al. *Spider-Man: Quality of Life*. New York: Marvel, 2002. ISBN: 0785 110119. Reprints *Spider-Man: Quality of Life 1–4*.

A high-powered corporation, Monnano, hires a snakelike assassin to kill Curt Connors. Connors's wife gets cancer and dies because of the chemicals that Monnano was spreading. Connors changes into the Lizard to exact his revenge against the CEO of Monnano. Spider-Man has to mediate between the Lizard and the Snake Woman.

This is a well written, but very sad tale. It is the first computerized Spider-Man graphic novel, and is beautifully done.

Stern, Roger, Gerry Conway, Steve Ditko, et al. *Spider-Man Megazine 1–6*. New York: Marvel, 1994–1995. Reprints *Amazing Spider-*

Man 16–21, 224–236; Marvel Team-Up 1–6.

Each issue in this volume is book-sized. It is a 96-page monster that contains reprints, in glorious color, of some of the most famous Spider-Man stories, many of which have been reprinted elsewhere. The stories include Spider-Man teaming up with the Human Torch against Morbius, and Spider-Man and the Thing fighting the Puppet Master. Other stories feature the Green Goblin, Black Cat, Will O' Wisp, Tarantula, Mr. Hyde, Cobra, the Vision, Foolkiller, Vulture, and Sandman fighting with/against Spider-Man. The story of the famous first meeting of Spider-Man and the Juggernaut, "Nothing Can Stop the Juggernaut," is also included. Others who Spider-Man meets in this book are Daredevil, for the first time; the original X-Men, who help save Spider-Man's life; and Jean Grey, whom he kisses.

Stern, Roger, Ron Frenz, Pat Olliffe, et al. *Spider-Man: Revenge of the Green Goblin.* New York: Marvel, 2002. ISBN: 0785108734. Reprints *Revenge of the Green Goblin 1–3; Amazing Spider-Man Vol. 2: 25; Peter Parker Spider-Man Vol. 2: 25.*

In this book, the original Green Goblin, Norman Osborn, tries to enlist Spider-Man as his heir and son, and Osborn, who becomes the leader of a religious cult, gives Peter Parker hallucinogenic drugs. This is one of the most intense Spider-Man stories ever written.

Stern, Roger, Ron Frenz, George Perez, et al. *Spider-Man: Hobgoblin Lives.* New York: Marvel, 1998. ISBN: 0785105859. Reprints *Spider-Man: Hobgoblin Lives 1–3.*

In this book, Jason Macendale is put on trial as the Hobgoblin, but someone else has taken on the mantle; many believe that Ned Leeds was the Hobgoblin, but he is thought to be dead. One of the greatest mysteries in the history of the Marvel Universe is revealed in this book. The foreword and afterword are by Roger Stern. An issue-by-issue timeline of the Hobgoblin saga is included.

Stern, Roger, Stan Lee, Steve Ditko, et al. *Spider-Man: The Secret Story of the Marvel's World Famous Wall Crawler.* Chicago: Children's Press, 1981. ISBN: 0516024140 (trd); 0824980115 (pbk). Reprints *Amazing Fantasy 15; Spider-Man 80; Spider-Man Annual 1.*

In this book, the Chameleon poses as Captain Stacy to steal some priceless artwork. He also pretends to be photographer Peter Parker. Narrative and graphic text are combined in this book about Spider-Man's origin, his powers, his friends, and his most famous opponents.

Stern, Roger, Bill Mantlo, Tom DeFalco, et al. *The Amazing Spider-Man: The Origin of the Hobgoblin.* New York: Marvel, 1993. ISBN: 0871359170. Reprints *Amazing Spider-Man 238–239, 244–245, 249–251; Spectacular Spider-Man 85.*

This book contains the entire origin of the Hobgoblin storyline. A small-time hood finds a secret underground storage area which belonged to the original Green Goblin, Norman Osborn. In the storage area there are notes, weapons, and costumes that the person for whom the hood works used to become the Hobgoblin. Included is an introduction by the author telling how the Hobgoblin came into being.

Stern, Roger, John Romita Jr., Pablo Marcos, et al. *The Amazing Spider-Man: Murder by Spider.* New York: Marvel, 2000. ISBN: 0785107622. Reprints *Amazing Spider-Man 224–230.*

Spider-Man teams up with the Black Cat for the first time, when she is trying to go straight. The Juggernaut tries to kidnap Madame Web, but when he rips her off of her life support machines, she becomes useless to him. Spider-Man investigates several mysterious murders by a group of spiders.

Villains in this book include the Vulture, Foolkiller (who kills anyone he considers a fool), and the Juggernaut. There is also a profile and history of the Black Cat. (*Backpack Marvel*)

Stern, Roger, John Romita Jr., Jim Mooney, et al. *The Sensational Spider-Man: Nothing Can Stop the Juggernaut.* New York: Marvel, 1989. ISBN: 0871355728. Reprints *Amazing Spider-Man 229–230.*

Spider-Man's first encounter with Cain Marko, the Juggernaut, occurs when the Juggernaut is trying to capture Madame Web, who is on life support. Spider-Man tries to stop him, but is unable to do so. When Cain realizes that Madame Web needs life support in order to function, he dumps her. Juggernaut sinks to the bottom of a cement pool.

Straczynski, J. Micheal, John Romita Jr., Scott Hanna, et al. *Amazing Spider-Man Vol. 1: Coming Home.* New York: Marvel, 2001. ISBN: 0785108068. Reprints *Amazing Spider-Man Vol. 2: 30–35.*

In this volume, Peter meets an old man, Ezekiel, who has powers that are similar to his, and the old man warns Peter about a creature that has been hunting superbeings for several centuries. This volume was critically acclaimed by *Entertainment Weekly* for Straczynski's storytelling ability.

Straczynski, J. Michael, John Romita Jr., Scott Hanna, et al. *Amazing Spider-Man Vol. 2: Revelations.* New York: Marvel 2002.

ISBN: 0785108777. Reprints *Amazing Spider-Man Vol. 2: 36–39.*

When Spider-Man deals with the tragic events of 9/11, helping rescue survivors, he realizes that the everyday people are the real heroes. He feels sorry for Captain America who is very somber over the event. Aunt May finds out that Peter Parker is actually Spider-Man, and they have a heart-to-heart discussion about honesty.

The volume also includes a wordless story featuring Aunt May and Mary Jane. There are endorsements by *Cinescape Magazine* and *Entertainment Weekly* in the back matter.

Straczynski, J. Michael, John Romita Jr., Scott Hanna, et al. *The Amazing Spider-Man Vol. 3: Until the Stars Turn Cold.* New York: Marvel, 2002. ISBN: 0785110755. Reprints Amazing *Spider-Man Vol. 2: 40–45.*

A group of teenagers, mostly junkies, are being sent to another dimension by the convict known as Shade. Spider-Man investigates, and comes in contact with Dr. Strange who tells him to sit in a chair and meditate. He saves the children, but in the process ends up missing a date with Mary Jane when she comes to New York for a photo shoot. Peter and Aunt May go to Los Angeles for a vacation, and for Peter to apologize to Mary Jane for missing their date. Spider-Man goes into action against a Dr. Octopus clone that stole Octavius's technology and designs. Doc Ock teams up with Spider-Man, and recognizes Aunt May. Aunt May starts a letter-writing campaign directed toward newspapers that print bad press about Spider-Man, including the *Daily Bugle.*

Straczynski, J. Michael, John Romita Jr., Scott Hanna et al. *The Amazing Spider-Man Vol. 4: The Life and Death of Spiders.* New York: Marvel 2003. ISBN: 0785110976. Reprints *Amazing Spider Vol. 2: 46–50.*

Dr. Strange visits Peter Parker to let him know that a wasp-like predator from another dimension is coming to kill him. Shanthra tries to "play" with Spider-Man, and in an attempt to spoil his reputation, goes on national television, talking about what a pervert he is. She stings him, and almost kills him, but Parker is rescued and taken to Africa by Ezekiel. He learns about the first Spider-Man and how destiny is linked to a tribal legend and spiders. Shanthra comes, and is destroyed by a nest of spiders. Parker then tries to patch things up with Mary Jane, and they meet in a Denver airport. Dr. Doom and Captain America make cameo appearances.

Straczynski, J. Michael, John Romita Jr., Scott Hanna, et al. *The Amazing Spider-Man Vol. 5: Unintended Consequences.* New York: Marvel, 2003. ISBN: 0785110984. Reprints *Amazing Spider-Man Vol. 2: 51–56.*

Much to his delight, Peter Parker and Mary Jane get back together. A group of mobsters were murdered in 1957 and buried out in the desert. In 2003, after gamma Bombs were tested near that site, a zombie, formed of the whole group, is brought back to life, and vows to kill the mobster, Forelli, who ordered the group's murder. Forelli hires Spider-Man to protect him and his family by arguing that innocents will be murdered by the zombie. Spider-Man figures out a way to destroy the zombie and also pin the murder on Forelli so that he goes to jail. Peter Parker shows an interest in one of his students, and Spider-Man follows her at night to make sure she is all right. Spider-Man stops her brother in a carjacking and sends him to jail. His friend Ezekiel plays a prominent role in this story, and Parker/Spider-Man learns some important lessons.

This volume is beautifully written and highly recommended.

Straczynski, J. Michael, John Romita Jr., Scott Hanna, et al. *Amazing Spider-Man Vol. 6: Happy Birthday.* New York: Marvel, 2004. ISBN: 0785113436. Reprints *Amazing Spider-Man Vol. 2: 57–58*; *Amazing Spider-Man 500–502.*

The Mindless Ones from Dormammu's dimension are unleashed on New York. Reed Richards figures out a way to send them back, but this is what Dormammu wants. Dr. Strange tries to stop them, and both he and Spider-Man are sent beyond space and time. Spider-Man relives various incidents in his life, including the death of Uncle Ben and the various villains he fought over the years. He even sees his future death at the hands of police officers. This all happens on Peter Parker's birthday. While Spider-Man is fighting a nut across town, Aunt May is at Ben's graveside, telling him about her daily life. A Jewish tailor with ties to Holocaust, who makes clothes for both villains and heroes, happens to tell Spider-Man about an assassination plan he overheard.

Straczynski, J. Michael, John Romita Jr., Scott Hanna, et al. *Amazing Spider-Man Vol. 7: Book of Ezekiel.* New York: Marvel, 2004. ISBN: 0785115250. Reprints *Amazing Spider-Man 503–508.*

While in another dimension with Dr. Strange, Spider-Man inadvertently lets out the chaos entity Morwen who had been banished hundreds of years ago by the Ancient One. Morwen uses one of Loki's daughters as a human hostage, and Loki and Spider-Man team up to stop Morwen. Loki eats his first hot dog. Mary Jane seems to have a big part in a movie, only to find out it is a bogus lead.

In this volume, the mysterious Ezekiel's purpose is revealed, as is his origin and the relationship between Spider-Man and the Spider entity.

Thomas, Jean, Win Mortimer, Mike Esposito, et al. *The Best of Spider-Man Super Stories.*

New York: Simon and Schuster, 1978. ISBN: 0671242202 (trd); 0671227653 (pbk). Reprints *Spider-Man Super Stories 1, 2, 4, 9, 10, 16, 18–19, 22–23.*

Spider-Man helps stop Dr. Doom from taking over the United Nations. The Hulk crashes a party that the cast of *The Electric Company* and Spider-Man are attending. Spider-Man meets the Silver Surfer for the first time, and he teams up with Ms. Marvel and Namor. Other villains include Green Goblin, and the Kingpin.

This is a joint publishing project between the Children's Television Workshop, including *Sesame Street, The Electric Company,* and Marvel. These stories are specifically written for children; they have fewer words per page, and the language is easy to understand. At the time these stories came out, they were considered revolutionary for comics. The book includes pin-ups and inside information about Spider-Man. This is one of the hardest to find Spider-Man–related books.

Thomas, Roy, Gerry Conway, Michael Bair, et al. *Spider-Man: Dr. Strange: The Way to a Dusty Death.* New York: Marvel, 1992. ISBN: 087135960X.

Spider-Man and Dr. Strange go to the Death Dimension and fight against the Xandu and other demons and spirits. While in the Death Dimension, Peter Parker sees visions of Uncle Ben and Gwen Stacy.

Thomas, Roy, Werner Roth, Dan Adkins, et al. *Spider-Man and the Uncanny X-Men.* New York: Marvel, 1996. ISBN: 0785102000. Reprints *Uncanny X-Men 27, 35; Amazing Spider-Man 92; Marvel Team-Up Annual 1; Marvel Team-Up 150; Spectacular Spider-Man 197–199.*

In this book the X-Men ask Spider-Man to officially join them in their first meeting, but Spider-Man declines the offer; the X-Men inadvertently think Spider-Man is a villain, and they fight against him; Ice Man and Spider-Man fight each other; and the X-Men and Spider-Man match wits against Professor Power. This is a nice, varied collection of Spider-Man and X-Men team-ups.

Thomas, Roy, Dann Thomas, Jeff Butler, et al. *Within Our Reach.* Canada: Star Reach Productions, 1991.

Marvel donated a Spider-Man cover and a short story for this benefit Christmas comic. In the Spider-Man story, "A Wolf at the Door," Spider-Man tries to get into the Christmas spirit by putting a greedy landlord, "El Lobo," in jail. He tries to help some poor, illegal immigrants, and breaks bread with them. This book contains numerous other Christmas-related stories in comic form.

Vaughn, Brian K, Staz Johnson, Danny Miki, et al. *Spider-Man/Doctor Octopus: Negative Exposure.* New York: Marvel, 2004. ISBN: 0785113304. Reprints *Doctor Octopus Negative Exposure 1–5.*

Doc Ock plays on Jeff Brasi's jealousy of Peter Parker, because he always seems to get the better photos of Spider-Man on the front page of the *Bugle.* Brasi is the *Daily Bugle* staff photographer whom Doc Ock uses to help him escape from jail. Brasi and his policewoman girlfriend almost get killed when Brasi helps Doc Ock get free. In the end, Ock and Brasi both end up in jail. Mysterio and the Vulture make appearances.

This is a nice look at Parker's early years as Spider-Man.

Vess, Charles, Gasper Saladino, Jim Salicrup, et al. *The Amazing Spider-Man: Spirits of the Earth.* New York: Marvel, 1990. ISBN: 0871356929.

Peter Parker and Mary Jane go to Scotland where Mary Jane inherits some land. When Spider-Man investigates the rumor that says a certain castle and its lands are haunted, he uncovers a conspiracy. A Hellfire Club member is trying to frighten the town's citizens into selling their lands.

This beautifully illustrated book contains a short account by the author of his experiences while traveling in Scotland. (*Marvel Graphic Novel 63*)

Way, Daniel, Francisco Herrera, Carlos Cuevas, et al. *Venom Vol. 1: Shiver.* New York: Marvel, 2004. ISBN: 0785112529. Reprints *Venom 1–5.*

Venom is being kept in the Canadian Arctic for study. He breaks loose, and kills nearly all of the scientists. A military unit that is close by investigates, and it also is destroyed by Venom who can change human hosts quickly. A Man in Black alien, who has his own agenda for Venom, is searching for him.

This story is very similar to John Carpenter's remake of the sci-fi classic *The Thing.*

Way, Daniel, Paco Medina, Francisco Herrera, et al. *Venom Vol. 2: Run.* New York: Marvel, 2004. ISBN: 0785115536. Reprints *Venom 6–13.*

Clones Frankie and Vic are trying to capture Venom to control him. The Man in Black is actually being controlled by spider-like nanonite aliens, who respond to the commands of Reed Richards. Wolverine is briefly possessed by Venom who uses Logan's claws in an epic battle scene. S.H.I.E.L.D. and Nick Fury take Venom into custody, but he, of course, escapes.

The volume contains flashback scenes featuring the Fantastic Four and Spider-Man. This is as confusing as any *X-Files* episode.

Way, Daniel, Skottie Young, Rick Ketham, et al. *Venom Volume 3: Twist*. New York: Marvel, 2004. ISBN: 0785115544. Reprints *Venom 14–18*.

A group of aliens want to combine Eddie Brock with their female version of Venom. Spider-Man tries to stop both versions from killing innocents, while also trying to save Brock's life. Nick Fury tries to kill both versions. The female Venom is taken captive by the Fantastic Four, but the two symbiotes end up combining.

This new version of Venom is different from the Eddie Brock Venom.

Wells, Zeb, Sam Keith, Francisco Herrera, et al. *Peter Parker Spider-Man Vol. 5: Senseless Violence*. New York: Marvel, 2003. ISBN: 0785111719. Reprints *Peter Parker Spider-Man Vol. 2: 51–57*.

When Hydro-Man and the Shocker are fired from Hammer Industries, they try to rob a bank, When Spider-Man foils their plans, the Shocker tries to have a heart-to-heart with him. Peter Parker tries to make excuses for his battered face to the principal of the school where he works. Several wealthy individuals who bet on battles hire Scorpion, Boomerang, and Rocket Racer to fight Spider-Man on a reality-based television program. The Sandman's personality gets split into different versions of himself, including a female, a child, and an evil one.

This is an interesting comic-book case study of multiple personality disorder.

Wells, Zeb, Ronnie Zimmerman, Duncan Fregredo, et al. *Spider-Man's Tangled Web Vol.*

3. New York: Marvel, 2002. ISBN: 078510 951X. Reprints *Spider-Man's Tangled Web 12–17*.

The Leapfrog gets out of prison, and his son has to bear jokes and abuse because his father was in prison. While sitting at a bar, the Vulture, Kraven Jr., and Norman Osborn discuss their hatred of Spider-Man. The Vulture's comments are especially funny and insightful. Crusher Hogan's boxing story is told up to the point where he battles Peter Parker for the first time. Tombstone has a heart attack, but still breaks out of jail and kills the nerdy Spot who helped him escape.

Yomtov Nel, Alex Saviuk, Steve Durto, et al. *Spider-Man Adventures*. New York: Marvel, 1995. ISBN: 0785101047. Reprints *Spider-Man Adventures 1–5*.

The Lizard captures his human family in an attempt to make them be like him. In hopes of capturing Spider-Man, Jonah Jameson helps create the Scorpion, and Norman Osborn works with Spencer Smythe to create the Spider Slayer who will be able to kill Spider-Man. Peter Parker continues to stand up Felecia Hardy. After Spencer Smythe is killed in a fight with the Slayer, his son Alistaire goes to work for the Kingpin to build a better Slayer which also fails to kill Spider-Man. Mysterio uses illusions to make Spider-Man appear to be a criminal, and to discredit him.

This collection is one of the rarest of all Marvel graphic novels. While it is based on the 1990s animated *Spider-Man* show, and much of the Spider-Man mythology remains the same, it contains a few different characters and ideas.

Thor

> I ain't just Crusher Creel, an ordinary con anymore! ... I'm the Absorbing Man
> ... The most dangerous guy in the world!! — *Crusher Creel*

> This is what I needed!! Action! Combat! A foe to lash out at!! — *Thor*

Buscema, John, Jerry Ordway, Dan Jurgens, et al. *Thor: Dark Gods*. New York: Marvel, 2000. ISBN: 0785107398. Reprints *Thor Vol. 2: 9–13*.

The Dark Gods have taken over Asgard, and Thor's father Odin is a prisoner. Thor has to fight for his father's kingdom, and is almost killed. He enlists the aid of the Destroyer, Hercules, and Replicus to defeat the Dark Lords. He constantly struggles between his obligations in his earthly guise as Jake Olson, and his obligations as the God of Thunder.

Danko, Dan, Mike Barr, George Perez, et al. *Godwheel: Wheel of Thunder*. Calabass, Ca: Malibu, 1995. Reprints *Godwheel 0–3*.

The mad god Argus brings Thor in to help him obtain the Three Keys to the Crucible of Life, which is in the realm of the Godwheel. Thor realizes that Argus is evil, and sides with the Ultras to defend the Crucible. Although Thor's appearance is brief, his deeds in the Ultraverse are important. Loki also gets to the Ultraverse, and plans to make himself ruler of the Godwheel.

This book contains a cover gallery, and explanation of the Godwheel, the heroes and villains of the Godwheel, the Crucible, the Keys, and Godhood. It has a glossary of the main Ultraverse characters and a lovely cover drawing of Thor and the Ultraverse characters, by George Perez. This series was part of Malibu's highly successful *Ultraverse* series.

DeFalco, Tom, Ron Frenz, Brett Breeding, et al. *The Mighty Thor: Alone Against the Celestials*. New York: Marvel, 1994. ISBN: 0871359340. Reprints *Mighty Thor 387–389*.

Thor goes to the world of Pangoria and tries to save it from destruction by two Celestials, Arishem and Exitar. Thor goes into the mind of Exitar, and scans his memory. The Celestials destroy all those on the planet who are morally corrupt.

Deodato, Mike Jr., Ellis Warren, William Messener-Loebs, et al. *Marvel Visionaries: Thor Mike Deodato Jr.* New York: Marvel, 2004. ISBN: 0785114084. Reprints *Thor Volume 1: 491–494, 498–500*; *Thor: the Legend*.

Thor, as the World-Ash, Yggdrasil, is dying. The Tree of Life is taken captive by a mad scientist, who is intent on creating a new world. The scientist creates new "post–Ragnarok humans," who quickly die when they breathe air. The Enchantress and Thor start a romantic relationship. Thor is hired to protect the daughters and wife of the owner of the Black Diamond sword, which was stolen from the evil Votan. Odin is homeless, and walks the streets with no memory. Loki wants to take the sword for his own purpose, but ends up helping Thor and the others fight against the gods in the Mirror World, which was created by the composer Wagner. Thor returns to Asgard.

This collection focuses on the work that artist Mike Deodato Jr. did on *Thor*. It contains the entire "WorldEngine" storyline.

Ellis, Warren, Mike Deodato Jr., Jonathan Babcock, et al. *Thor: WorldEngine*. New York: Marvel, 1996. ISBN: 0785102175. Reprints *Mighty Thor 491–494*.

Thor, the God of Thunder, is reduced to being a mortal man who is trying to figure out a way to stop the WorldEngine from destroying humanity. Thor is captured by the Enchantress, and they have a romantic interlude. Yggdrasil, the Tree of Life, is captured, and is forced to endure horrible experiments by the insane user of the WorldEngine. Odin rejects Thor's pleas for help. The Asgardians believe that Ragnarok is coming.

This book includes an essay by Warren Ellis on the writing of *Thor*.

Ennis, Garith, Glen Fabry, Paul Mounts, et al. *Thor: Vikings*, New York: Marvel, 2004. ISBN: 0785111751. Reprints *Thor: Vikings 1–5*.

An old curse keeps a group of Vikings alive for a thousand years, and turns them into zombies. Harald Jaekelsson and his band of Vikings pillage modern-day New York, turning it into a charnel house. Jaekelsson gives Thor several broken bones, and Thor is helpless to stop the zombies. With the aid of Dr. Strange and several warriors from the past, Thor is able to defeat the zombies, but Jaekelsson puts a sword through Thor's torso. Even the Avengers are no match for the zombies.

This book is part of Marvel's Max series for adults. It has terrific dialogue, and is very funny. It is one of the most original Thor stories ever written.

Jurgens, Dan, Joe Bennett, Jack Jadson, et al. *Mighty Thor Vol. 4: Spiral*. New York: Marvel, 2003. ISBN: 0785111271. Reprints *Mighty Thor Vol. 2: 60–67*.

Thor's human alter ego Jake Olson is not happy with the way Thor has been acting. He cuts off the leg of a young boy who'd been in a car wreck, saving his life, but the boy's mother refuses his help. She believes that the gods of Asgard will come and save her. Olson is fired from his EMT job. Thor meets his dead father Odin in the spirit realm, and asks for guidance. When Thor petitions the Council Elite for membership, the other members—Zeus, Osiris, Yu-Huang, Vishnu, Brahma, and Shiva—give him a character test which he must pass to become a member. Thor fails. A growing religious group known as the Asgardians, which worships Thor, comes into conflict with traditional religious groups, and violence erupts. An anti-Thor group manages to plant numerous bombs on Asgard. Jake Olson tries to reason with Thor about his behavior, but Thor refuses to listen. Olson picks up Thor's hammer, and fights him with it. Thor kills Jake, and no longer has the ability to pick up the hammer.

Jurgens, Dan, Scott Eaton, Drew Geraci, et al. *The Mighty Thor: Lord of Earth: Gods and Men*. New York: Marvel, 2004. ISBN: 0785115285. Reprints *Thor Vol. 2: 75–79*.

Although she had been banished, Sif returns to New Asgard. She tries to reason with Thor's son, Magni. The Scarlet Witch's daughter is hanged, but her spirit leads Magni to Thor's old hammer Mjolnir, and he picks it up. Magni tries to convince his father to leave the Earth and the tyranny he has put it under. He travels to the ruins of the original Asgard, and Thor and the other gods end up fighting the god killer Desak. Loki tries to persuade Thor to keep Earth, but Thor, with the help of Magni, Tarene, and the Destroyer, begins to realize that he was wrong in taking over Earth. Loki is very upset, because his reign of power is about to end. Thor realizes that he needs his human part in order to be whole.

Jurgens, Dan, Scot Eaton, Cam Smith, et al. *The Mighty Thor Vol. 5: The Reigning*. New York: Marvel, 2004. ISBN: 0785112472. Reprints *Thor Vol. 2: 68–74*; *Thor, Son of Asgard 1 Preview*.

In 2020, Jane Foster helps hide the Scarlet Witches' child from Asgardian identification, much to Thor's dismay. By 2170, Thor has instituted an Asgardian utopia on the Earth, and is its ultimate ruler. Loki,

Thor's chief of security, has an underhanded way of dealing with humans: the Asgardian's view humans as little more than pests or cattle to be swayed to the gods' way of thinking. The Scarlet Witch's daughter shows Thor's friend Thailfi, who returns from the past to Asgard, just how horrible life under Thor's rule is. Thor's son Magni falls for an Earth woman, and begins to see the error of his father's ways as dictator of Midgard. Thailfi tries to kill Thor during Odinsleep, but is stopped.

This volume also shows a previous fight, in which Thor basically destroyed all of the Avengers, including Captain America. This volume also introduces a new series, *Thor, Son of Asgard.*

Jurgens, Dan, Mike Grell, Scott Hanna, et al. *The Mighty Thor Vol. 3: Gods on Earth.* New York: Marvel, 2003. ISBN: 0785111263. Reprints *Mighty Thor Vol. 2: 51–58*; *Avengers Vol. 3: 63*; *Iron Man Vol. 3: 63*; *Marvel Double Shot 1.*

Thor moves Asgard above New York. He takes it upon himself to become Earth's official protector, and tries to eliminate hunger, disease, and other world problems. Thor intervenes in world affairs by disposing of tyrants and dictators, and the Absorbing Man becomes Thor's ally. The Tomorrow Man realizes that the world is headed for disaster, and tries to stop Thor. Volstagg tells young Asgardians a Thor legend. Many in the superhero community feel that Thor is overstepping his bounds, and is becoming a dictator. Iron Man, who fights Thor, enlists the aid of Dr. Doom. Thor also fights with Captain America, and even dents his shield.

This volume includes a story, told through letters written by someone who admires Thor.

Jurgens, Dan, Stuart Immonen, Joe Bennett, et al. *The Mighty Thor Vol. 1: Death of Odin.* New York: Marvel, 2002. ISBN: 07851092 50. Reprints *Thor Vol. 2: 39–44.*

Thor is mortally wounded, and in order for him to heal, Odin separates him from Jake Olson. With Thor incapacitated, Surtur uses the opportunity to attack the Earth. All of Asgard's warriors are summoned to fight Surtur and his demon legions. None of the warriors seem to be effective, and Odin comes to Earth for the battle. He defeats Surtur, but dies in the process. Thor, refusing to believe that Odin is dead, doesn't take on his father's leadership role.

Editor Tom Brevoort wrote the afterword.

Jurgens, Dan, Andy Kubert, Stuart Immonen, et al. *The Mighty Thor: Across All Worlds.* New York: Marvel, 2001. ISBN: 0785107967. Reprints *The Mighty Thor Vol. 2: 28–35.*

While Odin is sleeping, the dark elf Malekith tries to steal the power of Asgard from under Sif who is its ruler. The Wrecking Crew ambushes Thor and his buddies, and almost kills Hogun. Beta Ray Bill gains his cosmic powers back, and allies himself with Thor.

He meets Jake Olson's mother. Thor Girl, who wants to follow in Thor's footsteps, makes an initial appearance, and works with Thor against the Gladiator. The Gladiator seeks to kill Thor, and almost succeeds. The Trolls revolt, and Ulik almost succeeds in decapitating Odin who is asleep.

Jurgens, Dan, Tom Raney, Joe Bennet, et al. *The Mighty Thor Vol. 2: Lord of Asgard.* New York: Marvel, 2002. ISBN: 0785110208. Reprints *Thor Vol. 2: 45–50.*

Odin is dead, and Thor is ruling Asgard. Odin had divided Thor from Jake Olson, before he died. Thor asks Zeus for advice on how to rule. Tarene is turned to stone, and is shattered by Grey Gargoyle. Thor and his comrades battle the Frost Giants, and Thor battles Desak, who has sworn to destroy the gods. Jake Olson attempts to become Thor.

This volume includes the short story "Children of the Gods," which is about Thor's childhood.

Jurgens, Dan, John Romita Jr., Klaus Janson, et al. *The Mighty Thor Resurrection.* New York: Marvel, 1999. ISBN: 078510724X. Reprints *Thor Vol. 2: 1–2.*

A robot, the Destroyer, created by Odin for the Ultimate Celestial War, kills Thor and sends him to the Shadow Realm of Hela. Thor is revived in the person of paramedic, Jake Olson. Someone who claims to be Heimdall holds some children hostage, and asks that Thor take him to Asgard. Thor obliges, and shows him that Asgard is in ruins. The Avengers, Iron Man, Captain America, Scarlet Witch, and Hawkeye make appearances.

The book has an afterword by Tom Brevoort.

Oemnig, Michael Avon, Andrea Divito, Daniel Berman, et al. *Avengers Disassembled: Thor.* New York: Marvel, 2004. ISBN: 07851159 94. Reprints *Thor 80–85.*

The hour of Ragnarok is upon Asgard. Thor and his colleagues struggle against the destruction of the Golden Realm. Loki wants Asgard for himself, and makes "unholy" alliances to this end. The Enchantress, Balder, Warriors Three, and Sif all come to an end. Beta Ray Bill lends his hand to help in Asgard's time of need. Thor learns that he must undergo the same trials as Odin. His hammer Mjolnir has been shattered, and Thor must be Asgard's destroyer in order to be its savior. He actually gives Surtur free reign to destroy. Thor chops off Loki's head.

Olshevsky, George, Tony Frutti, Tim Conrad, et al. *The Marvel Comics Index 5: The Mighty Thor.* Ontario: G&T Enterprises, 1977. ISBN: 0943348501 (Marvel Index Set).

This is an index and history of *Thor*, up to 1977. It includes all the *Journey Into Mystery* Thor issues, as well as the annuals. Other titles indexed include *Mighty Thor, Tales of Asgard,* and *Giant-Size Thor.*

This index has detailed histories of the titles, a cross index, and a Marvel characters cross-index.

Shooter, Jim, Jim Owlsley, Paul Ryan, et al. *The Mighty Thor I, Whom the Gods Would Destroy.* New York: Marvel, 1987. ISBN: 0871352680.

In this novel, Thor, as Don Blake, is distraught over loosing a patient in the operating room. He tries to show his former love Sif why he remains on Earth and sometimes becomes mortal. The rest of the Gods in Asgard disapprove of Thor's human identity. (*Marvel Graphic Novel 33*)

Simonson, Walter, Terry Austin, Bob Wiacek, et al. *Thor Visionaries: Walter Simonson Book 1.* New York: Marvel, 2000. ISBN: 078510 7584. Reprints *Mighty Thor Vol. 1: 337–348.*

Balder the Brave, after going to the realm of Hela, and seeing all those he's killed, vows to give up fighting and violence. He becomes old, fat, and ill looking, but his courageous spirit remains. Thor loses his Dr. Donald Blake identity, and becomes Siguard Jarlson. He teams up with an old Viking, to fight the dragon, Fafnir. Malekith, the dark elf, seeks to find the Casket of Ancient Winters, and Thor fights alongside a human, against Malekith and the dark beings of the Fairie Realm. Nick Fury makes an appearance.

This groundbreaking collection of Thor stories, by Walt Simonson, has long been in demand by comic fans. It includes the Introduction of the Beta Ray Bill Thor.

Simonson, Walter, Sal Buscema, Al Milgrom, et al. *Thor Legends Vol. 3: Walt Simonson Book 3.* New York: Marvel, 2004. ISBN: 078511047X. Reprints *Mighty Thor Vol. 1: 360–369.*

Thor goes to Hela to free the souls of humans who were tricked by the dark elf Malekith from Earth. Hela and Thor have an epic battle in which Hela scars Thor's face. Loki plans to take over from Odin, and does everything in his power to stop Thor from becoming ruler of Asgard. Loki turns Thor into a frog. The Executioner dies trying to protect the Asgardian warriors from the hordes from Hela. Sif is upset that Thor slapped her, and considers going off with Beta Ray Bill. Thor suggests that Balder the Brave take the throne. Malekith wants to deceive Balder, but his plan fails. Thor and Balder battle one another under a spell of sorcery.

For several issues after Loki turns Thor into a frog, Thor, in frog form, helps in a war between the frogs and the rats in the park. Volume 4 is rumored to be coming in 2007 (ISBN: 0785127119).

Simonson, Walter, Sal Buscema, John Workman, et al. *Thor: Legends Vol. 2: Walt Simonson Book 2.* New York: Marvel, 2003. ISBN: 0785110461. Reprints *Mighty Thor Vol. 1: 349–355; 357–359.*

Odin tells the tale of his brothers and their run-in with Surtur. Odin takes Surtur's eternal flame from him, and hides in Asgard. Surtur plans to destroy the nine worlds, Earth, and the rest of the universe. Odin senses that Surtur is about to make war, and summons Beta Ray Bill. Surtur sends thousands of his demons to menace Earth, and Thor puts Beta Ray Bill in charge. With the help of the Avengers and Mr. Fantastic, they figure out a way to plug the dimension from which the demons are coming. Surtur attacks Odin and Asgard, and almost destroys Asgard. Thor, Loki, and Odin try to foil Surtur's plans, and Odin and Surtur fall into an endless pit. The Enchantress's sister Lorelei tries to win Thor's affections, while two-timing him with Loki. She tries to get Thor to announce that Loki will be ruler of Asgard. Thor believes Odin is not dead, and begins to search for him.

Simonson, Walter, John Workman, George Roussos, et al. *The Mighty Thor: Ballad of Beta Ray Bill.* New York: Marvel, 1990. ISBN: 0871356147. Reprints *Mighty Thor 337–340.*

An alien ship is headed toward Earth, and Nick Fury employs Thor to deal with it. Thinking Thor is an enemy, the alien, Beta Ray Bill, attacks Thor, and picks up his hammer. He beats Thor in several battles, before Odin calls a truce, and has dwarfs design a special hammer, with the same power as Mjolnir, for Bill. With the help of Thor and the Lady Sif, they fight demons that have plagued Bill's people. Lady Sif falls in love with Bill, and goes with him, when he leaves Asgard. In essence, there are now two beings with the power of Thor.

Yoshia, Akira, Greg Tocchina, Jay Leisten, et al. *Thor Son of Asgard Vol. 1: The Warriors Teen Digest.* New York: Marvel, 2004. ISBN: 0785113355. Reprints *Thor Son of Asgard 1–6.*

Odin sends the teenaged Thor, Sif, Loki, and Balder on a quest for elements to forge a magical sword. Loki tries to foil their quest, but is taken prisoner by Karnilla, Queen of the Norns. He escapes and warns his brother of Karnilla's pending attack on Odin and Asgard. Thor is almost killed by one of Karnilla's arrows, and she encounters Odin's wrath. Odin gives Balder the sword of Svadren.

This volume, part of the Marvel Age series, contains a sketchbook. Volume 2 was published in 2005 (ISBN: 0785115722).

Zelenetz, Alan, Charles Vess, Joe Rosen, et al. *The Raven Banner: A Tale of Asgard.* New York Marvel, 1985. ISBN: 0871350602.

This tale takes place in the godly realm of Asgard. In it, the son of a fallen god searches for the magical Raven Banner which was stolen by trolls. In the end, he meets a fate similar to that of his father. (*Marvel Graphic Novel 15*)

Transformers, G.I. Joe, and Death's Head

Humans get in the way when we fight Decepticons. — *Grimlock*

When my enemies lie dead at my feet, I shall resume my
rightful place as Decepticon leader. — *Megatron*

Budiansky, Bob, Ian Akin, Brian Garvey, et al.
Transformers Universe Vol. 1. New York:
Marvel, 1987. ISBN: 0871352966. Reprints
Marvel's *Transformers Universe 1–4.*

This guide to the Transformers who appear in the
Marvel comics includes information about their alle-
giances to either Decepticon or Autobot, and their
subgroups, functions, first appearances, illustrations,
profiles, abilities, and weaknesses. Some of the Transformers listed include BumbleBee, Drag Strip, Shockwave, and Megatron, among many others. The volume also includes a section on the Transformers from
Transformers: The Movie. This is one of the rarest of
the Transformers paperbacks.

Budiansky, Bob, Jose Delbo, Don Perlin et al.
Transformers: Treason. London: Titan,
2004. ISBN: 1840238453 (trd);
1840238445 (pbk). Reprints *Marvel's
Transformers 31–37.*

Ratbat has hypnotized Blackrock and others, including Sparkplug Witwicky, to help in stealing fuel
from the Wash and Roll car wash and gas station.
Buster foils the Decepticon's attempt at free enterprise. Grimlock becomes obsessed with punishing
Blaster and Goldbug for going AWOL. The Autobots try to hide at a car lot, but are found out, and
both Decepticons (Combaticons) and Autobots (Protectobots) battle over the two. Several Autobots, including Goldbug, are taken prisoner by the government, and Blaster is taken prisoner by the Autobots.
Some human children save him during a battle with
Defensor and Bruticus. Blaster takes them on a trip
through space, but the Ark is following and shooting
at them. Grimlock captures the children, and makes
them walk the plank into space, and Blaster surrenders.
The government destroys the Autobots that are held
captive, but a colonel saves the brains of the Autobots
and puts them into toy cars. Ratbat's Decepticon crew
comes to make sure the Autobots are dead, and finds
out that even though their bodies are smashed, they
still live.

The "Man of Iron" storyline from *Tranformers UK
33–34* is not reprinted in this collection, but its covers are. This story was published by Marvel UK, and
will be in a future collection, I hope. Gregg Berger, the
voice of Grimlock in the original animated series,
writes the introduction.

Budiansky, Bob, Jose Delbo, Frank Springer, et
al. *Transformers: Maximum Force.* London,
Titan, 2004. ISBN: 1840239700 (trd);

1840239557 (pbk). Reprints Marvel's
Transformers: 40–42, 44–45.

Optimus Prime is living in a video game, and believes he is a computer program. Zachary had up-
loaded Prime's personality and memory to disc before
he was killed by Megatron. Goldbug also helps try to
convince Prime that he is more than a video-game
program. While Prime is eavesdropping in the computer program, the Decepticon Scorponok creates the
Decepticon Pretenders. In a bizarre nod to Prince
Namor, one of the Pretenders is called Sub-Marauder.
The Autobots create six new warriors, and need to go
to the Ark, which is now commanded by Grimlock,
to get the parts to rebuild Optimus Prime. Grimlock
does not find the idea of giving leadership back to
Prime very appealing. He views Prime's peaceful
methods, and his caring about humanity, as signs of
weakness. Grimlock and Blaster have a duel to the
death, which is interrupted by the Decepticons. In
order to save Prime, the Autobots go to Nebulos to
find a human that Prime can binary-bond with. A
space carnival controlled by Jabba-the-Hut-lookalike
Mr. Big Top has the Autobot, Sky Lynx, and several
human children captive. The Decepticon Skullgrin,
becomes a movie star, and is defeated by Circuit
Breaker.

Budiansky, Bob, Jose Delbo, Frank Springer, et
al. *Transformers: Trial by Fire.* London:
Titan, 2004. ISBN: 1840239654 (trd);
1840239506 (pbk). Reprints Marvel's
*Transformers Headmasters 1–4; Transform-
ers Vol. 1 38–39.*

Autobots on Cybertron, led by Fortress Maximus,
go to the planet Nebulos in search of peace away from
the Decepticons. The Nebulans are skeptical, and declare war against the Autobots. Several Autobots take
off their heads and dismantle themselves to prove their
commitment to peace. One of the Nebulans, Lord
Zarak, believing the Autobots still want to conquer
the planet, contacts the Decepticons to come and destroy the Autobots. However, they have visions of
conquest, and would gladly take over the planet and
destroy the Autobots. In order to defeat the Decepticons, the Nebulans graft their minds with the head-
less Autobots, and become the Headmasters. The Decepticons graft themselves with Lord Zarak's group.
The Headmasters leave to go to Earth, believing the
Decepticons will follow. Buster Witwicky is taken
captive by Shockwave. His brother Spike becomes one
of the Headmasters when the Nebulan Autobot leader
Galen dies. Headmaster Spike defeats Shockwave,
but Buster is shot out into space.

Budiansky, Bob, William Johnson, Herb Trimpe, et al. *Transformers: New Order*. London: Titan, 2003. ISBN: 1840236256 (trd); 1840 236248 (pbk). Reprints Marvel's *Transformers 7–12*.

Shockwave has taken over the Decepticons. Ratchet makes a pact with Megatron to try to defeat Shockwave with the Dinobots, but Megatron betrays him. Optimus Prime has put the Creation Matrix inside of a boy, Buster Witwicky. Shockwave has taken Prime's head, and tries to create a new breed of Decepticons; the Constructicons are born. The Autobots make an ally of the industrialist, Mr. Blackrock. Prime defeats Shockwave who sinks into a tar pit.

This is first appearance of Circuit Breaker and Decepticon Devastator.

Budiansky, Bob, Graham Nolan, Don Perlin, et al. *Transformers: Cybertron Redux*. London: Titan, 2003. ISBN: 1840236612 (trd); 1840 236574 (pbk). Reprints Marvel's *Transformers 13–18*.

Megatron loses his memory and becomes a slave to a two bit crook. Jetfire becomes an Autobot, and Optimus Prime helps give life to five new Autobots. Bumblebee takes the new Autobots to a rock concert where they encounter the Decepticons. The government uses the comic book writer of *Robot Master* to quell public hysteria about the Transformer presence on Earth. The Robot Master ends up working for Megatron. Two car thiefs take Bumblebee from a car lot, and have the ride of lives. Cybertron receives the message that Shockwave sent to alert Cybertron of the Transformers' presence on Earth. The ruthless Decepticon leader Straxus is anxious to take over Earth, while the Autobot Blaster tries to foil their plan. Shockwave and Megatron are about to fight for control of the Decepticons, just as Straxus makes contact.

Budiansky, Bob, Don Perlin, Ian Akin, et al. *Transformers: Breakdown*. London: Titan, 2004. 1840238100 (trd); 1840237910 (pbk). Reprints Marvel's *Transformers: 25–30*.

Shockwave conspires against Megatron, and brings in the hunter Predaking from Cybertron. Megatron has a nervous breakdown, and obsesses about the death of Optimus Prime. Ratchet tries to save Optimus, but to no avail. A human mechanic who deals in stolen car goods ends up being in Ratchet, and sneaking into the Ark. Grimlock defeats a powerful Decepticon, Trypticon. The Dinobot Grimlock becomes the new leader of the Autobots, but causes all sorts of problems. He does not consider the welfare of humans to be important, and sets himself up as a dictator. Goldbug and Blaster go AWOL from the Autobots to get away from Grimlock. The Decepticons on Cybertron, under the leadership of Ratbat, send three Decepticons to find a space freighter carrying important cargo. The freighter and its Decepticon pilot are infected with the horrible Scraplet disease. Blaster and Goldbug, along with the Decepticons, are infected. Goldbug leaves Blaster to go get help. Ratbat sends three Autobots to discover what happened. The Scraplets merge and become a huge biological weapon. With the help of their industrialist friend G. W. Blackrock, they manage to kill the Scraplets, but the Decepticons get away.

Budiansky, Bob, Don Perlin, Herb Trimpe, et al. *Transformers: Showdown*. London: Titan, 2004. ISBN: 1840236817 (pbk); 18402368 76 (trd). Reprints Marvel's *Transformers 19–24*.

Omega Supreme is programmed to protect the Ark against the Decepticons. Optimus Prime invades the Decepticon camp to learn the secrets of Devastator. Shockwave relinquishes command back to Megatron. The Autobot Skids briefly becomes the family car for a human female. The Robot Master escapes from the Decepticons and tries to warn the Autobots of Megatron's plans. He ends up working for the government with the robot-hating Circuit Breaker. A listening bug is planted in Optimus Prime's brain. The Decepticons take control of a human to gain access to power from a dam, to open the bridge from Cybertron to Earth. Several Decepticons follow a human family, putting "Robot" graffiti all over important landmarks, including Mount Everest. Optimus Prime is killed after playing a computer game with Megatron. The Aerialbots, Stunticons, Insecticons, Menasor, Superion, Combaticons, and Protectobots make appearances.

Furman, Simon, Jeff Anderson, Dan Reed, et al. *Transformers: City of Fear*. London: Titan, 2003. ISBN: 184023671X. Reprints Marvel UK's *Transformers UK 132, 164–171, 188, 213–214*.

Ultra Magnus and several Autobots go back to Cybertron, to the city of Kalis. Autobots and Decepticons who have died there are arising from the dead as mechanical zombies who greet Ultra Magnus and his crew. They form an alliance with the Decepticon Flywheels to stop the zombies at the source. Underneath Cybertron, the Autobot Flame has taken over Megatron's old underground fortress. He reanimates the dead Transformers, and wants to use Cybertron as a ship to go through the universe. His plan, however, will not work, because in order to obtain his goal he has to start a nuclear reaction which will blow up Cybertron. The Decepticon Trypticon teams up with the Autobots to stop Flame. Ultra Magnus is captured and put in a gladiator-like arena to fight the Decepticon Hooligan to the death. A Firebug is menacing Earth, and the Autobots send him to Mercury. Megatron comes to Cybertron to renew his army.

This book also includes a short story featuring Kup, and a history of the Marvel UK *Transformers* strip.

Furman, Simon, Jeff Anderson, Dan Reed, et al. *Transformers: Legacy of Unicron*. London: Titan, 2003. ISBN: 1840235780. Reprints *Marvel UK's Transformers UK 133–134, 137–138, 146–153.*

The Decepticon Blot hires Death's Head to kill Rodimus Prime. When Death's Head is just about to kill Prime, Cyclonus and Scourge shoot Death's Head to settle an old score, and Prime gets away. Prime then lures Death's Head into a trap, and offers him more money to get the heads of Cyclonus and Scourge. Back on Earth, twenty years in the past, both Galvatron and Ultra Magnus are found petrified in volcanic stone. While human friends of Ultra Magnus and the Autobots try to save Ultra Magnus, Shockwave orders the Decepticons to destroy Galvatron. Unicron's head remained intact on the Junk planet, and has found a way to control the minds of any bot who lives on, or steps foot on, Junk. Unicron tries to make Death's Head, Cyclonus, and Scourge his servants. Unicron plans to start a full-scale war between the Autobots and Decepticons on Cybertron, so that they will both destroy each other, and he can then have his way with the universe. Death's Head kills Shockwave; Cyclonus and Scourge become the new leaders of the Decepticons. Death's Head defies Unicron, and even travels into Unicron's mind to try and find a way to defeat him. Death's Head and Prime team up against Unicron. Wreck-Gar figures out a way to blow him to pieces. Seacons are sent by Soundwave, under Shockwave's orders, to destroy Galvatron. The Firecons fight the Autobots.

This book includes a detailed introduction to the UK Transformer comics, and a synopsis of *Transformers: The Movie.* This volume is a direct sequel to *Transformers: The Movie.*

Furman, Simon, Jeff Anderson, Dan Reed, et al. *Transformers: Prey.* London: Titan, 2004. ISBN: 0840238313. Reprints Marvel UK's *Transformers UK 96–100, 103–104, 135–136; Transformers Annual 1987; Transformers Annual 1989.*

The Predacons rip Optimus Prime apart and he is left for dead. The Autobots believe he is dead. Prime had to go to Cybertron, and wanted the 'bots to think he was gone so they would not rely on him so much. Megatron also goes to Cybertron, and puts a spy in the Autobots' camp, who tells them that Optimus Prime is an Autobot traitor. Prime has to prove to the Autobots that he is on their side. Megatron makes a mess of the Decepticon camp, and tries unsuccessfully to take over. The Autobot Outback believes Prime, and stays with him till his death. Prime makes a loose alliance with the Decepticon Shockwave. The Autobot Divebomb seeks to take on the Decepticon who defeated him and stole his name. The Decepticon Pretenders try to take the fuel from an oil rig, but the Autobot Pretenders stop them.

This book includes background material that gives the history of *Tranformers UK* comics up to the last issue, issue 332.

Furman, Simon, Jeff Anderson, Geof Senior, et al. *Transformers: Dinobot Hunt.* London: Titan, 2004. ISBN: 1840237899. Reprints Marvel UK's *Transformers UK 45–50, 74–77; Transformers Annual 1986.*

The Autobots are searching for stray Dinobots who are running around wild. The Decepticons are also trying to find the Dinobots, to use them against the Autobots. Professor Morris develops a machine which can mentally control robots, and he takes hold of the Dinobot Swoop. Soundwave briefly takes over as the leader of the Decepticons, and wins several battles against the Autobots. Sludge falls in love with a woman reporter who wants to expose the stories about the Robot Masters. Neither the government nor the Decepticons want this story to hit the press. The Government kidnaps Professor Morris, and tries to use him to control their robot, the Centurion.

Several stories are told from the perspective of Dinobot consciousness. The book includes a narrative analysis of *Transformers UK 243–260,* published by Marvel UK.

Furman, Simon, Jeff Anderson, Will Simpson, et al. *Transformers: Fallen Angel.* London: Titan 2003. ISBN: 184023511X. Reprints *Marvel UK's Transformers UK 101–102; 113–120; Transformers Annual 1987.*

In 2007, Rodimus Prime puts a bounty on the head of Galvatron. The robot bounty hunter Death's Head wants to collect that bounty. He finds out that Galvatron has gone back to 1987, and travels back to find him, hoping to collect the bounty. Galvatron goes up against the Dinobots who don't have much success against him. Rodimus Prime goes back to 1987, even though there is a war against the Decepticons on Cybertron. Galvatron is hoping to harvest unlimited power with the help of an active volcano. Ultra Magnus makes friends with an Earth woman whose sister he saves. He fights Galvatron numerous times and loses. Death's Head almost kills Bumblebee. Wreck-Gar heals Bumble's wounds, and transforms into Goldbug. Death's Head and several other Autobots are sent to another time, but Galvatron has remained, and Ultra Magnus takes a stab at him once again.

This is the first appearance of Death's Head who went on to his own series. It includes a history of the Transformers UK, up to the beginnings of *Fallen Angel.* It also has a section about the movie and a little background history about Death's Head. These events tie in directly after *Transformers: The Movie.*

Furman, Simon, Jeff Anderson, Will Simpson, et al. *Transformers: Second Generation.* London: Titan, 2004. ISBN: 1840239352. Reprints Marvel UK's *Transformers UK 59–65, 93, 145, 198; Transformers Annual 1989.*

Buster Witwicky is given his own Autobot Robot suit in which to fight the Decepticons, but Optimus Prime vetoes the idea. He does not want Buster to fight alongside the Autobots in that costume. In his anger at Prime, Buster steals the suit and seeks out Decepticons to fight. He defeats Frenzy, but nearly dies at the hands of Shockwave. Buster begins to have bizarre nightmares which turn out to be prophetic visions of the Transformers' future and the second generation of Transformers. Buster is hooked up with Optimus Prime to help learn what these visions mean. Soundwave facilitates a truce between Megatron and Shockwave with the help of the Decepticons. Buster helps explain Christmas to the Autobot Jetfire. A young kid teaches the Decepticon Starscream the meaning of Christmas. The Autobots battle in the water with the Seacons.

Furman, Simon, Jeff Anderson, Will Simpson, et al. *Transformers: Target 2006.* London: Titan, 2003. ISBN: 1840235683 (trd); 1840235101 (pbk). Reprints Marvel UK's *Transformers UK 78–88.*

The Decepticon Galvatron comes back from 2006 to build a weapon to make him supreme in his time and destroy Unicron. When he appears in the past with two of his cronies, three Autobots disappear, including Optimus Prime. Three Autobots from 2006 come to bring Galvatron back to his time, and Ultra Magnus comes from Cybertron to help find Prime. He fights a great battle with Galvatron. Megatron and the Autobots form a loose alliance against Galvatron and his cronies. Hot Rod is badly wounded, and is being held prisoner. On Cybertron, an Autobot uprising against the Decepticons is in motion. Impactor is killed, saving his leader, Xaaron.

This book includes a history of the Transformers UK comic, and a synopsis of *Transformers: The Movie.* It is the first in the series of Titan's reprints from the rare UK Transformers series, which follows the continuity straight out of *Transformers: The Movie.*

Furman, Simon, Jose Delbo, Geoff Senior, et al. *Transformers: Matrix Quest.* London: Titan, 2002. ISBN: 1840235071 (trd); 184 0234717 (pbk) Reprints Marvel's *Transformers Vol. 1: 63–68.*

The Autobots search for their sacred life force, the Creation Matrix. The Decepitcon Thunderwing ends up commandeering the Matrix, with disastrous results, and the Matrix is exposed to true evil. An Autobout ends up destroying Vrobians, who are psychic vampires. Shockwave returns. Unicron's cronies Hook, Line and Sinker go to an alternate Earth where the Decepticons rule, and kidnap Galvatron.

This book has a who's who of the Transformers Universe.

Furman, Simon, Jose Delbo, Geoff Senior, et al. *Transformers: Primal Scream.* London: Titan, 2002. ISBN: 184023458X (trd); 1840234016 (pbk). Reprints Marvel's *Transformers Vol. 1: 56–62.*

Ratchet saves a number of Transformers as Pre-

tender shells. Several Autobots and Decepticons, including Grimlock and Bludgeon, are teleported to the center of Cybertron, and come in contact with their creator, Primus. Primus is awakened by a ricocheted blast. His scream is heard throughtout the universe, and it awakens Primus's caretaker Unicron who tells the origin of the Transformers. The Transformers go to the planet Pz-Zazz to seek the Matrix Life-force.

Furman, Simon, Manny Galan, Geoff Senior, et al. *Transformers: Rage in Heaven.* London: Titan, 2003. ISBN: 1840235772 (trd); 1840235284 (pbk). Reprints Marvel's *Transformers Generation 2, 7–12.*

Megatron and his Decepticons are beaten by Jhiaxus, and they almost die. Megatron makes offers to team up with Prime and the Autobots, and they form a loose alliance against Jhiaxus and his followers. The Swarm starts destroying Transformers with reckless abandon. The battle between Swarm and the Transformers ends up on Earth. Starscream ends up merging with the Matrix on the Warworld. At first Starscream tries to destroy both Prime and Megatron, but the Matrix turns him into a Decepticon who does good deeds. He gives the Matrix back to Prime who merges with the Swarm, and is reborn. Jhiaxus is destroyed, and an even greater threat, Liege Maximo, makes an appearance.

Furman, Simon, Manny Galan, Andrew Wildman, et al. *Transformers: Dark Designs.* London: Titan, 2003. ISBN: 1840235276 (trd); 184023525X (pbk). Reprints Marvel's *Transformers Generation 2, 1–6.*

Megatron is reborn with the help of Cobra. There is a new breed of Decepticons which has no ties to the Transformers' history, operating under Commander Jhiaxus. He prefers to conquer every planet that comes into their path. Bludgeon tries to take over the Decepticons, but Megatron kills him and takes the Life Matrix from Optimus Prime. The Ark is destroyed before Megatron could give the technology to Cobra. The Swarm arrives.

This storyline picks up right after *Transformers Vol. 1: 80.*

Furman, Simon, Bryan Hitch, Lee Sullivan, et al. *Life and Times of Death's Head.* London: Marvel UK, 1990. ISBN: 1854002384. Reprints *Death's Head 3–5, 7, 9–10.*

Spratt is attacked by a Plague Dog. The Understaker and the horse-like Dead Cert put a bounty on Death's Head, but both fail. In 1989, Death's Head ends up on top of the Baxter Building. He helps the Fantastic Four save the life of Mattie Franklin from Reed Richard's rogue defense robot. Richards sends him to 2020, where he fights with, and then teams with, the Arno Stark Iron Man. Death's Head is a robotic bounty hunter from the future.

This book includes an essay, "Death's Head: Past Present and Future," by Furman; and a narrative explanation of Death's Head's origin and his recreation with his bumbling buddy Spratt.

Furman, Simon, Dan Reed, Robin Smith, et al. *Transformers: Time Wars.* London: Titan, 2003. ISBN: 1840236477. Reprints Marvel UK's *Transformers UK 130–131, 189, 199–205; Transformers Annual 1988.*

Because Galvatron, Cyclonus, and Scourge's shared time displacement is causing havoc in 1989 and 2009, Galvatron seeks to conquer 1989 to stop Unicron in the future. He ends up teaming with Megatron to fight the Autobots. Shockwave has Megatron tear Cyclonus's head off, and he learns that both Cyclonus and Scourge will kill him in the future. Shockwave ends up going mad. In 2009, Soundwave is in charge of the Decepticons, and goes back in time to chase a group of Autobots who go back to make the time stream correct. Megatron learns that Galvatron is actually a future version of himself. Rhodiums Prime displaces Optimus Prime when he goes back to 1989, but through the Creation Matrix they are able to communicate. Highbrow briefly becomes enslaved by the Decepticons, and by Mindwipe. When Gort jumps out of Highbrow, and then back into him, he breaks the mind-control bond, and rips Scorponok's head off. Ravage finally gets Shockwave to cooperate, and lead him to the broken body of Cyclonus. The Horrorcons and Terrorcons make an appearance.

This book includes a narrative history of Marvel UK's run on the Transformers, an introduction to *Transformers: The Movie,* and annotations of previous Titan Marvel UK Transformers paperbacks.

Furman, Simon, Dan Reed, Lee Sullivan, et al. *Transformers: Space Pirates.* London: Titan 2003. ISBN: 1840236191. Reprints Marvel UK's *Transformers UK 160–161, 171–173, 180–187; Transformers Annual 1987.*

The remains of Megatron are pulled from the ocean, and Shockwave tries to revitalize him, through the use of a brain stimulator. Galvatron comes back to hound Ultra Magnus, and for once is beaten by him. Scourge and Cyclonus try to get Galvatron's time displacer to take them forward to 2008 and encounter the Autobot Wreckers. Wreck-Gar is captured by the Quintessons whose planet is dying. He is thrown in the Sharkticons' tank, but rescued in the nick of time. The Quintesson warriors ambush the Decepticons on Cybertron, with Soundwave in charge. The Autobots have to team up with the Decepticons to save them. The Quintessons also go to Autobot Earth and nearly destroy them. One of them even steals the Matrix from Prime, who turns back into Hot Rod. He awakens Metroplex, who defeats the Quintessons. Wreck-Gar manages to send a message to other planets throughout the galaxy, warning them of the Quintessons' plans to take over planets, and colonize them.

This book includes a cameo by Richard Branson of Virgin Records, an article on the Transformers UK series, and a synopsis of the *Transformers* movie.

Furman, Simon, Geoff Senior, Helen Stone, et al. *Death's Head: Body in Question.* London: Marvel UK, 1990. ISBN: 1854002171. Reprints *Marvel UK Strip 13–20.*

In 2020, Death's Head has been making a good living as a freelance peacekeeping agent. He is glad that his partner Spratt is left in 8162. Death's Head's wife and Big Shot, who both want to demolish Death's Head, time-travel back to 2020 with Spratt. Death's Head's father shows up, and wants to renew his energy by taking Death Head's body for his own. Death's Head almost loses their battle. He ends up overcoming his father, but he does not come out unscathed. It turns out that Death's Head's wife was actually his mother, searching for the original Death's Head, his father.

This book includes an origin sequence, and reviews from *Playdroid* and *Robot of Fortune* in the back matter.

Furman, Simon, Andres Wildman, Geoff Senior, et al. *Transformers: All Fall Down.* London: Titan 2001. ISBN: 1840233001 (trd); 1840233788 (pbk). Reprints Marvel's *Transformers Vol: 1 69–74.*

Unicron summons Galvatron to do his dirty work in taking him to Cybertron. Galvatron tries to deceive Unicron. A civil war occurs between the Decepticons, with Shockwave and Starscream on one side, and Scorponok on the other. Ratchet and Megatron have ben melded together from another dimension, and show up on the Autobots' ship. Grimlock goes in search of the unstable energy force called Nucleon which will save the dismantled Dinobots. Optimus Prime surrenders to Scorponok, and the Neo-Knights fight the Transformers.

Furman, Simon, Andrew Wildman, Geoff Senior, et al. *Transformers: End of the Road.* London: Titan, 2001. ISBN: 1840234199 (trd); 1840233729 (pbk). Reprints Marvel's *Transformers Vol. 1: 75–80.*

The Autobots and the Decepticons defeat Unicron who is trying to destroy their home world, Cybertron. Optimus Prime is killed, and he makes Grimlock the new leader of the Autobots. The human Neo-Knights are also transported to Cybertron, and help the Transformers save their world. The Transformers believe their world is dying and try to ecape, but the Decepticons betray the Autobots, through sabotage. Optimus Prime is reborn and defeats them.

Hama, Larry, Steven Grant, Mark Vosburg, et al. *G.I. Joe: A Real American Hero Vol. 2.* New York: Marvel, 2002. ISBN: 07851090 72. Reprints *G.I. Joe: A Real American Hero 11–20.*

For the Cobra, Dr. Venom creates a deadly virus which will kill thousands of people. The Joes try to stop Cobra's attempt to terrorize the world. Scarface ends up being infected, and is eventually taken captive by the Joes. The Cobra commander wants to find the Joes' headquarters by allowing Scarface to be captured. Venom makes a number of attempts on the lives of Snake Eyes and the Eskimo mercenary, Kwinn. Kwinn and Snake Eyes team up to find Venom and stop the infection. The Cobra Commander tries to have Destro assassinated by Major Bludd, and the Baroness is caught in an explosive blast, then taken to the Joe's headquarters. Destro and the Baroness have a romantic relationship. Major Bludd is captured by G.I. Joe, but escapes from the Joes' headquarters, the Pit. Bludd kills Colonel Flagg, and Dr. Venom is blown up by a grenade, as Kwinn is dying.

This volume introduces Joe regulars Cover Girl, Tripwire, and Snow Job.

Hama, Larry, Herb Trimpe, Jack Abel, et al. *G.I. Joe: A Real American Hero: Trojan Gambit*. New York: Marvel, 1983. ISBN: 0939766485. Reprints *G.I. Joe 3, 6*.

The Joes capture one of Cobra's battle robots. The Robot breaks free, and the Joes must do battle in the Pit. The Cobra Commander hopes the Robot will transmit the Joes' secret base location. A Russian spycraft lands in the Hindu Kush mountain range, and is captured by Afghani rebel tribesman. Hawk tells the Joes that the United States can have it for a price. The Russians also have plans for the aircraft, and come in direct conflict with the Joes.

This book contains two stories, "To Fail Is to Conquer ... to Succeed Is to Die" and "The Trojan Gambit."

Hama, Larry, Herb Trimpe, Joe Delbeato, et al. *G.I. Joe: Order of Battle Volume 1*. New York: Marvel, 1987. ISBN: 0871352885.

This is a guidebook to the world of G.I. Joe, similar to the *Official Handbook to the Marvel Universe*. Among the entries are Dr. Mindbender, Ace, Storm Shadow, Doc Ock, and Slugger.

Hama, Larry, Herb Trimpe, Steven Grant, et al. *G.I. Joe: A Real American Hero Vol. 1*. New York: Marvel, 2002. ISBN: 078510 9013. Reprints *G.I. Joe 1–10*.

This volume covers the origins of the elite, anti-terrorist G.I. Joe team, which includes the popular Snake Eyes, and it explains their conflict with the terrorist Cobra. It includes the first tours of the Pit, Joe's command center, and the first appearances of the October Guard and Kwinn, the Eskimo. In it, Snake Eyes is captured, and, while being tortured, gives interesting glimpses into his past. This book provides a definite comment on the Cold War of the 1980s.

Hama, Larry, Herb Trimpe, Bob Sharen, et al. *G.I. Joe: Special Missions*. New York: Marvel, 1988. ISBN: 0871354594. Reprints *G.I. Joe Special Missions 1–4*; *G.I. Joe: A Real American Hero 51*.

The Joes help to protect a Nazi war criminal who knows how to disable a dangerous bomb that was found, left from World War II. The Joes go to the Middle East to stop a crazy dictator. They also go to the South China Sea to go against some reds, only to be captured by river pirates who have their own bizarre code of honor.

This is a special collection describing G.I. Joe covert operations which are "classified." It provides a good look at the last years of the Cold War.

Hama, Larry, Mike Vosburg, Russ Heath, et al. *G.I. Joe: A Real American Hero Vol. 3*. New York: Marvel, 2002. ISBN: 0785109307. Reprints *G. I. Joe: A Real American Hero 21–30*.

The Cobra Commander is captured by the Joes but manages to escape. Snake Eyes goes to battle against Storm Shadow. The Joes attend Colonel Flagg's funeral which the Cobra Commander crashes. Bludd and the Baroness try to swindle the Cobra Commander out of millions of dollars. Destro learns that the Cobra Commander hired Bludd to kill him. When the Commander goes to Cobra headquarters in Springfield, he introduces the newest Cobra weapon, a deep-cover, All-American type of agent called the Crimson Guard.

This volume includes dossiers on Destro, Storm Shadow, and the Cobra Commande, and covers the days when Snake Eyes was a ninja and soldier in 'Nam. It also introduces Roadblock and Duke, new members of the G.I. Joe team. Cobra's master of disguise, Zartan, makes his debut.

Hama, Larry, Rod Whigham, Frank Springer, et al. *G.I. Joe: A Real American Hero Vol. 4*. New York: Marvel, 2002. ISBN: 07851095 52. Reprints *G.I. Joe: A Real American Hero 31–41*.

Airborne and Iron Knife are assigned to keep Snake Eyes under surveillance while on vacation. Firefly, a Crimson Guardsman, and Destro find Snake Eyes' cabin, and try to kill him. They blow up his cabin. With the help and old Ninja friend of Snake Eyes, the Joes take on the Cobra agents. Snake Eyes makes an escape through a hole in the floor. Cobra Commander's son is unknowingly set up to assassinate his father, but Destro stops him. He is put in prison and broken out by Storm Shadow. The Joes stop Cobra agents from blowing up a carnival, which is secretly serving as a Cobra hangout. The Cobra commander manages to make an island come out of the sea by blowing up a fault line in the Gulf of Mexico. This island becomes a sovereign state, recognized by the United Nations as Cobra Island.

Hama, Larry, Rod Whigham, Herb Trimpe, et al. *G.I. Joe: A Real American Hero Vol. 5*.

New York: Marvel, 2002. ISBN: 07851097
9X. Reprints *G.I. Joe: A Real American Hero
42–51.*

The Cobra Commander's son leaves Storm Shadow
and asks for forgiveness. A former Cobra agent, Wade
Collins, was also in 'Nam with Snake Eyes and
Stalker. They show him the error of his ways, by appealing to his reason rather than using force. Both
Storm Shadow and Snake Eyes go to Cobra Island in
search of revenge for the death of their comrade. It
turns out that the shape changer Zartan is the killer.
Ripcord goes to Cobra Island in search of his love;
Candy, whose father is a Cobra agent; he gets
wounded in the process. Zartan changes identities
with him, trying to find the location of the Joes' base.
Storm Shadow is killed, only to be resurrected. Destro
and Dr. Mindbender find graves of the ten greatest
warriors of all time, and create Serpentor, who will
become *the* greatest warrior of all time.

This book includes dossiers on Major Bludd,
Baroness, and Stalker, and a sneak preview of *G.I. Joe
Special Missions.* We learn more about Snake Eye's life
in Vietnam, and who killed his mentor.

Higgins, Michael, Herb Trimpe, Vince Colletta,
     et al. *G.I. Joe and the Transformers.* New
     York: Marvel, 1993. ISBN: 0871359731.
     Reprints *G.I. Joe and the Transformers 1–4.*

The Joes and the Autobots team up to stop the Decepticons from using a nuclear missile to destroy humanity. Cobra and the Decepticons also team up, but
when the Decepticons' devious plan is finally revealed,
Cobra teams with the Autobots and Joes to fight
them. A U.S. senator is found out to have been working with Cobra, and is assassinated by the Baroness.

Mantlo, Bill, Ralph Macchio, Jim Salicrup, et al.
     Transformers: Beginnings. London: Titan,
     2003. ISBN: 1840236426 (trd); 184023
     623X (pbk). Reprints Marvel's *Transform-
     ers 1–6.*

Optimus Prime saves Cybertron from an asteroid
disaster. The Decepticons ambush the Autobots.
Their ship, the Ark, crashes into Earth millions of
years ago. In 1984, both the Autobots and the Decepticons are awakened, and given the ability to transform into mechanical forms which the Ark's scout

thought were the life forms of Earth. The Decepticons
seek to rule Earth, and use nuclear power for their
fuel. During a battle at a drive-in theater, Bumblebee
is injured and Buster Witwicky takes him to his father,
Sparkplug, for repairs. The Autobots want to align
themselves with humanity, while the Decepticons seek
to conquer Earth. The Decepticons kidnap Sparkplug. Megatron forces him to make fuel for the Decepticons, but Sparkplug tricks them by making bad fuel.
Spider-Man aids the Autobots in a battle with the
Decepticons. Sparkplug gets hurt, and is taken to the
hospital. Shockwave is awakened, and nearly destroys
the Autobots. He tries to take over the Decepticons,
and usurps Megatron's leadership. Buster tries to help
heal Optimus Prime, who was incapacitated by
Shockwave's blast. Optimus transfers the Creation
Matrix to Buster.

Salicrup, Jim, Frank Springer, DeMulder Es-
     posito, et al. *Transformers: The Story Begins:
     Collected Comics 1.* New York: Marvel, 1985.
     ISBN: 0871350653. Reprints *Transformers
     1–3.*

After four million years, Mount St. Hilary erupts,
and the Transformers' ship, the *Ark,* awakens its robotic cargo. The Decepticons want to enslave the
Earth for fuel, while the Autobots want to ally themselves with humanity. Sparkplug gets taken captive
by the Decepticons. Spider-Man makes an appearance, and fights alongside the Transformers, against
Megatron and the Decepticons. Gears dies in the
fight.

This volume contains the story of the origin of the
Transformers on Earth. Sparkplug and Buster are introduced.

Salicrup, Jim, Frank Springer, John Workman,
     et al. *Transformers: The Battle Continues:
     Collected Comics 2.* New York: Marvel, 1985.
     ISBN: 0871350661. Reprints *Transformers
     3–5.*

After years of lying dormant, the Decepticon
Shockwave is awakened and wants to enslave the
Earth. He usurps Megatron's powers, and takes con-
trol of the Decepticons. The Decepticons defeat the
Autobots and are left for dead.

Wolverine, Deadpool, Sabretooth, and Weapon X

One more thing, bub. I'd take it real personal if anything happened to
my motor while I'm looking around upstairs. —*Wolverine*

Casey, Joe, Oscar Jimenez, Gina Going, et al.
     Wolverine: Black Rio. New York: Marvel,
     1998. ISBN: 078510674X.

Logan goes to Rio De Janeiro for Carnaval and
some R&R. He meets up with an old buddy of his
who is a detective. His friend is investigating a series
of brutal vampire-like murders, and Logan goes along

for kicks. He finds out that the perpetrator is a vampire who has joined himself to an alien parasite that has the power to raise the dead and create vampire-like beings. One of the vampires is the detective's missing wife, and she kills her husband.

Casey, Joe, Stephen Platt, Larry Strucker, et al. *Wolverine/Cable: Guts and Glory.* New York: Marvel, 1999. ISBN: 0785100032.

This book covers Cable's first encounter with the city of New York and the mutant Wolverine. They go up against D'Von Kray, a machine/mutant soldier from the future, bent upon destroying Cable.

Chaykin Howard, Shawn McManus, Gloria Vasquez, et al. *Wolverine/Nick Fury: Scorpio Rising.* New York: Marvel, 1994.

In this volume Wolverine, Nick Fury, and Fury's son, Scorpio, go to stop a civil war in Carpasia, an Eastern European country; Hydra is searching for the Scorpio key; and Mikel becomes president of Carpasia. This is a sequel to the graphic novel *Scorpio Connection.*

Chichester, D.G., Bill Sienkiewicz, Michael Heisler, et al. *Wolverine: Inner Fury.* New York: Marvel, 1992. ISBN: 0871359561.

Wolverine is infected with a high-tech virus which tears down his healing factor, and breaks down his adamantium skeleton. He goes with the criminal Big in search of former HYDRA operative the Whale whom he believes infected him. Big was actually the infector, and he just used Wolverine for his own ends.

Claremont, Chris, John Byrne, Frank Miller et al. *Wolverine: Triumphs and Tragedies.* New York: Marvel, 1995. ISBN: 0785101578. Reprints *Uncanny X-Men 109, 172–173; Wolverine Limited Series 4; Wolverine 41–42; 75.*

Shortly after he first joins the X-Men, Wolverine has his first encounter with a member of Alpha Flight, James Hudson, known as Weapon Alpha. Wolverine gets engaged to Mariko, but she calls off the marriage at the alter, with most of the X-Men present. Sabretooth tells Wolverine that he is his father, but, at the same time, he tries to rip his head off. Wolverine loses his adamantium skeleton and part of his healing factor because of Magneto, and he leaves the X-Men and Jubilee with a heartwarming note. Nick Fury and Storm's first punk outfit make appearances.

This is a collection of some fine and some not-so-fine moments in Wolverine's life. It needs to be reprinted.

Claremont, Chris, Frank Miller, Josef Ruinstein, et al. *Wolverine.* New York: Marvel, 2001. ISBN: 087135277X. Reprints *Wolverine Limited Series 1–4.*

In this book Wolverine voyages to Japan to be with his love Mariko. He fights the Hand and Japanese crime lords, samurai-style. This was the first Wolverine solo series, dating from 1987. This storyline shows a more human side to Wolverine, and is highly recommended. In 2007 Marvel will reprint this volume, as a special hardback—ISBN: 0785123296; 0785125728 (ltd).

David, Peter, Sam Keith, Steve Dutro, et al. *Wolverine: Blood Hungry.* New York: Marvel, 2002. Reprints *Marvel Presents 85–92.* ISBN: 0785100032 (1993).

Wolverine takes a vacation in Madripoor. He is staying with his lover Tyger Tiger. He encounters Cyber, the only man who gives him the creeps. Cyber beats him in battle, and drugs him with a hallucinogen. Eventually Logan beats Cyber at his own game.

Davis, Alan, Michael Heisler, Bernie Jaye, et al. *Wolverine: Bloodlust.* New York: Marvel, 1990. ISBN: 0871357054.

A group of normally peace-loving, mystical beings known as Neuri have become rogues, and are killing humans. They try to use Wolverine's animal psyche to make him believe he has killed innocent people, including children, in a fit of rage. Along with one of the peace-loving Neuri, Wolverine goes on the trail of the rogues, and eventually destroys them, bringing balance back to the race. (*Marvel Graphic Novel 65*)

DeFalco, Tom, John Buscema, Gregory Wright, et al. *Wolverine: Bloody Choices.* New York: Marvel, 1993. ISBN: 0871359804; 087135 7917 (1991).

Logan saves a small, frightened boy who attempts to assassinate the drug lord Bullfinch. Wolverine goes after a fat drug lord who enjoys sexually abusing little boys. One of Bullfinch's musclemen looks and fights like Wolverine, even to the point of having a claw. Blullfinch is willing to turn over evidence related to the cartel, in exchange for special protection under the command of Nick Fury. Fury and Wolverine clash over this point, and they end up in an intense fight which Wolverine wins. (*Marvel Graphic Novel 67*)

Edginton, Ian, John Ostrander, Jan Duursema, et al. *Wolverine: Knight of Terra.* New York: Marvel, 1995. ISBN: 0785101624.

Wolverine and Rahne are magically transported to the land of Geshem in a parallel universe. The Queen of Geshem is transported to Earth, and is with the X-Men. Wolverine and Rahne have to stop the Beast from taking over the kingdom and bringing about misery. Each of the X-Men has a counterpart in Geshem, including Charles Xavier, who is the Queen's council and a magician. The Beast, who is Sabretooth's double, is finally slain, and Wolverine is knighted.

Ellis, Warren, Leinil Francis Yu, Edgar Tadeo, et al. *Wolverine: Not Dead Yet.* New York:

Marvel, 1998. ISBN: 0785107045. Reprints *Wolverine 119–122.*

Wolverine drinks with an assassin, McLeish, who ends up killing the father of one of Wolverine's girl-friends. Logan tries to kill McLeish, but finds out, ten years later, that McLeish is still alive and is trying to assassinate him. McLeish kills Wolverine's old girlfriend, and sets several deadly traps, but Wolverine is "Not Dead Yet."

This is one of the most brutal of all Wolverine tales.

Gonzalez, Jorge, Frank Teran, Comic Craft, et al. *Sabretooth: Back to Nature.* Marvel: New York, 1998. ISBN: 0785106545. Originally *Sabretooth Volume 2: 1.*

Sabretooth and Warchild are chasing former KGB agents Yuri Yevgraf and Chop Chop who had turned serial killers, and who killed one of Warchild's former girlfriends.

Goodwin, Archie, Howard Chaykin, Richard Ory, et al. *Wolverine/Nick Fury: The Scorpio Connection.* New York: Marvel, 1989. ISBN: 0871355779 (trd); 0871356627 (pbk).

A new Scorpio is determined to kill Nick Fury. Wolverine investigates Scorpio's murder of a friend who turns out to be a mole. Fury learns that the new Scorpio, who is under the thumb of his mother, is the son of his brother, Mikel Fury. It turns out that Mikel is actually Nick Fury's son. Wolverine kills Mikel's mother Amber, and Scorpio gives up.

This book is a special hardback. (*Marvel Graphic Novel 50*)

Hama, Larry, Mark Texeira, Steve Buccellato, et al. *Sabretooth: Death Hunt.* New York: Marvel, 1994. ISBN: 0785100504. Reprints *Sabretooth 1–4.*

Sabretooth is kidnapped, and after a bomb is implanted in his body, he is ordered to kill Mystique. He barges in on Wolverine and Mystique who are out on a date together. He finds out that the person who ordered the assassination is the mutant-hating son of Mystique and Sabretooth.

This book includes a glimpse into Sabretooth's childhood.

Havanagh, Terry, Scott McDaniel, Keith Williams, et al. *Spider-Man/Punisher/Sabretooth: Designer Genes.* New York: Marvel, 1993. ISBN: 0871359898.

Several lab animals and homeless people are found dead and disemboweled. Apparently the Roxxon Corporation is trying to combine human and animal DNA as "designer genes" to create hybrid beings. Both the little brother of the doctor/scientist doing the experiments and the head of the department are hybrid beings. Apparently the scientist did experiments on Sabretooth and Wolverine in Canada, under Department H, and Sabretooth is seeking revenge against

the doctor. Spider-Man and the Punisher form an uneasy alliance, to bring Sabretooth in for murders they believe he has committed, but, all the while, Spider-Man wants to turn the Punisher in to the police.

One of the funniest parts of the book is when Spider-Man is trying to stop the Punisher from killing Sabretooth.

Jemas, Bill, Joe Quesada, Paul Jenkins, et al. *Origin: The True Story of Wolverine.* New York: Marvel, 2002. ISBN: 0785108661 (trd); 078510965X (pbk). Reprints *Wolverine Origin 1–6.*

This volume discloses Wolverine's real roots, and his transformation from a naïve, sickly boy into the person now known as Logan. It includes Wolverine's coming-of-age story, and tells how he inadvertently kills the one person he loves the most. This is one of the most anticipated graphic novels ever published, and has been praised as a cross between "*Great Expectations* and *Jane Eyre.*" It was twenty-six years in the making. The book contains the genesis for the project, idea sketches, and character designs.

Jones, Bruce, Scott Kolins, Lee Loughridge, et al. *Hulk Legends Vol. 1: Hulk/Wolverine: Six Hours.* New York: Marvel, 2003. ISBN: 0785111573. Reprints *Hulk/Wolverine, 6 Hours 1–4; Incredible Hulk 181.*

Bruce Banner and Wolverine get involved with saving the life of a teenager who was bitten by a coral snake, and is on the verge of death. They also inadvertently get involved in a drug deal gone bad, in which the Shredder is killing practically everyone he comes in contact with. Wolverine battles the Shredder who had previously beaten him. He finally triumphs over the Shredder, who is killed by a wild cat. The Hulk/Bruce Banner's blood is used to save the teenager. This book includes an extra reprint of the first Wolverine appearance, in which he battles the Hulk and the Wendigo.

Jones, Bruce, Jorge Lucas, Dave Sharpe, et al. *Wolverine Legends Vol. 4: Xisle.* New York: Marvel, 2003. ISBN: 0785112219. Reprints *Wolverine Xisle 1–5.*

Logan goes to the carnival with his stepdaughter Amiko. He goes into a violent rage, and shows a side of himself that scares Amiko and causes her to run away in fear. Wolverine battles a crazy, giant ape-man, which is own sub-consciousness. Amiko and Logan go to a human freak show.

Much of the book takes place inside Logan's mind, which gives it a hallucinogenic vibe.

Keith, Sam, Richard Isanovf, Richard Starkings, et al. *Wolverine Legends Vol. 1: Wolverine/Hulk.* New York: Marvel, 2003. ISBN: 0785111387. Reprints *Wolverine/Hulk 1–4.*

Wolverine comes across the spirit of little girl Po, who needs help from him and her uncle Bruce Banner to get out of a plane that her father had crashed twenty years previously. Po's spirit is forced to wander in limbo until they are found, and freed of the plane's safety belts. Wolverine and Hulk dig up the crashed plane and free Po's spirit. The Hulk cries at the end.

Kelly, Joe, Ed McGuinness, Nathan Massengill, et al. *Deadpool: Mission Improbable.* New York: Marvel, 1996. ISBN: 07851066 50 Reprints *Deadpool 1–5.*

Deadpool goes to the Antarctica to destroy a nuclear research facility, and fights Sasquatch. He ends up saving it, just before it is about to blow. He secretly watches X-Force's Siryn, while she sleeps. Weasel is taken prisoner by the Taskmaster, and is offered a job. Deadpool fights him and loses a finger which doesn't grow back. Deadpool and Siryn, whom Deadpool secretly loves, team up. They find Dr. Killbrew, the man responsible for much that went on in the Weapon-X project, including Deadpool. He tells Deadpool that he is dying, and needs the Hulk's blood to sustain himself. The Hulk is not very happy about Deadpool disturbing his peace, but Deadpool manages to get a blood sample anyway. Siryn stops Deadpool from killing Killbrew.

This trade paperback is the best of the Deadpool books, and it deserves to reprinted.

Leob, Jeph, Tim Sale, Comicraft, et., al. *Wolverine: Gambit: Victims.* Marvel Comics: New York, 1999. ISBN: 078510258 (1999): 0785 108963 (2002). Reprints *Wolverine/Gambit: Victims: 1–4.*

A series of Jack-the-Ripper–style murders take place in London, and Wolverine is blamed. Gambit and Wolverine team up to try to solve the murders. Arcade and Mastermind's daughter are the culprits. Arcade is put into a mental ward.

Mackie, Howard, Ron Garney, Al Milgrom, et al. *Ghost Rider, Wolverine, Punisher: The Dark Design.* New York: Marvel, 1994.

Blackheart has built up an army of possessed souls, and seeks Lucy's soul as well. Ghost Rider, the Punisher, and Wolverine are brought in to defeat Blackheart again, and stop his reign of terror. Blackheart also wants to assassinate his father Mephisto, and bring a new order to Hell. Ghost Rider is possessed by spirits, and is almost lost, but the desire to help the innocent prevails. Just as Ghost Rider is about to demolish Blackheart, Lucy comes and forgives him for his evil. Mephiso makes an offer to rule Hell with his son, but Blackheart commits patricide, stabbing him with a knife that is dipped in the blood of innocents. This is a direct sequel to *Hearts of Darkness.*

Mackie, Howard, Mark Jason, Tom Coker, et al. *Logan: Shadow Society.* New York: Marvel, 1996. ISBN: 0785102949.

Logan, Warbird, and Carol Danvers, the future Ms. Marvel, go on a top-secret government mission to in-

vistigate a "secret society" of mutants. This society is actually the Hellfire Club. Sebastian Shaw employs Sabretooth to take out Logan and Danvers, but Logan stabs him through the stomach. Another agent, one of Logan's friends, is killed. The Hellfire Club is not ready to make their presence or agenda known to the general populace.

This story takes place before Logan became Wolverine, and before he joined the X-Men.

Mackie, Howard, John Paul Leon, Gregory Wright, et al. *Logan: Path of the Warlord.* New York: Marvel, 1996. ISBN: 07851017 21.

This story takes place long before Weapon X and the X-Men. It is set in Japan where Logan fights several ninja. In the book, the espionage outfit he is with sends him to another dimension to stop an evil dictator, Kimora, who plans to use a special device to come to our dimension and conquer it.

Mackie, Howard, John Romita Jr., and Klaus Janson. *Ghost Rider: Wolverine: Punisher: Hearts of Darkness.* New York: Marvel, 1991. ISBN: 0871358735.

The Punisher, Wolverine, and Ghost Rider go to the city of Christ's Crown. They team up against the son of Mephisto, Blackheart. Blackheart is angry at his father for his diminished status as a petty deity. He tries to steal the souls of the innocents, including a young girl, Lucy. Ghost Rider learns a little bit about his past and the spirit that possesses him. Ghost Rider goes into the dark abyss to stop Blackheart from getting more innocent souls. The Punisher blows Blackheart into little pieces, and Mephisto comes to pick him up.

Mackie, Howard, Mark Texeira, Harry Candelario, et al. *Ghost Rider: Wolverine: Acts of Vengeance.* New York: Marvel, 1993. ISBN: 0785100229. Reprints *Marvel Presents 64–70.*

Wolverine and Ghost Rider meet for the first time, each one thinking the other is an enemy. Wolverine sticks one of his claws into one of Ghost Rider's eyes. A group of ninjas employed by Deathwatch want Wolverine and the fighter known as Brass. Deathwatch kidnaps several people, including one of Dan Ketch's friends, and Ghost Rider and Wolverine come to rescue them. Wolverine and Brass are thrown through several walls, and Ghost Rider finds the captives.

This is one of the most difficult Marvel graphic novels to find.

Matthews, Brett, Vatche Mavlian, Paul Morris, et al. *Spider Man Legends Vol. 4: Spider Man/Wolverine.* New York: Marvel 2003. ISBN: 0785112979. Reprints *Spider Man & Wolverine 1–4*; *Spider Man/Daredevil 1.*

Peter Parker is taken away from his teaching duties by Nick Fury who wants him to rescue a "special" person, who turns out to be Wolverine. They uncover a rogue government plot called "Stuff of Legends," in which a mutant-hating scientist has created a drug that make superhumans powerless. Because of the political nature of the job, Nick Fury's and S.H.I.E.L.D.'s hands are tied, and they can't do anything to stop the program. Spider-Man and Wolverine manage to shut the program down, but have to face the wrath of Aunt May, who was expecting Peter for dinner. Naturally, he missed his appointment with her. Wolverine stays to have supper with Aunt May and Peter Parker, and ends up carving the roast.

This book also contains a short story in which Spider-Man, Daredevil, and reporter Ben Ulrich help rescue a young girl who was kidnapped. The writing is very clever, and the book is well worth reading.

Milligan, Peter, Lee Weeks. Tom Palmer, et al. *Wolverine/Punisher Vol. 1*. New York: Marvel, 2004. ISBN: 0785114327. Reprints *Wolverine/Punisher 1–6*.

Criminals on the run from the Punisher find their "paradise" in the mythical Erewhon. This town is supposed to be a place where criminals are safe from the law and the Punisher. Both Wolverine and the Punisher follow the trail of murderer to Erewhon. They find that it is actually a trap set by the syndicate of the town, and both Logan and Castle are taken prisoner. Wolverine has an arrow shot through his head. The townspeople revolt against the elite of Erewhon who are really modern-day Nazis who have kept the body of Hitler preserved to inspire them.

Moench, Doug, Michal Dutkiewicz, Jimmy Palmiotti, et al. *Wolverine: Doombringer*. New York: Marvel, 1997. ISBN: 07851058 32.

A mysterious visitor from a thousand years ago brings tidings of the Doombringer who plans to destroy the world. The Yashida clan is some how mixed up in bringing the Doombringer from the past. Wolverine's love Mariko asks him to investigate the claim that the Yashidas were responsible for the dishonor of the Doombringer. Logan and Marko's brother, the Silver Samurai, form a loose alliance and go to the forgotten city of Tangkor Marat, to investigate the claims. Wolverine and the Silver Samurai fight the Doombringer, and Logan brings Marko a thousand-year-old white Chrysanthemum.

Nicieza, Fabian, Mark Brooks, Shane Law, et al. *Cable and Deadpool Vol. 1: If Look Could Kill*. New York: Marvel, 2004. ISBN: 078 5113746. Reprints *Cable & Deadpool 1–6*.

Deadpool is hired by the One World Church to get possession of a chemical, a biological agent which will turn humanity into a blue mass of one-conciousness, which is in line with the church's agenda. Cable interferes, goes head-to-head with Deadpool, and blows

his brains out. Deadpool becomes the church's assassin, and is cured of being a fleshy mess. Cable's techno-virus and Deadpool's cancer end up consuming them, because the biological agent they digested was defective. Cable swallows Deadpool and they both are cured, temporarily. Cable seeks to use the church's chemical for his own ends. He wants to change the world into his version of paradise. Professor X warns him that there will be those who will try to stop him, and Deadpool becomes a fleshy mess again.

Nicieza, Fabian, Joe Madureira, Mark Farmer, et al. *Deadpool: Circle Chase*. New York: Marvel, 1997. ISBN: 0785102590. Reprints *Deadpool: The Circle Chase 1–4*.

Deadpool and other mercenaries are searching for information about the arms-dealers' Tolliver's Will, which will lead them to the ultimate weapon. During the search, Deadpool encounters his ex-girlfriend Vanessa, known as Copycat; Garrison Kane; Black Tom; and Juggernaut. He ends up throwing Black Tom out of an airplane window. Juggernaut jumps to save his friend. When Deadpool finds the ultimate weapon, it turns out to be a weapon to ensure peace. Slayback, whom Deadpool thought he had killed ten years before, comes back for revenge, and almost kills Vanessa.

This was Deadpool's first solo adventure.

Nihei, Tsutomu, Guru Efx, Cory Petit, et al. *Wolverine Legends Vol. 5: Snikt!* New York: Marvel, 2003. ISBN: 0785112391. Reprints *Wolverine Snikt! 1–5*.

Wolverine is transported to a post-apocalyptic future by a young girl who knows his name and his powers. The remaining humans need Logan's help in fighting biomechanical beings known as the Mandates. Wolverine needs to eliminate the Queen Mandate. The Mandates have no power against the metal adamantium, which gives Logan the edge, and allows him to let his berserker rage go free.

This book is beautifully written and drawn.

Nocenti, Ann, Mark Texeira, Jon Royale, et al. *Wolverine Evilution*. New York: Marvel, 1994. ISBN: 087135943X.

Wolverine goes to the small town of Prescott where a cult called the DEVO is trying to destroy a nuclear power plant. He ends up saving the life of the mutant Boom Boom.

Nocenti, Ann, Steve Lightle, Michael Higgins, et al. *Wolverine: Typhoid's Kiss*. New York: Marvel, 1994. ISBN: 0785100563. Reprints *Marvel Presents 109–116*.

Wolverine and Mary have a romantic interlude, and try to find out who manipulated their minds. When the typhoid part of Mary comes out, however, problems begin to arise. Typhoid leaves many bodies in her wake, and even sets Logan on fire. Mary toys with Wolverine the entire time they are teamed. They find the scientist who was playing games with their personalities.

This book, which provides good insight into Mary's psyche and Wolverine's gullibility, deserves to be reprinted.

Owlsley, James, Mark Bright, Al Williamson, et al. *Spiderman vs. Wolverine*. New York: Marvel, 1990. ISBN: 0871356457. Reprints *Spiderman vs. Wolverine Vol. 1: 1*.

A group of former KGB agents end up dead in New York, and Peter Parker and Ned Leeds are sent to Germany to investigate. Wolverine's former lover and best friend Charlemagne is a former "free agent assassin/spy" who has a bounty on her head. Wolverine discovers that Peter Parker is Spider-Man. Ned Leeds is murdered. Wolverine and Spider-Man duke it out over Charlemagne, and she asks Wolverine to kill her.

This is one of the few stories that features Spider-Man in both his black and blue-and-red costumes.

Potts, Carl, Jim Lee, Jim Novak, et al. *The Punisher: Wolverine: The African Saga*. New York: Marvel, 1989. ISBN: 0871356112. Reprints *Punisher War Journal 6–7*.

The Punisher goes to Africa for some rest and relaxation, but winds up in the middle of a poaching trade. The Punisher goes as a bodyguard to help Professor Wyeth who is searching for rare animals and dinosaurs. When he meets Wolverine for the first time, they each think the other is fighting on the side of the poachers, and they have several intense battles between them. They almost destroy each other, but end up making a truce. They discover that there are dinosaurs are in Africa. A wealthy Texas man, who wants to make wall trophys of rare animals, hires Norma to become the professor's wife, in order to have her poach the animals.

Rieber, John Ney, Kent Williams, Bill Oakley, et al. *Wolverine: Killing*. New York: Marvel, 1993. ISBN: 0785100016.

Wolverine goes to the Himalayas for a vacation. He comes in contact with a religious cult of mutants that does not like outsiders. He falls in love with the daughter of one of the high priests. He has a difficult battle with a mutant whose power is to make one's darkest nightmares real.

Rucka, Greg, Leandro Fernandez, Studio F, et al. *Wolverine Vol. 2: Coyote Crossing*. New York: Marvel, 2004. ISBN: 0785111379. Reprints *Wolverine Vol. 3: 7–11*.

Logan goes to Mexico to bring down a drug lord and trader in illegal immigrants. It turns out that the drug lord is a woman and is pregnant. Wolverine does not kill her, but leaves her alone after he kills all the guards. She goes into labor, and dies giving childbirth.

Logan gives the child to her sister, who adopts it. The ATF agent, Cassie Lathrop, follows Logan and keeps popping up in his life.

Rucka, Greg, Darick Robertson, Tom Palmer, et al. *Wolverine Vol. 1: Brotherhood*. New York: Marvel, 2003. ISBN: 0785111360. Reprints *Wolverine Vol. 3: 1–6*.

Wolverine tracks down the killers of a young woman living next door to him. He goes to a small community Westfall, where a cult known as the Brotherhood has taken over. Logan goes after the cult that killed the young girl, and kidnaps a woman ATF agent. She is thrown in with other women who are used as sex slaves for the leader of the cult. Even the sheriff of Westfall is a member of the cult. The Brotherhood has built up a large arsenal of arms and weapons, and Wolverine takes them out. Wolverine has a heart-to-heart with Nightcrawler in a pub.

This book includes a cover sketchbook.

Rucka, Greg, Darick Robertson, Tom Palmer, et al. *Wolverine Vol. 3: Return of the Native*. New York: Marvel, 2004. ISBN: 07851139 75. Reprints *Wolverine Vol. 3: 12–19*.

Sabretooth is hired to capture the Weapon X project that got away, known as the Native, and he brings Wolverine in to help track her down. The agency that hired Sabretooth betrays him. Wolverine and the Native fall for each other, and she gets pregnant. The Native is captured, experimented on, and her eggs sold, to be cultivated as biological weapons. Wolverine rescues her, but Sabretooth tracks them down and kills the Native.

The book includes unused pages from *Wolverine 16*.

Sanderson, Peter, Larry Hama, Paul Benjamin, et al. *Wolverine Encyclopedia 1–2*. New York: Marvel, 1996. ISBN: 0785102965 (1); 0785102965 (2).

This is a very detailed, two-part guide that covers nearly everything in the world of Wolverine. It includes villains, allies, and even alternative universe characters. Volume 1 covers A–K, and Volume 2 covers L–R. Some of the entries included are Madripoor, with a map; Hussar; Lady Deathstrike; Lupo; Mojo; Microverse; Hobgoblin; Dark Riders; Clea; and Brood. Volume 2 contains a special art section that features Sauron, Omega Red, Sinister, and Hulk.

Sanderson, Peter, Janet Jackson, Rob Liefeld, et al. *The Wolverine Saga 1–4*. New York: Marvel, 1989.

These four volumes are written in novel-like prose, with reprints of various comic panels. The story covers the life of Wolverine from his time with the X-Men, to his time with Weapon X, and his time in Asia. These four volumes are based on the following comics: *Alpha Flight, 17, 33–34*; *Captain America Annual 8*; *Kitty Pryde and Wolverine 1–6*; *Marvel Comics*

Presents 1–10; Wolverine 1–10; X-Men Annual 4–7, 11; X-Men 94–96, 101–105, 107–116, 118, 120–129, 131–139, 145–147, 151, 156, 159, 162–166, 172–176, 178, 181, 183, 205, 207–208, 210, 212–213, 235–242, X-Men and Alpha Flight 1; Classic X-Men 1–22, 24, 26–33; Giant Size X-Men 1; Incredible Hulk 181–182; Wolverine Limited Series 1–4; Iron Fist 15; Marvel Treasury Edition 26; and Marvel Team Up Annual 1.

Silvestri, Marc, Larry Hama, Dan Green, et al. *Wolverine Legends Vol. 6: Marc Silvestri.* New York: Marvel, 2004. ISBN: 07851095 28. Reprints *Wolverine 31–34; 41–42; 48–50.*

Wolverine gets involved with stopping a Japanese yakuza gang which is harvesting a highly addictive drug from the brains of the Madripoorian spider monkey. Logan also comes in contact with the Hunter in the Darkness and an old man who remembers being a soldier in the same company in which Logan was a corporal. Professor X, Nick Fury, Jubilee, and Jean Grey help Logan in his quest to unlock his memories. They find, however, that helping him in this way may not have been beneficial to either Logan or the X-Men.

This book also contains a Sabretooth story in which Creed thinks he is Logan's father, as well as the sequel to the Weapon X story, *Memories Unbound.* It is a wonderful collection of Wolverine stories, highlighting the artistic work of Marc Silvestri.

Simonson, Walter, Mike Mignola, Bob Wiacek, et al. *Wolverine: The Jungle Adventure.* New York: Marvel, 1990. ISBN: 08713561 39.

Logan goes to the Savage Land, and becomes an honorary member of a local tribe whose members think he might be a god. He meets Apocalypse for the first time, in a lab where he is trying to breed superhumans, but the Apocalypse he meets is actually a robot pawn. Logan blows up the lab after destroying the robot and meeting the real Apocalypse.

Simonson, Walter, Louise Simonson, Jon J. Muth, et al. *Wolverine Legends Vol. 2: Meltdown.* New York: Marvel, 2003. ISBN: 0785110488; 0871357003. Reprints Epic's *Havok & Wolverine: Meltdown 1–4.*

Disgruntled Soviets General Meltdown and Dr. Neutron want to kidnap Havok. Meltdown wants to siphon Havok's power, to make him a living nuclear reactor. Wolverine and Havok are on vacation in South America, and they both get shot with bubonic plague. Wolverine is left for dead, but Havok is saved. A woman who is working for the Soviets nurses him back to heath. Wolverine is trying to follow the trail of Havok and the woman, but he ends up brainwashed and almost kills Havok. They eventually defeat Meltdown by using his own power against him. Havok's love interest, the nurse, is killed.

The watercolor-style artwork, drawn by Jon J. Muth and Kent Williams, is breathtaking. This volume is an interesting comment on the 1980s Cold War politics and glasnost. Graphitti Designs published a limited hardcover edition (ISBN: 0936211261).

Skroce, Steve, Lary Sucker, Steve Buccellato, et al. *Wolverine: Blood Debt.* New York: Marvel, 2001. ISBN: 0785107851. Reprints *Wolverine 150–153.*

In this book, Wolverine goes back to Japan and gets involved in the middle of a blood-clan war, which dates back to feudal times. He aligns himself with previous enemies, and fights to avenge the death of his beloved Mariko Yashida. This book was written by Steve Skroce, the story-board artist, for the popular science fiction movie *The Matrix.*

Sniegoski, Tom, Christopher Golden, Pat Lee, et al. *Wolverine/Punisher: Revelation.* New York: Marvel, 2000. ISBN: 0785107290. Reprints *Wolverine/Punisher Revelation 1–4.*

Wolverine teams up with the Punisher to help track down and contain a mutant morlock, Revelation, who unwittingly kills people who come near her. The mutant was in stasis for many years before being wakened in the tunnels of New York. They have to contend with robots that want to destroy Revelation. Wolverine's current girlfriend is killed, and the Punisher is observed by a band of angels, known as Council of Thrones. Storm and Daredevil make cameo appearances.

The graphics in this book are drawn in a manga style.

Tieri, Frank, Sean Chen, Georges Jeanty, et al. *Wolverine/Deadpool: Weapon X.* New York: Marvel, 2002. ISBN: 0785109188. Reprints *Wolverine 162–166; Deadpool 57–60.*

Wolverine is one of America's most wanted, for the murder of a prominent politician. He can't remember whether he actually committed the murder, but he goes on the run, with the Beast as his partner. He and Beast are captured by a S.H.I.E.L.D. agent before Nick Fury can find them and put them in a prison with other superbeings. They both have prices on their heads. The Beast is stabbed, and Wolverine is badly wounded. Weapon X is re-opened, with Sabretooth as one of their first recruits. Sabretooth rescues Wolverine and the Beast, and Wolverine is put through a series of tests. They want Wolverine to rejoin the Weapon X force. They ask Sabretooth to recruit Deadpool for Weapon X, which now has Sauron, Kane, and Wild Child as members. Deadpool learns that the Weapon X doctors can fix his face, and help his healing factor. He is asked to kill his former girlfriend Vanessa. He tries to save her, but Sabretooth gets to her first. Weapon X kills Deadpool for refusing to cooperate, and sends his hand to Wolverine at the X-Men's mansion.

Tieri, Frank, Sean Chen, Tom Palmer, et al. *Wolverine Legends Vol. 3: Law of the Jungle.* New York: Marvel, 2003. ISBN: 07851113 52. Reprints *Wolverine 181–186.*

This is a Sopranos-style Wolverine volume, in which he is the hit man for two warring mob factions. It reads almost like a crime pulp novel from the forties. It has excellent artwork.

Tieri, Frank, George Jeanty, Dexter Vines, et al. *Weapon X Vol. 1: The Draft.* New York: Marvel, 2003. ISBN: 0785111484. Reprints *Weapon X 1–2: 1–5; Weapon X: The Draft: War Child; Weapon X: The Draft Sauron; Weapon X: The Draft: Marrow; Weapon X: The Draft: Zero; Weapon X: The Draft: Kane.*

The new director of Weapon X is recruiting mutants. Zero is an old acquaintance of Wolverine's, and is asked to assassinate him, but he fails to do so. The other agents try to recruit members for Weapon X, and they kill the mutants who refuse recruitment. Sabretooth manages to get away from Weapon X, and steals a number of computer files. He proceeds to kill all the mutants before Weapon X agents can get to them. Mutants are being rounded up and put into concentration camps by Weapon X, in the name of security. The source of the Director's hate toward Wolverine and snippets about his past are revealed.

This volume also contains solo stories featuring Marrow, Sauron, War Child, Kane and Agent Zero. It is one of the darkest series that Marvel ever published.

Tieri, Frank, Dexter Vines, Scott Elmer, et al. *Weapon X Volume 2: The Underground.* New York: Marvel, 2003. ISBN: 0785112537. Reprints *Weapon X 6–13.*

Cable has assembled a team to investigate Neverland and the Weapon X program's covert activities against mutants. Agent Jackson secretly plots to take over Weapon X, and enlists the help of Cable and some of the Weapon X mutants. The Director falls in love with Aurora, and has plastic surgery to fix his scarred face. When agent Jackson jokingly calls the Director a "mutie lover," he freaks out, and ends up beating Aurora. Mesmero's mother dies, and he loses his power of mind control. A Weapon X mutant also dies. Sabretooth escapes and eventually Marrow dukes it out with him. The underground group led by Cable and agent Jackson attacks the Weapon X complex, and Washout makes an assassination attempt on the Director, but ends up dying.

The beginning of each issue in this volume is told from the Weapon X Director's point of view. This book is one of the rarest of Marvel's recent outputs; it is difficult to find.

Valentino, Jim, Chap Yaep, Rob Liefeld, et al. *Badrock/Wolverine.* Fullerton, CA: Image, 1996.

Tyrax wants to conquer both the Savage Land and Earth. He has the mutants, including Sauron, as his army. Sauron wants to be rid of his human side. Ka-Zar has been captured, and Wolverine is on vacation. Youngblood's Badrock receives a "mental" call for the X-Men/Wolverine to go the Savage Land, and Zabu gets Wolverine to help find Ka-Zar. Sauron puts Badrock under hypnotic control, and he fights Logan. Tyrax has mutated some of the wildlife into humanoid monstrosities, and Ka-Zar, Wolverine, Karl Lykos, and Badrock team up to defeat him.

This book includes a pin-up gallery.

Waid, Mark, Ian Churchill, Jason Minor, et al. *Deadpool: Sins of the Past.* New York: Marvel, 1997. ISBN: 0785105549. Reprints *Deadpool 1–4.*

Juggernaut breaks Black Tom out of prison. Tom sends his goons to capture Deadpool. The doctor who is working to heal him believes that regenerative cells from Deadpool will help cure the disease Tom is suffering from. Banshee and Syrin help Deadpool against Tom's goons. Banshee recounts his first encounter with Deadpool, while an agent of Interpol, Syrin, and Deadpool team up against Juggernaut. Deadpool's regenerative powers are fading. Banshee's former Interpol partner has a vendetta against Deadpool and tries to assassinate him. Black Tom grafts Deadpool's hand onto his own, but it is quite painful. Juggernaut steals Deadpool's mask, and Syrin finally sees Wade Wilson's scarred face. Syrin offers to become his partner.

Wein, Len, Herb Trimpe, Jack Abel, et al. *Wolverine Battles the Incredible Hulk.* New York: Marvel, 1986. ISBN: 0871356120. Reprints *Incredible Hulk 180–181; Marvel Treasury Edition 26.*

In this volume, Wolverine tries to get rid of the Hulk, but when he comes across the green behemoth battling Wendigo, he teams up with the Hulk to defeat Wendigo before he turns on the Hulk. This volume reprints the first appearance of Wolverine, as Weapon X, from the pages of the *Hulk.* It contains the story of a battle between Wolverine and Hercules which takes place in a bar and it includes a narrative history of the Wolverine character.

Wiesenfeld, Aron, Richard Bennett, Monica Bennett, et al. *Deathblow/Wolverine.* New York: Image/Wildstorm/Marvel, 1997. ISBN: 188727961X. Reprints *Deathblow/ Wolverine 1–2.*

While Logan is staying in San Francisco with his girlfriend, she is kidnapped by ninjas. While he is searching for her, Wolverine meets Deathblow, and they both set out on a journey to place a talisman on an urn which houses the spirits of dead souls who are to be reborn into an invincible army. When Wolverine finds out that his girlfriend was just using him to

complete this mission, and was never really kidnapped, he dumps her.

This book has great artwork which received two
Eisner nominations.

Windsor-Smith, Barry, Jim Novak, Mark Powers, et al. *Weapon X: Origin of Wolverine*.
New York: Marvel, 2000. ISBN: 07851013
14 (trd); 0785100334 (pbk). Reprints *Marvel Presents 72–84*.

This is the story of Wolverine's operation when he
had his adamantium metal bonded to his skeleton.
He was designed to be the ultimate killing machine for
the covert Weapon X Project. This story goes beyond
most Wolverine stories, into the minds of the people
who experimented on him, rather than into Wolverine's mind. It also relates how Wolverine escapes and
goes into a rampage. It is a very dark and twisted tale,
and one of the most popular Wolverine stories of all
time. Larry Hama wrote the afterword.

X-Men/Mutants and Related

I'm actually a terrible pessimist. I don't believe that humans and mutants are
such good souls that they can live in harmony simply because that is the best way
to live. That just isn't realty. I dream of a world where humans and mutants live
in harmony, that much is true. But I know if it happens, it will be because the
alternative is so terrifying that we have no other real choice.—*Charles Xavier*

Kids are so important ... they can be hurt so easily, their potential twisted
and warped.—*Doug Ramsey, Cypher of the New Mutants*

Adams, Arthur, Chris Claremont, Walter Si-
monson, et al. *X-Men Legends Volume 3:
Arthur Adams*. New York: Marvel, 2003.
ISBN: 0785110469. Reprints *New Mutants
Special Edition 1*; *X-Men Annual 9–10, 12*;
Fantastic Four 347–349.

The New Mutants go to Asgard to find Storm.
Loki wants Storm to be his queen, and seeks to rule
the kingdom in Thor's absence. The X-Men also come
to lend a helping hand against Loki. Mojo, whose ratings have fallen, wants the X-Men back, so both the
X-Men and the New Mutants go up against him. The
X-Men go up against Teminus, and seek the aid of
the High Evolutionary in the Savage Land. When
the Fantastic Four is believed to be dead, a new Fantastic Four is formed with Ghost Rider, Wolverine,
Hulk, and Spider-Man. A runaway Skrull seeks a
powerful egg that will help fight against the Skrull
Empire. The Skrull pretends to be Sue Richards, and
holds Reed under her spell. The Heroes briefly team
up with the Mole Man, who also wants the egg.

In this volume, Longshot makes his first appearance with the X-Men. It also has Fantastic Four
thumbnail sketches, and an introduction by Authur
Adams. This volume features the art of Adams.

Adams, Neal, Roy Thomas, Dennis O' Neil, et
al. *X-Men Visionaries Volume 2: Neal Adams
Collection*. New York: Marvel, 2000. ISBN:
0785101985. Reprints *Uncanny X-Men
56–63; 65*.

The original X-Men help save Alex Summers from
the Egyptian professor who seeks to utilize Summers's
powers to become the Living Monolith. Larry Trask,

the son of Sentinel creator Bolivar Trask, creates a
new breed of mutant-hunting Sentinels. They capture Polaris, Iceman, Beast, the Vanisher, Blob, Banshee, Quicksilver, Scarlett Witch, and Toad, among
others. When it is learned that Larry is a mutant, the
Sentinels stop obeying his commands. Cyclops dresses
as Quicksilver, Jean Grey as Scarlett Witch, and the
Beast as Toad to defeat the Sentinels. Cyclops poses
a philosophical question which makes the computerized Sentinels lock themselves in a logical conundrum,
and they end up flying into the sun. Magneto, who is
found alive, is changing Savage Land natives into
powerful mutants. Ka-Zar and the X-Men team up to
fight Magneto. The Angel's life is saved by Magneto.
Professor X is found alive, and the story of how the
Changeling took his place is revealed. X-Men fight
with Havok, and Polaris joins their team against the
alien Z'nox. The Angel changes costumes numerous
times.

This collection also features material that the origin of Havok and the reptilian Sauron. It has cover
gallery, a sketch gallery of Neal Adams's unused pages
for the graphic novel *God Loves Man Kills*, an afterword by Tom Palmer, and an introduction by Neal
Adams.

Austen, Chuck, Kia Asamiya, J.D. Smith, et al.
Uncanny X-Men Vol. 2: Dominant Species.
New York: Marvel, 2003. ISBN: 07851113
28. Reprints *Uncanny X-Men 416–420*.

Juggernaut and Sammy, who are becoming friends,
visit Cain's old house. A former mutant prostitute,
Stacy, makes a pass at Nightcrawler. The X-Men investigate the killing of several humans, and find out
that wolf-like mutants from Corporation Lobo are responsible. Lobo is a company that Angel Warren

Worthington owns, but he knew nothing about the killings. Polaris comes to visit Havok in the X-Men's infirmary. The Lobos wound Paige, Warren, and Logan. Angel, who is still distraught over the death of Psylocke, realizes that he also has the healing factor in his blood. Nightcrawler has a crisis of faith.

Austen, Chuck, Jim Calafiore, Mark McKenna, et al. *Exiles Vol. 7: Blink in Time.* New York: Marvel, 2004. ISBN: 0785112359. Reprints *Exiles 38–45.*

Blink comes back to the Exiles. The Weapon-X group, under Hyperion, try to take over various worlds they are sent to. The Tallus tells the Exiles that only six mutants will be allowed to continue fixing timelines. Vision, Magneto, Quicksilver, Magick, and other mutants are killed. Carol Danvers and Hyperion sleep together. Morph is upset at Mimic's killing of Sunfire. Morph gets to leave the Exiles, but opts to stay with the group. They go up against Apocalypse, and Cyclops leads his band of evil mutants against his former team.

In this volume we learn about Nocturne's past with the X-Men of her reality.

Austen, Chuck, Ron Garney, Philip Tan, et al. *Uncanny X-Men Vol. 3: Holy War.* New York: Marvel, 2003. ISBN: 0785111336. Reprints *Uncanny X-Men 421–427.*

Polaris tries to get Havok to marry her, but on the eve of their wedding Alex realizes that he is in love with his nurse, Annie. Polaris goes berserk, and puts on a costume like the one Magneto wore. It takes Juggernaut to stop her. Juggernaut joins the X-Men, and becomes very distraught when Alpha Flight takes his friend Sammy back to Canada. The anti-mutant Church of Humanity puts several X-Men, including Jubilee and Skin, on crosses in front of Xavier's school, and leaves them for dead. The X-Men investigate this atrocity, which leads them to Church of Humanity headquarters. Nightcrawler gives up his priesthood. Skin is killed, and Angel uses his blood to help heal sick children, including the child of a mutant-hating father.

This volume is highly recommended.

Austen, Chuck, Clayton Henry, Mark Morales, et al. *Exiles Vol. 5: Unnatural Instincts.* New York: Marvel, 2004. ISBN: 078511107. Reprints *Exiles 26–30. X-Men Unlimited 41.*

The Exiles are sent to kill the Avengers who are trying to stop Moses Magnum from taking over. Several Exiles object to helping the bad guys, so Magik does the dirty job of killing the Avengers. They are then transported to the regular Marvel Universe's world of the Uncanny X-Men, to stop an evil version of Havok from killing two mutant children. The Lobo Wolves make an appearance, and try to get the young mutant wolf-boy Nicholas to join their ranks. The Lobos rip Morph's arm off, and beat up Wolverine

and Husk. Nightcrawler meets his daughter, Nocturne, who destroys the evil version of Havok. Archangel ends up with one of Magik's swords, and admits his love for Hulk.

Watching Juggernaut become one of the X-Men is a gas. The volume also contains a short story that features Blink, Nocturne, and Wolverine who destroy the Spider god, and befriend a young Peter Parker. This is the best volume in the *Exiles* series.

Austen, Chuck, Salvador Larroca, Ron Garney, et al. *Uncanny X-Men Vol. 6: Bright New Morning.* New York: Marvel, 2004. ISBN: 0785114068. Reprints *Uncanny X-Men 435–436, 442–443; New X-Men 155–156.*

She-Hulk is hired to defend Juggernaut who is put on trial by the Canadian government, and they end up sleeping together. A false Juggernaut tries to claim the mantle of the true Juggernaut, but he turns out to be just a kid wearing the Juggernaut costume. The Rhino breaks out of prison, and Juggy helps the police restrain him. At the grave of Jean Grey, Cyclops and Emma Frost kiss. Cyclops wants to give up the school for mutants, but Emma wants to rebuild it. In Salem Center, mutant hysteria has become violent. The Cuckoos are saved by Emma Frost, and Cyclops and Beast lend them a hand, but one of their boyfriends is killed. Xavier goes back to Genoshia with Wolverine, to bury Magneto. Polaris tells Quicksilver and the Scarlet Witch that she is their sister. Wolverine rips out part of Toad's tongue. Nick Fury makes an appearance.

Austen, Chuck, Salvador Larroca, Danny Miki, et al. *Uncanny X-Men Vol. 5: She Lies with Angels.* New York: Marvel, 2004. ISBN: 0785111964. Reprints *Uncanny X-Men 431–437.*

The Guthrie family, which has mutant members, Cannonball and Husk, has been the object of persecution by the Cabot family, in a feud that has gone on for several decades. Julia Cabot is in love with Josh Guthrie, a mutant with wings. They love each other, but are afraid of reprisals. The Cabots put together Sentinel-like robots to try and destroy the Guthries and the X-Men who are visiting. Wolverine and Angel put aside their differences, and have a heart-to-heart. Warren Worthington, Angel, declares his love for Paige Guthrie, Husk. The story ends in a tragedy when Julia loses her life. X-Men, Nightcrawler and Polaris make appearances.

This is a Romeo-and-Juliet–style tale, which takes place in Cumberland, Kentucky.

Austen, Chuck, Phillip Tan, Takeshi Miyazawa, et al. *Uncanny X-Men Vol. 4: The Draco.* New York: Marvel, 2004. ISBN: 0785111 344. Reprints *Uncanny X-Men 428–434.*

Nightcrawler finds out his father is from another dimension, calls himself Azazel, and claims to be Satan. He learns that he apparently has other siblings.

Several X-Men go with Nightcrawler to the other dimension and have dinner with Azazel, which leads to disastrous results. Professor X and the human nurse Annie take a trip through Polaris's mind, and discover what made her go insane. Xavier and Cain Marko have a heart-to-heart about their life together as children. Marko goes to Canada with Northstar to check on his mutant friend Sammy, and things turn out badly when the Juggernaut discovers that Sammy is being beaten by his father. Juggernaut goes on a rampage, fights with Alpha Flight, and destroys Sammy's house. Sammy's mother is caught in the crossfire. Parts of the house fall on her, and she appears to be dead.

Austen, Chuck, Patrick Zircher, Larry Stucker, et al. *X-Men 2: Official Comic Book Adaptation*. New York: Marvel, 2003. ISBN: 078511162X. Reprints *X2 Movie Adaptation*; *X2 Movie Prequel Wolverine*; *X2 Movie Prequel Nightcrawler*.

Wolverine gets into a fight with Sabretooth, and sets Sabretooth on fire. They end up sharing a beer together after the fight, and are captured by a group of covert-operations thugs. The thugs refer to Sabretooth and Wolverine as experiments. Sabretooth dumps Wolverine out of an airplane. Nightcrawler is working in a circus, and falls in love with Amanda, the girl he grew up with, only to find out that their love relationship was just an illusion created by Stryker. Nightcrawler is captured by Stryker, and is put under a mind-control spell to assassinate the president.

This is a very loosely adapted version of the *X-2* movie in comic-book form. It includes two prequels to the movie, one featuring Wolverine, and the other featuring Nightcrawler.

Bedard, Tony, Mizuki Sakabibara, Jim Calafiore, et al. *Exiles Vol. 8: Earn Your Wings*. New York: Marvel, 2004. ISBN: 0785114599. Reprints *Exiles 46–51*.

Namora is brought into the Exiles team, and they are sent to the Marvel Universe proper. The Exiles go up against Namor and the Fantastic Four. Beak ends up leaving his family and becomes an Exile, but Nocturne is left behind. The Exiles have to free the Impossible Man from the Controller's mind control. Mystique, posing as Blink, deceives the Exiles into freeing a serial-killer version of Mimic and his Brotherhood of Evil Mutants. After coming in contact with the Exiles' Mimic, the evil Mimic changes his mode of thinking, and brings the Brotherhood on the right path.

This is an excellent series.

Bendis, Brian Michael, David Finch, Art Thiebert, et al. *Ultimate X-Men Vol. 8: New Mutants*. New York: Marvel, 2004. ISBN: 078511161. Reprints *Ultimate X-Men 40–45*.

Professor X brings Warren Worthington, the Angel, into his school. Many people believe he is a real angel from God, and they start a cult. A young mutant, whose powers started to manifest themselves inadvertently kills a whole town. Wolverine finds him, and the young mutant asks Wolverine to kill him. The president recruits a mutant education group featuring the Beast, who leaves Xavier's school; Havok; the White Queen; Karma; and Dazzler. A high-ranking general, who disagrees with giving mutants any headway, believes that Professor X is controlling the president. He tries to assassinate the president and the mutant group during a press conference. He brings out the Sentinels who cause a riot that results in the death of the Beast.

See "Vaughn" for Volume 9.

Bennett, Richard, Eliot Brown, Michael Golden, et al. *X-Men Survival Guide to the Mansion*. New York: Marvel, 1993.

This spiral-bound book is a guide to the inner workings of the X-Men mansion. Chapters include: X-Men Code of Ethics; X-Men Gear; sucurity; Layout of the Mansion; Hanger and Combat Operations; Cerebro and the Ready Room; Medical Lab; Danger Room; Muir Island; Massachusetts Academy; and What to Do in Case of Emergency. The introduction is by Professor X, aka Charles Xavier.

Bollers, Karl, Randy Green, Rick Ketcham, et al. *Emma Frost: Higher Learning*. New York: Marvel, 2004. ISBN: 0785114343. Reprints *Emma Frost 1–6*.

Emma Frost goes to an elite girls' school for the very wealthy. She falls in love with one of her teachers, but her father makes sure that this teacher is fired. Against her father's wishes, Emma wants to be a school teacher. Her father seeks to control every aspect of his family's lives. When it is revealed that her brother Christian is gay, her father gets Christian's partner sent to jail on drug charges, and sends Christian to a mental hospital. When Emma finds out that her father is having an affair, she exposes him, but it has no effect, and when Emma touches her mother, she falls into a coma-like state for a brief time.

This is the first series that tells the background history of Emma Frost, and how she first realized she had special powers. *Emma Frost* Volumes 2 and 3 (ISBN: 078511413; 0785114734)

Casey, Joe, Ian Churchill, Sean Philips, et al. *X-Men: Poptopia*. New York: Marvel, 2001. ISBN: 0785108017. Reprints *Uncanny X-Men 394–399*.

Chamber gets involved with a young pop star, Sugar Kane, who is always having the press hound her. When it is insinuated that she is pregnant with his baby, she dumps him. Nightcrawler, ArcAngel, Iceman, and Wolverine go to London, and encounter the mutant-slaughtering Mr. Clean. They also encounter a group of skinheads who are looking for a fight. Iceman stops them cold. Angel puts the lights out on a mutant brothel that his company was funding.

This book contains several X-Men stories which are told in tabloid style.

Casey, Joe, Steve Rude, Paul Smith, et al. *X-Men: Children of the Atom.* Marvel Comics: New York, 2001. ISBN: 078510805X. Reprints X-*men: Children of the Atom: 1–6.*

The FBI starts to do experiments on mutants, with the approval of hatemonger William Metzger. Hank McCoy becomes involved in the death of one of his classmates. Magneto also begins to recruit for his group, and even tries to get Warren Worthington, the Angel, to join with him. Jean Grey is captured, and would have been killed, were it not for the power of a mutant who heals.

This book provides a new take on how the original X-Men team was formed, consisting of Marvel Girl, Beast, Iceman, Cyclops, and Angel. The characters are high school students who learn about their mutant powers, and the prejudice the general populace has toward them. The author uses the early tales of Cyclops, Iceman and the others to craft a unique tale of how the X-Men came to be. There also is a sketchbook in this terrific tale of the original team.

Claremont, Chris, Arthur Adams, Terry Austin, et al. *Excalibur: Mojo Mayhem.* New York: Marvel, 1989. ISBN: 0871356252.

The X-Babies are on the run from Mojo's Agent, and come to Earth. Kitty Pryde seeks the aid of Excalibur to help her and the X-Babies. The X-Babies agree to be stars on Mojo's program, but only on their terms.

Reprinted in *Excalibur Classic Vol. 2* (ISBN: 07851 2201X).

Claremont, Chris, Arthur Adams, Scott Lobdell, et al. *X-Men Danger Room Battle Archives.* New York: Marvel, 1996. ISBN: 0785101950. Reprints *Incredible Hulk Annual 7*; *Uncanny X-Men Annual 3, 10, 17*; *New Mutants Annual 2.*

This collection features various X-Men in some of their biggest battles. The New Mutants go to Mojo's other-dimensional world. Captain Britain is reduced to a whimpering child, and it is up to Cypher and Warlock to save the New Mutants. Psylocke shares part of her being with Cypher. On a spaceship, the Hulk, Angel, and Iceman battle a bizarre Sentinel with a sense of humanity. Arkon kidnaps Storm to help save his other-dimensional world. The X-Men also lend a hand, but Mojo transforms them into X-Babies, and they have to fight the New Mutants who come to rescue them. Mastermind, who is dying, has Jean Grey, Bishop, and Iceman in his spell. Storm, Archangel, and Colossus have to contend with a being who calls himself the X-cutioner and is bent on destroying Mastermind.

Alan Davis wrote the introduction.

Claremont, Chris, Brent Eric Anderson, Tom Orzechowski, et al. *X-Men: God Loves, Man Kills.* New York: Marvel, 1994. ISBN: 0785100393; 0939766221 (1983).

An anti-mutant crusader, the Rev. William Stryker, uses the name of God to justify his racism and violence against mutants. His followers, the Purifiers, are slaughtering mutants. Stryker eventually gets shot while attempting to shoot Kitty Pryde.

This tale is one of the most intense, and relevant, X-Men stories. It is a "must have" for any fan of the X-Men and Marvel. In it, Magneto almost sways Professor X to his way of thinking. *Marvel Graphic Novel 5.*

Claremont, Chris, Juan Bobillo, Marcelo Sosa, et al. *Xtreme X-Men Vol. 4: Mekanix.* New York: Marvel, 2003. Reprints *Mekanix 1–6*; *X-Men Unlimited 36.*

Kitty Pryde, Shadowcat, is in college in Deerfield, a Chicago suburb. She has a hard time dealing with the racism against mutants, and ends up hitting several students who support the racist organization Purity. Because of her outburst, she is required to go to see a shrink. Kitty and several mutant friends, including Karma, have to fend off intelligent Sentinels who are trying to kill them. The Sentinels end up destroying the college's student union.

Claremont, Chris, Jon Bogdanove, Terry Austin, et al. *Fantastic Four vs. the X-Men.* New York: Marvel. 1994. ISBN: 0871356503. Reprints *Fantastic Four vs. The X-Men 1–4.*

Franklin Richards dreams that his father, Mr. Fantastic, and Dr. Doom are the same, and that Richards's diary revealed that he intended to have his ship go through the cosmic rays, and mutate Sue, Johnny and Ben. Sue finds the diary and reads that Reed apparently did know about the dangers of cosmic rays before they made their journey. This leads Reed to doubt everything his life is based on. Ben Grimm takes this news very hard, and feels betrayed by Richards. When the X-Men ask him to use his invention to help save Kitty Pryde's life, his insecurities stop him from helping her. The Fantastic Four and She-Hulk fight with the X-Men. Johnny Storm singes Storm's arm, and burns her badly. Magneto tries to gains the Fantastic Four's trust, and Dr. Doom offers to help the X-Men save Kitty from phasing into infinity. The X-Men go to Latveria, and take Doom up on his offer to help, despite their misgivings about his motives. During his dream state, Franklin visits Kitty with his astral projection. Reed must get over his insecurities and help Kitty, because Doom may actually do more damage than good.

This book is beautifully written. It has intense drama, human frailty, and good battle sequences.

Claremont, Chris, John Bolton, Tom Orzechowski, et al. *X-Men: Vignettes.* New

York: Marvel, 2001. ISBN: 0785108122. Reprints *Classic X-Men 1–13*.

This book contains stories detailing the day-to-day life situations of the X-Men. It includes Wolverine's first kiss with Jean Grey, Tag with Sabretooth, Storm dealing with her claustrophobia in the New York subways, Xavier's insecurities, and Cyclops's jealousy. It is a fun book of stand-alone stories.

Claremont, Chris, John Byrne, Terry Austin, et al. *X-Men Days of Future Past*. Marvel Comics: New York, 2000. ISBN: 0871355 825. Reprints *Uncanny X-Men Vol. 1: 141– 142*.

Kitty Pryde travels back into time to prevent a significant assassination, the repercussions of which spell the X-Men's and mutants' future doom. Mystique brings together the second Brotherhood of Evil Mutants.
This is a Small Bookshelf edition.

Claremont, Chris, John Byrne, Terry Austin, et al. *X-Men Days of Future Past*. New York: Marvel, 2004. ISBN: 0785115609. Reprints *Uncanny X-Men 138–143; X-Men Annual 4; Essential X-Men 3* (back cover); *Classic X-Men 44–47; Days of Future Past Bookshelf* (both covers).

Cyclops leaves the X-Men after Jean Grey's funeral. With Dr. Strange's help, the X-Men go to a hell that is based on *Dante's Inferno*. Nightcrawler, Wolverine, and Alpha Flight go up against the Wendigo. Because a presidential candidate is assassinated by the second Brotherhood of Evil Mutants, mutant hysteria affects the future. When the Sentinels are given carte blanche to take over the world, super-powered beings are killed. Kitty Pryde goes back in time to stop the assassination, and on Christmas Eve she is left alone at the X-Mansion where she has to fight a demon. Professor X brings her parents for a visit.
This book is a celebration of the work of the Claremont/Byrne team on the X-Men comics, which includes the famous "Days of Future Past" storyline, *X-Men 138*. It contains a complete history of the X-Men up to that point.

Claremont, Chris, John Byrne, Terry Austin, et al. *X-Men Legends Vol. 2: Dark Phoenix Saga*. New York: Marvel, 2003. ISBN 0939766965; Reprints *Uncanny X-Men 129–137*.

Jean Grey becomes her alter ego, the Dark Phoenix, due to a freak accident in space. Dark Phoenix has the power to incinerate worlds, and proves to be a worthy adversary to the X-Men. This volume, which was first published in 1984, includes appearances by the Hellfire Club, Dazzler, and the White Queen, among others.

Claremont, Chris, John Byrne, Terry Austin, et al. *X-Men Visionaries: Chris Claremont*. New York: Marvel, 1998. ISBN: 07851059 80. Reprints *Uncanny X-Men 114, 153, 186, 198, 268; Kitty Pryde and Wolverine 4; New Mutants 45; Excalibur 16*.

This is a collection of some of Chris Claremont's most famous one-shot X-Men stories, which he personally picked for the book, including an appearance by Captain America. Each story has a separate introduction. The collection was originally published as a hardback in the Marvel Limited series.

Claremont, Chris, Alan Davis, Dan Green, et al. *X-Men: Old Soldiers*. New York: Marvel, 2004. ISBN: 0785114637. Reprints *Uncanny X-Men 213, 215. 445; X-Men Annual 11; New Mutants Annual 11, 12; X-Men Fall of the Mutants; X-Men Danger Room Battle Archives*.

The New Mutants go to Mojo's other-dimensional world to save Psylocke. Captain Britain is also there. Cypher and Warlock become one. Warlock and the Impossible Man battle each other throughout the world. Sabretooth comes to Xavier Mansion to kill all the wounded mutants, and Psylocke diverts him until Wolverine shows up. Psylocke joins the X-Men. Storm fights a bunch of crazy World War II vets— Stonewall, Super Sabre, and Crimson Commando— in a dangerous game of cat and mouse. Horde gets the X-Men to find the Crystal of Ultimate Vision which bestows godhood. Wolverine experiences the cosmic awareness, and destroys the Crystal.

Claremont, Chris, Alan Davis, Scott Hanna, et al. *Uncanny X-Men: The New Age Vol. 1: The End of History*. New York: Marvel, 2004. ISBN: 0785115358. Reprints *Uncanny X-Men 444–449*.

One of the X-Men teams is now a world police force whose job it is to stop hostile mutants. Storm is the leader along with Sage, Nightcrawler, Bishop, Marvel Girl, and Cannonball. The X-Men play baseball, and Emma Frost and Rachel Grey get into a fight. Nightcrawler and Storm go out on a date. Bishop, Marvel Girl and Cannonball go to visit Captain Britain at Braddock Manor and find the robotic Fury there, waiting for them. Fury gets patched into Sage's feeds, and transformers her into an unstoppable machine that nearly destroys the X-Men. Through force of will, she purges Fury. Viper puts together her version of Murderworld, with revenge against Sage. Sage is seemingly killed in front of Viper, but it is actually Wolverine using the image inducer. Captain Britain and Sebastian Shaw make appearances.

Claremont, Chris, Alan Davis, Paul Neary, et al. *Excalibur: Sword Is Drawn*. New York: Marvel, 1988. ISBN: 0871353377.

Kitty Pryde is having nightmares. Rachel Summers is on the run from a being from another dimension, Gatecrasher, who reveals herself to be an agent from the Omniversal Majestrix. Rachel, Phoenix, is also on the run from Mojoverse's Warwolves, who intend to return her to Mojo. In order to save Shadowcat and Captain Britain's girlfriend Meggan, Nightcrawler and Captain Britain team up. Britain drowns himself in booze because of his sister's death. When the team defeats Gatecrasher's thugs, Excalibur is born.

Reprinted in 2006 in *Excalibur Classic Vol. 1* (ISBN: 0785118888).

Claremont, Chris, Michael Golden, Dave Cockrum, et al. *X-Men: Spider Man: Savage Land*. New York: Marvel, 2002. ISBN: 0785108912. Original ed., *The Savage Land* 1987. ISBN: 0871353385. Reprints *Marvel Fanfare 1–4*.

Spider-Man and the Angel go to the Savage Land to help find Kurt Lykos. Spider-Man and Angel are captured by Brainchild's machine, and turned into mutant beasts. Ka-Zar helps free them, and Lykos uses his energy-siphoning power to turn them back into their respective selves. As a result, Sauron is reborn, and the Angel requests help from the X-Men to stop Sauron. The X-Men are quickly taken hostage and transformed into beasts, and Ka-Zar and the Angel have to rescue them from Sauron's clutches. Professor X finds a cure for the Pteranodons virus which resulted in Lykos turning into Sauron.

Claremont, Chris, Igor Kordey, Greg Adams, et al. *X-treme X-Men Vol. 8: Prisoner of Fire*. New York: Marvel, 2004. ISBN: 078511 351. Reprints *X-Treme X-Men 40–46*; *X-Treme X-Men Annual 2001*.

Elias Bogan is doing his best to destroy the X-Men, and he takes Bishop prisoner. Sage, who is still distrusted by several collogues, leads the X-Men to Bogan's hideout, and Shadowcat is brought in to help. Various battles occur on the mental plane, and Bogan loses. Sunspot and Magma also are brought in. Bogan's empath is actually Rachael Summers, Young Phoenix. She was the one being used as a conduit for Bogan's revenge against the X-Men. Bogan's history with the Hellfire Club is revealed when several X-Men go into his underground headquarters and torch the place. Storm returns from Asia with Callisto, and makes the X-Men X-Marshalls. They also go up against the Shadow King, and it is learned that Bishop is related to Gateway. Gambit gets his powers back, and the Angel and Storm put aside their past differences, and bond as friends. Other New Mutants make appearances, and Rachel Summers changes her handle to Marvel Girl.

This is the best graphic novel in the X-Treme X-Men series.

Claremont, Chris, Igor Kordey, Scott Hanna, et al. *X-Treme X-Men Vol. 5: God Loves Man Kills II*. New York: Marvel, 2003. ISBN: 078511254. Reprints *X-Treme X-Men 25–30*; *God Loves Man Kills*.

The anti-mutant crusader the Rev. William Stryker escapes from prison with the help of Lady Deathstrike, and kidnaps Kitty Pryde from her job in Chicago. The X-Men Storm Bishop, Cannonball, Sage, and Wolverine go to Mount Haven, Washington, a secret town filled with mutant children, but no adults. Stryker's counterpart, the Rev. Paul, oversees the town in which only mutants are allowed to live, and humans are destroyed. In the town, the nannite virus, microbial machines that work on the central nervous system, affect the mutants' brainwaves, and make them slaves to nannite programming. Kitty and Bishop end up destroying the machines, and the Rev. Stryker merges with the Rev. Paul. The mutant children die when the nannite programming is destroyed. Deathstrike fights both Wolverine and Cannonball, and is supposedly killed.

This is the highly anticipated sequel to the original 1982 graphic novel. It includes the original, excellent "God Loves, Man Kills" story a bonus. It is a worthy sequel.

Claremont, Chris, Igor Kordey, Scott Hanna, et al. *X-treme X-Men Vol. 7: Storm the Arena*. New York: Marvel, 2004. ISBN: 078510 9366. Reprints *X-treme X-Men 36–39*.

Storm takes a vacation to Japan, and becomes involved in a high-dollar, mutant-fighting game called the Arena. Storm wins, but things are not always what they seem. Strong Guy, Guido, tries to warn Storm before it is too late, but Storm finds out on her own when she has to fight Callisto. Masque and cenobite-like minions try to take control of Storm and Callisto, forcing them to fight for Masque's amusement. Masque forces Storm to kill her friend Yukio, and Storm and Callisto team up to try to circumvent Masque's plans.

Claremont, Chris, Igor Kordey, Salvador Larroca, et al. *X-treme X-Men Vol. 6: Intifada*. New York: Marvel, 2004. ISBN: 07851123 08. Reprints *X-Treme X-Men 24, 31–35*.

Cannonball helps find people caught in the tunnel wreckage between England and France, after the Weapon Plus train is wrecked. Several mutant children caused a car carrying regular humans to wreck. The mutants are taken to court, but get off on a special discrimination plea. Although Rogue has lost her powers, she has lost none of her spunk and vigor. The Los Angeles branch of X-Corp is involved in unsavory activities, and Rogue crashes a party given by Sunspot. Elias Bogan is using Empath as a pawn in X-Corp, and plans to use the X-Men, especially Sage. Storm and Gambit go to a party where various political officials, including George Bush and Dick Cheney, are discussing the mutant problem. Gambit makes a pass at Storm.

Claremont, Chris, Salvador Larroca, Tom Orzechowski, et al. *X-Treme X-Men Vol. 1.* New York: Marvel, 2002. ISBN: 0785108416. Reprints *X-Treme X-Men 1–9.*

The X-Men go on a search for Destiny's books of prophecy. Psylocke and the new Thunderbird, Neal Shaara, have a little romance going. Vargas, who believes he is going to die at the hands of the X-Men, almost defeats them, and kills Psylocke in the process. Beast is almost mortally wounded, and Gambit is framed for a murder he did not commit.

The mutant Lifeguard is introduced in this volume, as are glimpses of Rogue's and Sage's pasts.

Claremont, Chris, Salvador Larroca, Tom Orzechowski, et al. *X-Treme X-Men Vol. 2: Invasion.* New York: Marvel, 2003. ISBN: 0785110186. Reprints *X-Treme X-Men 10–18.*

A group of dimension-conquering aliens led by Khan takes over Madripoor, using Gambit as an energy conduit. Storm is taken prisoner, and Khan asks her to be his queen. Rogue asks Sage to up her mutant powers so that every superbeing she touches will become manifest. Vargus is defeated by Rogue. As her powers manifest, Lifeguard learns she is actually of Shi'ar descent. Her brother, who is also a mutant, considers her a freak and rejects her.

Claremont, Chris, Salvador Larroca, Arthur Ranson, et al. *X-Treme X-Men Vol. 3: Schism.* New York: Marvel, 2003. ISBN: 0785110844. Reprints *X-Treme X-Men 19–23*; *X-Treme X-Men: X-Pose 1–2.*

Rogue and Gambit, who have lost their powers, take a road trip together. Storm is undergoing physical therapy under the care of Wolverine. Two television reporters interview a number of the X-Men to get their story on the rising mutant population. The television station wants to turn it into a negative expose on mutants, but the Angel, Warren Worthington, uses his influence to get the program squelched. Bishop and Sage investigate an unusual mutant murder, and find the suspect at Xavier's school. Emma Frost, the headmaster of the school, does not give them a warm welcome. A very powerful mutant, Elias Bogan, is behind the murders, and tries to get Storm, Emma Frost, and the young mutants at the school caught in his web of control.

Claremont, Chris, Jim Lee, Louise Simonson, et al. *X-Men: X-tinction Agenda.* New York: Marvel, 2001. ISBN: 0871359227. Reprints *Uncanny X-Men 270–272*; *X-Factor 60–62*; *New Mutants 95–97.*

Several of the New Mutants are kidnapped and taken to the Genosha. Cameron Hodge becomes a cyborg with a head. He enjoys torturing mutants, and with the Genegineer, Dr. Moraru, he turns mutants

into mindless servants of the state. Warlock is killed and Wolfsbane is turned into a mutant with no recollection of the New Mutants. The X-Men and X-Factor, along with Cable, go to Genosha to rescue them, and end up being caught. The X-Men are put on trial and end up being called enemies of the state. Eventually, through the help of Storm and Forge, they break free, and have a showdown with Hodge.

This is a weird but excellent tale.

Claremont, Chris, Jim Lee, Scott Williams, et al. *X-Men Legends Vol. I: Mutant Genesis.* New York: Marvel, 2002. ISBN: 0785108955. Reprints *X-Men Vol. 2: 1–7.*

Magneto organizes his fanatical followers the Acolytes, who are out for revenge against mankind. Fabian Cortez uses Magneto who takes revenge against Moria McTaggert for his own agenda. The X-Men split into two teams; several seem to join Magneto's cause. The X-Men also fight against Omega Red and Sabretooth, and Wolverine is captured.

This volume contains the launch of the second ongoing X-Men series, *New X-Men 1*, which was one of the most popular comics of all time.

Claremont, Chris, Scott Lobdell, Salvador Larroca, et al. *X-Men: Dreams End.* New York: Marvel, 2004. ISBN: 07851155X. Reprints *Giant Size X-Men 1*; *Uncanny X-Men 388–390*; *Cable 87*; *Bishop 16*; *X-Men 108–110.*

The Brotherhood of Evil Mutants tries to assassinate Senator Kelly who is once again running for president. Cable is his body guard. Mystique and Sabretooth raid Muir Island, and nearly kill Mora McTaggert. The X-Men try to stop them, but Mora dies. Xavier goes into Mora's mind before her death to try to get information about the cure she was working on for the Legacy virus. Mystique stabs Rogue, and a mutant-hating human kills Kelly. The details of Xavier and Mora's early romance are finally revealed. Based on the research Mora did, Henry McCoy is able to synthesize a cure for the Legacy virus. Colossus tests it on himself and dies from it, but the cure works after it is released into the atmosphere. The X-Men break into teams, and Storm leads one of them. Kitty Pryde reminisces about her love for Colossus, and leaves the X-Men to go to college.

This book has a two-page reprint of the first appearance of Colossus.

Claremont, Chris, Aaron Lopresti, Greg Adams, et al. *Excalibur Vol. 1: Forging the Sword.* New York: Marvel, 2004. ISBN: 0785115527. Reprints *Excalibur 1–4.*

Professor X is left in the war-torn and ravaged land of Genosha. He is left with the dead body of Magneto who it turns out was an imposter; the real Magneto and Xavier start to work together. Some of the mutants left on Genosha try to kill Professor X, but the mutants known as Wicked and Freakshow save him. Former Genoshan Magistrates try to kill all the mutants who are left by using a bio-organic Omega Sentinel. Xavier and Magneto save the Sentinel, and she helps them against the Magistrates. Storm sends Callisto to check on Professor X. Under Xavier's and Magneto's tutelage, Callisto, Wicked, Freakshow, the Omega Sentinel, and Synch help rebuild Genosha, and a new version of Excalibur is born.

I like the idea of Magneto and Xavier working together. This series has great potential (Vol. 2 ISBN: 0785114769)

Claremont, Chris, Simonson Louise, Mark Silvestri, et al. *X-Men: Inferno.* New York: Marvel, 2000. ISBN: 0785102221. Reprints *Uncanny X-Men 239–243*; *X-Factor 36–39*; *New Mutants 71–73*.

Madelyne Pryor, Cyclops's ex-wife, becomes the Goblin Queen and kidnaps their son. Sinister tells her that he created her as a clone of Jean Grey. Magick and the New Mutants witness countless horrors in Limbo where two demons are fighting to control her. Demons from Limbo are all over New York. At first, X-Men—who are under the Goblin Queen and the demon N'Astrih's spell—fight the X-Factor. Havok and Madelyne sleep together, and he becomes enchanted with her. As the Goblin Queen, Madelyne changes Jean Grey's parents into demons. Magick becomes Darkchilde, and, because of demons, various inanimate objects come alive and attack people. Mr. Sinister reveals to Cyclops his hand at work in Cyclops's early life, and the experiments he conducted on him. Cyclops blows Sinister to pieces.

This is a massive crossover volume.

Claremont, Chris, Bob McLeod. Tom Orzechowski, et al. *The New Mutants:* New York: Marvel, 1982. ISBN: 0939766205.

When Professor X thinks the X-Men have perished, he puts together a team of young mutants to carry on this dream. These include Rahne Sinclair, Roberto De Costa, Cannonball, Moonstar, and Karma. They stop Donald Pierce who kidnaps Professor X and tries to kill them. The young mutants learn the value of team work, and thus the New Mutants team is born.

This was reprinted in *New Mutants Classic* in 2006 (ISBN: 0785121943). (*Marvel Graphic Novel 4*)

Claremont, Chris, Whilce Portacio, Klaus Janson, et al. *X-Men: Crossroads.* New York: Marvel, 1998. ISBN: 0785106626. Reprints *Uncanny X-Men 273–277*.

Magneto, Rogue, Nick Fury, and Ka-Zar team up in the Savage Land to defeat Zaladane. The X-Men are transported to Shi'ar space to meet their mentor, Professor X. Wolverine kills Xavier. The X-Men unravel a plot by War Skrulls to take over the Shi'ar Empire where Xavier and Starjammers are held captive. Deathbird is the heroine of the tale.

Claremont, Chris, John Romita Jr., Dan Green, et al. *X-Men: Mutant Massacre.* New York: Marvel, 2001. ISBN: 0785102248. Reprints *Uncanny X-Men 210–212*; *New Mutants 46*; *Mighty Thor 373–374*; *Power Pack 27*; *X-Factor 9–11*.

A mutant-hunting group of assassins, the Marauders, go through the Morlock tunnels and exterminate everyone in sight. The X-Men try to stop the Marauders. When a young mutant boy whom X-Factor has been looking after goes into the tunnels to try to help, and meets with Leech, X-Factor goes looking for them. The Angel is left for dead, and his wings are pinned to a wall with ice picks. He is discovered by Thor who helps fight against several Marauders. The Power Pack also goes to the Morlock tunnels to help, and ends up fighting Sabretooth. The news comes out that X-Factor is financially backed by mutant Warren Worthington. Nightcrawler, Shadowcat, and Colossus are seriously wounded. X-Factor skirmishes with a version of the Brotherhood of Evil Mutants, now the government-sponsored Freedom Force. Magneto, who has supposedly reformed and is superintendent of the Xavier School, saves Colossus's life. Sabretooth has several showdowns with Wolverine, and, while Psylocke is watching over Xavier Mansion, Sabretooth infiltrates it. Psylocke becomes a full-fledged X-Man.

Claremont, Chris, Kevin Sharpe, Danny Miki, et al. *X-treme X-Men: Savage Land.* New York: Marvel, 2002. ISBN: 0785108912. Reprints *X-treme X-Men: Savage Land 1–4*.

In this book, the X-treme X-Men team, which features Storm, Bishop, Beast, Sage, Rogue, and Thunderbird, goes to the Savage Land to try to stop a race war between the Saurids and the humans. This series marks Chris Claremont's return to writing X-Men comics, after a lengthy absence.

Claremont, Chris, Bill Sienkiewicz, Tom Orzechowski, et al. *The New Mutants: The Demon Bear Saga.* New York: Marvel, 1990. ISBN: 0871356732. Reprints *New Mutants 18–21*.

Dani Moonstar encounters the spirit bear that killed her parents and wants to kill her. She ends up in the hospital after from her fight with the "demon bear." The New Mutants go to the spirit plane of the bear, and try to defeat it. Dani's parents, who were being held captive by the spirit, are returned to the earthly dimension. The techo-organic alien Warlock crashes to Earth, seeking escape from his world and sanctuary with the New Mutants. Professor X welcomes Warlock into the school.

Claremont, Chris, Marc Silvestri, et al. *X-Men vs. the Brood.* New York: Marvel, 1998. ISBN: 0785105581. Reprints *Uncanny X-Men 232–234* also published as *X-Men*

Earthfall; X-Men vs. Brood Day of Wrath 1–2.

The Brood crashes on Earth and lays eggs in mutant hosts, creating a super-powered Brood. The X-Men try to prevent the Brood from taking over the Earth, and in the process they realize that they must kill the Brood and their human hosts. The X-Men are caught in the middle of a war in which Brood assassins are trying to kill a renegade Brood Queen, Hannah. The Brood Queen is actually the wife of a prominent Christian preacher. The Queen's human side is emerging and rebelling against the Brood insider her, even though she created a Brood army. The X-Men try to save the human part of Hannah. The minister never loses faith in God throughout this ordeal.

Claremont, Chris, Marc Silvestri, Dan Green, et al. *X-Men: Fall of the Mutants.* New York: Marvel, 2001. Reprints *Uncanny X-Men 225–227; X-Factor 24–26; New Mutants 59–61.*

The X-Men fight disaster in Dallas, and go up against the Adversary. X-Factor goes up against Apocalypse and the Four Horsemen in New York. Warren Worthington is becomes ArchAngel, and the New Mutants go up against Dr. Animus on an isolated island. Animus is creating mutant/human/animal creations, similar to those of Dr. Moreau in the Wells novel. Cypher is killed.

Claremont, Chris, Paul Smith, Bob Wiacek, et al. *X-Men/Alpha Flight The Gift Vol. 2: 1.* New York: Marvel, 1998. Reprints *X-Men/Alpha Flight 1–2.*

Loki is asked to do one selfless act. When Scott Summers's plane is downed mysteriously, Rachel Summers has a vision of her father dying. The X-Men go to Canada, and Rachel attacks Alpha Flight. They eventually team up to figure out what happened. They find a virtual paradise in which disease can be eliminated and the world can be freed from famine through the use of magical beings. Cyclops and his wife Madelyne Pryor have been transformed into powerful, magical beings. The X-Men and Alpha Flight are also cured of their various problems, but all is not as it appears to be. The Shaman gets very sick and almost dies, and Loki tries to force this "gift" upon the world.

Claremont, Chris, Paul Smith, Bob Wiacek, et al. *X-Men: Asgardian Wars.* New York: Marvel, 1988. ISBN: 0871354349. Reprints *X-Men: Alpha Fight 1–2; New Mutants: Special Edition 1; X-Men Giant Sized Annual 9.*

Loki tries to do a selfless deed, giving the X-Men the power of the gods in a special land. Warpath and Narya almost die because their type of magic cannot survive. The X-Men reject Loki's gift, and Loki loses favor with the high Asgardian gods. Loki kidnaps

Storm. The New Mutants and the X-Men go to Asgard to try and save her.

Claremont, Chris, Paul Smith, Bob Wiacek, et al. *X-Men: Dark Phoenix Returns: Backpack Marvels.* New York: Marvel, 2000. ISBN: 0785107649. Reprints *Uncanny X-Men 167–173.*

Cyclops marries Madelyne Pryor; Mariko rejects Wolverine; and the Brother of Evil Mutants battles the X-Men. The Morlocks return, and Kitty Pryde goes to live with Caliban. Mystique tries to get Rogue away from the X-Men with her version of the Brotherhood of Evil Mutants which features Destiny, Blob, and Avalanche. Colossus is frozen, and Mastermind uses Madelyne Pryor as a new Dark Phoenix.

Claremont, Chris, Paul Smith, Bob Wiacek., et al. *X-Men from the Ashes.* New York: Marvel, 1993. ISBN: 0871356155. Reprints *Uncanny X-Men 168–176.*

Shortly after Cyclops leaves the X-Men, he meets Madelyne Pryor who seems to be uncannily similar to Jean Grey. Some even think she might be Phoenix reborn. Mastermind uses the X-Men and Madelyne to recreate Dark Phoenix. Rogue joins the X-Men. Kitty Pryde proves herself worthy to be a member of the X-Men rather than a New Mutant. The Morlocks kidnap the Angel, and Storm fights their leader for control of the Morlocks and the Angel's freedom. Wolverine brings the X-Men over to Japan for his wedding to Mariko, who dumps him on their wedding day. Storm and Yukio, an old friend and lover of Wolverine's, start a friendship and have several fun fighting adventures. Wolverine and Rogue fight side-by-side against the Silver Samurai. Storm gets a punk rock haircut and suit. Cyclops and Madelyne Pryor get married.

Claremont, Chris, Paul Smith, Bob Wiacek, et al. *X-Men: Target Angel: Backpack Marvels.* New York: Marvel, 2000. ISBN: 07851076 30. Reprints *Uncanny X-Men 167–173.*

The X-Men return from fighting the Brood. Professer X tries to walk in a new, cloned body. The Morlocks appear for the first time. Their leader Callisto has kidnapped the Angel for her husband, and Storm fights Callisto for leadership of the Morlocks. Rogue is admitted to the X-Men. Wolverine is dumped by Mariko on their wedding day. Kitty Pryde is demoted to the New Mutants, and calls Professor X a jerk.

Claremont, Chris, Len Wein, Michael Golden, et al. *X-Men: Famous Firsts.* New York: Marvel, 1996. Reprints *Avengers Annual 10; Hulk 181; Uncanny X-Men 221, 266.*

This collection brings together the first appearances of Rogue, Mister Sinister, Gambit, and Wolverine. Each of these characters has gone on to play an important role in the world of the X-Men. Rogue was originally a member of the Brotherhood of Evil Mutants. Gambit saves a young Storm from the Shadow King. Mister Sinister tells his Marauders to kill Madelyne Pryor, and humbles Sabretooth. Wolverine battles the Hulk.

Conway, Gerry, Syd Shores, Tom Sutton, et al. *X-Men: Mutations.* New York: Marvel, 1996. ISBN: 0785101977. Reprints *Amazing Adventures 11, 17; X-Factor 15, 24–25; Uncanny X-Men 256–258.*

This is a collection of stories detailing important transformations in the lives of the X-Men. The Beast's origin is described, along with his transformation into the blue-furred version. In one episode, Apocalypse turns the Angel into Archangel, and, in another, the Mandarin turns Elizabeth Braddock into an assassin.

Davis, Alan, Jamie Delano, Steve Craddock, et al. *Captain Britain.* London: Marvel Comics Ltd., 1988. ISBN: 1854000209. Reprints *Mighty World of Marvel 14–16; Captain Britain 1–13.*

Captain Britain finds Meggan just before she is about to scare a vagrant. As Meggan begins to understand her powers, she changes from being quite hideous into a beautiful woman with whom Captain Britain falls in love. Kaptain Briton, who is from another dimension, beats the real Captain, and attempts to rape Betsy. Gatecrasher takes the real Captain to a Nazi-like world, where he is the lover of Saturnyne. Betsy kills Kaptain. Slaymaster uses the Crazy gang to lure Brian Braddock into a trap for Vixen who wants to know the secret of the Captain's costume. Inspector Thomas figures out that Brian Braddock and Captain Britain are one and the same. The computer Mastermind, of Braddock Manor, takes the role of the butler Jeeves, and takes control of the manor. Captain UK, from another dimension, helps the secret government agency Resources Control Executive, RCX, bring a group of deformed, mutant children to live in the manor. When Britain's brother Jamie is kidnapped, he learns of the horrible things his brother did. Captain UK teaches Betsy how to take on the mantel of Captain Britain, and Brian quits for a brief time. During a fight with Slaymaster, Betsy is blinded.

This volume documents Captain Britain's life before he joined Excalibur. It describes his early adventures with his sister Betsy (Psylocke) and the were-woman Meggan. Chris Claremont writes the introduction, and gives the history behind the character, "dipped in magic and clothed in science." This is an amazing book.

Davis, Alan, Mark Farmer, Sophie Heath. et al. *ClanDestine versus the X-Men.* New York: Marvel Comics, 1997. ISBN: 0785105573. Reprints *ClanDestine: 1–8; ClanDestine X-Men 1–2.*

The ClanDestine family is an old family with superpowers. It has tried to keep itself from the public

eye for centuries. The father, Adam, can neither age nor die, and the mother is a mystical being who was locked in a gem until freed by Adam. The family's younger twins try to break out and become superheroes, much to the dismay of their guardian and brother. The youngsters steal the Gryphon, which is being sought by two interested parties. One of them is a scientist who was experimented on by Modok and A.I.M., and who wants the Gryphon to preserve his "race." The twins escape and go to New York where Spider-Man teaches them a lesson in being superheroes. The ClanDestine and the X-Men team up against the demon Synraith who seeks to enslave the Earth. Xavier had met two of the Destine clan years ago when Synraith wanted to come to Earth, and Wolverine and Adam had known each other years ago. At first the two teams fight one another, and then they join together to defeat the entity. Dr. Strange and the Invaders also make an appearance. Since the X-Men only show up in the last story, the title is misleading. Many consider this and *Captain Britain* to be Alan Davis's masterworks. The book deserves to be reprinted.

Davis, Alan, Terry Kavanagh, Howard Mackie, et al. *Astonishing X-Men: Deathwish.* Marvel Comics: New York, 2000. ISBN: 07851 07541. Reprints *Astonishing X-Men: 1–3; X-Men: 92, 95, and Uncanny X-Men: 375.*

The X-Men's mentor Charles Xavier turns on his team, and they splinter into several factions. Phoenix receives a telepathic distress call from a young girl, Nina, created in a laboratory. Cyclops, Nate Grey, Wolverine, and Cable investigate, and find a destroyed Hulkbuster base, with Bastion's head. A Skrull infiltrates the X-Men, posing as Wolverine, but his real name is Death. He is killed at the Hulkbuster base. Professor X plays a mind game with the X-Men, pitting them against one another. Angel goes in search of Pyslocke, and the X-Men infiltrate the Skrull mutant project.

DeFalco, Tom, Roger Stern, Marc Silvestri, et al. *Avengers vs X-Men.* New York: Marvel, 1993. ISBN: 087135967. Reprints *X-Men versus the Avengers 1–4.*

Several pieces of Magneto's former outer-space stronghold fall as meteorites throughout the Earth. Magneto goes to investigate, as do the Avengers and the Soviet Super Soldiers. The X-Men follow Magneto, and end up in a fight with the Avengers and the Soviets. Dr. Druid becomes a stowaway on the X-Men's jet. The Soviet Super Soldiers want Magneto to pay for his crimes against the Russian people, and the Avengers act as special deputies of the World Court, to rein Magneto in. In Singapore, the X-Men meet a group of mutants who seek their aid. Some members in the court conspire to have Magneto found guilty of crimes against humanity so that he could be held up as a martyr. This in turn would cause civil strife, and possibly war. The World Court frees him.

This story takes place after Magneto had reformed, when he was leading the X-Men.

DeFilippis, Nunzio, Christina Weir, Randy Green, et al. *New X-Men: Academy X Vol. 1: Choosing Sides*. New York: Marvel, 2004. ISBN: 0785115382. Reprints *New X-Men: Academy X 1–6*.

Emma Frost and Scott Summers, Cyclops, are the new headmasters for the Xavier Institute for Higher Learning. This school is designed to keep alive Professor X's dream to teach a new crop of teenage mutants how to control and use their powers for good. Former New Mutant Danielle Moonstar is an advisor and teacher. Each adviser, including the headmasters, has a team of young mutants to train. Frost has the Hellions; Moonstar, the New Mutants; and Cyclops, the Corsairs. Several of the kids break into the Danger Room, but end up working together as a team. The Hellions and the New Mutants are pitted against one another. Moonstar and Frost try to recruit the Whither, a mutant who kills organic matter when he touches it. The FBI wants to take Whither into custody for the death of his father, which actually was accidental. Several of the Hellions go after him, and almost get into a brawl with the FBI. The New Mutants stop them. Former New Mutant Rahne, known as Wolfsbane, is having an affair with one of the students. Whither, who was first assigned to the New Mutants team, joins the Hellions, and Jay Guthrie, Icarus, leaves the Hellions to join the New Mutants.) Several new characters are introduced in this volume. It starts out a little rough at the beginning, and is almost cheesy, but as the story progresses, the book is quite good. It is recommended for public, high-school, and middle-school libraries, and is appropriate for special collections. The book includes cover galleries.

Duffy, Jo, Chris Claremont, John Bolton, et al. *X-Men Rarities*. New York: Marvel, 1995. ISBN: 0785101594. Reprints *Bizarre Adventures 27*; *Classic X-Men 1*; *Marvel Fanfare 40*; *Amazing Adult Fantasy 14*.

This book is a collection of short stories which use mutant characters. It contains stories about Iceman's first solo adventure, while visiting a university; the new X-Men's first night at Xavier's mansion; Iceman's resentment of the new X-Men; Angel trying to get friendly with Storm; Wolverine trying to get friendly with Jean Grey; and a telepathic mutant who thinks he can help the world and gain people's appreciation for his powers, but who only encounters fear and resentment. There is a story featuring Mystique and Storm, and a copy of Marvel's first mutant story from 1962. There also is a promotional Generation-X story which was used for the 1994 San Diego comic convention.

Ellis, Warren, Ken Lashley, Roger Cruz, et al. *X-Men Age of Apocalypse: X-Calibre*. New York: Marvel, 1995. ISBN: 0785101322. Reprints *X-Calibre 1–4*.

Nightcrawler seeks passage to the sanctuary of Avalon where mutants and humans live in peace, away from Apocalypse. Cain Marko, who becomes a religious priest, dies. Mystique meets her son Nightcrawler on the way to Avalon where they seek the mutant Destiny. Apocalypse follows them and sends his mutant servants to destroy Avalon, and the Shadow King.

The entire *Age of Apocalypse* series was reprinted in four volumes 2005–2006. ISBN: 0785117148 (1); 0785118748 (2); 0785120513 (3); 0785120521 (4).

Faerber, Jay, Mark Mckenna, Karl Waller, et al. *X-Men: Beginnings*. New York: Marvel, 2000. ISBN: 0785107509. Reprints *X-Men Movie Prequel: Wolverine; X-Men Movie Prequel: Rogue; X-Men Movie Prequel: Magneto*.

Wolverine searches for some of his memories and helps an undercover cop, who also has amnesia, run from Silver Samurai and others who are trying to kill her. Rogue's powers start to appear, and everyone at her high school starts to reject her. The X-Men try to track Rogue down, but she had already run away from home. She is captured and put into a mutant prison where she helps organize a breakout. Erik meets Professor Xavier and they become friends. Together they build Cerebro, but then they start having differences of opinion. Erik becomes Magneto, and finds the Nazi who tortured him in Auschwitz. Magneto breaks Xavier's legs, and forms the Brotherhood of Evil Mutants.

This book contains three prequel stories which are related to the first X-Men movie.

Fingeroth, Danny, Larry Parr, Marvel Productions, et al. *X-Men Animation Special*. New York: Marvel, 1992. ISBN: 08713569 45 (pbk).

This is a graphic adaptation of the X-Men's first video, *Pryde of the X-Men*. In it, Kitty Pryde joins the X-Men who do battle with Magneto, Toad, and Juggernaut, among others.

Furman, Simon, Bryan Hitch, Joe Rubenstein, et al. *X-Men: Alterniverse Visions*. New York: Marvel, 1996. ISBN: 0785101942. Reprints *What If 40, 59, 62, 66, 69*.

This is a collection of X-Man "what if" stories in which Stryfe kills the X-Men, Rogue has the power of Thor, Storm remains a thief, and Wolverine battles the Weapon X project, and leads Alpha Flight. This book provides a unique perspective on the X-Men.

Grayson, Devin, Jay Faerber, Long Vo, et al. *X-Men Evolution Vol. 2*: New York: Marvel, 2003. ISBN: 0785113282. Reprints *X-Men Evolution 5–9*.

Mystique tries to deceive Rogue into believing that the X-Men don't care about her. They encounter a person who can mimic the X-Men's powers, but is not a mutant. Hank McCoy, the Beast, joins Xavier as a teacher, and helps with some of the new recruits. The X-Men go to the sewers and free the Angel who had been kidnapped by the Morlocks. When Professor X goes away for a few days, a party is held on his estate. The Brotherhood of Evil Mutants crashes the party.

This work is based on the hit animated television show, *X-Men Evolution.*

Grayson, Devin, Udon Studios, Long Vo, et al. *X-Men: Evolution.* New York: Marvel, 2002. ISBN: 0785109404; 0785113592 (Marvel Age Digest version, 2003); 078511 5811 (Marvel Age tpk, 2004). Reprints *X-Men Evolution 1–4.*

The X-Men are formed, with Wolverine and Storm as the adult leaders. Xavier and Magneto have a difference of opinion on mutant/human relations. Xavier finds Storm, Wolverine, Cyclops, and Jean Grey. Toad finally gets tired of being made fun of, and hits a student with his green slime. Nightcrawler uses his image inducer to disguise his elf-like appearance at school. He seems particularly sensitive about his looks.

This comic series is based on the hit X-Men television series. It details the exploits of the young X-Men team as high school students, trying to fit in. It is drawn in a manga style.

Hama, Larry, Steve Epting, Klaus Johnson, et al. *Team X: Team 7.* New York: Marvel/Image, 1996. ISBN: 0785102922.

Team X, a covert strike-force featuring Wolverine, Sabretooth and Maverick, join Team 7 to stop Omega Red.

Hama, Larry, Adam Kubert, Karl Kesel, et al. *X-Men: Age of Apocalypse: Weapon X.* New York: Marvel, 1995. ISBN: 0785101314. Reprints *Weapon X 1–4.*

Cyclops chops off one of Wolverine's hands. Logan and Jean Grey are romantically involved. The Human High Council decides to bomb the United States to prevent any further expansion, with Wolverine leading the mission. Brian Braddock turns out to be a mole working for Apocalypse. Cable also works for Apocalypse. Wolverine gets Gateway to come and help in the mission. Jean Grey leaves Wolverine.

Harris, Bob, Steve Epting, Tom Palmer, et al. *Avengers: X-Men: Bloodties,* New York: Marvel, 1995. ISBN: 0785101039. Reprints *Avengers 368–369; Avengers West Coast 101; Uncanny X-Men 307; X-Men 26.*

An Acolyte of Magneto, Exodus, seeks to purify Magneto's bloodline by killing his children and grandchildren. When Quicksilver's baby girl Luna is kidnapped by Acolyte Fabian Cortez, the X-Men team

up with the Avengers, and go to the mutant island of Genosha. Genosha is in the midst of a civil war between mutants and humans. Nick Fury makes an appearance and his S.H.I.E.L.D. forces take on the Avengers who are warned by the UN not to intervene in the civil war.

This is one of the darkest, most true-to-life stories ever published by Marvel.

Harras, Bob, Ron Lim, Michael Kraiger, et al. *Cyclops: Retribution.* New York: Marvel, 1994. Reprints *Marvel Comics Presents 17–24.*

Cyclops goes to Muir Island where he senses something has gone terribly wrong. Moria MacTaggert was brainwashed by the sentinel Master Mold into developing the mutant-destroying Retribution virus. Cyclops teams up with Callistro to save Banshee and a child mutant who is dying. The Retribution virus also is deadly to humans, so Master Mold's alter ego Conscience ends up helping to save the X-Men and mutant-kind.

Higgins, Michael, Tom Morgan, Justin Thyme, et al. *Excalibur: Weird War III.* New York: Marvel, 1990. ISBN: 087135702X.

Excalibur is caught between two realities that have converged. The group finds itself in a world where Hitler and the Nazis have taken over all of society. Professor X is a Nazi who conducts experiments on mutants. Hitler is very old, but with the help of the Phoenix force he becomes young again to the point of becoming a fetus, and is thrown back into the void. The same thing happens to the Red Skull. Kitty Pryde puts her hands into Xavier's head. Excalibur fights a bizarre version of the X-Men known has the Reichsmen. (*Marvel Graphic Novel 66*)

Hildebrandt, Greg, Tim Hildebrandt, John Francis Moore, et al. *X-2099: Oasis.* New York: Marvel, 1995. ISBN: 0785102345.

The mutant Ryu, once thought to be dead, has put together a secret mutant hideaway, with the Architect Memphis. The X-Men of 2099 visit this so called Oasis where mutants can live together in peace. All is not what it seems; Ryu plans to build the Oasis on the bones of humanity, and commit genocide. The Architect Memphis realizes that it's wrong to kill so many people in order to live in a so-called paradise. He destroys Oasis City, which allows the X-Men to escape and fight for the dream of a peaceful existence for both humans and mutants.

This work was beautifully painted by the famous fantasy team, Greg and Tim Hildebrandt. Bob Budiansky wrote a short biography of the team, and John Francis Moore wrote the afterword.

Jones, Bruce, Greg Rucka, Simon Bisley, et al. *X-Men Legends Vol. 4: Hated and Feared: The Best of X-Men Unlimited.* New York: Marvel, 2003. ISBN: 0785113509. Reprints

X-Men Unlimited 31, 35–36, 38, 40, 42, 46–49.

This is a terrific collection of short stories, each of which spotlights the adventures of a particular mutant. The characters include Cyclops, Psylocke, Wolverine, Mystique, Rogue, Jean Grey, the Blob, Nightcrawler, Lockheed, Sabretooth, Shadowcat, the Beast, and Magneto. The episodes include ones in which the Blob has a run-in with several hicks at a radio station; Jean Grey gets her second Marvel Girl costume from Professor X, for her birthday; Rogue and Jean Grey save a child from a serial killer; Mystique gets pregnant by Sabretooth; Kitty Pryde finds a Colossus look-alike who happens to be a police officer; and Nightcrawler saves a young girl who was kidnapped by ground dwellers.

Kavanagh, Terry, Dave Cockrum, Jeff Albrecht, et al. *X-Men Spotlight on the Starjammers.* New York: Marvel, 1990. ISBN: 08713565 89 (Vol. 1); 0871356589 (Vol. 2).

The Starjammers, a band of interstellar pirates, are devoted to Lilandra of the Shi'ar Empire. The Starjammers and Professor X help get Lilandra's royal throne back; it had been unlawfully taken by her sister Deathbird. Professor X merges with the Starjammers' ship, which is also alive, and he almost dies. His body at one point actually does die. The Starjammers search for the mysterious Phalkon planet which will help restore Lilandra's rightful place on the throne. On Earth, Professor X encounters Excalibur and is briefly endowed with a portion of the Phoenix. He becomes the Bald Phoenix. Deathbird sets her sights on conquering Earth. X-Factor makes a brief appearance.

Half of the story revolves around the Starjammers trying to find a Phalkon map which is scattered across the galaxy.

Kavanagh, Terry, Louise Simonson, Bob Layton, et al. *The Rise of Apocalypse.* New York: Marvel, 1998. ISBN: 0785105867. Reprints *X-Men: Rise of Apocalypse 1–4*; *X-Factor 4–6*; *Fantastic Four 19.*

When En Sabah Nur is left for dead, he is taken and raised by nomadic terrorists, the Sandstormers. His father instilled the idea of survival of the fittest, and taught Nur to rely only on himself. The Pharoah Rama Tut, a time traveler from the future, is fearful of Nur's rise to power which was prophesized. Nur learns the hard way to think only of himself and conquest, when he rescues a beautiful woman who rejects him after seeing his ugly face. Everyone Nur has ever loved has been killed, which eventually turns him into the bloodthirsty Apocalypse. In his chronicles, Tut's General Ozymandias tells the story of Apocalypse's origins as the first Homo-Superior and his rise to power. The Fantastic Four are kidnapped by Rama Tut, and taken back to Ancient Egypt. X-Factor helps rescue a mutant junkie who is strung out on smack. This mutant's power is to amplify power in other mutants, who then become addicted to the power surge. He tries to save

his wife from the mutant Alliance of Evil. The Alliance is working for Apocalypse.

The book relates Apocalypse's origin as En Sabah Nur who was born 5000 years ago in Ancient Egypt. This is Apocalypse's first appearance in the Marvel Universe.

Kelly, Joe, Alan Davis, Fabian Nicieza, et al. *Magneto: Rogue Nation.* New York: Marvel, 2002. ISBN: 0785108343. Reprints *Magneto Rex 1–3*; *X-Men: Magneto War 1*; *X-Men 85–87*; *Uncanny X-Men 366–367*; *Magneto Rex 1–3.*

Magneto tries to hold the world hostage by disrupting the Earth's magnetic sphere. The United Nations allows him to rule Genosha, a haven for all mutants. Magneto forms an uneasy alliance with his son Quicksilver who becomes a minister in his cabinet. The Magneto clone Joseph dies.

Kubert, Adam, Andy Kubert, Elan Cole, et al. *X-Men Visionaries: The Art of Adam and Andy Kubert.* New York: Marvel, 1995. ISBN: 0785101780. Reprints *Uncanny X-Men 279*; *X-Men 33*; *Wolverine 77–78.*

This four-issue collection features the art of the Kubert brothers. In these issues Professor X goes up against the Shadow King Wolverine goes up against both Lady Deathstrike and Bloodscream and Sabretooth tells Rogue about Gambit's shadowy and less than moral past.

Lee, Jim, Chris Claremont, Ann Nocenti, et al. *X-Men Visionaries: Jim Lee.* New York: Marvel, 2002. ISBN: 0785109218. Reprints *Classic X-Men 39*; *X-Men Annual 1*; *Uncanny X-Men 248, 252, 254, 256–258, 206–261, 264, 268–269, 273–277, 280, 286.*

The Mandarin forms an alliance with the Hand, and kidnaps Psylocke to make her their puppet. Jubilee and Wolverine have to defeat the Hand, Psylocke, and the Mandarin. Captain America and Wolverine have to save Natasha Romanoff who is a child during World War II, and Captain America asks Wolverine to be his sidekick. Rogue goes head-to-head with Ms. Marvel, from whom she stole her powers. Rogue, Magneto, Nick Fury, and Ka-Zar team up against Zaladane and her cronies in the Savage Land. The X-Men team up with Lady Deathbird of Shi'Ar, against her sister and Professor X. Wolverine apparently kills Charles Xavier, but it is actually a highly developed War Skrull, who had been holding the real Xavier hostage.

This volume showcases the artistic work of Jim Lee's tenure on the X-Men series.

Lee, Jim, Chris Claremont, Whilce Portaco, et al. *X-Men Wrath of Apocalypse.* New York: Marvel, 1996. Reprints *X-Factor 65–68.*

Apocalypse is very upset about the betrayal of his ship to X-Factor (the original X-Men). He sends his new team Riders of the Storm to attack X-Factor headquarters, and infect the ship with a mutated electronic virus. The team also kidnaps Cyclops's son Nathan. X-Factor tracks Apocalypse to the moon where it encounters the Inhumans. Most of the Inhumans have been taken prisoner, except for a few, like Black Bolt, Gorgon, Karnak, Crystal and Medusa. X-Factor teams up with Black Bolt and the remaining Inhumans to free the captives. X-Factor is defeated by Apocalypse, but quickly escapes and defeats him. X-Factor finds Nathan, who has been infected with the techno-virus, and takes him to the future and Mother Askani, in order to save his life.

This book includes a brief essay about Nathan and his history as Cable. It has a page spread of "images of Cable" and log entries for X-Factor that are taken from the *Apocalypse Manifesto*. Black Bolt actually speaks in this book.

Lee, Stan, Jack Kirby, Chris Claremont, et al. *Magneto Ascendent.* New York: Marvel, 1999. Reprints *Uncanny X-Men 11, 18, 104; Vision and Scarlet Witch 4.*

Magneto takes over the X-Men mansion, and it is up to Iceman to save the day. The Stranger takes Magneto away as his pet, and the new X-Men have to deal with the Stranger for the first time. Magneto learns that Quicksilver and the Scarlet Witch are his long lost children, and he has to deal with his grandchild being a human.

Some of the most famous Magneto stories appear in this volume.

Lee, Jim, Scott Lobdell, Art Thiebert, et al. *X-Men: Ghost Rider: Brood Trouble in the Big Easy.* New York: Marvel, 1993. ISBN: 087135974X. Reprints *X-Men 8–9; Ghost Rider Vol. 2: 26–27.*

Someone is killing the members of the Thieves Guild in New Orleans, and Gambit's wife goes to the X-Men for help. The Ghost Rider, seeking vengeance for the murderer, ends up going into the Brood's lair, and becomes infected. Psylocke goes into the being of Ghost Rider, and frees him from the Brood's infection. The X-Men and Ghost Rider team up against the Brood's minions, and Ghost Rider, with the help of Johnny Blaze, kills the Brood Queen. Gambit's wife Bella Donna dies.

Lee, Jim, Whilce Portacio, John Byrne, et al. *X-Men: The Coming of Bishop.* New York: Marvel, 1995. ISBN: 0785100997. Reprints *Uncanny X-Men 282–288.*

The Mutant policeman Bishop travels back a hundred years through a time portal from a dark future, to chase the insane, mutant-killing mutant Fitzroy and his band of criminals. At first Bishop believes that the X-Men are imposters, but eventually he joins the X-Men as a team member. Jean Grey puts her consciousness into the White Queen to save her own life.

Liefeld, Rob, Fabian Nicieza, Todd McFarlane, et al. *X-Force and Spider Man: Sabotage.* New York: Marvel, 1992. ISBN: 08713595 37. Reprints *Spider-Man 16; X-Force 3–4.*

Black Tom has taken a number of prisoners at the World Trade Center. Siryn teams up with X-Force, and Tom has the Juggernaut fight to keep X-Force and Spider-Man from rescuing the hostages. Black Tom defeats Sunspot, but Cable defeats Tom, and leaves him for dead. However, Deadpool rescues Tom, unbeknownst to Cable. Juggernaut takes on Warpath, Spider-Man, Shatterstar, Cannonball, and others, but none of them are able to make him move or take him down. Shatterstar stabs Juggernaut in the eye.

Most of the book revolves around the battle with Juggernaut, but Cable manages to tick off some folks as well.

Liefeld, Rob, Fabian Nicieza, Joe Rosen, et al. *Cable: Second Genesis.* New York: Marvel, 1999. Reprints *New Mutants 99–100; X-Force 1.*

Sunspot leaves the New Mutants, which breaks up. Cable's bedside manner with his students is upsetting. He wants to put together a new group of Mutants who will help in the coming mutant-human war which he believes is inevitable. When Warpath leaves the New Mutants to go back home to his school, he finds it has been destroyed, and the evidence points to the Hellfire Club. Warpath rejoins Cable. Shatterstar makes his appearance, running from Mojo and Spiral, and Feral is running from Masque and the Morlocks. Shatterstar and Feral also join Cable's new group X-Force, and almost immediately they have to fight Stryfe's Mutant Liberation Front.

X-Force also features Domino, Boom Boom, and Cannonball. These issues, along with *New Mutants 98*, also were reprinted in *X-Force Megazine, 1999.*

Lobdell, Scott, Chris Bachalo, et al. *X-Men Zero Tolerance.* New York: Marvel, 2000. ISBN: 078510738X. Reprints *Generation X 27; Cable 45–47; X-Men 65–70; X-Force 67–69; Wolverine 115–118.*

Bastion is in charge of Operation Zero Tolerance whose goal is to eliminate all mutants from the planet. Mutants are pursued by half-robot, half-human, mutant-hunting soldiers known as Prime Sentinels. The X-Men escape their capture by Bastion, and end up fighting the Sentinels in the desert. Cyclops has a bomb implanted in his chest. Iceman teams up with the Morlock Marrow and Dr. Celia Reyes. Senator Kelly changes from his mutant-hating ideas when he realizes that Zero Tolerance is genocide, and S.H.I.E.L.D. is called in to shut down the operation.

This is one of the most intense and best-written X-Men crossovers ever published. It is one of the largest X-Men collections ever printed.

Lobdell, Scott, Chris Bachalo, Mark Buckingham, et al. *X-Men: Road Trippin!* New York: Marvel, 1999. ISBN: 0785107347. Reprints *Generation X 5*; *Uncanny X-Men 138, 244–245, 323*; *X-Force 44, 70–71, 75*; *Wolverine 78*; *Marvel Treasury 26*, *New Mutants 99*, *Star Trek: Early Voyages 12* .

Generation X kids find some people brutally murdered in New York. Storm, Dazzler, Psylocke, and Rogue go shopping for clothes. At the mall they encounter the mutant-hating M-squad and Jubilee. Wolverine and Hercules get into a drunken brawl. Cyclops leaves the X-Men, and reminisces about his experiences. Wolverine encounters the deadly vampire Bloodscream in the Canadian wilderness, and Rogue and Iceman go on a road trip together. Havok, Wolverine, Colossus, and Longshot go out for a night on the town, and have to deal with a group of hostile aliens. X-Force breaks away from Cable and takes to the road. They get picked up by some hippies, and Dani Moonstar mentions that she hates the Grateful Dead. When they go to a Burning-Man–type festival, Selene tries to crash the party. Meltdown and Sunspot kiss, even though Meltdown is Cannonball's girlfriend. The members of X-Force do not know that Cable has been trailing them, making sure they are able to handle themselves. Cyclops leaves the X-Men; Generation X goes to New York; the X-Men ladies go shopping; the X-Men males have a night on the town; X-Force goes to a desert festival; and Wolverine and Hercules get into a bar fight.

This volume is made up of a hodgepodge of different stories about the X-Men and its various offshoots. It contains Jubilee's first appearance.

Lobdell, Scott, Mark Buckingham, Steve Buccellato, et al. *X-Men: Age of Apocalypse: Generation Next.* New York: Marvel, 1995. ISBN: 0785101306. Reprints *Generation Next 1–4.*

Colossus and his wife Shadowcat, along with the New Mutants, attempt to rescue his sister Illyana. They go up against Quietus. A number of the New Mutants are killed in the rescue attempt.

Lobdell, Scott, Peter David, Fabian Nicieza, et al. *X-Men: X-Cutioner's Song.* New York: Marvel, 1994. ISBN: 0785100253. Reprints *X-Force 16–18*; *X-Men 14–16*; *Uncanny X-Men 294–296*; *X-Factor 84–86.*

Someone who looks like Cable shoots Professor X at a pro-mutant rally. The X-Men and X-Factor capture X-Force, who they believe had something to do with the assassination attempt. Jean Grey and Cyclops are kidnapped by Stryfe. Bishop and Wolverine go looking for Cable who is attacked before he has a chance to explain himself. Eventually it is learned that Stryfe is Cable's "twin." In one of the most bizarre twists in an X-Men story, Apocalypse teams up with the X-Men to help defeat Stryfe who is acting like a

child. Stryfe and Cable duke it out, and seemingly blow up. Archangel leaves Apocalypse to die, like a wimp. Although Mr. Sinister has something to do with all these events, his role is never revealed. Iceman and Colossus go shopping for pork rinds.

This is a massive X-crossover, which contains much action and great fight scenes.

Lobdell, Scott, Trace Drury, Bill Sienkiewicz, et al. *X-Men: Books of Askani: A Guide to a New World of Mutants and Madness.* New York: Marvel, 1995.

This cardstock, one-shot book explains the mystical world of the Askani which includes entries about Mother Askani, the Sisterhood, Zero, Askani'Son, Stryfe, Unit Dayspring, and others.

Lobdell, Scott, Gene Ha, Jeph Loeb, et al. *Askani'Son.* New York: Marvel, 1997. ISBN: 0785105654. Reprints *Askani'Son 1–4.*

Apocalypse has been overthrown, but the world is almost plunged into civil war. The insincere New Canaanites are consolidating their power, and seek to destroy Nathan "Cable" Summers, who learns that he is the chosen Askani'Son. The professor, the computer in Cable, is awakened. The powerful mutant Stryfe plots his rise to power. The mysterious Blaquesmith helps Summers to continue the positive legacy of his family.

This book relates the early adventures of Nathan "Cable" Summers, 2000 years in the future. The Zero Unit android was created by Stryfe. Artist Gene Ha wrote the introduction.

Lobdell, Scott, Gene Ha, Al Vey, et al. *Adventures of Cyclops and Phoenix.* New York: Marvel, 1995. ISBN: 0785101713. Reprints *The Adventures of Cyclops and Phoenix 1–4.*

On their honeymoon, Scott Summers and Jean Grey are transported 2,000 years into the future by their future daughter Rachel, to help undermine the rule of Apocalypse. They raise their son Nathan Summers in the guise of surrogate parents, to hide his mutant powers. Nate eventually becomes Cable, and has to stop the Chaos Bringer from ruling the world.

Lobdell, Scott, Clayton Henry, Mark Morales, et al. *Alpha Flight Vol. 1: You Gotta Be Kidding Me.* New York: Marvel, 2004. ISBN: 0785114300. Reprints *Alpha Flight 1–6.*

Sasquatch recruits a new crop of super-powered beings to save Canada and the rest of the world. A group of aggressive aliens bent on galaxy conquest has captured the original Alpha Flight, and is holding them as hostages. The aliens attempt to clone the superhero group. After freeing the original Alpha Flight, they take unborn alien eggs back to their home world.

This new version of Alpha Flight includes Puck's daughter and a ninety-year-old man. Although this was one of the series which was vilified by comic fandom, I found the book to be quite funny and original in its sarcastic tribute to the new X-Men. The character Nemesis is pretty cool. As a tribute to *Giant X-Men 1*, this is the all-new, all-different Alpha Flight. Volume 2 ISBN: 0785115692.

Lobdell, Scott, Jim Lee, Scott Williams, et al. *WildC.A.T.S/X-Men*. New York: Wildstorm/Marvel. 1998. ISBN: 1582400229. Reprints *WildC.A.T.S/X-Men: The Golden Age*; *WildC.A.T.S/X-Men: The Silver Age*; *WildC.A.T.S/X-Men: The Modern Age*; *WildC.A.T.S/X-Men: The Dark Age*.

The X-Men and the WildC.A.T.S team up to fight the Daemonite menace. Grifter and Marvel Girl fight against Daemonite-Brood hybrids. The Hellfire Club's Blair Cameron offers Emp membership in the club, but ends up, with the mutant child, as a sacrifice to a demon. Sentinels and Daemonites combine to destroy mutants and humans in the future Dark Age. Nick Fury makes an appearance.

The first story takes place during World War II, and features Wolverine and Zelot against the Nazis. This volume contains variants and reprints of covers.

Lobdell, Scott, Ron Lim, Walter Simonson, et al. *Excalibur: Air Apparent*. New York: Marvel, 1991. ISBN: 0871358743.

A mad scientist is causing all kind of disasters, and the Weird Happenings Organization asks Excalibur to intervene. They have to deal with a former herald of Galactus, Air Walker, who is an android gone berserk. The team splits up, and each member has a different nemesis to conquer. Kitty's dragon Lockheed spooks two would-be thieves.

This story is divided into eight parts. Lobdell scripts the entire book, but a different artist gives a take on each chapter.

Lobdell, Scott, Jeph Loeb, Joe Madureira, et al. *X-Men: Age of Apocalypse: Astonishing X-Men*. New York: Marvel, 1995. ISBN: 0785101276. Reprints *Astonishing X-Men 1–4*.

The X-Men, including Sabretooth, go up against Holocaust. Sabretooth almost dies.

Lobdell, Scott, Ralph Macchio, Joe Bennett, et al. *A Tale from the Age of Apocalypse: By the Light*. New York: Marvel, 1996. ISBN: 0785102892.

Charles Xavier is dead, and Magneto has become the leader of the X-Men. Apocalypse is recovering on the Moon. Apocalypse has doubts about the loyalty of Cyclops who is his disciple. The Horseman Death wants power for himself. Sabretooth is one of the X-Men. With the help of Cyclops and Blink, X-Men save Sunfire from Death's experiments.

Lobdell, Scott, Joe Madureira, Fabian Nicieza, et al. *The Origin of Generation X: Tales of the Phalanx Covenant*. New York: Marvel, 2001. ISBN: 0785102167; 0785101969 (1986). Reprints *X-Factor 106*; *X-Force 38*; *Excalibur 82*; *Uncanny X-Men 316–317*; *X-Men 36–37*; *Wolverine 85*; *Cable 16*; *Generation X 1*.

The Phalanx are trying to capture or destroy as many mutants as they can in order to study them and learn how to assimilate them into their collective. Seven young mutants—Husk, Chamber, Skin, Jubilee, M, Synch and Blink—are captured and form the core of Generation X. They learn how to combat the Phalanx using their smarts and powers. X-Force, Excalibur, and X-Factor team up with Professor X, to find ways of defeating the Phalanx. Jean Grey, Cyclops, Wolverine, and Cable also join the team. Wolverine goes back to save Cable who almost gets assimilated, and they put their differences aside. The Generation X team is formed under the tutelage of Banshee and Emma Frost.

This epic tale deals with the alien Phalanx, and their conquest of Earth. The Phalanx is a techno-organic alien species, similar to the Borg on Star Trek, which can assimilate humans but has a hard time with mutants. The Phalanx rose up from the alien remains of the late New Mutant Warlock. The work includes a sketchbook of Generation X characters.

Lobdell, Scott, Joe Quesada, J.M. DeMatteis, et al. *X-Men: Fatal Attractions*. New York: Marvel, 1994. ISBN: 0785100652. Reprints *X-Factor 92*; *X-Force 25*; *Uncanny X-Men 304*; *X-Men 25*; *Wolverine 75*; *Excalibur 71*.

The X-Men reject Magneto's offer to join him on Avalon. Magneto almost kills Wolverine by turning his metal bones inside out. In retaliation, Xavier wipes Magneto's mind clean. Colossus gives up being an X-Man, and joins Magneto's group, the Acolytes. Cable almost dies. Kitty Pryde tricks Colossus into coming to see her. Moria and Professor can do surgery on Colossus's head. Wolverine leaves the X-Men, and Cable comes back to X-Force. Magneto is set up to be a lord and savior for mutants. The Acolytes slaughter human beings in Magneto's name, under Cortez. Cortez is seemingly killed.

This is a gigantic crossover collection in which the X-Men once again do battle with Magneto. It contains the first appearance of Exodus.

Lobdell, Scott, Mark Waid, Adam Kubert, et al. *Onslaught: The Awakening 1; To the Victor 2; Comrades in Arms 3; Eye of the Storm 4; The Front Line 5; Pyrrhic Victory 6*. New York: Marvel, 1996. ISBN: 0785102809 (1); 0785102817 (2); 0785102825 (3); 0785102833 (4); 0785102841 (5); 078510285X (6). Reprints *Uncanny X-Men 322, 334–336*;

X-Men 53–56; Wolverine 104; Onslaught X-Men; X-Man 18–19; X-Force 57–58; Fantastic Four 415–416; Cable 34–35; Hulk 444–445; Avengers 401–402; X-Factor 125; Amazing Spider Man 415; Green Goblin 12; Punisher 11; Spider Man 72; Onslaught: Marvel Universe.

Charles Xavier's astral form gains a quasi-physical existence of its own as the evil Onslaught. Onslaught gathers a team of extremely powerful beings and takes control of the U.S. government's entire fleet of Sentinel robots, and reprograms them to attack superhumans. With the assistance of his new minions, he sets out to take over Manhattan, and make it a haven for mutants. Most of Marvel's heroes are drawn into the battle. They discover that the only way to defeat Onslaught is for as many of the non-mutant heroes as possible to be absorbed into Onslaught. This causes him to become physical enough for remaining heroes to defeat him. The maelstrom this creates dissolves Onslaught into nothingness, but has the side effect of transporting all of the absorbed heroes to an alternate Earth created by Mr. Fantastic's son Franklin. Xavier's telepathic powers are destroyed.

Many thanks to Joel Hahn for help in tracking down this material and information.

Lobdell, Scott, Mark Waid, Fabian Nicieza, et al. *X-Men: Legionquest.* New York: Marvel, 1995. ISBN: 0785101799. Reprints *Uncanny X-Men 320–321; X-Men 40–41.*

Xaviers's son from another reality goes back in time to try to save his father from Magneto, whom he believes is going to cause Professor X untold grief. Legion tries to kill Magneto, but Xavier jumps in the way of Legion's blow, and dies. Several X-Men, including Strom, Iceman, and Bishop, are sent to this reality and witness this horrible event.

This story ushered in Marvel's *Age of Apocalypse* series.

Lobdell, Scott, Mark Ward, Roger Cruz, et al. *Twilight of the Age of Apocalypse.* New York: Marvel, 1995. ISBN: 0785101810. Reprints *X-Men: Omega; X-Universe 1&2.*

Magneto has a showdown with Apocalypse who at first beats Magneto down. Cable and the X-Men team up with Magneto to defeat Apocalypse. Magneto gives thanks to the memory of Charles Xavier. Gwen Stacy, Sue Storm, Ben Grimm, Anthony Stark, Donald Blake, and Victor Von Doom team up with humanity to defy Apocalypse. Matt Murdock is the human pawn of a very powerful mutant who is the prelate Mikhail Rasputin.

This Apocalypse story takes place at the end of the *Age of Apocalypse* storyline.

Loeb, Jeph, Steve Skroce, Mike Thomas, et al. *X-Men: Age of Apocalypse: X-Man.* New York: Marvel, 1995. ISBN: 0785101330. Reprints *X-Man 1–4.*

Nathan Grey, Forge, Toad, Sauron, Brute, and Mastermind go around the country as a touring theater group for entertainment, but also to thwart Apocalypse's forces. Nate is just beginning to know the power that exists within him. They meet another mutant, Essex, who befriends the troupe, but Essex turns out to be Sinister who wants Nate for his own purpose. Sinister nearly kills a number of Nate's friends, including Brute and Forge. Apocalypse sends out several bounty hunters to bring Nate in, but they are destroyed. Sinister tells Nate more about his past and his powers, but this falls on deaf ears. Nate kills Sinister, and meets his parents, Cyclops and Jean Grey.

Macchio, Ralph, Chris Claremont, Barry Windsor Smith, et al. *X-Men: The Movie.* New York: Marvel, 2000. ISBN: 0785107495. Reprints *X-Men: The Movie; Uncanny X-Men 112–113; 171; Marvel Comics Presents 72–75.*

Wolverine and Rogue come into the world of the X-Men when Cyclops and Storm rescue them from Sabretooth. Magneto wants to use Rogue as a conduit to turn people into mutants. The X-Men have to stop him, and battle with Mystique, Sabretooth, and Toad. Rogue shows up at the X-Mansion, asking for Xavier's help. Wolverine, Logan, is created in the deadly Weapon X project.

This volume features the adaptation of the first X-Men hit movie. Some of the back story, which did not appear in the movie, is provided in this book. It also contains several older stories in which Magneto captures the X-Men and holds them hostage beneath the Earth. In those stories he neutralizes their powers, and has a robotic nanny attend to their needs.

Macchio, Ralph, Andrew Wildman, Jeff Albrecht, et al. *X-Men Adventures Vol. 3: Irresistible Force: Muir Island Saga.* New York: Marvel, 1994. ISBN: 078510044X. Reprints *X-Men Adventures 9–12.*

The X-Men encounter Colossus who they believe trashed the mansion, and the Juggernaut who *did* do the damage to the school. Rogue seeks a cure from being a mutant, and when she hears about a doctor who developed a cure, she seeks him. In the process she meets Pyro, Avalance, and Mystique. This cure is really a ruse by Apocalypse to create an army to usher in his rule of Earth. Warren Worthington is transformed by Apocalypse from the Angel into the Angel of Death, Archangel. Apocalypse uses his Four Horseman to try to take over humanity, but the X-Men intervene. Archangel betrays Apocalypse after Rogue touches him, and Worthington realizes that he is not a killer.

This volume also features some brief scenes with Cable. It is based on the television show.

Macchio, Ralph, Andrew Wildman, Chris Batista, et al. *X-Men Adventures Vol. 2: Captive Hearts: Slave Island.* New York: Marvel,

1994. ISBN: 0785100288. Reprints *X-Men Adventures 5–8.*

A group of underground mutants capture Jean Grey and Cyclops. The X-Men learn about the underground mutants known as the Morlocks. Storm and the Morlocks leader Callisto battle to the death. Storm wins, and grants Callisto her life. Wolverine has a deadly fight with Sabretooth in the Arctic. Wolverine briefly finds peace and friendship with a tribe of Indians which Sabretooth terrorizes. Touted as a haven for mutants, several X-Men go to Genosha for a vacation. They find out that the so-called mutant paradise is actually a concentration camp. Mutants are herded for slave labor, and Sentinels are "keeping the peace." Gambit pretends to betray the X-Men when a breakout organized by Jubilee goes wrong. Storm is thrown into a small cage. Cable infiltrates the camp and helps to free the mutants.

Macchio, Ralph, Andrew Wildman, Robert Campanella, et al. *X-Men Adventures Vol. 1: Night of the Sentinels: Enter Magneto.* New York: Marvel, 1993. ISBN: 0785100067. Reprints *X-Men Adventures 1–4.*

Sentinels capture Jubilee. The X-Men break into a facility which houses information on Mutants, and they destroy the files. Morph is killed. The Beast is put on trial, and Magneto defeats the X-Men. Xavier tries to heal Sabretooth, who goes ballistic and ends up fighting Wolverine. Jubilee joins the X-Men, and Magneto offers to break the Beast out of jail. Rogue absorbs Cyclops's power during their battle with Magneto.

This was the first volume that was based on the animated television series.

Macchio, Ralph, Andrew Wildman, Nick Napalitano, et al. *X-Men Adventures Vol. 4: Days of Future Past: Final Conflict.* New York: Marvel, 1994. ISBN: 0785101136. Reprints *X-Men Adventures 13–15.*

The X-Men encounter the time-traveler Bishop who comes from the future. His mission is to stop the assassination of a U.S. senator. He believes Gambit will be the one to pull the trigger. The X-Men go to Washington to try to stop Mystique's band of cronies, including the Blob and Pyro, from killing Senator Kelly. The X-Men prevent the assasination, but do not prevent Magneto from kidnapping Kelly. Then Kelly is kidnapped again by the Sentinels. The Mastermold decides that the Sentinels need to control humanity. The X-Men take apart the Sentinels' manufacturing plant which is in the Appalachian Mountains. They defeat the head Sentinel, Mastermold.

This volume was based on the television series. Jaye Gardner, assistant editor, wrote the introduction.

Mackie, Howard, Lee Weeks, Klaus Janson, et al. *Gambit.* New York: Marvel, 1994. ISBN: 0785101098. Reprints *Gambit 1–4.*

Gambit has to intervene in a fight between the thieves and the assassins over the life-giving elixir. Gambit tries to save his ex-wife who is on the brink of death. Gambit's brother is killed, and Gambit takes Rogue with him to New Orleans. He has to choose between family loyalties and the life of his wife. He goes up against the "queen" of the guilds, Candra, and the mysterious Tithe Collector. Rogue tells Gambit she loves him.

Mackie, Howard, Mike Wieringo, Terry Austin, et al. *Rogue.* New York: Marvel, 1995. ISBN: 0785101403. Reprints *Rogue 1–4.*

Rogue tries to save Cody, the boy she put into a coma by kissing him. Gambit's ex-girlfriend/wife Bella Donna takes revenge against him because of his affection for Rogue. Bella Donna has kidnapped Cody who is on the brink of death. They go to New Orleans. Candra and her mutant Externals make a peace offering with Bella Donna and the Assassins Guild. Candra has her own reasons for wanting Rogue and Gambit captured. Rogue reminisces with the spirit of Cody.

This volume deserves to be reprinted with the first Gambit trade.

Mackie, Howard, Guang Yap, Bud LaRosa, et al. *Ghost Rider and Cable: Servants of the Dead.* New York: Marvel, 1992. Reprints *Marvel Presents 90–97.*

Cable and Ghost Rider try to save a young girl from being sacrificed to the Grateful Undead, Warriors of the Dead. It turns out this girl is one of the Grateful Undead, and can't be killed. This reality horrifies her, as she is to be the bride of a dead Master. She chooses true death, and the Master learns the truth about how his servants have become assassins.

Madureira, Joe, Tim Townsend, Steve Buccellato, et al. *X-Men Visionaries: The Joe Madureira Collection.* New York: Marvel, 2000. ISBN: 0785107487. Reprints *Uncanny X-Men 325–326, 329–330, 341–343.*

The X-Men and the Morlock Callisto go up against young Morlocks. When Sabretooth is at Xavier's, he goes berserk and almost kills Psylocke, Angel, and Wolverine. The X-Men and Magneto go up against the Phalanx in space to try to save the Shi'ar Empire.

McKeever, Sean, Manuel Garcia, Raul Fernandez, et al. *Mystique Volume 3: Unnatural.* New York: Marvel, 2004. ISBN: 07851155 60. Reprints *Mystique 14–18.*

Xavier has Mystique and Shortpack investigate a foreign cosmetic company, Dermafree, which is using mutants as guinea pigs. Mystique finds out that the company has been using her cloned cells to create their product. Thus the mission becomes much more personal. They are able to free some of the mutants from

Dermafree's headquarters, and, against Xavier's wishes, Mystique kills the person who has been kidnapping and selling mutants to the company. Short-pack slugs Mystique, and asks for a new assignment. Mystique scars the face of the Dermanfree's mutant-hating CEO.

Volume 4 completes the series (ISBN: 07851147 50).

McKeever, Sean, UDON Studios, Erik Ko, et al. *Marvel Age Sentinel Vol. 1: Salvage*. New York: Marvel, 2004. ISBN: 0785113800. Reprints *Sentinel 1–6*.

High school sophomore Justin Seyfert and his friends are the brunt of much abuse from their older classmates. His mother ran out on his family, and his father owns a junkyard. Justin's family is dirt poor, and as a result many in his school avoid him. One day, while salvaging in the junkyard, Justin finds the remains of an old Sentinel, a mutant-hunting robot. He brings the robot back online, and uses him to scare the abusive classmates. Justin meets a senior girl, Jessie, who becomes his friend.

This is the story of a "boy and his giant robot."

McKeever, Sean, UDON studios, Erik Ko, et al. *Sentinel Vol. 2: No Hero*. New York: Marvel, 2004. ISBN: 0785113681. Reprints *Sentinel 7–12*.

Jason Seyfert has second thoughts about using the Sentinel for his own selfish gains. Everybody, except for Jason, considers him to be a hero. Now that he is a celebrity, a girl who otherwise would not have given Jason the time of day, starts making passes at him. Several government agents try to find the Sentinel to stop it from doing any harm. Jason tries to use it to save people downed in an airplane crash. The Sentinel starts to go back to its old program, hunting mutants. Jason's brother becomes very ill and is taken to a hospital.

Millar, Mark, Chuck Austin, Adam Kubert, et al. *Ultimate X-Men: Vol. 3: World Tour*. New York: Marvel, 2002. ISBN: 07851096 17. Reprints *Ultimate X-Men 13–20*.

The X-Men go with Professor X on a world tour to promote his new book. Colossus goes back to Russia, believing that he really has no purpose in the X-Men. Cyclops and Jean Grey persuade him to come back. The mutant son of Xavier and Moria McTaggert, David (Proteus) has the ability to possess individuals and drain them of energy. Colossus ends up killing David, and Professor X thinks about disbanding the X-Men. Iceman is hurt badly in his battle with Proteus.

This volume includes a story featuring Gambit.

Millar, Mark, Chris Bachalo, Tim Townsend, et al. *Ultimate X-Men Vol. 5: Ultimate War*. New York: Marvel, 2003. ISBN: 0785112 98. Reprints *Ultimate War 1–4*.

Magneto is terrorizing New York, demanding that he become ruler, and humans become slaves. The X-Men are hiding because it was revealed that Xavier hid Magneto and kept him alive. The Ulimates are asked to find and take the X-Men. Quicksilver and Scarlet Witch join the Ultimates. Magneto destroys the Ultimates' office and Captain America swears a vendetta against Magneto and Professor X. Xavier tries to make a deal with Magneto, but is betrayed and led into the hands of the Ultimates. Iceman tries to help the X-Men in their battle, but Xavier is captured.

Millar, Mark, Brian Michael Bendis, David Finch, et al. *Ultimate X-Men Vol. 7: Block Buster*. New York: Marvel, 2004. ISBN: 0785112197. Reprints *Ultimate X-Men 34–39*.

A group of former Weapon X agents are after Wolverine. They shoot him in a public restaurant, which nearly puts him permanently out of commission. Logan goes to Peter Parker's house and asks to stay there so he can recover. The Weapon X agents stalk him, and their battle takes them to Hell's Kitchen where Daredevil is not amused by all the destruction and mayhem. Wolverine's amnesia keeps him from knowing who these people are who want him dead. Apparently the Weapon X agents were upset because Wolverine appeared on the cover of *Time*. Spider-Man calls the X-Men for help, and Xavier tries to help Wolverine. He also tells Wolverine that even though he is getting a second chance with the X-Men, he needs to earn their respect and trust. Nick Fury tells Xavier to keep the X-Men out of the engagement with the rogue Weapon X agents, but the X-Men do get involved. They destroy the group's headquarters, and take out some of the members, but fail to find out who was funding them. S.H.I.E.L.D. agent Dugan makes an appearance.

Ultimate X-Men Vol. 8: New Mutants appears under "Bendis" earlier in this chapter subsection.

Millar, Mark, David Finch, Adam Kubert, et al. *Ultimate X-Men Vol. 6: Return of the King*. New York: Marvel, 2003. ISBN: 0785110917. Reprints *Ultimate X-Men 26–33*.

Magneto and Professor X form their school for mutants, eight years hence. Magneto begins to shape his ideas of mutant domination during this period, and breaks with Xavier. Magneto cripples Xavier by throwing a metal spear through his spine. Mastermind and Multiple Man steal precious artwork for Magneto. Nick Fury shows the vice president new Sentinel agents. Wolverine leaves Cyclops to die in the Savage Land, because he wants to make time with Jean Grey. Magneto's group rescues him. Wolverine gets thrown off the team. Magneto is going to destroy all humanity by reversing magnetic polarities. The X-Men stop him, and are hailed in the press as heroes. They start working with Nick Fury and S.H.I.E.L.D., instead of against them. Magneto is put into a plastic prison, and Cyclops invites Wolverine to come back.

Millar, Mark, Adam Kubert, Danny Miki, et al. *Ultimate X-Men Vol. 4: Hellfire and Brimstone.* New York: Marvel, 2003. ISBN: 0785110895. Reprints *Ultimate X-Men 21–25.*

Kitty Pryde comes to the X-Men. Quicksilver tries to follow in his father's footsteps, but decides against it. A group of mutated-animal/human-mutant hybrids decide to try to find Magneto. Wolverine and Cyclops fight over Jean Grey. The Blob poses as a mutant woman on the Internet, and tricks the Beast into confiding in him. The Beast reveals where Magneto is located. Kitty is a stowaway on a trip to the Savage Land, with Cyclops and Wolverine. The X-Men learn that Hellfire Club is their financial backer. The Hellfire Club betrays the X-Men, and tries to awaken the Phoenix god in Jean Grey.

Millar, Mark, Adam Kubert, Tom Raney, et al. *Ultimate X-Men Vol. 2: Return to Weapon X.* New York: Marvel, 2002. ISBN: 07851 08688. Reprints *Ultimate X-Men 7–12.*

The X-Men are abducted by the Weapon X program. Wolverine averts being captured. He has to fight against Sabretooth to save the X-Men from being transformed into killing machines. The doctors at Weapon X transform Hank McCoy into the Beast. Nick Fury helps the X-Men break out of Weapon X.

In this volume, Nightcrawler, Rogue, Nick Fury, and Juggernaut make their debut appearance in the Ultimate Universe.

Millar, Mark, Adam Kubert, Art Thiebert, et al. *Ultimate X-Men Vol. 1.* New York: Marvel, 2003. ISBN: 9785107886. Reprints *Ultimate X-Men 1–6.*

Xavier puts together the team of Colossus, Beast, Marvel Girl, Cyclops, Storm, and Iceman. The Sentinels trash New York, and the X-Men try to save themselves and bystanders. Iceman is hit on the head with a bottle right after he saves some humans. Magneto, whose camp is in the Savage Land, wants humanity to let him rule, as a homo-superior. He sends Wolverine to infiltrate the X-Men and kill Xavier, but this plan backfires, and Wolverine joins the X-Men, and gets romantic with Jean Grey. Cyclops goes to Magneto's Brotherhood as a spy for Xavier. Wolverine stabs Magneto, and Xavier gets into his head, much to Magneto's dismay. Quicksilver acts very wimpy toward his father, and it seems as though Magneto has no respect for his son. Beast is almost killed.

This volume is the first in the re-launch of the X-Men for the Ultimate Universe series. It contains a sketchbook, secrets page, and an afterword by former chief Bill Jemas.

Milligan, Peter, Mike Allred, Laura Allred, et al. *X-Force: Final Chapter.* New York: Marvel, 2002. ISBN: 0785110887. Reprints *X-Force 121–129.*

X-Force gets several new members, including Spike and Dead Girl. The homoerotic relationship between Phat and Vivisector is explored in more detail. Lacuna is offered membership in X-Force, but uses them just to get her own Jerry-Springer–type talk show. X-Force is lured to a space station to contain a group of genetically-made mutants who are criminals. Spike betrays X-Force, and almost teams up with the criminals, but at the last moment comes through for the team. A bizarre, maggot-infested being points to one of the members of X-Force who will die, and it turns out to be U-Go-Girl. It is also learned that she has a daughter. X-Force has tryouts for new members. Orphan goes on Lucuna's television show to bare his heart to the world about his love for U-Go-Girl. X-Force changes its name, as requested by the dying U-Go-Girl.

Milligan, Peter, Mike Allred, Laura Allred, et al. *X-Force New Beginnings.* New York: Marvel, 2001. ISBN: 078510819X. Reprints *Reprints X-Force 116–120.*

X-Force is re-created to be media darlings under the payroll of a wealthy businessman. The missions are already planned for them, and various members die. Orphan saves a young mutant boy from pharmaceutical experimentation. Former members of X-Force, including Cannonball, criticize them for misusing the name X-Force, and regard them as an embarrassment to mutants and the name "X." Wolverine makes an appearance, and saves the Orphan and U-Go-Girl from death at the hands of the coach, as a favor for their camera operator Doop.

This comic series has been highly praised by filmmaker Kevin Smith for its "well observed scholarly analysis of media-manipulation."

Milligan, Peter, Mike Allred, Peter Bond, et al. *X-Statix Vol. 3: Back from the Dead.* New York: Marvel, 2004. ISBN: 0785111409. Reprints *X-Statix 11–18.*

X-Statix gets a new member, El Gaupa, who has a mutant bond with his skateboard. Dead Girl becomes a fashion symbol, and kills a coroner who likes necrophilia. Mutant pop sensation Henrietta Hunter comes back from the dead and joins X-Statix, but no one can stand her because she takes all of the limelight. Spike goes behind the team's back, and puts together the mutant assassin team Euro-Trash. Spider-Man comes to help out against Euro-Trash. Mr. Code puts into motion a random killing spree, all across the country. Spike Freeman is implicated, and is killed by Mr. Sensitive. X-Statix is seen as supporting terrorism, so the team has to win back America's favor. They go head-to-head with Mr. Code, and Henrietta dies again, as does Phat. El Gaupa loses his legs.

Milligan, Peter, Mike Allred, Darwyn Cooke, et al. *X-Statix Vol. 2: Good Guys & Bad Guys.*

New York: Marvel, 2003. ISBN: 0785111
395. Reprints *X-Statix 6–10*; *Wolverine/
Doop 1–2*; *X-Men Unlimited 41*.

Guy Smith, who leaves X-Statix, is the topic of all
the news shows. Venus Dee Milo's cousin starts rais-
ing trouble as the Bad Guy, who many think is Guy
Smith. The Anarchist takes over leadership of X-Statix. Professor X designs a new suit for Venus, to help
her experience human sensations. Guy rejoins X-Statix, but not as leader. Guy and Venus become romantically entangled. Wolverine and Doop team up to
find the Pink Mink. Each thinks the other is the disease Code X. Hunter Joe tries to eliminate Doop and
Wolverine. X-Statix put on a public event, a concert.
Venus and Dead Girl go shopping.

This volume includes a special story about the life
of the late Edie Sawyer. In it, we meet the Anarchist's
grandfather Tike. In parts, this volume is simply hilarious.

Milligan, Peter, Mike Allred, Nick Dragotta, et
    al. *X-Statix Vol. 4: X-Statix vs The Aven-
    gers*. New York: Marvel, 2004. ISBN: 0785
    115374. Reprints *X-Statix 19–26*.

Myles, Vivasector, is dating Bradon, a teen heart-
throb. He participates in an experiment that will free
him of his wolf-like mutant powers. The scientist
working with him, who used to work for Professor X,
is secretly draining Myles of his powers, so that he
can take them. He leaves X-Statix. Myles goes to visit
his father for his sixtieth birthday party. The "fake"
Vivasector crashes the party, and takes Myles' father
hostage. They duke it out, with help of the rest of the
X-Statix. Captain America tells the press that he
thinks X-Statix is irresponsible, and that they are not
serious crime fighters. A group of terrorists kidnap
Doop, and are using him for weapon. The X-Statix ask
the Avengers for help in rescuing Doop, but his brain
blows up, and parts of it are all over the world. Rather
than work together, X-Statix and the Avengers are
now at odds. Captain America fights the Anarchist;
the Scarlet Witch fights against Dead Girl; Hawkeye
fights. Vivasector; and Venus Dee Milo fights Ant-
Man. Iron Man and Mr. Sensitive take on each other,
at the Church of the Naked Truth. Both have to get
naked, fight each other, and then take on Surrender
Monkey. The last piece of Doop's brain ends up in
Asgard. Doop swallows Mjolnir, Thor's hammer.
Doop's back-up brain, stored in his butt, starts to burn
out, and the Avengers and X-Statix put him back together. Captain America relents and agrees that
X-Statix is responsible. He puts Doop back in their
care. They decide to break up, but take on one last
mission which goes horribly wrong.

The reader learns a little about Doop's history, but
not much.

Milligan, Peter, Mike Allred, Paul Pope, et al.
    X-Statix Vol. 1: Good Omens. New York:
    Marvel, 2003. ISBN: 0785110593. Reprints
    X-Statix 1–5.

The former members of the mutant media darlings
X-Force change their name to X-Statix. Phat loses
his powers, and then regains them when he finally admits he is gay, but not attracted to Vivisector. The
Anarchist, with the help of Dead Girl, tries to make
it without the team, but eventually goes back to them.
Another mutant team, O-Force, tries to steal the
thunder and media attention away from X-Statix.
X-Statix is brought in to save a town from a young
mutant, Arnie, who has been terrorizing the town
where he lives. Arnie is obsessed with Edie Sawyer,
and blames Guy Smith for her death. Arnie ends up
joining X-Statix as Fanboy, but Guy has Arnie killed
prematurely by Lacuna.

Milligan, Peter, John Paul Leon, Shawn Mart-
    inbrough, et al. *The Further Adventures of
    Cyclops and Phoenix*. New York: Marvel,
    1997. ISBN: 0785105565. Reprints *The
    Further Adventures of Cyclops and Phoenix
    1–4*.

Scott Summers and Jean Grey go back to the Victorian Age and meet scientist Nathaniel Essex who is
working on mutation theories. He is considered to be
a quack by the scientists of his day. He discusses his
theories with Charles Darwin who is not unsympa-
thetic. However Essex's ideas are a little too far out,
even for the man who espouses survival of the fittest.
En Sabah Nur, Apocalypse, also comes to Victorian
England, and tells the scientist that he can reach his
goal, but he must choose between it and his love for
his wife. Apocalypse also uses the Hellfire Club as his
pawns. Out of Essex he creates Mr. Sinister. Jean Grey
and Cyclops do their best to thwart Sinister and
Apocalypse. Cyclops even misses a chance to kill
Essex who as Sinister caused so much pain and
suffering for the Summers family.

This book includes an early version of the Marauders, a sketch book, and a forward and afterword by
Peter Milligan. This is one of the best X-Men solo
stories, and it deserves to be reprinted along with the
first series.

Moore, Alan, Alan Davis, Jose Villarrubia, et
    al. *Captain Britain*. New York: Marvel,
    2002. ISBN: 00785108556. Reprints *X-Men
    Archives 2–7*.

Captain Britain travels through various dimensions
and worlds to save Earth from robot superhero-killer
the Fury and catastrophe. Merlin the magician dies.

This rare collection has long been sought by Moore
aficionados. One of Moore's first works, it was originally available only from Marvel UK.

Moore, John Francis, Steve Epting, Terry Dod-
    son, et al. *Age of Apocalypse: Factor X*. New
    York: Marvel, 1995. ISBN: 0785101284.
    Reprints *Ultimate Factor X 1–4*.

Cyclops is freeing prisoners from Apocalypse's
stronghold. When he fights Northstar and Aurora, he
is found out. Mr. Sinister is planning his betrayal of

Apocalypse. Jean Grey and Cyclops are captured, and given to the Beast to experiment on. Havok and Cyclops fight, almost to the death.

Moore, John Francis, Brian K. Vaughan, Steve Epting, et al. *Tales from the Age of Apocalypse: Sinister Bloodlines*. New York: Marvel, 1997. ISBN: 0785105840.

Mr. Sinister, acting as a foster father, raises Cyclops and Havok. Their real father, Christopher Summers, comes back from space to meet them, but is taken captive by his sons who do not know him. The Beast and Sinister perform all kinds of experiments on him. Christopher Summers breaks free and meets his children, but he becomes Brood, and Cyclops is forced to kill him.

Morrison, Grant, Phil Jiminez, Chris Bachalo, et al. *New X-Men Vol. 5: Assault on Weapon Plus*. New York: Marvel, 2003. ISBN: 0785111190. Reprints *New X-Men 139–145*.

Jean Grey finds out that her husband has been having a mental affair with Emma Frost. She goes into Frost's mind, and forces her to relive painful events. Cyclops leaves the X-Men. Somebody shoots Emma Frost while she is in her glasslike state, and Bishop and Sage are called in to investigate the attempted murder. Beak and Flygirl have mutant-insect children. Cyclops and Wolverine get drunk at a special Hellfire Club bar. Fantomex and Wolverine recruit Cyclops to help them find the truth about a covert place known as Weapon Plus, or the World. This is a special place were reality is not always real, and where there are files on Wolverine's past. Mutants are being experimented on, and a new breed of mutant-killing Sentinels is being created.

Morrison, Grant, Phil Jimenez, Andy Lanning, et al. *New X-Men Vol. 6: Planet X*. New York: Marvel, 2004. ISBN: 0785112014. Reprints *New X-Men 146–150*.

Shaking the world of the X-Men, Xorn is actually Magneto in disguise. Magneto, posing as the healer Xorn, has infiltrated Xavier Mansion and the school by poisoning the minds of the special class and others. He put up an elaborate ruse to destroy the X-Men from within. He destroys Cerebro, tries to kill the rest of the X-Men, and cripples Xavier again. Magneto uses Esme as a means to an end, and brushes her off when she wants romance from him. Toad is back with Magneto as his henchman. Magneto becomes addicted to the mutant drug Kick. The Phoenix force is once again awakened in Jean Grey, which saves her life and Wolverine's while in space. Magneto goes crazy, and the people who were once his disciples realize just how off the wall he really is. He kills Jean Grey, and Wolverine, goes feral and kills Magneto. Later, it is learned that this Magneto was an imposter.

This volume includes Phil Jimenez's cover sketchbook.

Morrison, Grant, Igor Kordey, John Paul Leon, et al. *New X-Men Vol. 3: New Worlds*. New York: Marvel, 2002. ISBN: 0785109765. Reprints *New X-Men 127–133*.

Xorn tries to protect a young, sick, deformed mutant from an advancing mob. A mutant terrorist, Fantomex, seeks refuge with Xavier. Scott Summers begins to confide in Emma Frost, who has her own agenda with Cyclops. Archangel tries to train some young mutants. The X-Men go to Genosha and meet up with Quicksilver. Magneto's essence is very much alive, and there is a monument built to him. Xavier's former lover Lilandra tries to assassinate him, and she dumps him. Jean Grey's Phoenix force is reawakened.

Morrison, Grant, Frank Quitely, Keron Grant, et al. *New X-Men Vol. 4: Riot at Xavier's*. New York: Marvel, 2003. ISBN: 0785110674. Reprints *New X-Men 134–138*.

A very powerful telepathist, Quentin Quire, who is a student at the Xavier school, starts to believe that there can be no peaceful coexistence between humans and mutants. He starts to question Professor X, and leans more about Magneto's teachings. Quentin gathers a group of students who want to cause chaos during the school's Open Day when humans are allowed in. The group kidnaps Xavier, and holds him hostage. Humans kill the mutant Jumbo Carnation. Quentin's group also starts using an addictive, mutant drug Kick. Xorn takes a group of mutants out on a camping trip, and mutant organ hunters, the U-Men, attack them. The mutant girl Sophie sacrifices herself to save Xavier, and the other X-Men. Jean Grey catches her husband Cyclops fooling around with Emma Frost.

Morrison, Grant, Frank Quitely, Igor Kordey, et al. *New X-Men Vol. 2: Imperial*. New York: Marvel, 2002. ISBN: 0785108874. Reprints *New X-Men 118–126*.

Professor X's conscience is trapped within the broken body of his evil twin Cassandra Nova. Nova is controlling Xavier's body, and declares all-out war on mutants. During a previous battle, the X-Men were exposed to Nano-Sentinels, which act as a virus in the bloodstream to destroy mutants. Jean Grey puts Xavier's consciousness into her own. Xorn, who helps heal the X-Men, heals Xavier's legs.

This is the sequel to the "E is for Extinction" storyline.

Morrison, Grant, Frank Quitely, Mark Powers, et al. *New X-Men: E Is for Extinction*. New York: Marvel, 2001. ISBN: 0785108114. Reprints *New X-Men 114–117*.

A very powerful telepathic mutant-hating mutant, Cassandra Nova, finds a "lost" series of Sentinels to use in her plans of eradicating all mutants. She uses them to destroy the mutant state of Genosha, where Magneto supposedly dies. Nova takes control of Professor X's psyche.

This volume includes the Morrison Manifesto, in which the author gives his ideas for the X-Men, complete with story arc.

Morrison, Grant, Marc Silvestri, Tim Townsend, et al. *New X-Men Vol. 7: Here Comes Tomorrow*. New York: Marvel, 2004. ISBN: 0785113452. Reprints *New X-Men 151–154*.

The Beast wants to use the Phoenix egg to create his own master race. The X-Men, Wolverine, E.V.A., Beak, Cassandra Nova, Tom Skylark, and his giant robot Sentinel named Rover try to stop the Beast from getting and using the egg. It turns out that the Beast had been using the mutant drug Kick. Emma Frost and Scott Summers, Cyclops, kiss and decide to start a new mutant school.

This is Grant Morrison's last X-Men story arc, and one of his worst in the series. It is very derivative of earlier X-Men storylines, "Days of Future Past" and the "Age of Apocalypse." This story takes place 150 years in the future when the Beast is evil and seeks to blot out everyone who does not conform to his perfect gene pool.

Nicieza, Fabian, Mark Brooks, Shane Law, et al. *Cable and Deadpool Vol. 1: If Looks Could Kill*. New York: Marvel, 2004. ISBN: 0785 113746. Reprints *Cable & Deadpool 1–6*.

Deadpool is hired by the One World Church to get possession of a chemical biological agent which will turn humanity into a single blue mass of consciousness, which is in line with the church's agenda. Cable interferes and goes head-to-head with Deadpool, blowing out his brains. Deadpool becomes the church's assassin, and is cured from being a fleshy mess. Cable's techno virus and Deadpool's cancer end up consuming them, because the biological agent they digested was defective. Cable ends up swallowing Deadpool, and they both are cured, temporarily. Cable seeks to use the church's chemical agent for his own ends, to change the world into his version of paradise. Professor X warns him that there will be those who will try to stop him. Deadpool ends up being a fleshy mess again.

Nicieza, Fabian, Andy Kubert, Matt Ryan, et al. *Age of Apocalypse: The Amazing X-Men*. New York: Marvel, 1995. ISBN: 07851012 68. Reprints *Amazing X-Men 1–4*.

Magneto is kidnapped by Apocalypse. Banshee, Iceman, Exodus, Storm, and Quicksilver go up against Sentinels and the Abyss. The Abyss captures Bishop, and they rescue him. Rogue punches Gambit when she finds out her son Charles has been kidnapped by Apocalypse's henchmen.

Nicieza, Fabian, Salvador Larroca, Tony Daniel, et al. *X-Men: Age of Apocalypse: Gambit and the X-ternals*. New York: Marvel, 1995. ISBN: 0785101292. Reprints *Gambit and the X-ternals 1–4*.

Magneto recruits Gambit and his group of thieves to steal the precious M'Krann Crystal. They fight with the Imperial Guard and meet up with the Starjammers who help them in their quest. Gambit and the X-ternals actually go into the Crystal, and meet with the guardian living within. Sunspot gives his life in the quest. They manage to bring back a shard from the Crystal, but are betrayed by strongman, Guido Carosella, who is in league with Apocalypse. Magneto's child is kidnapped.

Nocenti, Ann, Arthur Adams, Whilce Portacio, et al. *Longshot*. New York: Marvel, 1989. ISBN: 087135568X. Reprints *Longshot 1–6*.

Longshot comes to Earth through a dimensional portal, with no memory of who he is. Dr. Strange helps him understand his purpose and background. Mojo and Spiral come through the portal, and try to recapture him. Mojo sets a up a church to worship him. Spider-Man and She-Hulk make appearances.

Nocenti, Ann, Rick Leonardi, P. Craig Russell, et al. *Colossus: God's Country*. New York: Marvel, 1994. Reprints *Marvel Presents 10–17*.

The X-Man Colossus takes a vacation into America's Heartland. He winds up having to deal with a group of cold warriors dedicated to keeping America pure. The group is out to destroy Colossus and the family who befriended him. Colossus demolishes a pornography newsstand.

This is a masterful piece of prose.

Olshevsky, George, Tony Frutti, Brent Anderson, et al. *The Marvel Comics Index: X-Men 9A*. San Diego: G&T Enterprises, 1981. ISBN: 0943348501 (*Marvel Index Set*).

This is an index and history of the X-Men through 1981. Comics indexed include *X-Men, X-Men Annual, Giant Size X-Men, Amazing Adventures, Ghost Rider*, and *Champions*. It includes a synopsis, personnel and major-character cross indexes, and a Golden Age cover gallery.

Olshevsky, George, Tony Frutti, John Romita Jr., et al. *The Official Marvel Index to the X-Men 1–7*. New York: Marvel, 1987–1988. ISBN: 0871352168 (Vol. 1).

The *X-Men Index* was Volume 4 of Marvel's Official Index series. The Avengers index series was the only other set done in Prestige Format. All other issues in the series were done as regular, floppy comic books. Each entry has character cross-references; synopses of issues, authors and artists; and date. This series covers *Uncanny X-Men 1–138*. Other titles indexed include *Classic X-Men, Amazing Adventures, Marvel Treasury Edition* featuring X-Men, *Ka-Zar, Marvel Tales, Incredible Hulk & Wolverine, King-Size X-Men, Giant Size X-Men, Phoenix:The Untold Story*, and *King Size Annual X-Men*. The book contains beautiful reproductions of the original covers.

Ostrander, John, Carlos Pacheco, Cam Smith, et al. *X-Men: Bishop the Mountjoy Crisis.* New York: Marvel, 1996. ISBN: 07851021 16. Reprints *Bishop 1–4.*

The time traveler Bishop has to stop an evil mutant, Mountjoy, from destroying the X-Men and rampaging in New York.

Raab, Ben, Terry Dodson, Rachel Dodson, et al. *Nate Grey: The X-Man: All Saints Day.* New York: Marvel, 1997. ISBN: 0785105999.

Nate Grey, the genetically engineered mutant whose powers are slowly killing him, goes to Transylvania to seek a doctor who can supposedly cure all illness. Grey goes in search of a cure for a young boy dying of leukemia. Dr. Absynthia is not as she appears to be, and has diabolical plans of her own.

This is a very good, heartwarming story of faith against all odds.

Shooter, Jim, Frank Springer, Vince Colletta, et al. *Dazzler: The Movie.* New York: Marvel, 1984. ISBN: 0871350009.

Dazzler gets involved with a Hollywood big-shot producer who promises her fame and fortune. Everything goes wrong when anti-mutant hysteria becomes a problem on the set. The financial backer of the film was once jilted by Dazzler, and wants his revenge by forcing her to become his property. She refuses, and destroys the last print of the movie, thus preventing it from being seen by the public.

This is one of the weirdest books Marvel ever published. It was the first graphic novel to feature the mutant Dazzler. (*Marvel Graphic Novel 12*)

Simonson, Walter, Jackson Guice, Geof Isherwood, et al. *X-Men: Days of Future Present.* New York: Marvel, 1991. ISBN: 08713573 99. Reprints *Fantastic Four Annual 23*; *New Mutants Annual 6*; *X-Factor Annual 5*; *X-Men Annual 14.*

Franklin Richards comes from the future as a grownup. In his future all mutants are dead, destroyed by the mutant-hating Ahab. The Fantastic Four, X-Men, New Mutants, and X-Factor all team up to help stop Ahab from destroying them in the present. Ahab turns Cyclops and the Invisible Woman into his mutant-hunting hounds. Rachel reveals to Jean Grey and Scott Summers that she is their daughter from the future.

This is the sequel to the famous "Days of Future Past" storyline.

Simonson, Louise, Rob Liefeld, Hilary Barta, et al. *Cable and the New Mutants.* New York: Marvel, 1990. ISBN: 0871359375. Reprints *New Mutants 86–91; 93–94; 100.*

Cable's brother Stryfe tries to poison the world's water supply, and thus destroy humanity. New Mutants get new costumes. The Blob, Mystique, Angel, and Pyro make appearances, as Freedom Force. Cable is introduced to the New Mutants, and takes over their training. The Mutant Liberation Front kidnaps two of the New Mutants. Stryfe heads the MLF. There is a battle of epic proportions between Cable and Wolverine. Cannonball, Sunfire, Boom Boom, and Warlock are taken captive by the MLF.

Starlin, Jim, Jackson Guice, Michael Heisler, et al. *X-Factor: Prisoner of Love.* New York: Marvel, 1990. ISBN: 0871356953.

A beautiful female who is on the run from the Dark Ones rescues the Beast from some hoods. Iceman and Angel try to rescue Beast. Beast falls in love with the mysterious female who drains his life energy like a vampire. In fact she even bites him, but has to leave. The Beast aids her against the Dark Ones.

This is one of the few solo stories featuring the Beast.

Stephenson, Rick, Roger Cruz, Larry Stucker, et al. *X-Force/Youngblood: Smokin' Mojo.* Fullerton/New York: Image/Marvel, 1996.

Youngblood's Shaft gets transported to Xavier's mansion. His Youngblood colleagues are taken to Mojo's world of television and ratings for reality-based-danger shows. Cable and X-Force agree to help Shaft find his comrades, and save them from Mojo's schemes.

Stern, Roger, John Buscema, Kurt Busiek, et al. *X-Men Phoenix Rising.* New York: Marvel, 1999. ISBN: 0785107188. Reprints *Avengers 263*; *Fantastic Four 286*; *X-Factor 1.*

The body of Jean Grey is found at the bottom of the ocean. The Fantastic Four is called in to help at the Avenger's mansion. Jean Grey is revived and recalls the sordid past of the entity Phoenix. The original five X-Men are reunited as X-Factor, posing as mutant investigators. Sub-Mariner is asked to be a member of the Avengers.

Stern, Roger, Tom DeFalco, Marc Silvestri, et al. *X-Men Versus the Avengers.* New York: Marvel, 1993. ISBN: 0871359677. Reprints *X-Men Versus the Avengers 1–4.*

Magneto is headmaster at Xavier's school, and wants to find a meteor which fell to Earth. The Avengers doubt his motive, given Magneto's villainous past. The Avengers come into conflict with the X-Men. They also have to deal with the Crimson Dynamo and the Soviet Super Soldiers.

Thomas, Roy, Neal Adams, Tom Palmer, et al. *Greatest Battles of the X-Men.* New York: Marvel, 1994. ISBN: 0785100423. Reprints *Uncanny X-Men 57–59; 137, 141–142, 277.*

This volume collects stories in which the X-Men do battle with the Sentinels, the Imperial Guard of

Lilandra, the Brotherhood of Evil Mutants, and a doppelganger of Xavier. The Watcher makes an appearance.

Thomas, Roy, Werner Roth, Dan Adkins, et al. *Spider Man and the Uncanny X-Men*. New York: Marvel, 1996. ISBN: 0785102000. Reprints *Uncanny X-Men 27, 35*; *Amazing Spider Man 92*; *Marvel Team-Up Annual 1*; *Marvel Team-Up 150*; *Spectacular Spider Man 197–199*.

This is a nice collection of Spidet-Man team-ups with the X-Men. In one issue, the X-Men ask Spider-Man to join them in their first meeting, but Spider-Man declines the offer. In another issue, the X-Men inadvertently think Spider-Man is a villain, and fight him. Ice Man and Spider-Man fight each other in a third story, and the X-Men and Spider-Man match wits against Professor Power.

Tischman, David, Igor Kordey, Chris Sotomayor, et al. *Cable Vol. 1: The Shining Path*. New York: Marvel, 2002. ISBN: 078510 9099. Reprints *Cable 97–100*.

Cable goes Peru to stop a communist terrorist organization, the Shining Path, from taking over the country. In the future, the Shining Path's actions have disastrous results. Cable rids himself of the techo-organic virus, and teaches a young boy about the Askani philosophy and discipline.

This volume's special features include a "nuff said" full script for issue 100, by Tischman, and an introduction, by artist Igor Kordey.

Tischman, David, Darko Macan, Igor Kordey, et al. *Cable: The End*. New York: Marvel, 2002. ISBN: 0785109633. Reprints *Cable 101–107*.

Cable goes to Kosovo and Macedonia to help ease the tension in those war-torn countries. He teams up with a famous lady scientist. The Albanians are cloning soldiers in order to wipe out opposing forces and "clean" the gene pool. Cable gets shot in the head, but his mutant power helps him recover. He goes to Rio de Janeiro, and tries to stop a mutant boxing match. He wipes the minds of the spectators, and runs away. He goes to buy arms with a S.H.I.E.L.D. agent. The S.H.I.E.L.D. agent is killed, and Cable's rage takes out the dealers. Mr. Singapore wants Cable as a pawn for one of his political games, but Cable shows him the true depth of his power.

Torres, J., Makoto Nakatsuka, Hiromi Nakatsuka, et al. *Marvel Mangaverse Vol. 4: X-Men Ronin*, New York: Marvel, 2003. ISBN: 0785111158. Reprints *X-Men: Ronin 1–4*.

Xavier is the evil leader of the Hellfire Club. The Hellfire club, through Emma Frost, tries to forcibly get Jean Grey to join their ranks. The X-Men consists of Wolverine, Jean Grey, Storm, Cyclops, and Toad, who is their sensei. Forge is a member of the police force.

This volume includes appearances by the Manga, Wolfsbane, Gambit, Iceman, Pyro, Mastermind, Sentinels, and Psylocke, among others.

Vaughn, Brian K., Jorge Lucas, Daniel Perez Sanchez, et al. *Mystique Vol. 1: Drop Dead Gorgeous*. New York: Marvel, 2004. ISBN: 07851132405. Reprints *Mystique 1–6*.

One of Xavier's top, covert, mutant operatives is killed. He contacts Forge to help find Mystique. She agrees to help Xavier by becoming an undercover agent for him. She goes to Cuba to find out where several Soviet Sentinels are being kept. Mutants in Cuba have been disappearing, and are being used as guinea pigs to test out the Sentinels. She meets a three-inch-tall operative named Shortpack. Mystique agrees to do undercover work for Xavier and another mysterious client.

Vaughn, Brian K., Brandon Peterson, Justin Ponsor, et al. *Ultimate X-Men Vol. 9: The Tempest*. New York: Marvel, 2004. ISBN: 0785114041. Reprints *Ultimate X-Men 46–49*.

Angel and Nightcrawler try to recruit the mutant who becomes Northstar for the X-Men, but he refuses. The Beast's funeral commences, and Storm takes it really hard. Mutants are being killed throughout New York. Mr. Sinister debuts as a disciple of Apocalypse. Dazzler pops into the Danger Room, drunk. The X-Men split up trying to find the mutant serial killer, leaving Professor X and the younger mutants alone. Sinister goes to the X-Mansion. He throws Xavier down a flight of stairs, and smashes Iceman.

This volume includes Vaughn's outline for Mr. Sinister, and Peterson's cover pencils.

Vaughn, Brian K., Michael Ryan, Manuel Garcia, et al. *Mystique Vol. 2: Tinker, Tailor, Mutant, Spy*. New York: Marvel, 2004. ISBN: 0785115552. Reprints *Mystique 7–13*.

Professor X has Mystique go after a new strain of smallpox which is spread telepathically. She goes to Johannesburg and finds a disease-loving mutant called the Host who also wants the virus. The Host threatens Shortpack's life, and lets the virus free. The virus only attacks people who have been vaccinated against smallpox. Mystique pretends to get sick from the disease, and then electrocutes the Host. Another group tries to get Mystique to play both sides and eventually kill Professor X. When Forge asks her out for coffee, they hear of a young mutant boy who has been captured. It turns out that this three-eyed mutant can control men. Mystique and Force duke it out. Xavier sends Mystique to Brazil to find a dead mutant's hand. She ends up helping a woman who seeks to be a man.

Whedon, Joss, John Cassaday, Laura Martin, et al. *Astonishing X-Men Vol. 1: Gifted.* New York: Marvel, 2004. ISBN: 0785115315. Reprints *Astonishing X-Men 1–6.*

Emma Frost and Cyclops start the school over again with a new team featuring Cyclops, The White Queen, Shadowcat, Wolverine, and the Beast. Kitty Pryde rejoins at the request of Emma Frost. Kitty explains why she hates Frost so much. It is because the first time she ever met the X-Men, Frost had captured and caged them. A mutant cure has been discovered, and the alien Ord wants it because a mutant will destroy his world in the future. It turns out that part of this project has been under the supervision of S.H.I.E.L.D. However, much of the experimentation on mutants was unknown to Nick Fury, but not to his extraterrestrial liaison. Apparently they stole Colossus's body, revived him, and have been experimenting on him ever since his death. The Beast wants to try the cure on himself, but Logan disagrees, and they end up fighting in the school. Ord gives the cure to a student at the school, and nearly kills him when he looses his flying power. As Ord tries to leave, Colossus throws Wolverine as a fastball, and he does not escape. Colossus rejoins the X-Men. Cyclops and Wolverine fight over Jean Grey.

Winick, Judd, Jim Calafiore, Kev Walker, et al. *Exiles Vol. 4: Legacy.* New York: Marvel, 2003. ISBN: 0785111093. Reprints *Exiles 20–25.*

The Exiles go to an Earth where the Legacy Virus has mutated with a sentient computer force which originated from the New Mutant Warlock. The Exiles team up with the Avengers, which include Doc Ock, Spider-Woman, Frog, Rhino, Beast, and the Blob, among others. Blink is infected with the virus, and almost dies. Rachel Summers, with Morph's help, asks the Asgardian Gods to use their blood in the antidote. Blink gets to go home, back to her time. Tony Stark, Iron Man, becomes a power-hungry dictator. The Weapon X Exiles are brought in, to help Stark attack the Inhumans. He wants to use their DNA as a prototype for new Super Soldiers to conquer the Universe. Weapon X fights against Wonderman, Scarlet Witch, and Dr. Strange. Black Bolt is married to Sue Storm, Invisible Woman, and sacrifices himself to save his race. Sue ends up killing Stark just before she is shot. She-Hulk gets to go home, and Colossus replaces her in Weapon X.

Exiles Vol. 5: Unnatural Instincts appears among the entries for "Austen" earlier in this chapter.

Winick Judd, Tom Mandrake, Clayton Henry, et al. *Exiles Vol. 6: Fantastic Voyage.* New York: Marvel, 2004. ISBN: 0785111972. Reprints *Exiles 31–37.*

The Exiles are transported to a planet on which the Avengers are vampires and Captain America is the King of Vampires. They seek out the original Union Jack for help in defeating the Avengers. When they are defeated, and Union Jack reveals himself also to be a vampire, Sunfire kills him. Morph and Sasquatch go up against a feral Wolverine, and Sunfire and Nocturne go back to a world they have already saved. Spider-Girl and Sunfire rekindle their romantic affair, but then Sunfire is whisked away. The Exiles go with the Fantastic Four on the fateful day when they are bombarded with comic rays. Mimic is transformed into a Brood, and it takes the rest of the Exiles and the Thing to stop him. Sunfire is killed and Blink returns.

Winick, Judd, Mike McKone, Jim Calafiore, et al. *Exiles Vol. 2: A World Apart.* New York: Marvel 2002. ISBN: 0785110216. Reprints *Exiles 5–11.*

The Exiles team up with Alpha Flight to subdue the Hulk. Sabretooth, Deadpool, and Weapon X try to thwart their plans, but to no avail. Sabretooth smells Blink. John Proudstar meets an alternate version of himself in Alpha Flight. They end up on an Earth which has been taken over by Skrulls. Nearly all superhumans are imprisoned and forced to fight each other for the entertainment of Skrulls. Galactus comes to Earth, and the Skrulls leave. The Exiles, along with Earth's superhumans, are forced to fight him. T-Bird fights Galactus until he is in a coma. Nocturne is pregnant with T-Bird's child, but T-Bird is on Earth in a coma, and Sasquatch is his replacement. Sunfire admits to Morph that she is gay, even though he is in love with her.

Winick, Judd, Mike McKone, Jim Calafiore, et al. *Exiles Vol. 3: Out of Time.* New York: Marvel 2003. ISBN: 0785110852. Reprints *Exiles 12–19.*

The Exiles, with their new member Sasquatch, meet the time-traveling counterpart of Weapon X, which includes Sabretooth, She-Hulk, Vision, Spider, and Storm. Sabretooth and Blink are happily reunited from the Age of Apocalypse timeline. They are commanded to kill a child who will grow up to be evil. The Exiles have to side with Dr. Doom against the Sub-Mariner who is trying to take over the world. Mimic ends up defeating Namor. Nocturne loses her baby through the time warp, and reveals how she fell in love with the late Thunderbird. Mojo brings the Exiles to Mojoverse, to use Morph for his television show to get higher ratings. Mojo tortures and jails Nocturne, as collateral for Morph's cooperation. The rest of the Exiles break Longshot out of jail, and try to rescue Morph and Nocturne from Mojo's clutches. The Exiles also deal with the world of the Lizard.

Winick, Judd, Mike McKone, Mark McKenna et al. *Exiles.* New York: Marvel, 2002. ISBN: 0785108335. Reprints *Exiles 1–4.*

Led by Blink, the Exiles consist of mutants that were pulled from alternate timelines and universes to correct problems in Multiverse. This book has been described as a comic version of "*Mission Impossible* meets *Quantum Leap*." Some of the characters include Mimic, Morph, and Nocturne, the daughter of Nightcrawler, among others. Their travels take them back to the trail of Phoenix, where they are instructed to kill Jean Grey. Magnus, Magneto's son, dies in an effort to free his father. Mimic destroys an evil version of Professor X.

4

Minor Characters and
Minor Character Combos

Minor Characters

Have you noticed an aura of strangeness in your life?
—*Damion Hellstorm to Johnny Blaze*

Nothing living is meant to remain the same.—*Jude, the Entropic Man*

Abnett, Dan, Andy Lanning, Igor Kordey, et al. *Tales of Marvels: The Wonder Years 1–2*. New York: Marvel, 1995.

Cindy Knutz, a young woman, becomes obsessed with Simon Williams after he saves her from destruction at the hands of Red Ronin. She accidentally commandeers his glasses. Cindy joins the Wonder Man fan club, and even moves to L.A. to be near him. Shortly after the West Coast Avengers disbanded, Cindy and her friend Bernie go to the Mansion, hoping to find a collectible trinket. The Kree come and attack the remaining Avengers, and Wonder Man is killed. Cindy is invited to the funeral, but she refuses to believe that Simon is dead. She leaves the funeral when she realized that Bernie, who was also invited, may have killed herself in despair over Wonder Man's death.

These beautifully painted volumes looks at Marvel's Wonder Man through the eyes of Cindy Knutz. The volumes include news clippings which are excerpts from the *Wonder Fan Newsletter*. This Marvel Select imprint is recommended.

Austen, Chuck, Bruce Jones, David Finch, et al. *The Call of Duty Vol. 1: The Brotherhood and the Wagon*. New York: Marvel, 2002. ISBN: 5552444930 (trd); 0785109714 (pbk). Reprints *Call of Duty: The Wagon 1–4*; *Call of Duty: The Brotherhood 1–6*.

This is the story of several firefighters, a police officer and an ambulance medic whose lives become intertwined again and again because a mystical young girl keeps appearing and telling them that some horrible accident is about to occur. It is a realistic tale of the day-to-day lives of civil-service workers, with a bit of fantasy thrown in.

Azzarello, Brian, Richard Corben, Jose Villarrubia, et al. *Cage Vol. 1*. New York: Marvel, 2002. ISBN: 0785109668 (trd); ISBN: 078 5113010 (pbk). Reprints *Cage 1–5*.

Luke Cage, the Hero for Hire and the second Power Man in the Marvel Universe, is hired to help find out who killed a thirteen-year-old girl in a drive-by shooting. Cage finds himself embroiled in the middle of a gang/drug war between Hammerhead and Tombstone. Cage plays both sides against each other.

This "Boys in the Hood equivalent told in comics format for adults," is part of Marvel's adult Max line. It is very graphic in the execution of the story, well written and beautifully illustrated. Recommended, but not for the faint of heart. The introduction is by postmodern novelist Darius James.

Baron, Mike, Shawn Martinbrough, Carl Potts, et al. *Tales of the Marvels: Blockbuster*. New York: Marvel, 1995.

A former police officer, now a private detective, stalks the Silver Surfer. His parents died in a battle between the Surfer and Tyros. The detective falls in love with a graduate student who is studying the Surfer scientifically. A small-time crook attempts to take on the Kingpin, with disastrous results.

This is a sequel, of sorts, to the *Marvels* series. It is beautifully written and drawn.

Barr, Mike, Rob Ortaleza, Ken Lopez, et al. *Mandrake the Magician 1–3*. New York: Marvel, 1995.

Mandrake, with the help of a female archaeologist, is searching for the 13th scroll. The Black Wizard steals the 12th scroll, and kidnaps Mandrake. Octon is using the Black Wizard as his pawn. Both Mandrake and his enemies are imprisoned by the Guardian in the mystical prison of Theugia.

This cardstock series was part of the Marvel Select line, and features Lee Falk's famous magician Mandrake. We learn about Mandrake's sister and a bit about Mandrake's past.

Bendis, Brian Michael, Michael Gaydos, Mark Bagley, et al. *Alias Vol. 4: The Secret Origin of Jessica Jones*. New York: Marvel, 2004. ISBN: 0785111670. Reprints *Alias 22–28*.

Jessica Jones becomes as a super-powered being after a car wreck which kills her family and exposes her to experimental government material. As a teenager she has a crush on Peter Parker. She stops the Scorpion in a laundromat robbery. She becomes Jewel, but gets entrapped for eight months under the Purple Man's spell. She is hired to talk with the Purple Man, and get him to admit to some murders. He escapes, and attempts to control Jessica again, but she fights back with a psychic-defense trigger put into her psyche by Jean Grey. She is pregnant with Luke Cage's baby, and Scott Lang dumps her. Avengers, Nick Fury, and Clay Quaterman make appearances.

Bendis, Brian Michael, Michael Gaydos, David Mack, et al *Alias Vol. 1*. New York: Marvel, 2003. ISBN: 0785111417. Reprints *Alias 1–9*.

Jessica Jones, a former superhero who has given up the cape and tights, has her own private-investigator service. She sleeps with Luke Cage. While working on a case, she inadvertently captures Captain America's secret identity on film. A political opponent wants to use the film against Captain America, and murders Captain America's girlfriend. Jones is questioned as a suspect in the murder. The wife of a man impersonating Rick Jones hires Jessica to find her husband. She finds him, and also finds out that he is not the real Rick Jones. She is hired to spy on a husband who's been having gay cybersex.

This is part of Marvel's adult Max line.

Bendis, Brian Michael, Michael Gaydos, David Mack, et al. *Alias Vol. 2: Come Home*. New York: Marvel, 2003. ISBN: 0785111230. Reprints *Alias 11–15*.

Jessica Jones is hired to find a missing teenager in a small backwoods town that is plagued by racism. It is believed that the young teenage girl might be a mutant, and that her disappearance might be a hate crime. Jones has a one-night stand with the sheriff of the town. His sister-in-law murders the teenage girl's father. The girl, who ran away, is found by Jones who goes out with Ant-Man, Scott Lang, on a date. Luke Cage and Matt Murdock make an appearance.

Bendis, Brian Michael, Michaell Gaydos, Cory Petit, et al. *Alias Vol. 3: The Underneath*. New York: Marvel, 2003. ISBN: 0785111 654. Reprints *Alias 10, 16–21*.

Jessica Jones is hired by Jonah Jameson to find out the identity of Spider-Man. Teenager Mattie Franklin, the third Spider-Woman, shows up at Jones's apartment stoned out of her mind. Franklin, who has been adopted by Jameson, has been missing. When Jones confronts Jameson, he accuses her of kidnapping Mattie. Jones searches for Franklin who is being used as drug source. Her boyfriend has her hooked on some kind of drug. The original Spider-Woman, Jessica Drew, also thinks Jones has kidnapped Franklin, and a fight ensues. They eventually work together to save Mattie from the drug pushers. The New Warrior, Speedball, makes a cameo. Scott Lang and Jessica get into a fight, but Lang eventually admits his love for her.

Bendis, Brian Michael, Mike Avno Oeming, Peter Pantazis, et al. *Powers Vol. 6: The Sellouts*. New York: Marvel, 2004. ISBN: 078 511582X; 1582403449 (Image). Reprints *Powers 25–30*.

Homicide detectives Christian Walker and Deena Pilgrim investigate murders specific to enhanced humans. A famous former member of the superhero group Unity is involved in a sex scandal, and is murdered. The police have a tape of the murder, but the murderer appears to be invisible. The detectives investigate the history of the Unity group, only to find that other members of Unity are also being murdered. A huge explosion happens in Story, Utah. It turns out that one of the former members of Unity, disillusioned, is killing the heroes. Detective Pilgrim is put into the hospital.

This resembles a *noir*, comic-book version of the movie *48 hours* and similar films. It is the equivalent of an R-rated movie, for adults only, but highly recommended. The volume is part of the Icon imprint, and reprints some of Bendis and Oeming's creator-owned, award-winning Powers series. It contains a detailed interview with artist Oeming, pencil sketches, and a cover gallery. The picture-perfect, sensationalist newsletter *Under the Cape* appears throughout the comic.

Bendis, Brian Michael, Michael Avon Oeming, Peter Pantazis, et al. *Powers Volume 7: Forever*. New York: Marvel, 2004. ISBN: 0785116567. Reprints *Powers 31–37*.

Walker is an immortal Power who can't be destroyed. His nemesis, the man with the red, who is pure evil, tries to destroy his spirit at every turn. Walker struggles with morality and ethics throughout the ages. He joins an ancient, hermetic, Eastern sect of like individuals, but eventually leaves, to help humanity. Eventually Walker looses his powers, and becomes a detective. The "red" man disembowels Walker's wife.

This volume of the Icon series is the biggest *Powers* trade collection to date. It is a bizarre book which looks into the inner life of Detective Walker, and contains the infamous, controversial, monkey anal-sex scenes, with very little dialogue. It includes a prologue and script for the "infamous monkey issue," and a sketch and cover gallery.

Busiek, Kurt, Joe Clifford Faust, L. Neil Smith, et al. *Open Space 1–4*. New York: Marvel, 1989–1990. ISBN: 0871356384 (3); 0871356694 (4).

This series was part of the *Marvel Graphics* imprint. It is a bizarre "Shared Universe" story set in the late twenty-first century in which science-fiction writers and artists who don't normally write comics come together and tell a short tale. Each book has four stories. In this future dystopia, corporations like AstroNet have almost complete control of humanity on Earth, and seek to make outer space profitable as well. Two families, the Brodys and Ethcisons, are always at odds. This was supposed to be on an ongoing series, but only four issues came out. Artist Alex Ross did his first artwork for Marvel in *Wizard's Open Space 0*. Despite the fact that *Open Space* only contains four issues, it is an intelligent work that any fan of utopian/dystopian literature should read.

Busiek, Kurt, Alex Ross, Stan Lee, et al. *Marvels*. New York: Marvel, 2001. ISBN: 0785100490 (pbk); 078510061X (trd, 1994); 0752206451 (pbk, 1994); 0613536886 (ltd, 2003). Reprints *Marvels 0–4*.

This is the greatest Marvel story ever produced, showcasing the artwork of Alex Ross. The story follows a newspaper photographer, Phil Sheldon, from his first encounter with two superbeings, the original Human Torch and the Sub-Mariner during World War II, to the death of Gwen Stacy. Sheldon gives his perspective on the Fantastic Four's "marriage" and on Galactus, Silver Surfer, Mutants, and Power Man. He produces a book of photography called *Marvels*, which features them in action. That story is the inspiration behind this book. It includes an introduction by Stan Lee, and commentary by Kurt Busiek, John Romita Sr., Scott McCloud, and Alex Ross. Nearly every event is documented by an earlier Marvel comic, starting with the Golden Age *Marvel Comics* and *Marvel Mystery Comics*, and going to the Silver and early Bronze Age Marvel Comics. Each comic is cited. Ross demonstrates and comments on his drawing technique. He also discusses his real-life models for various scenes. The original four-issue series was in Prestige Format, and had beautifully produced covers.

Byrne, John, Mark Gruenwald, Sal Buscema, et al. *The Pitt*. New York: Marvel, 1987. ISBN: 0871353369.

After the "White Event," some people in the general population start developing paranormal powers. Pittsburgh disappears, and falls into a pit—the Pitt. A ghost, the Witness, sees the destruction and the cause of Pittsburgh's demise. A human-controlled robot, Spitfire, tries to save human life while the army tries to declare martial law.

The book includes an introduction by the Witness, and an afterword by Colonel Browning. A schematic of the Pitt is also included. This is the first graphic novel published as part of Marvel's New Universe experiment.

Claremont, Chris, Terry Austin, Bill Mantlo, et al. *Amazing Adventures: Tales of Exotic Places, People, and Times*. New York: Marvel, 1988. ISBN: 0871353393.

This collection of graphic short stories is taken from various genres, including science fiction, pulp, fantasy, and historical fiction. One story deals with a Jew who learns how to fight back against the Nazis as they kill his loved ones, and another deals with the Polish pogroms against the Jews in the 1600s. Other stories deal with the Holy Grail; the first submarine, known as the Turtle, which was launched during the Revolutionary War; and the female spy Mata Hari.

Claremont, Chris, John Bolton, Tom Orzechowski, et al. *Marada: The She-Wolf*. New York: Marvel, 1985. ISBN: 0871351536.

A demon has his way with the young Marada, and rapes her. Eventually she faces the demon who wants his way with her again, and she kills him. She and her goddaughter are taken prisoner by a queen who wishes to play the "most dangerous game," and hunts Marada and her goddaughter. Marada defeats the queen in combat, and the spirit of the "She-Wolf" is restored.

Marada is the story of a young girl with the fierce power of a warrior, who has been beaten down through sorcery. Stories featuring Marada were originally published by *Epic Illustrated* as short adventures (*Marvel Graphic Novel 21*)

Claremont, Chris, John Byrne, Terry Austin et al. *Starlord Megazine*. New York: Marvel, 1996. Reprints *Marvel Preview 11*.

Peter Jason Quill is an enhanced being who fights for the rights of people, and loves to explore space. His ship is sentient. Star-Lord rescues the prisoners of a group of Slavers, taking them to the planet Wind-hölme. Kip and Sandy then join Peter, two recent slaves who wish vengeance on those who had sent the Slavers. Their search brings them to the planet Cinnibar where they find out about a conspiracy that is taking place on Sparta. They learn that the profits from the worlds stripped by the Slavers are being used to replace the Emperor with an evil prince, Gareth. Quill confronts Gareth and his associate Rruothk'ar whom he recognizes as the one who slew his mother. Star-Lord fights and kills Rruothk'ar and Gareth. He meets the Emperor, who reveals himself to be Quill's father Jason, and who also reveals his origins. Jason offers Peter the role as heir to the throne of Sparta, but Peter declines, preferring the freedom of space. Instead, Quill recommends that Jason adopt Kip, and take him as heir to the throne. Eventually, Star-Lord and his father go out into space together, and Kip is left to rule.

This is a bizarre science-fiction story in the spirit of Flash Gordon and Buck Rogers. This book includes a brief preview of the Star-Lord limited series.

Claremont, Chris, Oscar Jimenez, Michael Ryan, et al. *Contest of Champions II*. New York: Marvel, 2001. ISBN: 0785108130. Reprints *Contest of Champions Vol. II: 1–5.*

The Heroes of Earth are transported by the Coterie into space. The Coterie wishes to see the Heroes battle one another in a seemingly benign contest. Iron Man soon learns the sinister plans of the Coterie are actually from the Brood Queen, who wishes the best of the Earth's heroes to become royal hosts. The Coterie is actually the Brotherhood of Badoon. Some of the contests include the Hulk against Mr. Fantastic, in which the Hulk wins by eating Mr. Fantastic and spitting him out; the new Spider-Woman against the Human Torch; Daredevil against Deadpool; Thor against Storm; the Thing against Phoenix; and Captain America against the Black Panther. Carol Danvers has a reconciliation of sorts with Rogue. The Brood Queen tries to take on Rogue's persona.

The book includes a history of Marvel battles by Robert Greenberger, going back to the Timely Comic days. See the entry for Volume I under "Mantlo" in this chapter subsection.

Cockrum, Dave, Jim Novak, Paty, et al. *The Futurians*. New York: Marvel, 1983. ISBN: 09379766817.

The Ghron go back in time to the twentieth century in order to change the timeline so they will be victorious in the future. The wisest and most powerfull Terminus, General Callistrax, also goes back in time to stop the attacks on Earth. He puts together a group of super-powered beings to stop the invasion. These include Sunswift, Avatar, Werehawk, Terrayne, Blackmane, Mosquito, Silkie, and Silver Shadow.

This is a science-fiction story about the battle between two warring groups: the Ghron (*Inheritors*) and the Terminus. (*Marvel Graphic Novel 9*)

Colon, Ernie, A. A. Perry, Sid Jacobson, et al. *AX*. New York: Marvel, 1988. ISBN: 0871 35490X.

This a weird science-fiction story about a young boy who is on a medieval planet, and is a prophesied savior on another, technologically sophisticated planet. They are at war with the aboriginal inhabitants of another world, and it is up to the boy to bring all the worlds together in a harmonious way. (*Marvel Graphic Novel 43*)

David, Peter, Salvador Larroca, Art Thiebert, et al. *Return of the Heroes*. New York: Marvel, 1999. ISBN: 0785107053. Reprints *Heroes Reborn: The Return 1–4.*

After the death of many of Marvel's greatest heroes at the hands of Onslaught, Franklin Richards imports them to another Earth, in another dimension, with no memory of the incidents. A Celestial visits Franklin to test him. Franklin decides to go ahead and transport the heroes back to Earth. The heroes include the Fantastic Four, Dr. Doom, the Hulk, Iron Man, and She-Hulk. There are two Hulks, one of which goes to the other dimension. Spider-Man is also transported. Dr. Doom unsuccessfully tries to harness Franklin's powers for himself. Captain America's partner Bucky is a woman whom he leaves behind. Man Thing, Eternity, and others make appearances.

DeFalco, Tom, Barry Windsor-Smith, Herb Trimpe, et al. *Machine Man*. New York: Marvel, 1988. ISBN: 0071354581. Reprints *Machine Man 1–4.*

In the year 2020, Machine Man is found in a junkyard by some looters. They reactivate him, and are forced to run from Baintronics robot soldiers. They go to a special hideout where Machine Man is reunited with his friend Gears Gavin. Machine Man fights and defeats Arno Stark, the Iron Man of 2020.

Delano, Jamie, David Lloyd, Jenny O'Conner, et al. *Night Raven: House of Cards*. London: Marvel UK, 1992.

A vigilante who poses as a maintenance man and cab driver tries to clean up the various mobs throughout the city. He puts a Night Raven mark on his kills. He falls in love with a young woman who is being forced into prostitution. Her boyfriend betrays her, and she is ultimately killed. The Night Raven exposes a corrupt congressman.

This is a crime *noir* graphic novel, similar to many of the pulp stories from the thirties and forties. It is beautifully written and drawn.

DeMatteis, J.M., Mark Badger, Ann Nocenti, et al. *Greenberg, the Vampire*. New York: Marvel, 1986. ISBN: 0871350904.

Oscar Greenberg gets an offer to write a screenplay for one of his novels that is to be made into a movie.

He believes that a serial killer, someone who is killing women, is Adam's first wife Lillith. Lillith's spirit tries to deceive Oscar into becoming her mate, but she has no love or affection. A rabbi is brought in to exorcise Lillith, but it is Oscar's love for his vampire companion that triumphs over her.

The book contains several narrative texts, including "Confessions of a Vampire," "Second Book of Genesis," a screenplay draft, and a letter to Greenberg's dead mother. This is a beautifully written story about a Jewish vampire, Oscar Greenberg, who is also a horror novelist. (*Marvel Graphic Novel 20*)

DeVries, Dave, Glen Lumsden, John Costanza, et al. *The Phantom Ghost Who Walks 1–3.* New York: Marvel 1995.

In the African state of Bangala, certain mining interests want to mine in an area where, in order to protect their land and lives, the traditional chiefs refuse to allow mining. But the companies, along with a greedy general, seek to destroy the chiefs and allow mining to run rampant. The Phantom comes in to stop the greedy capitalists.

This cardstock-cover mini-series features Lee Falk's the Phantom. In it we learn some of the history behind the various Phantoms, and how the mantle is passed from father to son—how, as one phantom dies, another takes over. The book includes various Phantom Journal Disk entries.

Dixon, Chuck, Tristan Shane, Brad Parker, et al. *Code of Honor 1–4.* New York: Marvel, 1997.

This is a sequel to *Marvels* told from the perspective of a police officer who lives in a world of super-powered beings. The officer resents the superbeings, and considers them to be show-offs, who save the world every other day. When his car is stopped, the Kingpin "accidentally" leaves a $1,000 bill, and the officer takes it. The trials of dealing with corruption, marriage, and family are woven throughout this story. It includes several important events in the history of the Marvel Universe, including Secret Wars, the arrest of the Punisher, and the Dark Phoenix saga. There are appearances by the Silver Surfer, Daredevil, the Abomination, and Luke Cage, among others.

Dixon, Chuck, Timothy Truman, Gary Kwapisz, et al. *Ka-Zar: Guns of the Savage Land.* New York: Marvel, 1990. ISBN: 087135 6414.

Lord Kevin Reginald Plunder, Ka-Zar, is being driven to madness because he is living within the confines of civilization. Wyatt Wingfoot hires Ka-Zar and his wife Shanna to find out about a secret passage in the Southwestern American desert that leads to a hidden land, the Savage Land. They find the Savage Land, and Ka-Zar declares himself Lord. Pluto Fuel has been exploiting the land and its people, but Ka-Zar rallies the natives against the fuel company, and they drive it out. Shanna leaves Ka-Zar,

because she believes he is too old to play Lord of the Jungle. (*Marvel Graphic Novel 62*)

Dunn, Ben, Kevin Gunstone, C.B. Cebulski, et al. *Marvel Mangaverse Volume II.* New York: Marvel, 2002. ISBN: 0785110062. Reprints *Marvel Mangaverse 1–6.*

Galactus has come to destroy Earth, and the Watcher asks the Fantastic Four to find Captain Marvel's son. Marvel goes into Galactus, and frees the Inhumans. He defeats a Skrull-like creature in the heart of Galactus. Dr. Strange, Tigra, and Scarlet Witch go up against Dr. Doom. Doom kills the president, Captain America, in his quest to have the world join in her plans. The Black Panther infiltrates Doom's stronghold, only to find out that his sister T'Channa is Doom.

The dialogue is exceptionally good in the first story, "Hungry Planet." These stories are rooted in Marvel history, and told in the Japanese manga style.

Ellis, Warren, Cliff Nielsen, Terese Nielsen, et al. *Ruins 1–2.* New York: Marvel, 1995.

The Avengers' plane blows up. Nick Fury shoots Jean Grey who is a prostitute, and then shoots himself. Cyclops and Nightcrawler are in jail where Wilson Fisk is the warden. Magneto blows himself up, and Peter Parker infects Sheldon who almost dies from a horrible virus.

Ruins is a two-part story: "Men on Fire" and "Women in Flight." It takes place in an alternative Marvel Universe where photographer Phil Sheldon from the *Marvels* series writes a book about Marvel's various super-powered beings. This is one of the darkest, most gruesome stories Marvel ever published. Nothing but hopelessness and pain are conveyed in its pages. The artwork and the writing are excellent, despite the dismal content. This is part of Marvel's Alterniverse.

Gerber, Steve, Val Mayerik, et al. *Void Indigo.* New York: Marvel, 1984. ISBN: 0871350 017.

The barbarian is killed by the sorcerers, but is reborn as an alien who inadvertently ends up on Earth. He is searching for something, which he cannot quite understand nor comprehend. He befriends a harlot, and changes his appearance to look more acceptable to other humans.

This bizarre science fiction tale deals with an age long war, between a group of evil sorcerers and a valiant barbarian. The story was continued in a two comic issue, published by Epic Comics. (*Marvel Graphic Novel 11*)

Gerber, Steve, Whilce Paortacio, Scott Williams, et al. *Legion of the Night.* New York: Marvel, 1991. ISBN: 087135750X (Vol. 1); 087135751 (Vol. 2).

This is an uncanny horror story which involves a religious cult that awakens the dragon Fin Fang Foom to destroy the Earth. Unrelated people are brought together as a group through an entity known as the Omen who has taken over the body of a dead lawyer, and they go to the dream world to defeat the dragon.

Gerber, Steve, Phil Winslade, Glen Fabry, et al. *Howard the Duck*. New York: Marvel 2002. ISBN: 0785109315. Reprints *Howard the Duck Vol. 2: 1–6*.

Beverly's ex-husband Dr. Bong, who is cloning people illegally, turns Howard into a mouse. Howard and Bev end up at the "boarding house of mystery" where wishes come true and craziness abounds. They befriend a Hunter S. Thompson journalist wannabe and are guests on America's talk show, hosted by Irpah, the spiritual guru for those who cannot think for themselves. Irpah ends up fighting with the spirit of Sigmund Freud. Howard ends up meeting with God while he is having a beer with Jesus and the Holy Spirit in the bar of Heaven. God tells Howard some interesting tidbits about the creation of the world.

This volume was written by Howard creator Steve Gerber, for Marvel's Max line of adult comics. Gerber writes intense satire, taking pokes at everything from cookie-cutter society, to Oprah, to religion. This is one of the most cleverly written books Marvel has ever published, but it is definatley not for children or those who are easily offended.

Glanzman, Sam, Phil Felix, Don Daley, et al. *A Sailor's Story Book Two: Winds, Dreams and Dragons*. New York: Marvel, 1989. ISBN: 0871355566.

This is Glanzman's sequel to *A Sailor's Story*. It looks at the logistics of living on a destroyer, the USS *Stevens*, and includes stories about Glanzman's first experience with Japanese kamikazes, which he calls dragons. It also contains travel logs for 1944 and 1945, and detailed information about various atolls, tanks, guns, and other destroyers at Okinawa. The author tells humorous stories about having trouble sleeping on deck, and problems with homemade "firebricks" used to keep coffee warm. It includes original sketches drawn while he was on the *Stevens*. (*Marvel Graphic Novel 48*)

Glanzman, Sam, Phil Felix, Larry Hama, et al. *A Sailor's Story*. New York: Marvel, 1987. ISBN: 0871352982.

This is the true story of Glanzman's time in the Navy aboard the USS *Stevens*. It takes place during World War II, in the Pacific. The author describes the everyday grind aboard the vessel, as well as the battles with the Japanese. The volume includes a list of destroyers and escorts at Okinawa. (*Marvel Graphic Novel 30*)

Goulart, Ron, Lee Sullivan, Pat Brousseau, et al. *William Shatner's Tek World*. New York: Marvel, 1993. ISBN: 0871359855. Reprints *Tek World 1–5*.

Jake Cardigan, a cop, is framed for illegal peddling and use of. Tek, a highly addictive brain stimulant. Working for a private investigative agency, Jake goes to Mexico to find some missing persons, and to get revenge on the Tek-lord who framed him.

This is a graphic adaptation of the popular book series by William Shatner.

Grant, Alan, John Wagner, Ian Gibson, et al. *The Chronicles of Genghis Grimtoad*. London: Marvel Comics Ltd, 1990. ISBN: 1851 00228.

Ranald and Grimtoad's sorcerer uncle Karbunkle Grimtoad was killed by hordes of Kang the Awful. Quanah, one of the warriors who was sworn to protect the queen and prince, gives his soul to Boab, the Devil Toad, in exchange for a narrow escape.

This is a funny, *Lord of the Rings*–style tale about a Toad sorcerer, Genghis Grimtoad, and his attempts at saving the wife and son of King Ranald.

Gruenwald, Mark, Fabian Niceieza, Herb Trimpe et al. *The Draft*. New York: Marvel, 1988. ISBN: 0871353954.

Nightmask, Keith Remsen, is asked to psychologically evaluate a group of paranormals for a special fighting force. Blow Out becomes a loose cannon after Pit Bull eats his some of his private notebooks. He transports out of the army base, and tries to assassinate the president.

The story revolves around the basic training of Pit Bull, Sgt. Haldeman, Gridlock, Blur, Mastodon, Metallurgist, and Blow Out. It is a sequel to *The Pitt*, and a part of Marvel's New Universe.

Gruenwald, Mark, Alex Ross, Paul Ryan, et al. *Squadron Supreme*. Marvel Comics: New York, 2003. ISBN: 078510576X. Reprints *Squadron Supreme: 1–12*; *Captain America 314*.

A group of super-powered beings control society and their planet. They outlaw war and violence, and force criminals to undergo a brainwashing technique to make them good citizens. Nighthawk quits the Squadron Supreme, believing that their tactics, while well intentioned, are wrong. He recruits his previous enemies, and forms his own group to defeat the Squadron Supreme. Several "new recruits" infiltrate the Squadron, and through spying bring about the Squadron's downfall. There are mortally wounded casualties on both sides. Nighthawk goes to Earth and seeks the help of Captain America and the Avengers.

In 1985, this ground-breaking series set a high standard for graphic storytelling. It predates *Dark Knight Returns*, *Kingdom Come*, *Watchman*, and *Marvels*. This comic series was one of the first to set up a utopian/dystopian world. The story takes place on a parallel Earth, and some of the characters are different versions of mainstream Marvel heroes, e.g., Whizzer and Nighthawk. There are also some loose similarities between the Squadron Supreme characters and DC's

JLA. The book contains essays by Catherine Gruenwald, Tom DeFalco, Mark Carlin, Alex Ross, Mark Waid, and Kurt Busiek, and an afterword by Ralph Macchio.

Gruenwald, Mark, Paul Ryan, Al Williamson, et al. *Squadron Supreme: Death of a Universe.* New York: Marvel, 1989. ISBN: 0871355 981.

A giant being with the ability to ingest whole universes is making its way toward the Squadron Supreme's Earth. The future warlord, Scarlet Centurion, is bored with all of his conquests, and goes back in time to see if he can help the Squadron Supreme save the Earth. When the Squadron is busy dismantling their utopian program, and giving political power back to the politicians, they learn of the horrible fate awaiting them. The Squadron makes an alliance with their oldest enemies, Scarlet Centurion and Master Meance, to save the Earth. Although they team up, nothing seems to work, and even Overmind is not able to stop the entity. Benjamin Thomas, the son of Sorceress Arcanna, plays an important role.

This graphic novel (*Marvel Graphic Novel 55*) is one of Marvel's rarest and most sought. It was reprinted in 2006 (ISBN: 0785120912).

Gruenwald, Mark, Peter Sanderson, Josef Rubinstein, et al. *Official Handbook of the Marvel Universe Vols 1–10.* New York: Marvel, 1986–1987. ISBN: 0871352087 (1); 08713 52095 (2); 0871352109 (3); 0871352117 (4); 08713521325 (5); 08713521336 (6); 08713 52141 (7); 087135215X (8); 0871353539 (9); 0871353660 (10). Reprints *Official Handbook of the Marvel Universe Deluxe Edition 1–20.*

This series of trade paperbacks covered the history of the Marvel Universe and its characters, up to the point of publication. These books are high on detail. Each entry contains a picture or diagram, first appearance information, and a historical essay. The characters covered include the following, by volume: (1) from the Abomination to the Circus of Crime, (2) from Clea to Gaea, (3) from Galactus to Kang, (4) from Karakas to Mister Fantastic, (5) from Mister Fear to Quicksilver, (6) from Radioactive Man to Stiltman, (7) from Stingray to Wendigo, (8) from Werewolf to Zzzak (9) Book of the Dead, from Dorma to Patriot, and (10) Book of the Dead, from Phantom Eagle to Zuras. Marvel reissued these as *Essential* trade paperbacks in 2006: ISBN: 0785119345 (1); 0785119353 (2); 0785119361 (3).

Hama, Larry, Roy Wilson, Whilce Portacio, et al. *Wolfpack.* New York: Marvel, 1987. ISBN: 0871353067.

A group of high school students form a martial arts fighting force under the leadership of Mr. Mack. Mack is murdered by an evil ninja society known as the Nine. The Wolfpack is formed to stop the Nine from doing any more harm. (*Marvel Graphic Novel 31*)

Hudnall, James, Mark Bagley, Carlos Garzon, et al. *Strikeforce Morituri: Electric Undertow 1–5.* New York: Marvel, 1989–1990. ISBN: 0871355604 (1); 0871355612 (2); 08713 55620 (3); 0871355639 (4); 0871355671 (5).

The strikeforce Morituri fights evil aliens, the Horde, with the help of a mysterious race called the "New Ones." The New Ones seem to leave the planet, but they never really do. They manipulate human events, and create more enhanced humans. They also are behind numerous spontaneous combustions of people around the globe. The old Morituri is brought out of retirement by a "computer ghost" who is trying to get the strikeforce to stop the "New Ones" from destroying what is left of humanity. Morituri ends up on the alien's ship with its hybrid of technology and organic material.

This is a well-written, surrealistic tale that contains as many questions as it does answers. One is never quite sure about the motivations of the characters or the computers. This story of super-powered humans, the Morituri, is set in the middle of the twenty-first century.

Hudnall James D, John Ridgway, Koven Kindzierski, et al. *Rick Mason: The Agent.* New York: Marvel, 1989. ISBN: 0781355450.

Rick Mason is an information broker who is hired by Nick Fury to survey a military coup in Costa Brava. The coup was engineered by super-powered beings. The Kingpin also has his hand in the drug trade coming out of Costa Brava. The Tinkerer is Mason's father. His teacher, Master Teng, is the mastermind behind the Costa Brava coup, and betrays Mason. They end up fighting to the death. Mason dismantles the super-powered government, and helps usher in a democratic government. (*Marvel Graphic Novel 57*)

Jenkins, Paul, Jae Lee, Stan Lee, et al. *The Sentry.* New York: Marvel, 2001. ISBN: 0785 107991. Reprints *Sentry 1–5*; *Sentry Fantastic Four*; *Sentry X-Men*; *Sentry Spider-Man*; *Sentry Hulk*; *Sentry vs. The Void.*

This *Blair Witch* comic equivalent is about an early Marvel Hero, the Sentry, about whom no one can remember anything. The Sentry, Stan Lee's first superhero, was created by Lee and Artie Rosen before the Fantastic Four. Bob Reynolds, the Sentry, was a Silver Age hero and one of the few friends of the early Hulk. He had retired from crime fighting, but comes back into action when his nemesis the Void makes his presence known. This work includes team-ups with the Fantastic Four, Thor, Avengers, Captain America, X-Men, and Spider-Man. It also contains reprints of interviews between Marvel editor in chief Joe Quesada and Stan Lee about the creation of the Sentry, and reprints from *Wizard Magazine* about the Sentry controversy. This is a deconstructionist story, if there ever was one. Great Kirby-style artwork is scattered throughout the book, and there is an afterword by Stan Lee. This book includes reprints from the early Sentry covers from *Startling Stories*, *The Hulk* and other publications.

Jones, Bruce, Deny's Cowan, Tom Palmer, et al. *Moon Knight: Divided We Fall*. New York: Marvel, 1992. ISBN: 087135909X.

Because of Marc Spector's arrogance, his partners Marlene and Frenchie leave. They are brought under the spell of one of the Bushman's henchman, Blaine. The Bushman plans to assassinate President Bush and Moon Knight in the process. Frenchie gets shot.

Jones, Bruce, Tom Mandrake, David Finch, et al. *Call of Duty 2: The Precinct*. New York: Marvel, 2003. ISBN: 0785109749. Reprints *Call of Duty: Precinct 1–6*.

Police officer Frank Gunzer is on the trail of a high-powered drug dealer who is actually the leader of a bizarre drug cult. The dealer puts a hit on Gunzer. Gunzer's wife almost ends up sleeping with his brother who wants to quit the priesthood.

Jones, Bruce, Paul Mounts, Jack Morelli, et al. *Arena*. New York: Marvel, 1989. ISBN: 0871355576.

A mother and daughter end up alone in the forest where they come across a group of inbred savages who want them for breeding purposes. The mother ends up killing herself rather than be raped by the deformed savages. The daughter meets a future version of herself, and attempts to stop her mother from killing herself.

In this book, the characters travel back and forth from the time of the dinosaurs and cavemen, to the near future. (*Marvel Graphic Novel 44*)

Kaminski, Len, Anthony Williams, Andy Lanning, et al. *Squadron Supreme: New World Order*. New York: Marvel, 1998. ISBN: 078 5106715.

The Squadron returns to Earth from exile, and finds it under the rule of the Blue Eagles. They enlist the aid of former comrades Nighthawk, Amphibian, and Skymax, to fight against the totalitarianism of the Blue Eagles, only to find out that they were elected by the people.

This was reprinted in 2006 (ISBN: 0785120912).

Lee, Elaine, Michael William Kaluta, Todd Klein, et al. *Starstruck: The Luckless, the Abandoned and the Forsaken*. New York: Marvel, 1984. ISBN: 0871350017.

This is a very bizarre, but equally witty comedy and science fiction story. It was originally a play that was turned into a graphic novel. The work includes a glossary of terms. (*Marvel Graphic Novel 13*)

Mantlo, Bill, Mark Farmer, Sal Velluto, et al. *Power Pack & Cloak and Dagger: Shelter from the Storm*. New York: Marvel, 1989. ISBN: 0871356015.

Two teenagers run away to New York where they are assisted by Cloak and Dagger. Dagger gets hurt, and goes with the teenagers to a shelter. They are kidnapped by a group that works for the sinister Cadaver. Cloak seeks the aid of the Power Pack to find Dagger and save the teenagers. (*Marvel Graphic Novel 56*)

Mantlo, Bill, Mark Gruenwald, Steven Grant, et al. *Contest of Champions Vol. 1*. New York: Marvel, 2001. ISBN: 0785107266. Reprints *Contest of Champions Vol. 1: 1–3*; *West Coast Avengers Annual 2*; *Avengers Annual 16*.

The Gamemaster gathers Earth's heroes together to play a game of chance so that his brother, the Collector, can return from Death. The safety of Earth is at stake. The Collector does return from Death, but the Gamemaster has to forfeit his life in exchange. The East Coast and West Coast Avengers are pitted against each other in the real game of death. The Gamemaster has captured Death, and intends to destroy the entire universe, and rebuild it to his liking. However, a game of chance put forth by Hawkeye frees Death from her bond to the Gamemaster, and he is ultimately defeated. The Avengers are forced to fight the Swordsman, Bucky, the Executioner, Captain Marvel, Nighthawk, the original Black Knight, the Green Goblin, Dracula, and others, who are already in Death's hands.

This book also focuses on many of the low-rent, more obscure superbeings, including the Talisman, Arabian Knight, Defensor, Vanguard, Le Peregrine, Collective Man, Shamrock, and Blitzkrieg. Many fans believe that this series sets the stage for the Secret Wars massive crossover. See the entry for Volume II under "Claremont" in this chapter subsection.

Mantlo, Bill, Jackson Guice, Ken Bruzenak, et al. *Swords of the Swashbucklers*. New York: Marvel, 1984. ISBN: 0871350025.

A young girl goes into a coma when she finds a mysterious object in the sand. A group of pirates from another galaxy come to Earth to stop another group of colonizer aliens. The young girl learns that her parents have been kidnapped, and she is transformed into a superbeing. She finds that the pirates' captain is related to her. (*Marvel Graphic Novel 14*)

Mantlo, Bill, Larry Stroman, Al Williamson, et al. *Cloak and Dagger: Predator and Prey*. New York: Marvel, 1988. ISBN: 087135 1250.

Cloak and Dagger go up against the spirit of Jack the Ripper. The Predator uses Jack the Ripper and Cloak to feed on the light of individuals.

The book includes the origin story of the duo, and describes them as victims of an experiment for developing a synthetic substitute for heroin. (*Marvel Graphic Novel 35*)

McDuffie, Dwayne, Gregory Wright, Jackson Guice et al. *Deathlok 1–4*. New York: Marvel, 1990. ISBN: 0871356686 (1); 0871356775 (2); 0871356783 (3); 0871356791 (4).

The Roxxon Corporation transplants Michael Collins's brain into the cyborg Deathlok. He is designed to be the perfect killing machine for hire. During the test run against native South Americans, Collins's moral ideology overrides Deathlok's programming to kill. He goes AWOL from the corporation, and becomes a free agent. Deathlok's former boss Harlan Ryker, who instigated the brain transplant, is a constant thorn in Deathlok's side. He befriends a circus worker, Jesus, and lives with him for a while, but Roxxon finds him and sends its soldiers to apprehend him. Nick Fury and S.H.I.E.L.D. become involved, and want to find information about the creation of Deathlok. Deathlok returns to South America to stop Roxxon from exterminating an Indian village and razing the rainforest. Ryker offers Deathlok a chance to become human again, if he will do Ryker's bidding.

McGregor, Don, P. Craig Russell, H.G. Wells, et al. *Killraven: Warrior of the Worlds*. New York: Marvel, 1983. ISBN: 0939766590.

Killraven, who came to Earth after the Martian invasion and conquest of Earth, is a warrior who has the power to invade other minds and places, telepathically. He kills his brother who had become a wolf, and invades the Martian commander's mind.

This work, which is a sequel of sorts to the H. G. Wells novel *War of the Worlds*, contains some beautiful collage work. (*Marvel Graphic Novel 7*)

Michelinie, David, Greg La Rocque, Jim Shooter, et al. *The Aladdin Effect*. New York: Marvel, 1985. ISBN: 0871350815.

A hidden force field imprisons the citizens of Venture Ridge, Wyoming. A young girl with extraordinary powers wills Storm, Tigra, She-Hulk, and the Wasp to come to the aid of the town. A.I.M. sets up a base to try to harness the power of the young girl, and they kidnap her. (*Marvel Graphic Novel 16*)

Michelinie, David, Marc Silvestri, Geof Isherwood, et al. *Revenge of the Living Monolith*. New York: Marvel, 1985. ISBN: 087135 0831.

Ahmet Abdol, the Living Monolith, seeks revenge on humanity for the way it has treated him in the past, and plans on blowing up New York. He kidnaps the Fantastic Four, and uses them as a conduit for power. He ends up killing his daughter, and fighting with the She-Hulk, Thor, Captain America, and Spider-Man. Spider-Man rescues the Fantastic Four, and Reed

Richards eventually reasons with Ahmet, who sees the error of his ways. Using Thor's hammer, the Living Monolith throws himself into space, and becomes a living planet.

Because it tells the early history of Ahmet Abdol and his origin as the Living Monolith, this book is a loose sequel to *X-Men 58*. (*Marvel Graphic Novel 17*)

Morrison, Grant, J.G. Jones, Sean Parsons, et al. *Marvel Boy*. New York: Marvel, 2001. ISBN: 0785107819. Reprints *Marvel Boy 1–6*.

Noh-Varr is a member of a diplomatic team of the alien Kree. His colleagues are blown out of the sky, and only Noh-Varr survives. He is tortured by the mystifying Midas Organization. Marvel Boy's enemy is Exterminatrix.

In this book, the evil Midas looks like a futuristic Iron Man. The book provides a new take on a Marvel character from the fifties.

Mumy, Bill, Miguel Ferrere, Gray Morrow, et al. *Dreamwalker* New York: Marvel, 1989. ISBN: 0871355507.

An ex–secret agent walks in his father's footsteps as the new Dreamwalker, to stop a corrupt DA and his crime lord partner. The Dreamwalker watches as the crime lord has his father and stepmother killed, and he learns the truth about the death of his mother.

This is very similar to the *Shadow*. (*Marvel Graphic Novel 47*)

Murphy, Warren, Richard Sapir, et al. *The Destroyer*. New York: Marvel, 1991. ISBN: 0871358441. Reprints *Destroyer 1–4*.

This book covers the origin of Remo Williams, an assassin of a covert government agency, who becomes known as the Destroyer. According to one story, a Sinnaju master, Chiun, teaches Williams how to use his body as a weapon against ninja and other threats. In another story, the Destoyer defeats a greedy gold broker who is turning lead into radioactive gold. Filled with action and humans, this graphic novel is one of the best adaptations of well-known novel characters. It includes a short section, "How to Draw Chiun the Marvel Way."

Murray, Doug, Tom Morgan, Paul Mounts et al. *The War Book 1–4*. New York: Marvel, 1989–1990.

Several powers want to see the world destroy itself, and seek to cause a nuclear war between Russia, the United States, and the rest of the world. The paranormal special-forces team, first introduced in the *Draft*, is called to go to South Africa to try to capture the person who they believe is responsible for sinking Pittsburgh. The whole thing was actually a trap, an attempt for certain parties to send the world into chaos. Blow Up becomes a pawn of the Ayatollah, who uses him to kill "American devils" all over the world. Nightmask, who feels guilty about claiming that Blow

Up was sane during his evaluation, is brought in to kill him. First goes into Blow Up's dreams, and then kills him with a gun. Nuclear devices are deployed all over the world, but do not go off because Starbrand makes them inoperative, calling for world peace.

This volume includes an appearance by Fidel Castro. This series provides a nice subtext for the Cold War of the 1980s. *The War* is one of the last stories published from Marvel's New Universe. It is a sequel to *The Draft*.

Nicieza, Fabian, Tom DeFalco, Mark Bagley et al. *New Warriors: Beginnings*. New York: Marvel, 1992. ISBN: 0871359162. Reprints *Might Thor 411–412*; *New Warriors 1–4*.

This book covers the origin of the New Warriors who got together to help Thor battle Juggarnaut. In this book they do battle against Terrax, Mad Thinker, and Psionex. The New Warriors team includes Thrasher, Nova, Marvel Boy, Namorita, Firestar, and Speedball.

Nicieza, Fabian, Christian Gorney, Michael Halbeib, et al. *The Two-Gun Kid: Sunset Riders Vol. 1–2*. New York: Marvel, 1995.

The Two-Gun Kid, who knows the future after an adventure with the Avengers, saves an African-American man from hanging for murder. The Kid blows up the law offices of Matt Hawk, his alter ego, in an effort to distance himself from him. The Kid and his group hook up with an Indian warrior, Running Fish, and a samurai, Hijiro Nguri. The government, under Grover Cleveland's presidency, has a bounty on the Kid and his group. The posse comes into the possession of some important minks, which politically could star a major war.

This book includes a history of the Two Gun Kid, *Two Guns Three Faces*, by Paul J. Becton. The book is part of the Marvel Select imprint.

Nicieza, Mariano, Bob Wakelin, Jim Novak, et al. *Tales of the Marvels: Inner Demons*. New York: Marvel, 1995.

This is the story of the friendship that exists between the Sub-Mariner and a homeless man, when Sub-Mariner loses his memory. In the story, Johnny Storm recognizes Sub-Mariner in the homeless shelter, and throws him into the water, hoping to awaken him from his amnesia. This is a new telling of some events from *Fantastic Four 4*.

O'Neil, Denny, Michael W. Kaluta and Russ Heath. *The Shadow: Hitler's Astrologer*. New York: Marvel, 1988. ISBN: 0871353415 (trd); 0871356643 (pbk).

Nazis kidnap one of the daughters of a mystic/astrologer from the Ministry of Propaganda. The Shadow and some of his entourage go into Nazi Germany to save her life, and she learns the awful truth about her heritage and family. The Shadow has to make sure that Hitler keeps his pact with the Soviet Union.

This is an amazing book that captures the spirit of the 1940s and World War II. It is loosely based on the story that Hitler supposedly consulted an astrologer before invading Russia, rather than attacking Britain. (*Marvel Graphic Novel 35*)

Ostrander, John, Leonardo Manco, Paul Tutrone, et al. *Apache Skies*. New York: Marvel, 2003. ISBN: 0785110860. Reprints *Apache Skies 1–4*.

The Apache Kid's Indian wife and the Rawhide Kid seek retribution for the death of the Apache Kid. The Apache Kid's wife, fearful that Geronimo will be killed, wants to find him and stop him from going to the reservation. The man responsible for shooting the Apache Kid is killed, but his father now wants revenge. He starts by getting his cronies to burn and kill men, women, and children in the town where his son lived. The Rawhide Kid befriends a former slave who is now working on the railroad. Rawhide and the Apache Kid's wife smuggle some young children out of the reservation, and take them to a place where they have a freer life, and are not taught the gospel of the "white devils."

This series is part of Marvel's adult Max line. It is a very good western story with all of the traditional elements. It would not have been out of place in a Zane Grey novel.

Ostrander, John, Lenardo Manco, Sharpefont, et al. *Blaze of Glory*. New York: Marvel, 2002. ISBN: 0785109064. Reprints *Blaze of Glory 1–4*.

This is a Western graphic novel featuring Rawhide Kid, Kid Colt, Caleb Hammer, Red Wolf, and the Two-Gun Kid, who go to the aid of Wonderment, Montana, against the Nightriders who are terrorizing the town. The original Ghost Rider makes an appearance at the end of the story, and reveals that he is the African-American Remo Jones. The book is beautifully drawn and well written.

Parkhouse, Steve, John Bolton, David Lloyd, et al. *Nightraven: The Collected Stories*. London: Marvel Comics Ltd, 1990. ISBN: 185 4002279.

This book reprints five-page stories which originally ran in the Marvel UK magazine *Hulk Weekly*. It is written and drawn in the style of the traditional pulp stories and comics of the thirties and forties. In this volume, Nightraven, who fights crime on his own terms, has no problem killing evil doers, and leaving the mark of the Raven on his victims. He is similar to the Shadow, Zorro, and the Green Hornet.

Rodi, Rob, John Higgins, Sandu Floera, et al. *Identity Disc*. New York: Marvel, 2004. ISBN: 0785115676. Reprints *Identity Disc 1–5*.

Crime lord Tristan Silver has dirt on Sabretooth, Bullseye, Juggernaut, Deadpool, the Vulture, and the

Sandman. Silver's agent, who is actually the Vulture's daughter, coerces them to take an assignment to find the Identity Disc. The Identity Disc is a computer file that lists the alter egos, addresses, and personal information of everyone who wears tights and a cape, heroes and villains alike. This disc is in the hands of A.I.M., and the group of villains is supposed to infiltrate A.I.M. headquarters in New York, and take the disc. However, nothing is what it appears to be. The Sandman is turned into "goo" and Bullseye is beaten up when he hints that he wants to pull out. The Vulture shoots Juggernaut, and is captured by S.H.I.E.L.D. Nick Fury interrogates the Vulture, and believes that Sabretooth is covertly behind the whole operation.

This fun book is highly recommended.

Rosemann, Bill, Guy Davis, Greg Horn, et al. *Deadline.* New York: Marvel, 2002. ISBN: 0785110100. Reprints *Deadline 1–4.*

An ambitious, cape-hating reporter goes after a prize-winning story dealing with an allegedly deceased lawyer who is on a serial-killing rampage throughout New York. She noses around, and comes into contact with Bullseye and the Tinker. It turns out the Tinker is using the lawyer as his pawn, and actually he is the one who killed the lawyer's family.

Severin, John, Ron Zimmerman, Steve Buccellato, et al. *Rawhide Kid Vol. 1: Slap Leather.* New York: Marvel 2003. ISBN: 078511 0690. Reprints *Rawhide Kid 1–6.*

The Rawhide Kid comes into the town of Wells Junction where the sheriff is being bullied by a band of outlaws. The Kid is made a deputy to help the sheriff. The sheriff's son believes his father is a coward, and has no respect for him. When the bandits finally have a showdown in Wells Junction, the Kid takes them all out.

In *Rawhide Kid*, which was published as part of Marvel's mature Max series, the Kid is retooled to be gay. This is a very enjoyable, hilarious read, which stays true to the Rawhide Kid's mystique. The drawings are by the original Rawhide Kid artist, John Severin, who drew the comic in the 1950s. This series was highly praised by various media outlets, including *Entertainment Weekly*, the *New York Post*, the *Advocate*, and the *New Yorker*. This book is not to be missed.

Simonson, Louise, June Brigman, Bob Wiacek, et al. *Power Pack: Origin Album.* New York: Marvel, 1988. ISBN: 0871353857. Reprints *Power Pack 1–4.*

Jack Powers's four children are given special powers by the alien Whitey as he is dying. Another alien species, the Snark, kidnap the elder Powers to get the formula for a weapon of great potential which involves anti-matter conversion. The Power Pack must rescue their parents, and stop a demonstration of the weapon on Earth.

This book covers the origin of the superhero children known as the Power Pack.

Simonson, Walter, Louise Simonson, Deborah Pedler, et al. *Star Slammers:* New York: Marvel, 1983. ISBN: 0939766213.

The Starslammers are a group of well-trained mercenaries from a planet where the inhabitants are hunted by Orions. They seek to learn a mind-bridging technique which will unite them against their Orion oppressors. The "Grandfather" of the Starslammers was from Orion, but realized their evil ways. (*Marvel Graphic Novel 6*)

Slate, Barbara, L. Lois Bhualis, Bobbie Chase, et al. *Yuppies from Hell.* New York: Marvel, 1989. ISBN: 0871356090.

This is a hilarious collection of strip cartoons which poke fun at yuppie life during the eighties and early nineties. Primarily concentrating on women and New York, it contains biting social satire. One of the stories is about a busy couple who leave messages for one another on their answering machines instead of talking to each other. Two sequel collections were also published, and are just as good: *Son of Yuppies from Hell* (1990; ISBN: 0871357372); and *Sex, Lies, and Mutual Funds of the Yuppies from Hell* (1992; ISBN: 087135893X). These collections provide a fun look at the decade of greed and indulgence. They are recommended.

Smith, Jim, John K., Shane Glines, et al. *Spumco: Comic Book (Volume 1: 1).* New York: Marvel, 1995.

This oversize, Prestige-format comic was written by one of the early Ren and Stimpy television show writers. It features the misadventures of Jimmy, the Turtle Food Collector, who fights with various insects, and ends up being abducted by aliens. There are also essays on the biology of farting and comic books as part of a child's education, and a membership card for the Spumco secret membership lodge. Marvel only printed one issue. Dark Horse comics released two issues. This book is very rare.

Starlin, Jim, Tom Orzechowski, Archie Goodwin, et al. *Dreadstar: The Metamorphosis Book Three.* New York: Marvel, 1982. ISBN: 0939766159.

The warrior Vanth Dreadstar is left for dead on Delta 219. The cat-like aliens take him to the city's only human inhabitant, Delilah. Dreadstar recovers, falls in love with Delilah, and lives a simple life as a farmer. He meets with the sorcerer Syzygy Darklock who seeks to help Dreadstar hone his warrior abilities, to stop the centuries-old war between the Monarchy and the Instrumentality. When the Monarchy kills Delilah and the other inhabitants, Dreadstar takes revenge against the King, and vows to stop the senseless war. He infiltrates the military ranks of the Monarchy, becomes one of their most valued soldiers, and rises in the ranks. He eventually has his revenge, and kills the King to start the process of stopping the war.

The introduction is by Steve Englehart. (*Marvel Graphic Novel 3*)

Straczynski, J. Michael, Gary Frank, John Saul, et al. *Supreme Power Vol. 2: Power and Principalities.* New York: Marvel, 2004. ISBN: 0785114564. Reprints *Supreme Power 7–12.*

Hyperion learns that his whole life has been a lie, and tries to find out his origin. Hyperion finds out that the United States is using another superbeing for covert missions, and engages him in a fight. A female version of Hyperion, Zarada, is awakened and walks around the city naked. In an attempt to destroy Hyperion, the government detonates a nuclear bomb. A super-powered serial killer is loose. An aquatic alien saves Colonel Ledger, and the government scientists plan to use the alien's DNA on humans.

Straczynski, J. Michael, Gary Frank, Jon Sibal, et al. *Supreme Power Vol. 1: Contact.* New York: Marvel, 2004. ISBN: 0785112243. Reprints *Supreme Power 1–6.*

A baby crashes to Earth in a spaceship. The government raises him, hoping to use him as a propaganda tool, and learns about his various powers. Mark Milton, Hyperion, does covert work in Iraq during the Desert Storm war. He searches for others with special powers, and finds the Speedster, Blur, and an African-American Punisher named Nighthawk, among others.

This is a reworking of the Squadron Supreme characters, by award-winning writer Mike Straczynski. It is part of Marvel's adult Max line. *Entertainment Weekly* praises the book's realism and "paranoiac suspense."

Straczynski, J. Michael, John Romita Jr., Scott Hanna, et al. *NUFF SAID.* New York: Marvel, 2002. ISBN: 0785109811. Reprints *Amazing Spider-Man Vol. 2: 39*; *Peter Parker: Spider-Man Vol. 2: 38*; *New X-Men 121*; *X-Force 123*; *Incredible Hulk 35*; *Thor Vol. 2: 44*; *Punisher Vol. 4: 7.*

This is an innovative collection of wordless stories that Joe Quesada and Bill Jemas challenged the writers and artists to put together. In various stories, Spider-Man fights Mimes of Crime, Professor X fights with his twin sister in the womb, and the Punisher kills some mobsters. The book contains panel-by-panel scripts, and a cover gallery for the individual issues.

Thomas, Roy, P. Craig Russell, Michael Morcock, et al. *Elric: The Dreaming City.* New York: Marvel, 1982. ISBN: 0939766124.

Elric goes to the city of Imrryr to overthrow his evil cousin Yyrkoon. He and his band of Sea Lords are successful. Elric has to come to terms with his sword Stormbringer.

This is an adaptation of the "Dreaming City" story about the wizard Elric. (*Marvel Graphic Novel 2*)

Valentino, Jim, Steve Montano, Evelyn Stein, et al. *Guardians of the Galaxy: Quest for the Shield.* New York: Marvel, 1992. ISBN: 087 1358794. Reprints *Guardians of the Galaxy 1–6.*

A group of superheroes from the thirty-first century, known as the Guardians of the Galaxy, search for an artifact from the twentieth century, Captain America's lost shield. They have to battle a group that found some of Tony Stark's Iron Man technology, which he sent into space from Earth during a war with the Martians. This group calls themselves the Stark, and has distorted Tony Stark's original intent to one of conquest and pillaging. The Guardians eventually defeat the Stark, but Vance Astro, Martinex, and Yondu are almost killed. Starhawk and Aleta are separated during the battle. When the Guardians seek Captain America's shield, they are forced by the sentient computer ship Mainframe to battle a group of pillagers, the Force. The Mainframe turns out to be the Vision. Yondu's heart is broken when he meets a female of his race who has no interest in him or the culture they come from. Each Guardian is forced to battle a member of the Force. Vance Astro is found to be worthy of taking the Shield.

Vaughn, Brian K., Adrian Alphona, Takeshi Miyazawa, et al. *Runaways Vol. 2: Teenage Wasteland.* New York: Marvel, 2004. ISBN: 0785114157. Reprints *Runaways 7–12.*

The Runaways stop a robbery at a convenience store, and take in another distraught teenager who causes romantic strife among them. The robbery was captured on video tape, and the parents get their first clue as to their children's activities. The Pride has its hands in everything in the town of Los Feliz, California, including the police and all of the local government. The Runaways' new friend is actually a vampire, and tries to kill them. Cloak and Dagger are brought in to find the Runaways. There is a mole among the Runaways.

This book is even better than the first one.

Vaughn, Brian K., Adrian Alphona, David Newbold, et al. *Runaways Vol. 1: Pride and Joy.* New York: Marvel, 2004. ISBN: 0785 113797. Reprints Runaways 1–6.

A group of teenagers discover that their parents are part of a secret, evil organization, the Pride. They witness the sacrificial death of a teenage girl, and try to get their parents arrested, but the Pride is too well organized. They engage several of their parents in combat, in an attempt to expose the fact that they are supervillains. The teens find out that they each have a special power, and one teen discovers she is not even human.

This is part of the Marvel Age series for teens. It is a well written, interesting book.

Vaughan, Brian K., Kyle Hotz, Eric Power, et al. *The Hood: Blood from Stones.* New York: Marvel, 2003. ISBN: 078511058. Reprints *The Hood 1–6.*

Parker Robbins, whose father was once one of the Kingpin's soldiers, wants to follow in his father's footsteps into a life of crime. He and his cousin John go to an abandoned warehouse, and shoot at what appears to be a demon. Parker takes the shoes and hood off of the monster, and ends up with certain powers. Parker and John try to hijack diamonds from a smuggling operation that is run by a mobster, the Golem. The Golem hires the Shocker, Constrictor, and Jack O' Lantern to protect the stolen diamonds. When Parker accidentally shoots a police officer who dies, the press dubs him "The Hood," and the FBI gets involved. The Golem's hench-lady Rapier is killed.

This is one of Marvel's Max imprints, and has very explicit content.

Veitch, Rick, Jim Novak, Archie Goodwin, et al. *Heartburst.* New York: Marvel, 1984. ISBN: 0939766825.

The inhabitants of Epsilon find the sacred word of the "sponsor," from broadcasts of old Earth television programs and commercials from the fifties. Humans are not allowed to mate with the original inhabitants of Epsilon, the Ploo. Humanity wages an all-out genocide against the Ploo, while the main character Sunoco breaks the taboo against interspecies relations.

This is a bizarre science fiction story set in the future on the planet of Epsilon. The book is filled with mysticism, and shows the triumph of spirit against impossible odds. (*Marvel Graphic Novel 10*)

Vess, Charles, Elaine Lee, John Ridgway, et al. *Prince Valiant 1–4.* New York: Marvel, 1994–1995.

King Arthur is dead, and it is up to Prince Valiant to help restore good in the kingdom of Camelot. The evil Queen Morgause, who has taken the mystical sword Excalibur from Sir Gawain, also has captured

Valliant's granddaughter Ingrid and is torturing his son Galan. She is trying to teach Ingrid the evil ways of her sorcery.

This was a special *Marvel Select*, cardstock-cover series, which tells the story of the fall of Camelot. There is much adventure and action throughout this tale, which would have made series creator Hal Foster proud.

Wildey, Doug, Cindy Emmert, Eric Fein, et al. *Rio Rides Again.* New York: Marvel, 1990. ISBN: 0871356562.

Rio is pardoned by the president, and cleared of previous offenses. He goes to the town of Limestone, Missouri, and is asked to become acting sheriff. He meets a woman named Zee who is the wife of Jesse James. James's son is mistakenly kidnapped, and after his rescue the town fathers want to take him away from the family. Zee holds the town officials back at gunpoint, while Rio does nothing. The mayor fires Rio. After word gets out that Jesse James is living in Limestone, the town is overrun by the media and curiosity seekers. Rio leaves the town to its own devices, and refuses to take back the job of sheriff. *Marvel Graphic Novel 60.*

Wilson, Roy, John Byrne, Armando Gil, et al. *Super Boxers.* New York: Marvel, 1983. ISBN: 0939766779.

In this science fiction tale set in the near future, corporations and the police control everything. In this culture, the measure of a corporation is taken through boxing matches which deterermine who wins or loses. In this book, a non-corporation fighter from the underground fights the corporate champion. (*Marvel Graphic Novel 8*)

Zelenetz, Alan, Charles Vess, Joe Rosen, et al. *The Raven Banner: A Tale of Asgard.* New York: Marvel, 1985. ISBN: 0871350602.

This tale takes place in the godly realm of Asgard. In it, the son of a fallen god searches for the magical Raven Banner which was stolen by trolls, but he meets a fate similar to that of his father. (*Marvel Graphic Novel 15*)

Minor Character Combos

Brevot, Tom, ed., Scott Lobdell, Stan Lee et al. *Best of Marvel 1996.* New York: Marvel, 1996. ISBN: 0785102205. Reprints *Generation X 17; Fantastic Four 416; Captain America 454; Untold Tales of Spider-Man 13; Wolverine 102; Daredevil 353; Sensational Spider-Man 8; Thor 502; Onslaught Marvel Universe.*

Skin fights the X-Cutioner who believes that he murdered Angelo Espinosa, Skin's alter ego. Captain America and Sharon Carter go on another mission together. He tries to rekindle their relationship, and her loyalty to S.H.I.E.L.D., to no avail. Spider-Man goes up against the Looter in a hilarious story. Daredevil goes up against Mr. Hyde; Matt Murdock reappears in the law firm and in the life of Foggy; Bluebird dies; and Spider-Man fights the Black Knight. Nearly all of Marvel's heroes try to defeat Onslaught, with little luck. Thor reminisces about his childhood and Loki.

This book contains the "Onslaught Primer" and highlights the best comics published in 1996, which include Stan Lee's appearance in the pages of *Generation X*.

Bryne, John, Frank Miller, Bill Mantlo, et al. *Marvel Super-Heroes Megazine 1–6*. New York: Marvel, 1994–1995. Reprints *Fantastic Four 232–237; Daredevil 159–163; Iron Man 47,115–117, 159; Incredible Hulk 314–319; Marvel Two-in-One 50*.

Daredevil is taunted by Bullseye, and Dardevil's identity is revealed to reporter Ben Ulrich. The Hulk gets married; the Thing fights himself, in a bizarre twist; Doc Samson destroys a Hulk robot; Daredevil fights with the Hulk; and the Fantastic Four contend with Ego, the Living Planet.

In these books, the evil mystic Diablo has Iron Man fight various versions of his armor, including my favorite, the early Gray suit. In a separate story, the book also provides a glimpse back in time to Iron Man's creation of the Gray suit. There are many other exciting stories in these six issues.

Claremont, Chris, Stan Lee, Steve Ditko, et al. *The Very Best of Marvel Comics*. New York: Marvel, 1992. ISBN: 0871358093. Reprints *Uncanny X-Men 112–113; Amazing Spider-Man 8, 39–40; Doctor Strange 55; Daredevil 7, 47; Mighty Thor 337; Fantastic Four 5, 51*.

Norman Osborn reveals to Spider-Man that he is the Green Goblin. Daredevil entertains the troops in Viet Nam, and helps a blind veteran in a trial. Daredevil meets with the Sub-Mariner who seeks Matt Murdock's legal advice. Dr. Strange is mourning the loss of his love Clea, and the Fantastic Four go back in time as pirates. Magneto captures the X-Men, and chains them up in a room in which their powers are neutralized.

This book also contains a famous Fantastic Four story, "This Man This Monster," featuring the Thing, and introductions to Beta Ray Bill and Dr. Doom. Many heavyweights in the comic industry—including Todd McFarlane, Stan Lee, J. M. De Matteis, Art Adams, and Rob Liefeld—picked their favorite Marvel stories for this book and added their commentaries.

DeFalco, Tom, Roy Thomas, Chris Claremont, et al. *Marvel Holiday Special 2004*. New York: Marvel, 2004. ISBN: 0785116257. Reprints *Marvel Holiday Special 2004; Marvel Team-Up 1; Uncanny X-Men 143; Amazing SpiderMan 314; Incredible Hulk 378*.

Emma Frost and Cyclops stay over during Christmas break with a young mutant who has nowhere to go. In an original adaptation of "The Christmas Carol," Jonah Jameson is visited by Captain America, the Thing, and Spider-Man. Franklin Richards learns how his family celebrates the holidays. Spider-Man and the Human Torch go after the Sandman while he visits his mother on Christmas Day. Kitty Pryde has to deal with a demon that is loose in the Mansion, and Peter Parker and Mary Jane are thrown out of their apartment on Christmas Day. The Rhino becomes a Santa for a department store, and the Grey Hulk ends up being a very large elf.

This special collection of Marvel Christmas tales features both new and old stories.

Jemas, Bill, Mark Bright, Paul Neary, et al. *Marville*. New York: Marvel, 2003. ISBN: 0785110429. Reprints *Marville 1–6*.

This was the pet project of former Marvel president Bill Jemas, and it shows his ability to link sarcasm, humor, and serious philosophical issues in comic-book form. The book is essentially a treatise on the nature of the universe, told in comic format. It pokes fun at AOL, DC Comics, political issues, and even Marvel. Batman, Superman, Iron Man, Punisher, the Kingpin, Spike Lee, Paul Levitz, Ted Turner, Jane Fonda, Wolverine, and Spider-Man, all make appearances. It includes a prologue, "Insiders Guide to Marville," and Jemas's open letter to comic book creators.

Kaminski, Len, Mike McKone, Mark McKenna, et al. *2099: Manifest Destiny*. New York: Marvel, 1998. ISBN: 0978510657X.

The original Captain America, who is in suspended animation, is found by Miguel O'Hara. He is revived and is given the hammer of Thor. The heroes of this age, along with the Watcher, save the Earth from a threat from space, and Captain America and the Watcher sacrifice themselves for the sake of the others. The hammer of Thor is given to Miguel.

This story is about Marvel superheroes a hundred years in the future. It shows changes that occur in 2199, 2399, 2799, and 3099.

Kane, Gil, Stan Lee, Jack Kirby, et al. *Marvel Visionaries: Gil Kane*. New York: Marvel, 2002. ISBN: 078510882. Reprints *Tales to Astonish 76; Tales of Suspense 88–91; Captain Marvel Vol 1: 17, 23; Marvel Premiere 1, 15; What If Vol. 1: 3, 24; Amazing Spider-Man 99; Marvel Comics Presents 116; Mighty Marvel Western 44; Kid Colt Outlaw 161; Western Gunfighters 31; Sub-Mariner 44*.

This is a massive collection that celebrates the art of Gil Kane. The collection includes Rick Jones's first encounter with Captain Marvel, Adam Warlock's rebirth at the hands of the High Evolutionary, Bulleye's defeat at the hands of Daredevil while at a television studio, and two famous "what if" stories. In these "what if" stories, the Avengers split up, and Iron Man dies. Gwen Stacy lives, and the press discovers Spider-Man's secret identity. The work includes original cover artwork and sketches.

Larson, Eric, Peter Gillis, Frank Miller, et al. Marvel Collection Vol. 3. New York: Marvel, 1992. Reprints *Spider-Man 23*; *Adventures of the Thing 3*; *Wonder Man 10*; *Bill and Ted's Excellent Comic Book 7*; *Marvel Presents 105*; *Alpha Flight 110*; *Ghost Rider Vol. 2: 26*; *Pirates of Dark Water 7*; *Punisher War Zone 4*; *Silver Sable and the Wild Pack 1*; *Silver Surfer Vol. 3: 66*; *Moon Knight Divided We Fall Graphic Novel*; *Marvel Age 113*; *Avengers 348*; *Nightbreed 16*; *Conan the Barbarian 257*; *Marvel Tales Featuring Spider-Man 262*; *Doctor Strange: Sorcerer Supreme 42*; *Nick Fury: Agent of S.H.I.E.L.D. Vol. 2: 37*; *Epic Anthology 4*; *Defenders of Dynatron City 5*; *Terror Inc 1*; *Original Ghost Rider 1*; *Cage 4*; *Punisher War Journal 44*.

This is the third and last bound collection of Marvel comics, with cover dates of June/July 1992. It combines both regular Marvel and Epic titles, and is quite rare.

Lee, Stan, Steve Ditko, Jack Kirby et al. *100 Greatest Marvels of All Time Vol. 1–9*. New York: Marvel, 2001. Reprints *Amazing Fantasy 15*; *Fantastic Four 1*; *Uncanny X-Men 137*; *Giant Size X-Men 1*; *X-Men 1*; *Ultimate Spider Man 1*; *Uncanny X Men 1*; *Avengers 4*; *Amazing Spider-Man 121*; *Incredible Hulk 1*; *Ultimate X-Men 1*; *Daredevil 227*; *Wolverine 75*; *Spider-Man 1*; *Amazing Spider-Man 33*; *Incredible Hulk 181*; *X-Men 25*; *Avengers 1*; *Uncanny X-Men 350*; *Amazing Spider-Man 122*; *Captain America 109*; *Uncanny X-Men 141*; *Fantastic Four 48*; *Amazing Spider-Man 1*; *Daredevil 181*.

When the fans voted on the one hundred best Marvel comics of all time, Marvel collected the first twenty-five in these nine volumes. The first four volumes are individual comic issues, while volumes 5–25 are collected in books of four issues each. These are some of the greatest stories in the history of the Marvel Universe.

Lee, Stan, Jack Kirby, Dick Ayers, et al. *Fantastic Firsts*. New York: Marvel, 2001. ISBN: 0785108238. Reprints *Fantastic Four 1, 4*, *Fantastic Four Annual 1*; *Tales to Astonish 27, 35*; *Hulk 1*; Amazing Fantasy 15; *Journey into Mystery 83*; *Tales of Suspense 39, 63*; Sgt.

Fury 1; *Strange Tales 110, 115, 135*; *Avengers 1, 4*; *X-Men 1*; *Daredevil 1*; *Silver Surfer 1*; *Origin 1*.

This paperback book was originally published as a limited hardcover edition, without Origin 1. (See chapter 5 in this book.) In addition to the acclaimed Wolverine origin story, it contains some of the first and most famous, stories featuring Captain America, Sub-Mariner, Ant-Man, Sgt. Fury/Nick Fury, Thor, Ant-Man, Daredevil, Iron Man, Dr. Strange, Silver Surfer, and the X-Men. This is an essential collection for anyone who is wants to understand the Silver Age of Marvel and its origins.

Lee, Stan, Jack Kirby, G. Bell, et al. *Marvel's Greatest Superhero Battles*. New York: Simon and Schuster, 1978. ISBN: 067124 5449 (trd); 0671243918 (pbk). Reprints *Fantastic Four 25–26*; *Daredevil 7*; *X-Men 3*; *Silver Surfer 4*; *Tales of Suspense 79–80*; *Tales to Astonish 82*; *Strange Tales 139–141, 188*; *Amazing Spider-Man 69*.

This is a collection of some of the titanic, early battles in the Marvel Universe. They include the Hulk vs. the Thing; Dr. Strange vs. Dormammu; Iron Man vs. Sub-Mariner; X-Men vs. the Blob; Silver Surfer vs. Thor; Daredevil vs. Sub-Mariner; and Spider-Man vs. the Kingpin.

Lee, Stan, Jack Kirby, Sol Brodsky, et al. *Grandson of Origins*. New York: Marvel, 1998. ISBN: 078510593X. Reprints *Fantastic Four 4*; *Namor 1*; *Uncanny X-Men 117, 309*; *Captain America 255, 350*; *Nick Fury: Agent of SHIELD 5*; *Marvel Spotlight 31*; *KA-ZAR: The Savage 1*; *KA-ZAR 1*.

This book contains debut and origin stories for Sub-Mariner, Captain America, Nick Fury, Professor X, and Ka-Zar. Newer stories involving these characters appear alongside of the earlier ones. Each story is preceded by an essay that explains it.

Lee, Stan, Jack Kirby, John Byrne, et al. *Origins of Marvel Comics*. New York: Simon and Schuster, 1974. ISBN: 0671218646 (trd); 0671218638 (pbk). Reprints *Fantastic Four 1, 55*; *Hulk 1, 118*; *Amazing Fantasy 15*; *Amazing Spider-Man 72*; *Journey into Mystery 83*; *Mighty Thor 143*; *Strange Tales 110, 115*.

This was the first book-size collection of Marvel comics. It tells the origin of the Fantastic Four, Hulk, Spider-Man, Thor, and Dr. Strange. Each story has a separate essay by Stan Lee, explaining how the ideas for the characters came to him. This is essential reading for anyone who is interested in knowing the foundations of the Marvel Universe.

Lee, Stan, Jack Kirby, John Byrne, et al. *Origins of Marvel Comics: Revised Edition*. New York: Marvel, 1997. ISBN: 0785105514. Reprints *Fantastic Four 1, 243*; *Hulk 1, 373*; *Amazing Fantasy 15, Spider-Man Torment 1*; *Journey into Mystery 83*; *Mighty Thor 143*; *Strange Tales 110, 115*; *Doctor Strange 56*.

This collection contains the original stories for Fantastic Four, Spider-Man, Hulk, Thor, and Dr. Strange. The original essays by Stan Lee are reprinted, and there are short, new essays that accompany the revisions.

Lee, Stan, Jack Kirby, Gene Colon, et al. *Son of Origins of Marvel Comics*. New York: Simon and Schuster, 1974. ISBN: 0671221701 (trd); 0671221663 (pbk). Reprints *Uncanny X-Men 1*; *Tales of Suspense 39, 97*; *Avengers 1*; *Daredevil 1, 47*; *Strange Tales 135*; *Silver Surfer 1*.

This work contains stories of the origins of Nick Fury, Silver Surfer, X-Men, Avengers, Daredevil, and Iron Man. Of special interest is the origin of the Watcher, which first appeared in *Silver Surfer 1*. Each story has an introduction by Stan Lee.

Lee, Stan, Jack Kirby, Stan Ditko, et al. *Marvel Team-Up Thrillers*. New York: Marvel, 1983. ISBN: 0939766604. Reprints *Tales of Suspense 58*; *Marvel Team-Up 79*; *X-Men 9*; *Marvel Feature 11*; *Silver Surfer 4*.

This is a nice collection of various team-up tales featuring popular Marvel characters. It includes Spider-Man with Red Sonja; Iron Man and Captain America; the Hulk with the Thing; Daredevil and Spider-Man; Thor and the Silver Surfer; and the X-Men and the Avengers. In nearly ever story, the main heroes fight each other before teaming up.

Lee, Stan, Jack Kirby, Steve Ditko, et al. *Target Marvel Classic Origins*. New York: Marvel, 2004. ISBN: 078511579X. Reprints *Amazing Fantasy 15*; *X-Men Vol. 1: 1*; *Daredevil Vol. 1: 1*; *Avengers Vol. 1: 1*; *Hulk Vol.1: 1*; *Strange Tales 110*.

This collection contains re-mastered versions of the stories of the origins/first appearances of some of Marvel's heavyweights, including the Hulk (back to the grey), Spider-Man, Daredevil, Dr. Strange, the X-Men, and the Avengers. This book was part of the Marvel Age series for young readers, designed to introduce them to the original stories. It includes pin-ups of Spider-Man and Dr. Strange.

Lee, Stan, Jack Kirby, Don Heck, et al. *Bring Back the Bad Guys*. New York: Marvel, 1998. ISBN: 0785105913. Reprints *Uncanny X-Men 4, 161*; *Marvel Tales 190*;

Daredevil 172; *Avengers 8*; *Giant Size Avengers 2*; *Tales of Suspense 50*; *Iron Man 275*; *Fantastic Four 341*.

This work contains origin stories and some other of the first stories that starred the villain: Magneto, Kingpin, Bullseye, Kang, Rama-Tut, Fin Fang Foom, Mandarin, and Galactus. Each issue is preceded by an essay explaining the concepts behind the villains. This collection contains the rare Avengers story in which the Swordsman dies.

Lee, Stan, Jack Kirby, Pual Reinman, et al. *Son of Origins of Marvel Comics: Revised Edition*. New York: Marvel, 1997. ISBN: 078510559X. Reprints *Uncanny X-Men 1*; *X-Men 3*; *Tales of Suspense 39*; *Iron Man 231*; *Avengers 1, 347*; *Daredevil 1, 232*; *Silver Surfer 1*.

This is a reprint of the 1975 edition, with newer stories added for comparison with the old stories. Stan Lee's original introductions are included, and there are new introductions for the added issues. The work contains origin stories for X-Men, Iron Man, Avengers, Daredevil, and Silver Surfer.

Lee, Stan, Jack Kirby, Chic Stone, et al. *Bring on the Bad Guys: Origins of Marvel Villains*. New York: Simon and Schuster, 1976. ISBN: 0671223542 (trd); 0671223550 (pbk). Reprints *Fantastic Four 5*; *Fantastic Four Annual 1*; *Strange Tales 126–127*; *Journey Into Mystery 112–113, 115*; *Tales of Suspense 66–68*; *Amazing Spider-Man 40*; *Tales to Astonish 90–91*; *Silver Surfer 3*.

This book contains origin/first appearance stories for Dr. Doom, Loki, the Red Skull, Dormammu, Mephisto, Green Goblin, and the Abomination.

Lee, Stan, Jack Kirby, Chic Stone et al. *Bring On the Bad Guys: Origins of Marvel Villains*, revised edition. New York: Marvel, 1998. ISBN: 0785105972. Reprints *Fantastic Four 5, 278–279*; *Strange Tales 126–127*; *Journey Into Mystery 112–113, 115*; *Tales of Suspense 66–68*; *Amazing Spider-Man 40*; *Tales to Astonish 90–91*; *Silver Surfer 3*.

Nearly all the tales from the original 1976 version are reprinted in this work. In addition, it contains a modern-day origin story for Dr. Doom, and a story in which the She-Hulk is a member of the Fantastic Four.

Lee, Stan, John Romita, Don Heck et al. *Superhero Women*. New York: Simon and Schuster, 1977. ISBN: 0671227661 (trd); 067122928 (pbk). Reprints *Amazing Spider-Man 62*; *Marvel Feature 4*; *Fantastic*

Four 22; *Ms. Marvel 1*; *Mighty Thor 189–190*; *Cat 1*; *Tales to Astonish 44*; *Savage Tales 1*; *Shanna, the She Devil 2*; *Amazing Spider-Man 86.*

This is a groundbreaking collection showcasing Marvel's superheriones, including Medusa, Shanna, the Cat, Red Sonja, Invisible Woman, Wasp, Ms. Marvel, Hela, Femizons, and the Black Widow. Of special interest is the story of the origin of the Wasp, and the rare reprint of *The Cat.* It is a shame that this collection, which highlights the fact that all superbeings are not men in spandex tights, is no longer in print. A similar book, *Women of Marvel*, was published in 2006 (ISBN: 0785122192).

Liefeld, Rob, D. G. Chichester, John Bryne, et al. *Marvel Collection Volume 1.* New York/Canada: Marvel, 1992. Reprints *X-Force 11*; *Namor the Sub-Mariner 27*; *Darkhawk 16*; *Daredevil 305*; *NFL Superpro 9*; *Avengers West Coast 83* ; *Captain America 401*; *Marc Spector Moon Knight 39*; *Nomad Vol. 2: 3*; *Hellraiser 13*; *Sensational She-Hulk Vol. 2: 41*; *Warlock Vol. 2: 3*; *Captain Planet and the Planeteers 8*; *Quaser 35*; *Sleepwalker 13*; *Wolverine 55*; *X-Factor 79*; *WCW World Championship Wrestling 3*; *Warheads 2*; *Groo 90*; *Kid n' Play 5*; *Guardians of the Galaxy 25*; *Pendragon 1*; *Web of Spider-Man 89.*

This bizarre three-volume collection binds together various comics from June/July 1992. It is quite rare, and there is no indication as to why this set was produced. Perhaps it was a promotional item. *Marvel Collection Vol. 1* collects both mainstream Marvel comics, and those published by the Epic imprint.

Lobdell, Scott, Peter David, Dan Abnett et al. *Marvel Collection Vol. 2.* New York: Marvel, 1992. Reprints *Uncanny X-Men 289*; *Incredible Hulk 394*; *Punisher Vol. 2: 64*; *What If Vol. 2:38*; *Toxic Crusaders 2*; *Death's Head II 4*; *Excalibur 52*; *Warlock and the Infinity Watch 6*; *Barbie 18*; *Doctor Strange: Sorcerer Supreme Annual 2*; *Fantastic Four 365*; *Iron Man 281*; *New Warriors 24*; *G.I. Joe: A Real American Hero 125*; *Silver Surfer Annual 5*; *Mighty Thor 448*; *Hellraiser: Book of the Damned 2*; *X-Men Classic 72*; *Deathlok 12*; *James Bond Jr. 6*; *Nick Fury: Agent of S.H.I.E.L.D. Vol. 2: 36*; *Spectacular Spider-Man 189*; *The 'Nam 69*; *Hell's Angel 1*; *Amazing Spider-Man 363.*

This bound collection is the second volume of Marvel comics with cover dates of June/July 1992. This volume combines both regular Marvel titles and selected Epic titles.

McLaurin, Marc, Scott Lobdell, Chris Bachalo, et al. *The Best of Marvel: 1995.* New York: Marvel, 1995. Reprints *Generation X 5–6*; *Amazing Spider-Man 400*; *Spectacular Spider-Man Super Special 1*; *Avengers 384*; *Incredible Hulk 426*; *Tales of Marvels: Blockbuster*; *Doom 2099*; *X-Men 45.*

Bruce Banner struggles to stay sane, as Betty Ross's life hangs in the balance. The Dr. Doom of 2099 conquers North America, and Generation X and Emma Frost go up against Marrow and her cronies. Hercules fights his stepmother for the life of a mortal woman, and ends up going against his father Zeus who banishes him. Rogue goes crazy after bonding with Gambit who has dark secrets of his own, including working with Mr. Sinister. A former police officer stalks the Silver Surfer.

This work contains some memorable quotes from 1995, and some of the best stories that Marvel published that year. It includes the emotional story of the death of Aunt May.

Nicieza, Mariano, Tom DeFalco, Ron Linn et al. *Best of Marvel: 1994.* New York: Marvel, 1994. ISBN: 0785100717. Reprints *Doom 2099 13*; *Incredible Hulk 419*; *Thunderstrike 8*; *Night Trasher 6*; *Punisher 93*; *X-Factor 101*; *Uncanny X-Men 303*; *Wolverine 82*; *X-Men 30.*

Doc Ock steals radioactive medicine for AIDS patients, to help save a former lover. Doom 2099 goes up against the Demon Necrotek. The Hulk fights a Skrull, seeking to restore his honor. The Hulk gives up to the Skrull, and becomes a pathetic wimp. Thunderstrike tries to help his son who is hostage to the lover of his ex-wife. He only makes the problems worse by butting in. Night Trasher and his partner try to stop a racial war. A block on East Tenth in New York is being overrun by thugs, and a young boy asks the Punisher for help in cleaning up the neighborhood. X-Force is mourning the death of Madrox, and the X-Men are mourning the loss of Illyana. Jubilee begins to understand the relationship between Kitty Pryde and Illyana, and why it was special. Wolverine takes a young girl, whom he promised to take care of, away from her abusive foster parents, and Jean Grey and Scott Summers get married.

In this book we learn a great deal about Ock's past and his relationship with his mother who disapproved of his lover. The volume also includes quotes to remember from various 1994 Marvel comics. The introduction is by Mariano Nicieza who also was the editor.

Ross, Alex, Jim Krueger, Dougie Braithwaite, et al. *Earth X Vol. 3: Universe X: Book 2.* New York: Marvel, 2002. ISBN: 0785108 858. Reprints *Universe X 8–12*; *Universe X: X*; *Universe X: Beasts*; *Universe X: Iron Men*; *Universe X: Omnibus.*

Mar-Vell kills the Kree's Supreme Intelligence on the Moon. Mephisto is revealed to be Satan, and his daughter is Death. Mar-Vell helps start a rebellion in the Land of the Dead, Limbo, trying to kill Death. The X-Men go up against the Wendigo, and it is revealed that Multiple Man is Wendigo reincarnated. The Gargoyle dies after he is allowed to feel again. Dracula is actually a mutant, and Belasco is a Nightcrawler deceived by Mephisto. Immortus reverts back to Kang, and he realizes his mistakes. Iron Maiden, the Black Knight, and Cable help Magneto get back his powers, and Toad tries to kill himself. The Absorbing Man, Crusher Creel, is reanimated to keep the New York torch burning. The Silver Surfer is in the torch, and his wife is killed by Creel. The Vision appeals to Creel's goodness. Captain America's face is sculptured into Mount Rushmore. Reed Richards plans to leave Earth, with his Sue. The "dead" army that rebels in Limbo includes Bucky, Blazing Skull, Bloodstone, 3-D Man, and the original Vision, among others. Loki redeems himself for all his deceitful behavior. The Surfer gets into Mar-Vell's cloak, and becomes normal again.

This volume, which should be in every library, contains discussions about reality, the nature of the universe, and alternative Earths. It also contains a history of the Kree/Skrull connection.

Ross, Alex, Jim Krueger, Dougie Braithwaite, et al. *Earth X: Volume 5: Paradise X Book 2.* New York: Marvel, 2004. ISBN: 0785111 212. Reprints *Paradise X Devils*; *Paradise X A*; *Paradise X: X*; *Paradise X 6–12*; *Paradise X Ragnarok 1–2*.

Reed Richards tries to find a way to free Jude, the Entropic Man, who can bring death to the suffering. Desguised as Daredevil, Mephisto has been playing all the heroes along. Marv-vell's Paradise of the Dead, in the Neutral Zone, is causing all kinds of problems. Reed Richards and numerous other heroes, including Hyperion, go into the negative zone, to try to balance the scales. Frank Castle tries to make his family understand that they are dead, and Captain America tries to convince Bucky, whom he killed, to help. Thor, Loki, and others bring about the day of Ragnarok, and beat up Odin. He had deceived Thor and company into believing they were real, when they were actually just constructs from his mind, and not real gods. In fact, Odin is not the real Odin; he gained his prestige by making a pact with Mephisto. X-51, Machine Man, has detailed conversations with Jude and Deathlok, and Mephisto kills Captain Britain with the sword Excalibur. The original Marvel Boy and 3-D Man make cameo appearances.

This volume contains both narrative and graphic text, and a sketchbook by Alex Ross. It is the conclusion of this epic retelling of the Marvel Universe in the distant future.

Ross, Alex, Jim Krueger, John Paul Leon, et., al. *Earth X Vol. 1.* New York: Marvel, 2000.

ISBN: 078510755X. Reprints *Earth X Vol. 1: 0–12* and *Earth X: X.*

The Red Skull is a young man, who attempts to take over the Earth. Thor is a woman. The Celestials plan to take over the Universe, and bring forth the Celestial embryo from the Earth, destroying Earth in the process. Black Bolt released the Terrigen Mists into the air, thus mutating everybody on Earth. Bolt calls for Galactus to save the Earth, and Celestials destroy him. It turns out that the Watcher was a pawn of the Celestials, and Black Bolt had blinded him.

This is the greatest Marvel epic tale ever told, describing a time when Marvel's traditional heroes are older. Most of the Marvel characters are involved in this tale of the latest menace to take over Earth. Machine Man is featured prominently, and there is an intense dialog between him and the Watcher who is blind.

Ross, Alex, Jim Kruger, Steve Pugh, et al. *Earth X Vol 4: Paradise X: Book 1.* New York: Marvel, 2003. ISBN: 0785111204. Reprints *Paradise X: The Heralds 1–3*; *Paradise X: 0–5*; *Paradise X: Xen.*

In the aftermath of the death of Death, people on Earth do not die. They may live in excruciating pain, due to accidents, but death eludes them. Captain America becomes an angel, along with Phoenix, Black Bolt and others, to bring the souls from the realm of the dead into Paradise. Captain America wants to bring his family into Paradise. Dr. Strange brings the Xen group from Japan to Asgard to find his love Clea who was taken prisoner by Odin. Thor offers himself to the land of Hel in exchange for Clea. Wolverine is not actually a mutant, but the spawn from a race of beings who are not manipulated by the Celestials. Moon Boy is actually Wolverine's descendant. Using the monolith from *2001*, X-51 brings Deathlok, Hyperion, Bloodstorm, Spider-Girl, Wolverine, Iron Man 2020, and Killraven from alternate Earths. He warns the Earths in other realities about the Celestial manipulation, and urges them to seek out the Reed Richards of each world. On one Earth, Richards is actually IT, the Living Colossus. The Watchers come to kill Uatu. X-51 uses the monolith to send the other Watchers into worlds they have watched, thus exposing themselves to the populace, and breaking their vow of noninterference. Kyle Richmond becomes the 4-D Man. Both of Peter Parker's daughters meet, fight, and then become friends. Captain Britain marries Medusa, but the Grey Gargoyle brings his wife Megaan back to life. In the land of death, the Punisher's family sees him murder criminals, and disapproves.

This volume includes appearances by Fing Fang Foom, Ulysses Bloodstone, Surfer, White Tiger, Jigsaw, Kingpin, and Guardians of the Galaxy, among many others. There is narrative and graphic text throughout the volume which belongs in every academic and public library.

Ross, Alex, Jim Krueger, Al Williamson, et al. *Earth X Vol. 2: Universe X: Book 1,* New

York: Marvel 2002. ISBN: 078510867X. Reprints *Universe X: 0–7*; *Universe X: 4*; *Universe X: Spider-Man*; *Universe X: Cap.*

Reed Richards tries to burn out all the torches and Terrigen Mists, to free humanity of mutation. Mar-vell is reborn through Warlock and Eve. Captain America takes Mar-Vell under his wing to try to protect him, and dies in the process. Sue Storm is brought back to life from the land of the dead, through the use of Warlock's Soul Gem and Reed Richards's arm. Nighthawk can see the future through eyes given to him by Mephisto, and the Gargoyle is chronicling history. Magneto is under the thumb of Toad. Peter Parker goes through a dream sequence in which Uncle Ben does not die, nor does Gwen Stacy, his wife. Spider-Man deceives him, and his daughter Venom, what is happening. Captain America learns that he was a tool of the Nazi government and the Red Skull.

This volume, which is an epic sequel to *Earth X*, includes graphic and narrative text, and belongs in every library. The authors make extensive use of "peripheral" Marvel Universe characters, such as the Living Mummy, Moon Knight, the Micronauts, Machine Man, Captain Universe, Nighthawk and the Gargoyle.

Shooter, Jim, Mike Zeck, Bob Layton, et al. *Marvel Super Heroes: Secret Wars.* New York: Marvel, 1999. ISBN: 0785107274; 0871359030 (1992). Reprints *Secret Wars 1–12.*

The Avengers, Spider-Man, and the X-Men, among other characters, fight their foes on the planet Battleworld. Spider-Man gets his black costume, and the Wasp and Magneto have a romantic interlude. The Beyonder, an all-powerful being, wants to know the difference between good and evil, and Galactus makes an appearance in an unexplained mystery.

This has long been considered one of the best crossover books in the Marvel Universe. It was reprinted in 2005 (ISBN: 078511873X).

Smith, Brian, Ralph Macchio, Ben Dunn, et al. *Marvel Mangaverse.* New York: Marvel, 2002. ISBN: 0785109358. Reprints *Marvel Mangaverse New Dawn 1*; *Avengers Assemble 1*; *Fantastic Four 1*; *Ghost Riders 1*; *Punisher 1*; *Spider-Man 1*; *X-Men 1*; *Eternity Twilight 1.*

Hellstorm is trying to convince Ghost Rider that they are brothers, and they go up against their sister Satana. The Avengers go up against Apocalypse, and Spider-Man has to go up against a bunch of demon ninja. The Punisher is a woman samurai, and head-mistress of a school. The X-Men have to face the mystical Mangus, and Dr. Strange and Baron Strucker also fight on the mystical plane. The Hulk is the size of Godzilla.

All the titles republished in this collection are under the Marvel Mangaverse imprint. The main charac-ters are reimagined using the Japanese manga style of comic drawing and writing. This book uses some lesser-known characters such as Son of Satan. It is a fun book.

Steranko, Jim, Arnold Drake, Stan Lee, et al. *Marvel Visionaries: Steranko.* New York: Marvel, 2002. ISBN: 0785109447. Reprints *Western Gunfighters 14*; *Creatures on the Loose 21–22*; *Tex Dawson Gunslinger 1*; *Nick Fury and his Agents of S.H.I.E.L.D. 1–2.*; *Nick Fury: Agent of S.H.I.E.L.D. Vol. 2: 1*; *X-Men 49–51*; *Captain America 110–111, 113*; *Fantastic Four 130–131*; *Tower of Shadows 1*; *Our Love Story 5*; *Supernatural Thrillers 1–2*; *Incredible Hulk Special 1.*

The X-Men go up against Mesmero who has trapped Lorna Dane. Magneto claims that Lorna is his daughter. Captain America saves Rick Jones from the Hulk, and Jones puts on Bucky's old uniform to be Captain America's partner. He stages his death, in order to defeat Hydra.

This book includes a love story about an actress who falls for a director. It also has a cover gallery. The book is a tribute to artist Jim Steranko. It includes some of his best stories, and reproductions of various covers.

Thomas, Roy, Jim Craig, Pablo Marcos, et al. *The Best of What If.* New York: Marvel, 1991. ISBN: 0871358573. Reprints *What If Vol. 1: 1, 8, 24, 27–28, 32, 34, 36.*

This is a collection of alternate universe stories, in-cluding "What If Spider-Man had joined the Fantas-tic Four, and Sue Richards had left the group to live with Sub-Mariner?" Other stories include "What if Gwen Stacy had lived?" "What if the Fantastic Four had not gained their powers?" and "What if Phoenix had not died?" The volume also contains some bits of humor, such as Aunt May becoming a superhero and Iron Man having an eating problem.

Thomas, Roy, Stan Lee, Jack Kirby, et al. *Marvel's Greatest Super Battles.* New York: Marvel, 1994. ISBN: 07851002318. Reprints *Journey into Mystery 112*; *Uncanny X-Men 112–113*; *Amazing Spider-Man 318–319*; *Punisher War Journal 10*; *Marvel Two in One Annual 7.*

This is a collection of great battle stories including Thor's titanic battle against the Hulk; Wolverine against Sabretooth; Spider-Man against the Scorpion; the Punisher against one of his old enemies from his 'Nam days; and the Thing against the alien Cham-pion, who also defeats the Hulk, Sub-Mariner, Doc Samson, Thor, Wonder Man and Sasquatch. The Thing loses, but his fighting spirit impresses the Champion.

Thomas, Roy, Jim Shooter, Gil Kane, et al.
   What If Classic Vol. 1. New York: Marvel,
   2004. ISBN: 0785117024. Reprints *What
   If Vol. 1: 1–6*.

In the seventies Marvel put together a comic which told stories outside of the continuity of the Marvel Universe. These stories are what might have happened if certain events were changed. The Watcher is the host for each of the tales. If Spider-Man had joined the Fantastic Four to make the Fantastic Five, Sue Storm would have left Reed Richards for Namor, the Sub-Mariner, and she would have become his wife instead of Reeds. If the Hulk had retained Bruce Banner's intelligence, he would have married Betty. Reed Richards, Professor X, and Bruce Banner would have become the X-Man to stop Galactus. If the Avengers had never formed, the Hulk and Namor would have killed Iron Man, while Rick Jones and Henry and Janet Pym would have donned a bizarre set of Iron

Man outfits. If Bucky had survived World War II, eventually he would have put on the Captain America costume and died. If the Fantastic Four had different powers, Reed Richards would have become just a brain, the Thing would have wings, Invisible Woman would have stretching powers, and Johnny Storm would become a living robot. Dr. Doom would kidnap Reed's brain, but the brain would be so powerful that Reed would take over in Doom's body, wearing the armor. One story, however, did happen. In *What If 4*, when the Invaders stay together after World War II, Captain America and Bucky are lost at sea, but the Spirit of '76 takes over in Captain America's costume, with another Bucky. The Invaders become the All Winners Squad. The Spirit of '76 dies, and the Patriot takes his place as Captain America. This book includes several of Roy Thomas's essays, and an ad for Marvel Premiere, featuring the coolest Marvel Character, the 3-D Man. It also includes a *What If* checklist, 1–114.

5

Special Hardbacks and
Marvel Masterworks

No, Horton, I'll be free and no one will ever use me for selfish
gain or crime.—*Original Human Torch to his creator in 1939*

What fools these mortals be! Warring among each other to satisfy
the arrogant egos of a few stupid governments! I'll show them what war is
like—war to preserve the safety and happiness of the civilian population.
—*Prince Namor, the Sub-Mariner, 1940*

Special Hardbacks

Azzarello, Brian, Richard Corben, Jose Villarrubia, et al. *Cage Vol. 1.* New York: Marvel,
2002. ISBN: 0785109668 (trd); ISBN:
0785113010 (pbk). Reprints *Cage 1–5.*

Luke Cage, the Hero for Hire and the second
Power Man in the Marvel Universe, is hired to help
find out who killed a thirteen-year-old girl in a drive-
by shooting. Cage finds himself embroiled in a
gang/drug war between Hammerhead and Tombstone. Cage plays each side against the other.

This volume is a *Boys in the Hood* equivalent told
in comics format for adults, part of Marvel's adult Max
line. The story is very graphic, well-written and beautifully illustrated. This volume is recommended, but
not for the faint of heart. The introduction is by postmodern novelist Darius James.

Beazley, Mark, Syd Barney-Hawke, Eric J.
Moreels, et al. *Marvel Encyclopedia Vol. 2:
X-Men.* New York: Marvel, 2003. ISBN:
0785111999.

This is a very detailed character guide to the X-
Men, with chapters ranging from the Acolytes, Alpha
Flight, Savage Land Mutates, Weapon X, to X-Statix and the X-Corporation. It spans the years from
the very first *X-Men* comic to Grant Morrison's *New*

X-Men books. Each entry contains a picture, written
text, and a chart that explains the character's powers,
etc. Even characters who only appear in a book once,
are listed with supporting information. There are also
chapters on Xavier Institute, Xavier Mansion, Cere-
bra Files, and Ultimate X-Men. The volume includes
a bibliography of all *X-Men* graphic novels in print,
and a section on power ratings. The only mutant missing in this encyclopedia is Deadpool. Note: Entries
for Volumes 3, 4, and 5 of *Marvel Encyclopedia* appear
in this section under "Kiefer." Volume 7 appears under
"Christiansen." In 2006 Marvel partnered with
Scholastic to publish a two-volume version of the *X-
Men Encyclopedia*—ISBN: 0785121994 (1); 0785123
962 (2) These volumes are only available through
Scholastic bookstores.

Beazley, Mark, Marvel Staff, Marvel Entertainment Group, et al. *The Marvel Universe
Role Playing Game: Guide to the X-Men
Universe.* New York: Marvel, 2003. ISBN:
0785110356.

This special hardcover covering the X-Men includes character profiles, group profiles, new actions
and modifiers, supplemental rules and clarifications,
a gamemaster section, adventure briefings, and sam-

ple adventures. The appendix includes weapons, vehicles, and a character-actions display foldout.

Beazley, Mark, Jeff Younquist, Matt Brady, et al. *Marvel Encyclopedia Vol. 1.* New York: Marvel, 2002. ISBN: 0785109846.

This volume contains a newer look at the characters who make up the Marvel Universe. Each chapter looks at a specific group of characters, both heroes and villains. The Avengers chapter contains entries that range from Ant-Man, Hulk, Wonder Man, and Jarvis, to Loki and the Red Skull. The chapter on the Fantastic Four contains Namor, Silver Surfer, Galactus, and Doom, among others. The entries in the Marvel Knights/Max chapter go from the Punisher, Blade, Ghost Rider, Daredevil, and Kingpin, to Marvel Boy and Jessica Jones. Spider-Man's chapter contains mostly villains, including Green Goblin, Vulture and Mysterio, along with a few "good" folks like Aunt May, Black Cat, and Mary Jane. X-Men entries range from Agent X, Soldier X, Beast, and Jubilee, to Cassandra Nova and the Sentinels. There are also chapters on the Ultimate Marvel Universe and the *Call of Duty* series. In 2006, DK published their version of the *Marvel Encyclopedia* (ISBN: 0756623588).

Bendis, Brian Michael, Mark Bagley, Art Thiebert, et al. *Ultimate Spider-Man Collection.* New York: Marvel/Barnes and Noble, 2004. ISBN: 0760761337. Reprints *Ultimate Spider-Man 1/2, 1–39; Amazing Fantasy 15.*

This collection is a massive, 500+ page limited edition of the first thirty-nine issues of *Ultimate Spider-Man.* It was available only at selected Barnes and Noble stores.

Bendis, Brian Michael, Mark Bagley, Art Thiebert, et al. *Ultimate Spider-Man Vol. 2.* New York: Marvel, 2003. ISBN: 0785110 615. Reprints *Ultimate Spider-Man 14–27.*

After he is captured, Doc Ock figures out the connection between Parker and Spider-Man. Justine Hammer dies of a heart attack. Kraven, who tries to battle Spider-Man on live television, ends up being arrested, and his show is cancelled. Norman Osborn threatens Spider-Man, and tries to force him to do his bidding. He kidnaps Mary Jane who is almost killed.

This deluxe hardcover contains storylines from the paperback Volumes 3–4 and short essays by the author, artist, and editor, as well as original sketches.

Bendis, Brian Michael, Mark Bagley, Art Thiebert, et al. *Ultimate Spider-Man Vol. 3.* New York: Marvel, 2003. ISBN: 0785111565. Reprints *Ultimate Spider-Man 1/2, 28–39.*

The Rhino is creating havoc in New York, and Peter rushes out from school to help, only to see that Iron Man has the situation well in hand. A fake Spider-Man has been committing robberies, and the "real" Spider-Man has the cops looking for him. The cops shoot Spider-Man in the arm. Captain Stacy gets killed in the line of duty, and Mary Jane breaks up with Peter. Peter Parker learns that his father and Eddie Brock's father were working on a cure for cancer before they died. They created a symbiotic life form which was supposed to bond with the host and destroy the disease. Peter seeks out Brock and learns that Brock has been trying to keep his father's dream alive. Peter tries to get a sample of the symbiotic form, but is transformed into a Spider-Man with a live suit. The suit tries to control Peter, and kills an innocent bystander. Brock joins with it, and becomes Venom. They have a huge battle at Peter's school, and Peter asks Nick Fury to rid him of the Spider powers. Curt Connors discovers that Parker is Spider-Man. Spider-Man comes to the rescue of a lady shoplifter, and inadvertently punches Danny Rand.

The introduction was written by the *Evil Dead* and *Spider-Man* movie star Bruce Campbell. The volume also contains a one-act play by Bendis and former Marvel president Bill Jemas, as well as the Venom script.

Bendis, Brian Michael, Mark Bagley, Art Thiebert, et al. *Ultimate Spider-Man Vol. 4.* New York: Marvel, 2004. ISBN: 0785112496. Reprints *Ultimate Spider-Man 40–45, 47–53.*

A mutant from a sister high school, Geldoff, is causing havoc by blowing up cars. Peter tries to reason with him, to no avail. The X-Men show up and take both Spider-Man and Geldoff to the X-Mansion. The X-Men find out Spider-Man's secret identity, and they learn that Geldoff was experimented on while he was in the womb. X-Man member Kitty has a crush on Spider-Man. Aunt May, who has very strange notions about Spider-Man and her nephew Peter, sees a therapist. May and Peter go see a movie. Peter Parker loses his job when he asks Jonah why they let Kingpin, who had murdered someone, out of jail, and he gets kicked out of his classes when he questions his teacher about a justice system that would let a murderer go free. Sam Bullit runs for the office of district attorney, and when the *Daily Bugle* questions his ties to the Kingpin and organized crime, Jonah Jameson is almost beaten up by thugs. Spider-Man saves him. The Black Cat steals a precious historical tablet, and Spider-Man tries to stop her. She puts a personal ad in the *Bugle,* asking Spider-Man for a date. Elektra is hired by Wilson Fisk to take down both Spider-Man and the Black Cat. The Cat is captured and beaten senseless, but escapes, with Spider-Man's help. Jonah apologizes to Parker, gives him his job back, and tells the story of his missing son. Mary Jane runs away from home when her father forbids her to date Peter Parker.

This volume contains an interview with Bendis, sketch art, and a deleted script from *Ultimate Spider-Man 53.*

Bendis, Brian Michael, Mark Bagley, Art Thiebert, et al. *Ultimate Spider-Man Vol. 5.* New

York: Marvel, 2004. ISBN: 0785114017. Reprints *Ultimate Spider M an 46*; *54–59*; *Ultimate Six 1–7*.

The Green Goblin, Doc Ock, the Sandman, Electro, and Kraven are put into a special S.H.I.E.L.D. prison for illegally experimenting on themselves and being a danger to society at large. Nick Fury updates the Ultimates on the situation. Hank Pym is the special-liaison psychologist to the supervillains. With the help of Doc Ock, they all break away and form a team to take Fury down, but Norman Osborn, the Green Goblin, wants Spider-Man, whom he refers to as his son, to join in their evil pursuits. Spider-Man's identity is revealed to the Ultimates. A film company is in New York to film a fictional account of Spider-Man and his adventures. Peter Parker, who is not very happy about this, visits the set. Doc Ock breaks out of prison by using his mental telepathy to control his mechanical arms. He kidnaps Spider-Man from the movie set, and takes him to Brazil. Ock's widow is being used as a consultant for the movie. Gwen Stacy figures out that Peter Parker is Spider-Man, and comes to grips with it.

This volume contains special appearances by director Sam Rami; producer and CEO of Marvel Studios, Avi Arad; and star Tobey Maguire. It includes a sketchbook, a cover gallery, and a removed page from *Ultimate Spider-Man 46*. *Ultimate Spider Man Volumes 6–8*—ISBN: 0785118411 (6); 078512148X (7); 078512 604X (8).

Bendis, Brian Michael, Michael Gaydos, David Mack, et al. *Alias.* New York: Marvel, 2002. ISBN: 0785108726 (trd); 0785111417 (pbk). Reprints *Alias 1–9.*

Jessica Jones is a private investigator who was once a costumed hero. While working on a case, she inadvertently videotapes Captain America changing from his secret identity. A political group is after the tape and some murders are committed. She tracks down unfaithful wives/husbands, and searches for Rick Jones who is afraid of Skrulls lurking in the darkness. It turns out that this is not the real Rick Jones but a person obsessed with him.

The volume includes sections from Bendis's book *Sidekick*. In 2006 Marvel published the *Alias Omnibus* (ISBN: 0785121218) which included the whole series in one volume. This hardcover is a crime *noir* graphic novel for adults.

Bendis, Brian Michael, Bill Jemas, Mark Bagley, et al. *Ultimate Spider-Man Vol. 1.* New York: Marvel, 2002. ISBN: 078510898X. Reprints *Ultimate Spider-Man 1–13*; *Amazing Fantasy 15.*

This deluxe hardcover covers the first thirteen issues of Marvel's award-winning *Ultimate Spider-Man*. It includes Bill Jemas's rationale for creating the Ultimate Marvel Universe, and Brian Bendis's discussion of how he got the job to write it. Jemas and Bendis's email discussions are included, as are sketchbooks,

character descriptions, pieces of deleted script material, and written narrative of issues 1–6.

Bendis, Brian Michael, Alex Maleev, Manuel Gutierez, et al. *Daredevil Vol. 3.* New York: Marvel, 2004. ISBN: 0785111069. Reprints *Daredevil Vol. 2: 38–50*

Matt Murdock defends the White Tiger who is blamed for the death of a policeman. The Tiger is found guilty, and goes berserk. The void left by Kingpin's absence, because he is near death, is bringing out all kinds of low-rate hoods, waiting to fill his shoes. The Owl and a band of the Kingpin's former employees want to take Daredevil down. Daredevil saves a young blind girl from being run over. She hears that Matt Murdock is accused of being Daredevil, and visits him. She recognizes him as Daredevil by listening to his voice. Murdock becomes a suspect in the brutal slaying of publisher, Mr. Rosenthal. Luke Cage snubs Murdock when he visits. The Kingpin returns to New York, and wants to set up his empire again. He employs Typhoid Mary to weed out anyone who would oppose him, including Matt Murdock. Mary takes on Jessica Jones and Luke Cage, and sets Matt's face on fire. Bullseye attempts to assassinate Matt's new girlfriend while she is at his apartment. Daredevil catches him, and uses a knife to carve scars into Bullseye's head in retribution for the death of two of his former girlfriends. The Kingpin kills anyone who opposed him when he fell from power, and attempts to take back Hell's Kitchen. Daredevil takes the Kingpin on in hand-to-hand combat, and beats the stuffing out of him. Daredevil declares that he is now running Hell's Kitchen. Boomerang sues Matt Murdock. Luke Cage and Iron Fist make cameo appearances.

The stories in this deluxe hardcover resemble pulp fiction, and are *noir* at its finest. The volume includes a sketchbook from *Daredevil 48 and 49,* by Alex Maleev. Bendis reprints his letter to the guest artists, and writes his thoughts on working with Maleev, Gene Colan, Lee Weeks, Klaus Janson, John Romita, Joe Quesada, Michael Avon Oeming, and David Mack. Bendis also includes deleted scenes. *Daredevil Vols. 4–6* were published in 2005 and 2006, with ISBN 0785113428 (4); 0785121102 (5); and 0785121110 (6).

Bendis, Brian Michael, Alex Maleev, Matt Hollingsworth, et al. *Daredevil Vol. 2.* New York: Marvel, 2002. ISBN: 0785109269. Reprints *Daredevil Vol. 2: 26–37.*

This is a deluxe hardcover that includes the "Under Boss" and "Out" storylines in which Daredevil is revealed to the world at large as Matt Murdock. *Daredevil* screenwriter and movie director Mark Stephen Johnson wrote the foreword. Bendis wrote the afterword in which he states that this volume is a tribute to Frank Miller's earlier work on *Daredevil*. It has a sketchbook by Alex Maleev and an article by Matt Hollingsworth on painting Daredevil. There is also a *Newsarama.com* article, including an interview with Bendis about "outing" the "pulp hero of Hell's Kitchen."

Bendis, Brian Michael, Matt Wagner, Comicraft, et al. *Ultimate Marvel Team-Up*. New York: Marvel, 2002. ISBN: 078510870X. Reprints *Ultimate Marvel Team-Up 1–16*; *Ultimate Spider-Man Super Special 1*.

Spider-Man teams up with the Ultimate versions of Hulk, Wolverine, Iron Man, Man-Thing, Daredevil, Fantastic Four, Punisher, Dr. Strange, Black Widow, Electra, Shan Ci Master of Kung Fu, and Blade. The X-Men encounter Parker in a shopping mall, and Wolverine refers to Parker as his cousin. Spider-Man asks Shan Ci to teach him how to fight. He also goes to the Baxter Building, to see if the Fantastic Four could use a fifth member. Daredevil tells him he is too young to be a superhero, and he should give it up.

This deluxe hardcover includes a cover gallery and an afterword by Bendis.

Bisley, Simon, Alex Ross, Vince Evans, et al. *The Art of Marvel Comics*. New York: Marvel, 2000. ISBN: 078510769X.

This is a wonderful collection of the works of some of the hottest artists in the industry, picturing various characters in the Marvel Universe. In it Spider-Man, the Hulk, Ghost Rider, and X-Men are pictured alongside lesser-known characters like Polaris and Wonder Man. This is a must-have for libraries and fans. Two later volumes were also published under this title.

Burgos, Carl, Bill Everett, Roy Thomas, et al. *Marvel Comics: Action Mystery Adventure*. New York: Marvel, 1990. ISBN: 087135 729. Reprints *Marvel Comics 1*.

This a hardback reprint of the very first Marvel Comic ever produced, in 1939. In it, Professor Horton creates the Human Torch as a human android, and the Sub-Mariner learns from his mother about his unique heritage. Other character featured include the Angel, Masked Raider, and Ka-Zar. The book contains an adventure story "Jungle Action," and the original prose story "Burning Rubber." It includes essays by Roy Thomas, reminiscing about Human Torch creator Carl Burgos and Sub-Mariner creator Bill Everett. Comics historian Les Daniels wrote the introduction.

Busiek, Kurt, Len Kaminski, George Perez, et al. *Avengers Assemble*. New York: Marvel, 2004. ISBN: 0785115730. Reprints *Avengers Vol. 3: 1–12*; *Avengers Annual 1998*; *Avengers Morgan Conquest*; *Avengers Supreme Justice*; *Wizard 81*; *Avengers Vol 3: 1 Rough Cut*.

The Avengers go back to medieval times to battle the spells of the villainess Morgan LeFay. She has commandeered the Twilight Sword, and attempts to remake reality in her image. Thirty-nine Avengers are called together to defeat LeFay, and the Scarlet Witch is the key to this. Through force of will, the Scarlet Witch summons Wonder Man. Firestar and Justice join the Avengers, but Carol Danvers is booted off the team because of her problems with alcohol and incidents in which she endangered the team. The Squadron Supreme and the Avengers gang up against Imus Champion. Moses Magnum tries to win the mutant Apocalypse's, favor by detonating a very destructive bomb. Jarvis's sponsored "daughter," from Costa Verde, is actually Silverclaw, who is briefly in the employ of Magnum.

This volume contains the first appearance of Triathlon. Wonder Man is brought back to the land of the living. Other villains who make appearances include Wonder Man's brother, Grim Reaper; and "dead" versions of Captain Marvel, Swordsman, Thunderstrike, and Hellcat. The Scarlet Witch learns much more about her magical powers in this, Kurt Busiek's first effort after taking over the Avengers. The book also includes the biggest gathering of Avengers in the history of the series; Perez's penciled pages for *Avengers 1 Rough Cut*; Busiek's plot pages and notes; and reproductions of the 30th Anniversary poster and the poster included with *Avengers 4*. ISBNs for Volumes 2–4: 0785117733 (2); 0785121307 (3); 0785123474 (4).

Busiek, Kurt, George Perez, Tom Smith, et al. *JLA/Avengers: Collector's Edition*. New York: DC/Marvel, 2004. ISBN: 1401202071. Reprints *JLA/Avengers 1–4*; *Marvel Age 19*.

The Grandmaster and Metron play a game in which the stake is reality in both the DC and Marvel universes. Krona starts a wave of destruction through various universes, seeking the meaning of life, only to become lured by the power of a demigod. He believes that he is the cause of the phasing of reality between the DC and Marvel Earths, and briefly kills the Grandmaster. Both the Avengers and the JLA are sent to various Earths to seek objects including the Cosmic Cube, Soul Gems, Wand of Watoomb, the Eternity Book, and Power Battery, among others. At first, all the JLA and the Avengers fight, except for Captain America and Batman, who seem to realize that there is more than meets the eye to their encounter. When the Avengers and the JLA decide to pool their resources to stop a common enemy, Superman gives up leadership to Captain America, and Captain America gives Superman his shield for safekeeping.

Nearly everyone who has been a JLA or Avenger, and their respective foes, makes a cameo appearance, but the focus is on the heavies like Wonder Woman, Batman, Superman, Flash, Captain America, Iron Man, Thor, Yellowjacket, and the Wasp. A deluxe slipcase contains two volumes, one of which is the story itself; the other contains a history of DC/Marvel crossovers, which includes a bibliography of individual and collected editions. The set includes George Perez's original pencil, from the 1983 aborted crossover; a key to every character (there are so many that it is confusing); a breakdown of the story; Kurt Busiek's original outline for the 2003 series; and the JLA/Avengers you never saw. This is a beautiful set, well worth seeking. It is the epic crossover of the decade in which the two Universes, Marvel and DC, come together to stop a greater threat.

Busiek, Kurt, Alex Ross, Stan Lee, et al. *Marvels 10th Anniversary Edition.* New York: Marvel, 2004. ISBN: 0785113886. Reprints *Marvels 0–4; Marvels Hardcover, Marvels TBC 1st and 2nd printing; Fantastic Four 1; Amazing Fantasy 15; Avengers 5; Uncanny X-Men 1; Marvel Age 130.*

This is a special Tenth Anniversary hard cover edition of *Marvels* that features the same content as previous printings, as well as the complete script; reprints of various covers; the original proposals for the series; the full text of some newspaper articles, scattered throughout the series; classic covers series; and a book behind the scenes of the series, including where certain guests appear in the series. These guests include the Beatles, Pete Townshend and Roger Daltry, Timothy Dalton, Martin Goodman, Clark Kent and Lois Laine, Bill Batson, Badfinger, Dick Van Dyke, Mary Tyler Moore, Nick Fury, and Bea Arthur, among others. This book was the inspiration for the book you hold in your hands.

Busiek, Kurt, Alex Ross, Stan Lee, et al. *Marvels.* New York: Marvel, 1994. ISBN: 0785 10061X. Reprints *Marvels 1–4.*

This was the original hardback in this groundbreaking series. The introduction is by Stan Lee.

Busiek, Kurt, Alex Ross, Richard Starkings, et al. *Marvels: Deluxe Autographed Hardcover.* Anaheim, CA: Graphitti Designs, 1994. ISBN: 0936211474. Reprints *Marvels 0–4.*

This volume was published as a special limited edition of 8,000 copies, an autographed hardcover of the groundbreaking series. It contains Alex Ross's original vision for the series, *Marvels 0*, and a new introduction by Kurt Busiek explaining the genesis of the series. Ross contributes his Marvels paintings of X-Women, Namor, Ben Grimm, Doom, Tony Stark, the Black Widow, Gwen Stacy, Black Panther, Inhumans, and Hobgoblin, among others. The book is dedicated to Jack Kirby.

Christiansen, Jeff, Kit Kiefer, Ronald Byrd, et al. *Marvel Encyclopedia Volume 6: Fantastic Four.* New York: Marvel, 2004. ISBN: 0785114807.

This collection gives an in-depth look at Marvel's first family, the Fantastic Four. Chapters cover a history of the Fantastic Four; the Fantastic Four in animated television and movies; Fantastic Four action figures and toys; and the Fantastic Four A–Z. This last section includes entries on such heavyweights such as the Negative Zone, Galactus, Dr. Doom, Silver Surfer, Namor, Inhumans, Annihilus, and the Watcher, among many others. It also has entries on obscure characters like the Aquarian, Goody Two Shoes, Infant Terrible, Texas Twister, the Rogue Watcher, and Doctor Weird. The collection also contains a detailed look at alternate Earths and the various Fantastic Fours on those Earths. There is a general appendix and an appendix for the alternate Earths. DK books published their own guide to the Fantastic Four, written by Tom Defalco, and published in 2005 (ISBN: 1405309962).

Claremont, Chris, John Byrne, Terry Austin, et al. *Wolverine: Wizard Masterpiece Edition.* Congers, NY: Wizard/Marvel, 2004. ISBN: 097432535X. Reprints *Uncanny X-Men 139–140, 172–173, 268; Incredible Hulk 340; Classic X-Men 25; Wolverine 150–153.*

Wolverine and Nightcrawler help Alpha Flight against the Wendigo. Mariko dumps Logan at the wedding altar. The Gray Hulk battles Wolverine in a fantastic fight sequence, and a hunter hunts Wolverine, thinking he is an animal. Wolverine gets stuck in the middle of a blood feud between various Yakuza members.

This collection is a special limited edition that was published by the comic news source *Wizard* in conjunction with Marvel enterprises. It contains ten of the best comics featuring Wolverine, and a World War II story featuring Captain America, the Black Widow, and Baron Strucker. Supplementary material includes a list of all the women Wolverine has been involved with, called Weapon Sex, and the Hulk's history with Wolverine. The volume also includes Wolverine's fight scores against villains such as the Sentinels, Sabretooth, and Lady Deathstrike; an interview with artist Jim Lee; and "Wolverine: The True Hollywood Story." Avi Arad wrote the introduction.

Claremont, Chris, John Byrne, Terry Austin, et al. *X-Men Visionaries: Chris Claremont Collection.* New York: Marvel Limited, 1994. ISBN: 0785100733. Reprints *Uncanny X-Men 114, 153, 186, 198, 268; Kitty Pryde and Wolverine 4; New Mutants 45; Excalibur 16.*

The X-Men are stranded in the Savage Land. Kitty tells Illyana a fairy tale about pirate Kitty, featuring all the X-Men in various roles. Storm loses her powers, and finds out Forge was behind her loss, just as she was falling in love with him. She helps deliver a baby while visiting Africa. When the New Mutants go to a mixer, Kitty becomes friends with a mutant who ends up committing suicide. Wolverine and Captain America save a young Black Widow from Baron Strucker during World War II.

This is a collection of some of Chris Claremont's most famous one-shot X-Men stories which he personally picked for the volume. Each story has a separate introduction. The collection, which was limited to several hundred copies, also contains a fairy tale featuring Excalibur. Marvel also published a *Chris Claremont Visionaries* in 2005 (ISBN: 078511887X).

Claremont, Chris, John Bryne, Dave Cockrum, et al. *Wizard X-Men Masterpiece Edition: The 10 Greatest X-Men Stories Ever.* Congers NY: Wizard Entertainment/Marvel 2003. ISBN: 0974325317. Reprints *Uncanny X-Men 126–128, 135–137, 141–142, 143, 150.*

This special limited edition hardcover contains some of the most famous stories in X-Men history, including "Mutant X, Proteus"; "The Dark Phoenix Saga"; "Days of Future Past"; and "Demon and I Magneto." Created just for this book are essays which describe the process that Chris Claremont and John Byrne went through to create the story. The original, never before seen, alternate Dark Phoenix ending is reprinted, in which Phoenix lives but has a psychic lobotomy performed on her. Magneto's psychiatric evaluation is reprinted, and eleven reasons why Wolverine should be dead are presented. Greg Horn signed 190 books in this special edition. X-Men artist Jim Lee wrote the introduction.

Couper-Smartt, Jonathan, Kit Kiefer, Tom Mavelli, et al. *The Amazing Spider-Man 500 Covers 1962–2003.* New York: Marvel, 2004. ISBN: 0785114211.

This is a beautiful hardcover book that contains the complete collection of *Amazing Spider-Man* covers from issue 1–500, as well as covers from the annuals and king-sized issues. Each cover has been painstakingly reproduced in full color to make a beautiful coffee-table book. The volume also includes a year-by-year, 1963–2003 commentary on Spider-Man's activities.

David, Peter, George Perez, Tom Smith, et al. *Hulk: Future Imperfect.* New York: Marvel Limited, 1994. ISBN: 0785100709. Reprints *Hulk: Future Imperfect 1–2.*

This is a special limited edition hardcover of several hundred copies. It is a ground-breaking collaboration between writer Peter David and artist George Perez, in which the Hulk meets an alternate version of himself in the distant future. Bobbie Chase wrote the introduction which details how the writer/artist collaboration came about, and Peter David contributes a special afterword detailing how *Future Imperfect* fits into the Marvel Universe. The volume includes a key to the infamous Trophy Room.

Ennis, Garth, Steve Dillon, Jimmy Palmiotti, et al. *Punisher: Vol. 1.* New York: Marvel, 2002. ISBN: 078510982X. Reprints *Punisher Vol. 3: 1–12; Punisher Kills the Marvel Universe; Marvel Knights Double Shot 1.*

This special hardback reprints the entire "Welcome Back Frank" saga, along with the intense *Punisher Kills the Marvel Universe* graphic novel in which the Punisher kills all the Marvel heroes for their crimes against humanity. In this volume the Punisher also kills a mob boss who is getting dental work. The volume contains a cover gallery and essays "In Defense of the Punisher" and "The Punisher Manifesto," by Garth Ennis. It also includes an original Punisher script.

Ennis, Garth, Steve Dillon, Jimmy Palmiotti, et al. *Punisher: Vol. 2.* New York: Marvel, 2003. ISBN: 0785111700. Reprints *Punisher Vol. 4: 1–7; 13–18.*

Once again, Frank Castle goes up against the Russian, who this time is wearing the body of a woman. He fights General Kreigkopf on Grand Nixon Island. Spider-Man and the Punisher team up against the Russian. The Punisher goes to South America to rescue a Mafia don from terrorists. After he rescues the Mafia boss, when they have a meeting of the bosses back in the states, the Punisher kills them all. He gets into a fight with Wolverine while both are on the trail of a leg-chopping maniac. It turns out that a group of Mafia-style midgets and dwarfs are trying to take over crime in New York, and are cutting people down to size. The Punisher blows Wolverine's face off, and drives a steam roller over him. Frank also goes to Ireland.

This volume includes a full script for *Punisher 18,* and an introduction by writer Mark Millar.

Ennis, Garth, Steve Dillon, Jimmy Palmiotti, et al. *Punisher: Vol. 3.* New York: Marvel, 2004. ISBN: 0785113177. Reprints *Punisher Vol. 4: 19–27.*

Frank Castle does surveillance on two crooked cops. One of the police officers beats his wife, and the other is involved in cocaine dealing to pay off his mob debts. The Punisher finds the cocaine and blows up the warehouse. Ghosts torment a hood to kill the Punisher who ends up being eaten by a giant squid. Frank teams up with a social worker to find and destroy a cannibal who is recruiting the homeless to find him more homeless people to eat. The underground of New York is turned into a charnel house. Castle asks Elektra out to dinner after she's been scoping and killing all of his hits.

Vol. 3 includes the script from *Punisher 19* and unused pages from *Punisher 25 & 27.*

Ennis, Garth, Darick Robertson, Tom Palmer, et al. *The Punisher: Born.* New York: Marvel, 2004. ISBN: 0785112316 (trd); 078511 0259 (pbk). Reprints *Born 1–4.*

This is the story of Frank Castle during his third tour of duty in Vietnam and Cambodia in 1971. Frank is a fearless army captain who will kill anything that moves, including his own men if they get out line. He begins punishing those he feels deserve punishment. The story is brutal, but it portrays what life was like for soldiers toward the end of the war. This story behind the birth of the Punisher includes sketches, character designs, layouts, a Vietnam photo reference, and Ennis's original proposal for the series. This volume is part of Marvel's Max adult line. Other Ennis Max Punisher hardcovers include ISBN: 0785118403 (1); 078512022X (2); 0785122761 (*Punisher from First to Last*).

Gaiman, Neil, Andy Kubert, Richard Isanove, et al. *Marvel 1602*. New York: Marvel, 2004. ISBN: 0785110704. Reprints *Marvel 1602 1–8*.

Queen Elizabeth is betrayed, and assassinated by Doom. The evil King James takes the reigns of England and Scotland, declares that all Witchbreed mutants are to be killed, and commands Fury to carry this out. Fury helps the Witchbreed, and helps free the Fantastic Four from Doom's clutches. Magneto is the Grand Inquisitor who searches out and kills those who don't agree with him, including Witchbreed. He tries to kill the Angel, but Carlos Javier's group rescues him. The Grand Inquisitor is betrayed by King James, and is to be burned at the stake, but when he is brought his helmet, he is able to save himself. Fury and the superpowered X-tra brethren go to America to find freedom from hate and distrust. The Inquisitor Enrique and his group take to the sea, as does Banner and Parquah, Spider-Man. James commands them to kill Fury and the Witchbreed. Strange goes into a trance, and learns from the Watcher that a superbeing from the future has come back in time. It turns out this superbeing is Steve Rogers, Captain America, and he must be sent back into the future, or the Universe will collapse. Rogers, who is a shape shifter, poses as the Indian protector of Virginia Dare, the first-born white settler born in Roanoke, Virginia. Rogers and Fury duke it out and both are sent back into the future. Javier asks for Enrique's help, and they form a loose alliance. Both agree that they will stay out of each other's way, and that Javier will take care of his children, Wanda, the Scarlet Witch, and Petros (Quicksilver).

Gaiman presents a new take on the Marvel Universe in 1602, at the dawn of America. Only characters from the Silver Age, before 1970, are used in this tale, so we have versions of Nick Fury, Stephen Strange, Fantastic Four, Spider-Man, Daredevil, Black Widow, the Watcher, X-Men, and the Brotherhood of Evil, among others. There are also versions of Thor, Clea, Toad, and the Hulk. This is the most original "modern" take on the Marvel Universe. The introduction is by Marvel historian Peter Sanderson, and the afterword is by Gaiman. There is also a sketchbook and script with this issue. (2007 edition ISBN: 0785125698).

Jemas, Bill, Joe Quesada, Paul Jenkins, et al. *Origin: The True Story of Wolverine*. New York: Marvel, 2002. ISBN: 0785108661 (trd); 078510965X (pbk). Reprints *Wolverine Origin 1–6*.

This deluxe hardcover edition discloses the real story of Wolverine's roots, in which he is transformed from a naïve, sickly boy to the person known as Logan. It also contains Wolverine's coming-of-age story, in which he ends up inadvertently killing the one person he loves most in all the world. This is one of the most anticipated graphic novels ever published, and has been praised as a cross between *Great Expec-*

tations and *Jane Eyre*. The volume, which was twenty-six years in the making, includes material that the genesis for the project, idea sketches, and character designs. (2006 edition ISBN: 0785124381).

Jones, Bruce, Stuart Immonen, Mike Deodato Jr., et al. *Incredible Hulk Vol. 2*. New York: Marvel, 2003. ISBN: 0785111425. Reprints *Incredible Hulk 44–54*.

Bruce Banner is being pursued by a secret organization that is desperate for the Hulk's blood. He is hit by a car, and taken in by a young woman. Then he is framed for the murder of the same woman. Agent Pratt, who has been genetically modified, fights with Banner, almost beating him a pulp. Banner Hulks-out and smashes Pratt into the ground. The Abomination's ex-wife takes in Banner, in another conspiracy to trap the Hulk. The Abomination gets out of his prison, and goes straight for his ex-wife and Banner. In a titanic battle, the Abomination and the Hulk duke it out, and the Hulk throws the Abomination into the air.

This special hardcover edition includes an alternate cover concept by Kaare Andrews and an introduction by Bruce Jones. It also includes material about the process behind *Hulk 50*, by Kaare Andrews, as well as promo posters, character studies, layouts, and commissioned pieces.

Jones, Bruce, John Romita Jr., Tom Palmer, et al. *The Incredible Hulk Vol. 1: Return of the Monster*. New York: Marvel 2002. ISBN: 0785110224, Reprints *Incredible Hulk Vol. 2: 34–43*; *Startling Stories: Banner 1–4*.

This is a beautiful, green, hardcover edition of three stories, "Return of the Monster," "Boiling Point," and "Banner." The book includes an introduction by Bruce Jones, the evolution of a cover design, and a Richard Corben sketchbook. Science fiction scribe Harlan Ellison endorses the book. (2007 edition ISBN: 0785112375).

Kiefer, Kit, *Marvel Encyclopedia Vol. 3: Incredible Hulk*. New York: Marvel, 2003. ISBN: 0785111646. Reprints *Hulk 1*; *Incredible Hulk 34*; *Ultimates 5*.

This is a beautifully illustrated hardback dedicated to the world of the Hulk. It includes "Why the Hulk Matters"; "The Hulk's Salad Days"; and chapters on the Hulk on the small screen, including the live-action and animated television series; the 2003 Hulk movie; and how the current *Hulk* comic was reborn into one of the best-written Marvel comics on the market today. There are separate sections on the "Top Ten *Hulk* Comics"; the top ten Hulk battles; Hulk toys, board, and video games; the Hulk in the history of comics; and the top ten most collectible issues of *Hulk*. It is written in a lively, humorous style that is accessible to younger readers, as well as those who have collected comics for years.

Kiefer, Kit, Jonathan Couper-Smartt, Syd Barney-Hawke, et al. *Marvel Encyclopedia Vol.
4: Spider-Man.* New York: Marvel, 2003.
ISBN: 0785113045.

This volume contains an exhaustive look at the
world of Spider-Man. It includes chapters on "Why
the Wall Crawler rules comics" and is the world's
number one superhero; Spider-Man on television;
Spider-Man at the movies; Spider-Man toys and action figures; and "Spider-Man A to Z—His Friends,
Family, and Foes." This latter section is all-inclusive,
from Spider-Man's beginnings to the present day, and
covers all the various Spider-Man titles through the
years. Even the most obscure Spider-Man villains and
acquaintances are mentioned. The volume covers all
the Spider-Man permutations, including the Spider-
Man clone his doppelganger, Spider-Man Hulk, Cosmic Spider-Man, various Spider-Man costumes, Ultimate Spider-Man, Mangaverse Spider-Man,
Spider-Man 2099, Spider Woman, and Spider Girl.
There is a detailed appendix, and a Web address for
more information. The volume is profusely illustrated,
well written, and highly recommended.

Kiefer, Kit, Jeff Christiansen, Barry Reese, et al.
Marvel Encyclopedia Vol. 5: Marvel Knights.
New York: Marvel, 2004. ISBN: 0785113
851.

This book contains essays dealing with the history
of Daredevil/Elektra, the Punisher, and Ghost Rider/
Blade. Each of the related films is given a chapter, including a preview of the upcoming Ghost Rider film,
and there is a discussion of action figures based on the
characters. Encyclopedic chapters are here for Daredevil, the Punisher, and Ghost Rider/Blade. There
are also entries for Echo, Pope, the Eel, Fixer, Castle's
War, Jigsaw, Hitman, Punisher, Moon Knight, Werewolf by Night, Dracula, Hellstorm, and Morbius,
among many others. There is an appendix which details some of the lesser-known characters. Although
the original western Ghost Rider is mentioned briefly,
there is no full entry for him or the Blazing Skull.

Kirby Jack, Stan Lee, Joe Simon, et al. *Marvel
Visionaries: Jack Kirby.* New York: Marvel,
2004. ISBN: 0785115749. Reprints *Red
Raven Comics 1; Marvel Mystery Comics 13;
Captain America Comics 1; Yellow Claw 3;
Rawhide Kid 17; Amazing Adventures 1;
Strange Tales 94; Hulk 3; Amazing Spider-
Man 8; Avengers 4; Sgt. Fury 6; Fantastic
Four 48–51; Mighty Thor 134–136; Fantas-
tic Four Annual 5; Amazing Adventures Vol.
2: 1–2; Captain America 200; Eternals 7;
What If 11; National Detective Cases Maga-
zine, May 1941.*

This deluxe hardcover book, a tribute to the genius
of artist Jack Kirby, covers his Marvel work from the
Golden Age of the forties to his last work from the

seventies Bronze Age. Some of the characters included
in this volume are the god Mercury, Dr. Doom, the
Yellow Claw, Pildorr, and the Inhumans. The volume
covers the origins of the Golden Age Vision and Captain America, the Hulk, and the Rawhide Kid, who,
like Spider-Man, has an Uncle Ben who was killed.
Some of the most famous Marvel stories reprinted in
the volume include Captain America joining the
Avengers; the Fantastic Four Galactus/Silver Surfer
Saga; Thor and his dealings with the High Evolutionary; Jane Foster going to Asgaard, and Odin be-
stowing godhood on her; Captain America and the
Falcon stopping the Madbomb; the Celestials decid-
ing the fate of humanity; the original Marvel bullpen
becoming the Fantastic Four; and Sgt. Fury dealing
with racism in his platoon, while trying to go after
General Rommel. The volume also includes a Kirby
Fantastic Four sketch and pencils, a self portrait, and
a humorous cartoon. Other titles in this series include
Jack Kirby Visionaries Vol. 2 (ISBN: 0785120947), *Stan
Lee* (ISBN: 0785116931); *John Romita Sr.* (ISBN:
0785117806); *John Romita Jr.* (ISBN: 0785119647);
Roy Thomas (ISBN: 0785120882); *Steve Ditko* (ISBN:
0785117830); and *John Buscema* (ISBN: 0785121617).

Kirby, Jack, Joe Simon, Tom DeFalco, et al.
Marvel Presents the Fighting American. New
York: Marvel, 1989. ISBN: 0871356007.
Reprints *Fighting American 1–7* (1954–55);
Giant Size Fighting American 1 (1966).

The team that created Captain America in the forties created the Fighting American and Speedboy in
the fifties. Instead of battling the Nazis like Captain
America did, the Fighting American does battle with
the communists, "the red menace," and those who
want to overthrow the U.S. government. In this book,
Nelson Flagg takes on the guise of his dead brother
Jack, who was a newscaster who spoke out against
traitors and swindlers. As the Fighting American, he
does battle with those who are anti–American, including Poison Ivan, Hotsky Trotski, and Super
Khakalovitch, whose power is extreme body odor and
flatulence. This is an excellent commentary on the
state of America during the fifties, and a fine example of heroes from the end of the Golden Age. The introduction is by Joe Simon and Jack Kirby. The book
also includes the never-before published story, "The
Beef Box."

Kirby, Jack, Joe Simon, Mork Meskin, et al. *Kid
Cowboys of Boy's Ranch.* New York: Marvel,
1991. ISBN: 087135859X. Reprints *Kid
Cowboys of Boy's Ranch 1–6.*

This volume contains reprints of the celebrated
western series, originally published by Harvey comics
in the fifties. The stories here focus on three young
orphan boys, Wabash, Dandy, and the gun-slinging
Angel, who are watched over by the "White Indian,"
Clay Duncan. In the book, they inherit a ranch, which
they open as a boy's ranch for orphaned children. They
go up against hostile Indians, robbers, and various

types of outlaws, and Duncan is made a marshal in one of the issues. Each issue has informative lessons pertaining to the Old West, including riding a horse, making western moccasins, learning types of cowboy lingo and western lore, learning Texas Rangers' history, spinning a rope, and making a tom-tom and Indian war rattle. President Andrew Jackson makes a cameo appearance. The introduction is by Jack Kirby and Jim Simon.

Kirby, Jack, Joe Simon, Alex Schomberg, et al. *Captain America: The Classic Years Slipcase.* New York: Marvel Limited, 1995. ISBN: 087135649X (Slipcase); 0871356473 (Vol. 1: 1–5); 0871356481 (Vol. 2: 6–10) Reprints *Captain America Comics 1–10.*

This limited slipcase edition reprints Simon and Kirby's complete run on the first ten issues of the 1940s *Captain America Comics.* The collection contains Captain America's original origin story, as well as the stories of his various fights against Nazi spies and saboteurs, including Sando, Oriental Giants, the Unholy Legion, and the Hunchback of Hollywood. Captain America and Bucky foil their opponents' plans in every case. Captain America and Bucky also meet Hitler. In other stories, in volume 1, the Red Skull makes his first appearance, is seemingly killed, and revealed to be industrialist George Maxon; Steve Rogers and Bucky are extras in a movie in which a hunchback is killing folks (this movie stars Goris Barloff); Bucky is hurt and taken to a hospital, where all is not what it seems to be and horrible experiments are being performed; and the Red Skull comes back to continue his reign of death and terror. In volume 2, Captain America and Bucky still fight Nazis and spies, but more emphasis is on solving seemingly supernatural murders; they continue to assist FBI agent Betty Ross, who is realizing the connection of Captain America and Steve Rogers; Cap exposes a female German spy, whom he sends back to Germany because "your kind don't deserve to be in a free land"; and at a carnival, impostors of Captain America and Bucky are swindling people out of money, and the Red Skull believes them to be the real thing. Some of the ghouls they expose include the Camera Fiend, Fang, the Black Talon, Man Who Could Not Die, Black Witch, and the White Death. There is also the Agatha Christie–like murder mystery, "The Strange Case of the Who Killed Doctor Vardoff," and the Sherlock Holmes–like mystery, "The Phantom Hound of Cardiff Moor."

Kruger, Jim, Jeffery Simon, Evan Jones, et al. *The Marvel Universe Role Playing Game: Guide to the Hulk and the Avengers.* New York: Marvel, 2003. ISBN: 0785111581.

This guide to Marvel role playing, using the Hulk and the Avengers, contains a complete written history of both the Hulk and the Avengers, along with various statistics. It also contains sections about members of the Avengers and opponents of both the Avengers and the Hulk. There is an actions section, supplemental rules and clarifications, a gamemaster section, and adventure briefings. The volume has schematics of Avengers Mansion, Wundagore Mountain, Blue Area of the Moon, Kang's Time Machine, and Chronopolis. It also contains a time-traveling, three-issue, Marvel Universe adventure, "Hulk Runs Through It," complete with maps.

Lee, Stan, John Buscema, Max Scheele, et al. *The Silver Surfer: Judgment Day.* New York: Marvel, 1988. ISBN: 0871354276 (trd) 0871356635 (pbk).

Mephisto tricks Nova into bringing Galactus to feed on worlds where life abounds. The Silver Surfer intervenes, and fights Nova. Galactus banishes the Surfer and Nova from space. Mephisto tries to trick the Surfer into giving him his soul, but the Silver Surfer suggests to Galactus that he feed on Mephisto's dark domain.

Lee, Stan, Steve Ditko, *Birth of Spider-Man Box Set.* Singapore: Applewood Books, 1997. ISBN: 1557093350. Reprints *Amazing Fantasy 15.*

This hardbound, box-set edition, which was limited to 2,500 copies, reprints *Amazing Fantasy 15* in its entirety. It contains a certificate of authenticity, a Spider-Man ring, and a spider-shaped CD on which Stan Lee reads *Amazing Fantasy 15* and talks about the creation of Spider-Man. The other Lee/Ditko stories in the set involve the fantastic and supernatural. In one of the stories, a living mummy helps a criminal on the run, but the criminal finds out things are not what they seem. In other stories, a bell ringer, who is on an island about to be rocked by an erupting volcano, is swept up in the eternal light; and a Martian concerns himself with his wife, who gets caught by authorities. The original *Amazing Fantasy* fifteen-issue run is one of the Masterworks most requested by fans. One can only hope that it is forthcoming.

Lee, Stan, Jack Kirby, Dick Ayers, et al. *Fantastic Firsts.* New York: Marvel Limited, 1994. ISBN: 0785100369; 0785108238 (pbk) Reprints *Fantastic Four 1, 4, Fantastic Four Annual 1; Tales to Astonish 27, 35; Hulk 1; Amazing Fantasy 15; Journey into Mystery 83; Tales of Suspense 39, 63; Sgt. Fury 1; Strange Tales 110, 115, 135; Avengers 1, 4; X-Men 1; Daredevil 1; Silver Surfer 1.*

This limited edition hardcover comes with slipcase, a bookmark, and silkscreen pages which divide the chapters. Limited to around 350 copies, originally it was available only through comic-book stores. It contains some of the first and most famous stories featuring Captain America, Sub-Mariner, Sgt. Fury/ Nick Fury, Thor, Ant-Man, Daredevil, Iron Man, Dr. Strange, Silver Surfer, and the X-Men. With beautiful color reproductions on acid free paper, this is an essential collection for anyone wanting to understand the Silver Age of Marvel and its origins. It has chapter introductions by various Marvel writers and artists, and was reprinted in 2001 as a paperback with extra material.

Lee, Stan, Jack Kirby, Christ Claremont, et al. *The Best of Marvel Comics*. New York: Marvel, 1987. No ISBN. Reprints *Uncanny X-Men 183*; *Fantastic Four 52–53*; *Amazing Spider-Man 31–33, 248*; *Captain America 255*; *Thor 159, 171*; *Doctor Strange 56*;. *Hulk Annual 8*.

The Fantastic Four meet the Black Panther. Peter Parker reveals his identity to a young, terminally ill boy who idolizes him. Parker helps save Aunt May who is in the hospital, and deals with the Master Planner. Donald Blake learns much about his past identity and his relationship to Thor, from Odin. Thor has to deal with the Wrecker. A television crew tries to deceive Dr. Strange into revealing some of his secrets, but the crew members are really evil demons in disguise. Colossus breaks it off with Kitty Pryde who is heartbroken. Wolverine, who is angry about this, takes Colossus and Nightcrawler to a bar where Juggernaut is also having a drink. Eventually there is a brawl, and Juggernaut and Colossus have a mammoth fight in which Colossus is defeated.

This red-leather hardback collection puts together some of the most memorable tales in the Marvel Universe. It contains the origin story of the Black Panther and a retelling of Captain America's origin. It also contains a new X-Men story, "He'll Never Make Me Cry," which features Wolverine, and was written for this volume by Chris Claremont. The introduction is by Ralph Macchio.

Lee, Stan, Jack Kirby, Chris Claremont, et al. *The Very Best of the X-Men*. New York: Marvel Limited, 1994. ISBN: 0785100598. Reprints *Fantastic Four 28*; *Uncanny X-Men 35, 57–59, 66, 105, 107–108, 120–121, 190–191*; *X-Men Annual 5*.

The Fantastic Four battle the X-Men, along with the Puppet Master and the Mad Thinker. Spider-Man and the X-Men duke it out. The Sentinels kidnap Lorena Dane, and begin their assault against mutants under Bolivar Trask's son, who himself is mutant. Cyclops dons Quicksilver's costume. The X-Men enlist the help of Bruce Banner to save Professor X, but the Hulk will have none of it. Alpha Flight kidnaps the X-Men to try to take Wolverine, and the X-Men and the Fantastic Four go up against the alien Badoon. The Avengers, the Starjammers, Dr. Strange, and the wizard Kulan Gath, among others, make appearances.

This beautiful, deluxe, hardcover box set contains some of the best X-Men stories from their thirty-year history. It was limited to several hundred copies, as part of Marvel's Limited hardcover program.

Lee, Stan, Jack Kirby, Chris Claremont, et al. *X-Men: Famous Firsts*. New York: Marvel Limited, 1995. ISBN: 0785101187. Reprints *Uncanny X-Men 1, 50, 54, 129, 244, 266, 283*; *Incredible Hulk 181*; *Giant Size X-Men 1*; *Avengers Annual 10*; *New Mutants 87*.

This is a specially handcrafted leather-lover volume which was limited to 650 copies. It contains landmarks in X-Men history, which include the first appearances of the X-Men, Polaris, Gambit, Bishop, Jubilee, Rogue, Wolverine, Nightcrawler, Storm, Colossus, Kitty Pryde, Cable and Havok.

Lee, Stan, Jack Kirby, Joe Sinnott, et al. *The Silver Surfer*. New York: Marvel Limited, 1995. ISBN: 0785101179. Reprints *The Silver Surfer Fireside Book*.

This is a reprint of the original 1978 Fireside book by Kirby and Lee. It was limited to 750 copies, and has a silver, handcrafted, embossed cover. In the book, the Surfer has to save the Earth from Galactus. There is a new introduction by Stan Lee. This was Lee and Kirby's last collaboration.

Lee, Stan, Moebius, Dan Hosek, et al. *Silver Surfer: Parable*. Marvel Comics: New York, 1998. ISBN: 0871354918 (trd, Epic Comics, 1988: 0785106561). Reprints *Silver Surfer Parable 1–2*.

In this spiritual tale of saving the Earth, the Surfer encounters his maker, Galactus. Galactus comes to Earth where the people see him as God, and he even has his own televangelist and espouses a Crowley-esque, "Do what you will" philosophy. This hardback edition includes essays by Stan Lee and Moebius on the creation of the project and the difficulty Moebius had in drawing it. This is an excellent morality tale.

Lee, Stan, Keith Pollard, Jose Rubinstein, et al. *The Silver Surfer: The Enslavers*. New York: Marvel, 1990. ISBN: 0871356171.

The Silver Surfer has to defend Earth against an alien, Mrrungo-Mu, bent on enslaving the populace. Even Earth's most powerful superbeings cannot beat him. The Surfer uses cunning, instead of brute force, to defeat the alien threat. He is reunited with his love Shalla-Bal after many years of separation.

This is a beautiful hardcover edition.

Lee, Stan, Alex Ross, Jim Steranko, et al. *Captain America: Red White and Blue*. New York: Marvel, 2002. ISBN: 078511033X. Reprints *Marvel Fanfare 18*; *Captain America Vol. 1: 111*; *Tales of Suspense 66*; *Captain America Marvel Knights 1*.

This is a special volume commemorating Captain America's sixtieth anniversary. For the most part, it contains new material composed specifically for this volume. There are a total of twenty stories which range from Captain America's adventures in World War II, to 9/11, and the credits read like a who's who of modern comics. One story includes a Captain America adventure from the fifties, in which he is fighting communism. The only thing missing from this deluxe hardcover is an original Jack Kirby/Joe Simon story from the forties.

Lee, Stan, Syd Shores, Alan Sulman, et al. *Secrets Behind the Comics.* New York: Marvel Limited, 1994. ISBN: 0785100725.

This beautiful reprint of a 1947 pamphlet by Stan Lee was one of the first of the Marvel Limited hardcovers. It features fourteen secrets for those who want to get into the business of comics. Lee goes through the whole detailed process of producing a comic, from the writing, through the lettering and drawing, to the finished product, and reveals what goes on behind the scenes at a comic publishing house. Some of the characters featured in the book include Blonde Phantom, Millie the Model, Georgie, Tessie, Namor, Hedy Devine, Rusty, Powerhouse Pepper, and, of course, Captain America. Lee credits the publisher and founder of Timely Comics, Martin Goodman, with having the foresight to publish comics that told the world the "truth about the Nazi menace" in Marvel Comics. There is a section on the creation of Captain America, but it includes no mention of creators Simon & Kirby. Stan Lee offered to personally look at the work of would-be comic writers and artists, if they would send in $1.00. This is a fun and worthwhile piece of comic-book history. Apparently, there were only 700 copies of this hardback published, but another pamphlet-sized version was also printed.

Loeb, Jeph, Tim Sale, Richard Starkings, et al. *Daredevil: Yellow.* New York: Marvel, 2002. ISBN: 0785108408. Reprints *Daredevil Yellow 1–6.*

This volume chronicles Daredevil's early crime fighting career, when he donned a yellow costume. In the book, Foggy Nelson wants to propose to the secretary, Karen, but Matt Murdock loves her as well. Daredevil saves Karen from the Owl, and she suggests that he change his costume from yellow to red. This is one of the best-written and best-drawn books of 2002. It was published as a paperback with the title *Daredevil Legends Vol.1* in 2003 (ISBN: 0785109692).

Loeb, Jeph, Tim Sale, Richard Starkings, et al. *Hulk: Gray.* New York: Marvel, 2004. ISBN: 0785113142; 0785113460 (pbk). Reprints *Hulk: Gray 1–6.*

Bruce Banner, in a therapy session with Doc Samson, tells him the story of the first forty-eight hours after becoming the Hulk. The Hulk kidnaps Betty Ross, while her father, General Ross, starts his campaign to subdue the Hulk. Iron Man, while still in his gold costume, is brought in to try to bring the Hulk down, to no avail. The Hulk nearly kills Iron Man and General Ross. He accidentally slugs Betty during his fight with Iron Man, and then tries to give her first aid.

This is a beautifully painted and well-written volume. It includes a sketchbook with commentary by Sale and Loeb in which they discuss the original *Hulk* comics by Stan Lee and Jack Kirby, as well as "The Bulk," by Marie Severin, who also wrote the introduction. The events in this book take place between *Hulk 1* and 2, when the Hulk was still gray.

Loeb, Jeph, Tim Sale, Richard Starkings, et al. *Spider-Man: Blue.* New York: Marvel, 2003. ISBN: 0785110623; 0785110712 (pbk, 2004) Reprints *Spider-Man: Blue 1–6.*

This is a beautiful hardcover with a previously untold tale of Spider-Man and his love affair with Gwen Stacy during his early career. It contains a wonderful story and artwork, and is a moving tribute to the original comics. In this story, Peter Parker tells his feelings about his first meetings with both Gwen and Mary Jane, documenting this on tape. Parker's insecurities about both Gwen and Mary Jane are a defining point in the story. Also in the story, Peter moves out of Aunt May's house into Harry Osborn's apartment for the first time. Artist Tim Sale draws Spider-Man as a tribute to John Romita, who provides an introduction to the book in which he discusses how much he liked this untold story about Parker and Gwen. The volume also includes a tribute to the original issue in which Mary Jane utters the line, "You just hit the jackpot." Villains in the book include the Vulture, Green Goblin, Rhino, the Lizard, and Kraven.

Marvel Editors, et al. *The Marvel Universe Role-playing Game.* New York: Marvel, 2003. ISBN: 0785110283.

This illustrated guide was Marvel's first foray into publishing role-playing games. It contains the basic information for beginners and Game Masters, and has a special section for Game Masters. There are chapters about various Marvel characters, and chapters on how to create your own character and how to play Marvel. The authors also included Marvel Universe briefings, and a sample Marvel role-playing adventure. The appendices detail weapons, vehicles, and equipment. This volume is a good choice for public libraries.

McLaughlin, Jim. *2000–2001: Fanboys and Bad-girls: Bill and Joe's Marvelous Adventure.* New York: Marvel, 2002. ISBN: 078510 9277.

This illustrated hardcover documents how former president Bill Jemas and editor in chief Joe Quesada turned Marvel Comics around, and made it the number one comics company in the industry. It contains interviews with Jemas and Quesada who discuss the reasoning behind the Ultimate Universe, the slashing of the X-books, the Marvel Knights series, and more. Bill Jemas wrote the introduction and Joe Quesada wrote the afterword. This fun read also has a glossary of abbreviations.

Michelinie, David, Mark Bagley, Randy Emberline, et al. *Spider-Man: Carnage*. New York: Marvel Limited: 1993. ISBN: 0871 359715. Reprints *The Amazing Spider-Man 344–345, 359, 360–363*.

The symbiote breaks Eddie Brock out of jail, and leaves its offspring there. The offspring bonds with serial killer Cletus Kasady, and Carnage is born. Carnage escapes from prison and starts a rein of terror, killing people all over New York. Spider-Man decides to free Venom, who thinks Spider-Man is dead, from his island paradise. With the Human Torch, Spider-Man and Venom come to New York, to try to stop Carnage's onslaught. Carnage kidnaps Jonah Jameson, and raids a heavy metal concert.

This special hardcover came with the *Maximum Carnage* Super Nintendo videogame, itself in a limited edition red cartridge. It also came with a certificate of authenticity and three pins, depicting Carnage, Venom, and Spider-Man. The video game came with code and instruction books. There were just 5,000 of these sets printed. David Michelinie wrote the introduction, which discusses how Carnage was created.

Millar, Mark, Chuck Austen, Adam Kubert, et al. *Ultimate X-Men Vol. 2*. New York: Marvel, 2003. ISBN: 0785111301. Reprints *Ultimate X-Men 13–25*.

This is the second deluxe *Ultimate X-Men* hardcover. It contains the World Tour storyline, which includes Xavier's son, and the birth of Phoenix at the Hellfire club. It also includes Beast's online love affair with the Blob, the return of Magneto, and a Gambit solo story. Volume 2 contains stories in which the X-Men go, with Professor X, on a world tour to promote his new book; Colossus goes back to Russia, believing that he really has no purpose in the X-Men, but Cyclops and Jean Grey persuade him to come back; Davis, Proteus, the mutant son of Xavier and Moria McTaggert, has the ability to possess individuals, and drain them of their energy, but Collossus ends up killing David; Professor X thinks about disbanding the X-Men; Iceman is hurt badly in his battle with Proteus; Kitty Pryde comes to the X-Men; Quicksilver tries to follow in his father's footsteps, but decides against it; a group of mutated animal/human hybrids decide to try to find Magneto; the Blob poses as a mutant woman on the Internet, and tricks the Beast into revealing where Magneto is located; Wolverine and Cyclops fight over Jean Grey; Kitty is a stowaway on a trip to the Savage Land, with Cyclops and Wolverine; the X-Men learn that Hellfire Club is their financial backer; and the Hellfire Club betrays the X-Men, and tries to awaken the Phoenix god in Jean Grey. Volume 2 includes a storyboard for "Resignation," by Millar and Kubert, from *Ultimate X-Men 20*. Ralph Macchio wrote the introduction.

Millar, Mark, Chris Bachalo, David Finch, et al. *Ultimate X-Men Vol. 3*. New York: Marvel, 2003. ISBN: 078511131X. Reprints *Ultimate War 1–4; Ultimate X-Men 26–33*.

Magneto is terrorizing New York, demanding that he become the ruler and humans become his slaves. The X-Men are hiding, because it was revealed that Xavier hid Magneto, and kept him alive. The Ultimates are asked to find and take the X-Men, and Quicksilver and Scarlet Witch join the Ultimates. When Magneto destroys the Ultimates' office, Captain America swears a vendetta against him and Professor X. Xavier tries to make a deal with Magneto, but he is betrayed, and led into the hands of the Ultimates. Iceman tries to help the X-Men in their battle, but Xavier is captured. Magneto and Professor X form their school for mutants, eight years hence. Magneto begins to shape his ideas of mutant domination during this period, and breaks with Xavier. He cripples Xavier by throwing a metal spear through his spine. Mastermind and Multiple Man steal precious artwork for Magneto. Nick Fury shows the vice president new Sentinel agents. Wolverine leaves Cyclops to die in the Savage Land, because he wants to make time with Jean Grey, but Magneto's group rescues him, and Wolverine gets thrown off of the team. Magneto plans to destroy all humanity by reversing magnetic polarities, but the X-Men stop him, and are hailed as heroes in the press. Cyclops invites Wolverine to come back.

Abbie Bernstein's interview with Ian McKellen, who plays Magneto in the *X-Men* movies, is included in this volume. Volumes 4–6 have the following ISBNs: 0785112510 (4); 078512103X (5); 0785121048 (6).

Millar, Mark, Bryan Hitch, Andrew Currie, et al. *The Ultimates Vol. 1*. New York: Marvel, 2004. ISBN: 0785110828. Reprints *The Ultimates 1–13; Wizard 123*.

Tony Stark and Nick Fury put together a group of super–villain-fighters, which includes Captain America, Giant Man, the Wasp, Iron Man, Nick Fury, Bruce Banner, and Thor. Captain America is found frozen after more than fifty years, and when he is revived, he meets up with his old partner Bucky who is now old and feeble. Thor is a socialist, and all of the heroes do not have secret identities. When Banner combines his Hulk serum with the Super Soldier formula, he becomes the Hulk, and goes rampaging through New York. In the wake of the Hulk's destruction, Captain America gives a eulogy for those who died. The Wasp, Janet Pym, is put in the hospital after she is beaten up by her husband, Giant Man, and Captain America, who tracks him down, beats the stuffing out of him. Groups of shape-shifting aliens who were Hitler's allies, have been influencing human affairs since World War II. The Hulk is brought out to smash the aliens. Black Widow, Hawkeye, Quicksilver, and the Scarlet Witch are introduced to the team. Thor and Iron Man help save the world from the aliens' bomb, and the Hulk tries to eat Hawkeye.

This is the Ultimate Universe's answer to the

Avengers. In this volume we learn a little more about Captain America's life during the forties, and the war in which he almost died because of the aliens. This volume also contains commentaries on issues 1–13 of *The Ultimates*, written by the authors, and a Bryan Hitch gallery of unused covers and other art.

Millar, Mark, Adam Kubert, Andy Kubert, et al. *The Ultimate X-Men.* New York: Marvel, 2002. ISBN: 0785110089. Reprints *Ultimate X-Men 1–12; Giant Size X-Men 1.*

This deluxe hardcover reinvents the X-Men's origin and story for the millennium and new readers. It contains plot lines by Millar in which the X-Men are abducted by the Weapon X program; Wolverine avoids being captured, and has to fight against Sabretooth to save the X-Men from being transformed into killing machines; the doctors at Weapon X transform Hank McCoy into the Beast; Nick Fury helps the X-Men break out of Weapon X; and Nightcrawler, Rogue, Nick Fury, and Juggernaut make their debuts in the Ultimate Universe. The afterword is by former Marvel chief Bill Jemas.

Miller, Frank, Klaus Janson, Dr. Martin, et al. *Daredevil: Frank Miller Visionaries Vol. 2:* Anaheim, CA: Graphitti Designs, 2001. ISBN: 0936211652. Reprints *Daredevil 168–182.*

Matt Murdock first meets Elektra while in college, and they become lovers. Elektra figures out that Daredevil is Matt Murdock, but Bullseye goes crazy believing everyone is Daredevil. Daredevil saves Bullseye's life from an oncoming train, which he later regrets. Matt Murdock infiltrates the Kingpin's gang. The Kingpin's wife Vanessa is nearly killed and ends up missing. The Gladiator, who goes crazy, ends up teaming with Elektra to help Daredevil. When Daredevil loses his radar sense due to an explosion, he goes back to his sensei Stick for training. Everybody starts looking for Murdock, and Power Man and Iron Fist become his bodyguards, but he is trying to find ways to ditch them so that he can become Daredevil again. Daredevil finds Vanessa living in the sewers with other transients, and has to fight the King of the Sewers. The Kingpin hires Elektra to kill Foggy Nelson. Bullseye kills Elektra, but Matt refuses to believe she is dead. Daredevil drops Bullseye from a ledge and leaves him for dead, and Matt digs up Elektra's grave. This special limited hardcover edition, which covers Elektra's origin as an assassin, was limited to 2,500 copies.

Miller, Frank, Klaus Janson, Denny O'Neil, et al. *Daredevil: Frank Miller Visionaries Vol. 3.* Anaheim, CA: Graphitti Designs, 2001. ISBN: 0936211695. Reprints *Daredevil Vol. 1: 183–191; What If Vol. 1: 28, 35; Bizarre Adventures 28.*

The Punisher shoots Daredevil with a tranquilizer. Both the Punisher and Daredevil are trying to stop drug dealers, who are pushing their dope to kids. Murdock ends up representing a murderer, inadvertently, and as Daredevil he stops a kid from killing. Matt Murdock asks Heather to marry him, after he has nearly ruined her life. Heather finds out that her business is building bombs, and that the Kingpin is involved. When Foggy goes undercover as hit-man Guts Nelson, he even intimidates the Kingpin. Turk steals the Stiltman's costume. Daredevil's hearing is injured, and everything sounds too loud. He seeks out his old sensei Stick who is in the middle of a war with the Hand. The Hand resurrects the warrior Kirigi, but when he is defeated by Stick and his disciples, he helps Daredevil heal. The Black Widow is poisoned by the Hand, and Stick ends up combusting after their battle in which the Black Widow helps. Foggy and the Widow help split Matt and Heather apart. The Hand resurrects Elektra, and Daredevil spends some time playing Russian roulette with Bullseye, in the hospital.

In this limited hardcover edition, we also learn about Elektra's early training under Stick, and her subsequent banishment; and what would happen if Daredevil was a S.H.I.E.L.D. Agent, and Bullseye had not killed Elektra. The volume also contains a reprint of the classic storyline "Child's Play," featuring Daredevil and the Punisher; a black-and-white Elektra story; an art gallery from the *Elektra Saga* trade paperback; and an introduction by Klaus Janson. This edition was restricted to 2,500 copies. This is the third and final volume in Marvel's tribute to artist/writer Frank Miller's classic run on *Daredevil*. In 2007 Marvel published a complete omnibus of all the Frank Miller/Kaus Janson material (ISBN: 078512 3431).

Miller, Frank, Bill Mantlo, Frank Springer, et al. *The Complete Frank Miller Spider-Man.* New York: Marvel, 2002. ISBN: 078510 8998; 0785100547 (1994). Reprints *Spectacular Spider-Man 27–28, 46, 48, 50–52, 54–57, 60; Amazing Spider-Man Vol. 1: Annual 14–15; Marvel Team Up 95, 99–100, 102, 106; Marvel Team Up Annual 4; Amazing Spider-Man Vol. 1 203, 218–219, Spider-Man/Daredevil Special Edition.*

Spider-Man loses his sight, and teams up with Daredevil against the Masked Marauder and his Tri-Man. The death-dealing Carrion knows that Parker is Spider-Man, and breaks into his apartment. Dr. Doom and the dreaded Dormammu seek to bring the evil Bend Sinister upon mankind, and Dr. Strange and Spider-Man work together to stop them. Spider-Man and the Fantastic Four fight each other. The mutant Karma takes over Spider-Man, and attempts to rescue her younger siblings. When the Kingpin hires the Purple Man to kill Spider-Man and Daredevil, Moon Knight, Luke Cage, and Iron Fist help defeat the Purple Man, who also has put Jonah Jameson under his spell. Doc Octopus threatens to kill over five million New Yorkers, and Spider-Man and the Punisher try to stop him. The Punisher is almost killed by Doc Ock, but Spider-Man saves his and Jonah Jameson's lives, and the Punisher is arrested.

This book, which contains many of the wonderful covers that Miller drew, was limited to only a few hundred copies, and was originally published as part of Marvel's limited hardcover program in 1994. Frank Miller wrote the introduction.

Miller, Frank, Roger McKenzie, Klaus Janson, et al. *Daredevil: Frank Miller Visionaries Vol. 1.* Anaheim, CA: Graphitti Designs, 2000. ISBN: 0936211630. Reprints *Daredevil Vol. 1: 158–161; 163–167.*

This limited hardcover edition was Frank Miller's first work as a young artist on *Daredevil.* It contains famous Daredevil stories in which Bullseye hires Slaughter to assassinate Daredevil; the Black Widow is kidnapped, and when she realizes that Matt Murdock loves Heather Glen, she leaves New York to go back to Russia; Foggy Nelson gets married and Daredevil fights with the Gladiator; reporter Ben Ulrich figures out that Matt Murdock is Daredevil; and the Death-Stalker and the Mauler die. This volume includes schemata of Murdock's living quarters and an explanation of his powers. This edition was limited to 2,500 copies.

Miller, Frank, John Romita Jr., Al Williamson, et al. *Daredevil: The Man Without Fear.* New York: Marvel Limited, 1994. ISBN: 0785100601. Reprints *Daredevil: Man Without Fear 1–5.*

This special edition was limited to several hundred copies as part of Marvel's limited hardback program. It contains a retelling of Daredevil's origin, and the story of Matt Murdock's revenge against the Fixer and those who killed his father. In this latter story, Matt rooms with Foggy Nelson, and has an affair with Elektra, while still in college. The first costume Murdock wears is very similar to the one worn in the television special *Trial of the Incredible Hulk.* The book includes an art gallery with a special script, and a behind-the-scenes look at the making of the series. Ralph Macchio wrote the introduction.

Miller, Frank, Bill Sienkiewicz, Jim Novak, et al. *Daredevil/Elektra: Love and War.* New York: Marvel, 2003. ISBN: 0785110321. Reprints *Daredevil: Love & War: Marvel Graphic Novel 24; Elektra Assassin; Elektra Volume 1: 1–8.*

Because Kingpin's wife is sick, he kidnaps a medical specialist and the specialist's blind wife. Daredevil rescues the doctor's wife, but the doctor takes the Kingpin's wife Vanessa away from him. Elektra kills the president of San Concepcion in South America. She also kills a number of S.H.I.E.L.D. agents

and brainwashes a cyborg agent into following her. S.H.I.E.L.D. has been making cyborg soldiers out of killers and molesters in their ExTech Op Division. Elektra and her cronies seek to kill presidential hopeful Ken Wind who they believe will start World War III with the Soviets by pushing the button for a nuclear missile attack.

This collection highlights the collaborations between writer Frank Miller and artist Bill Sienkiewicz. In this volume, Miller writes in a non–narrative style. The work contains a very intense, psychological drama: a surreal tale about various aspects of Elektra's past and present. It showcases areas of Elektra not covered in previous comics. The writing is thought-provoking, and the artwork is quite beautiful. The work also contains an essay by Jo Duffy.

Miller, Frank, Lynn Varley, Steve Miller, et al. *Elektra Lives Again.* New York: Marvel, 2002. ISBN: 0785108904.

Matt Murdock has Elektra-related nightmares night after night, and seeks solace in his faith, and through confession. Bullseye is killed while in prison, but he and Elektra are brought back to life by the evil ninja cult, the Hand. Bullseye slices Murdock's face. Matt tries to purge Elektra of the evil within.

This is a beautiful hardcover reprint of the graphic novel which was originally published in the Epic line. (See the Epic Comics graphic novels chapter in this book.). Really it is a horror story, complete with zombies, gore, and death.

Milligan, Peter, Mike Allred, Laura Allred, et al. *X-Force: Famous Mutant and Mortal.* New York: Marvel, 2003. ISBN: 0785110232. Reprints *X-Force 116–129.*

This deluxe hardcover documents the X-Force whose new media darlings are prone to dying on every mission, and are always in need of replacement. In this story, the X-Force is owned by a young punk millionaire who rents the X-Force out to the highest bidder for each of their missions. The most mysterious member, Doop, a green blob who flies around, documents each of their missions with a camera for a reality-television show. There is also a story in which Doop pops a pimple, and the bizarre events that surround the popping. The book contains an introduction by Peter Milligan, an X-Force sketchbook, and X-Force pin-ups.

Morrison, Grant, Chris Bachalo, Andy Lanning, et al. *New X-Men Vol. 3.* New York: Marvel, 2004. ISBN: 0785112006. Reprints *New X-Men 142–154.*

Cyclops and Wolverine get drunk at a special Hellfire Club bar. Fantomex and Wolverine recruit Cyclops to help them find the truth about a special covert place known as Weapon Plus, or the World, where reality is not always real, and files exist on Wolverine's past. Mutants are being experimented on, and a new breed of mutant-killing Sentinels is being created. Shaking the world of the X-Men, Xorn is actually Magneto in disguise. Magneto, posing as Xorn, has infiltrated Xavier Mansion and the school by poisoning the minds of the special class and others. He puts up an elaborate ruse to destroy the X-Men from within. He destroys Cerbero, tries to kill off the rest of the X-Men, and again cripples Xavier. Toad is back with Magneto, as his henchman. A hundred and fifty years in the future, the Beast is evil, seeking to blot out everyone who does not conform to his perfect gene pool. He wants to use the Phoenix egg to create his own master race. Wolverine, E.V.A., a new Beak, Cassandra Nova, a human named Tom Skylark, and his giant robot Sentinel Rover, try to stop the Beast from using the mutant drug Kick and getting the egg. Emma Frost and Scott Summers, Cyclops, kiss, and decide to open a new mutant school.

Marvel also published a *New X-Men Omnibus* (ISBN: 0785123261) as a classic *Uncanny X-Men Omnibus* (ISBN: 0785121013).

Morrison, Grant, Frank Quitely, Igor Kordey, et al. *New X-Men Vol. 1.* New York: Marvel, 2002. ISBN: 0785109641. Reprints *New X-Men 114–126; New X-Men 2001.*

This volume contains the "E is for Extinction" storyline, in which Xavier's evil twin destroys Genosha and Magneto. It also contains the "Imperial" storyline, in which the X-Men go up against Xavier's twin, and Xorn frees Xavier from his disability. In another story, Cyclops, Emma Frost, the Beast, Domino, and Wolverine free the mutant healer Xorn from captivity. This is a fine collection of Morrison's groundbreaking work on the *X-Men.*

Morrison, Grant, Frank Quitely, Igor Kordey, et al. *New X-Men Vol. 2.* New York: Marvel, 2003. ISBN: 0785111182. Reprints *New X-Men 127–138.*

Mr. Xorn tries to save a young mutant boy who is transforming into a monster, goes berserk, and is set on fire. Xorn tries to heal him, but is too late. The mutant Dark Star is also killed. Xorn takes a group of mutants on a field trip into the woods and stops the U-Men from harming any of them. Xavier goes to Genosha with the X-Men, after the mutant holocaust. Somebody tries to assassinate Emma Frost by shooting her while she is in her glasslike state. McCoy and Jean Grey try to put her back together, even though she wants to have an affair with Cyclops. Bishop and Sage are brought in to investigate the shooting. The gaseous Mutant Dummy's suit is shot, and he escapes into the air. Beak and Fly Girl have children.

This special hardcover edition includes the "Riot at Xavier" storyline, and a script for *New X-Men 138.*

Rieber, John Ney, John Cassaday, Dave Stewart, et al. *Captain America Vol. 1: The New Deal.* New York: Marvel, 2003. ISBN: 078510 9781 (trd); 0785111018 (pbk). Reprints *Captain America Vol. 4: 1–6.*

Captain America tries to help survivors after the 9/11 attack, and vows to fight terrorists. Fury tries to get Captain America to stop helping the survivors of 9/11, and take on a mission, but Captain America tells him to go by himself. The tiny town of Centerville is being held hostage by terrorists, and Captain America goes to rescue the hostages and fight the terrorists. He unmasks himself on live television while talking about killing the terrorists, and tells the world that he is Steve Rogers. He goes to Dresden to fight against another terrorist group. Mysterious tags that have a strange technology seem to show up on the terrorists wherever Captain America appears.

This hardcover contains an introduction by Max Allan Collins, an original script, a character study of Captain America (by John Cassaday), and reprints of various Wizard *Captain America* covers.

Romita John, Sr., Stan Lee, Art Simek, et al. *Art of John Romita.* New York: Marvel, 1996. ISBN: 0785102736. Reprints *Amazing Spider-Man 109; Strange Tales 4; Menace 6.*

This hardcover book features an extensive interview with artist/writer John Romita Sr., in which he talks about the early days working for Atlas Comics, and why he chose working in comics. He describes feeling desperation that working in comics was just a passing fad, and it almost was during the fifties implosion. He goes on to discuss working on romance comics for DC, and how the Comics Code almost ruined comics. He talks about the rebirth of Marvel Comics, his work on Spider-Man, and his work as editor/art director at Marvel. He describes working with Jim Shooter, the problems behind that controversial period, and the failure of the New Universe. Romita talks about the creation of the Punisher, his son John Jr.'s work in comics, and how he regrets that the Femizons, from *Savage Tales*, never become the epic it should have been. This interview contains a wealth of comics history and knowledge. Stories reprinted in this volume include Spider-Man and Dr. Strange trying to save Flash Thompson from some Asian priests, who seek to kill him; an alien, disguised as a baby, plotting his conquest of the world; and Flying Saucers appearing on the Earth for an invasion, but human beings not realizing that the saucers themselves are the Martians. There is a reprint of the cover of *Captain America 77*, in which the "commie smasher" Captain America and Bucky look on as the atomic bomb is detonated, and Captain America remarks that, as long as it is used for America's struggle for world peace, it's a "glorious sight." The work also has character designs for the Punisher, Brother Voodoo, and Wolverine, among many others. One hundred and eighty volumes of this hardcover featured an autographed, penciled Spider-Man. In 2005, Marvel published a special hardcover devoted to John Romita Sr., which also contained some of the above material. There are character designs for the Punisher, Brother Voodoo, and Wolverine, among many others.

Ross, Alex, Jim Krueger, John Paul Leon, et al. *Earth X*. Anaheim, CA: Graphitti Designs, 2001. ISBN: 0936211679. Reprints *Earth X 1/2, 0–12; X*.

This is a beautiful, signed, 8¼" x 12⅛", deluxe hardcover in a silver slipcase. It features a full-body outline of X-51, Machine Man, on the cover. The book was limited to 6,000 copies and came with a two–CD soundtrack that should be played while reading the book. The CDs also contain animation, live-action segments, and more. The volume also includes a beautiful color poster. The soundtrack was composed by Scott Vladimir Licina. The two compact discs contain twenty-five musical compositions, sixteen dialogue tracks, and the first fully-realized *Earth X* video. The book itself is in black and white, however there is also a sixteen-page color section which contains various *Earth X* covers, and reproductions of T-shirt artwork. This volume features a five-page epilogue of art by Alex Ross, painted over pencils by John Paul Leon. It also includes a unique, illustrated, sequentially-numbered signature page signed by Ross, Krueger, Leon, and Reinhold, and is well worth seeking. Despite its rarity, it can be found for a reasonable price. In 2005, Marvel decided to produce their special, hardcover, color edition of *Earth X* (ISBN: 0785118756).

Rucka, Greg, Yoshitaka Amano. *Elektra and Wolverine: The Redeemer*. New York: Marvel, 2002. ISBN: 0785109110. Reprints *Elektra and Wolverine: The Redeemer 1–3*.

Elektra is hired to kill a scientist, and the scientist's daughter Avery who witnesses the murder. A former Weapon X boss hires Wolverine as Avery's bodyguard. Elektra ends up kidnapping Avery from him, and puts two sais straight through Wolverine's chest. Avery has a power-healing factor similar to Wolverine's, and the government wants her for experiments. Elektra and Avery form a unique bond and friendship. Wolverine and Elektra eventually team up to thwart the plans of the "secret" government men.

This beautiful, deluxe hardcover is illustrated by the famous Japanese artist Yoshitaka Amano. It includes an interview with Greg Rucka and an endorsement by author Brad Meltzer. It is a wonderfully written graphic novel.

Simonson, Walter, Terry Austin, Bob Wiacek, et al. *Thor Visionaries: Walt Simonson*. Anaheim, CA: Graphitti Designs, 2001. ISBN: 0936211660. Reprints *Mighty Thor 337–348*.

Thor gives up his mortal guise as Dr. Donald Blake, and becomes Sigurd Jarlson. He comes under the love enchantment spell of the sorceress Lorelei. The dark elf Malekith captures Lorelei, and Thor will do anything to rescue her while he is under her spell. Odin tells Balder to take an important message to Loki, and finds Loki teamed up with Malekith.

This special, limited, signed, numbered hardcover edition was restricted 1,500 copies. It contains groundbreaking work on Thor by writer/artist Walt Simonson, and introduces Beta Ray Bill. There are sketch pages, an introduction by Simonson, and an afterword by *Seinfeld* writer Dave Mandel.

Smith, Kevin, David Mack, Joe Quesada, et al. *Daredevil Vol. 1*. New York: Marvel, 2003. ISBN: 0785110151. Reprints *Daredevil Vol. 2: 1–11, 13–15*.

A baby, who some see as the savior of mankind, is brought into Matt Murdock's life. He wants to protect it from those who would seek to kill it. Daredevil, who is drugged into seeing a conspiracy to harm the child, hits his former lover, the Black Widow, and visits Dr. Strange to find out what supernatural forces are working against him. Karen Page learns that she has AIDS. Murdock goes to the church where his mother, a nun, lives, and asks her to take care of the baby. Bullseye destroys the church, and kills numerous nuns and parishioners. During his fight with Daredevil, Bullseye kills Karen Page. Mysterio has been playing Daredevil for a fool in his game to break Matt Murdock's spirit. Matt Murdock falls in love with a client who is deaf. The Kingpin deceives this person into believing that Daredevil killed her father, and, as Echo, she seeks revenge against Daredevil, until she learns that the Kingpin has been playing her for a dupe. A disgruntled former employee shoots the Kingpin, Wilson Fisk, and Echo shoots Fisk in the eyes, blinding him.

This volume contains sketches by Quesada and an introduction by actor Tom Sullivan.

Smith, Kevin, Joe Quesada, Jim Palmiotti, et al. *Daredevil Visionaries*. Anaheim, CA: Graphitti Designs, 1999. ISBN: 0936211555. Reprints *Daredevil Vol. 2: 1–8*.

This special hardcover was limited to 2,500 copies. It is numbered and signed by Kevin Smith, Joe Quesada, and Jim Palmiotti. The book came with a CD-Rom which includes commentary from the author and artists, rough unedited scripts, original pencil art, and *Daredevil 0*, and *Daredevil 1/2*, among other goodies. The volume is part of the award-winning Guardian Devil storyline. This is a one-of-a-kind collector's item.

Stern, Roger, David Michelinie, Todd McFarlane, et al. *Wizard Spider-Man Masterpiece Edition Vol. 1*. Congers, NY: Wizard Publishing, 2004. ISBN: 0974325368. Reprints *Amazing Spider-Man 229–232, 248, 315–317; Spectacular SpiderMan 107–110*.

Spider-Man meets Mr. Hyde for the first time. Spider-Man captures the Cobra, but Hyde is not far behind. His officemate, Debra Whitman, suspects that Peter Parker is really Spider-Man. It takes a fall from a skyscraper to finally stop Hyde, who wants to kill the Cobra for betraying him. Venom goes after Spider-Man again, and even meets with Aunt May when he shows up at the Parker household. Finally Peter Parker gives up, and gives himself back to the alien costume. However the bond between the costume and Eddie Brock is too strong to break.

This special volume features the ten greatest Spider-Man tales ever published, including "Nothing Can Stop the Juggernaut," "Kid Who Collects Spider-Man," and "Death of Jean DeWolfe." Each story features an introductory essay with factual tidbits. Some of the interesting bonus material includes the legion of lamest villains ever to grace the pages of Spider-Man, and the best tales featuring Spider-Man's main cast of foes: Doc Ock, Kraven, Mysterio, Vulture, Green Goblin, Hobgoblin, and others. A double-page spread features all the costumes Spider-Man has worn including Spider Ham, Captain Universe Spider-Man, Spider Clone, Spider-Man 2099, Scarlet Spider, and all the others. The introduction is by Brian Bendis.

Straczynski, J. Michael, John Romita Jr., Fiona Avery, et al. *Best of Spider-Man Vol. 3*. New York: Marvel, 2004. ISBN: 0785113398. Reprints *Amazing Spider-Man 500*; *Amazing Spider-Man Vol. 2: 46–58*.

Dr. Strange visits Peter Parker to let him know that a wasp-like predator, Shanthra, is coming from another dimension to kill him. Shanthra tries to "play" with Spider-Man and wants to spoil his reputation. She goes on national television and talks about what a pervert Spider-Man is. She stings Spider-Man, and almost kills him, but Parker is rescued by Ezekiel and taken to Africa. A group of mobsters were killed in 1957 and buried in the desert. After gamma bombs were tested near the site, a zombie, who is composed of a whole group of zombies, is brought to life in 2003, and vows to kill Forelli, the mobster who ordered the hit. Forelli hires Spider-Man to protect him and his family, arguing that innocents will be murdered by the zombie. Spider-Man figures out a way to destroy the zombie and pin the murder on Forelli who goes to jail for the hit he ordered all those years ago. Spider-Man relives various incidents in his life, including the death of Uncle Ben, and the many villains he has fought over the years. He even sees his future death at the hands of police officers. This all happens on Peter Parker's birthday.

The book contains several Spider-Man/Villain pin-ups. The script from issue 500 is included, along with the panels from the original *Spider-Man* issues that were the basis of the script. Panels from *Amazing Fantasy 15*; *Amazing Spider-Man 2, 4, 6, 9, 11, 12, 14, 33*, and *121* are included. Volume 4–5 ISBN: 0785118276 (4) 0785121285 (5).

Straczynski, J. Michael, John Romita Jr., Scott Hanna, et al. *The Best of Spider-Man Vol. 1*. New York: Marvel, 2002. ISBN: 0785109 005. Reprints *Amazing Spider-Man Vol. 2: 30–36*; *Spider-Man's Tangled Web 4–6*; *Peter Parker Spider-Man Vol. 2: 35*; *Ultimate Marvel Team Up 6–8*.

This is a beautiful hardback edition of some of the groundbreaking Spider-Man stories from 2001, including the story about how Spider-Man dealt with the events of 9/11/2001. This book includes appearances by the Rhino, Kingpin, Punisher, Captain America, and Daredevil. This collection belongs in every library.

Straczynski, J. Michael, John Romita Jr., Scott Hanna, et al. *Best of Spider-Man Vol. 2*. New York: Marvel, 2003. ISBN: 0785111 00X. Reprints *Amazing Spider-Man Vol. 2: 37–45*; *Peter Parker: Spider-Man Vol. 2: 44–47*; *Spider-Man's Tangled Web 10–11*.

This deluxe hardcover edition contains stories from recent Spider-Man titles, including the story in which Aunt May finds out that Peter Parker is Spider-Man. It also contains the Return of the Green Goblin storyline, and the "Insect Man" and "Valentine's Day" stories. The Introduction was written by Marvel executive editor Axel Alonso.

Waid, Mark, Mike Wieringo, Karl Kesel, et al. *Fantastic Four Vol. 1*. New York: Marvel, 2004. ISBN: 0785114866. Reprints *Fantastic Four Vol. 3: 60–70, 500–502*.

Johnny Storm admits to his sister Sue Richards that all the gags mailed to Ben Grimm from the Yancy Street Gang were actually from him. Grimm goes on a rampage to track down the culprit of the pranks. Sue, wanting Johnny to act more mature, gives him a job handling the finances of the Fantastic Four's corporation. Mr. Fantastic's mathematical computer, driven by jealousy, comes to life and threatens the Fantastic Four. Insects from another dimension find their way into the Baxter Building. Franklin is jealous of his sister, and Reed has tests run on her to make sure she is normal. Victor Von Doom tracks down an old lover, and destroys her soul in return for the powers of a sorcerer. He has a bond with Reed and Susan's daughter Val, and kidnaps her to lure the Fantastic Four to his home. He sends Franklin Richards to a place inhabited by demons, Hell. The Fantastic Four try to rescue Richards, to no avail. Doom uses his magical powers to torture the Fantastic Four, and has the Thing fight the Mindless Ones. Doom locks Reed Richards in a room to humble him by forcing him to study magic. Reed, a scientist who does not believe in magic, finds this most difficult. Dr. Strange, in his astral form, tries to teach Reed some basic lessons in sorcery. Reed is finally able to use magic against Doom, but Doom manages to scar his face. Franklin is saved, but he has a real hard time adjusting to normalcy, seeing demons everywhere he goes.

This hardback contains a special section with deleted scenes, outtakes, a commentary by Waid, scripts, Stan Lee's original synopsis for Issue 1, Fred Hembeck's five-hundred-issue tribute, and a "printography" of the cover of every *Fantastic Four* issue up to issue 50. It also includes Mark Waid's brilliant "Fantastic Four Manifesto," and the Wizard Ace edition covers for *Fantastic Four 48*. Volumes 2–3 ISBN: 078511775X (2); 0785120114 (3); *Fantastic Four Omnibus* ISBN: 0785118705; *Best of the Fantastic Four* ISBN: 0785117822.

Wein, Len, Herb Trimpe, Chris Claremont, et al. *Best of Wolverine Vol. 1*. New York: Marvel, 2004. ISBN: 0785113703. Reprints *Incredible Hulk 181*; *Wolverine 1–4*; *Captain America Annual 8*; *Uncanny X-Men 205*; *Wolverine 167*; *Marvel Comics Presents 72–84*.

Logan goes to Japan to seek his girlfriend Marko. She has not replied to any of his letters or telephone calls. She is married to a man who beats her to pay off a debt of her father's. Her father sets himself up as the new Yakuza crime lord. Her father captures and defeats Logan, and shows Marko what an animal he is. Logan meets Yukio, who is also hired to kill him, but saves his life. They have a whirlwind romance, but are continually harassed by the Hand. When Logan calls out Marko's name, Yukio leaves him. He finally has a duel to the death with Marko's father, Shingen, and kills him. Wolverine and Captain America have to fight against a very powerful robot, and a madman who is trying to destroy all U.S. nuclear weapons.

This collection features some of the most historic Wolverine stories ever published, including his first appearance fighting the Hulk. It also features the creation of Lady Deathstrike from Power Pack, and her cronies. She is defeated by Wolverine with the help of Katie Powers. The entire Weapon X Creation of Wolverine storyline is reprinted here as well. There is a cover gallery, cover reprints of the Wizard Ace *Incredible Hulk 181* and *Wizard 149*, and a Wolverine lithography by Dynamic Forces. The introduction is by Chris Claremont.

Wood, Wally, Roy Thomas, Artie Simek, et al. *Marvel Comics Art of Wally Wood*. New York: Thumbstack Books, 1982. ISBN: 0942480023. Reprints *Tower of Shadows 5–7*; *Astonishing Tales 1–3*.

This is a nice hardback tribute to the work of Wally Wood. It contains several of his sword-and-sorcery tales, including one in which the legendary Beowulf is featured, and a solo Dr. Doom story. In the Dr. Doom story, Doom creates an android using cosmic power and his own brain patterns; Prince Rudolpho tries to usurp Doom's rule with the help of an alien known as the Faceless One and Doom's creation, Doomsan; and an earthquake destroys Doom's castle.

Youngquist, Jeff, Mark Beazley, Alex Ross, et al. *The Art of Marvel Volume Two*. New York: Marvel, 2004. ISBN: 0785113614.

This lovely coffee-table book features Marvel artwork, mostly covers from the Golden Age to the present day. It is divided into two sections: "The Golden Age," which includes the sixties through the nineties, and "Today," which is the largest section. Marvel characters are represented, from the original Human Torch and Captain America, through the Fantastic Four, X-Men, Daredevil, Wolverine, She Hulk, and new characters like NYX and Arena. There are quotes from Warren Ellis, Brian Bendis, and Stan Lee. This volume is even better than the first one.

Youngquist, Jeff, John Romita Jr., Alex Ross, et al. *Art of Marvel Volume One*. New York: Marvel, 2003. ISBN: 0785111638.

This collection updates a previous art collection by focusing on several years of Marvel art up to 2003. It contains chapters on Spider-Man; X-Men, including Wolverine; Daredevil, including Elektra; the Hulk, including She Hulk; and Marvel heroes, including Captain America, Iron Man, Thor, and the Fantastic Four. There also are chapters which feature other Marvel heroes and villains, including the Marvel Knights/Max, with Black Widow, Punisher, Jessica Jones, Cage, Inhumans, Fury, and the Black Panther. Writers Stan Lee, Mark Waid, Bruce Jones, and others give their opinions of the artwork.

Marvel Masterworks

Burgos, Carl, Bill Everett, Ben Thompson, et al. *Golden Age Marvel Comics Masterworks Vol. 1*. New York: Marvel, 2004. ISBN: 0785116095; 0785116109 (ltd). Reprints *Marvel Comics 1*; *Marvel Mystery Comics 2–4*.

In late 2004, Marvel began to reprint Golden Age books from the Timely era. Volume 1 reprints the very first Marvel comic ever published, which includes stories of the origins of two superhero heavyweights: the original Human Torch and the Sub-Mariner. Lower-rate heroes, including the Golden Age Angel, Ka-Zar, and the western hero, Masked Rider, are also introduced. By its second issue, renamed *Marvel Mystery Comics*, the very bizarre American Ace was introduced, but only lasted through issue 3. Some stories in this volume involved the Human Torch taking out gangsters who have been involved with murders at the races. Professor Horton's original data on the Human Torch is reprinted. Also in this volume, the Torch takes up his Jim Hammond identity and fights the cold Green Flame men, who threaten to destroy New York; the Sub-Mariner meets policewoman

Betty Dean, who convinces Namor to give the "White American devils" another chance; Dean convinces Namor to help the British in the war effort against the Germans, two years before the U.S. enters the war; and Ka-Zar saves numerous animals from being taken to the zoo, and encounters the man who killed his father, and whom he had sworn vengeance against. Issue 4 features the introduction of the Golden-Age Electro, an indestructible robot created by Professor Zog to benefit mankind. Each issue contains a story in text, and a story that features the Golden-Age Angel. Marvel plans to continue publishing Golden Age Masterworks, with *Captain America, Human Torch, All Winners Comics.* and other titles. They also plan to publish Atlas Era Masterworks. Roy Thomas wrote a detailed introduction for this volume. Recommended. (*Marvel Masterworks 36*)

Claremont, Chris, John Byrne, Terry Austin, et al. *Uncanny X-Men Masterworks Vol. 3.* New York: Marvel, 2004. ISBN: 0785111 948; 0785112952 (ltd). Reprints *Uncanny X-Men 111–121.*

Magneto takes the X-Men from Mesmero's clutches to his secret base under ground in Antarctica. In the ensuing battle, the Beast and Jean Grey escape through the top, while the rest of the X-Men tunnel through to the Savage Land, each believing the other dead. Professor X goes with Lilandra to her planet. The X-Men fight Sauron and help Ka-Zar defeat the tyranny of the god Garnok. They help Sunfire against Moses Magnum. Alpha Flight tries to take Wolverine from the X-Men by force, and Wolverine meets Mariko. (*Marvel Masterworks 24*)

Claremont, Chris, John Byrne, George Perez, et al. *The Uncanny X-Men Masterworks Vol. 4.* New York: Marvel, 2004. ISBN: 078511 6303; 0785116311 (ltd). Reprints *X-Men Vol. 1: 122–133; X-Men Annual 3.*

Wolverine forces Colossus to use his powers in the Danger Room. Storm goes to a house full of junkies and meets up with Luke Cage and Misty Knight. Acarde, who is hired to kill the X-Men, kidnaps them and forces them to go through his Murderworld. Arkon comes from his dimension and kidnaps Storm. The X-Men follow and help the Imperions restore the life-giving energy rings. Mastermind begins to groom Jean Grey for the Hellfire club. The Beast and Jean find out that the other X-Men are alive, after their fight with Magneto. The X-Men go to Muir Island where Moria McTaggert's son, Mutant X, also known as Proteus, escapes. He takes over his father, and nearly defeats the X-Men. Emma Frost, the White Queen, captures the X-Men for the Hellfire Club. Kitty Pryde is left to help free them from White Queen's clutches. She is particularly cruel to Storm.

Kitty Pryde and Dazzler make their first appearances in this volume. This volume includes Frank Miller's original cover for *X-Men Annual 3.* (*Marvel Masterworks 37*)

Claremont, Chris, Dave Cockrum, John Byrne, et al. *Uncanny X-Men Masterworks Vol. 2.* New York: Marvel, 2004. ISBN: 0785111 93X; 0785112901 (ltd) 0871356287 (1990). Reprints *Uncanny X-Men 101–110.*

Jean Grey turns into the Phoenix. The X-Men take a vacation to Cassidy Keep, only to find Black Tom and Juggernaut waiting for them, but with the help of the "little people" and Nightcrawler, the X-Men escape. Xavier keeps having disturbing images and nightmares that originate from outer space. Magneto returns to take on the new X-Men, who retreat, and Jean Grey learns that the Starjammer's leader is actually Cyclops's father. Weapon Alpha tries to kidnap Wolverine.

This volume contains the story of the origin of Storm, and the first appearance of the Starjammers. (*Marvel Masterworks 12*)

Claremont, Chris, Len Wein, Dave Cockrum, et al. *Uncanny X-Men Masterworks Vol. 1.* New York: Marvel. 2003. ISBN: 078511 921; 0785112855(ltd); 0871355973 (1989). Reprints *Giant Size X-Men 1; Uncanny X-Men 94–100.*

The new X-Men team investigates the disappearance of the old X-Men team on the island of Krakoa. The island itself turns out to be a giant mutant who feeds off the energy of other mutants. Thunderbird is killed while on a mission against Count Nefaria, and the X-Men fight robot versions of the old team on an orbiting satellite. The Sentinels return.

This volume contains the groundbreaking stories of the assembly of the new X-Men team, which features Wolverine, Sunfire, Banshee, Storm, Thunderbird, Colossus and Nightcrawler. (*Marvel Masterworks 11*)

Everett, Bill, Stan Lee, Roy Thomas, et al. *Sub-Mariner Masterworks Vol. 1.* New York: Marvel, 2002. ISBN: 0785108750; 078511 2898 (ltd). Reprints *Marvel Comics 1; Daredevil 7; Tales to Astonish 70–87.*

Subby meets and fights with Daredevil, Krang takes over Atlantis. Namor, who goes on a quest to find the trident of Neptune, defeats Krang. Lady Dorma tries to woo Namor. Dorma is banished to face the Faceless Ones who are an underwater version of the mystical Mindless Ones from the dreaded Dormammu's domain. Namor rescues her, but almost dies in the process. Namor banishes Krang who vows revenge. The Puppet Master takes control of the Sub-Mariner briefly, and with Krang's help awakens the Behemoth. Krang forces Lady Dorma to marry him by promising to spare Namor's life. He tries to take control of the surface world, but Namor defeats him. The Sub-Mariner and Iron Man have an action-packed battle based on a misunderstanding. The fallen Leader of the Secret Empire tries to coerce Namor into battling the Hulk, with less than satisfactory results. The Sub-Mariner goes into a jealous rage over Dorma.

This book includes the original origin story of the Sub-Mariner. (*Marvel Masterworks 32*)

Lee, Stan, John Buscema, Jack Kirby, et al. *Silver Surfer Masterworks Vol. 2*. New York: Marvel, 2003. ISBN: 0785111778; 078511 2774 (ltd); 0871358085 (1991). Reprints *Silver Surfer 7–18*.

One of Frankenstein's heirs creates a "monster" version of the Surfer, intent on destroying him. Mephisto has the Flying Dutchman, as a super–powerful ghost, attempt to destroy the Surfer, but the Surfer's innate kindness outwits Mephisto, and saves the Dutchman's soul. The Surfer gets involved in a political struggle in a Latino country. When Shalla Bal, the Surfer's love, comes to Earth, she is shot and is sent back to Zenn-La. Mephisto kidnaps Shalla Bal, and does his best to get the Surfer's soul. He even has the Surfer attack Nick Fury and S.H.I.E.L.D. Both Spider-Man and the Human Torch fight the Surfer. They mistakenly think he is guilty of a crime. The Surfer gets in the middle of a fight with the Inhumans, and Maximus makes it look like the Silver Surfer is fighting on his side. In the end, the Surfer swears his vengeance upon humanity. (*Marvel Masterworks 19*)

Lee, Stan, John Buscema, Sam Rosen, et al. *The Silver Surfer Masterworks Vol. 1*. New York: Marvel, 2003. ISBN: 0785111875 (2003); 0871356317 (1990). Reprints *Silver Surfer 1–5*; *Silver Surfer 1–6* (1990); *Fantastic Four Annual 5*

In order to save his home world, Zenn-La, from being destroyed by Galactus, Norrin Radd sacrifices himself. He becomes Galactus's herald, the Silver Surfer, who is supposed to find worlds for Galactus to feed upon. After he finds Earth, and works with the Fantastic Four in Earth's defense, the Surfer rebels against his former master. As punishment for going against Galactus's will, the Silver Surfer is marooned in Earth's atmosphere, never again to fly through the galaxy. Loki tries to deceive the Surfer into fighting with Thor, and Mephisto seeks to imprison the Surfer's soul.

This is an epic tale of the Silver Surfer's early adventures, which takes place shortly after Galactus maroons him in Earth's atmosphere. In a similar story, the Surfer saves the Earth from the Stranger, who also seeks to destroy it. (*Marvel Masterworks 15*)

Lee, Stan, Steve Ditko, Jack Kirby, et al. *Incredible Hulk Masterworks Volume 2*. New York: Marvel, 2004. ISBN: 0785116559 (ltd); 078 5116540. Reprints *Tales to Astonish 59–79*.

Giant Man goes on a search for the Hulk. The Human Top tries to intervene, but the Hulk saves Giant Man's life. Banner designs an indestructible robot which is stolen by an agent of the Leader. The military believes that Banner may be a traitor, and Major Talbot is assigned to investigate. The Hulk

finally is captured, but when he changes into Banner, he is able to get out of the bonds that hold him. The Chameleon, who is the Leader's agent, tries to sabotage the military base. The Leader, who wants the Hulk to be his ally, creates pink humanoids to try and subdue the Hulk, and take over the military base's secrets. Talbot begins to suspect not only that Banner is a traitor, but that there is a connection between him and the Hulk. Banner is taken captured by the reds and is forced to work with other captured scientists. Rick Jones goes to the president, and explains that Banner is actually the Hulk. When Banner is shot in the head and almost dies, the Leader saves his life and sends the Hulk to the Watcher's "blue" area on the moon to steal the Ultimate Machine. The Leader supposedly dies after wearing the Machine, because it proves to have too much knowledge. The Hulk is sent to the future where he battles the Executioner. Rick Jones, believing Banner/Hulk to be dead, admits that Bruce Banner is actually the Hulk. The Hulk faces Hercules in a titanic battle.

In this volume, Leader's origin is revealed and Major Talbot is introduced. (*Marvel Masterworks 39*)

Lee, Stan, Steve Ditko, John Romita, et al. *Amazing Spider-Man Masterworks Vol. 4*. New York: Marvel, 2003. ISBN: 078511 1891; 078511288X (ltd); 0871357305 (1991). Reprints *Amazing Spider-Man 31–40*.

Peter Parker starts college. Aunt May gets sick and is put into a hospital. Spider-Man tries hard to help cure her, but Doc Ock wants the radioactive material needed to cure Aunt May. Many of Parker's college classmates think he is a stuck-up snob. The Robot Master tries to kill Norman Osborn. The villains Molten Man, Kraven, Meteor, and the Green Goblin make appearances.

This volume contains the final Spider-Man issues worked on by Steve Ditko, and the first issues by John Romita. The introduction is by Stan Lee. The original 1991 Masterworks contained *Annual 2*. (*Marvel Masterworks 16*)

Lee, Stan, Steve Ditko, Sam Rosen, et al. *Amazing Spider-Man Masterworks Vol. 3*. New York: Marvel, 2003. ISBN: 0785111 883; 0785112839 (ltd); 0871355965 (1989). Reprints *Amazing Spider Man 20–30*; *Amazing Spider-Man Annual 2*.

Spider-Man teams up with the Human Torch to fight the Beetle. Johnny Storm thinks Peter Parker is trying to make time with his girl. Peter Parker graduates from high school. Spider-Man outwits Jonah Jameson, who is trying to capture him with a spider-sensing robot. The Green Goblin and the Crime Master both try to control the gangster rackets. When the Crime Master is killed, the Ringmaster's gang tries to go on without him. Dr. Strange and Spider-Man meet for the first time, to battle wits with Xandu.

The villains in this volume include the first Cannonball, Vulture, and the Cat Burger, among others. The volume also contains Mary Jane's first appearance, the origins of the Scorpion and the Molten Man, and pin-ups for Spider-Man's most famous foes. The introduction is by Stan Lee. (*Marvel Masterworks 10*)

Lee, Stan, Steve Ditko, Art Simek, et al. *Amazing Spider-Man Masterworks Vol. 1*. New York: Marvel, 2003. ISBN: 0785112561; 0785107037 (1998); 0785108645 (2002); 0871353059 (1987). Reprints *Amazing Fantasy 15*; *Amazing Spider-Man 1–10*.

This volume covers the origin of Spider-Man, and Peter Parker's first battles with the Vulture, Sandman, Doc Ock, Chameleon, Electro, Lizard, and Doctor Doom. Spider-Man has a tiff with the Human Torch, and Jonah Jameson gets into an argument with the Vulture. Many of the key players in the Spider-Man saga are introduced, including Jonah Jameson, Aunt May Flash Thompson, Liz Allen, and Betty Brant. The introduction is by Stan Lee. (*Marvel Masterworks 1*)

Lee, Stan, Steve Ditko, Art Simek, et al. *Amazing Spider-Man Masterworks Vol. 2*. New York: Marvel, 2002. ISBN:0785109242 (2003); 0871354802 (1988). Reprints *Amazing Spider-Man 11–19*; *Amazing Spider-Man Annual 1*.

The Green Goblin hires the Enforcers for a movie in which they kill Spider-Man. They all go to Hollywood, where the Hulk ruins the Goblin's plans. Spider-Man meets Daredevil, and helps foil the Ringmaster's plans. Flash Thompson impersonates Spider-Man, and gets hurt in the process. Spider-Man has to leave a fight with the Green Goblin, because Aunt May gets sick, and then everyone thinks Spider-Man is a coward. The Sandman hires the Enforcers, and they kidnap the Human Torch in an effort to lure Spider-Man.

The Introduction is by Stan Lee. (*Marvel Masterworks 5*)

Lee, Stan, Steve Ditko, Art Simek, et al. *Marvel Masterworks: Dr. Strange Vol. 1*. New York: Marvel, 2003. ISBN: 0785111808; 0785111276 (ltd); 0871359154 (1990). Reprints *Strange Tales: 110–111, 114–141*.

Stephen Strange goes from being a selfish, money-grubbing doctor to master of the mystic arts. Strange loses the use of his surgical hands in an accident, and seeks out the Ancient One who is said to have healing powers. The Ancient One's former disciple, Baron Mordo, wants to use the mystic arts to usurp the Ancient One, and enslave mankind. Dr. Strange battles with various occult forces through mystical dimensions. He helps a group of people who are stuck in a somnambulistic state, by entering the dream world to fight Nightmare. In an epic drama where Dr. Strange battles Baron Mordo and the dreaded Dormammu, Strange meets with Eternity, and learns that wisdom

can be as potent a force as special powers. (*Marvel Masterworks Volume 23*)

Lee, Stan, Bill Everett, Wally Wood, et al. *Daredevil Masterworks Vol. 1*. New York: Marvel, 2003. ISBN: 078511257X; 078511 2618 (ltd); 0785107142 (1999); 0871358069 (1991). Reprints *Daredevil 1–11*.

Matt Murdock is blinded by radioactive material while saving a man from getting run over. His father is killed by the Fixer when he refuses to throw a fight. The Thing tries to hire Murdock in his civilian guise as a lawyer. The Sub-Mariner wants to sue the human race for crimes against his people, and Daredevil tries rein him in. Daredevil goes up against a bizarre group of thugs, who are under the control of the Organizer.

Other villains who appear in this volume include Stilt Man, Owl, El Toro, and Purple Man. In the volume, Daredevil goes from wearing his yellow costume to wearing the red one. The introduction is by Stan Lee. (*Marvel Masterworks 17*)

Lee, Stan, Don Heck, Steve Ditko, et al. *Iron Man Masterworks Vol. 1*. New York: Marvel, 2003. ISBN: 0785111867; 0785112820 (ltd); 087135912X (1992). Reprints *Tales of Suspense 39–50, 55*.

Billionaire industrialist Tony Stark is taken prisoner and mortally wounded in Vietnam. With the help of another scientist, he creates the Iron Man armor, and defeats the communist overlord who took him captive. During a car race, Stark wipes out and Happy Hogan saves his life. He hires Happy and introduces him to his future wife, Pepper Potts. The Angel from the X-Men gets caught in a radioactive storm, and becomes evil. He leaves the X-Men, and Iron Man has to help him fight the evil transformation.

The Mandarin is introduced in this volume, and he and Iron Man fight an early, evil Dr. Strange, who is not the supernatural mystic of *Strange Tales*. By the second Iron Man story, Stark has changed his gray suit to a golden one. Throughout his early years as Iron Man, he kept changing the style of his suit, and updating it with useful transistors and gadgets. These stories read like a commentary on the Cold War, with Premier Khrushchev making a number of appearances. Some of the other villains that fight Iron Man in this volume include the Melter, Mister Doll, Jack Frost, and the Red Barbarian. The bonus feature, "All About Iron Man," from *Suspense 55*, and a Pepper Potts pin-up page, are included in the new edition. Stan Lee wrote the introduction. (*Marvel Masterworks 20*)

Lee, Stan, Don Heck, Art Simek, et al. *Avengers Masterworks Volume 3*. New York: Marvel, 2004. ISBN: 0785111794; 0785112936 (ltd); 0871359936 (1993). Reprints *Avengers 21–30*.

The Avengers are defeated by the Enchantress and the original Power Man. Power Man frames them for crimes they did not commit, which causes them to them fall out of favor with the public, and they are asked to disband. Captain America leaves the Avengers. Hawkeye baits Captain America, and Kang kidnaps the remaining Avengers, minus Captain America, to the future. Captain America finds out about Kang's plans, and goes to the future to stop him. Kang's guard commander betrays him, and Kang has to align himself with the Avengers. The Princess, whose love Kang has long sought, finally agrees that she loves him, only to be killed. For the first time, the remaining Avengers encounter Dr. Doom, who lures them to Latveria, and quickly captures them. The Wasp is captured by the evil Attuma who plans to flood the Earth in his never-ending desire to take over the surface world. The Wasp calls on the Avengers for help, and they too, minus Hawkeye, are captured. The Beetle breaks into the Avenger's mansion and has a showdown with Hawkeye who defeats the Beetle and seeks out his captured comrades. They finally defeat Attuma, and Captain America destroys Attuma's flood tide machine. Both the Wasp and Giant-Man rejoin the Avengers. Scarlet Witch designs a new costume for Giant-Man, who becomes Goliath. The Collector tries to capture the Avengers, and he and his crony the Beetle are defeated. Goliath nearly dies trying to size down, and is now stuck at a height of ten feet; he considers himself a freak. The Black Widow, who has been brainwashed by the Soviets, recruits the Swordsman and Power Man to help destroy the Avenger. Goliath goes off by himself, and finds the Keeper of the Flame, while searching for a famous doctor who might be able to cure him. Goliath is captured. Quicksilver and the Scarlet Witch go back to their homeland when they find out their power is waning. The Fantastic Four makes a cameo appearance. The introduction by Stan Lee. (*Marvel Masterworks 27*)

Lee, Stan, Don Heck, Roy Thomas, et al. *Avengers Masterworks Vol. 4.* New York: Marvel, 2004. ISBN: 0785116389; 078511 6397 (ltd). Reprints *Avengers 31–40.*

While seeking Dr. Anton for a cure to his problem of being ten feet tall, Goliath goes to South America and gets involved in a civil war between two political factions who are trying to be the keepers of the Cobalt fire. Hank Pym gets a new assistant, the African-American Bill Foster. The Avengers go up against a racist organization, the Serpent Society, which is trying to divide America. Goliath makes a speech against the society, but Captain America is seemingly duped by them, as a disciple. The Living Laser kidnaps the Wasp, in an early example of obsessive stalking. The Laser captures Hawkeye and Captain America. The Avengers and the Black Widow are captured by the alien Ultriods. Quicksilver and the Scarlet Witch return to the fold, and they fight against the colossal Ixar the Invincible. Hercules fights the Avengers under a spell of the Enchantress. Instead of being at

odds with Captain America, Hawkeye is now bickering with Goliath. Hawkeye wants the Black Widow to be accepted for membership in the Avengers, but Nick Fury and S.H.I.E.L.D. have her go undercover. Hercules is exiled on Earth, and stays with the Avengers. Black Widow becomes a traitor to America. When the Sub-Mariner learns about the powerful Cosmic Cube, he goes head to head with the Avengers for it.

Hercules, Hammerhead, and several low-rent villains are introduced in this volume. Roy Thomas wrote the introduction. (*Marvel Masterworks 38*)

Lee, Stan, Jack Kirby, Dick Ayers, et al. *Fantastic Four Masterworks Vol. 1.* New York: Marvel, 2003. ISBN: 0785111816; 078511 260X (ltd); 0785105891 (1997); 0871353 075 (1987). Reprints *Fantastic Four 1–10.*

This is the comic series that began the Marvel Universe and the Age of Marvel. This volume contains the story of the origins of the Fantastic Four and their first encounters with Namor/Sub-Mariner, Dr. Doom, the Mole Man, the Puppet Master, Kurgo, Miracle Man, and the Skrulls. Golden Age character the Sub-Mariner was reintroduced to the Marvel Universe in the pages of the *Fantastic Four*. The volume includes pin-ups of the Human Torch and Sue Storm. The introduction is by Stan Lee. (*Marvel Masterworks 2*)

Lee, Stan, Jack Kirby, Dick Ayers, et al. *Fantastic Four Masterworks Vol. 2.* New York: Marvel, 2003. ISBN: 0785109803; 0785112 758 (ltd); 0871354810 (1988). Reprints *Fantastic Four 11–20; Fantastic Four Annual 1.*

Ben and Reed reminisce about being in the big war together. The Hulk is accused of sabotaging government experiments, and the Fantastic Four is brought in to investigate. The Red Ghost and his simian friends are bathed in cosmic rays, and he is given special powers. The Watcher is introduced when the Fantastic Four and the Red Ghost discover his home on the moon. The Puppet Master controls the Sub-Mariner, and has him kidnap Sue Storm. The Yancy Street gang eggs the Thing on, and even calls him a sissy. The Mad Thinker gets the Fantastic Four to break up for a brief time. Ant-Man assists the Fantastic Four in defeating Dr. Doom in the micro world. Namor, who declares war on humanity again, saves Sue Storm's life, and still pines for her love.

Other villains introduced in this volume include the Molecule Man, Rama Tutt, and the Super Skrull. The bizarre alien from the planet Poppup, the Impossible Man, and Willy Lumpkin, the mailman, also are introduced. In one of the stories in the book, Willy Lumpkin asks to be a member of the Fantastic Four because he can wiggle his ears, and, in another, Spider-Man's first meeting with the Fantastic Four is retold. The volume contains pin-up pages that feature Fantastic Four villains, and unused covers for *Fantas-*

tic Four 3 and *Fantastic Four Annual 1*. Stan Lee's original synopsis for *Fantastic Four* also is reprinted. Lee also wrote the book's introduction (*Marvel Masterworks 6*)

Lee, Stan, Jack Kirby, Dick Ayers, et al. *Marvel Masterworks: The Mighty Thor Vol. 1*. New York: Marvel, 2003. ISBN: 0785112677; 0785112731(ltd); 0785107339 (1999). 08713 58077 (1991) Reprints *Journey Into Mystery Annual 1; Journey Into Mystery 83–100*.

This volume contains classic color reprints of Thor's earliest adventures, his origin story, and his first battles with his half brother Loki. In the volume: JFK has a cameo appearance; Thor tries to sway his father Odin into letting him marry Jane Foster; and Merlin, the magician, comes back as a power-hungry tyrant. Other characters include the Lava Man, Human Cobra, Carbon Copy Man and Mr. Hyde. The volume also contains two tales of Asgard, a map of Asgard, and tales of the origins of the Frost Giants, Odin, and the Buri, the first of the Norse Gods. (*Marvel Masterworks 18*).

Lee, Stan, Jack Kirby, Steve Ditko, et al. *The Incredible Hulk Masterworks Vol. 1*. New York: Marvel. 2003. ISBN: 0785111859; 0785112588 (ltd); 0871355949 (1989). Reprints *Hulk Vol. 1: 1–6*.

This volume includes the original Hulk stories, and it reprints the original "Grey" Hulk. If one reads between the lines, these stories can be seen as statements on the Cold War and the evils of communism. Written during the early sixties, the stories mirror popular culture's concern at the time about communism and the preservation of the American way of life This volume has the Hulk's origin story. Some of the characters he goes up against include Tyrannus, Toadmen, Gargoyle, the U.S. Army, the Metal Master, and General Fang. While saving Rick Jones's life, Bruce Banner is bathed in gamma radiation, and ends up becoming the incredible Hulk. During these early stories, the Hulk only appears at night. (*Marvel Masterworks 8*)

Lee, Stan, Jack Kirby, Don Heck. *Avengers Masterworks Vol. 1*. New York: Marvel, 2002. ISBN: 0785108831 (2002); 0785105905 (2000); 0871354799 (1997). Reprints *Avengers 1–10*.

Captain America is found frozen in suspended animation. He is revived after twenty years, and ends up joining the Avengers. He forms a bond with the youth Rick Jones. Sub-Mariner and the Hulk team up against the Avengers. Captain America's old nemesis Baron Zemo founds the Masters of Evil with the Enchantress. Simon Williams is transformed into Wonder Man to trick the Avengers into Zemo's hands, but he ends up helping the Avengers, and dies in the process.

This volume features Stan Lee's and Jack Kirby's second groundbreaking superhero team, which includes the Hulk, Iron Man, Thor, Ant-Man, and the Wasp. The Hulk leaves by issue 2 because he is too much for the Avengers to handle. (*Marvel Masterworks 4*)

Lee, Stan, Jack Kirby, Don Heck, et al. *Avengers Masterworks Vol. 2*. New York: Marvel, 2003. ISBN: 0785111786; 0785112871 (ltd); 0871355957 (1989). Reprints *Avengers 11–20*.

Rick Jones continues to want to be an Avenger, despite Captain America's protests. Spider-Man tries to join the Avengers, but he turns out to be a robot employed by Kang. Iron Man is missing from an important Avengers meeting. Giant-Man gets an alarm from his ants, which upsets Thor greatly, but it turns out that the ants are correct, as the Mole Man once more tries to take over the surface world. Count Nafaria has the press and the government turn against the Avengers. During a battle with his Maggi, the Wasp is badly injured, and the Avengers search for the doctor who can save her, but aliens have kidnapped him. The U.S. Army engages the Avengers in battle. Steve Rogers, Captain America, writes to Nick Fury, asking to join Fury's espionage organization. Zemo puts together another version of the Masters of Evil, adding the Black Knight and the Melter. During a battle with Captain America and Rick Jones, Zemo is killed. Thor, Iron Man, Giant-Man, and the Wasp leave the Avengers, and Captain America sets about putting together a new team that features Hawkeye, Quicksilver, and the Scarlet Witch. They ask Sub-Mariner to join, but he declines. The "new" Avengers search for the Hulk, to ask him to consider joining the team once again. They have to fight the Mole Man. The Swordsman tries to join for his own nefarious purpose, and aligns himself with the Mandarin. Captain America's letter to Fury falls into the wrong hands.

This volume also features a communist villain, the Commissar. The introduction is by Stan Lee. (*Marvel Masterworks 9*)

Lee, Stan, Jack Kirby, Phil Lord, et al. *X-Men Masterworks Vol. 1*. New York: Marvel, 2002. ISBN: 0871353083; (1987); 078510 6642 (1997); 0785108459; 0785112634 (ltd, 2002). Reprints *Uncanny X-Men Vol. 1: 1–10*.

The X-Men travel to the Savage Land and encounter Ka-Zar for the first time. The Vanisher tries to take over organized crime, and Magneto tries to use government missile tests against the country, but the X-Men stop him. Professor X muses to himself that he loves Jean Grey. Xavier finds the Blob working at a carnie show, and tries to get him to join the X-Men; Magneto tries to get the Sub-Mariner to join the Brotherhood of Evil Mutants; and Professor X tries to get the Blob to join the X-Men. The X-Men fight the Avengers, while Professor X is trying to subdue Lucifer. The Beast leaves the X-Men briefly, and becomes a wrestler.

This volume contains the first appearance of the X-Men, and their first encounters with Magneto, Sub-Mariner, Avengers, and the Toad, among others. It also contains the first appearance of the Silver-Age Ka-Zar, who becomes a long-term ally of the X-Men and the Savage Land. Several of the covers included in the volume show Quicksilver in a blue costume, and the Scarlet Witch in a green one. The new edition contains an afterword by Peter Sanderson. (*Marvel Masterworks 3*)

Lee, Stan, Jack Kirby, George Roussos, et al. *Fantastic Four Masterworks Vol. 3.* New York: Marvel, 2003. ISBN: 0785111824; 0785112812 (ltd); 0871356295 (1990). Reprints *Fantastic Four 21–30*.

When the Hate Monger turns the Fantastic Four against each other, Nick Fury, who was in the war with Reed, helps the Fantastic Four come back together. It turns out that the Hate Monger is actually Hitler. The Mole Man has the tenants of the Baxter Building turn against the Fantastic Four, and lures them to his private island. The Fantastic Four foils Dr. Doom's capture plans, and he is thrown into space. A bizarre alien youngling, the Infant Terrible, menaces the Earth. The Hulk is angry because Captain America has replaced him on the Avengers, and the Fantastic Four are drawn into the fight, as the Thing and the Hulk duke it out. The Sub-Mariner kidnaps Sue Storm in an attempt to get her to love him instead of Reed, and Dr. Strange is brought in to help locate the Sub-Mariner and Sue. The Mad Thinker and the Puppet Master team up and use the X-Men against the Fantastic Four. The Fantastic Four goes back to the moon to stop the Red Ghost. The Watcher's home and scientific equipment fascinate Reed. Diablo is able to change the Thing back into Ben Grimm, briefly. The Thing betrays the Fantastic Four, and starts serving Diablo.

The introduction is by Stan Lee. (*Marvel Masterworks 13*)

Lee, Stan, Jack Kirby, Art Simek, et al. *Fantastic Four Masterworks Vol. 4.* New York: Marvel, 2003. ISBN: 0785111832; 0785112863 (ltd); 0871359138 (1992); Reprints *Fantastic Four 31–40; Fantastic Four Annual 2.*

Dr. Doom believes that by killing Reed Richards, he finally defeats the Fantastic Four. Rama Tutt may be a relative of Doom, or Doom himself. The Mole Man kidnaps Sue Storm, and the Avengers and the Fantastic Four duke it out. The Super Skrull pretends to be Dr. Storm, and terrorizes the Fantastic Four as the Invincible Man. The Skrulls kidnap him and send him back to Earth, but Dr. Storm dies. The Fantastic Four aid Namor against the mad Attuma without him knowing they have helped. The rich industrialist Gideon pits the Fantastic Four against each other. When Reed Richards speaks at the university where he and Ben went to school, Diablo crashes the party with Dragon Man. The Fantastic Four helps the Skrull Empire against a power hungry warlord. After another battle with the Frightful Four, the Fantastic Four lose their powers, and Daredevil comes to their aid against Dr. Doom.

In this volume, Dr. Doom's origin is told, and Dr. Franklin Storm, the Storms' father, and the Frightful Four are introduced. The introduction is by Stan Lee. (*Marvel Masterworks 21*)

Lee, Stan, Jack Kirby, Art Simek, et al. *Marvel Masterworks: Fantastic Four Vol. 5.* New York: Marvel, 2004. ISBN: 0785111840; 078511291X (ltd); 0871359901 (1993). Reprints *Fantastic Four 41–50; Fantastic Four Annual 3.*

The Watcher tells the Fantastic Four about the coming of Galactus and the arrival of the Silver Surfer. Galactus seeks to digest Earth's energy, but his herald, the Silver Surfer, rebels because he sees value in humanity. The Watcher goes against his creed and tells the Fantastic Four about the Ultimate Nullifier. The Frightful Four and the Wizard get the Thing to turn against Reed Richards and the Fantastic Four. Dr. Doom tries to destroy the wedding of Mr. Fantastic and the Invisible Woman, but the Watcher intervenes, and saves the wedding from disaster. When Gorgon seeks to take Medusa back to her people, the Fantastic Four and Dragon Man try to stop him. Black Bolt has to defeat his insane brother Maximus. The Human Torch goes to college and meets Wyatt Wingfoot, who becomes his longtime friend.

This volume contains some of the most memorable storylines in the history of the Fantastic Four. The first Punisher makes his debut, and the Inhumans are introduced in this volume. The introduction is by Stan Lee. (*Marvel Masterworks 25*)

Lee, Stan, Jack Kirby, Art Simek, et al. *Marvel Masterworks: The Mighty Thor Vol. 2.* New York: Marvel, 2003. ISBN: 0785111913; 0785112790 (ltd); 0871359928 (1993) Reprints *Journey Into Mystery 101–110* .

Thor becomes the slave of Zarrko, the Tomorrow Man. Odin is still very upset that Thor loves the human Jane Foster, and finds this love to be insubordinate. The Enchantress and the Executioner try to get Thor away from Jane Foster. Odin comes to Earth to reason with Thor, and Loki lets out Skagg, the storm giant, and Surtur, the fire demon. Thor, Balder, and Odin fight them, while Odin casts a spell so that the humans on Earth will not know that such a fight is taking place. Thor fights against the team of the Cobra and Mr. Hyde, and it seems like Donald Blake sells out Thor to Hyde and Cobra. Thor asks for the help of Dr. Strange against the magic of Loki. Magneto, thinking Thor is another mutant, asks Thor to join him. When Jane Foster is almost killed, Odin helps to heal her. A group of kids are fighting over who is stronger, Hulk or Thor, and Thor tells them the story of his various battles with the Hulk. He also fights Grey Gargoyle. The Avengers make a cameo appearance.

This volume contains the Gargoyle's origin story and various "Tales of Asgard" supplements, including "Death comes to the Thor"; "Thor's Mission to Mirmir"; "Himdall, Guardian of the Mystic Rainbow Bridge"; "Balder, the Brave"; and "The Defeat of Odin," among others. The volume also contains a Thor pin-up and an introduction by Stan Lee. (*Marvel Masterworks 26*)

Lee, Stan, Jack Kirby, Joe Sinnott, et al. *Fantastic Four Masterworks Vol. 7*. New York: Marvel, 2004. ISBN: 0785115846; 0785115 854 (ltd). Reprints *Fantastic Four 61–71*; *Fantastic Four Annual 5*.

The Four go up against the team of Blastaar and the Sandman, and eventually even the Sandman sees that Blastaar is nuts. The Silver Surfer breaks out of Doom's prison. Crystal interrupts a football game to find Johnny Storm, and talks to Wyatt Wingfoot. Reed gets thrown into the Negative Zone. The Fantastic Four find and destroy an old Kree sentry that was left dormant for thousands of years. The Kree Supreme Intelligence forces all the Fantastic Four members to have the same disturbing dream, and Ronin, the Accuser, is sent to punish the Fantastic Four for destroying the sentry. The Citadel of Science kidnaps Alicia because they believe she can help them in their quest to control HIM. The Thing goes berserk, and lashes out against his team and the world at large when the Mad Thinker exposes him to an experiment that brings out Ben's inner hate for his condition. The Mad Thinker's android nearly kills the Thing, Mr. Fantastic and the Torch. The Thinker discovers many of Reed's scientific secrets, including the Negative Zone. Sue Storm announces that she is pregnant, and Reed and Sue leave the team. The Silver Surfer frees Quasimodo from his computer prison. The Inhumans, the Black Panther, and the Fantastic Four team up against Psycho Man.

This volume contains the first appearance and the origin story of HIM, who becomes Adam Warlock. It also contains pin-ups of the Inhumans and various Fantastic Four villains and friends; unused cover pencils for Issues 64 and 71; and story notes/boards for *Fantastic Four 61, 63, 66*. Joe Sinnott wrote the introduction. (*Marvel Masterworks 34*)

Lee, Stan, Jack Kirby, Joe Sinnott, et al. *Marvel Masterworks: Fantastic Four Vol. 6*. New York: Marvel, 2004. ISBN: 0785112669; 0785112960 (ltd); 0785107525 (2000). Reprints *Fantastic Four 51–60*; *Fantastic Four Annual 4*.

A mad scientist transforms himself into Ben Grimm in order to destroy the Fantastic Four, but he saves Mr. Fantastic, as a last heroic deed. The Thinker

and Quasimodo bring the original Human Torch back to life to defeat the Fantastic Four. John Storm and Jim Hammond have a titanic fight. The original Human Torch sacrifices himself to save the Fantastic Four. Dr. Doom deceives the Silver Surfer by befriending him, and then stealing his powers. Doom tries to take over the planet. The Black Panther teams up with the Fantastic Four to defeat Klaw, but first the Black Panther tests the Fantastic Four with a great fight against the Thing, to see if they would be worthy allies. The secret of the Inhuman Black Bolt is revealed. The Fantastic Four admit defeat to Dr. Doom, which Doom's ego loves, and the Sandman, who gets a new costume, almost defeats the Fantastic Four. Reed Richards is shot out into the Negative Zone, and the Inhuman, Triton, saves him. Blastaar is released from the Negative Zone, and attempts to defeat the Fantastic Four, with the Sandman as his partner. Klaw also nearly destroys the Fantastic Four. The Thing becomes jealous when the Silver Surfer befriends his girlfriend Alicia. The Thing goes berserk, and fights the Surfer.

This volume contains the first appearance of the Black Panther, the first African-American superhero, and Jack Kirby's original, unused costume art of the Black Panther. The Introduction is by Stan Lee. (*Marvel Masterworks 28*)

Lee, Stan, Jack Kirby, Chic Stone, et al. *Captain America Masterworks Vol. 1*. New York: Marvel, 2003. ISBN: 078511176X; 078511 2715 (ltd); 0871356309 (1990). Reprints *Tales of Suspense 59–81*.

While Captain America is demonstrating a fitness exercise at Avengers Mansion, Baron Zemo's goons attack him. The Red Skull, who is Hitler's right-hand man, captures Bucky and Captain America during World War II. Twenty years later, the Skull is awakened and is working for A.I.M. A.I.M. creates the Cosmic Cube, and the Skull seeks to rule the galaxy with it. Captain America appeals to the Skull's vanity, and tricks him into dropping the Cube into the ocean. Nick Fury and Captain America fight against an android from THEM.

In this volume, several Golden Age stories are reenvisioned, including Captain America's origin, "The Red Skull Strikes," and "Sando and Omar." In addition to World War II stories, the volume contains present-day stories in which Captain America has to fight several Nazi sleepers whom the Red Skull designed to destroy the Earth twenty years after the war. The original version contains a pin-up. (*Marvel Masterworks 14*)

Lee, Stan, Jack Kirby, Chic Stone, et al. *Marvel Masterworks: The Mighty Thor Vol. 3*. New York: Marvel, 2003. ISBN: 0785112685; 0785112847 (ltd); 0785108149 (2001). Reprints *Journey into Mystery 111–120*; *Mighty Thor Annual 1*.

In this volume, Thor fights the Hulk in an epic battle, and reveals his identity to Jane Foster. He also does battle with the Destroyer, Loki, and Absorbing Man, among others. The volume includes the epic story, "Trial of the Gods," and several mythological "Tales of Asgard." (*Marvel Masterworks 30*)

Lee, Stan, Jack Kirby, Roy Thomas, et al. *X-Men Masterworks Vol. 2*. New York: Marvel, 2003. ISBN: 0785109838; 078511274X (ltd); 0871354829 (1988). Reprints *Uncanny X-Men Vol. 1: 11–21*.

The Stranger kidnaps Magneto and Toad, and takes them to his planet. Professor X explains his origin as his brother, Cain Marko, the Juggernaut, is making his way to the school to destroy it. The Human Torch is brought in to help defeat Juggernaut. The Sentinels are created, and the X-Men are taken captive by them. Mastermold, the chief Sentinel, tries to get Dr. Trask, their creator, to make many more of them so that they can take over and protect humanity. Iceman gets badly hurt in the battle. Magneto defeats the X-Men at the school, and uses DNA from the Angel's parents to create his own army of mutants. It is up to a sickly Iceman to help defeat Magneto, and save the X-Men. The Blob and Unus pose as the X-Men, and begin a series of robberies. They are secretly under the control of the alien Lucifer. Professor X tells the story about how Lucifer took the use of his legs away by dropping a giant slab on him. The X-Men have to defeat the great machine Dominu.

This volume also includes the Juggernaut's origin story and the first appearance of Mimic. Entries for *X-Men Masterworks Vol. 3*. and *X-Men Masterworks Vol. 4*. are located in this chapter subsection under "Thomas." (*Marvel Masterworks Volume 7*)

Lee, Stan, John Romita, Gene Colan, et al. *Daredevil Masterworks Vol. 2*. New York: Marvel, 2004. ISBN: 0785112650; 078511 2928 (ltd); 0785108041 (2001).

Daredevil meets Ka-Zar under unusual circumstances. Ka-Zar's brother, the Plunderer, seeks to create the ultimate weapon. He frames Ka-Zar for murder, and Matt Murdock asks Foggy and Karen to come to England to defend him. The Ox gains some smarts in a weird mind transformation. A group of fake Daredevils attack Spider-Man, and the real Daredevil also ends up fighting Spider-Man, while the Masked Marauder commits his crime. Foggy Nelson pretends to be Daredevil to impress Karen Page, but his plan backfires when the Gladiator wants to fight for real. The Owl kidnaps Matt Murdock to force Murdock to defend him in a mock trail against the judge who sent Owlsley to prison. (*Marvel Masterworks 29*)

Lee, Stan, John Romita, Mickey Demeo, et al. *Spider-Man Masterworks Vol. 6*. New York: Marvel, 2004. ISBN: 0785113622; 0785114 53X (ltd). Reprints *Amazing Spider-Man 51–61*; *Amazing Spider-Man Annual 4*.

Spider-Man meets the Kingpin. The Kingpin takes Jonah Jameson and Spider-Man hostage, and tries to kill them both. Foswell gives his life for Jameson. Peter and Gwen go to a science demonstration for the nullifier, which Dr. Ock steals. Spider-Man looses his memory, and Dr. Ock convinces him that they are partners. Doc Ock moves in with Aunt May, much to Peter's horror, and he attempts to show Aunt May that he is really Spider-Man. Ka-Zar come to New York for the first time, and battles Spider-Man. Jameson uses a new and improved Spider Slayer. Colonel Jameson and Captain Stacy are convinced that Spider-Man is innocent of any crimes. Mary Jane becomes a dancer at the Gloom Room A-Go-Go, which is really a hideout for the Brainwasher. The Kingpin, who is really the Brainwasher, gets Captain Stacy under his spell. Peter slaps Captain Stacy, and Gwen breaks up with him. Peter ends up taking pictures of Stacy robbing police files. Norman Osborn begins to crack, and he begins to remember his past. Spider-Man and the Human Torch team up against Mysterio and the Wizard. They are both lured to a fake movie set.

This volume contains a look at the Coffee Bean, Spider-Man's suit, and his various talents. The introduction is by John Romita Sr. (*Marvel Masterworks 33*)

Lee, Stan, John Romita, Don Heck, et al. *Amazing Spider-Man: Masterworks Vol. 5*. New York: Marvel, 2004. ISBN: 0785111 905; 0785112944 (ltd); 0871359146 (1992). Reprints *Amazing Spider-Man Vol. 1: 41–50*; *Amazing Spider-Man Annual 3*.

Betty Brant and Ned Leeds announce their marriage. Spider-Man has to fight with a broken arm, and Peter Parker meets Mary Jane for the first time. Flash Thompson is going to Vietnam. Spider-Man fights John Jameson who wants to be a superhero, and he eventually gets sick from Space Spores which also him some special powers. Daredevil suggests that Spider-Man would be a good Avenger, and Spider-Man is asked to join, but he fails the test the Avengers give him. Spider-Man ends up fighting the Hulk. Kraven comes back and almost kills Norman Osborn, but Spider-Man saves him, and Peter Parker moves in with Harry Osborn. Curt Connors becomes the Lizard again. A new Vulture starts prowling around New York, and teams up with Kraven. When Foswell tries to take over the mob, the Kingpin is not amused. Parker decides to quit being Spider-Man.

The Shocker and the Rhino are introduced in this volume, and the Rhino's origin story is told. Stan Lee wrote the introduction. (*Marvel Masterworks 22*)

Thomas, Roy, Werner Roth, Dick Ayers, et al. *X-Men Marvel Masterworks Vol. 3*. New York, Marvel, 2003. ISBN: 0785112693; 0785112804 (ltd); 0785108092 (2001). Reprints *X-Men Vol. 1: 22–31*.

Count Nefaria captures the X-Men and holds the Washington, D.C. hostage for $100,000. He tries to get the X-Men to join his criminal organization, the Maggia. He has already recruited the Eel, Porcupine, Plantman, Scarecrow, and the Unicorn. The X-Men pretend to join his organization. A research entomologist unleashes a chemical which can make insects huge. He dons a costume and calls himself the Locust. The X-Men have to go to Central America to fight the Mayan god Kukulcan. Jean Grey's parents force her to leave Xavier's school and the X-Men, and go to a regular college in New York. The Puppet Master tries to control Mimic against the X-Men, with little success. Spider-Man is asked to join the X-Men. Mimic briefly joins the X-Men, and becomes leader when Cyclops steps down after inadvertently shooting Angel during a battle. Banshee, who is under the power of the Ogre and Factor Three, tries to capture Professor X.

Other villains in this volume include the Super Adaptoid, the first Warlock, and a Blue Iron Man look-alike, Cobalt Man. The volume also contains Banshee's first appearance, cover sketches for *X-Men 25* and *33*, and an X-Men pin-up. Roy Thomas wrote the introduction. The 2001 edition contained pin-ups of Beast and Cyclops, which have now been moved to Vol.1. (*Marvel Masterworks 33*)

Thomas, Roy, Werner Roth, Don Heck, et al. *X-Men Masterworks Vol. 4.* New York: Marvel, 2004. ISBN: 0785116087 (ltd); 0785116079. Reprints *Uncanny X-Men Vol. 1: 32–42.*

The Juggernaut breaks free of his imprisonment at the Xavier school. Professor X is wounded, and Juggernaut is sucked into the Cyttorak jewel. Jean Grey learns that the Ancient One dealt with the Cyttorak demon hundreds of years earlier. The X-Men are caught in the middle of a battle between Tyrannus and the Mole Man. Factor Three captures Professor X and Banshee, and the X-Men fight Spider-Man, thinking that he is a part of Factor Three. The X-Men are put on trial for treason against their fellow mutants, by the leader of Factor Three who is really an alien, Homo Superior. The Blob, Mastermind, the Vanisher, and Unus are all being used by Factor Three against the X-Men. The X-Men get new costumes, and fight an android version of the Frankenstein monster. While saving the world from the Sub-Human Grotesk, Professor X dies, but it is actually the Changeling who is impersonating Xavier who dies.

This volume also contains stories in which Professor X brings Cyclops aboard as the first of the X-Men; the first evil mutant, the Living Diamond, wants to use Scott Summers for his own purpose; the FBI/secret government becomes aware of mutants; the prototype for the mutant-finding machine Cerebro, known as Cyberno, is first used by Xavier. The volume includes the banned cover for *X-Men 33* and the unused cover for *X-Men 38*. The introduction is by Roy Thomas. (*Marvel Masterworks 35*)

Paperback Masterworks

Claremont, Chris, Len Wein, Dave Cockrum, et al. *All New All Different X-Men Masterworks Vol. 1.* New York: Marvel, 1993. ISBN: 087135988X. Reprints *X-Men: Giant Size 1; X-Men 94–97.*

This paperback version of the *X-Men Masterworks 11* does not contain reprints all of the issues, but it does contain a behind-the-scenes look at creating the new X-Men, and an introduction by Chris Claremont, two things which are not in the hardback version.

Lee, Stan, Steve Ditko, Art Simek, et al. *Spider-Man: Masterworks Volume 1.* New York: Marvel, 1992. ISBN: 0871359022. Reprints *Amazing Fantasy 15; Amazing Spider-Man 1–5.*

This volume contains the origin story of Spider-Man, and his first battles with the Chameleon, Vulture, Sandman and Doctor Doom. In the book, Spider-Man saves the Earth from aliens, who form an alliance with the Tinker to take over the Earth. The volume includes a special section on "How Stan Lee and Steve Ditko Create Spider-Man," and a Masterwork pin-up page.

Lee, Stan, Steve Ditko, Art Simek, et al., *Spider-Man: Masterworks Volume 1.* New York: Marvel, 1992. ISBN: 0871359022. Reprints

Amazing Fantasy 15; Amazing Spider-Man 1–5.

This volume contains the original story of Spider-Man, and his first battles with the Chameleon, Vulture, Sandman and Doctor Doom. In the book, Spider-Man saves the Earth from aliens, who form an alliance with the Tinker to take over the Earth. The volume includes a special section on "How Stan Lee and Steve Ditko Create Spider-Man," and a Masterwork pin-up page.

Lee, Stan, Jack Kirby, Steve Ditko, et al. *Monster Masterworks.* New York: Marvel, 1989. ISBN: 0871355922. Reprints *Where Monsters Dwell 2–3, 6, 10, 15–16, 21, 35; Journey Into Mystery 10; Where Creatures Roam 1, 4, 7; Creatures on the Loose 3; Fear 2–3; Uncanny Tales from the Grave 12; Amazing Fantasy 4; Tales of Suspense 28.*

This is a wonderful collection of early monster stories, featuring Groot, the Glop, Vandoom, the Blip, Sporr, Zzutak, Titan, Gigantus, and Iron Man's nemesis, Fin Fang Foom, among others. Monsters created from atomic tests, like Grottu, King of Insects, or those used to stop communist aggression, like

Fin Fang Foom, provide interesting insights into the Cold War during the sixties. The book includes the famous Lee/Kirby story, "A Martian Walks Among Us," which is about a Martian invasion of Earth, thwarted by a Venusian. The introduction is by Jack Kirby. The book is highly recommended.

Lee, Stan, Jack Kirby, Don Heck, et al. *Avengers: Masterworks Volume 1*. New York: Marvel, 1993. ISBN: 0871359839. Reprints *Avengers 1–5*.

This paperback volume contains reprints of the first five issues of *Avengers*, which include the formation of the team and Captain America's first appearance.

The book also contains an introduction by Stan Lee, and a reprint of Jack Kirby's original, unused artwork for page 22 of *Avengers 3*.

Lee, Stan, Jack Kirby, Paul Reinman, et al. *The Uncanny X-Men: Masterworks Vol. 1*. New York: Marvel, 1993. ISBN: 0871359642 (pbk). Reprints *Uncanny X-Men 1–5*.

This volume features the origin of the X-Men and their first encounter with Magneto. It includes their first encounters with the Blob and the Brotherhood of Evil Mutants, Quicksilver, the Scarlet Witch, and the Vanisher. In the book, the Angel gets trapped in a scrap with Magneto.

Barnes and Noble Paperback Masterworks Reprints

Claremont, Chris, Dave Cockrum, John Byrne, et al. *Uncanny X-Men Masterworks Vol. 2*. New York: Marvel/Barnes and Noble, 2004. ISBN: 0760755663. Reprints *Uncanny X-Men 101–110*.

In this volume Marvel Girl turns into Phoenix; the X-Men battle Eric the Red and Firelord; the X-Men do battle with mental constructs of the old X-Men, dressed in their old uniforms; the X-Men help Princess Lilandra stop her brother from gaining power from the M'Krann Crystal, which has the potential to wipe the Universe; Warkhawk infiltrates the Xavier mansion; and Magneto returns. The volume includes appearances by the Fantastic Four, Clark Gable, Groucho Marx, and Douglas Fairbanks.

Claremont, Chris, Len Wein, Dave Cockrum, et al. *Uncanny X-Men Masterworks Vol. 1*. New York: Marvel/Barnes and Noble. 2003. ISBN: 0760749582. Reprints *Giant Size X-Men 1*; *Uncanny X-Men 94–100*.

In this volume, the new X-Men team is formed to help save the old X-Men from a mutant island; the Sentinels return; Thunderbird dies; Havok, under the influence of Eric the Red, fights his brother Cyclops and the rest of the X-Men; and Jean Grey pilots a ship through a radiation storm. The volume also contains other classic stories, plus appearances by Stan Lee, Jack Kirby, and Geraldo.

Lee, Stan, John Buscema, Jack Kirby, et al. *The Silver Surfer Masterworks Vol. 1*. New York: Marvel/Barnes and Noble, 2003. ISBN: 0760746974. Reprints *Silver Surfer Vol. 1: 1–6; Fantastic Four Annual 5*.

This volume contains the story of the origin of the Silver Surfer and his early adventures in which he deals with Thor, Loki, the Stranger, and Mephisto. In a bonus story, the Surfer frees Quasimodo, a sentient computer whose program is mass destruction, from his electronic prison, only to find out that he has un-

leashed a terror upon mankind. This is epic storytelling at its finest. In the introduction, Stan Lee describes the Surfer as his favorite character.

Lee, Stan, Steve Ditko, John Romita, et al. *Amazing Spider-Man Masterworks Vol. 4*. New York: Marvel/Barnes and Noble, 2004. ISBN: 0760763038. Reprints *Amazing Spider-Man 31–40*.

This volume contains Steve Ditko's final run on Spider-Man. In it Gwen Stacy appears for the first time; she thinks that Peter Parker was snubbing her when he was concerned about his sick aunt, and not paying attention to her; Betty Brant quits the *Daily Bugle*; the Green Goblin learns Spider-Man's secret identity; and Spider-Man learns the Goblin's identity.

Lee, Stan, Steve Ditko, Sam Rosen, et al. *The Amazing Spider-Man Masterworks Vol 2*. New York: Marvel/Barnes and Noble, 2003. ISBN: 0760749574. Reprints *Amazing Spider-Man 11–19*; *Amazing Spider-Man Annual 1*.

In this volume, Spider-Man has encounters with the Green Goblin; the Hulk; the Sandman; the Sinister Six, which includes first-time encounters with Mysterio, Daredevil, and Kraven; and the Human Torch. In addition to a gallery of Spider-Man's famous foes, this volume contains the secrets of Spider-Man, his house, his classmates, and his girlfriend. There is a special section on how Stan Lee and Steve Ditko create Spider-Man.

Lee, Stan, Steve Ditko, Sam Rosen, et al. *Amazing Spider-Man Masterworks Vol. 3*. New York: Marvel/Barnes and Noble 2004. ISBN: 0760755655. Reprints *Amazing Spider-Man Vol. 1: 20–30*; *Amazing Spider-Man Annual 2*.

This volume contains stories in which the Human Torch and Spider-Man get into a fight; the Green Goblin tries to take over the gangster rackets; Aunt May finds the Spider-Man costume, and Peter Parker has to buy an ill-fitting costume from a costume shop; the Scorpion tries to kill J. J. Jameson; and Peter Parker and Betty Brant break up. It also contains the origins of the Scorpion, the first Spider Slayer, and the Molten Man.

Lee, Stan, Steve Ditko, Art Simek, et al. *The Amazing Spider-Man Masterworks Vol. 1.* New York: Marvel/Barnes and Noble, 2003. ISBN: 0760737932. Reprints *Amazing Fantasy 15; Amazing Spider-Man 1–10.*

This volume contains the origin of Spider-Man, and it introduces several key villains, including Sandman, Vulture, Dr. Doom, Doctor Octopus, and the Lizard. Some main characters who are introduced, include Aunt May, Betty Brant, J. J. Jameson, and Flash Thompson. The volume also contains unused cover art from *Amazing Fantasy 15*, and *Amazing Spider-Man 10*. It has a special pin-up by Steve Ditko.

Lee, Stan, Bill Everett, Wally Wood, et al. *Daredevil Masterworks Vol. 1.* New York: Marvel/Barnes and Noble, 2003. ISBN. 0760737940. Reprints *Daredevil 1–11.*

In this volume Daredevil goes from his yellow costume to his red one; Karen Page starts to fall in love with Daredevil's alter ego, the blind Matt Murdock, and tries to get him to have eye surgery; Matt visits a doctor who may be able to help him, buts ends up in the clutches of a dictator; and Matt's partner Foggy Nelson is asked by the Reform Party to run for the office of district attorney of New York. The book also contains appearances by Mr. Fear, the Ox, and the Eel; Daredevil's origin story; and the origins of various villains, including the Owl, the Purple Man, and the Stilt Man.

Lee, Stan, Jack Kirby, Dick Ayers. *Fantastic Four Masterworks Vol. 1.* New York: Marvel/Barnes and Noble, 2003. ISBN: 0760737 959. Reprints *Fantastic Four 1–10.*

This is a special paperback printing of Marvel's flagship title which ushered in the Marvel Age of Comics. In this volume, the Sub-Mariner returns out of the pages of the Golden Age of Timely/Atlas Comics. The stories in the book include the Fantas-

tic Four's origin; the Skrulls impersonating the Fantastic Four, in order to turn the world against them; the Fantastic Four, who are broke, being hired by the Sub-Mariner, who is wealthy, to star in a movie that is very successful; the Sub-Mariner losing a fight that he tricked the Fantastic Four into; and Dr. Doom assuming Richards's body to trick the Fantastic Four into defeat.

Lee, Stan, Jack Kirby, Steve Ditko, *Marvel Masterworks: The Incredible Hulk Vol. 1.* New York: Marvel/Barnes and Noble, 2003. ISBN: 0760737967. Reprints *Hulk Vol. 1: 1–6.*

This volume includes the original Hulk stories by Stan Lee. If one reads between the lines, these stories can be seen as statements on the Cold War and the evils of communism. Although written during the early sixties, the stories mirror popular culture's concern at that time about communism and the preservation of the American way of life.

Lee, Stan, Jack Kirby, Don Heck. *Avengers Masterworks Vol. 1.* New York: Marvel/Barnes and Noble, 2003. ISBN: 076074808X. Reprints *Avengers 1–10.*

This volume contains the early, classic stories that feature one of Marvel's flagship titles. It reprints the tale of the formation of the Avengers with Thor, Iron Man, Hulk, Wasp, and Ant-Man. By issue 2, the Hulk leaves, and in Issue 4, Captain America joins the Avengers. Featured villains include Space Phantom, Lava Mean, Baron Zemo, Wonder Man, Kang, Immortus, and the Masters of Evil.

Lee, Stan, Jack Kirby, Phil Lord, et al. *The X-Men: Masterworks Vol. 1.* New York: Marvel/Barnes and Noble, 2003. ISBN: 07607 37975. Reprints *X-Men 1–10.*

This special paperback edition features the first adventures of the X-Men, and includes the story of the formation of the initial X-Men team under Professor X. The volume also features the first appearance of Magneto and the Brotherhood of Evil Mutants, and future Avengers Quicksilver and Scarlet Witch. In this volume the X-Men journey to the Savage Land, Magneto gets the Blob to join the Brotherhood of Evil Mutants, and Magneto betrays the Blob. The book also includes special pin-ups of Cyclops, the Beast, and Jean Grey. Stan Lee wrote the introduction.

6

Marvel's Essentials Series

Use your crucifixes! Save yourselves! Believe in your God—He is your only
Salvation now.... Do what I say, otherwise you will be slain.—*Dracula, to a group
of young children about to be killed by his former followers*

If one wishes to rule with a hand of iron, one must make it appear that the hand
holds only sugar.... Today the fight is between cold inanimate weapons.... [T]he
soldiers of today know little of true warfare.—*Dracula*

In order to save the universe we have to destroy it.—*Wolverine*

Avengers, Ant-Man, Captain America, Iron Man, and Thor

Avengers

Lee, Stan, Jack Kirby, Don Heck, et al. *Essential Avengers Vol. 1.* New York: Marvel, 2001. ISBN: 0785107010; 0785118624 (2005). Reprints *Avengers 1–24.*

The Hulk, not really a team player, leaves the Avengers. Captain America, who is found frozen in suspended animation after twenty years, is revived and joins the team. Sub-Mariner and the Hulk team up against the Avengers. The Masters of Evil team is formed by Baron Zemo who gives Simon Williams the power of Wonder Man. Wonder Man befriends the Avengers, but is secretly working for Zemo. He ends up helping the Avengers, and dies in the process. Despite Captain America's protests, Rick Jones wants to be an Avenger. Kang uses a robotic Spider-Man to deceive the Avengers. Iron Man misses an important Avengers meeting. When Giant Man gets an alarm from his ants, Thor finds it hard to believe. The ants' warnings are correct, and once again the Mole Man tries to take over the surface world. During a battle, the Wasp is terminally injured. The Avengers search for the only doctor who can save her, but aliens have kidnapped him. The U.S. Army engages the Avengers

in a battle. Steve Rogers, Captain America, writes to Nick Fury, asking to join his espionage organization, S.H.I.E.L.D. Zemo adds the Black Knight and the Melter to the Masters of Evil. During a battle with Captain America, Zemo is killed. Thor, Iron Man, Giant Man, and the Wasp leave the Avengers and Captain America to put together a new team. This new team features Hawkeye, Quicksilver and the Scarlet Witch. They ask Sub-Mariner to join, but he declines. The "new" Avengers search for the Hulk, to ask him to consider joining the team once again. The Swordsman, while aligning himself with the Mandarin, tries to join the "new" Avengers, for his own nefarious purposes. Captain America's letter to Fury falls into the wrong hands. The Avengers are defeated by the Enchantress and the original Power Man who frames them for crimes they did not commit. This causes them to fall out of favor with the public, and they are asked to disband. Captain America leaves the Avengers, and Kang kidnaps the remaining Avengers to the future. Captain America finds out about Kang's plans, and goes to the future to find out why. Kang's guard commander betrays him, and Kang has to align himself with the Avengers. Kang's love, the Princess, is killed.

Stan Lee and Jack Kirby's second, groundbreaking superhero team featured the Hulk, Iron Man, Thor, Ant-Man, and the Wasp. This volume also features communist villain the Commissar.

Lee, Stan, Don Heck, Roy Thomas, et al. *Essential Avengers Vol. 2*. New York: Marvel, 2001. ISBN: 078510741X. Reprints *King Size Avengers 1*; *Avengers 25–46*; *Tales to Astonish 27*.

The Avengers meet Dr. Doom. He lures them to Latveria, and quickly captures them. The Wasp gets captured by the evil Attuma, who plans to flood the Earth in his never-ending desire to take over the surface world. She calls on the Avengers for help, and they too are captured, except for Hawkeye. The Beetle breaks into the Avengers' mansion and has a showdown with Hawkeye. He defeats the Beetle, and seeks out his captured comrades. Captain America destroys Attuma's tide machine. The Wasp and Giant Man rejoin the Avengers, and Scarlet Witch designs a new costume for Giant Man, who becomes Goliath. The Collector tries to capture the Avengers, but he and his crony the Beetle are defeated. Goliath nearly dies trying to size down, and is now stuck at ten feet. He becomes self-absorbed and insecure. The Black Widow, who is working for the Soviets, recruits the Swordsman and Power Man to destroy the Avengers. While searching for Dr. Anton, who might be able to cure him, Goliath finds the Keeper of the Flame, and is captured. Quicksilver and the Scarlet Witch go back to their homeland when they find out their power is decimating. Goliath goes to South America and gets involved in a civil war between two political factions who both are trying to be the keeper of the Cobalt fire. Hank Pym, Goliath, gets a new assistant, the African-American Bill Foster. The Avengers go up against a racist organization, the Serpent Society, that is trying to divide America. Goliath makes a speech against the society, but Captain America, who is seemingly duped by them, is a disciple. The Living Laser kidnaps the Wasp, in an early example of obsessive stalking. The Laser also captures Hawkeye and Captain America, and the Avengers and the Black Widow are captured by the alien Ultroids. Quicksilver and the Scarlet Witch return to the team, and fight against the colossal Ixar the Invincible. Under a spell cast by the Enchantress, Hercules fights the Avengers. Instead of always baiting Captain America, Hawkeye is now bickering with Goliath. Hawkeye wants the Black Widow to be accepted for membership in the Avengers, but Nick Fury and S.H.I.E.L.D. ask her to go undercover. Hercules is exiled on Earth, and stays with the Avengers. Black Widow becomes a traitor to America. The Sub-Mariner learns about the powerful Cosmic Cube, and goes head to head with the Avengers for it. The Avengers fight a Soviet version of Captain America. The Red Guardian turns out to be the Black Widow's long-lost husband. The Black Widow is hurt in the battle, and is hospitalized. Hercules, who is sweet on the Scarlet Witch, becomes the newest member of the Avengers. Thor and Iron Man join the new Avengers in a battle against the Mandarin and his "team of evil," which features Power Man, Enchantress, Execution, Living Laser and the Swordsman. Janet Van Dyne, the Wasp, inherits several million dollars. The Fantastic Four make a cameo.

Other villains in this volume include Super Adaptoid, Dragon Man, and Whirlwind, among others. The book also includes an inside look at Avengers Mansion, pin-ups of Hercules and the Avengers, and the original story about Hank Pym, "Man in the Ant Hill."

Thomas, Roy, Neal Adams, John Buscema, et al. *Essential Avengers Vol. 4*. New York: Marvel, 2004. ISBN: 0785114858. Reprints *Avengers Vol. 1: 69–97*; *Incredible Hulk Vol. 2: 140*.

The Avengers are transported to Kang's future, where they have to play a game with the Grand Master. In this game, the Earth's future hangs in the balance. The Avengers fight the Squadron Sinister for the first time, and they also fight the Invaders who think the three Avengers are Nazis. The Black Knight becomes an Avenger. The Zodiac captures the Avengers, and the Sons of the Serpent, who capture the Black Panther, attempt to discredit him as a criminal. The Panther takes a day job teaching at a school, and meets Monica Lynne who will become his girlfriend. The Avengers, with Quicksilver back in the fold, try to rescue the Scarlet Witch who has been taken to an alternate world by Arkon. Arkon promptly defeats Quicksilver, the Witch and the Toad. He wants Wanda as his wife, but she is not interested in loving a conqueror. The Black Widow dumps Goliath, who is now Hawkeye. The Avengers hire themselves out to do basic labor for an evil land monger. The Lethal Legion is formed, featuring an old enemy of Black Panther, Man-Ape. The Legion's goal is to take down the Avengers. Red Wolf, one of the first Native American heroes, allies himself with the Avengers to save his land from real estate developers. Briefly, Daredevil aids the Avengers. The Wasp, Black Widow, Medusa, Scarlett Witch, and Valkyrie form a women's lib superhero group, the Liberators. They defeat the male Avengers, along with Klaw, Whirlwind, and the Melter. Arkon, a spell of the Enchantress, tries to defeat the Avengers again, but the Black Knight helps the Avengers against Arkon. The Avengers go to an alternate universe and help the Squadron Supreme save their Earth from Brain Child. T'Challa seeks to go back to Africa. The Hulk is taken prisoner by Psyklop, who wants to use the Hulk's power to help feed the Dark God's powerful energies. The Hulk is reduced and sent to the Microverse, where he falls in love with Jarella.

In this volume we learn Red Wolf's and the Black Panther's origins. This volume also includes the epic story, "The Kree-Skrull War." *Essential Avengers Vol. 5* (ISBN: 0785120874) was published in 2005.

Thomas, Roy, John Buscema, Don Heck, et al. *Essential Avengers Vol. 3*. New York: Marvel, 2001. ISBN: 0785107878. Reprints *Avengers 47–68*; *Avengers Annual 2*.

The Avengers meet Magneto and the Toad. Dane Whitman, nephew of the "evil" Black Knight who has died, takes on the mantle of the Black Knight, but is a force for good. He tries to aid the Avengers, but initially they spurn him. Captain America leaves the Avengers. Hercules goes back to Olympus, and finds it deserted. Typhon has taken control of Olympus, and Hercules tries to defeat him. Quicksilver and Scarlet Witch are taken prisoner by Magneto. Hawkeye and Goliath are always arguing. Hercules leaves the Avengers and goes back to live with the gods. The Collector gets Thor to fight against the Avengers. Captain America recommends that the Black Panther be admitted to the Avengers roster, and the Grim Reaper takes revenge on them for the death of his brother Wonder Man. The Avengers fight the original X-Men. Quicksilver, and the Scarlet Witch stay

with Magneto. Magneto tries to reason with the United Nations. A new group, the Masters of Evil, is formed, and Jarvis ends up betraying the Avengers. Captain America goes back in time to see if he could have saved Bucky. The new Avengers fight the original Avengers, which included the Hulk, under the machinations of the Scarlet Centurion. Ultron creates a synthoid, the Vision, who is used to kill the Avengers. The Vision has Simon Williams's brain patterns. Yellowjacket is introduced, and marries the Wasp. Dr. Strange seeks the aid of the Avengers against Surtur and Ymir. One of the Black Panther's subjects tries to usurp the Panther's power. The Vision helps create another version of Ultron made of admantium. Hawkeye becomes Goliath, and his brother dies.

In this volume, we learn the origin of both Vision and Ultron. This volume also contains the funny "Avenjerks Assemble," starring Roy Thomas.

Ant-Man

Lee, Stan, Jack Kirby, Don Heck, et al. *The Essential Astonishing Ant-Man Vol. 1*. New York: Marvel, 2002. ISBN: 078510822X. Reprints *Tales to Astonish 27*; *35–69*.

Henry Pym meets his future wife and crime-fighting partner, Janet Van Dyne, the Wasp. One of the more colorful villains in the Marvel pantheon, Egghead, tries to best Ant-Man by turning the ants against him. When Henry Pym discovers his ability to shrink, he also learns how to communicate with ants and other insects. Pym uses a wide variety of bugs in his crime fighting, including alien bugs, termites, bees and wasps. Egghead pits Spider-Man against Ant-Man in a big misunderstanding. Pym's special ant, Korr, is killed. When Pym tries to get the Hulk

to rejoin the Avengers, they just end up fighting, but ultimately the Hulk saves Giant Man's life from a nuclear explosion. Ant-Man fights against such characters as Porcupine, the Black Knight, Trago, the Human Top, Wrecker, an early Colossus, Attuma, and Madam Macabre, among others. Captain America, Thor, and Iron Man make cameos.

This volume covers Henry Pym's origins as Ant/Giant Man. These stories contain a soap-opera type of romance between Pym and Janet Van Dyne, who as the Wasp has her own feature stories which tell little morality and solo crime-fighting tales. One of these is a great story in which she fights against the Magician. The Ant-Man stories are fun to read, even though they might seem cheesy to the modern reader.

Captain America

Lee, Stan, Jack Kirby, Sam Rosen, et al. *The Essential Captain America Vol. 1*. New York: Marvel, 2000. ISBN: 0785107041. Reprints *Tales of Suspense 59–99*; *Captain America 100–102*; *Captain America Comics 10*.

Captain America has to fight several Nazi sleepers, designed by the Red Skull to destroy the Earth twenty years after World War II. The Skull is awakened and starts working for A.I.M. A.I.M. creates the Cosmic Cube, and the Skull seeks to rule the galaxy with it. The Skull continues to return, even though seemingly he is always being killed. Captain America meets the Black Panther, and they both have to fight against a fake Baron Zemo. Steve Rogers falls in love, briefly decides to give up being a costumed hero, and reveals himself to the world. The Red Skull awakens a fourth Sleeper, and another Master Planner is introduced.

In this volume, there are several stories that revolve

around Captain America's role in the Avengers, as well as stories about his adventures during World War II. Several Golden Age stories are "re-envisioned," including Captain America's origin, the Red Skull's origin as Hitler's right-hand man, and "Sando and Omar." Captain America was reintroduced to the Marvel Universe in the sixties. In addition, there are present day stories, and a bonus, short forties adventure story.

Lee, Stan, Jack Kirby, Jim Steranko, et al. *Essential Captain America Vol. 2*. New York: Marvel, 2002. ISBN: 0785108270. Reprints *Captain America 103–126*.

Steve Rogers and Sharon Carter have ups and downs in their relationship. Steve wants her to leave S.H.I.E.L.D., or at least take less dangerous assignments. When the Red Skull captures Carter, Rogers as Captain America has to swing into action. Carter finally agrees to stop the dangerous espionage assignments, but does put herself in danger in an attempt to save Captain America from a trap. He misunderstands her motives, and accuses her of lying to him. He also believes that Nick Fury lied to him. Captain America fights Batroc, the Living Laser, and the Swordsman, while a dangerous bomb is about to go off. The Asian communists attempt to replicate Steve Rogers and Captain America, and a psychiatrist tries to drive Steve Rogers insane. Captain America reminisces about his beginnings, and about Bucky. He meets the Hulk and Rick Jones for the first time. Rick Jones wants to train with Captain America, and be his sidekick like Bucky was, but Captain America is very reluctant. He eventually relents, and allows Jones to fight by his side. Captain America is believed dead, and the Red Skull exchanges bodies with him through

the use of the Cosmic Cube. As the Red Skull, Captain America tries to convince the Avengers he is the real thing. The Red Skull, as Captain America, makes Rick Jones feel less than useful, and preys on his insecurities, and Jones believes he will never be able to compete with Bucky. Captain America meets the Falcon, and they form a bond of friendship. Modok tries to kidnap a scientist, while infiltrating a student radical group, and Suprema tries to take over S.H.I.E.L.D. Captain America visits Vietnam for the first time. The Falcon is framed for a crime he did not commit, and Captain America tries to clear him.

This volume contains the Falcon's origin story. Other villains who appear in this volume include Diamond Head, Man Brute, the Trapster, and the Scorpion. *Essential Captain America Vol. 3* was published in 2006 (ISBN: 0785121668).

Iron Man

Lee, Stan, Don Heck, Steve Ditko, et al. *Essential Iron Man Volume 1.* New York: Marvel, 2002. ISBN: 078511002X; 0785107592 (2000). Reprints *Tales of Suspense 39–72.*

Billionaire industrialist Tony Stark is taken prisoner and mortally wounded in Vietnam. With the help of another scientist, he creates the Iron Man armor and defeats the communist overlord who took him captive. The Angel from the X-Men gets caught in a radioactive storm, and becomes evil. He leaves the X-Men, and Iron Man has to help him fight the evil transformation. The Mandarin captures Iron Man, and almost kills him. Hawkeye and the Black Widow are introduced as villains. Hawkeye falls in love with the Black Widow, and both try to destroy Iron Man. Iron Man fights an odd version of Captain America, masterminded by the Chameleon. Tony Stark is believed dead, and Iron Man is the prime suspect. Happy Hogan decides that Stark is Iron Man. When Iron Man's armor is stolen, Stark has to use his old gold suit to defeat the villainous new Iron Man. Iron Man has a difficult run-in with the evil Black Knight. During a battle between Titanium Man and Iron Man, Happy Hogan is badly wounded.

Some of the other villains that fight Iron Man in this volume include the Melter, Mister Doll, Jack Frost, the Red Barbarian, Scarecrow, Unicorn, Crimson Dynamo, and the Mad Thinker. By the second Iron Man story, Stark has changed his gray suit for a gold one. Throughout his early years as Iron Man, Stark kept changing the style of his suit, and updating it with useful transistors and gadgets. These stories read like a treatise on the Cold War, with Premier Nikita Khrushchev making a number of appearances. The Mandarin is introduced in this volume, and his origin story is told. The evil Dr. Strange, whom Iron Man

fights in this volume, has no connection to the supernatural mystic of *Strange Tales.* This volume includes a brief essay on unused *Suspense* covers. ISBN: 0785118608 (2005).

Lee, Stan, Don Heck, Gene Colan, et al. *Essential Iron Man Volume 2.* New York: Marvel, 2004. ISBN: 0785114874. Reprints *Tales to Astonish 82; Tales of Suspense 73–99; Iron Man and Sub-Mariner 1; Iron Man 1–11.*

Happy Hogan is transformed into the Freak, and Tony Stark tries to find a way to bring him back to normal. Pepper Potts and Happy get married. The Mandarin tries to defeat Iron Man by using Ultimo. He also suspects that Tony Stark is Iron Man, and has Stark accused of acting like a "commie pinko." Sub-Mariner and Iron Man have a titanic battle. Titanium Man kidnaps Pepper Potts, and Iron Man surrenders. Happy Hogan dons the Iron Man armor, and fights the Mandarin. The Mole Man makes a portion of Stark's complex collapse into the ground. Tony Stark goes back to Vietnam, and has to contend with Half Face. The young Jasper Sitwell is introduced as S.H.I.E.L.D.'s representative at Stark's lab. Sitwell falls in love with a woman, who is actually the head of the criminal empire Maggia. A.I.M. boards the Maggia ship in an attempt to steal Iron Man's armor and destroy the Maggia crime syndicate. Iron Man fights an android version of the Hulk, but goes easy on him, because the Hulk used to be an Avenger. Iron Man slaps Jasper Sitwell.

Several other villains who appear in this volume include the Gladiator, Cerebrus computer, the Crusher, Demolisher, Unicorn, and Grey Gargoyle. This volume was reprinted in 2006.

Thor

Lee, Stan, Jack Kirby, Larry Leiber, et al. *The Essential Thor Vol 1*. New York: Marvel, 2001. ISBN: 0785107614; 0785118667 (2005). Reprints *Journey into Mystery 83–112*.

Thor tries to persuade his father Odin to let him marry Jane Foster. Merlin the magician comes back as a power-hunger tyrant. Thor becomes a slave to Zarrko, the Tomorrow Man. Odin is still very upset that Thor gives his love to the human Jane Foster, and finds this love to be insubordinate. The Enchantress and the Executioner try to get Thor away from Jane Foster, and Odin comes to Earth to reason with Thor. While Odin is gone, Loki frees Skagg, the storm giant, and Surtur, the fire demon. On Earth, Thor, Balder, and Odin fight them, while Odin casts a spell so that humanity does not know that such a fight is taking place. Thor fights against the team of the Cobra and Mr. Hyde. Donald Blake seemingly sells out Thor to Hyde and Cobra. Thor asks for Dr. Strange's help against the magic of Loki. Magneto asks Thor to join him, thinking Thor is another mutant. Jane Foster is almost killed, and Odin helps to heal her. Thor comes across a group of kids who are arguing over who is stronger, Hulk or Thor, and he tells them the stories of his various battles with the Hulk. The Avengers and JFK make cameo appearances.

Other characters that make appearances in this volume include the Lava Man, Carbon Copy Man, and Grey Gargoyle. This volume reprints the stories of Thor's origin, his earliest adventures, and his first battles with his half brother, Loki. It also presents the origins of the Frost Giants, Odin and the Buri, the first of the Norse gods. The tales that feature the early life of Thor include the origin of Loki; Balder's first adventure, showing his purity of heart; the secret of Sigurd; Thor trapped by trolls; Thor getting his hammer; and Heimdall's first time guarding the Rainbow Bridge. The volume also contains two tales of Asgard, a map of Asgard, Thor and Loki pin-ups, a Thor biography, and a weapons and paraphernalia outline. These stories are a joy to read. *Essential Thor Vol. 2* (ISBN: 0785115919) was published in 2005, and *Essential Thor Vol. 3* (ISBN: 0785121498) was published in 2006.

Daredevil

Lee, Stan, Gene Colan, Artie Simek, et al. *Essential Daredevil Vol. 2*. New York: Marvel, 2004. ISBN: 0785114629. Reprints *Daredevil 26–48*; *Daredevil Special 1*; *Fantastic Four 73*.

The Masked Marauder's identity is revealed, and he takes Matt, Foggy and Karen hostage. Daredevil helps Spider-Man with some two-bit hoods. Stilt Man and the Marauder team up. Matt reveals that his brother Mike is Daredevil, and he plays this charade throughout most of the book. Daredevil fights a group of aliens. Matt pretends to be Daredevil, to rescue Karen Page who has been taken captive by the Boss. Mr. Hyde and the Cobra team up, and Daredevil dons a Thor costume, and pretends to be Thor. Thor, of course, is not amused. Hyde attacks Daredevil with a chemical that blinds him, and results in all of his radar senses being turned off. Foggy makes a brave attempt to stop the Beetle. Electro puts together the Emissaries of Evil, featuring the Gladiator, Leap Frog, Matador, and the Stilt Man. The Trapster dons a Daredevil costume, and breaks into the Baxter Building, wanting to fight the Fantastic Four. Foggy starts dating Deborah Harris, a former convict. He initially dates her in secret, because he is running for the office of district attorney of New York and he is afraid of what the press would say and what effect the publicity would have. Dr. Doom takes Daredevil hostage, and switches bodies with him in order to fight the Fantastic Four. Daredevil warns the Fantastic Four that Doom is in his body, and when Daredevil returns to his normal self, the Fantastic Four believe it is Doom, and try to take him down. Spider-Man and Thor help in the fight. The Exterminator hires the Unholy Three to do his dirty work to fight Daredevil. Exterminator comes up with a device which will immobilize people for a brief period of time. Foggy's girlfriend Debbie and Daredevil are shot; in his battle with the Exterminator, Mike Murdock dies and a new Daredevil is born. A new villain similar to the Joker is introduced, the bizarre Jester who frames Daredevil for murder. Matt sends Karen away because he can't reveal his love to her. Daredevil fights Captain America in Madison Square Garden. He entertains some soldiers in 'Nam, and befriends Willie Lincoln. Karen comes back to the office, and Matt finally kisses her. Foggy Nelson wins the election for D.A.

This volume contains the Beetle's origin story, and pin-up pages for the cast of characters. There is a story conference between Stan Lee and Gene Colon, showing how they write and draw Daredevil. *Essential Daredevil Vol. 3.* was released in 2005 (ISBN: 0785 117245).

Lee, Stan, Wally Wood, John Romita, et al. *The Essential Daredevil Vol. 1*. New York: Marvel, 2002. ISBN: 0785109498; 0785118616 (2005). Reprints *Daredevil: Man Without Fear 1–25*.

Karen Page falls in love with Daredevil's alter ego, the blind Matt Murdock. She tries to get him to have eye surgery. Matt visits a doctor who may be able to help him, but the doctor ends up in the clutches of a dictator. Matt's partner Foggy Nelson is asked by the Reform party to run for district attorney of New York. The Thing tries to hire Murdock as a lawyer, and the Sub-Mariner wants to sue the human race for crimes against the Atlantean people. Daredevil tries to stop Namor's temper tantrums. He goes up against a bizarre group of thugs led by the Organizer. Ka-Zar meets Daredevil under unusual circumstances. Ka-Zar's brother, the Plunderer, seeks to create the ultimate weapon, and he frames Ka-Zar for murder. Matt Murdock asks Foggy and Karen to go with him to England to defend Ka-Zar. The Ox gains some smarts in a weird mind transformation. A group of fake Daredevils attack Spider-Man, and the real Daredevil also ends up fighting Spider-Man. This allows the Masked Marauder to commit crimes. Foggy Nelson pretends to be Daredevil to impress Karen Page, but his plan backfires when the Gladiator wants to fight for real. The Owl kidnaps Matt Murdock to have him defend a judge in a mock trail. This was the judge who sent Owlsley to prison.

This volume also includes appearances by Mr. Fear and the Eel, along with the story of the origin of Daredevil who had two different costumes. In addition, it covers the origins of various villains, including the Owl, the Purple Man, the Stilt Man, and Leap Frog.

Fantastic Four, Dr. Doom, Human Torch, and Inhumans

Lee, Stan, Dick Ayers, Jack Kirby, et al. *Essential Human Torch Vol. 1*. New York: Marvel, 2003. ISBN: 0785113096. Reprints *Strange Tales 101–134*; *Strange Tales Annual 2*.

At first, the Torch tries to keep his identity a secret, but he learns that everyone knows who he is anyway, including his high school classmates. He dates Doris, a girl who seems to care less about his super powers than about him. The Torch disguises himself as Spider-Man to fight the Sandman. He also meets Iceman and teams up with Spider-Man. He has a number of battles with the Wizard.

This volume contains all of the Fantastic Four's solo Human Torch stories, one (from *Strange Tales 123*) drawn by original Human Torch creator Carl Burgos. The later stories feature the Torch and the Thing pairing up against such foes as Paste Pot Pete, Sub-Mariner, Terrible Trio, Quicksilver, the Scarlet Witch, Puppet Master, Kang and, in a stroke of writing genius, their own comrade, Mr. Fantastic, Reed Richards. The Beetle is a villain, and the Human Torch and the Thing get to meet the Beatles, the rock group.

Lee, Stan, Jack Kirby, Dick Ayers, et al. *The Essential Fantastic Four Vol. 1*. New York: Marvel, 2001. ISBN: 0785106669. Reprints *Fantastic Four 1–20*; *Fantastic Four Annual 1*.

The Fantastic Four is broke, and they are hired by the wealthy Sub-Mariner to star in a movie. Namor tricks the Fantastic Four into fighting him, and ultimately loses, but the movie is released and is very successful. Dr. Doom takes over Reed Richards's body, and tries to trick the Fantastic Four into defeat. Ben and Reed reminisce about being in the big war together. The Hulk is accused of sabotaging government experiments, and the Fantastic Four is brought in to investigate. The Red Ghost and his simian friends are bathed in cosmic rays, and given special powers. The Puppet Master controls the Sub-Mariner, and has him kidnap Sue Storm. The Yancy Street gang eggs the Thing on, and even calls him a sissy. The Mad Thinker gets the Fantastic Four to break up briefly, and the Ant-Man assists the Fantastic Four in defeating Dr. Doom in the micro world. Namor, who declares war on humanity, saves Sue Storm's life, and still pines for her love.

This volume collects the ground-breaking series which ushered in the Marvel Universe and the Silver Age of Comics. It contains the stories of the Fantastic Four's origins and their first encounters with the Mole Man, Sub-Mariner, the Skrulls, the Puppet Master, Cyclops, Doctor Doom, Impossible Man, Hulk, and Mad Thinker, among many others. Other villains introduced include the Molecule Man, Rama Tutt, and the Super Skrull. The bizarre alien from the planet Poppup, the Impossible Man, and the Watcher are introduced, and the Sub-Mariner is returned from the pages of the Golden Age of Timely/Atlas Comics. By the second issue, Skrulls are impersonating the Fantastic Four to turn the world against them. The volume also contains a Fantastic Four pin-up. This is essential reading for anyone with an interest in popular culture. A 2005 edition (ISBN: 0785118284) was also published.

Lee, Stan, Jack Kirby, Vince Colletta, et al. *The Essential Fantastic Four Vol. 3*. New York: Marvel, 2001. ISBN: 0785107827. Reprints *Fantastic Four 41–63*; *Fantastic Four Annual 3–4*.

The Watcher tells the Fantastic Four about the coming of Galactus, and the arrival of the Silver Surfer. Galactus seeks to digest Earth's energy, but his herald, the Silver Surfer, rebels because he sees value in humanity. The Watcher goes against his creed and tells the foursome about the Ultimate Nullifier. The Frightful Four and the Wizard get the Thing to turn against Reed Richards and his friends. Dr. Doom tries to destroy the wedding of Mr. Fantastic and the Invisible Woman. Again, the Watcher intervenes, and saves the wedding from disaster. Gorgon wants to take Medusa back to her people, but the Fantastic Four, along with Dragon Man, try to stop him. Black Bolt has to defeat his insane brother Maximus. The Human Torch goes to college and meets Wyatt Wingfoot who becomes his longtime friend. Johnny Storm falls in love with the Inhuman Crystal. A mad scientist transforms himself into Ben Grimm to destroy the foursome, but saves Mr. Fantastic as a last, heroic deed. Klaw nearly destroys the team. The Thinker and Quasimodo bring the original Human Torch back to life, to defeat the Fantastic Four. Johnny Storm and Jim Hammond have a titanic fight. The original Human Torch sacrifices himself to save the foursome. Dr. Doom deceives the Silver Surfer by befriending him and then stealing his powers. Doom tries to take over the planet. The Four team up with the Panther to defeat Klaw. The secret of Black Bolt is revealed. The team admits defeat to Dr. Doom, which greatly inflates Doom's ego. Sandman gets a new costume, and nearly defeats the whole team. Reed Richards is shot out into the Negative Zone, and the Inhuman Triton saves him. Blastaar is released from the Negative Zone, and attempts to defeat the Fantastic Four, with the Sandman as his partner.

This volume includes stories of Galactus and the Silver Surfer. The first Punisher makes his debut, and the Inhumans and the Black Panther are introduced. *Essential Fantastic Four Vol. 4.* was published in 2005 (ISBN: 078511484X) and *Essential Fantastic Four Vol. 5.* was published in 2006 (ISBN: 0785121625).

Lee, Stan, Jack Kirby, George Roussos, et al. *The Essential Fantastic Four Vol. 2.* New York: Marvel, 1999. ISBN: 0785107312. Reprints *Fantastic Four Vol. 1: 21–40*; *Fantastic Four Annual 2*; *Strange Tales Annual 2.*

The Hate Monger turns the Fantastic Four against each other, but Nick Fury helps them come back together. Fury and Reed were in the war together. It turns out that the Hate Monger is actually Hitler. The Mole Man has the tenants of the Baxter Building turn against the Fantastic Four, and lures them to his private island. The Fantastic Four foil Dr. Doom's capture plans, and he is thrown into space. A bizarre alien youngling known as the "Infant Terrible" menaces the Earth. The Hulk gets angry that Captain America has replaced him in the Avengers. The Fantastic Four are drawn into the fight as the Thing and the Hulk duke it out. The Sub-Mariner kidnaps Sue Storm in an attempt to get her to love him instead of Reed. Dr. Strange is brought in to help locate Namor and Sue. The Mad Thinker and the Puppet Master team up, and use the X-Men against the foursome. They go back to the moon to stop the Red Ghost. The

Watcher's home and scientific equipment fascinate Reed Richards. Diablo is briefly able to change the Thing back into Ben Grimm. He betrays the Fantastic Four and starts to serve Diablo. Dr. Doom believes that he will finally defeat the Fantastic Four, by killing Reed Richards. Rama Tutt may be a relative of Doom, or Doom himself. The Mole Man kidnaps Sue Storm, and he dukes it out with Avengers. The Super Skrull pretends to be Dr. Storm, and terrorizes the team as the Invincible Man. The Skrulls who kidnap him send him back to Earth, but Dr. Storm dies. The group aids Namor against the mad Attuma, without him knowing. The rich industrialist Gideon pits the foursome against each other. Reed Richards speaks at the university where he and Ben went to school. Diablo crashes the party with Dragon Man. The Fantastic Four help the Skrull Empire against a power-hungry warlord. After a battle with the Frightful Four, the team loses their powers, and Daredevil comes to their aid against Dr. Doom. Spider-Man and the Torch team up.

This volume contains Dr. Doom's origin story. The Storms' father, Dr. Franklin Storm, and the Frightful Four are introduced.

Thomas, Roy, Wally Wood, Artie Simek, et al. *Essential Super Villain Team Up.* New York: Marvel, 2004. ISBN: 0785115455. Reprints *Astonishing Tales 1–8*; *Avengers 154–156*; *Champions 16*; *Giant Size Super Villain Team Up 1–2*; *Super Villain Team Up 1–17*; *Marvel Super Heroes 20.*

Doom wants Namor's help to take over the world. Doom and Namor fight against Attuma's hordes, and Namor's people are freed from their cryogenic sleep, with Doom's help. Henry Kissinger gives Doom diplomatic immunity and forbids Americans from trespassing in Latveria. The Champions fight against Magneto and the Beast, while under Doom's controlling influence. The Red Skull takes over Latveria, and Doom shrinks them. After the Skull tries again to oust him, Doom leaves the Red Skull for dead on the Moon, but the Hate Monger rescues the Skull. Along with Arnim Zola, the Skull and Hate Monger attempt to use the Cosmic Cube to build the Fourth Reich. It turns out that the Hate Monger is none other than Adolph Hitler himself.

This collection of reprints features Dr. Doom and the Sub-Mariner in most of the stories. Sometimes they work together, but other times they are at odds. The covers for *Super Villain Team Up 15* and *Marvel Super Heroes 20* are reproduced. This volume includes appearances by the Avengers, Black Panther, the Shroud, and the Fantastic Four. There also is an unused art spread.

Hulk

Lee, Stan, Jack Kirby, Paul Reinman, et al. *The Essential Incredible Hulk Vol. 1*. New York: Marvel, 1999. ISBN: 0785107126; 0785123 741 (2005). Reprints *Incredible Hulk 1–6*; *Tales to Astonish 60–91*.

Bruce Banner, while conducting a gamma bomb test, saves a teenage Rick Jones who stumbles onto the test site, and due to radiation exposure Banner becomes the Hulk. When Giant Man goes on a search for the Hulk, the Human Top tries to intervene, but the Hulk saves Giant Man's life. Banner designs an indestructible robot which is stolen by an agent of the Leader. The military believes that Banner may be a traitor, and Major Talbot comes to investigate. The Hulk finally is captured, but when he changes into Banner he is able to get out of the bonds. The Chameleon, who is the Leader's agent, tries to sabotage the military base. The Leader, who wants the Hulk as his ally, creates pink humanoids to try and subdue the Hulk and learn the military's secrets. Talbot begins to suspect that Banner is not only a traitor, but that there is a connection between him and the Hulk. Banner is taken captive by the reds, and is forced to work with other captured scientists. Rick Jones goes to the president and explains that Banner is actually the Hulk. Banner is shot in the head and almost dies. The Leader saves his life, and sends the Hulk to the Watcher's blue area on the moon, to steal the Ultimate Machine. The Leader is supposedly killed after wearing the Machine, because it provides too much knowledge. The Hulk is sent to the future where he battles the Executioner. Rick Jones, believing that Banner/Hulk is dead, reveals that Bruce Banner is actually the Hulk. The Hulk also faces Hercules in a titanic battle.

This collection includes the Hulk's first encounters with the Gargoyle, the Leader, General Fang, and Betty Ross. The Leader's origin story is included.

Lee, Stan, Herb Trimpe, Marie Severin, et al. *The Essential Incredible Hulk Vol. 2*. New York: Marvel, 2001. ISBN: 0785107959. Reprints *Tales to Astonish 92–101*; *Incredible Hulk 102–117*; *147*; *Hulk Annual 1*.

The Silver Surfer tries to befriend the Hulk, but the Hulk refuses his attempts at friendship. Bruce Banner discovers that he loves Betty Ross, despite the fact that she wants to destroy the Hulk. The High Evolutionary kidnaps the Hulk to use him as a weapon against his New Men and their revolt. The Evolutionary evolves into a being such as humans will become in a million years. The Legion of Living Lightning tricks the Hulk into fighting for them. The Hulk kidnaps Betty Ross. For a short time, the Puppet Master controls the Hulk and forces him to fight the Sub-Mariner. Loki sends the Hulk to Asgard, but things don't turn out as Loki planned. The Hulk inadvertently helps Odin, and squashes a Troll revolt. Rick Jones testifies against the Hulk on national television. The Hulk is believed to have committed a murder. He fights a radioactive "Beast Man" from eons past. The Mandarin puts the Hulk through a series of tests. The bizarre Space Parasite attempts to feed on the Hulk's energies. The Rhino gets a new suit and fights the Hulk. The Hulk ends up in the land of the Inhumans. Maximus and his rebels attempt to use the Hulk in their coup against Black Bolt. Black Bolt offers the Hulk sanctuary, but the rest of the Inhumans are afraid of him. The Hulk ends up in the Savage Land, where he meets Ka-Zar. The Hulk comes into conflict with a giant alien UMBU. Bruce Banner has to use his brains and scientific skill to disable a computerized planet destroyer. Banner dies, but is revived by a group of aliens just so he can be killed again by the Galaxy Master. The Hulk ends up destroying the Galaxy Master. The Sandman attempts to get the Hulk to join him, and the Mandarin and the Sandman team up. In his delusional goal of world conquest, the Leader wants to launch a special missile which will start World War III. While in the desert, the Hulk sees a mirage, a city that accepts him and welcomes him.

Essential Hulk Vol. 3. was published in 2005 (ISBN: 0785116893), and in 2006 *Vol. 4*. was published (ISBN: 0785121935). Marvel also published *Essential Savage She Hulk* in 2006 (ISBN: 0785123350.

Spider-Man

Conway, Gerry, John Romita, Gil Kane, et al. *Essential Amazing Spider-Man Vol. 6*. New York: Marvel, 2004. ISBN: 0785113657. Reprints *Amazing Spider-Man 114–137*; *Giant Size Super Heroes 1*; *Giant Size Spider-Man 1–2*.

Spider-Man goes to Canada and has to deal with the Hulk. The Smasher attempts a smear campaign against a candidate for mayor of New York. Luke Cage is hired by Jameson to destroy Spider-Man. Spider-Man and Johnny Storm, the Human Torch, build a Spidermobile. Mary Jane sees the Vulture commit a murder, and knows he is after her. It is up to Spider-Man to be her protector. The Molten Man reappears.

The Punisher and Spider-Man take on the Tarantula. Morbius figures out how to control Man Wolf for his own nefarious purposes. Spider-Man meets Dracula and teams up with Shang Chi.

This collection features some of the most historic Spider-Man stories of all time. These include the death of Gwen Stacy and the subsequent death of the Green Goblin; the introduction of the Punisher to the Marvel Universe; Jonah Jameson's son, John, becoming the Man-Wolf; Harry Osborn taking on the mantle of the Green Goblin; Aunt May almost marrying Doctor Octopus; and the origin of Hammerhead. *Essential Spider-Man Vol. 7.* was published in 2005 (ISBN: 0785118799).

Conway, Gerry, Len Wein, Gil Kane, et al. *Essential Marvel Team-Up Vol. 1.* New York: Marvel, 2002. ISBN: 0785108289. Reprints *Marvel Team-Up 1–24.*

This was the premier team-up title. It features Spider-Man teaming up with an assortment of heroes and monsters, including Human Torch, X-Men, Vision, Thing, Thor, Werewolf, Brother Voodoo, Ghost Rider, Captain Marvel, Mr. Fantastic, Black Panther, the Cat, Iron Man, Inhumans, Captain America, Ka-Zar, Dr. Strange, and Hawkeye. The Human Torch also stars in a few issues in which he teams up with Iceman and the Hulk. The villains who are featured range from more famous characters, like the Mole Man, Gray Gargoyle, and Morbius, to more obscure villains like Stegron and Equinox Basilisk. Another edition was published in 2006 (ISBN: 0785121633), as was *Essential Marvel Team-Up Vol. 2.* (ISBN: 0785121633).

Lee, Stan, Steve Ditko, Art Simek, et al. *The Essential Spider-Man Vol. 1.* New York: Marvel, 1996. ISBN: 078510286; 0785109 889 (2002). Reprints *Amazing Fantasy 1; Amazing Spider-Man 1–20; Spider-Man Annual 1.*

Jonah Jameson begins his crusade against Spider-Man, and he meets with the Green Goblin for the first time. Spider-Man has a tiff with the Human Torch, and Jonah Jameson gets into an argument with the Vulture. The Green Goblin hires the Enforcers for a movie in which they will actually kill Spider-Man. They all go to Hollywood, where the Hulk ruins the Goblin's plans. Spider-Man meets Daredevil and helps foil the Ringmaster's plans. Flash Thompson impersonates Spider-Man, and gets hurt in the process. Because Spider-Man has to leave a fight with the Green Goblin when Aunt May gets sick, everyone thinks Spider-Man is a coward. The Sandman hires the Enforcers who kidnap the Human Torch in an effort to lure Spider-Man.

This volume contains Spider-Man's origin story and his first battles with the Vulture, Doc Ock, Sandman, Dr. Doom, Living Brain, and Electro, among others. These are some of the most influential comic storylines ever written. A new edition was published in 2006 (ISBN: 0785121927).

Lee, Stan, Steve Ditko, Art Simek, *The Essential Spider-Man Vol. 2.* New York: Marvel, 2002. ISBN: 0785109897; 078510299X (2001). Reprints *Amazing Spider-Man 21–43; Spider-Man Annual 2–3.*

Peter Parker's identity is unmasked by the Green Goblin. Spider-Man battles with the Scorpion, Kraven, Molten Man, Meteor, and the Rhino, among others. Parker transfers his affections from Betty Bryant to Gwen Stacy, and he graduates from high school. Spider-Man outwits Jonah Jameson who is trying to capture him using a spider-sensing robot, the Spider Slayer. The Green Goblin and the Crime Master both try to control the gangster rackets. The Crime Master is killed, but the Ringmaster's gang tries to go on without him. Dr. Strange and Spider-Man meet to battle wits with Xandu. Peter Parker starts college. Aunt May gets sick and is put into a hospital. Spider-Man tries to help cure her, but Doc Ock wants the radioactive material needed to cure her. Many of Parker's college classmates think he is a stuck-up snob. The Robot Master tries to kill Norman Osborn.

This volume contains the origin stories of Scorpion and the Molten Man, and Mary Jane makes her first appearance in it.

Lee, Stan, John Romita, John Buscema, et al. *Essential Spider-Man Vol. 4.* New York: Marvel, 2002. ISBN: 0785107606. Reprints *Amazing Spider-Man 69–89; Amazing Spider-Man Annual 4–5.*

The Kingpin is trying to steal a rare Tablet, and tries to frame Spider-Man and some teenage college protesters for the crime. The Kingpin makes the police think that he is in league with Spider-Man. Peter Parker's constant disappearing is making the love of his life, Gwen Stacy, question their relationship. She asks Flash Thompson out, for a heart to heart talk, which Peter sees as a threat. He goes bananas, and nearly ruins his entire relationship with her. The Kingpin breaks out of jail. Quicksilver, believing Spider-Man is a villain, tries to rein him in, to show the public that he is a hero and to be able to rejoin the Avengers. Silvermane gets Man-Mountain Marko to steal the Tablet from the Shocker's girlfriend. Silvermane kidnaps Curt Connors to help make the potion from the Tablet, which contains the secret to the fountain of youth, but after Silvermane drinks it, he becomes so young that he goes beyond the baby stage. Harry Osborne gets a Fu Manchu mustache. The stress of the kidnapping causes Curt Connors to become the Lizard again. Spider-Man fights the Human Torch to save the Lizard from being hurt, but all this while the Lizard is trying to bring about Spider-Man's fall. Mysterio and the Wizard team up to try to destroy both the Human Torch and Spider-Man. The Prowler nearly kills Peter Parker, or so it seems; the Chameleon impersonates Captain Stacy; and Electro tries to defeat Spider-Man on television. The Schemer tries to take down the Kingpin, but there is more here than meets the eye; the Schemer has a sordid history with

Wilson Fisk. Peter Parker admits to his friends that he is Spider-Man, and he finally learns that the Red Skull was behind his parents' death. Doc Ock returns.

This volume contains the origin story of the Prowler. It also offers a glimpse into how the Marvel Bullpen works. The 2005 edition contains *Amazing Spider-Man 66–89* and *Spider-Man Annual 5* (ISBN: 0785118659).

Lee, Stan, John Romita, Sam Rosen, et al. *The Essential Spider-Man Vol. 3*. New York: Marvel, 2001. ISBN: 0785106588. Reprints *Amazing Spider-Man 44–68*.

Kraven comes back and almost kills Norman Osborn whose life is saved by Spider-Man, and Peter Parker moves in with Harry Osborn. Curt Connors becomes the Lizard again. A new Vulture starts prowling around New York, and he teams up with Kraven. Peter Parker gets a very bad cold and decides to quit being Spider-Man. Foswell tries to take over the mob, but the Kingpin is not amused. Spider-Man meets the Kingpin, and Kingpin takes both Jonah Jameson and Spider-Man hostage, and tries to kill them. Foswell gives his life for Jameson. Peter and Gwen go to a science demonstration of the nullifier, which Dr. Ock steals. Spider-Man loses his memory, and Dr. Ock convinces him that they are partners. Doc Ock moves in with Aunt May, much to Peter's horror. He attempts to show Aunt May that he is really Spider-Man. Ka-Zar comes to New York for the first time, and he battles Spider-Man. Jameson gets to use a new, improved Spider Slayer. Colonel John Jameson and Captain Stacy are convinced that Spider-Man is innocent of any crimes. Mary Jane becomes a dancer at the Gloom Room, A-Go-Go, which is really a hideout for the Brainwasher. The Kingpin, who is revealed to be the Brainwasher, puts Captain Stacy under a hypnotic spell, and when Peter slaps Captain Stacy, Gwen breaks up with him. He ends up taking pictures of Stacy robbing police files. Norman Osborn begins to crack, and starts to remember his past. The Vulture lives, and fights his newer namesake. Spider-Man is arrested and helps save Captain Stacy's life from some escaping convicts. Peter is asked to get involved with a demonstration on the ESU campus.

This volume includes the famous story, "Where Crawls the Lizard," and the Shocker is introduced. The 2005 edition contains *Amazing Spider-Man 44–65* and *Spider-Man Annual 4* (ISBN: 0785118640).

Lee, Stan, John Romita, Roy Thomas, et al. *Essential Spider-Man Vol. 5*. New York: Marvel, 2002. ISBN: 0785108815. Reprints *Amazing Spider-Man Vol. 1: 90–113*.

Captain Stacy is killed while saving the life of a child. Doc Ock is the ultimate cause of his death, but Spider-Man is blamed. Iceman and Spider-Man duke it out because Iceman thinks Spider-Man has kidnapped Gwen. The Prowler is also after Spider-Man. The Beetle kidnaps Aunt May, and Gwen goes to Europe. Parker, as Spider-Man, gets an assignment in Europe to find Gwen, but ends up helping Scotland Yard foil a terrorist plot. Norman Osborn becomes the Goblin again. Harry Osborn gets hooked on drugs. Spider-Man helps quash a prison riot, and Gwen and Parker make up. Peter ends up with six arms due to a drug miscalculation, and becomes a real human spider. Spider-Man seeks the help of Dr. Curt Connors to turn him back into a normal human, but the Lizard reappears. Spider-Man ends up fighting both the Lizard and Morbius. Gwen, Peter, and J. J. Jameson go to the Savage Land to learn the story of Gog. It turns out the alien Gog has teamed up with Kraven to take over the Savage Land. A new, more efficient Spider Slayer is introduced. Flash Thompson got into "mystical trouble" in Vietnam, and Spider-Man and Dr. Strange have to help save him. Kraven tries to make the insecure Gibbon his pawn against Spider-Man. Peter's Aunt May ends up leaving Peter, and vanishes after Gwen tells her to stop mothering him so much.

In this volume, Morbius the vampire is introduced, and his origin story is told. This volume also contains a groundbreaking set of issues that the Comics Code refused to approve. There is also a 2005 edition (ISBN: 0785123792). The entry for volume 6 of this series appears under "Conway" in this chapter subsection.

Wolverine

Claremont, Chris, John Buscema, Klaus Janson, *The Essential Wolverine Vol. 1*. New York: Marvel, 2002. ISBN: 0785102574. Reprints *Wolverine 1–23*.

Logan, who is known as Patch in the city of Madripoor, decides to make that eastern city his home base, away from the X-Men. The rest of the world at this time believes the X-Men are dead. An evil crime lord is searching for the mystical Black Blade, and the Silver Samurai fights for the Blade which has the

power to possess people, including Logan. The crime lord, General Coy, who is New Mutant Karma's uncle, wants all rivals to be eliminated. He hires Bloodsport and Roughhouse to do his dirty work. Logan protects rival crime lord Tyger, as a friend and as her conscience, and they eventually become lovers. Coy and Tyger seem to be battling to the death, until a compromise is reached in which Madripoor has two crime lords. Logan teams up with former Spider-Woman Jessica Drew to protect actress Lindsay McCabe. The Grey Hulk, Joe Fixit, comes to Madripoor to do a mob job, unknown to the Hulk. He changes to Bruce Banner during the day. Someone leaves a bunch of purple pants for the Hulk to find, much to his dismay. Logan and the Hulk free several kidnapped women who are being held for the sex slave trade, and the Hulk is upset because he believes that Banner is doing all the partying. Logan stalks a couple of soldiers who did nasty things in Iraq. After Silver Fox is murdered, Wolverine fights with Sabretooth for the first time. A power-mad dictator in Central America seeks to use a bizarre form of cocaine to make his own national superhero, and kidnaps Roughhouse for this purpose. Logan goes to Central America to free Roughhouse, and meets up with a former advisor to Hitler, Geist. The cocaine is poisoned by an alien entity, Spore. This volume includes appearances by Gateway, Storm, Daredevil, Tiger Shark, the Celestials and Magneto.

The six-part "Gehenna Stone Affair" is included in this volume. This story deals with a supernatural stone that the demon Ba'al needs to allow him to unleash a reign of terror. A 2005 edition was issued (ISBN: 0785118675).

Hama, Larry, Mark Texeria, Mark Silvestri, et al. *Essential Wolverine Vol. 3*. New York: Marvel, 2002. ISBN: 0785105956. Reprints *Wolverine 48–69*.

Wolverine attempts to grapple with his past. With the help of Professor X, he tries to sort out what is real and what has been implanted into his mind. He goes back to the Weapon X complex and relives some of his adventures with Sabretooth while he was a member of Team X. He has to go up against Shiva, the computerized destroyer from Weapon X, and at times Nick Fury helps Wolverine in his quest, but he also uses him. Mojo kidnaps Jubilee, and wants her to do his bidding; he creates a model of her. When Wolverine forms a loose alliance with Mystique and Spiral against Mojo, they have to fight a very difficult plasma wraith. Logan meets with Shattestar, and they have an interesting discussion about the merits of television. Jubilee is arrested in Tokyo. Gambit also goes along for the ride, in Tokyo, against the Hand and Matsuo. Jubilee meets Yukio and Sunfire, who help the two X-Men in their battle against the Hand. Because of Matsuo, Logan's one true love Mariko is killed, and Wolverine's heart broken yet again when he is forced to end her suffering. Logan has a vendetta against Matsuo, and makes sure he suffers. Logan and Terror team up, much to Jubilee's disgust. All the previous members of Team X get back together to learn more about their past. Logan learns that the death of Silver Fox at the hands of Sabretooth was just something

implanted in his brain. However, he is never quite sure that the love and romance they shared in the past was real. Then he has to witness the real death of Silver Fox. Mastodon dies all over Jubilee, actually turning to mush in her hands. Wolverine relives a mission from the 1960s and the Team X days against Terry Adams. He finds out certain truths about his past, but never the whole picture. Wolverine, Jubilee, and Rogue go to the Savage Land, and end up meeting Sauron.

This whole collection is well written and full of action and intrigue, but it is sometimes difficult to follow what is imaginary and what is "real" in the world of the Wolverine. The reader actually experiences some of what Logan goes through. This volume also includes the narrative "Weapon X: Origin of Wolverine," from the *Official Handbook of the Marvel Universe. Essential Wolverine Vol. 4*. was published in 2006 (ISBN: 0785120599).

Silvestri, Marc, Larry Hama, Peter David, et al. *The Essential Wolverine Vol. 2*. New York: Marvel, 2001. ISBN: 0785105506. Reprints *Wolverine 24–47*.

Logan helps a couple of street urchins who steal an important bag from a lady assassin. He tries to learn why a good friend of his was murdered in Japan. Jessica Drew fights a robot known as Pinocchio. Jessica is sent back to the United States with her actress friend. A wholesale slaughter of spider monkeys in Madripoor sets Wolverine off on an investigation. The monkeys are being used for their chemical drug properties. However, the drug made from the spider monkeys has a fatal side effect. Jean Grey appears to Wolverine in a dream. Logan fights the Hunter in the Darkness. Lady Deathstrike, in her mad lust for the death of Logan, travels back to the Spanish Civil War. Logan is a Freedom Fighter, along with Puck. An android version of Logan, Albert, and a young girl android, Elsie Dee, are filled with explosives, because their creators want to kill Wolverine once and for all. Things go haywire when both Albert and Elsie gain self-awareness, and decide they want to live. Logan saves Elsie's life. Sabretooth believes that he is Logan's father, but still wants to kill him. While on a pleasure cruise, Logan investigates the murders of several young girls, and comes in contact with an otherworldly beast. While living with Silver Fox, Logan can hardly bring himself to kill his rabid dog. Karma, Cable, Jubilee, Storm, and Nick Fury make appearances.

This collection includes gallery pictures and the famous "Lazarus Project" storyline, which is something a lot of people look for.

X-Men

Claremont, Chris, Jon Byrne, Terry Austin, et al. *The Essential X-Men Vol. 2*. New York: Marvel, 2000. ISBN: 0785102981. Reprints *Uncanny X-Men 120–144*.

Alpha Flight tries to take Wolverine from the X-Men by force. Wolverine meets his longtime love Mariko. The Beast and Jean Grey find out the other X-Men are alive after their fight with Magneto, but Jean Grey dies. Wolverine forces Colossus to use his powers in the Danger Room. Storm goes to a house full of junkies, and she meets with Luke Cage and Misty Knight. Acarde, who is hired to kill the X-Men, kidnaps them and forces them to go through his Murderworld. Mastermind begins to groom Jean Grey for the Hellfire club. The X-Men go to Muir Island, to which Moria McTaggert's son Proteus escapes. Proteus, Mutant X, takes over his father's body, and nearly defeats the X-Men. Emma Frost, the White Queen, captures the X-Men for the Hellfire Club, and Kitty Pryde is left to help free them from White Queen's clutches. The Queen is particularly cruel to Storm. The Wendigo and Wolverine duke it out. Man Thing makes a guest appearance.

This volume contains the first appearances of Dazzler and Kitty Pryde, and the first battles with Proteus and Alpha Flight. It also has some of the major X-Men stories, including "Dark Phoenix Saga" and "Days of Future Past," and an X-Man roster. The 2005 edition adds *X-Men Annual 3–4* (ISBN: 07851 20076).

Claremont, Chris, Dave Cockrum, Joe Rubinstein, et al. *The Essential X-Men Vol. 3* New York: Marvel, 1998. ISBN: 0785106618. Reprints *Uncanny X-Men 145–161*; *X-Men Annual 3–5*.

The X-Men have to invade Dr. Doom's home to save Arcade, otherwise their friends and family will be killed. Storm and Dr. Doom fight, and Doom freezes Storm. When Storm is released, her power is like a fury. Cyclops and his boss are shipwrecked on an island that turns out to be Magneto's base. Magneto threatens the world with nuclear destruction if they don't heed his rule. The X-Men try to stop him, but he has an inhibitor that hinders their powers. Storm approaches him while he is sleeping, and nearly slits his throat, but she hesitates. Kitty is nearly killed by Magneto, and the White Queen sends Kitty to a new school. The Hellfire Club starts using Sentinels, who kidnap the X-Men.. Storm and Emma Frost exchange bodies and powers. Kitty tells an X-Men fairy tale to Illyana. Illyana is taken to the netherworld of the demon Belasco, and loses a good part of her childhood in the process. Corsair reveals that he is the father of Cyclops and Havok. The X-Men have to help the Sh'ar imperial, Lilandra. Her sister Deathbird has made a deal with the Brood to set herself up as the ruler. Colossus is stabbed through the chest, and al-most dies. Storm is bitten by Dracula, and nearly becomes a vampire. Professor X, who is in a catatonic state, reminisces about his first meeting with Magneto, and the days when they were friends and had a very unpleasant encounter with Baron Strucker. When Arkon comes from his dimension and kidnaps Storm, the X-Men follow them, and help the Imperions restore the life-giving energy rings. Nightcrawler is whisked away to a hell-like world, and Dr. Strange comes to help the X-Men deal with this crisis. The X-Men and the Fantastic Four work together against the alien Badoon. The Angel leaves the X-Men because he can't stand Wolverine. Caliban tries to kidnap Kitty during a performance by Dazzler, and Spider-Woman and Storm help rescue her. Kitty builds herself a costume. Ronald Reagan makes an appearance.

Claremont, Chris, Dave Cockrum, Paul Smith, et al. *The Essential X-Men Vol. 4*. New York: Marvel, 2001. ISBN: 0785107754. Reprints *Uncanny X-Men 162–179*; *X-Men Annual 6*.

Kitty Pryde battles against a weird alien, and Professor X nearly dies. The X-Men have to battle the Brood, and are infected with the Brood virus. Wolverine, because of his healing factor, is able to kill the Brood embryo within him, but he may have to kill the other X-Men in order to save them from becoming Brood. Carol Danvers becomes Binary. The Brood's sentient ship, the *Acanti*, is freed from its slavery. The Morlocks kidnap the Angel and torture him. Callisto views the Angel as the most beautiful man in the world, and wants him as her consort. Storm and Callisto battle, almost to the death, and Storm becomes leader of the Morlocks. Caliban wants to marry Kitty, and keep her with him and the Morlocks forever. Cyclops and Madelyne Pryor begin their romance, and Madelyne becomes a form of the Dark Phoenix. Rogue comes to the X-Men seeking help, and joins the team. Wolverine almost gets married, but he is dumped at the altar. Storm gets a Mohawk hairdo. Mystique want to get her adopted daughter Rogue back, and makes a deal with Arcade. Colossus is covered in liquid nitrogen. Rachel Van Helsing, who has been turned into a vampire, dies at the hands of Wolverine. Professor X is allowed the use of his legs for a brief period, and Kitty is transferred to the New Mutants.

The 2006 edition contains *Marvel Graphic Novel 5: God Loves, Man Kills* (ISBN: 0785122958).

Claremont, Chris, John Romita Jr., Barry Windsor-Smith, et al. *Essential X-Men Vol. 5*. New York: Marvel, 2004. ISBN: 078511 3665. Reprints *Uncanny X-Men 180–198*; *X-Men Annual 7–8*.

Kitty and Cypher, Doug Ramsey, become friends. She accompanies him to the school where Emma

Frost is headmistress. Lockheed's dragon friend becomes huge and attacks Tokyo. Rogue is framed for killing a S.H.I.E.L.D. agent. Colossus claims he doesn't love Kitty anymore. Colossus and Juggernaut, Cain Marko, have a nice little brawl. Rachel Summers comes from another timeline, into what she at first believes is her world in the past. Selene, the Dark Queen, wants to use Rachel for nefarious purposes. Rachael admits to the X-Men that Jean Grey is her mother. Forge, who makes his first appearance, designs a gun which neutralizes mutant powers, and which is used on Storm. She loses her power over the weather, and falls in love with Forge, even though she hates his guts. The X-Men have to fight the Wraiths. Nightcrawler threatens to leave the X-Men, and Rachel explains why the X-Men are needed more than ever in a world that hates mutants. Selene captures Rachel and Magma. The old sorcerer Kulan Gath takes New York hostage, and it is transformed into a world of magic and evil. Storm saves Callisto's life, and they start a friendship, despite being old enemies. Juggernaut and Nimrod duke it out. Kitty and the dragon Lockheed have an adventure, and ROM makes a cameo appearance.

In this volume, the X-Men meet Power Pack; the Sentinel, Nimrod, and Warpath are introduced; there are appearances by the Avengers, Spider-Man, Galactus, and the Impossible Man, the weirdest guest in an *X-Men* title. This volume also contains the *Secret Wars II* crossover, and two fantastic stories with Barry Windsor-Smith's amazing art. *Essential X-Men Vol. 6.* was published in 2005 (ISBN: 078511727X), and *Essential X-Men Vol. 7.* was published in 2006 (ISBN: 0785120556).

Claremont, Chris, Len Wein, Bob McLeod, et al. *The Essential X-Men Vol. 1.* New York: Marvel, 1996. ISBN: 0785102566; 0785123 768 (2006). Reprints *Giant Size X-Men 1*; *Uncanny X-Men 94–119.*

The X-Men are still battling the Sentinels and racism against mutants. Several of the original X-Men decide to retire, but Cyclops stays on. They investigate the disappearance of the old X-Men team on the island of Krakoa. The island turns out to be a giant mutant who feeds off the energy of other mutants. Thunderbird is killed on a mission against Count Nefaria. The X-Men fight robot versions of the old team on an orbiting satellite. Jean Grey turns into the Phoenix. The X-Men take a vacation to Cassidy Keep, only to find Black Tom and Juggernaut waiting for them. With the help of the "little people" and Nightcrawler, the X-Men escape. Xavier starts having disturbing nightmares and visions which originate from outer space, and Magneto returns to take on the new X-Men. The Starjammers make their first appearance, and Jean Grey learns that their leader is actually Cyclops's father. Weapon Alpha tries to kidnap Wolverine, and Magneto takes the X-Men from Mesmero's clutches to his secret base underground in Antarctica.

In the ensuing battle, the Beast and Jean Grey escape, and the rest of the X-Men tunnel through to the Savage Land. Professor X goes with Lilandra to her planet. The X-Men fight Sauron and help Ka-Zar defeat the tyranny of the god Garnokk. They also help Sunfire against Moses Magnum.

This volume collects those milestone issues in which the new X-Men were introduced. The new X-Men included Wolverine, Banshee, Storm, Nightcrawler, Sunfire, Colossus, and Thunderbird. The volume also contains Storm's origin story.

Lee, Stan, Jack Kirby, Roy Thomas, et al. *The Essential Uncanny X-Men Vol. 1.* New York: Marvel, 1999. ISBN: 0785107304; 078510 9919 (2002). Reprints *Uncanny X-Men 1–24.*

The X-Men travel to the Savage Land, and encounter, Ka-Zar who will become their longtime ally. The Vanisher tries to take over organized crime. Magneto tries to use government missile tests against the country, but the X-Men stop him. Professor X muses to himself that he loves Jean Grey. Xavier finds the Blob working at a carnie show, and tries to get him to join the X-Men, and Magneto tries to get the Sub-Mariner to join the Brotherhood of Evil Mutants. The X-Men fight the Avengers, while Professor X is trying to subdue Lucifer. The Beast leaves the X-Men for a short time, and becomes a wrestler. The Stranger kidnaps Magneto and Toad to his planet. Professor X explains his origin, while his brother Cain Marko, the Juggernaut, is making his way to the school to destroy it. The Human Torch helps defeat the Juggernaut. The Sentinels are created, and the X-Men are taken captive by them. Mastermold, the chief Sentinel, tries to get Dr. Trask, their creator, to make many more Sentinels so that they can take over and protect humanity. Iceman is badly hurt in the battle, and Magneto defeats the X-Men at the school. He takes the Angel's parents and uses their DNA to create his own army of mutants. It is up to a sickly Iceman to help defeat Magneto, and save the X-Men. The Blob and Unus pose as the X-Men, and begin a series of robberies. They are secretly under the control of the alien Lucifer. Professor X tells the story about how Lucifer took the use of his legs away by dropping a giant slab on him. The X-Men have to defeat the great machine Dominu.

This volume has been hailed as "pop culture at its best." The collection includes origin stories of the X-Men and their first encounters with longtime X-Men foes, including Magneto, the Blob, the Sentinels, Ka-Zar, Sub-Mariner, the Brotherhood of Evil Mutants, Juggernaut, Count Nefaria, the Eel, and Unicorn, among others. It tells the origins of Professor X and the Beast, and contains the first appearances of Mimic, the Silver-Age Ka-Zar, and the Savage Land. These stories are very well written and fun to read. *Essential Classic X-Men Vol. 2.* was published in 2006 (ISBN: 0785121161).

Essential Monsters

Friedrich, Gary, Mike Ploog, Doug Moench, et al. *Essential Monster of Frankenstein Vol.1.* New York: Marvel, 2004. ISBN: 0785116 346. *Reprints Monster of Frankenstein 1–5; Frankenstein's Monster 6–18; Giant Size Werewolf 2; Monsters Unleashed 2, 4–10; Legion of Monsters 1.*

The Monster ends up in all sorts of unique situations in his never ending quest to find relatives of Victor Frankenstein. He battles Dracula and ends up losing a portion of his vocal cords after being bitten by a female vampire with whom the Monster falls in love. The Monster ends up in modern times, in a carnival sideshow. Several people are after him, including a member of the Frankenstein family and a group that wants to build a legion of monsters to use as an army. The Monster comes in contact with a Satanist group who is about to sacrifice the Werewolf's sister.

Mary Shelley's creation comes alive in this collection which details the life of Victor Frankenstein's Monster. The first several issues are a tribute to the original Frankenstein, and fairly accurately retells Shelley's story. This volume includes several black-and-white pin-ups, and the entry from the *Handbook of the Marvel Universe.* It is recommended reading. Several other monster/horror *Essential* collections were published in 2005 and 2006, including *Essential Horror* (ISBN: 078512196X); *Essential Man-Thing* (ISBN: 0785121358); *Essential Ghost Rider Vol. 1* (ISBN: 0785118381); *Essential Ghost Rider Vol. 2* (ISBN: 0785121641); *Essential Werewolf by Night* (ISBN: 078511839X; and *Essential Godzilla* (ISBN: 0785121 536).

Wolfman, Marv, Gene Colon, Chris Claremont, et al. *Essential Tomb of Dracula Vol. 2.* New York: Marvel, 2004. ISBN: 0784114610. Reprints *Tomb of Dracula 26–49; Giant Size Dracula 2–5; Dr. Strange 14.*

Dracula fights Garon whom he believes killed his wife. He meets a young Jewish man, and learns that even the Star of David is repulsive to him. Taj goes back to India to kill his vampire son. A blind woman who has supernatural powers vows vengeance against Dracula, because he murdered her father who had murdered the Count's wife. Dracula starts to act very strange; his powers are being diminished; and, once again, he is on the verge of death. Dr. Sun is causing Dracula to slowly lose his powers, and to be transformed into a raving lunatic. During the Depression, Dracula goes to a small town where he encounters a living heart that has a demon's soul. Frank Drake goes to Brazil to search for himself, but he encounters a group of zombies who are set on killing him. Brother Voodoo saves Drake's life, and instills a new sense of confidence in him. Dracula and Quincy Harker have a terrific battle in Harker's mansion. Dracula's minions

have been torturing Rachel Van Helsing, and Harker allows Dracula to go free to save Van Helsing's life. Dracula goes to Boston to seek Dr. Sun, as do the vampire hunters. Harold H. Harold finds Dracula on the street, and takes him back to his apartment. Dr. Sun kidnaps Harker's band of vampire hunters, and brings Dracula to them. Sun kills Dracula, and it is up to Harker to bring Dracula back to life, in order to defeat Dr. Sun. Blade joins in their efforts against Sun. Dracula kills Wong, Dr. Strange's servant, and Strange vows vengeance. Dracula tries to turn Strange into a vampire. Hannibal King and Blade meet, and team up to find Deacon Frost. Dracula becomes the leader of satanic cult, and marries the bride that the cult has put before him. Blade fights a vampire double of himself, created by Deacon Frost. Dracula invades the fantasies of an insane young woman, in which he meets Frankenstein, D'Artagnan, Tom Sawyer, and other characters from literature.

This volume includes original art by Gene Colon and a Dracula sketch by Bill Sienkiewicz.

Wolfman, Marv, Gene Colan, Gerry Conway, et al. *Essential Tomb of Dracula Vol. 1.* New York: Marvel, 2003. ISBN: 078510920X. Reprints *Tomb of Dracula 1–25; Giant Size Chillers 1; Werewolf by Night 15.*

Quincy Harker, a relative of Frank Drake, Dracula, and Rachel Van Helsing form a group whose sole purpose is to track down Dracula and kill him. The vampire hunter Blade appears and aids Harker's group. Blade even manages to kill Dracula, temporarily. He also gets bitten by Dracula, and left for dead. The Werewolf by Night goes to Transylvania to search for his family history, and battles Dracula on several occasions. Dracula is taken captive by Dr. Sun, and battles the vampire for the title Lord of the Vampires. Dracula's daughter Lillith makes her first appearance.

This is the first collection of this excellent horror series which document Dracula's adventures in modern times.

Wolfman, Marv, Gene Colan, Steve Ditko, et al. *Essential Tomb of Dracula Vol. 3.* New York: Marvel, 2004. ISBN: 0875115587. Reprints *Tomb of Dracula 50–70; Tomb of Dracula Magazine 1–4.*

Dracula meets the Silver Surfer; Dracula kills the vampire hunter, Blade; and Dracula meets a foe who is heaven-spawned. The Son of Satan, Damian Hellstrom, helps resurrect Blade, who, with Hannibal King's help, destroys Deacon Frost, the vampire who killed Blade's mother. Dracula's son Janus is born, and Harold H. Harold writes his opus, *The Vampire Conspiracy.* Blade helps a friend whose wife has almost been turned into a vampire. The satanic high priest Lupenski teams up with Quincy Harker and his vampire-hunting group, to slay Dracula. The plot backfires, and Lupenski ends up killing Dracula's son. Dracula's wife Domini resurrects Janus from the dead. Janus combines with the golden heaven-sent man. He is now on a mission to kill his father. Janus and Dracula duel, while the woman Topaz witnesses this. Dracula and Topaz meet Satan, who strips Dracula of all his power, and makes him human again. He goes to New York to seek help, only to be turned back into a vampire by his daughter Lilith, who then spurns him. Dracula ends up back in Transylvania. He actually commits a heroic act by using a cross to protect a group of children from the other vampires. The new Lord of Vampires, Torgo, has a duel to the death with Dracula. Quincy Harker and Dracula finally have their duel to the death in which Harker kills Dracula as Castle Dracula blows up. Dracula, however, is resurrected by a woman seeking his help to bring her sorcerer husband back to life. A little girl somehow is possessed with Dracula's blood, most likely through sa-

tanic intervention, and is draining Dracula, almost to the point of death, in a story that is reminiscent of the *Exorcist*. An innocent lady artist is corrupted by Dracula's influence, and young children are being sought to be corrupted by Dracula.

The great Steve Ditko helped with the story of Dracula fighting the Dimensional Man. This book finishes the general run of the *Tomb of Dracula* comic, and starts reprinting the tales from the unrated *Tomb* magazine. This series has been long considered to be one of the finest comics ever published, both in art and narrative, and this particular collection makes a good case for that argument. I consider these comics to be among the top ten best-written series of all time. 2005 saw the release of *Essential Tomb of Dracula Vol. 4* (ISBN: 0785117091). Roy Thomas's adaptation of Stoker's *Dracula* was also published by Marvel (ISBN: 0785114777).

Other Essentials

Claremont, Chris, John Bryne, Roy Thomas, et al. *Essential Iron Fist Vol. 1.* New York: Marvel, 2004. ISBN: 0785115463. Reprints *Marvel Premier 15–25*; *Iron Fist 1–15*; *Marvel Team-Up 63–64*; *Power Man 48–49*; *Power Man and Iron Fist 50.*

Danny Rand's parents are killed in Tibet while they are searching for the mythical city of K'Un-Lun. Danny is raised in K'Un-Lun where he is taught to be a master of martial arts, and receives the mythical power of the Iron Fist. It turns out that his father was killed by a business associate. Danny first meets Luke Cage as an enemy, but then they team up as crime-fighting partners. Iron Fist seeks revenge against the man who murdered is father, but finds the taste of revenge bitter.

Some of the other characters in the volume include Misty Knight, Wrecking Crew, Batroc, Atomic Man, Angar the Screamer, Iron Man, Captain America and Spider-Man. This is a well-written, and entertaining volume.

Conway, Gerry, Len Wein, Marv Wolfman, et al. *Essential Punisher Vol. 1.* New York: Marvel, 2004. ISBN: 07/85113649. Reprints *Amazing Spider-Man 129*; *134–135*; *161–162*; *174–175*; *201–202*; *Amazing Spider-Man King Sized Annual 15*; *Marvel Super Action Featuring the Punisher 1*; *Marvel Preview Presents the Punisher 2*; *Giant Sized Spider-Man 4*; *Captain America 241*; *Daredevil 182–184*; *Peter Parker: Spectacular Spider-Man 81–83*; *Punisher Limited Series 1–5.*

This volume contains the Punisher's introduction into the Marvel Universe in the pages of *Spider-Man*. The Jackal convinces the Punisher, Frank Castle, that Spider-Man is actually a villain, and the Punisher tries to kill Spider-Man. Even after several encounters with Spider-Man, the Punisher is not convinced that Spider-Man fights on the side of justice. The Tarantula and his cronies take over a ship, and the Punisher, who just happens to show up, believes at first that Spider-Man is in league with Tarantula. Spider-Man and the Punisher team up to stop Moses Magnum from distributing a deadly gas to the highest bidder. Magnum has been kidnapping innocent citizens, and killing them to demonstrate the power of his chemical weapon. Nightcrawler and Spider-Man meet, and the Punisher gets involved in their little conflict. A leftist group decides to kidnap Jonah Jameson, and hires the Hitman. Captain America and Daredevil meet the Punisher, and Daredevil is not very approving of the Punisher's methods. Doc Ock plans to use the *Daily Bugle* as a means of distributing a deadly poison throughout New York. Ock defeats the Punisher a number of times, drugs him, and leaves him for dead. The Punisher goes to jail, and Jigsaw tortures him while he is behind bars. When he tries to kill the Kingpin, the Punisher ends up meeting with Cloak and Dagger.

This volume contains the famous "Circle of Blood" storyline, in which the Punisher learns the deadly secrets of the Trust. It also contains the origin of the Punisher, which explains how Castle's one-man war on crime started. This is comic *noir* at its finest; it includes the *Handbook of Marvel Universe* Punisher entry.

Gerber, Steve, Val Mayerik, Sal Trapani, et al. *The Essential Howard the Duck Vol 1.* New

York: Marvel, 2002. ISBN: 0785108319. Reprints *Fear 19*; *Man Thing 1*; *Giant-Size Man Thing 4, 5*; *Howard the Duck 1–27*.

Howard the Duck comes to Earth from another dimension in which everyone is a duck. He teams up with Man Thing a number of times, to fight mystical forces. He meets Beverly who will become his long-time friend and companion, and learns Quack Fu, to fight against a bully who was terrorizing his friends. He teams up with the Defenders ands helps them against a mystical band of criminals. Howard runs for president against Jimmy Carter. He goes to court where an old lady who lost her kidneys presses charges against him. Then he ends up in a mental ward with his friend Winda. Damien Hellstrom, the Son of Satan, is brought in to exorcise the demon from Winda, but the demon ends up inside of Howard. Dr. Bong kidnaps Howard and Beverly, and forces Beverly to marry him. Howard goes to work for Beverly's relatives. He destroys a bizarre religious cult whose adherents wear citrus fruit masks and want to impose their morality on the world. He begrudgingly joins the Ringmasters Circus of Crime, but eventually defeats them. Some of the other colorful characters Howard fights include the rock group Kiss, Turnip Man, the Sleep Walker, the Incredible Cookie Creature, and the giant Le Beaver.)

The volume contains the story of Bong's origin. The stories in this book contain a great deal of social satire related to the decade of the seventies, including a presidential race and the Hare Krishnas. *Howard the Duck 16* is Gerber's essay on "Zen and the Art of Comic Book Writing."

Lee, Stan, John Buscema, Jack Kirby, et al. *Essential Silver Surfer*. New York: Marvel, 2001. ISBN: 078510271X; 0785120084 (2005). Reprints *Silver Surfer Vol. 1: 1–18*; *Fantastic Four Annual 5*.

In order to save his home world, Zenn La, from being destroyed by Galactus, Norrin Radd sacrifices himself. Radd agrees to become Galactus's herald, and is transformed into the Silver Surfer. His job is to find worlds for Galactus to feed on. Upon finding Earth and working with the Fantastic Four in Earth's defense, the Surfer rebels against his former master. As punishment for going against Galactus's will, the Silver Surfer is marooned in Earth's atmosphere, never to fly through the galaxy. The Surfer saves the Earth from the Stranger who was seeking to destroy it. Loki tries to deceive the Surfer into fighting with Thor, and Mephisto seeks to imprison the Surfer's soul. The Surfer contends with the Overlord. One of Frankenstein's heirs creates a monster version of the Surfer which is intent on destroying him. Mephisto has the Flying Dutchman, as a super–powerful ghost, attempt to destroy the Surfer. The Surfer's innate kindness outwits Mephisto, and saves the Dutchman's soul when a tear is shed on the Dutchman's behalf. The Surfer gets involved in a political struggle in a Latin-American country. Shalla Bal, the Surfer's love, comes

to Earth, and when she is shot, she is sent back to Zenn-La. Mephisto kidnaps Shalla Bal, and tries his best to get the Surfer's soul. He even has the Surfer attack Nick Fury and S.H.I.E L.D.. Both Spider-Man and the Human Torch fight the Surfer, thinking he is guilty of a crime. The Surfer gets in the middle of a fight with the Inhumans, and Maximus deceives the Inhumans into believing that the Surfer is fighting for him. The Surfer swears his vengeance upon humanity, and the "living computer," Quasimodo, is given a body of sorts by the Surfer.

These epic tales feature the Silver Surfer's early adventures, shortly after Galactus marooned him in Earth's atmosphere. In my opinion these eighteen Silver Surfer stories are the best, most thoughtful, and most creative stories that Stan Lee ever wrote.

Lee, Stan, Steve Ditko, Terry Szenics, et al. *The Essential Dr. Strange Vol 1*. New York: Marvel, 2002. ISBN: 0785108165; 0785123164 (2006). Reprints *Strange Tales 110–111, 114–168*.

Stephen Strange learns the true value of selflessness, and becomes the Sorcerer Supreme of Earth. He battles Nightmare, Loki, Umar, Voltorg, and the Mindless Ones, among others. Dr. Strange has an interesting philosophical discussion with Eternity, as well discussions with the Ancient One. Dormammu and Dr. Strange battle, in hand-to-hand combat, and Dr. Strange wins. Loki tries to deceive Strange. Dr. Strange frees Zom to defeat Umar. The Ancient One is seemingly killed. The Living Tribunal decides to destroy the Earth, unless Strange can change the wind of black magic that has overcome the Earth. Baron Mordo is released from a mystical prison. The Scientist Supreme, Yandroth, uses his science against Strange's mysticism.

The use of enigmatic symbols, like the Crimson Bands of Cyttorak, the Omnipotent Oshtur, the eternal Vishanti and the all-seeing Eye of Agamotto, are scattered throughout all of the issues in this volume. The volume includes the origins of Dr. Strange and the Ancient One. *Essential Dr. Strange Vol. 2.* was released in 2005 (ISBN: 0785116680).

Thomas, Roy, Barry Windsor-Smith, Robert Howard, et al. *The Essential Conan*. Marvel Comics: New York, 2000. ISBN: 0785107 517. Reprints *Conan the Barbarian: 1–25*.

After Conan is taken prisoner and made a slave by the Beast Men, he starts a rebellion which frees the human slaves. He meets the Grim Grey War God, Borri, and frees the alien elephant god from the sorcerer who is holding him captive. The daughter of the wizard Zukala, a former god who terrorizes a village in the form of a tiger, is in love with Conan. She refuses to hurt him, even on the command of her father. Conan kills several supernatural gods, including the bat-like Night-God and the Medusa-like Lurker Within who is a servant of Thoth-Amon. Conan also kills the Serpent God who uses zombies to protect its treasures. Conan's concubine Jenna betrays him while in a Corinthian city state. Conan breaks out of prison, and throws Jenna in a pile of feces. He fights against the man beast Thank, and kills the red priest Nabonidus. Conan's friend Burgun is hanged. Seeking retribution, Conan goes to the priest who betrayed his friend and who summons the bull-god Anu. He fights the Lovecraftian Octopus, "Dweller in the Dark," and the Spider God. The Frost Giant's daughter tries to lure Conan to his death, but he ends up killing her brothers. Conan meets Michael Moorcock's Elric of Melnibone during an inter–dimensional war against the Green Empress. Conan befriends the red-headed Fafnir, and they help to dethrone Gothan,

the Priest of the Dark God, at the bequest of a scheming princess. She betrays them to the bat-like Dark God. Conan and Fafnir go to war for the Turans against the city of Makkalet. Fafnir has his arm cut off, and is left for dead. Conan fights the Black Hound of Makkalet's high priest. He also fights against the frog-like Monster of the Monolith.

This volume adapts many of Robert Howard's original Conan stories in graphic format. Marvel lost the rights to the Conan character, and now full-color reprints of these original Marvel stories are being published by Dark Horse. See the Conan subsection of chapter 3 in this book.

7

Epic Comics Graphic Novels

If ya get 'nuff nuclear stuff ... like uranium ... together in one place,
ya get critical mass!—*Freddy Fisson*

Deities do NOT impress us—*Pinhead-Cenobite, from Hell*

The Universe itself is a mystery and my life is but a mystic entity within
that great mystery!—*Charlie Chin, in the "The Sleeze Brothers"*

If the Universe is infinite and no matter is either created or destroyed,
what happens to all the bogeys [boogers] I pick?—*El Ape Sleeze*

That's a fascist-instigated lie designed to discredit the revolution....
[N]ow talk or we'll multiply the number of your elbows.
—*Revolutionary wannabe, from "The Sleeze Brothers"*

Allred, Michael, Bernie E. Mireault, Richard Ashford, et al. *The Everyman.* New York: Epic, 1991. ISBN: 0871358654.

A witch who was raped and murdered rises from the dead as an androgynous being, to seek her revenge on her killers.

Aragones, Sergio, Mark Evanier, Bob Chapman, et al. *Sergio Aragones: the Groo Chronicles.* Anaheim, CA: Graphitti Designs/ Epic, 1990. ISBN: 0936211180. Reprints *Groo Chronicles 1–6.*

This beautiful limited-edition hardcover documents the early adventures of Groo. Limited to 1,500 copies, it includes a detailed explanation by Mark Evanier about Groo's creation and the author's attempts to publish a creator-owned strip.

Aragones, Sergio, Mark Evanier, Stan Sakai, et al. *The Death of Groo.* New York: Epic, 1987. ISBN: 0871352907.

The King Krag hates Groo, and wants him dead. When he thinks Groo is actually dead, he becomes bored and his life has no meaning. Groo poses has a hero and has many adventures saving people before he is found out. During his "funeral," nobody has a good thing to say about Groo, except a young waitress.

This graphic novel also was published by Graphitti Designs as *Life of Groo* (ISBN: 0936211741), and as *Marvel Graphic Novel 32.*

Aragones, Sergio, Mark Evanier, Stan Sakai, et al. *The Groo Adventurer.* New York: Epic, 1990. ISBN: 0871357038. Reprints *Groo the Wanderer 1–4.*

Groo becomes a soldier and has two kingdoms fighting against one another. He kidnaps the Minstrel and goes to battle a dragon called Mocosa. It turns out the dragon was nothing but an old man. He also rescues the lady folk from a kingdom in the sky. The women, however, don't want to be rescued.

This volume introduces the Minstrel.

Aragones, Sergio, Mark Evanier, Stan Sakai, et al. *The Groo Bazaar.* New York: Epic, 1990. ISBN: 087135766. Reprints *Groo The Wanderer 5–8.*

Groo helps two different slave traders in their quest for slaves. He helps recover the ruby of Kabula, only to get into trouble. He goes undercover as a woman. Groo goes to the elephant graveyard to find ivory.

This graphic novel includes a short Sage segment, and a history of the electron microscope.

Aragones, Sergio, Mark Evanier, Stan Sakai, et al. *The Groo Carnival*. New York: Epic, 1991. ISBN: 0871357712. Reprints *Groo the Wanderer 9–12*.

The Sage and Groo go on an adventure, and try to find some food. Each town they visit is in poverty, with everyone starving. One town protects sacred apples, and another town protects sacred pigs. Groo gets the towns to fight each other, and then eat the sacred food. Groo and Sage end up sick because the apples and swine are poisoned. Groo then goes on an adventure with the Minstrel and the hero Arcadio. Groo kills the dragon and fights battles, while the Minstrel sings of Arcadio's greatness. Of course Groo does all the work, and is rewarded with rancid cheese dip. Groo becomes part of an actors' troupe, and despite his being a crowd pleaser there is mayhem wherever he goes.

The introduction and afterword are by Mark Evanier.

Aragones, Sergio, Mark Evanier, Stan Sakai, et al. *Groo Dynasty*. New York: Epic, 1992. ISBN: 0871359065. Reprints *Groo the Wanderer 13–16*.

The Sage becomes a king, but Groo turns the people against him. Groo instructs everyone to become farmers, under King Sage's rule. He tries to become a quarryman in the building of a pyramid, which, of course, falls to pieces once Groo touches it. Groo joins a group of silent monks and has his hair cut, but the monks do their best to get rid of him. He attempts to help build an ark, and inadvertently aids Taranto in stealing from the shipbuilders.

This collection includes a short story that features the Minstrel, "Ten Reasons To Buy Groo Dynasty," and an afterword by Mark Evanier in which he explains that this particular Groo book is a tribute to the Prince Valiant comic strip.

Aragones, Sergio, Mark Evanier, Stan Sakai, et al. *Groo Expose*. New York: Epic, 1993. ISBN: 0871359073. Reprints *Groo the Wanderer 17–20*.

Groo almost gets eaten by piranhas, but he manages to get himself to a city in the middle of the lake, which is surrounded by piranhas as protection against warring tribes. Groo causes all sorts of problems for this group of folks, and war breaks out. Groo attempts to help his sister Grooella keep her empire, only to find out that he has lost it for her. When Groo tries to get it back, he causes mayhem again. Groo even ruins her beautiful hair, twice.

This is a hilarious three-part adventure in which the reader learns a great deal about Groo's early life with his sister, and her constant problems because of Groo's blatant stupidity. This volume includes a cover gallery, as do all Groo volumes, and has a thoughtful afterword by Mark Evanier.

Aragones, Sergio, Mark Evanier, Stan Sakai, et al. *The Groo Festival*. New York: Epic, 1993. ISBN: 0871359952. Reprints *Groo the Wanderer 21–24*.

Groo meets two witches who need a brave warrior to go up against the Wizard. Groo goes in search of the Waters of Poderes to help restore the old witch's powers. Groo meets a king's peace ambassador named Gru, and becomes his bodyguard, but of course all hell breaks out. Groo tries to help the village of Aracido, with disastrous results, and even the Minstrel wants to kill Groo by the end of the story.

This volume contains some of the funniest Groo stories ever published.

Aragones, Sergio, Mark Evanier, Stan Sakai, et al. *Groo Garden*. New York: Epic, 1993. ISBN: 0785100261. Reprints *Groo the Wanderer 25–28*.

Groo attempts to lead some troops against a town beset with bandits. One of the bandit groups includes Groo's "friend," Taranto. Groo tries to train a group of soldiers, but ends up beating them all to a pulp. Groo is sent by the witch on a quest for a magical object. He is shrunk, tames a bat, and of course he makes a mess of the quest. When the Minstrel and the Sage are taken prisoner, the Minstrel sings songs of Groo's blunders in order to save their lives, and Groo ends up saving them. Groo attempts to learn how to be a chef, and steals one king's chef for another king. Groo eats some laundry.

The afterword is by Mark Evanier.

Aragones, Sergio, Mark Evanier, Stan Sakai, et al. *Groo: Houndbook*. Milwaukie, OR: Dark Horse, 1999. ISBN: 1569713855. Reprints Marvel/Epic's *Groo the Wanderer 29–32*.

Groo meets a dog in the forest who he initially wants to eat, but ends up becoming friends with. There is a reward for the dog, Rufferto, which Groo tries to get for himself, as do others. Groo ends up becoming rich and everyone tries to trick him out his dough. Groo ends up giving the money to some monks. Groo is so stupid that this actually works in his favor. Evanier writes an afterword.

Aragones, Sergio, Mark Evanier, Stan Sakai, et al. *Groo Inferno*. Milwaukie, OR: Dark Horse, 1999. ISBN: 1569714304. Reprints Marvel/Epic's *Groo the Wanderer 33–36*.

Groo becomes leader of a band of pirates. Rufferto gives Groo an amulet which makes his wishes come true instantly. Needless to say, Groo gets into all kinds of trouble with the Sage, the witches and warlocks, and the Minstrel, among others.

This is one of the funniest Groo stories published.

Aragones, Sergio, Mark Evanier, Stan Sakai, et al. *The Groo Jamboree*. Milwaukie, OR: Dark Horse, 2000. ISBN: 1569714622.

Reprints Marvel/Epics's *Groo the Wanderer 37–40.*

Groo announces he is coming to a village, and all hell breaks out before he even gets to the town. He mistakenly thinks he ate Rufferto, who was stolen by some thieves. Groo attempts to find another Rufferto, but without much luck. Eventually Groo stumbles upon Rufferto, and they are joyfully reunited. Groo searches the world over for a replacement for a glass carafe.

Aragones, Sergio, Mark Evanier, Stan Sakai, et al.. *Groo: Kingdom.* Milwaukee, OR: Dark Horse, 2001. ISBN: 1569714789. Reprints Marvel/Epic's *Groo the Wanderer 41–43, 46.*

Groo is hired to remove a band of gypsies from a town. The Gypsy's queen is Groo's grandmother. Granny Groo uses him in several schemes, including marrying him off for the dowry. Granny also sells him into slavery. Groo is given money for new clothes.
This book includes insights into Groo's childhood dealings with Granny Groo.

Aragones, Sergio, Mark Evanier, Stan Sakai, et al. *The Groo Library.* Milwaukie, OR: Dark Horse, 2001. ISBN: 1569715718. Reprints Marvel/Epic's *Groo the Wanderer 44–45, 47, 49.*

Rufferto has a daydream in which he is a fearless warrior. He is captured by dog catchers, while guarding Groo's swords. Groo goes to work for free, and meets up with the Minstrel. He also meets with his sister Grooella to obtain the sapphire jewel. Groo becomes a protector of a city, but ends up destroying it, and eventually meets up with Chakal.

Aragones, Sergio, Mark Evanier, Stan Sakai, et al. *Groo: Maiden.* Milwaukie, OR: Dark Horse, 2002. ISBN: 1569717567. Reprints Marvel/Epic's *Groo the Wanderer 50–53.*

Groo falls in love with the warrior goddess Chakall. He constantly follows her and asks her to marry him, but she ignores him. Together they fight various battles in which Groo always does something stupid. One of their adventures involves getting a giant spider drunk in order to kill it. Groo's dog Rufferto is jealous of Chakall.

Aragones, Sergio, Mark Evanier, Stan Sakai, et al. *Groo: Nursery.* Milwaukie, OR: Dark Horse, 2002. ISBN: 156971794X. Reprints Epic/Marvel's *Groo the Wanderer 54–56.*

Groo totally demolishes two kingdoms in which he was unknown. His heart was in the right place, but he ends up destroying everything. The Minstrel is thrown in jail for singing stories about Groo. Groo goes to a city where there are anti–Groo signs.

Aragones, Sergio, Mark Evanier, Stan Sakai, et al. *Groo Odyssey.* Milwaukie, OR: Dark Horse, 2003. ISBN: 156971858X. Reprints Epic/Marvel's *Groo the Wanderer 57–60.*

Groo becomes captain of a ship, and all he does is eat. He relinquishes his captaincy to Ajax, and ends up sinking the ship. The ship's crew finds an island which they name Grooland, and some natives make an idol of Rufferto. The town of Susto builds a wall to keep Groo out, which brings thieves and many others who leave the town in greater chaos. Groo is employed by a king to get rid of the jobless and homeless, and he goes to Malydor to find work for a whole town.

Aragones, Sergio, Mark Evanier, Stan Sakai, et al. *The Life of Groo.* New York: Epic, 1993. ISBN: 0871356422.

This novel contains the origin story of Groo who was born without the ability to think, and has a knack for setting things on fire, and causing mayhem and madness wherever he goes. In the book, Groo eventually gets revenge on the Wizard who cursed his family. The book was reprinted by Graphitti Designs, as *Graphic Album No. 1.* (ISBN: 0936211520). It also was published with *Death of Groo* (ISBN: 0936211741).

Barker, Clive, et al. *Clive Barker's Hellraiser Collection.* New York: Epic, 1991. ISBN: 08713 57488. Reprints *Hellraiser 1–4.*

This is a special hardback that contains the first four issues of *Hellraiser*, based on the mythos created by Clive Barker. Graphitti Designs also published three deluxe hardcover reprints of *Hellraiser 1–6.* ISBN: 0936211199 (1); 093621130X (2); 0936211369 (3).

Barker, Clive, Dave Dorman, Larry Wachowski, et al. *Clive Barker's Hellraiser Collected Best II.* Centerville, OH: Checker, 2003. ISBN: 0971024979. Reprints Marvel/Epic's *Hellraiser1–4*; *15–16*; *Hellraiser Spring Slaughter* (ISBN: 0785100350); *Hellraiser Summer Special* (ISBN: 0871359235); *Hellraiser Dark Holiday Special* (ISBN: 0871359324).

An old-lady cat lover exacts her revenge against a neighbor who abused and tortured her cat, by making a deal with the Cenobites. A young Jewish boy takes revenge on those who killed his father, by calling on the Cenobites, who he believes represent the Golem of legend. A blind composer writes music from Hell to be played by the man who ruined his ability to play the piano. A young poet goes to a Parisian house for artists, which is really a doorway to the Cenobite world. A doctor finds an AIDS vaccine, which is actually a doorway into Hell.
These tales are based on Barker's Hellraiser mythos. *Summer Special, Spring Slaughter,* and *Dark Holiday Special* are all out of print. This fine collection of stories is even superior to Checker's first *Hellraiser* collection. It is the second reprint collection of the best Hellraiser stories originally published by Marvel. The story "Razing Hell" was written by one of the Wa-

chowski brothers, of *The Matrix* fame, in which three tortured souls try to wage war on Leviathan's kingdom.

Barker Clive, Neil Gaiman, Alex Ross, et al. *Hellraiser 1–20.* New York: Epic, 1989–1992. ISBN: 0871357615 (6); 0871357623 (7); 0871358298 (8); 0871358301 (9); 0871 358670 (10); 0871358699 (11); 0871358697 (12); 0871358700 (13); 0871358719 (14); 0871358727 (15); 0871359278 (16); 0871359 286 (17); 0871359294 (18); 0871359308 (19); 0871359316 (20).

This is a collection of twenty volumes, all dealing with the Hellraiser mythos which was created by Clive Barker. The guardians of Hell, the Cenobites, are featured prominently in many of the stories, as is the evil puzzle box. Marvel/Epic also published an adaptation of the third movie *Hellraiser III: Hell on Earth* in 1992 (ISBN: 0871359081).

Barker, Clive, Alan Grant, John Wagner, et al. *Nightbreed Genesis.* New York: Epic, 1991. ISBN: 0871357574. Reprints *Nightbreed 1–4.*

A young man, Boone, is framed for some grisly murders that his psychiatrist committed. He goes to the land of Midian, and is shot down. Underneath the ground in Midian is a civilization of misfits, outcasts, and monsters. Boone is rescued by the Nightbreed, and brought back to life. After talking with the god Baphomet, who transforms him into Cabal, he becomes the Nightbreed's savior. The Nightbreed have to fight the local residents and police force, and Cabal is responsible for finding them a new home.

This is the rare graphic-novel adaptation of the movie *Nightbreed* which contains material that was in the original shooting script, but not in the film. The introduction is by actor Malcolm Smith who plays the priest in the movie, and the afterword is by writer D. G. Chichester. This volume includes photos of the film's production models.

Barker, Clive, Erik Saltzgaber, Mike Manley, et al. *WeaveWorld 1–3.* New York: Epic, 1991–1992. ISBN: 0871358506 (1); 0871358 514 (2); 08713585252 (3).

This is a very surreal and bizarre adaptation of Barker's second and most ambitious novel. The story has a fairy-tale feel to it, and is based around a magic carpet which is the gateway to a world of folks known as the Seers. They view the humans as Cuckoos. The carpet, which was initially placed in the care of a Cuckoo woman, is referred to as the Fugue. The woman tries to pass the Fugue on to her granddaughter when she dies, but nemesis Immacolata and her two disgusting sisters, one of whom is called Mother Puss, are trying to destroy the Fugue and all of Seerkind.

Barker, Clive, Mark Thompson, Alex Ross, et al. *Hellraiser: Collected Best I.* Centerville, OH: Checker, 2002. ISBN: 0971024928. Reprints stories from Marvel's Epic line including *Hellraiser 1; 4; 5; 8; 13; 17; 18; 19; 20.*

This is a collection of some of the best horror stories from the early nineties *Hellraiser* books, including "The Harrowing 1&2," "Dead Things Rot," "Death Where is Thy Sting," and "Mazes of the Mind." These stories are all based on the Hellraiser mythos created by Clive Barker.

Barker, Clive, Larry Wachowski, D.G. Chichester, et al. *Clive Barker's: Book of the Damned: A Hellraiser Companion 1–4.* New York: Epic, 1991–1993. ISBN: 0871358417 (1); 0871358964 (2); 0871359332 (3); 087 1359766 (4).

This is a collection of stories, spells, and prose, combined with various images that tell about aspects of the Hellraiser's world and the puzzle box. The book includes "The Testament of Peter" "Of Hell," by Isadore Klauski; "Blades of Boros Uratu"; "The Journals of Philip Lemarchan"; and "The Revelation of Johnny John." This series provides a unique glimpse into the Hellraiser mythos, and is highly recommended.

Barker, Clive, Larry Wachowski, Bernie Wrightson, John Bolton, et al. *Clive Barker's Hellraiser: Collected Best III.* Miamisburg, OH: Checker, 2004. ISBN: 097538080X. Reprints Epic/Marvel's *Hellraiser 1, 2, 4–5, 9–10, 14, 19.*

A man with leprosy lures hospital staff to the Cenobites. A man gets pregnant by a Cenobite. Jack the Ripper helps in a modern-day Ripper-style murder series. The court of the Cenobites becomes a chaotic mess, and Pinhead has to bring order back. A group of war veterans play Russian roulette every year. A rich boxer seeks a challenge, and makes a deal with the Cenobites which allows him to continue to box throughout eternity.

Barker wrote the introduction. This is the third and best collection in Checker's series of reprints of the original *Hellraiser* comics. This book abounds in good stories and fantastic artwork. It includes a story which is a tribute to Lon Chaney Sr., about a man who kills his victims, and steals their faces.

Bester, Alfred, Howard Chaykin, Bryon Preiss, et al. *The Complete Alfred Bester's Stars My Destination.* New York: Epic, 1992. ISBN: 0871358816. Reprints *Stars My Destination 1–2.*

This book, which contains narrative and graphics, is a beautiful adaptation of the famous science fiction novel. The plot revolves around a hero named Gulliver Foyle who teleports himself out of a tight spot, and creates a great deal of chaos. After stealing a fortune on his former ship, the *Nomad*, and taking a volatile substance, Pyre, he is considered a high-risk criminal, but he eludes authorities at every turn. In the story, corporations are even more powerful than governments; people can reshape their bodies any way they want, including cybernetically; and humans can "jaunte," or teleport, from point to point. Foyle has an innate ability to "jaunte" through space, and even time. The story deals with contemporary and timeless issues—atomic menace, corporate madness, falling in love—with a sinister twist showing the dark side of humanity. Foyle is also on a mission of revenge to find out who left him stranded when the space ship *Vorga*, went by the Nomad. The answer to this question is one of the most interesting parts of the story. The first part of the story was originally published as a separate book in 1978, and parts of the second section were published in *Heavy Metal*. The volume includes an introduction and a biography of Alfred Bester. This adaptation took over ten years to complete, and is highly recommended.

Bolton, John, Chris Claremont, Jo Duffy, et al. *Back Down the Line*. Forestville, CA: Eclipse Books, 1991. Reprints Marvel/Epic's *Epic Illustrated 7, 18, 25*.

The Lleh's sister was killed by a Coke can. A monster wants the services of Joanna Marlowe, but is told that business hours are over. A lovely young girl is thrown out of her town by her father, the mayor, to be sacrificed to (and eaten by) an ogre. The ogre, however, is not interested eating the girl, but in fighting his enemy. The ogre and the young woman form a friendship, and carry on down the road.

This collection also reprints material from *Pathways to Fantasy*, including a story about the spurned love of sentient female octopi, by a small humanoid creature called a Lleh. There are a number of really bizarre science fiction stories in this volume. This book also includes a version of a famous Christina Rosetti poem, "Goblin Market."

Carnell, John, Andy Lanning, Dave Hine, et al. *The Sleeze Brothers File*. London: Marvel/Epic, 1990. ISBN: 1845002422. Reprints *Sleeze Brothers 1–6*.

Officer Pigheadski and El Ape have a conversation. El Ape is released from prison, and he and his brother Deadbeat form a P.I. business. They guard, and destroy, a cosmic egg which contains information that could give peace to the galaxy. A minister has a virtual-reality television show that is slowly killing people, and the Sleezes are brought in to investigate.

This trade paperback documents the first six cases of El Ape and Deadbeat Sleeze. These are parodies of stories from popular culture, including *Alien, Then There Were None* (also known as *Ten Little Indians*), and *Tom and Jerry*, among others. The sarcasm and humor in these stories is biting, and the stories are filled with adventure and delight. This book should be read by everyone.

Carnell, John, Andy Lanning, Helen Stone, et al. *The Sleeze Brothers: Some Like It Fresh*. New York: Epic, 1991.

The Sleeze Brothers, dressed as women, pose as Air Temperance advocates, in a world where "fresh air" is considered to be an evil drug. President Sinatra tries to woo the Temperance Society into electing him for a third term, all the while hitting on one of the Sleeze Brothers who is dressed as a woman. The Mafia is also trying to take care of the brothers. Eventually, the entire Temperance Society conference is exposed to the "fresh air," and everybody parties.

This is a cardstock volume.

Chaykin, Howard, Mike Mignola, Al Williams, et al. *Fritz Leiber's Fafhrd and the Gray Mouser 1–4*. New York: Epic, 1990–1991. ISBN: 0871357194 (1); 0871357208 (2); 0871357216 (3); 0871357224 (4).

Fafhrd and Grey Mouser vow to destroy the very powerful thieves' guild that killed their girlfriends. They go to the haunted tower, and fight wolves in the spirit world. They do the bidding of two wizards in order to stop the pain of losing their girlfriends. Mouser and Fafhrd have a falling out, and Fafhrd becomes a religious fanatic, but their true friendship wins out. They visit the Sea King's kingdom, which is underneath the sea, in an attempt to make love to his various concubines.

This four-part Prestige series is based on Fritz Lieber's sword-and-sorcery swashbuckling duo, Fafhrd and Gray Mouser. These two thieves meet for the first time in the story, "Ill Met Lankhmar." Other stories in this volume include the "Bazaar of the Bizarre" story, in which Fafhrd and Gray Mouser fight against evil capitalist ghosts.

Chichester, D. G., Margaret Clark, Klaus Janson, et al. *Critical Mass: A Shadowline Saga 1–7*. New York: Epic, 1989–1990. ISBN: 0871356023 (1); 0871356031 (2); 087135 604X (3); 0871356058 (4); 0871356066 (5); 0871356074 (6); 0871356082 (7).

In this volume, one of the Shadow Dwellers, Doctor Zero, is Earth's protector and superhero. However, an ancient order of monks, the Order of St. George, sees Zero's work as a manipulation of humanity, and they know him as the Dragon. They use a human saint, clothed in mystical armor, to defeat the Dragon. Zero, the Order of St. George, and Power Line, another group of Shadow Dwellers who are seen as heroes, have to put aside their differences to defeat Professor Henry Clerk, who killed Zero's mate Sheila. Clerk plans to ignite and overload all of the nuclear power plants in America, so that the whole country is bathed in nuclear mist. *Critical Mass* is part of the Shadowline Saga that was created by Archie Goodwin. This is an epic story that has many twists and is quite difficult to follow in places. There are way too many subplots for me to even begin to explain how complicated this series is. The basic premise is that there is a race called Shadow Dwellers whose members have incredible powers which made them the basis for monster mythology. Some of them look quite different from humans. Within the seven volumes, there are thirteen chapters. This series also features Terror Inc., Shreck, who has appeared in the mainstream Marvel Universe, and worked with Wolverine on occasion. Terror gains his powers from digesting body parts from the living or the dead.

Chichester, D.G., Paul Johnson, Bill Oakley, et al. *Hellraiser/Nightbreed: Jihad 1–2.* New York: Epic, 1991. ISBN: 0871357682 (1); 0871357690 (2)

The Lord of Hell, Leviathan, demands that the Nightbreed be exterminated. Much to Pin-Head's dismay, the Cenobite Alastor and his lover are given leave to "burn out the rot of ANARCHY the Nightbreed spread." Alastor has his own agenda, aspirations to become his own deity, and he slaughters Nightbreed in a disorderly fashion, which disturbs Pin-Head. He and his loyal Cenobites team up with the Nightbreed to help "rebuild" Baphomet, the deity of the Nightbreed, with Cabal's essence. Alastor needs the child of a Nightbreed, Peloquin, and his human lover in order to expedite his goals. After defeating Alastor, Baphomet allows Peloquin to feast on human flesh.

In this satanic opus, two different worlds from the mind of Clive Barker meet.

Chichester, Dan, Mark Verheiden, Lewis Shiner, et al. *Epic: An Anthology 1–4.* New York: Epic 1992. ISBN: 087135845X (1); 0871358 468 (2); 0871358476 (3); 0871358484 (4).

This is a four-part mini series featuring new stories from characters/series in the Epic line. Volume 1 features Hellraiser, Stalkers, Dreadlands, and Wild Cards; volume 2 features Nightbreed, Stalkers, Wild Cards, and Sleeze Brothers; volume 3 features Alien Legion, Stalkers, Wild Cards, Cholly, and Flytrap; and volume 4 features Dinosaurs, Stalkers, Wild Cards, Cholly, and Flytrap. The Stalkers and Wild Cards stories run through all four volumes, and the Cholly and Flytrap stories appear in Volumes 3 and 4. In 2004, a new *Epic Anthology* was published, in comic book form. It features Sleepwaker and the Young Ancient One. Unfortunately there was only one issue, and it quickly became a collector's item.

Claremont, Chris, John Bolton, Anne McCaffery, et al. *The Black Dragon.* Milwaukie, OR: Dark Horse, 1996. ISBN: 1569710422. Reprints Marvel/Epic's *The Black Dragon 1–6.*

In 1193, James Dunreith, following the death of King Henry, returns to Britain after a long exile. Henry's widow, Queen Eleanor of Acquintaine, employs James to seek out an old ally who is practicing black arts and seeks to claim the kingdom for his own.

Dunreith learns that he is actually part fairy folk; he is actually the Black Dragon, who must save the land before Edmund De Valere uses his sorcery to take it over. James's mother is Morgan Le Fay. Robin Hood, Little John, Friar Tuck, and others make cameo appearances.

Longtime X-Men scribe Chris Claremont shows he knows traditional British and Celtic mythology in this beautifully illustrated and well-written volume. The introduction is by Anne McCaffrey.

De Haven, Tom, Bruce Jensen, Alex Jay, et al. *William Gibson's: Neuromancer Vol. 1.* New York: Epic, 1989. ISBN: 0871355744.

This is a graphic novel adaptation of the famous science fiction novel by William Gibson. Volume 1 covers the first part of the novel in which Case, an information thief, fears and runs from Wage, from whom he stole information. Wage does not actually want to kill him. A bounty hunter, Molly, comes to collect Case, to put him to work for her employer, Armitage, who wants to plug Case into the Matrix to steal some information. Volume 1, which contains an introduction by William Gibson, was the only volume published. However a "lost" portion from volume 2, by Frank Henkel and Givens Long, was published in *Ultimate Cyberpunk*, which was edited by Pat Cadigan, and published by Ibooks. ISBN: 0743452399 (2002); 0743486528 (2004).

DeMatteis, J. M., Jon Muth, Kevin Nowland, et al. *Moonshadow.* New York: Epic, 1989. ISBN: 0871355558. Reprints *Moonshadow 1–12.*

This is a difficult book to describe and annotate, except to say that it describes a variety of human experiences, and is excellent. It tells the story of a Moonshadow human, an alien hybrid, and his adventures around the universe. Moonshadow experiences war, prison, sex, love, family, loyalty, prejudice, insanity, isolation, death, and full adventure, in search of some kind of cosmic truth. The volume is beautifully painted, and should be read by everyone who wants to read a graphic novel that could be considered "high literature," as good as anything Dickens, Tolstoy, Kerouac, or Hemingway ever wrote. The book has been endorsed by such luminaries as Ray Bradbury, and the *New York Daily News* called it a "spectral literate tone-poem." Graphitti Designs published a hardcover version (ISBN: 0936211164). In 1998, Titan and DC both reprinted this version, with a continuation. ISBN: 1852869178; 1563893436.

DeMatteis, J. M., Kent Williams, Gasper Saladino, et al. *Blood: A Tale.* New York: Epic, 1989. ISBN: 0871354926; Reprints *Blood: A Tale 1–4.*

This beautifully painted book is one of the most bizarre and surreal graphic novels ever published. In it, Blood, a young vampire who does not want to admit that he is a vampire, is on a never-ending quest for "truth." The story revolves around love, desire, loss, and death, which are all human characteristics that Blood feels despite being a vampire. In this volume, redemption, a fever dream of an already dead king, and a children's fairy tale are all woven into a tapestry of words and pictures. *Blood: A Tale* is unlike traditional vampire stories. DC/Vertigo Comics reprinted the book in 2004 (ISBN: 1401202632).

Dixon, Chuck, Scott Hanna, Hoang Nguyen, et al. *Alien Legion: One Planet at a Time 1–3.* New York: Epic, 1993. ISBN: 0871358980 (1); 0871358998 (2); 0871359782 (3).

Nomad is sent to Bakel II, which has been conquered by the mythical Vreel that no one has ever actually seen. They discover that the Vreel is actually a bacterium which contaminates and controls whole races of people. Nomad and the *Piecemaker* just barely escape and contain the soldiers infected with the Vreel. The new Nomad commander, Spal-Volma, sabotages the *Piecemaker*, and calls the Brotherhood of the S'Thanth to destroy the Legion. Grimrod comes up with an idea to subdue Spal-Volma, by using Legionnaire Spellik. He is poured through a crack as sand, and reforms when liquid is added. Spellik, with the help of No'or, subdues the commander. No'or sacrifices himself to save the Legion, when the Brotherhood attacks.

Dixon, Chuck, Mike McMahon, Dave Sharpe, et al. *Alien Legion: Jugger Grimrod.* New York: Epic, 1992. ISBN: 0871358972.

Grimrod gets tricked into taking an assignment on the planet Ocadus. Grimrod, thinking he is going to a paradise, finds out that he is left on a methane-infested dirtball under the command of Belvooters. He helps the locals rise up against their nomad oppressors by using tactical advantages, along with strength.

This is a solo tale of the most popular alien character, Grimrod. It was reprinted by Titan Comics in 2004 (ISBN: 1840238119).

Dixon, Chuck, Larry Stroman, Mark Farmer, et al. *Alien Legion: On the Edge.* London: Titan, 2003. ISBN: 1840237651. Reprints *Alien Legion: On the Edge 1–3*; *Epic Anthology 3.*

The Legion helps the Alvarians against an enemy that is plundering their land. They use the gift of song to shatter a mountain on their enemy. The introduction is by *Alien Legion* creator Carl Potts.

Dixon Chuck, Larry Stroman, Mark Farmer, et al. *Alien Legion: On the Edge 1–3.* New York: Epic, 1990–1991. ISBN: 0871357062 (Vol. 1); 0871357070 (Vol. 2); 0871357089 (Vol. 3).

Force Nomad and their ship, the *Piecemaker*, get drawn into an Event Horizon, Black Star. They are caught between two races, the B'Be No N'GTH, who worship the Star as a god, and the cannibal race,

VARN/HROTH. Force Nomad tries to enlist the help of the N'GTH to escape. The alien, the protoplasmic Spellik, whom many of the Nomad considered useless, becomes the most valued member of the ship. When Nomad comes back through the Star, it is fifteen years in the future, and they are delegated to be a suicide squad.

Dixon, Chuck, Larry Stroman, Mark Farmer, et al. *Alien Legion: Piecemaker.* Centerville, OH: Checker, 2002. ISBN: 0971024944. Reprints Epic's *Alien Legion Vol. 2: 12–18.*

Jugger Grimrod does fighting-skills training. Meico commands a mission on the planet Momja, and his party almost dies in the stomach of a Momojain Kndrel, but Meico saves the group through a physical bond with the creature. Grimrod's father is leader of a terrorist group on Mmrosdia. Grimrod ends up killing his father, and giving Sarigar a glimpse of his past life. Sarigar is reunited with his sister. Tamara has a baby.

This is a reprint of the original *Alien Legion* comics from the Epic line.

Dixon, Chuck, Larry Stroman, Mike McMahon, et al. *Alien Legion: Tenants of Hell.* London: Titan, 2004. ISBN: 1840238119. Reprints Marvel/Epic's *Alien Legion: Tenants of Hell 1–2*; *Alien Legion: Jugger Grimrod.*

This edition contains two stories in their entirety, and includes extra "Legion Files," a glossary of terms, "Galactic Primer," and an essay about Hellscape. The introduction is by Chuck Dixon. This book is recommended.

Dixon, Chuck, Larry Stroman, Dan Panosian, et al. *Alien Legion: Tenants of Hell.* New York: Marvel, 1991. ISBN: 087135764X (1); 0871357658 (2).

Force Nomad 18, after being cast fifteen years in the future, is assigned to the planet Combine IV as a peacekeeping force. The corporation Halicorp is just using the Legion as cannon fodder, and is going to destroy Combine IV with them on it. Montroc's father finds out his son is still alive, and warns the Legion about Halicorp's plans. The Legionnaires escape with a young kid who wants to join.

This graphic novel was reprinted by Titan Comics in 2004 (ISBN: 1840238119).

Dixon, Chuck (Charles), Jorge Zaffino, Julie Michael, et al. *Seven Block: An Experiment in Terror.* New York: Epic, 1990. ISBN: 0871356988.

Three prison inmates are subjected to a secret government medical experiment. The government wants its own Super Soldier who will be useful in a war. The inmates, however, rebel; they kill the doctors and take over the prison.

Elliot, Dave, Garry Leach, Peter Milligan, et al. *A1 Volume 2: 1–4*. New York: Epic, 1991–1992. ISBN: 0871359499 (1); 0871359502 (2); 0871359510 (3); 0871359529 (4).

This is an excellent anthology of stories by various comic-industry talents. One story has Cyrano De Bergerac visiting the moon. Another story, which goes through three of the issues, deals with a young black man learning of his royal British heritage, only to be killed at the end. The amazing bird detective Cheek Wee Budgie Boy solves a case in which opera sopranos are being killed systematically. There also is a philosophical treatise in which Frankenstein meets Shirley Temple; this runs through all four issues,. Each issue also contains environmentally conscious information about endangered and hunted animals. The introduction is by Ninja Turtles creator Kevin Eastman.

Ellison, Harlan, Ken Steacy, Archie Goodwin, et al. *Night and the Enemy*. Norristown, PA: Comico/Graphitti Designs, 1987. ISBN: 0936211075 (trd) 0938965069 (pbk). Reprints Marvel/Epic's *Epic Illustrated 4, 6, 11*.

This collection puts together numerous short stories based on Ellison's stories, "Sleeping Dogs," "Run for the Stars" and "Life Hutch," which are about the future war between humans and a humanoid race, the Kyben. Ellison's stories were originally published by *Epic Illustrated*. One of the best stories in the collection deals with Earth prisoners who implant a bomb inside the body of a junkie, who then uses it to get the Kyben to do his bidding. He seeks revenge against the humans who put the bomb inside him. This limited edition of 1,500 copies that were signed by Ellison and Steacy. It also contains a new sequel story, "The Few, the Proud."

Goff, Cindy, Rafael Nieves, Seitu Hayden, et al. *Tales from the Heart of Africa: Bloodlines*. New York: Epic, 1992. ISBN: 0871358638.

In this book, Cathy Grant becomes interested in the story of a former dictator, and asks questions of her physician friend who was a prisoner under the dictator's regime. Although the story is fictional, the dictator is not. Emperor Jean-Bedel Bokassa was the "African Napoleon," who killed children and natives, and apparently kept human bodies in his freezer for meat. This is a gut-wrenching tale, realistically told in the "Butcher of Bangui." The afterword contains information relating to Bokassa and his rule, including the massacre at Ngaragba Prison. This is a sequel to *Temporary Natives*.

Goff, Cindy, Rafael Nieves, Seitu Hayden, et al. *Tales from the Heart of Africa: The Temporary Natives*. New York: Epic, 1990. ISBN: 0871356511

Cathy Grant befriends another worker, Jack Glasher, who is trying to build a school. He enlists the help of Cathy, only to disappoint her and the Africans with his arrogance and request for help. Cathy has to struggle with her purpose for being in Africa, and questions whether she is actually doing more harm than good.

This is the story of Peace Corps worker, Cathy Grant, and her time in Central Africa.

Grant, Alan, Tony Luke, Motofumi Kobayashi, et al. *Psychonauts 1–4*. New York: Epic, 1993–1994. ISBN: 0871359660 (1); 0871359979 (2); 0871359987 (3); 0871359995 (4).

In a desolate future, 2199, Earth has seemingly been destroyed by war and nuclear holocaust, and humanity has taken to the stars. Because of problems on the satellite planets, a group of six ESP-enhanced individuals is forced to come back to Earth, to see if it is inhabitable. They encounter intelligent dinosaurs, cyborgs, humans, weird wildlife, and a hybrid human/alien being which preys psychically on living beings. This hybrid being plans to eat the humans, and it is up to the Psychonauts to stop him.

This series was one of the first Japanese/American-produced comics. This is a well-written, interesting volume.

Hudnall, James, Paul Johnson, Steve Craddock, et al., *Espers: Interface*. Fullerton, CA: Image, 1998. ISBN: 1582400504. Reprints Marvel/Epic's *Interface 1–6*.

Linda Williams wants to keep the orignal Espers team together, but nobody is sure they want to continue, until they realize their lives may be on the line. Numerous people, including an Italian crime lord respnsible for JFK's death, and those from the Inner Circle, are gunning for the lives of the Espers team. Maria Rivas is not dead, but regains her memory just in time to save the lives of some of her colleagues. Several Esper assassins are brought in to kill them. Another Esper group, S.E.A., had offered to keep the Espers away from the Inner Circle.

This amazing series, which is a cross between the X-Files and Mission Impossible, continues to adventures of the Espers team. Hudnall writes a very detailed explanation of how this series came about. It is highly recommended for those who love thrillers and spy stories.

Hudnall, James, David Lloyd, John M. Burns, et al. *Espers*. New York: Epic, 1990. ISBN: 0871356937. Reprints *Espers 1–5*.

A team of psychically enhanced humans form a group to rescue Linda Williams's father from terrorists in the Middle East. It turns out that his kidnapping is not a terrorist act, but a cover-up for an organization doing secret experiments on psychic humans. The Espers infiltrate the "terrorist" compound, but Williams's father is dead. They free the other prisoners.

This volume, which was originally published by Eclipse Comics, combines narrative and graphics. The author gives biographical background essays on each character. Caliber republished a slightly abridged form of the first four issues in 1995, and Image Comics republished the first five issues as *Espers: The Storm*.

Hudnall, James, Robert P. Ortaleza, Michael Heisler, et al. *Sinking*. New York: Epic, 1992. ISBN: 0871359480.

This volume is a well-written case study of Ted Smith who believes the world is coming to an end. It traces his insanity and schizophrenia from his childhood when a golf ball broke in half and the acid from its middle worked its way into his brain and through the core of the Earth. This is a realistic portrait of a schizophrenic individual.

Hudnall, James, John Ridgway, John Workman, et al. *Chiller 1 & 2*. New York: Epic, 1993. ISBN: 0785100008.

A demon from the past is let loose on the world. A secret society of influential and wealthy men seeks to harness the demon's power for their purposes. A magician is hired to seek the demon, and bring back the spirit of sorcerer Aldo Roth. Roth and the secret society are actually in league with one another, for political and spiritual domination of the world. The magician has to figure out a way to stop them.

This was reprinted in a single volume by Image Comics in 2001 (ISBN: 1582400601).

Jewell, Stephen, Gary Chaloner, Gary Martine, et al. *The Olympians 1–2*. New York: Epic Comics, 1991–1992.

This two-part, cardstock-cover miniseries is a sarcastic look at superheroes who are attempting to protect Britain from all evildoers. The only problem is that nobody will save society from the Olympians, who are causing chaos everywhere. Many of the characters seem to be humorous stabs at DC Comics heroes, particularly the Justice League. This is a very funny book.

Jodorowsky, Alexandro, Moebius, Jean-Marc Lofficier, et al. *The Incal 1, 2, 3*. New York: Epic 1988. ISBN: 0871354365 (1); 0871354 373 (2); 0871354381 (3).

John DiFool is a private investigator who lives in the "Great Buried City." He stumbles upon the living gem, the Incal, in a strange encounter, and ends up being the reluctant hero who saves the universe from an age of darkness.

This is a beautifully written and drawn surreal science fiction epic that was originally published as a serial in *Heavy Metal*. Parts of the story are similar to Jodorowsky's film *Holy Mountain*. The series was republished and continued by Humanoids/DC Publishing as *Incal Epic Conspiracy* (ISBN: 1401206298); *Incal: Epic Journey* (ISBN: 1401206468); *Incal: Orphan of the City Shaft* (ISBN: 1930652348); *Incal: John Di-*

fool, Class "R" Detective (ISBN: 1930652852). Moebius's artistic designs also can be seen in the film *Fifth Element*.

Jones, Gerard, Steve Mattsson, Ron Randall, et al. *The Idol 1–3*. New York: Epic, 1992.

This three-issue cardstock-cover series is one of the more fascinating titles that Epic produced during their tenure. It concerns a movie crew making an action flick, *Idol of Slime 2*, on a defunct underwater military complex. One by one, strange things start happening, and it is learned that a bio-weapon is being tested on both the military crew and the film crew. This story is filled with adventure and intrigue. The onscreen super-woman, Rachel Ahmed, learns how to conquer her fears, and become a real live Super Woman.

Kubert, Joe. *Abraham Stone 1–2*. New York: Epic, 1995. ISBN: 078510608 (1); 0785101 632 (2).

Stone saves a rich lady from being robbed. She is the owner of a film studio, and she takes Stone to California, to be her "kept man," and to work in silent films. He acts in a number of films, but finds Hollywood to be a hollow, cold place. He goes to Mexico, and ends up in Pancho Villa's army. Villa recruits Stone to take part in his raid on the United States at Columbus, New Mexico, April 9, 1918. Stone refuses to fight against his country, and turns a machine gun on the Mexican army. Just as Villa is about to shoot Stone, the American Calvary comes.

This is Kubert's tale of a young wanderer, just as the American West was dying out. It is based on actual events.

Kubert, Joe, Kevin Somers, Carl Potts, et al. *Tor 1–4*. New York: Epic, 1993.

This is an oversize cardstock-cover series that was part of Epic's Heavy Hitters imprint. Tor is a super agile caveman, who has the strength and cunning to defeat various dinosaur-like creatures and bestial men who would seek to oppress him. In the volume, we learn about his origin and how he takes revenge against the "beast men" who killed his father and mother. There also is a story in which Tor saves a lovely woman from sacrifice, and ends up being captured himself. Although one might try to lump Tor with other jungle heroes like Tarzan and Ka-Zar, Kubert's creation is quite different.

Kurtzman, Harvey, Robert Crumb, Rick Geary, et al. *Harvey Kurtzman's Strange Adventures*. New York: Epic/Byron Preiss, 1990. ISBN: 0871356759 (trd); 0871357992 (pbk).

Originally a hardcover book, this collection of fun stories was written by *Mad* artist/writer Harvey Kurtzman. It features tributes by various artists, including Moebius, Dave Gibbons, Sergio Aragones, and Tomas Bunk; and Robert Crumb writes an ode to Harvey, in which he discusses their relationship over the years. In this volume, a caveman teaches his tribe to throw stones; Captain Bleed gets captured; the vampire, Mel, wants to be cured; and Sassy, the dog, sets his neighbors' houses on fire. The story of Mel is interesting because of all the hidden item placements. The stories include guest appearances by the Watchmen, an elderly Superman, Batman, Shazam, and Wonder Woman, among many others. The Super Surfer is Kurtzman's parody of the Silver Surfer. The volume also includes a Halloween parody, artists' biographies, penciled pages, and an introduction by Art Spiegelman.

Lanning Andy, Steve White, Phil Gascoine, et al. *Dreadlands 1–4*. New York: Epic, 1991–1992.

In post-apocalyptic America 2033, human scavengers are raiding a group of scientists/military officers, underground. The scientists have created a time machine, and intend to go into the future. The group goes to the pre-historic era of dinosaurs, where they break up into two factions: a civilian faction and a military one which has a megalomaniac who would rather shoot first. A group of nonviolent aliens has been herding dinosaurs, and when the military attacks its base, all hell breaks loose.

This is a cardstock-cover series that contains actions that take place in both the past and the future.

Lee, Elaine, James Sherman, Third Eye Studio, et al. *Transmutation of Ike Garuda 1 & 2*. New York: Epic, 1991–1992. ISBN: 08713 57755 (1); 0871357763 (2).

This is a surreal science fiction tale about a private eye, Ike Garuda, who is searching for the daughter of the CEO of the corporation Diamond Mines. There is an interview with Garuda on the back of the book.

Lovece, Frank, Mike Okamota, Al Williamson, et al. *Atomic Age 1–4*. New York: Epic, 1990–1991. ISBN: 0871357097 (1); 0871357 100 (2); 0871357119 (3); 0871357127 (4).

In 1957, an alien who is a slave on her home planet comes to Earth to destroy the Mother Seed, which will result in "geneticide" of her species. The Nimbus alien, a bounty hunter, is sent to Earth to kill the clone-slave, but he leans that he once was a clone-slave as well, and the two aliens fall in love. An army general who wants to maintain his glory keeps the existence of the aliens to himself, but he is almost court-martialed. He kills himself before he can be taken prisoner. A journalist wants to make a name for himself by writing the story about the aliens.

This work revolves around four main characters: two aliens, an army general, and a Hispanic journalist. The historical fifties feel of the text and artwork is authentic. This is a fun science fiction tale, but at times it is quite complicated.

Macklin, Ken, Raymond E. Feist, Lela Dowling, et al. *Dr. Watchstop: Adventures in Time and Space*. Forestville, CA: Eclipse Books, 1989. ISBN: 0913035858. Reprints Marvel/Epic's *Epic Illustrated 14, 17, 24, 29, 33–34*.

This a wonderful collection of short vignettes featuring the scientist, Dr. Watchstop. Watchstop, a physicist and archeologist, is fascinated with the universe and its history. His bizarre adventures are quit quirky and indescribable, except to say that they are very *Far Side*–ish and a hoot to read.

McKeever, Ted, et al. *Metropol A.D.* Canada: Sorhenn Grafiks, 2000. ISBN: 2914406 037. Reprint's Marvel/Epic's *Metropol Vol. 1: 1–3*.

This bizarre horror comic has a very interesting visual and narrative premise, but it is difficult to describe; even McKeever says it defies characterization and description. In the book, the Metropol Universe is filled with dead bodies, odd characters, surreal landscapes, and bizarre erotic happenings. The main character, everyman Jasper Notochord, is taken to jail, and accused of a crime he knows nothing about, and no one will tell him anything about the crime. A limited-edition hardcover was produced by Blue Eyed Dog in 1995, featuring all twelve issues of volume 1, and the first three issues of the volume 2 series, with no ISBNs.

McKeever, Ted, Phil Felix, Robbin Brosterman, et al. *Plastic Forks 1–5*. New York: Epic, 1990.

A scientist who is working on a way to eliminate the need for both a male and a female in the reproductive process, creates a technological device which, when grafted onto the genitalia of either male or female, allows reproduction in either sex. The result is a monstrous being, with little or no resemblance to a regular human. The scientist, after unwillingly being subjected to the experiment by his former partner, realizes the evil he has wrought on humanity. When others kidnap his pregnant wife, and try to subject her to the experiment, a strange soldier of fortune comes to his aid, blows up the medical facilities, and saves his wife and child.

This bizarre cyberpunk tale deals with the dangers of genetic and technological manipulation. It is well written, and illustrated with a dark atmospheric touch. Graphitti Designs published a cloth-cover version in 1990 (ISBN: 0936211245).

Miller, Frank, Bill Sienkiewicz, Jim Novak, et al. *Elektra: Assassin*. New York: Epic, 1987. ISBN: 0871353091. Reprints *Elektra Volume 1: 1–8*.

Elektra kills the president of San Concepcion, South America. She also kills a number of S.H.I.E.L.D. agents, and brainwashes a cyborg agent into following her. S.H.I.E.L.D. has been making cyborg soldiers out of killers and molesters, in their ExTech Op Division. Elektra and her cronies seek to kill presidential hopeful Ken Wind, who they believe will start World War III with the Soviets by pushing the button for a nuclear missile attack.

This is a surrealistic tale about various aspects of Elektra's past and present, in which many details about Elektra not covered in previous comics are showcased. The non-narrative writing style in this volume is thought-provoking, and the artwork is quite beautiful. This book was also published as a special, signed hardcover by Graphitti Designs (ISBN: 0936211148).

Miller, Frank, Lynn Varley, Jim Novak, et al. *Elektra Lives Again.* New York: Epic/ Graphitti Design, 1990. ISBN: 0936211 27X; 0871357380; 0813573807 (1991); 087 1357984 (1993).

Matt Murdock struggles with his faith, and the death of his love Elektra. He has nightmares which are both surreal and horrifying. Bullseye is seemingly murdered while in prison.

This graphic novel was reprinted in 2003 as a hardback. See the Marvel Masterworks chapter for more information.

Mills, Pat, Kevin O'Neill, Steve Buccellato, et al. *Pinhead vs. Marshal Law: Law in Hell 1–2.* New York: Epic, 1993.

Marshal Law, his girlfriend, and other heroes take a journey into Hell. Pinhead makes Marshal feel pain, but is eventually defeated when he is confronted with his past. Pinhead realizes that Marshal can do more good in the world, and they shake hands before departing to their respective domains.

These issues were printed in cardstock-cover format.

Mills, Pat, Kevin O Neill, Phil Felix, et al. *Marshal Law: Fear and Loathing.* New York: Epic, 1990. ISBN: 0871356767. Reprints *Marshal Law 1–6.*

Genetically enhanced superhumans are running through the streets of San Futro, causing violence and mayhem because of a government-sponsored genetics program. Marshal Law protects the remaining humans, and brings justice by killing the killers. Marshal Law hates the world's leading superhero, Public Spirit, with a vengeance. He tries to discredit Spirit anyway he can, believing him to be a murderer. A murdering creep who calls himself the Sleepman is killing women who dress like his mother Virgo. Sleepman kills Law's girlfriend, Lynn. Law eventually finds out that Spirit's past is unkosher.

Marshal Law is Marvel's answer to Judge Dredd, and San Futro is a futuristic and violent version of San Francisco. This volume was reprinted by Titan Books in 2003 (ISBN: 1840234520), and Graphitti Designs published a hardcover version, which combined *Fear and Loathing* and *Crime and Punishment*, in 1990 (ISBN: 0936211237).

Mills, Pat, Kevin O'Neill, Mark A. Nelson, et al. *Crime and Punishment: Marshal Law Takes Manhattan.* New York: Epic, 1989.

Marshal Law is sent to a mental institution for deranged superheroes, where his nemesis, the Persecutor, is admitted. Law's boss sets him up by revealing Law's identity to the Persecutor. Law was actually a student of Persecutor's when they worked for the C.I.A.. Law totally demolishes all the so-called heroes in the institution, and his former teacher.

This novel was reprinted in the *Marshal Law: Fear Asylum* collection from Titan Books in 2003 (ISBN: 184023699X).

Moebius (Jean Giraud), Jean-Michel Charlier, Jean-Marc Lofficier, et al. *Blueberry 1: Chihuahua Pearl.* New York: Epic 1989. ISBN: 087135569.

Blueberry is asked to go undercover as an outlaw to find a half million dollars in gold for the U.S. government. His problems become insurmountable when others find out about the gold's existence. He goes into Mexico and meets up with a woman known as the Chihuahua Pearl whose husband knows where the gold is hidden. Blueberry breaks her husband out of jail, only to be caught by a group of bandits who also want the gold.

In 1996, Mojo Press reprinted some of the Blueberry saga as *Confederate Gold* (ISBN: 1885418086).

Moebius (Jean Giraud), Jean-Michel Charlier, Jean-Marc Lofficier, et al. *Blueberry 2: Ballad for a Coffin.* New York: Epic, 1989. ISBN: 0871355701.

Lieutenant Blueberry helps a group of roughnecks find a coffin full of gold in Mexico. A Mexican army officer and a group of bandits pursue the band of roughnecks. The Mexican government steals the gold, and Blueberry is arrested.

In "The Outlaw," Blueberry escapes from prison. This volume includes Moebius's environmentally conscious "Words of Chief Seattle."

Moebius (Jean Giraud), Jean-Michel Charlier, Jean-Marc Lofficier, et al. *Blueberry 3: Angel Face.* New York: Epic, 1989. ISBN: 087135571X.

Blueberry is framed for the attempted assassination of President Grant. His friend Guffie Palmer is killed, and Grant places Blueberry on the most-wanted list, with a hefty reward on his head. Blueberry poses as a fireman in order to get out of the town, and thwarts another attempt on Grant's life by the assassin Angel Face. He also tries to save his Apache friends from a massacre at the hands of the U.S. Army. Blueberry gives himself up to the authorities, in order to save the life of the Indian princess he loves.

Moebius (Jean Giraud), Jean-Michel Charlier, Jean-Marc Lofficier, et al. *Blueberry 4: The*

Ghost Tribe. New York: Epic, 1990. ISBN: 0871355809.

Blueberry is to be taken to Durango, to be put on trial and hanged. Red and Mac seek the aid of Chihuahua Pearl to help them free Blueberry. They succeed, and Blueberry goes to help the Apaches and Chief Cochise get to Mexico. The army wants to take them to San Carlos, where they will die of starvation and disease. Blueberry and the Apaches outsmart the Army and the U.S. government by causing them to miss their trail; Blueberry and the Apaches appear to be ghosts. They even go so far as to commandeer an "iron horse," a train, from under the army's noses. Blueberry, Red, and Mac go into Mexico to find Vigo.

Moebius (Jean Giraud), Jean-Michel Charlier, Jean-Marc Lofficier, et al. *Blueberry 5: The End of the Trail.* New York: Epic, 1990. ISBN: 0871355817.

Blueberry and his friends go to Chihuahua where they are promptly put in jail by Vigo. Vigo is overthrown and put in jail himself; he is to stand before the firing squad. He is the only one who can prove Blueberry is innocent of stealing the Confederate gold. Vigo is sprung, but killed, and Blueberry, who finds the gold, goes back to the States. He proves his innocence, and foils another plan to kill President Grant. His old nemesis, General Golden Mane, is behind the assassination plot. Angel Face returns, but with a scarred face. Blueberry intends to marry Chihuahua Pearl.

Graphitti Designs published a collection of Blueberry stories (ISBN: 0936211210). Other epic Moebius books from Graphitti Designs are assigned the following ISBNs: 0936211288; 0936211113; 0936211385; 0936211105; 0936211121; 0936211202; 0936211229; 0936211342; 0936211334; and 0936211350.

Moebius (Jean Giraud), Jean-Michel Charlier, Jean-Marc Lofficier, et al. *Lieutenant Blueberry Book 1: The Iron Horse.* New York: Epic, 1991. ISBN: 0871357402

In 1867, General Dodge brings Blueberry in, to help relations with the Indians. Two railroad companies, the Union Pacific and Central Pacific, are both trying to link the Atlantic to the Pacific via a transcontinental railroad. Steelfingers is brought in by Central Pacific, to make sure the Indians are not a problem. He starts a fight with Blueberry, and then with the Indians. There is a mole working in General Dodge's camp for the rival company.

This takes place in 1867, two years before the regular Blueberry series.

Moebius (Jean Giraud), Jean-Michel Charlier, Jean-Marc Lofficier, et al. *Lieutenant Blueberry Book 2: Steelfingers.* New York: Epic, 1991. ISBN: 0871357410.

A spy for the Central Pacific Railroad Company has infiltrated the Union Pacific camp in Omaha. All the food, water, and supplies have been destroyed, and camp is surrounded by Cheyenne Indians. Blueberry is sent out to get supplies and help. His enemy, Steelfingers, makes a pact with the Indians to raid the supply train with Blueberry and $200,000 on it. The train is destroyed, but Blueberry escapes, and hides the money.

Moebius (Jean Giraud), Jean-Michel Charlier, Jean-Marc Lofficier, et al. *Lieutenant Blueberry Book 3: General Golden Maine.* New York: Epic, 1991. ISBN: 0871357429.

Blueberry is framed by Steelfingers for stealing the payroll. He is being pursued by the army, but is a prisoner of the Indians. He manages to break away, but Steelfingers follows him, takes the money, and beats Blueberry senseless. He puts a few thousand dollar bills in Blueberry's shirt, to make it look like he stole the money. Steelfingers kills his posse to keep the money for himself. The Indians find out that he has betrayed them, and kill him. Blueberry sets up a meeting with General Dodge, and he negotiates a peace treaty. General Golden Mane sees no validity in the treaty, and puts together a regiment to kill all the Indians. Blueberry is left to rot with the sick and wounded, but he manages to survive, as does General Golden Mane when Dodge shows up with reinforcements.

Moebius (Jean Giraud), Jean-Michel Charlier, Jean-Marc Lofficier, et al. *Marshal Blueberry: The Lost Dutchman's Mine.* New York: Epic, 1991. ISBN: 0871355698.

Blueberry is now the town marshal in Palomito, Arizona. A man claiming to be the Dutch Baron Luckner is causing trouble, and Blueberry arrests him. A number of people in the town want the Baron's blood, for various things, including murder. The Baron tricks Blueberry's partner Jimmy into freeing him, with a promise to share the gold from his "lost" mine. Several bounty hunters are after the Baron and Jimmy, as are Blueberry and several others. They have to contend with hostile Indians, and, once they go into the mining area, the Indians stop their chase. The Indians believe it is cursed by a ghost who haunts the caves and mountains. It turns out the real Baron is the "ghost," and the one posing as the Baron is the Baron's assistant. The Baron was attacked and left for dead, and his identity taken by his former employee.

This volume is filled with action, humor, and suspense, and is one of the best in the series. It contains an early, 1958, pro–Indian strip by Moebius, "King of the Buffalo," with a short introduction. This volume also includes a short essay, "General Who Never Was," about a character who appears in previous Blueberry books.

Moebius (Jean Giraud), Jean-Michel Charlier, Jean-Marc Lofficier, et al. *Moebius 8: Mississippi River.* New York: Epic, 1991. ISBN: 0871357151.

Union officer Jim Cutlass comes into an inheritance. While traveling to New Orleans, he helps a slave break free and get off of the boat. He becomes a wanted man throughout the South, where he is considered a traitor. Cutlass ends up killing his cousin's fiancé. When the war is over, Cutlass goes back to New Orleans to claim his inheritance, and helps his cousin against carpetbaggers who want to buy the plantation. After several brawls, and time in jail, Cutlass decides to go back into the army, and he leaves his cousin and the plantation.

This tale, which takes place during the Civil War, is very similar to the Blueberry stories.

Moebius (Jean Giraud), Jean-Michel Charlier, Jean-Marc Lofficier, et al. *Moebius 9: Stel.* New York: Epic, 1994. ISBN: 0785100202.

The Paternum is chasing Stel, as a dinosaur. A group of Nesters on patrol know nothing about the overthrow of the Nest. The leader of the group kills the radio operator, and ends up being controlled by the Paternum. Stel is captured by the Nesters after fixing their vehicle, and, along with another "out-nester," he is taken to another Nest underneath a volcano. Stel meets with an old friend who turns out to be the Paternum. Stel's brain is probed.

This is the sequel to *Moebius 7,* in which Stel searches for Atan on Aedena. This is the fourth chapter of the Aedena cycle.

Moebius (Jean Giraud), Jean-Marc Lofficier, Randy Lofficier, et al. *Chaos.* Epic, 1991. ISBN: 0871358336.

This is a collection of artwork and comic musings. Chapters are separated three sections: "Parapsychology," "Wonders of the Universe," and "Something Inside Something."

Moebius (Jean Giraud), Jean-Marc Lofficier, Randy Lofficier, et al. *Fusion.* New York: Epic, 1995. ISBN: 0785101551.

This is a beautiful, hardcover collection of science fiction—related artwork, both in color and in black and white. It includes pictures of Wolverine, Spider-Man, the Punisher, Elektra, the Thing, Iron Man, and a very aged Silver Surfer. This volume also includes a philosophical short story, "Oracle," about the meaning of life.

Moebius (Jean Giraud), Jean-Marc Lofficier, Randy Lofficier, et al. *Metallic Memories.* New York: Epic, 1992. ISBN: 0871358344.

This is a collection of sketches, short comics, doodlings, a science fiction book, and magazine covers.

Moebius (Jean Giraud), Jean-Marc Lofficier, Randy Lofficier, et al. *Moebius 1: Upon A Star.* New York: Epic, 1987. ISBN: 087135 2788.

This is a collection of mystical science fiction tales, originally published in the *Heavy Metal* magazine. It

is the first in a series known as the Aedena Cycle, about the mystery of the universe. The Aedena Cycle tales feature two characters, Stel and Atan, who find an abandoned ship and land on a strange planet where they meet different races from different parts of the galaxy. Each tale has an introduction by Moebius, documenting his thought processes. A biography, "The Life and Times of Jean 'Moebius' Giraud," is included in this volume, plus the short prequel, "The Repairmen."

Moebius (Jean Giraud), Jean-Marc Lofficier, Randy Lofficier, et al. *Moebius 2: Arzach and Other Science Fiction Stories.* New York: Epic, 1987. ISBN: 0871352790.

This volume contains one of Moebius's most famous series of science fiction stories. It was originally published in book form in *Métal Hurlant,* and later in *Heavy Metal* magazine. The original stories, which were wordless, deal with Arzach, the pterodactyl-riding warrior. A new Arzach short story, created just for this volume, "Legend of Arzach," has words. This collection also includes the Lovecraft-inspired Ktulu. A novel version, which was written by Randy and Jean Lofficier, with illustrations by Moebius, was published by iBooks. ISBN: 0743400151 (trd, 2000); 074349 2994 (plbk, 2004). There also are reprints by Titan (ISBN: 1852860456) and Dark Horse, (ISBN: 15697 11321).

Moebius (Jean Giraud), Jean-Marc Lofficier, Randy Lofficier, et al. *Moebius 3: Airtight Garage.* New York: Epic, 1987. ISBN: 087135280X.

This volume contains the humorous space-opera adventures of Major Grubert, told in separate chapters. In these stories Grubert attempts to stop the plans of his enemies who are trying to take over the world. The Grubert stories were originally serialized in the European magazine *Métal Hurlant.* The volume is filled with humor and different planes of reality which remind me of Douglas Adams's *Hitchhiker's Guide to the Universe.* This is a witty and surreal science fiction piece that was four years in the making.

Moebius (Jean Giraud), Jean Marc Lofficier, Randy Lofficier, et al. *Moebius 4: The Long Tomorrow and Other Stories.* New York: Epic, 1987. ISBN: 0871352818.

This is a collection of short science fiction stories. The title story features private detective Pete Club who is a cross between Blade Runner and Raymond Chandler. This story also features the inspiration behind the Imperial Probe that was used in *Star Wars: The Empire Strikes Back.* Moebius gives his takes on a nuclear holocaust and hunting.

Moebius (Jean Giraud), Jean-Marc Lofficier, Randy Lofficier, et al. *Moebius 5: Gardens of Aedena.* New York: Epic, 1988. ISBN: 087 1352826.

Stel and Atan end up on a planet filled with wildlife, fruit, and grass. They try eating fruit and meat, and drinking water for the first time. Stel and Atan go through some physical transformations, from being androgynous to male and female. Stel, who realizes that he is attracted to Atan, wants to make love, but Atan will have none of it, and runs away.

This is a continuation of the Stel and Atan's story from *Upon a Star*. Parts of this are very similar to the Garden of Eden and Adam and Eve stories from the Bible. The volume also includes a Major Grubert short story, and the famous "Hit Man" series.

Moebius (Jean Giraud), Jean-Marc Lofficier, Randy Lofficier, et al. *Moebius 6: Pharagonesia and Other Strange Stories*. New York: Epic, 1988. ISBN: 0871352834.

This collection of weird science fiction stories features the wordless "Absoluten Calfeutrail," and a story about hunting a vacationing Frenchman. It features the first appearance of Major Grubert. Moebius comments on racism in "The White Nightmare." The title story, "Pharagonesia," gives a humorous look at transmitted viruses.

Moebius (Jean Giraud), Jean-Marc Lofficier, Randy Lofficier, et al. *Moebius 7: The Goddess*. New York: Epic, 1990. ISBN: 087135 7143.

Atan searches for Stel in a society called the Nest in which no one is allowed to show one's face, and everyone has to wear a mask, called a face, oddly enough. The Nest is ruled by an all-powerful father who gives them their ideas. When an Atan shows up naked, with no mask, several believe she is the goddess who will deliver them to freedom. When their god, the Paternum, can not guarantee their safety, the citizens of the Nest revolt.

This is Moebius's version of *Brave New World*, a dystopian society, and it is the third chapter in the Aedena Cycle. The volume has an afterword by Moebius.

Moebius (Jean Giraud), Byron Preiss, Jean-Marc Lofficier, et al. *The Art of Moebius*. New York: Epic, 1989. ISBN: 0871356104.

This is a collection of Moebius's artwork, with a personal reflection by the artist on each piece. Filmmaker George Lucas wrote the introduction.

Moench, Doug, Paul Gulacy, Gasper Saladino, et al. *Six from Sirius*. New York: Epic, 1988. ISBN: 0781353342. Reprints *Six from Sirius 1–4*.

A group of interstellar heroes from the planet Sirius tries to stop a war between two planets, Axellon and Balsamo, over the moon, Heavenstone. Heavenstone is inhabited by a group of spiritualists who follow the teachings of five founders who have died, yet live. The groups from Sirius break Ambassador Phaedra out of prison, to help with peace negotiations.

They go up against years of bad blood, and have to fight androids known as Fax-Men/Women.

This mystical science fiction tale was reprinted in trade form by Dynamite Entertainment (ISBN: 1933305037).

Murray, Doug, Russ Heath, Jim Novak, et al. *Hearts and Minds: A Vietnam Love Story*. New York: Epic, 1990. ISBN: 0871356996.

When a Vietnamese village is ransacked by the Americans, a married couple, each believing the other is dead, go their separate ways. One becomes a Viet Cong soldier, while his wife becomes a prostitute. She meets with an American soldier, who buys her, and promises to take care of her. The American asks her to marry him. Her husband ends up killing the American soldier while he is in a loving embrace with his wife-to-be. She pulls a gun on her husband, but he shoots her first. Then, he is shot by the Americans.

This is realistic portrayal of the Vietnam War, told through the lives of three people: a Viet Cong, an American, and a prostitute, who all die in the end.

Nocenti, Ann, John Bolton, Jo Duffy, et al. *Someplace Strange*. New York: Epic, 1988. 087135439X.

This is a bizarre fantasy story, similar to *Alice in Wonderland*, in which two brothers and a gothic teenager are transported to a magical realm. Ideas and drawings become real and dangerous. A hybrid of Spider-Man, Popeye, Captain America, and Iron Man is drawn to fight a huge monster. Graphitti Designs published a hardcover version of this volume (ISBN: 0936211121).

Otomo, Katsuhiro. *Kaba: Artwork*. Tokyo, Japan: Kodansha, 1989. Reprints Epic's *Farewell to Arms*; *Watermelon Messiah*.

This collection of Otomo's artwork was distributed by Marvel. It features Otomo's work for *You Magazine* and various comic and television commercial illustrations, along with movie storyboards. Otomo shows off his collection of memorabilia, his cat, and his studio, and provides personal commentaries. This hardcover book is well worth seeking, for any true student of anime/manga.

Otomo, Katsuhiro, Steve Oliff, Jo Duffy, et al. *Akira 1–10*. New York: Epic, 1991–1993. ISBN: 087135697X; 999123344X (1); 087 1357828 (2); 087135831X (3); 0871358328 (4); 0871359006 (5); 0871359014 (6); 087 1359391 (7); 0871359405 (8); 0871359413 (9); 0785100024 (10).

Marvel reproduced some of the Prestige *Akira* edition, as trade paperbacks in a ten-volume series collection. These trade paperbacks are extremely rare and costly, should you be able to find them. *Akira* has been republished many times all over the world since the first Epic series; there are far too many to cover them all here. Dark Horse Comics produced six black-and-white trade paperbacks covering the whole series: ISBN: 1569714983 (1); 1569714991 (2); 1569715254 (3); 1569715262 (4); 1569715270 (5); 1569715289 (6). There is a Barnes and Noble edition of Vol. 1 (076 075859X). Graphitti Designs also published five beautiful, limited-edition, hardcover volumes: ISBN: 0936211318 (1); 0936211377 (2); 0936211407 (3); 093621144X (4); 0936211458 (5).

Otomo, Katsuhiro, Steve Oliff, Jo Duffy, et al. *Akira 1–38*. New York: Epic, 1988–1995. ISBN: 0871355841 (1); 087135585X (2); 0871355841 (9); 0871355868 (11); 087135 5876 (12); 0871355884 (13); 0871355892 (14); 0871355906 (15); 0871355914 (16); 087135618X (17); 0871356198 (18); 087135 6021 (19); 087135621X (20); 0871356228 (21); 0871356236 (22); 0871356244 (23); 087135683X (24); 0871356848 (25); 08713 56856 (26); 0871356864 (27); 0871356872 (28); 0871356880 (29); 0871356899 (30); 0871356902 (31); 0871357933 (32); 08713 57941 (33); 087135795X; 0785101616 (34); 0871357976; 0785101659 (35); 0871359103; 0785101667 (36); 0871359103; 0785101675 (37); 0875101683 (38).

This is a postmodern look at a dystopia, set thirty-eight years after World War III. In it, Neo-Tokyo once again comes under the threat of annihilation by superpowered children who have the mental capacity to destroy with just a thought. The most powerful of them, Akira, has been suspended animation for twenty years. *Akira*, a massive epic of over 1,600 pages set the standard for modern day manga. It was made into a successful animated film, and began in the pages of *Young Magazine* in Japan. The story concerning young Kaneda and his girlfriend Kay, revolves around what happens after Akira is awakened. How do you deal with children who have the power of God? These volumes also contain extra information about the film, Otomo, and the process of making *Akira* for western audiences, among other special features. The last several volumes contain tributes to *Akira* by Moebius, Mike Allred, John Romita, and Alex Toth, among others.

Otomo, Katsuhiro, Yoko Umezawal, Robert Spaulding, et al. *Memories*. London: Mandarin Paperbacks, 1995. ISBN: 0749396 873. Reprints Marvel/Epic's *Farewell to Weapons*; *Memories*.

This is a collection of short science-fiction stories by *Akira* creator Otomo. Stories include "Minor Swing," which has cameos by Godzilla and Ultraman; "Flower"; "Chronicle of Planet Tako"; "Fireball"; and "Farewell to Weapons," among several others. "Fireball" is about a computer-controlled society and "Farewell to Weapons" is an interesting story about a fight against the war machine Gonk.

Pini, Wendy, Richard Pini. *Elfquest*. Poughkeepsie, NY: Father Tree Press/Warp Graphics/Wolfrider Books/DC, 1993–2003. Reprints Marvel/Epic's *Elfquest 1–32*.

Elfquest was originally published by Warp Graphics as *Elfquest 1–20*, which contains the first part of the Elfquest saga. Marvel reprinted this first part of the saga in 1983, and the issues were reprinted by Warp in four volumes, as hardcover and softcover books: *Fire and Flight* (1), ISBN: 0936861169 (trd); 0936861061 (pbk); 093686155X (pbk); *Forbidden Grove* (2), ISBN: 0936861185 (trd); 093686107X (pbk) 0936861568 (pbk); *Captives at Blue Mountain* (3), ISBN: 09368 61193 (trd) 0936861088 (pbk); 0936861576 (pbk); and *Quest's End* (4), ISBN: 0936861150 (trd) 093686109X (pbk); 0936861096 (pbk); 0936861584 (pbk). DC recently republished the first five Warp issues in a special hardcover edition, as *Elfquest Archives 1* which is currently in print (ISBN: 1401201288). It continues in three more volumes, *Elfquest Archives 2–4* (ISBNs: 1401201296; 1401204120; 1401207731). The story of Cutter and his search for his elf ancestors was also published, both as a novel and as a book on tape.

Potts, Carl, Chuck Dixon, Larry Stroman, et al. *Alien Legion: Force Nomad*. Centerville, OH: Checker, 2001. ISBN: 0971024901. Reprints Marvel/Epic's *Alien Legion Vol. 2: 1–11*.

Major Sarigar searches for lost members of Nomad on the planet Quaal. Jugger Grimrod is promoted and given his own command, which he hates. A bunch of new recruits join Nomad. Grimrod finds an illegal trade agreement between the Harkilons and the Orestans. Someone tries to assassinate Grimrod in prison. Montroc enlists the aid of his father to unravel this alien conspiracy. Several in Nomad are captured, but the conspiracy is brought into the open.

A complete reprint of this wonderful science fiction saga is needed.

Potts, Carl, Dennis O' Neil, Terry Austin, et al. *The Last of the Dragons*. New York: Epic, 1988. ISBN: 0871353350.

Groups of evil ninjas train the usually peaceful dragons to be instruments of destruction in their war to claim the New World. It is up to a wise old ninja, Masanobu, and his young ally to stop the war of the dragons.

Potts, Carl, Alan Zelenetz, Frank Cirocco, et al. *Alien Legion: A Grey Day to Die:* New York: Marvel, 1986. ISBN: 0871352079.

The Legion is called in to stop the antagonistic race of Technoids, by assassinating their leader. Their leader turns out to be the legendary Legion hero Captain Vektor, who had been swayed to the way of the Technoid. Captain Sarigar does the assassination.

The story explores morality, greed, loneliness, and

the significance of a legend in which fact is less important than myth. (*Marvel Graphic Novel 24*)

Potts, Carl, Alan Zelenetz, and Frank Cirocco, et al. *Alien Legion: Slaughterworld*, New York: Epic, 1991. ISBN: 0871357631. Reprints *Alien Legion Vol. 1: 1, 7–11.*

The Legion is called out to protect the ecosystem of a world which is been ransacked by pirates. Both the Alien Legion and their enemies, Harkilons, are stranded on a seemingly desolate planet. At first, the Legion and the Harkilons fight each other in a gruesome battle, but then they make an uneasy alliance and pool their resources to get off the planet. They have to contend with a brainwashing plant which uses a carnivorous symbiotic being to kill both the Legion and the Harkilons for food. The Legion and the Harkilons end up turning on each other in a horrible slaughter. The medical officer Mecio is hurt, and has to have an arm amputated.

This is an excellent science fiction story. The introduction is by Carl Potts and the afterword is by Marc McLaurin.

Purcell, Steve, Lois Buhalis, et al. *Sam and Max: Freelance Police: Special Color Collection.* New York: Epic, 1992. ISBN: 0871359383. Reprints *Sam and Max Show 1–3.*

Sam and Max go to the Philippines to stop an evil cult, and almost get sacrificed themselves. Mack Salmon tries to kill them, but the Rubber Pants Commandos come to their rescue. They catch a hot-dog vendor at the fair, who is selling bootleg corndogs. They go back in time to ancient Egypt, and stop aliens from invading Earth. They save the world's largest prairie dog. Sam and Max are called upon to stop a demon that is terrorizing the cereal a isle in a local supermarket.

Sam and Max's philosophy of life is explained in this novel, in the short section, "Ponderings of the Ages." There are many crazy tales in this volume. It was reprinted by Marlowe: ISBNs: 1569248125 (trd); 1569248141 (pbk); 1569248370 (ltd).

Robinson, James, Steve Yoewell, Gloria Vasquez, et al. *67 Seconds.* New York: Epic, 1992. ISBN: 0871358646.

This is a bizarre love story about a photographer and the reporter he loves, and their adventures as they try to get the most interesting story. They both have various brushes with death, and never really come to terms with the romance in their relationship. This is a well-written, futuristic tale, in which the photographer has only sixty-seven seconds in which to make a choice between life or death, and the story of the century.

Russell, Craig P., Patrick Mason, Bill Pearson, et al. "Ein Heldentraum" in *Opera Adaptations Vol. 3.* New York: NBM, 2004. ISBN: 1561633887 (trd); 1561633895 (pbk). Reprints Marvel/Epic's *Epic Illustrated 33.*

"Ein Heldentraum," Hugo Wolf's operatic adaptation of a poem by Goethe, tells the story of a daydreaming young man who wishes he could be a hero. This collection also has adaptations of "Pelleas & Melisande," "The Godfather's Code," and "Salome."

Saenz, Mike, William Bates, Archie Goodwin, et al. *Iron Man: Crash.* New York: Epic, 1988. ISBN: 0871352915.

Iron Man is in his seventies, and he sells his Iron Man weapon schematics to a firm in Japan who outbid S.H.I.E.L.D. for the information. An industrial spy group, the Digital Dreadnoughts, intercepts the information, and Iron Man has to go and clean up the damage. Nick Fury makes a cameo appearance.

This is the first completely computer-generated graphic novel. It provides a surrealistic look at a future in which information is the basis of power, not military might. This also is the first cyberpunk graphic novel. It includes a section, "The Making of *Crash*," by the author.

Schultz, Mark, Vince Rush, Al Williamson, et al. *Cadillacs & Dinosaurs.* Princeton, WI: Kitchen Sink Press, 1989. ISBN: 087816 0701 (trd); 087816071X (pbk). Reprints Marvel/Epics's *Cadillacs and Dinosaurs 1–4.*

This book reprints, in black and white, the original series *Cadillacs and Dinosaurs*, which was published by Kitchen Sink Press as *Xenozoic Tales 1–4*; *Death Rattle 8.* The series is set five to six hundred years in the future, after an apocalypse. Humanity, which had been underground for many years, comes to the surface, but is stuck in mid–twentieth-century technology. Dinosaurs, mammoths, and bizarre creatures are commonplace. The stories revolve around the characters Jack Tenrec and Hannah Dundee. Hannah is a scientist and diplomat for one tribe, while Jack is a mechanic, nature mystic, and the unofficial leader of a rival tribe. Their adventures together are as interesting as one could imagine. The Grith, who are humanoid reptile-like creatures that Jack has known about for some time, reveal themselves to Hannah. I was horrified when, in one story, a library of thousands of ancient twentieth-century books is flooded. In 2003, Dark Horse Comics reprinted *Cadillacs and Dinosaurs 1–6* and *Death Rattle 8* as *Xenozoics Tale Vol. 1: After the End* (ISBN: 1569716900) and *Xenozoic Tales Vol. 2: The New World* (ISBN: 1569716919). Al Williamson wrote the introduction.

Schultz, Mark, Steve Stiles, Jack Jackson, et al. *Dinosaur Shaman: Nine Tales from the Xenozoic Age.* Princeton, WI: Kitchen Sink Press, 1990. ISBN: 0878161171 (trd); 08781 6118X (pbk). Reprints Epic/Marvel's *Cadillacs and Dinosaurs 5–6.*

While fishing, Jack Tenrec and Hannah Dundee almost are killed by some kind of large, aquatic crustacean. Hannah looks for a lost boy who has been trained by the Girth. A dog protects sheep from a T-Rex–like dinosaur, and some scientists find some biological ooze, "archeoplasm," left over from 2010. Although Jack tries to stop the ooze from being spread, it is let loose, and changes the ecosystem. Some large sea vipers ruin a fishing expedition. Jack and Hannah have a hallucinatory dream, and almost die in an area with deadly vapors.

This volume continues the adventures of Jack Tenrec and Hannah Dundee. It includes a sketchbook and an introduction by Jack Jackson. It reprints Kitchen Sink's *Xenozoic Tales 5–8.*

Shiner, Lewis, Melinda Snodgrass, Howard Waldrop, et al. *Wildcards.* New York: Epic, 1991. ISBN: 0871357887. Reprints *Wildcards 1–4.* ISBN: 0871356961 (1); 0871357164 (2); 0871357178 (3); 0871357186 (4).

This is a peculiar science fiction story in which an alien gene bomb has been dropped on Earth. The bomb's virus kills 90 percent of the people. Those who are left are infected, and are known as jokers and aces. The jokers are mutated and disfigured, while the aces are given some kind of super power. This story follows the exploits of an ace, Jay Ackroyd, who is hired to find out who destroyed Jetboy's tomb.

Sienkiewicz, Bill, James Novak, Carl Potts, et al. *Stray Toasters.* New York: Epic, 1991. ISBN: 0871357135. Reprints *Stray Toasters Model 1–4.*

In this volume, a criminal psychologist who has recently been in a mental institution is called in to investigate a series of gruesome murders. None of his previous women want anything to do with him. This volume is also known as the *Stray Toasters Designer Collection.* The original four-issue series was printed in Prestige editions, without ISBNs. On the back page of each issue there is an ad for the Bolle-Happel Appliance Company, for various types of toasters. This novel contains a mix of narrative, poetry, collage art, and graphic illustration. It is a very surrealistic and beautiful horror story. Graphitti Designs reprinted a special edition in 2000, which was limited to 1,000 copies, and they reprinted a paperback edition in 2003 (ISBN: 0936211997).

Starlin, Jim, Jim Novak, Archie Goodwin, et al. *Dreadstar Vol. 1: Metamorphosis Odyssey.* San Jose, CA: Slave Labor Graphics, 2000. ISBN: 0943151287. Reprints Marvel/Epic's *Epic Illustrated 1–9.*

The godlike Osirosian Akanton seeks to find several other beings whose destiny is to help give rebirth to the Universe. The beings known as the Zygoteans have taken over many planets and solar systems, and have enslaved them. No military force can fight against them. Akanton seeks the warrior Dreadstar to help in his quest. Dreadstar is the one who commands the icy fire sword. Once the Infinity Horn is blown,

the solar system is destroyed, and a new one is reborn. Akanton has a talk with God. Dreadstar kills Akanton in a rage, after realizing the magnitude of his having destroyed the Milky Way galaxy. Dreadstar is left on Caldor to continue the work of guiding other species so that they won't breed their own Zygoteans.

Starlin, Jim, Jim Novak, Archie Goodwin, et al. *Dreadstar Vol. 2: The Price.* San Jose, CA: Slave Labor Graphics, 2000. ISBN: 0943151309. Reprints Marvel/Epic's *The Price Graphic Novel; Dreadstar Marvel Graphic Novel 3; Epic Illustrated 18.*

The Lord Papal tells Darklock that his brother was murdered by a demon. He finds and defeats the demon, and becomes the slayer of Dark Gods. He resigns from his religious office, which relieves the Lord Papal. Dreadstar ends up on planet Delta 219 where the cat farmers live. He marries and lives as a humble, mystic farmer, very happily, until the Monarchy destroys the planet, and kills his wife. He meets Darklock, and sets upon the journey of killing the man responsible for the death of his wife. Oedi and Willow become part of his team, to stop the war.

This volume contains the origin story of Darklock Syzygy who seeks revenge on his brother's murderer. It includes a detailed history of Dreadstar, by Jim Starlin, an essay for all Dreadstarophiles.

Starlin, Jim, Jim Novak, Archie Goodwin, et al. *Dreadstar Vol. 3: Plan M.* San Jose, CA: Slave Labor Graphics, 2001. ISBN: 094315135X. Reprints Marvel/Epic's *Dreadstar 1–6.*

The war between the Church of the Instrumentality and the Monarchy rages on. Dreadstar's rebels steal money from one of the Instrumentality's church coffers, which inflames the Lord High Papal so much that he completely destroys a city and millions of people, just to kill Dreadstar. The Rebels end up forming a loose alliance with the Emperor of the Monarchy, and Oedi, who despises the Monarchy, saves the emperor from being poisoned. Instrumentality agents almost capture Darklock; Skeevo joins the rebels; and Dreadstar introduces Maxilon, Plan M, to the world.

This volume contains the origins of Cat Man, Oedi, and the blind psychic Willow.

Starlin, Jim, Jim Novak, Archie Goodwin, et al. *Dreadstar Vol. 4: The Secret of Z.* San Jose, CA: Slave Labor Graphics, 2001. ISBN: 0943151465. Reprints Marvel/Epic's *Dreadstar 7–12.*

The Monarchy Emperor's right-hand advisor, Z, is suspected by Dreadstar of being the Osirosian Lord Aknaton, who Dreadstar had killed in a moment of anger. Z sells out the Monarchy to the Church of the Instrumentality, which then proceeds to crush the Monarchy throughout the galaxy. The Inquisitors kill millions of people who won't comply with the church.

Dreadstar falls into a trap set by the Instrumentality, but is saved by Willow. Z shoots Oedi. The Rebels gain a physician as part of their group, when they visit this doctor to help heal Oedi's wounds. Dreadstar's band goes to the commune, seeking aid in their fight. The giant Tuetun tries to destroy Skeevo, and falls off a building.

This volume contains the origin story of the Lord High Papal.

Starlin, Jim, Jim Novak, Archie Goodwin, et al. *Dreadstar Definitive Collection 1*. Runnemede, NJ: Dynamic Forces, 2004. ISBN: 0974963801 (trd); 097496381X (Book 1, pbk); 0974963828 (Book 2, pbk). Reprints Marvel/Epic's *Dreadstar 1–12*.

This is the first collection in a series dedicated to reprinting all of Starlin's terrific, twelve-issue Dreadstar series, in glorious color. These reprints come in one hardback, or two paperbacks. Starlin has signed five hundred hardbacks. There are introductions by Walt Simonson and Al Milgrom.

Suydam, Arthur, John Workman, Eric Fein, et al. *The New Adventures of Cholly And Flytrap: Till Death Do Us Part 1–3*. New York: Epic, 1990–1991. ISBN: 0871357313 (1); 0871357321 (2); 087135733X (3).

Cholly and Flytrap are plied with alcohol. A greedy businessman who wants Flytrap to be a boxer shanghais him. Flytrap is taught by a former robot boxing champ. Cholly meanwhile is trying to find Flytrap, and a hit man is hired to eliminate him. Flytrap becomes famous as the faceless Mr. Ho, and is set to fight the Champ to the death. Flytrap had beaten the Champ once before, in a bar. Flytrap is defeated, and almost dies, but Cholly is able to revive him.

There is also a subplot involving a gay/deformed/crippled gangster and the Champ. This is a fun read.

Suydam, Arthur, John Workman, Eric Fein, et al. *The Original Adventures of Cholly and Flytrap*. New York: Epic, 1991. Reprints *Epic Illustrated 8, 10, 13–14, 34*.

Cholly and Flytrap are two aliens trapped on an alien world. They play a game, "A Little Love, A Little Hate," in which they try to destroy each other with the other aliens. Cholly finds a bug in his food at a restaurant, and totally demolishes the place.

The surrealistic science fiction feel of the story and the artwork are similar to what was published in *Heavy Metal* magazine.

Veitch, Rick, John Lind, Ven Yann, et al. *The One: Last Word in Superheroics*. King Hell Press, 2003. ISBN: 0962486450; 0962486 40X (1989). Reprints Marvel/Epic's *The One 1–6*.

A wealthy industrialist tricks the United States and the Soviets into launching their nuclear missiles. Instead of nuclear devastation, a secret cosmic force is released. The two world powers unleash their lab-created superbeings against each other, which makes the threat of nuclear war seem tame by comparison.

The One takes on the appearance of Geeky Man who has a fifties haircut. He embodies the collective souls of mankind. His goal is to lead humanity into its collective evolution, beyond physical existence. This volume includes an introduction by Alan Moore and an original article from the February 12, 1984, *New York Times* stating that the A-bomb might actually be good for humanity. This book was originally published in the mid-eighties, near the end of the Cold War. Rick Veitch writes the afterword. The book also includes his Puzz Fundles.

Wolfman, Marv, Gene Colan, Al Williamson, et al. *Tomb of Dracula: Day of Blood, Night of Redemption*. New York: Epic, 1991. ISBN: 0871358379 (1); 0871358387 (2); 0871358 395 (3); 0871358409 (4).

Dracula's relative Francis Drake inadvertently helps Professor Smirnoff revive Dracula. Dracula then haunts Drake's wife, and tries to make her a vampire. Smirnoff wants to become a vampire, in order to have everlasting life, and, using the college he has formed a cult around Dracula. Blade helps Drake try to destroy Dracula. The vampire's face is burned with a cross. Psychic energy eventually destroys Dracula, and Blade ends up in a mental hospital.

Zelenetz, Alan, John Pierard, Kurt Hathaway, et al. *Steve Brust's Jhereg: The Graphic Novel*. New York: Epic, 1990. ISBN: 0871356740.

This graphic novel is based on Steve Brust's fantasy series about an assassin, Vlad Taltos, and a Jhereg, Loiosh. Jheregs are miniature dragon-like creatures who can communicate telepathically.

8

Marvel and
Marvel-Related Paperbacks

Can a man with green skin and petulant personality find
true happiness in today's newly-liberated society?—*Stan Lee*

I'm bigger, I'm stronger than anybody! That's why they fear me.
That's why they all hate the Hulk. There's no place on Earth for me to go!
Men will hunt me ... hound me ... forever"—Hulk

The Chinese say: before you set out on revenge, dig two graves....
[W]hen you kill for revenge something in you dies—*James Bond*

I am a good judge of men. You have guts, Mr. Bond—*Milos Columbo*

Binder, Otto, E. R. Cruz, Jules Verne, et al.
Mysterious Island (*Pocket Classics C19*).
Westport, CT, 1984. ISBN: 0883017180.
Reprints *Marvel Classic Comics 11*.

In this book, a group of men are shipwrecked on a
mysterious island where unexplained good things start
happening to them. It is as though someone else on the
island is looking out for their welfare. It turns out that
Captain Nemo himself is the unknown benefactor.
This is a black-and-white sequel, of sorts, to *20,000
Leagues Under the Sea*. It was also published by Pen-
dulum, 1973 (ISBN: 0883011387; 0883011069); Lake
Illustrated Classics, 1994 (ISBN: 1561037975); and
American Guidance, 1994 (ISBN: 0785407219).

Binder, Otto, Romy Gamboa, Jules Verne, et al.
20,000 Leagues Under the Sea (*Pocket Classics C12*). Westport CT: Academic Industries, 1984. ISBN: 0883017113. Reprints
Marvel Classic Comics 4.

This black-and-white book recounts the story of
Captain Nemo and his crew who sail the seas away
from the rest of humanity in the *Nautilus*. In the tale,
Captain Nemo kidnaps several high-society people,
and takes them on the adventure of a lifetime, in
which they fight a giant squid, and encounter many
other creatures. The book was also published by Pen-

dulum in 1973 (ISBN: 0883011042); American Guid-
ance, 1994 (ISBN: 0785406735); Lake Illustrated
Classics, 1994 (ISBN: 1561034479); and Random
House, 1973 (ISBN: 0394847229).

Binder, Otto, Alex Nino, H. G. Wells, et al.
Time Machine (*Pocket Classics C9*). Westport, CT: Academic Industries, 1984. ISBN:
0883017083. Reprints *Marvel Classic Comics 2*.

This is the famous story that features the time traveler who goes thousands of years into the future. The
future world seems like a virtual paradise, but there is
a dark secret that the inhabitants, the Eloi and the
Morlocks, are hiding. This is a black-and-white book
which was also published by Random House (ISBN:
0394847210); Pendulum, 1973 (ISBN: 0883011026);
American Guidance, 1994 (ISBN: 0785406700); and
Lake Illustrated Classics, 1994 (ISBN: 156103438X).

Brennert, Alan, Martin Pasco, Luke McDon-
nell, et al. *Star Trek: The Further Adventures
of the Starship Enterprise: Marvel Illustrated
Books*. New York: Marvel, 1981. ISBN:
0939766000. Reprints *Star Trek 7, 11–12*.

Janice Rand gets an exploratory ship all her own, the
USS *Icarus*, and she marries a Phaetonian who is of

pure mind and thought. The *Icarus* penetrates a mysterious energy field, which makes the Phaetonians go insane. Kirk and company have to rescue Rand and stop the senseless aliens. The *Enterprise* picks up a cult under the mind-control of Dr. Wentworth. His assistant, a former lover of Scotty, has the ability to conjure horrible creatures from Scottish mythology. Kirk, McCoy, and Spock go the planet Andrea IV, which is about to be bombarded with radiation. They go to try and convince the inhabitants to evacuate. Apparently their coming was foretold, as they find monuments themselves there.

These stories take place shortly after the first *Star Trek* feature film.

Buscema, John, Michael Fleisher, Earl Norem, et al. *Conan: The Movie*. New York: Marvel Illustrated Books, 1982. ISBN: 093976 6078. Reprints *Conan the Barbarian: The Movie Special 1–2*; *Marvel Super Special 21*.

Conan's parents were killed when he was a child, and he was sold into slavery. As an adult, he seeks to kill the man who was responsible, Thulsa Doom. Along the way, Conan finds several companions, including a lover, and he kills a giant serpent. When Doom has Conan nailed to a cross, his companions free him, and, in the final showdown between Doom and Conan, Doom is beheaded.

This is the comic adaptation of the Conan movie which starred Arnold Schwarzenegger and was based on the character created by Robert Howard. This is one of the rarest Marvel paperbacks ever published.

Claremont, Chris, John Byrne, David Hunt, et al. *SpiderMan Team-Up 2 (Marvel Illustrated Books)*. New York: Marvel, 1982. ISBN: 0939766132. Reprints *Marvel Team Up 68–70*.

Spider-Man saves Man Thing from being put in a circus side show, and they team up against the black wizard D'Spayre. The Living Pharaoh kidnaps Havok to harness his power. Spider-Man and Thor fight him in the middle of New York. The Pharaoh has Havok encased in a casket-like structure that is rigged with a bomb. Spider-Man figures out how to free Havok in order to defeat the Living Pharaoh. Polaris is almost killed, and the Beast goes to help her.

This is a black-and-white Marvel Illustrated book.

Claremont, Chris, Dave Cockrum, John Bolton, et al. *X-Men: Enter the Phoenix*. New York: Torkids, 1996. ISBN: 0812543254. Reprints *X-Men 100–101*; *Classic X-Men 8*.

The X-Men battle robot copies of the original X-Men. Jean Grey dies while saving the X-Men from burning up, from radiation in the atmosphere. When she is reborn as the Phoenix, she collapses and is taken to the hospital. Xavier orders the X-Men to take a vacation, and they go to Banshee's Mansion, where Black Tom and Juggernaut are waiting.

This volume includes the story about the merging of Phoenix and Jean Grey. It contains the Xavier files, with entries on the various X-Men, and one long entry on the Sentinels.

Claremont, Chris, Dave Cockrum, Bob Wiacek, et al. *X-Men: The Brood Saga Part 1*. New York: Torkids, 1996. ISBN: 081254 4056. Reprints *Uncanny X-Men 162–163*; *Classic X-Men 67–68*.

A horrendous alien species known as the Brood can transform other species into their own kind. Wolverine has to step in and battle the Brood to save his teammates and the Universe, from transforming.

This paperback, which is in black and white, only contains the first part of the Brood saga.

Claremont, Chris, Tony DeZuniga, Annette Kawwecki, et al. *The Uncanny X-Men*. New York: Torkids, 1990, 1995. ISBN: 0812510216. Reprints *X-Men 110, 123, 124*.

This is a black-and-white paperback which contains three stories: "The X-Sanction," "Listen—Stop Me If You Heard I—But This One Will Kill You," and "He Only Laughs When I Hurt." The latter is a tale in which the X-Men go up against the madmen Arcade who is being paid a million dollars a head to destroy the X-Men. Spider-Man makes a cameo.

Claremont, Chris, Walter Simonson, Terry Austin, et al. *X-Men and the Teen Titans*. New York: Warner books, 1983. ISBN: 0446305294. Reprints *X-Men and the Teen Titans*.

In this book, DC's Teen Titans and Marvel's X-Men go up against Darkseid, who resurrects a version of the Dark Phoenix, and Slade becomes an agent of Darkseid.

Duffy, Joe, Bob Hall, Joe Rosen, et al. *Marvel Comics Presents Willow: The Illustrated Version*. New York: Del Rey, 1988. ISBN: 0345357760. Reprints *Willow 1–3*.

A Nelwyn, known as Willow, finds a young baby. Willow is entrusted to take care of the baby, who is actually a princess. He encounters many dangerous situations and ends up imprisoned along with his companions.

This is Willow's coming of age story, in which he learns how to become a great sorcerer. It is a comic adaptation of the hit movie, *Willow*, by George Lucas. This was also published as a *Marvel Graphic Novel*.

Ellison, Harlan, Roy Thomas, Sal Buscema, et al. *Incredible Hulk (Marvel Illustrated Books)*. New York: Marvel, 1982. ISBN: 0960414 69X. Reprints *Incredible Hulk 140, 142*; *Avengers 88*.

The Avengers are trying to stop the insect-like Psyklop who wants to harness the power of the Hulk.

The Hulk is shrunk and sent to the subatomic sphere, where he meets and falls in love with Queen Jarella. They plan on ruling together, but Psyklop cuts the Hulk's happiness short. The Hulk becomes the darling cause of rich philanthropists.

This color paperback is a loose adaptation of Tom Wolfe's *Radical Chic and Mau-Maying the Flak Catchers.* Tom Wolfe makes a cameo appearance in it.

Fago, John Norwood, E. R. Cruz, Jonathan Swift, et al. *Gulliver's Travels (Pocket Classics C14).* West Haven, CT: Academic Industries, 1984. ISBN: 088301713X. Reprints *Marvel Classic Comics 6.*

This is a satirical story about Captain Gulliver and his sea adventures in which he encounters bizarre societies. They include worlds of thumb-sized beings, giants, horses that talk, wizards, and ape-like beings. This story was also published by Lake Illustrated Classics, 1994 (ISBN: 1561034827); Pendulum Press, 1974 (ISBN: 0883011425); and American Guidance Services, 1994 (ISBN: 0785407162).

Farr, Naunerle, Jon Lo Famia, Victor Hugo, et al. *Hunchback of Notre Dame (Pocket Classics C15).* Westport, CN: Academic Industries, 1984. ISBN: 0883017148. Reprints *Marvel Classic Comics 3.*

This black-and-white paperback tells the heart-wrenching story of the bell ringer Quasimodo who falls in love with the young gypsy girl, Esmeralda. The perverted cardinal wants Esmeralda for himself, despite her being labeled a witch. The story also has been published by Pendulum, 1974 (ISBN: 0883011395); American Guidance, 1994 (ISBN: 0785407170); and Lake Illustrated Classics, 1994 (ISBN: 1561034851).

Farr, Naunerle, Rudy Nebres, Anna Sewell, et al. *Black Beauty (Pocket Classics C1).* Westport, CN: Academic Industries, 1984. ISBN: 0883017008. Reprints *Marvel Classic Comics 5.*

This black-and-white paperback tells the life story of a horse named Black Beauty, and the various owners, trials, and tribulations this horse endured during its life. This story also has been published by Pendulum, 1973 (ISBN: 0883010941); American Guidance, 1994 (ISBN: 078540662X); and Lake Illustrated Classics, 1994 (ISBN: 1561034142).

Farr, Naunerle, Alex Nino, Alexander Dumas, et al. *Three Musketeers (Pocket Classics C-23).* West Haven, CN: Academic Industries, 1984. ISBN: 0883017229. Reprints *Marvel Classic Comics 12.*

This black-and-white paperback tells the classic story of young D'Artagnan who wishes nothing more than to be one of the King of France's elite Musketeers.

This has been published numerous times, including by Pendulum Publishing, 1974 (ISBN: 0883011336); Random House, 1974 (ISBN: 0394847237); and Lake Illustrated Classics, 1994 (ISBN: 1561035092).

Farr, Naunerle, Nestor Redondo, Bram Stoker, et al. *Dracula (Pocket Classics C-4).* West Haven, CN: Academic Industries, 1984, ISBN: 0883071032. Reprints *Marvel Classic Comics 9.*

This is the classic story of the famous vampire Dracula and his attempt to spoil London and the Harker family with his evil intentions. In this story, the famous Dr. Ábraham Van Helsing becomes Dracula's nemesis when he figures out a way to destroy the evil vampire forever. The story also has been published by American Guidance Systems, 1994 (ISBN: 0785406654); Lake Illustrated Classics, 1994 (ISBN: 15610 34231); Star Stream Productions/Pendulum, 1973 (ISBN: 088301100X); and Happy House Books, 1981 (ISBN: 039484727X). This is a black and white paperback.

Gately, George, *Heathcliff: The Big Sport.* New York: Torkids, 1991. ISBN: 0812510879. Reprints *Heathcliff 2, 7, 23, 25, 27–28; Heathcliff's Funhouse 2, 5.*

Heathcliff gets into all kinds of trouble, from being expelled from obedience school, to stopping a game of baseball being played by ghosts. He tries to stop a mouse from taking all the fish from a market, only to take them for himself. Heathcliff also stars in his own videogame.

Gately, George, *Heathcliff: The Many Lives of Heathcliff.* New York: Torkids: 1990. ISBN: 0812510232. Reprints *Heathcliff 37; Heathcliff Funhouse 4, 9, 11, Heathcliff Annual 1.*

Heathcliff and Iggy have an adventure with dinosaurs. Heathcliff becomes invisible by drinking invisible ink, and stops a robbery at his home. He is the giant in a modern take on the Jack and the Beanstalk tale, and Muggsy and Spike draft him into the army.

Goodwin, Archie, Chris Claremont, Carmine Infantino, et al. *Star Wars Vol. 2: World of Fire (Marvel Illustrated Books).* New York: Marvel, 1982. ISBN: 939766140. Reprints Marvel UK's *Star Wars Weekly 107–115.*

Luke, Princess Leia, Artoo Detoo, C-3PO, and Mici steal a special ship, the *Staraker,* from the Empire. They end up on the planet Alashan where an unseen force has been killing anyone who comes to investigate the planet. An Imperial battle cruiser orbiting above the planet is destroyed. The Rebels have to team up with the Imperials in order to survive. They encounter an underground city and find out that the protector of the planet is a monster that can change its shape, and seemingly has unlimited power.

This black-and-white paperback is the second Marvel *Star Wars* book which reprints stories that only appeared in the UK.

Goodwin, Archie, Carmine Infantino, Marie Severin, et al. *Star Wars 1* (*Marvel Illustrated Books*). New York: Marvel, 1981. ISBN: 0960414681. Reprints Marvel UK *Star Wars Weekly 60, 94–97, 104–106.*

This paperback features four full-color Star Wars stories in which Han Solo learns the "way of Wookie" when Chewbacca kidnaps a Wookie prisoner that his family is feuding with, from right under the noses of the Imperial guards; Princess Lela learns to use a weapon; after the destruction of the Death Star, Luke encounters a lone Tie-Fighter, and learns that the enemy is not as different as he appears to be; and Luke commandeers a Tie-Fighter during a battle.

Goodwin, Archie, Al Williamson, Carlos Garzon, et al. *Star Wars: Return of the Jedi* (*Marvel Illustrated Books*). New York: Marvel, 1983. ISBN: 0939766582. Reprints *Return of the Jedi 1–4; Marvel Super Special 27.*

Luke Skywalker becomes a real hero. He helps rescue Han Solo from Jabba the Hut, and gets wisdom from Yoda, and the spirit of Obe Wan. He meets Ewoks and fights with Darth Vader and the Emperor. Anakin Skywalker/Darth Vader dies.

This paperback is the official comic adaptation of the third *Star Wars* film, *Return of the Jedi.*

Goodwin, Archie, Al Williamson, Bob Larkin, et al. *Star Wars: The Empire Strikes Back* (*Marvel Illustrated Books*). New York: Marvel, 1980. ISBN: 0960414606. Reprints *Star Wars 39–44: Marvel Super Special 16; Marvel Special Edition Vol. 2: 2.*

This color paperback is the official comic adaptation of the second *Star Wars* film, *The Empire Strikes Back.* In this book, the Empire gains a strong political foothold and declares martial law. Luke meets Yoda, and he finds out that Darth Vader is his father. Lando turns Han Solo over to Boba Fett, the bounty hunter, and the rebels over to Vader.

Goodwin, Archie, Al Williamson, Steranko, et al. *Blade Runner* (*Marvel Illustrated Books*). New York: Marvel 1982. ISBN: 093976 6108. Reprints *Blade Runner 1; Marvel Super Special 22.*

A policeman, Deckard, comes out of retirement to stop several androids that revolt against their maker, the Tyrell Corporation. Deckard, known as a Blade Runner, follows the droids to kill them. One particular droid, Roy Batty, is causing a great deal of trouble and remains elusive until the final showdown with Deckard. The androids want to live indefinitely.

Deckard falls in love with Rachel, who also is an android, and he flees from the city with her.

This is the comic adaptation of *Blade Runner*, a science fiction film, based on the Philip K. Dick book *Do Androids Dream of Electric Sleep.* The Super Special edition contains photographs from the movie. This paperback is in black and white, and is one of the rarest of the Marvel paperback editions.

Goodwin, Archie, Marv Wolfman, Carmine Infantino, et al. *Spider-Woman.* New York: Pocket Books, 1979. ISBN: 0671830260. Reprints *Marvel Spotlight 32; Spider-Woman 1–8.*

Young Jessica Drew is Spider-Woman who was raised by the High Evolutionary. She searches for her identity and her past, as well as for the killer of her real father. She is used by Hydra to break into S.H.I.E.L.D. and rescue the man she thinks she loves. While in England searching for her identity, she has run-ins with the law and a S.H.I.E.L.D. agent falls in love with her. She meets a wise old man, an ancient sage who wants to help her find her past, and they go to America. While fighting the ancient witch Morgan LaFay, Spider-Woman gets help from the Werewolf by Night, and defeats her. Some of the other villains include Brother Grimm and the Hangman. Ultimately, Jessica finds the man who is responsible for the death of her father, a prominent U.S. congressman.

This seems to be the rarest of all the Marvel pocket paperbacks.

Hama, Larry, Howard Chaykin, Vince Colletta, et al. *For Your Eyes Only* (*Marvel Illustrated Books*). New York: Marvel, 1981. ISBN: 0960414649. Reprints *For Your Eyes Only 1–2; Marvel Super Special 19.*

Bond stops a smuggler from giving a special weapons transmitter, A.T.A.C., into Russian hands. Bond also meets his old nemesis, Ernst Stavro Blofeld, who attempts to kill him on the eve of tenth anniversary of Teresa Bond's death. Bond intentionally befriends the man in Greece who is trying to kill him and make a deal with the Russians. Bond helps a woman whose parents were killed in the mad rush to get the A.T.A.C.

This is another of the rare color Marvel Illustrated paperbacks. It is the graphic adaptation of the popular James Bond film.

Lee, Stan, Rich Buckler, Frank Glacola, et al. *Incredible Hulk Vol 3.* New York: Tempo Books, 1982. ISBN: 0448168375.

Jack McGee pays a lady friend to befriend David Banner, to get close to the Hulk. She ends up falling for Banner, and discovers that he actually is the Hulk. Banner starts working at a lab in order to use gamma radiation and possibly stop Hulking out. As he is drifting across America, Banner comes across a circus that needs some workers. Mysterious accidents start happening at the circus. Several attempts on the lives of the carnies fail, thanks to Banner. The would be murderer tranquilizes the Hulk, and attempts to keep him locked up. It turns out that the circus clown is the villain.)

This is the third volume of reprints from the Hulk newspaper strips.

Lee, Stan, John Buscema, Marie Severin, et al. *Incredible Hulk Vol. 2*. New York: Pocket Books, 1979. ISBN: 0671825593. Reprints *Tales to Astonish 85–99*.

Rick Jones finds the Hulk in New York. General Ross orders the launch of the Orion missile, and the army captures the Leader's Hulk Killer. The Hulk fights the comical Boomerang. The Stranger manipulates the Hulk's anger, to get him to turn against the Earth. The Silver Surfer attempts to befriend the Hulk, but it turns out badly. The Hulk also meets the High Evolutionary, and has to go up against the legions of Living Lightning.

This volume contains the origin story of the Abomination, and two bonus pin-up pages.

Lee, Stan, Steve Ditko, et al. *Amazing Spider Man: Collector's Album*. New York: Lancer, 72–112, 1966. Reprints *Amazing Spider-Man 1, 13, 16*; *Amazing Spider Man Annual 1*.

Spider-Man meets Daredevil. The Ringmaster hypnotizes everyone, including Spider-Man who at first fights Daredevil. Astronaut John Jameson's father, Jonah, starts his anti–Spider-Man ranting in the *Daily Bugle*. Jonah works with Mysterio who seeks to frame Spider-Man for crimes with which he had nothing to do.

This volume includes an origin tale and Spider-Man's adventure helping the astronaut John Jameson. This volume includes a number of pin-up pages and an endorsement from the *Village Voice*.

Lee, Stan, Steve Ditko, Don Rico, et al. *Dr. Strange Vol. 1*. New York: Pocket Books, 1978. ISBN: 0671814478. Reprints *Strange Tales 110–111, 115–129*.

Dr. Strange goes up against his nemesis Baron Mordo several times. Mordo kidnaps Dr. Strange, and attempts to destroy the Ancient One. Strange also has to contend with Nightmare, the Purple Veil, and the dreaded Dormammu. Loki tries to outwit Dr. Strange by making him believe that Thor is evil. Strange goes back in time to help Cleopatra get back to her own time. The screaming idol from Peru becomes the evil god Tiboro.

This full color paperback contains the early adventures of Dr. Strange, including his first appearance and origin story. It also features a Dr. Strange pin-up.

Lee, Stan, Steve Ditko, Art Simek, et al. *Amazing Spider Vol. 1*. New York: Pocket Books, 1977. ISBN: 0671814435. Reprints *Amazing Fantasy 15*; *Amazing Spider Man 1–6*.

This volume features Spider-Man's early adventures, including his origin. In it Spider-Man has trouble cashing a check; he saves John Jameson from an accident; and he meets Dr. Doom, Chameleon, Vulture, Tinker, Dr. Octopus, Sandman, and the Lizard. The volume also contains a special Spider-Man feature which tells the secrets of his mask and webbing.

Lee, Stan, Steve Ditko, Art Simek, et al. *Amazing Spider-Man Vol. 2*. New York: Pocket Books, 1978. ISBN: 0671814443. Reprints *Amazing Spider-Man 7–13*.

In this volume Spider-Man fights the Vulture, the Living Brain, Electro, Doc Ock, the Enforcers, and Mysterio. When Mysterio first appears, committing crimes, he is dressed as Spider-Man, and. J. Jameson hails Mysterio as a hero. The volume also contains a boxing match between Peter Parker and Flash Thompson. The introduction is by Stan Lee.

Lee, Stan, Steve Ditko, Art Simek, et al. *Amazing Spider-Man Vol. 3*. New York: Pocket Books, 1979. ISBN: 0671825798. Reprints *Amazing Spider Man 14–20*.

The Green Goblin tricks Spider-Man into appearing in a movie, fighting the Enforcers, but the Hulk shows up and spoils the Goblin's plan. The Ringmaster puts a large circus audience, including Spider-Man, into a trance. Daredevil happens to be there, and they fight. Flash Thompson puts on a Spider-Man suit, and ends up getting beaten up pretty badly, while Peter Parker was looking after sick Aunt May and so out of action as Spider-Man. The Human Torch makes an appearance.

The volume includes the origin story of the Scorpion.

Lee, Stan, Steve Ditko, Artie Simek, et al. *Dr. Strange Vol. 2*. New York: Pocket Books, 1979. ISBN: 06718218528. Reprints *Strange Tales 130–144*.

Dr. Strange is defeated by Baron Mordo. Mordo has added extra powers to his magic, by forming an alliance with the dreaded Dormammu. Clea, a woman in Dormammu's dimension, helps Strange, and is put into prison for her betrayal. Strange helps unseat the evil Shazana from her throne, so that the rightful heir, Shazana's kind sister, can rule. The Ancient One is sick, and Dr. Strange seeks and finally meets Eternity. Dormammu is jealous, and seeks to find out what knowledge Eternity imparted to Dr. Strange. Strange and Dormammu end up in hand-to-hand combat, with neither using their mystical powers, but Mordo intervenes at the last moment. They continue their combat, and Strange wins. Mordo's disciples continue to hound Dr. Strange, and he ends up wearing a bizarre mask. The entities Asti and Tazza also make appearances.

This full-color volume also features a pin-up page.

Lee, Stan, Bill Everett, Johnny Romita, et al. *Here Comes Daredevil: Mighty Marvel Collector's Album*. New York: Lancer, 72–170, 1967. Reprints *Daredevil 1, 16–17, 20–21*.

Daredevil goes after the Fixer for killing his father. Spider-Man is pitted against Daredevil, and he tracks Daredevil to the law offices of Nelson and Murdock. Spider-Man believes that Foggy Nelson is Daredevil. Daredevil fights with Spider-Man, who thinks he's in league with the Masked Marauder. Nelson lets his secretary, Karen, believe that he is Daredevil. Spider-Man and Daredevil finally team to take down the Masked Marauder. The Owl kidnaps Matt Murdock to have him preside at a kangaroo court against Judge Lewis, who sent Owlsley to prison. Daredevil intervenes, while keeping his secret identity, and winds up a prisoner of the Owl.

This book also contains the origin story of the blind superhero from the first *Daredevil*.

Lee, Stan, Jack Kirby, et al. *The Fantastic Four Vol 1*. New York: Pocket Books, 1977. ISBN: 0671814451. Reprints *Fantastic Four 1–6*.

This volume contains full-color reprints of the first six issues of the *Fantastic Four* in paperback. It has the origin story of the Fantastic Four, and various other stories in which the Human Torch, while staying in a Salvation Army type facility, finds the Sub-Mariner who has amnesia; the Fantastic Four and Dr. Doom meet; the Sub-Mariner returns and starts a war against New York and the human race; and Dr. Doom teams up with Namor against the Fantastic Four. Villains in the volume include Mole Man, the Skrulls, and Miracle Man. This volume features an introduction by Stan Lee.

Lee, Stan, Jack Kirby, et al. *Incredible Hulk Vol. 1*. New York: Pocket Books, 1978. ISBN: 067181446X. Reprints *Incredible Hulk 1–6*.

This volume presents the Hulk's origin and his battles with the Gargoyle, Toad Man, Mongu, Metal Master, General Fang, and the Ringmaster. In this great Cold War volume, the Gargoyle captures Bruce Banner and learns the secret of the Hulk. When the Gargoyle is changed back into a real person, through Banner's work, he sacrifices himself.

The book contains an introduction and an epilogue, both written by Stan Lee, and a special Hulk miniature pin-up, in color.

Lee, Stan, Jack Kirby, Dick Ayers, et al. *The Fantastic Four Collector's Album*. New York: Lancer, 72–111, 1966. Reprints *Fantastic Four 1, 6, 11, 31*.

The Sub-Mariner and Dr. Doom team up against the Fantastic Four. The Impossible Man makes a pest of himself to the Fantastic Four, and Reed tricks him into thinking that the Earth is boring. Sue Storm is put in the hospital after from a battle with the Mole Man. Her father escapes from prison, and he comes to the hospital to meet with his children when he finds out Sue has been injured.

This is the first paperback collection of Marvel comic stories. It includes the origin story of the Fantastic Four, and reproductions of various pin-ups. It is printed in black and white.

Lee, Stan, Jack Kirby, Dick Ayers, et al. *The Fantastic Four Return: Mighty Marvel Collector's Album*. New York: Lancer, 72–169, 1967. Reprints *Fantastic Four Annual 2; Fantastic Four 33, 35*.

The Fantastic Four are invited to a celebration at the Latverian Embassy. Doom drugs their drinks, and everyone but Reed hallucinates their worst nightmare. Doom challenges Reed to a duel to the death, but Reed tricks Doom into drinking the drugged punch. Doom imagines that he has destroyed Reed. The Fantastic Four come to the aid of the Sub-Mariner, helping him fight against Attuma. Attuma is trying usurp Namor's power in Atlantis. The Fantastic Four go to Reed and Ben's old college, where Reed is giving a speech. Diablo breaths life back into the Dragon Man, and tries to destroy the Fantastic Four.

This black-and-white book includes the reproduction of a Namor pin-up.

Lee, Stan, Jack Kirby, Steve Ditko, et al. *The Incredible Hulk: The Strangest Man of All Time: Collector's Album*. New York: Lancer, 72–124, 1966. Reprints *Hulk 3; Tales to Astonish 60–63*.

General Ross tricks Rick Jones into allowing the Hulk to be captured and sent into space. When the Hulk crashes back to Earth, he briefly becomes a slave to Rick. Rick goes to the circus and is hypnotized by the Ringmaster. The Hulk is captured and put in a cage by the Ringmaster, but when he regains his own will he destroys the Ringmaster's operation. The Leader employs the Chameleon to infiltrate gamma Base, and commandeer the work Bruce Banner has been doing. Ross uses Major Talbot to spy on Banner. Banner realizes that his transformation into the Hulk happens when he is upset. Ross and Talbot capture the Hulk, and Ross begins to suspect there is a connection between Banner and the Hulk.

This black-and-white volume contains the origin story of the Leader, and includes Hulk pin-ups.

Lee, Stan, Jack Kirby, Don Heck, et al. *The Mighty Thor: Mighty Marvel Collector's Album*. New York: Lancer, 72–125, 1966. Reprints *Journey Into Mystery 97, 104, 114–115*.

Thor battles the Lava Man. Donald Blake decides to propose to Jane Foster against Odin's wishes, but she leaves him for another doctor. Odin comes to Earth to see what his son has been doing for himself. Loki lets

loose the storm giant Skagg and the fire demon Sur-
tūr on Earth. Odin, Thor, and Balder take care of
them, and disclose Loki's treachery. The Absorbing
Man, Crusher Creel, is created by Loki to be a thorn
in Thor's side. After losing several battles, Creel is
transformed into the element helium and sent to wander the universe.

This black-and-white book includes a Thor pin-
up and a bonus feature in which he tries to free Jane
Foster, who is kidnapped by his half brother. It also includes bonus feature which shows the typical Asgardian street.

Lee, Stan, Jack Kirby, Art Simek, et al. *Captain
America.* New York: Pocket Books, 1979.
ISBN: 067182581X. Reprints *Avengers 4;
Tales of Suspense 59–71.*

Captain America is revived from suspended animation and joins the Avengers, and thugs attack the
Avengers' mansion. The Red Skull was just a simple
hotel bellboy until Hitler molded him into the most
feared man in Germany. The Red Skull captures Captain America. He tries to make him a slave to Nazi
interests, and almost succeeds.

This book contains the origin stories of Captain
America, Bucky, and the Red Skull. It is printed in
color.

Lee, Stan, Jack Kirby, Joey Sinnot et al., *Fantastic Four: Marvel Illustrated Books.* New York:
Marvel, 1982. ISBN: 0939766027. Reprints *Fantastic Four 55, 66–67.*

The Silver Surfer befriends Alicia, and tries to understand more about humanity. Ben Grimm, the
Thing, thinks the Surfer is making time with his girlfriend, and a titanic battle ensues. The Surfer, bewil-
dered at Grimm's behavior, loses the battle with the
Thing. Alicia is whisked away by scientists attempting to create the perfect being. The being's radiated
glow, however, is too much for the scientists to bear,
so they send the blind Alicia to confront the being,
known as Him.

This black-and-white sequence of stories is thought
to contain Adam Warlock's first appearance in the
Marvel Universe.

Lee, Stan, Larry Lieber, *Incredible Hulk Vol. 1.*
New York: Tempo, 1980. ISBN: 0448171
97X.

David Banner goes to Professor Danby for help and
insight into his alter ego. The Hulk is being pursued
by both the CIA and an international crime boss who
wants to harness the Hulk's power. The crime boss kidnaps the Hulk and the CIA agent. Both the agent and
Banner manage to escape, while the Hulk is strangely
absent. An ex-con wants to terrorize the police officer,
and his daughter who David Banner is dating.

This is the first paperback reprint of the newspaper
strip stories of the Hulk. It is tied directly to the television *Hulk* series, rather than the comic book. This
is a very rare Marvel related paperback.

Lee, Stan, Larry Lieber, *Incredible Hulk Vol. 2.*
New York: Tempo Books, 1981. ISBN: 044
817314X.

The Hulk witnesses a murder, and the person who
committed the murder is trying to frame the Hulk for
it. David Banner works at a monster carnival, while the
CIA is continuing to try to track down the Hulk.
Banner gets involved in a political fight between a corrupt candidate and an honest candidate for president of a dockworkers union. Banner supports the
honest candidate, and gets into all kinds of brawls
which result in his changing into the Hulk. Reporter
Jack McGee makes an appearance.

This is the second volume of newspaper-strip Hulk
reprints.

Lee, Stan, Larry Lieber, *Incredible Hulk Vol. 4.*
New York: Tempo, 1983. ISBN: 0448168
588.

The Hulk befriends a blind woman who is working
on a novel, and David Banner goes to work for her.
Newspaperman Jack McGee is hot on his trail, and
actually ends up capturing the Hulk, right under the
noses of law officials. McGee gets very sick, and almost dies, but Banner, with the help of a local doctor,
performs surgery and saves his life. The Hulk befriends two homeless women, and Banner befriends a
mountain family who is trying to stop the building of
a lodge.

This is volume 4 of the black-and-white reprints
of the Hulk newspaper strips.

Lee, Stan, John Romita, et al. *The Amazing Spi-
derMan #1: The Great Newspaper Strip in
Full Color,* Pocket Books: New York, 1980.
ISBN: 0671834894.

The *Daily Bugle* sponsors Dr. Doom's presence at
the United Nations as an advocate to stop terrorism.
Doom requires that all nations bow down to his iron
rule, by taking the UN hostage. Spider-Man stops
him. Dr. Ock uses Aunt May as a decoy to steal a rare
Chinese dragon idol of pure gold. Her association with
Otto bothers Peter Parker to no end.

This volume is the first reprint of the Spider-Man
newspaper strip done by the classic team of Lee and
Romita. The introduction is by Lee and Romita, and
the afterword is by Lee.

Lee, Stan, John Romita, et al. *The Amazing Spi-
der-Man #2: The Great Newspaper Strip in
Full Color.* New York: Pocket Books, 1980.
ISBN: 0671834908.

While taking photographs of Mary Jane, Peter
Parker inadvertently photographs a new villain, the
Rattler. The Rattler, who has the power and ability of
a rattlesnake, knocks out Mary Jane, Flash Thompson,
and Harry Osborn, and nearly defeats Spider-Man. In
an attempt to keep his powers, the Rattler seeks a special venom, but he doesn't get it, and he dies. The
Kingpin asks Spider-Man to sponsor his bid for mayor

of New York. When Spider-Man refuses, the Kingpin tries to shoot him, but ends up hitting his own wife, Vanessa.

This is the second volume of reprinted Spider-Man newspaper strips.

Lee, Stan, John Romita, Gil Kane, et al. *The Amazing Spider-Man*. New York: Torkids, 1992. ISBN: 0812510194. Reprints *Amazing Spider-Man 88–90*.

Dr. Octopus breaks out of jail, and almost defeats Spider-Man. Captain Stacy saves a young boy from apartment rubble which topples onto him. Stacy dies in Spider-Man's arms, asking him to take care of Gwen and revealing that he knew that Peter Parker and Spider-Man were one and the same.

This work contains the stories, "The arms of Doctor Octopus!"; "Doc Ock lives!" and "And death shall come."

Lee, Stan, John Romita, Jim Mooney, et al. *Spider-Man: His Greatest Team-Up Battles: Marvel Illustrated Books*. New York: Marvel, 1981. ISBN: 0960414673. Reprints *Amazing Spider-Man 71*; *Amazing Spider-Man Annual 2*; *Marvel Team-Up 27*.

Spider-Man meets Dr. Strange, and they team up against Xandu. Quicksilver and Spider-Man end up fighting each other, with Quicksilver thinking Spider-Man is a criminal. The Hulk and Spider-Man do battle, while the Chameleon tries to frame Spider-Man for crimes he didn't commit. The Chameleon pretends to be Rick Jones, to get the Hulk to do his bidding and break a friend, Joey, out of prison. Joey takes a bullet that was meant for the Chameleon.

This color paperback is one of rarest of the Marvel paperbacks.

Lee, Stan, Wally Wood, Sam Rosen, et al. *Daredevil: The Man Without Fear: Marvel Illustrated Books*. New York: Marvel, 1982. ISBN: 0939766183. Reprints *Daredevil 6, 8*.

Daredevil goes up against the Eel, the Ox, and Mr. Fear. He is accused of being a coward, but clears his name when he catches the crooks. Daredevil goes up against the Stilt Man who is a client of Matt Murdock. Murdock bemoans the fact that he loves Karen Page, and puts off her urgings to get eye surgery.

This book is printed in black and white.

Lieber, Larry, Frank Giacoia, Charles Nicholas, et al. *The Incredible Hulk Vol. 5*. New York: Tempo Books, 1983. ISBN: 0441348602.

David Banner becomes the trainer for a washed-up boxer who gets a chance to fight with a young upstart. The boxer's daughter is kidnapped by some hoods who try to convince him to throw the fight. With the help of the Hulk, the daughter breaks gets free, and the boxer wins. David Banner gets amnesia, and is be-

friended by a rich young women whose brother is trying to kill her for an inheritance. Banner and the woman fall in love and stop her brother's plans, but Banner leaves her after he reveals that he is the Hulk. Reporter Jack McGee continues to hound Banner and the Hulk.

This is the last black-and-white volume in the series that reprints the Hulk newspaper strips. It too is based on the *Hulk* television show.

Macchio, Ralph, Bill Sienkiewicz, Bob Budiansky, et al. *Dune*. New York: Berkeley Publishing, 1984. ISBN: 0425076237. Reprints *Dune 1–3*; *Marvel Super Special 36*.

The Duke's son Paul becomes an unlikely hero in the world of Dune. Dune is the source of a much-coveted spice, melange. Both the Emperor and the Baron Harkonnen seek to rule the planet, and control the spice. Paul Maud'Dib becomes the Messiah, for whom the planet Dune has been waiting.

This paperback is a nice adaptation of the David Lynch epic film. It is based on the works of Frank Herbert.

Marvel Mini Books. New York: Marvel, 1966.

This is a collection of very rare and fragile books. They are each about the size of a thumbnail, and contain text and pictures. There were six mini books in the series: *Captain America, Millie the Model, Spider-Man, Thor, Nick Fury*, and the *Hulk*.

McKenzie, Roger, Ernie Colon, Jim Novak, et al. *Battlestar Galactica Vol. 1*. New York: Tempo, 1978. ISBN: 0441048765. Reprints *Battlestar Galactica 1–2*; *Marvel Super Special 8*.

A group of lone human survivors search for a new world where they can live in peace, while the alien Cylons are seeking the death of all humans. The Cylons despise humanity's independent spirit, and seek to crush any life-form that will not conform to Cylon ways and lifestyles. The crew learns how humans are being processed for food by the Ovions.

This volume includes an interview with producer John Dykstra, and several essays which provide an overview of life in the world of *Battlestar Galactica*: a look at the alien life-forms and robots; battle tactics of the ship; and the hardware and spaceships which inhabit this universe. This is the direct adaptation of the original television movie *Battlestar Galactica*.

McKenzie, Roger, Walt Simonson, Jim Novak, et al. *Battlestar Galactica Vol. 2*. New York: Tempo, 1979. ISBN: 0441048773. Reprints *Battlestar Galactica 3–5*; *Marvel Super Special 8*.

The crew goes to the planet Kobol to learn of their history and to find out about a planet called Earth. Apollo's wife Sernia is killed, and there are some dirty political dealings going on behind Commander

Adama's back. Adama seeks to learn some hidden knowledge by using the memory machine.

This is the continuation of the adaptation of the television movie *Battlestar Galactica.*

O'Neil, Dennis, Marie Severin, John Tartaglione, et al. *DragonSlayer: Marvel Illustrated Books.* New York: Marvel, 1981. ISBN: 0960414657. Reprints *DragonSlayer 1–2; Marvel Super Special 20.*

A young magician goes off to kill a dragon which has been tormenting a kingdom for many years. Young women are chosen by lottery to be sacrificed to the dragon. Much to the chagrin of her father, the king's daughter offers herself to the dragon.

This is the official, color, comic adaptation of the movie *DragonSlayer.*

Platt, Kin, Nester Redondo, R.L. Stevenson, et al. *Dr. Jekyll and Mr. Hyde (Pocket Classics C3).* Westport, CT: Academic Industries, 1984. ISBN: 0883017024. Reprints *Marvel Classic Comics 1.*

This is a black-and-white reprint of Robert Louis Stevenson's story about Dr. Henry Jekyll and his experiments with the good and evil in human nature. By taking a special potion, Jekyll is able to unleash the murderous, dark side of humanity in the guise of Mr. Hyde. This story also was published by Lake, 1994—ISBNs: 1561034207 (pbk), and 1561034215 (cassette); by Pendulum, 1973—ISBNs: 0883010968, 0883010933, 0883010968 (1991), and 0872320022; and by American Guidance, 1994—ISBN: 0785406646.

Shapiro, Irwin, E. R. Cruz, Stephen Crane, et al. *Red Badge of Courage (Pocket Classics C8).* Westport. CT: Academic Industries, 1984. ISBN: 0883017075. Reprints *Marvel Classic Comics 10.*

This is the story of a young Union solider whose bravery is tested during the Civil War. At first the soldier runs away, afraid of being killed, but eventually he proves his bravery on the battlefield by being fearless in the face of death. While realistically portraying the horrors of war, the story also shows the romance of bravery on the battlefield. It also was published by Pendulum Press, 1973 (ISBN: 0883011018); American Guidance, 1994 (ISBN: 0785406697); and Lake Illustrated Classics, 1994 (ISBN: 1561034355 (pbk.)).

Shapiro, Irwin, E. R. Cruz, Mark Twain, et al. *Tom Sawyer (Pocket Classics C10).* Westport, CT: Academic Industries, 1984. ISBN: 088 3017091. Reprints *Marvel Classic Comics 7.*

This black-and-white book tells the story of Tom Sawyer and his friend Huck Finn, and their adventures. In the story they witness a murder, find a huge amount of gold, and become rich. This story also was published by American Guidance, 1994 (ISBN: 0785406719); Pendulum, 1981 (ISBN: 0883011794); and Lake Illustrated Classics, 1994 (ISBN: 1561034 41X).

Shapiro, Irwin, Alex Nino, Herman Melville, et al. *Moby Dick (Pocket Classics C7).* Westport, CT: Academic Industries, 1984. ISBN: 0883017067. Reprints *Marvel Classic Comics 8.*

This is the story of Captain Ahab and his consuming revenge against the great white whale, Moby Dick, no matter the cost to his crew. It was also published by Pendulum, 1973 (ISBN: 0883010992); American Guidance, 1994 (ISBN: 0785406689); and Lake Illustrated Classics, 1994 (ISBN: 1561034320). This book is in black and white.

Shooter, Jim, John Buscema, Joe Sinnott, et al. *Superman and Spider-Man.* New York: Marvel/DC, 1981. ISBN: 0446917575. Reprints *Superman and Spiderman.*

Dr. Doom has teamed up with the Parasite with a plan to turn all of the world's fuel into sand. Clark Kent starts working for the *Daily Bugle* in New York, and Peter Parker works for the *Daily Planet* in Metropolis. Lana Lang turns down Parker for a date. Superman goes to Latveria. Doom captures both the Hulk and Wonder Woman, and Spider-Man learns firsthand, how the Parasite's power works. The Parasite has the hots for Wonder Woman.

This is the story of the second pairing of Superman and Spider-Man, published in paperback form. This paperback also contains the Parasite's origin story.

Stern, Roger, John Byrne, Joe Rubinstein, et al. *Captain America Battles Baron Blood (Marvel Illustrated Books).* New York: Marvel, 1982. ISBN: 0939766086. Reprints *Captain America 250, 253–254.*

A series of slasher murders in England causes the Falsworth family to become suspicion, and to ask Captain America to investigate. Baron Blood, who is Lord Falsworth, the first Union Jack's brother, is alive and well, and is committing vampire-type murders. Joey Chapman dons the Union Jack costume as bait for Blood. Captain America decapitates the vampire, and Lord Falsworth dies peacefully, knowing that his family curse is eliminated. Captain America is coerced into running for president on the Populist Party ticket, but he declines the nomination.

This book, part of the Marvel Illustrated Book series, contains black-and-white reprints.

Thomas, Roy, Howard Chaykin, George Lucas, et al. *The Marvel Comics Illustrated Version of Star Wars.* New York: Ballantine, 1977. ISBN: 034527492X. Reprints *Star Wars 1–6; Marvel Special Edition 1–3.*

This black-and-white paperback presents reprints of the Marvel's *Star Wars* movie adaptation. It contains Luke Skywalker's coming-of-age story in which he learns about the special role he is going to play in defeating the Empire. It includes a pin-up gallery and an introduction by Stan Lee.

Thomas, Roy, Kenneth Johnson, et al. *The Incredible Hulk: A Video Novel.* New York: Pocket Books, 1979. ISBN: 0671828274.

David Banner is distraught over the death of his wife, and his helplessness at trying to save her. He and his partner Elaina are studying various forms of radiation, including gamma radiation, which can possibly improve a person's strength. Banner does some experimenting on himself, and ends up overloading himself with gamma rays. He turns into the Hulk who scares a little girl and her father. Tabloid reporter Jack McGee keeps hounding Banner and Elaina. A fire at the research lab kills Elaina and Banner, but Banner's body is never found. McGee believes this green Hulk is responsible for the deaths.

This is a picture novel which presents the first episode of the television show *Incredible Hulk* in book form. The introduction is by Stan Lee.

Thomas, Roy, Michael Moorcock, Barry Smith, et al. *The Complete Marvel Conan Vol. 6.* New York: Grosset & Dunlap, 1979. ISBN: 04741116973. Reprints *Conan The Barbarian 12, 14–15; Giant Sized Conan 5.*

The wizard Zukala sends his daughter Zephra to join Conan on his journey. Conan and Elric form an uneasy alliance against the black queen Xiombarg. They defeat Prince Gaynor of the Damned. Kulan Gath resurrects the evil Green Empress, whose power is almost limitless. She becomes engulfed in a blue-white flame, and is defeated.

This color volume contains the first combination of the fantasy worlds of Moorcock's Elric and Howard's Conan. It includes a short history of the Hyborian Age, "Tales of the Hyborian Age," similar to the "Tales of Asgard" in the *Thor* comic. This story details the early history of the world in which Conan lives. Thomas and artist Gil Kane recount the legend of the Hydragon. The volume has a Hyborian Age map and an introduction written by Thomas.

Thomas, Roy, John, Sam Rosen, et al. *The Avengers: Origin of the Vision: Marvel Illustrated Books.* New York: Marvel, 1982. ISBN: 093976694. Reprints *Avengers 57–56; 83.*

Ultron builds the Vision to destroy the Avengers, but the Vision turns against Ultron and saves the Avengers. Ultron is supposedly destroyed and thrown into a junkyard where a young boy finds his head. Vision, who wants to join the Avengers, is tested. When he is accepted, he shows that even an android can cry. The Enchantress poses as Valkyrie, and gets all of the women Avengers to fight the men Avengers, and they stop the Masters of Evil.

Thomas, Roy, Barry Smith, Robert Howard, et al. *The Complete Marvel Conan the Barbarian Vol. 1.* New York: Grosset & Dunlap, 1978. ISBN: 0441116922. Reprints *Conan the Barbarian 1–3.*

Conan deals with Sharkosh, the Shaman, and his fortune-telling star stone. Conan is taken prisoner by the apelike Beast Men, and helps to launch a revolt by their human prisoners against the Beast Men jailers. He gets caught in a battle between the Brythunian and Hyperborean camps. Borr, the "Grey War God," and his "Choosers of the Slain" figure into this war epic. King Kull makes a cameo appearance.

In this volume, the Hyborian Age and Conan the Cimmerian are introduced, in color. The introduction is by Roy Thomas.

Thomas, Roy, Barry Smith, Robert Howard, et al. *The Complete Marvel Conan the Barbarian Vol. 2.* New York: Grosset & Dunlap, 1978. ISBN: 0441116930. Reprints *Conan the Barbarian 4–6.*

Yara, the sorcerer, enslaves the brilliant, elephant-like alien Yag Kosha. Yag Kosha requests that Conan kill him to put him out of his misery. Conan fights the bat-like Night God to save his lover Jenna who in turn saves Conan's life. While he slept, she robbed him of the gold he had.

This color volume includes an adaptation of the famous Robert Howard story "Tower of the Elephant"; "Zukala's Daughter," which is based on Howard's poem "Zukala's Hour"; and a map of the Hyborian Age, based on Howard's design. The introduction is by Roy Thomas.

Thomas, Roy, Barry Smith, Robert Howard, et al. *The Complete Marvel Conan the Barbarian Vol. 3.* New York: Grosset & Dunlap, 1978. ISBN: 0441116949. Reprints *Conan the Barbarian 7–9.*

Conan saves the life of Lady Aztrias who sends him on a journey to steal the contents of a golden bowl. The Sons of Set's serpent god is awakened and slain. Conan sees the face of Thoth-Amon in the bowl. Conan kills a giant Gila-like lizard. He finds the treasure crypt of Lanjau and the demons that guard the treasure. Conan runs into Jenna and has to save her from the winged, manlike demon Garakaa, whom he slays.

The introduction is by Roy Thomas. The volume is in color.

Thomas, Roy, Barry Smith, Robert Howard, et al. *The Complete Marvel Conan the Barbarian Vol. 4.* New York: Grosset & Dunlap, 1978. ISBN: 0441116957. Reprints *Conan the Barbarian 10–11.*

Conan meets the bull-god Anu who, while in solid form, destroys his own priest. Conan is betrayed by his lady friend Jenna, and taken to prison. He does battle with Nabonidus, the Red Priest, and his apelike apprentice Thak.

Thomas, Roy, Barry Smith, Sam Rosen, et al. *The Complete Marvel Conan Vol. 5*. New York: Grosset & Dunlap, 1978. ISBN: 0441116965. Reprints *Conan the Barbarian 12–13, 16; Savage Tales 1, 4*.

Conan becomes a queen's "kept man." When he rebels, he is forced to do battle with a giant octopus-like creature. After being robbed, he is left for dead in the desert. He is saved by an old man, but then he is caught and thrown in a dungeon with other slaves. He destroys the Spider God after an intense battle with it. He is lured into a trap by the Ymir's beautiful daughter Atali. Her brothers attempt to kill Conan. After defeating Ymir's sons, Conan turns to Ymir's daughter who is then bathed in a blue flame.

This color volume contains a map of the Hyborian age. Thomas wrote the introduction.

Wein, Len, Dave Cockrum, Chris Claremont, et al. *The X-Men (Marvel Illustrated Books)*. New York: Marvel, 1982. ISBN: 0939766 019. Reprints *Giant Size X-Men 1; Uncanny X-Men 117*.

This is the landmark story that reintroduced the X-Men to the public. In it, Professor X recruits a new X-Men team to save the original X-Men from the living mutant island Krakoa. While in Cairo during his younger years, Professor X met the first evil mutant, Amahl Farouk, the Shadow King, and they battled on the psychic plane. Storm, as a child, guests in this issue. This book reprints the stories in black and white.

Wein, Len, Jose Luis Garcia Lopez, Dick Giordano, et al. *Batman vs. The Incredible Hulk*. New York: Warner Books, 1982. ISBN: 0446302449. Reprints *Batman vs. The Incredible Hulk*.

Bruce Banner works for Wayne Industries, seeking a cure for his alter ego. The Joker tries to steal the gamma device that Banner is working on, which causes the Hulk to appear and go ballistic. The Shaper of Worlds needs the gamma radiation to help with an ailment. He promises the Joker the ability to make a world in his image in exchange for his assistance. They quickly learn that the Hulk is the key to healing the Shaper. The Hulk and Batman have a couple of battles, almost getting pulverized. Eventually the Joker and Batman, out of necessity, team up to find the Hulk. The Joker is granted his wish, but all the choices are too much for him to handle, and he is sent back to the asylum.

This color paperback was original published as an oversize comic, a team-up of DC and Marvel.

Wein, Len, Herb Trimpe, Marie Severin, et al. *The Incredible Hulk: A Man-Brute Berserk*. New York: Torkids, 1991. ISBN: 0812511 727. Reprints *Incredible Hulk 189–191*.

The Hulk ends up in a paradise in his subconscious, given to him by the Shaper of Worlds, and he meets Glorian. The Toad Men come over into this world, and kidnaps the Hulk and his friends. The Hulk goes berserk and the Toad Men are defeated. The Hulk also helps a blind girl and fights the Mole Man. The Hulk actually cries.

Wolfman, Marv, Harold Livingston, Gene Roddenberry, et al. *Star Trek: The Motion Picture*. New York: Pocket Books, 1980. ISBN: 0671835637. Reprints *Star Trek 1–3; Marvel Super Special 15*.

The crew of the original *Enterprise* faces living machine which is destroying everything in its past. It turns out that this machine is actually the Voyager satellite from the twentieth century. Commander Decker and Lieutenant Ilia become one with the machine.

This is an adaptation of the first *Star Trek* movie in which the crew of the original *Enterprise* comes back together.

9

Marvel/DC Crossovers

Huh? What has white-face done to Hulk now!—*Hulk, to the Joker*

There is a form of oriental fighting in which you don't resist your opponent!
Instead you allow him to make his move first and then you use that move against
him.—*Superman, to Spider-Man*

I'm a clone, try to grasp the concept.—*Superboy, to the Ben Reilly Spider-Man*

Busiek, Kurt, Keith Griffen, Barbara Kesel, et al. *Return to the Amalgam Age of Comics: The Marvel Comics Collection.* New York: Marvel, 1997. ISBN: 0785105808. Reprints *Challengers of the Fantastic 1; Exciting X-Patrol 1; Iron Lantern 1; Magnetic Men Featuring Magneto 1; Spider-Boy Team Up 1; Thorion of the New Asgods 1.*

The Challengers of the Fantastic Four have to deal with Galactica who turns Ben Grimm into a four-armed punisher. "Red," Storm's clone, is killed while saving the Earth, and the Silver Racer claims his death. X-Patrol has to contend with Brother Brood, and Iron Lantern fights the Great White in space. Magneto resurrects the Metallic Men, and turns them loose into the world. Spider-Boy keeps going through the timeline, meeting with the Legion of Galactic Guardians 2099. Thorian becomes the Celestial.

This combination of Marvel and DC characters tells a new story. The characters include the Green Lantern/Iron Man; X-Men/Doom Patrol; Challengers of the Unknown/Fantastic Four; Thor/Orion; Superboy/Spider-Man; and Magnetic Men/Metal Men.

Busiek, Kurt, George Perez, Tom Smith, et al. *JLA/Avengers Collector's Edition.* New York: DC/Marvel, 2004. ISBN: 141202071. Reprints *JLA/Avengers 1–4; Marvel Age 19.*

The Grandmaster and Metron play a game in which the stake is reality in both, DC and Marvel universes. Krona starts a wave of destruction throughout various universes, seeking the meaning life, only to become lured by the power of being a demigod. He believes that he is the cause of the phasing of reality between the DC and Marvel Earths, and even kills the Grandmaster, briefly. Both the Avengers and the JLA are sent between the Earths to seek various objects, including the Cosmic Cube, Soul Gems, the Wand of Watoomb, the Eternity Book, and the Power Battery, among others. All of the JLA and the Avengers fight, except for Captain America and Batman. They seem to realize there is more to the encounter than meets the eye. Nearly everyone who has been a JLA/Avenger, and their respective foes, makes a cameo, but the focus is on the heavies like Wonder Woman, Batman, Superman, Flash, Captain America, Iron Man, Thor, Yellowjacket, and the Wasp. When the Avengers and the JLA decide to pool their resources to stop a common enemy, Superman gives up leadership to Captain America, and Captain America gives Superman his shield for safekeeping.

This is the epic crossover of the decade, in which the Marvel and DC Universes come together to stop a greater threat. This deluxe slipcase contains two volumes, one of which is the story itself; the other contains a history of DC/Marvel crossovers, including a bibliography of individual and collected editions, called the *Avengers/JLA Compendium.* The work also has George Perez's original pencils from the 1983 aborted crossover; a key to every character—there are so many that it is confusing; a breakdown of the story; Kurt Busik's original outline for the 2003 series; and the JLA/Avengers you never saw. This is a beautiful set that is well worth seeking.

Byrne, John, Terry Austin, Patricia Mulvihill, et al. *The Amalgam Age of Comics: The DC*

Comics Collection. New York: DC/Marvel, 1996. ISBN: 1563892952. Reprints *Amazon 1; Doctor Strangefate 1; JLX 1; Legends of the Dark Claw 1; Super Soldier 1.*

The Amalgam Universe is peopled with characters that are combinations of Marvel and DC characters. For example, Storm and Wonder Woman are Amazon; Red Skull and Lex Luthor are the Green Skull; Captain America and Superman are the Super Soldier; Dr. Strange, Dr. Fate, and Professor X are Dr. Strangefate; Jubilee and Robin are Sparrow; and Wolverine and Batman are Dark Claw. In this, the first collected edition of these bizarre stories, Amazon/Wonder Woman battles Poseidon, the sea god; Dare and Catsai fight against Enigma Fisk, and Dare is killed; Bruce Banner becomes a combination of Solomon Grundy and the Hulk, Skulk; Luther, the Green Skull, is the head of Hydra, and it is up to the Super Soldier to stop him from using Ultra-Metallo against the world; the JLAX go up against an amalgamated version of Sentinels, including the female Jocasta; and the Huntress, Carol Danvers, finds out that Logan is the Dark Claw. The appendix includes a synopsis of the various Amalgam issues.

Byrne, John, Graham Nolan, Karl Kesel, et al. *DC/Marvel Crossover Classics Vol. 4.* New York: Marvel/DC, 2003. ISBN: 141201695. Reprints *Green Lantern/Silver Surfer: Unholy Alliances; Darkseid vs. Galactus: The Hunger; Batman and Spider-Man: New Age Dawning; Superman/Fantastic Four.*

Thanos seeks to take over the mystical power of the Green Lantern's ring. Silver Surfer fights the Superman cyborg. Thanos enlists the aid of Kyle Rayner whom Thanos deceives. Hal Jordan tries to enlist the aid of the Silver Surfer. Galactus seeks to devour the energies of Darkseid's world, Apokolips. The Surfer is still the herald of Galactus. Orion goes to the aid of Darkseid to fight the Surfer and Galactus. Galactus finds the world to be devoid of any life-giving energy. Batman and Spider-Man team up with the Kingpin against Ra's Al Ghul who wants to control the elements and sink New York. The Kingpin's wife is dying from a disease that Ra has created. Galactus tries to get Superman to become his herald, and the Cyborg Superman seeks to be the one Galactus picks. The Fantastic Four and Cyborg Superman briefly team up against Galactus. Superman realizes that Galactus's amoral stance is not a good one. Galactus transforms the cyborg into a perfect alloy.

Byrne, John, Rick Taylor, Electric Pickle, et al. *Darkseid vs. Galactus: The Hunger.* New York: Marvel/DC, 1995. ISBN: 1563891 824.

In this book, the Silver Surfer is still the herald of Galactus who goes to Apokolips to feed. Darkseid defends his world; Orion battles the Surfer; and Galactus finds Darkseid's world devoid of life force.

David, Peter, Stuart Immonen, Joe Rosas, et al. *Spider-Man/Gen 13.* New York: Marvel/DC, 1996. ISBN: 0785102914.

Spider-Man and Gen 13 team up to defeat Glider and her band of goons.

DeMatteis, J. M., Mark Begley, Scott Hanna, et al. *Spider-Man/Batman: Disordered Minds.* New York: DC/Marvel, 1995. ISBN: 0785 101926.

Spider-Man and Batman team up to fight Carnage who is loose in Gotham. Carnage tries to team up with the Joker, but is rejected.

DeMatteis, J. M., Graham Nolan, Karl Kesel, et al. *Batman & Spider-Man: New Age Dawning.* New York: DC/Marvel, 1997. ISBN: 1563893088.

Batman and Spider-Man make a loose alliance with the Kingpin against Ra's Al Ghul, the Demon.

Dixon, Chuck, John Ostrander, Gerard Jones, et al. *The Amalgam Age of Comics: The Marvel Collection.* New York: Marvel, 1996. ISBN: 078510240X. Reprints *Bruce Wayne: Agent of S.H.I.E.L.D. 1; Bullets and Bracelets 1; Magneto and the Magnetic Men 1; Speed Demon 1; Spider Boy 1; X-Patrol 1*

This is a collection of Amalgam comics which combine Marvel and DC characters in their own separate Universe. In the best story of the collection, Speed Demon is Ghost Rider, the Demon, and the Flash, all in one character. In other stories, Spider-Boy is Superboy and Spider-Man, and the Magnetic Men are the Metal-Men. Some of the stories work real well, but others are abysmal.

Gibbons, Dave, Alan Grant, Larry Hama, et al. *Return to the Amalgam Age of Comics: The DC Comics Collection.* New York: DC/Marvel, 1997. ISBN: 1563893827. Reprints *Bat-Thing 1; Lobo the Duck 1; Generation Hex 1; Super-Soldier Man of War 1; Dark Claw Adventures 1; JLX Unleashed 1*

Bat-Thing destroys some thugs who would kill his family. Dark Claw and Sparrow have to face Claw's old flame Talia who has a "mad on" for him. Generation Hex takes revenge on the town of Humanity which ostracized its leader Jono when his Malform powers started to manifest. Amazon frees JLX from prison to face Fin Fang Flame. Lobo has various escapades with women, while his lady, Bevarlene, keeps catching him cheating on her. Lobo faces the Gold Kidney Lady, and Super Soldier faces Zemo's War Wheel, along with Sgt. Rock and the Howling Commandos. The All-Star Winners Squadron also makes an appearance.

This book, from the Golden Age of Amalgam, is another collection of amalgamated Marvel and DC characters. For example, Manbat and Man Thing are Bat Thing; Generation X and Jonah Hex are Generation Hex; Lobo and Howard the Duck are Lobo the Duck; and the JLA and the X-Men are JLX.

Grant, Alan, Eduardo Barreto, Matt Hollingsworth, et al. *Batman/Daredevil: King of New York.* New York: Marvel/DC, 2000. ISBN: 1563893835.

Batman and Daredevil team up and go against the Kingpin and the Scarecrow.

Jurgens, Dan, Art Thiebert, Greg Wright, et al. *Superman/Fantastic Four: Infinite Destruction.* New York: DC/Marvel, 1999. ISBN: 1563894432.

Superman finds out that Galactus had a hand in devouring Krypton. He goes to the Marvel Earth to seek the aid of the Fantastic Four to deal with Galactus. Against his will, he is turned into the herald of Galactus. Uneasily, the Fantastic Four team-up with the Cyborg Superman, to find and deal with the devourer of worlds. Superman breaks free, with the help of the Fantastic Four, and Galactus destroys the cyborg.

This is an oversize graphic novel.

Lee, Stan, John Buscema, Joe Kubert, et al. *Just Imagine Stan Lee Creating the DC Universe Vol. 1.* New York: DC Comics, 2002. ISBN: 1563898918. Reprints *Just Imagine Stan Lee with Joe Kubert Creating Batman; Just Imagine Stan Lee with Jim Lee Creating Wonder Woman; Just Imagine Stan Lee with John Buscema Creating Superman; Just Imagine Stan Lee with Dave Gibbons Creating Green Lantern; Just Imagine Stan Lee ... Secret Files and Origins.*

This is the first of three volumes in which Mr. Marvel, Stan Lee, gives his take on the key heroes from DC comics: Batman is a black man who was framed and sent to jail, then, after being released, becomes a famous wrestler; Superman is an alien police officer, in pursuit of his wife's killer; Batman and Superman end up on Earth, with Superman vowing vengeance; Superman gets a job as a circus performer, and wows audiences; Lois Lane becomes his agent; Green Lantern is a professor of archaeology who finds the Tree of Life, Yggdrasil, which transforms him into the Lantern, and he fights an old-style, Marvel-type monster, Gargantua; Maria Mendoza finds the Golden Staff of the Incan Sun Goddesses, and becomes the protector of light and goodness, Wonder Woman. The one theme that runs through all of these stories, is the malevolent Church of Eternal Empowerment, led by Rev. Dominic Darrk.

Lee, Stan, Carmine Infantino, Gerry Conway, et al. *Crossover Classics: The Marvel/DC Collection.* New York: Marvel: DC, 1991.

ISBN: 0781358581. Reprints *Superman vs. Spider-Man; Superman and Spider-Man; Batman vs. Incredible Hulk; Uncanny X-Men and the New Teen Titans.*

Lex Luthor teams up with Doctor Octopus to build a weapon so strong that it will destroy parts of the Earth. Even Dr. Octopus realizes that Luther is insane, and turns against him. Luthor builds a fake Superman which causes Clark Kent to freak out. Dr. Doom teams up with the Parasite, with a plan to turn all of the world's fuel into sand. The Joker uses the Hulk against Batman in his attempt to get the Shaper of Worlds to create a world in which he is king. Darkseid revives the Dark Phoenix in his attempt to conquer the universe, and, with her at his side, he feels confident that he will succeed. However, the X-Men and the Teen Titans manage to foil his plans. Slade becomes Darkseid's pawn.

This is the first collected edition of some of the most historic crossover stories ever published in comics form. This volume reprints the first DC/Marvel superhero crossover, featuring the meeting of Superman and Spider-Man. It also contains a reprint of the cover of the first Marvel/DC copublication, *Wizard of Oz.* Each story has a preface explaining the background of the story, written by a prominent writer or editor.

Lee, Stan, Jerry Ordway, John Byrne, et al. *Just Imagine Stan Lee Creating the DC Universe Vol. 2:* New York: DC Comics 2003. ISBN: 1563899876. Reprints *Just Imagine Stan Lee with Kevin Maguire Creating the Flash; Just Imagine Stan Lee with Jerry Ordway Creating the JLA; Just Imagine Stan Lee with John Byrne Creating Robin; Just Imagine Stan Lee with Gary Frank Creating SHAZAM; Just Imagine Stan Lee Secret Files.*

Mr. Marvel gives his take on various characters from the DC Universe in this the second volume of a three-volume series. In this volume, the Flash is a young girl who wishes for adventure in her life, and when she finds out her scientist father is wanted by a covert organization, he injects her with serum from a hummingbird, and she becomes the Flash; Flash has her own comic book, based on her real-life adventures; Green Lantern brings together Flash, Wonder Woman, Superman, and Batman, to form the JLA, against Lee's version of the Doom Patrol; the JLA have a showdown with Rev. Dominic Darrk who tries to use the Doom Patrol to take down Green Lantern and the JLA; Robin was raised in an orphanage, controlled by the Church of Eternal Empowerment, and Darrk, who tries to control him, wants him to fight with Batman; an Interpol agent helps an old Indian mystic, and just before the mystic dies he passes the power of SHAZAM on to the agent; the agent's partner is captured by Gunga Khan who plans to shrink the United States; when the agent says the "SHAZAM," he turns into a huge, red/pink monster who has super strength and a pure heart, but is not too bright. This character harkens back to Lee's monster stories from the fifties and early sixties. The volume contains a detailed explanation of the Church of Eternal Empowerment.

Lee, Stan, Michael Ulsan, Walt Simonson, et al. *Just Imagine Stan Lee Creating the DC Universe Book 3*. New York: DC, 2004. ISBN: 1401202284. Reprints *Just Imagine Stan Lee with Scott McDaniel Creating Aquaman; Just Imagine Stan Lee with Walter Simonson Creating Sandman; Just Imagine Stan Lee with John Chris Bachalo Creating Catwoman; Just Imagine Stan Lee with John Cassaday Creating Crisis; Just Imagine Stan Lee ...Secret Files.*

This is the third volume in which Stan Lee gives his take on characters from the DC Universe. In this volume, he presents his take on Aquaman, Catwoman, Sandman, and Crisis. In it, a young biologist, who also is an environmentalist, injects himself with various underwater DNA and becomes Aquaman; his brother, a police officer, inadvertently becomes involved with the Church of Eternal Empowerment; Catwoman is a famous model who, along with her cat, is accidentally hit with mysterious green lightning and gains various feline powers; Catwoman has to contend with a super-powered mobster and his cronies; the Sandman gains a mystical power through the dream dimension after he crashes during a routine space mission; the Sandman has a very negative encounter with Rev. Darrk who wants him to convert and use his power for evil; the evil entity known as Crisis is loosed upon Earth; Stan Lee's Batman, Superman, Sandman, Robin, Catwoman, Wonder Woman, Green Lantern, Flash, Aquaman, and Shazam come together and form the JLA to try to stop Crisis; after the last groundbreaking battle, the Tree of Life, Yggdrasil, helps give birth to a new leader, the Atom. Each story contains Lee's humorous "On the Street" short take, and each artist writes a brief blurb on working with Stan Lee. The introduction is by Michael Uslan and the afterword by Lee, in which he describes how wonderful working on this project was. This volume is recommended.

Maguire, Kevin, Karl Story, Richard Starkings, et al. *Fantastic Four/Gen 13: Queelocke's Really Big New York Adventure*. New York: Marvel/DC 2001.

Gen 13 visit New York and things get out of hand when Freefall's pet Queelocke grows huge. Spider-Man and Human Torch capture him, and take him to the Baxter Building. Gen 13 and the Fantastic Four fight for the pet's release.

Marz, Ron, Darryl Banks, Terry Austin, et al. *Green Lantern/Silver Surfer Unholy Alliances*. New York: Marvel/DC, 1995. ISBN: 1563892588.

The Silver Surfer comes up against the Cyborg Superman who just tore off a part of the planet. Parallax, Hal Jordan, a former Green Lantern, tries to get the Surfer to agree to go back in time to right certain wrongs. Thanos deceives the Green Lantern, Kyle Rayner, into aiding him, and the Lantern and the Surfer fight against one another, as Hal Jordan and Thanos duke it out. Hal Jordan siphons some of the Surfer's power, but it's too strong, even for Parallax.

Marz, Ron, Peter David, Dan Jurgens, et al. *DC Versus Marvel Comics*. New York: Marvel/DC, 1996. ISBN: 1563892944. Reprints *DC Versus Marvel Versus DC 1, 4; Marvel Versus DC Versus Marvel 2, 3; Doctor Strangefate 1.*

Two brothers, one from the DC Universe and the other from the Marvel Universe, suddenly become aware of each other, and they start to fight. This causes havoc in their respective universes, with characters from Marvel and DC popping in and out. As a result, the brothers decide that there should be a battle between the universes; the winners will save their universe; the losers will lose their universe, and all life within it. In the ensuing battle, Thanos fights Darkseid; the Spectre goes against the Living Tribunal; Bane fights Captain America; Jubilee and Robin start to fall for each other, but they also are forced to fight; Captain Marvel fights Thor; Quicksilver fights the Flash, and loses; Aquaman fights the Sub-Mariner, and wins; Wonder Woman picks up Thor's hammer; Green Lantern goes against the Silver Surfer, and loses. Elektra fights Catwoman, and wins; Peter Parker asks Lois Lane out on a date, and gets turned down; Jonah Jameson runs the *Daily Planet*, and the Kingpin pushes Perry White out and becomes the new owner; Wolverine fights Lobo, and wins; Wonder Woman fights Storm, and loses; Spider-Man fights Superboy, and wins; Superman defeats the Hulk, and then they go up against the Mole Man. Rick Jones meets Snapper Carr. Batman and Captain America are so well matched, that they decide to put their brains together to figure out a solution to the conflict. In this book we learn that the combination of Dr. Fate and Dr. Strange is Charles Xavier, and we get to read Jubilee's dairy.

This was the crossover that created the Amalgam age of comics and its characters. The volume includes a character sketch of each of the characters of *DC Versus Marvel Comics*.

O'Neil, Dennis, Chuck Dixon, George Perez, et al. *Marvel/DC Crossover Classics Vol. 2*. New York: Marvel/DC, 1998. ISBN: 1563893991. Reprints *Batman/Punisher: Lake of Fire*. ISBN: 1563891611; *Batman/Punisher: Deadly Knights*; *Silver Surfer/Superman: Pop*; *Batman & Captain America*. ISBN: 156389291X.

Azrial, as Batman, meets the Punisher and saves his life. At first he wants to take the Punisher to jail, but decides on working with the lesser evil against Jigsaw. Jigsaw comes to Gotham to see if he can become a bigwig in the crime world, and forms an alliance with the Joker. Azrial seeks the guidance of St. Dumas. The Punisher comes back to Gotham and meets the real Batman who has nothing but disdain for Frank Castle. But again they briefly work together to stop the Joker and Jigsaw. The Joker gets Jigsaw a corrupt plastic surgeon who fixes his face, but the Punisher destroys it again. Captain America and Bucky meet Batman and Robin towards the end of World War II. Apparently the Joker is working with a mysterious crime lord who is trying to get "Fat Man," the A-bomb, in his custody. Captain America and Batman stop the kidnapping of Robert Oppenheimer. The Joker finds out that he had been working with the Red Skull. The Joker is a crook, but he is an American crook and is horrified that he has been working with a Nazi. The Skull plans to drop the bomb on Washington, D.C.

Perez, George, Roy Linn, Terry Austin, et al. *Silver Surfer/Superman: Pop.* New York: Marvel/DC, 1996. ISBN: 0785102930.

The Impossible Man and MXYZPTLK play a game with Superman and the Silver Surfer, and send them to their respective universes where their worlds collide. Neither Superman nor the Surfer are amused. Metropolis ends up in a glass case, and people blame the Surfer. Impossible Man becomes Galactus, and tries to chew MXYZPTLK like a piece of chewing gum.

Stern, Roger, Steve Rude, Al Milgrom, et al. *The Incredible Hulk vs. Superman: Double Lives.* New York: Marvel/DC, 1999. ISBN: 0785107363.

Lex Luthor tries to use the Hulk to defeat Superman. Clark Kent interviews Bruce Banner.

Stern, Roger, Steve Rude, Al Milgrom, et al. *Marvel DC Collection— Crossover Classics Vol. 3* New York: Marvel/DC, 2002. ISBN: 0785108181. Reprints *Superman/Incredible Hulk*; *Spider-Man/Gen 13*; *Team X/Team 7*, ISBN: 0785102922; *Daredevil/Batman*, ISBN: 0785105522; *Spiderman/Batman*; *Generation X/Gen 13*.

Lex Luthor tries to build a robot Hulk in order to get the real Hulk to destroy Superman. Batman and Daredevil meet and immediately start fighting. Matt Murdock knew Harvey Dent in law school. Mr. Hyde and Two-Face form a loose alliance, and Batman and Daredevil have to take them down. The Joker and Carnage form a brief alliance when chips implanted in their brains in order to control them, go bad. Batman and Spider-Man have to rein them in. Batman and Spider-Man actually shake hands at the end. Gen 13 and Spider-Man go up against assassin Glider and her cronies. Generation X and Gen 13 meet in Mexico at a very bizarre hotel/castle. Its proprietor, a mad scientist, wants to use the genes and internal organs of both super-powered groups to create his own brand of animal/human hybrids. Team X, which features Wolverine, Sabretooth, and Maverick, during their early cover-op missions, joins Team 7 to defeat Omega Red and get the info on a special Soviet Super Soldier program. Mystique also makes an appearance.

This action takes place during the height of the Cold War. The original book, *Team X/Team 7*, includes profiles of Team X and Team 7.

10

Children's Books

Never fear, Spidey's here.—*Spider-Man*

Give it up—your plan to steal the secrets in this building has failed.—*Chuck Norris, to Super Ninja*

Alan, Geoffrey, Rob Lee. *SuperTed in Cookie Capers*. London: Marvel, 1990. ISBN: 18540 01779.

This book was published by Marvel in association with Redan.

Anastasio, Dina, Cathy Beylon. *All Year Long*. New York: Marvel/Fisher Price, 1987. ISBN: 0871351846.

This sticker book features the Little People.

Anastasio, Dina, Cathy Beylon. *Roger Goes to the Doctor*. New York: Marvel, 1988. ISBN: 0871351064.

Roger goes to the doctor with his dog Hero who becomes mischievous at the doctor's office.

Anastasio, Dina, Dick Codor, Carol Bouman, et al. *The Fisher-Price Picture Dictionary*. New York: Marvel/Fisher-Price, 1987. ISBN: 0871351730.

This dictionary goes from Able to Zoom. It includes definitions and pictures for words that young children should be learning.

Anastasio, Dina, Tom Cooke. *Weekly Reader Presents Baby Piggy and the Giant Bubble*. New York: Marvel/Muppet Press, 1987. ISBN: 0871350963.

Baby Miss Piggy daydreams about flying around in a giant bubble.

Anastasio, Dina, Ann Losa. *Marvin's Invention*. New York: Marvel, 1987. ISBN: 0871351 889.

The Little People household is in chaos when Marvin the inventor comes.

Anastasio, Dina, John Speirs. *One Big Balloon: A Board Book About Numbers*. New York: Marvel, 1987. ISBN: 0871351986.

This book helps children learn about numbers and how to count; it features the Puffalumps.

Anastasio, Dina, John Speirs, et al. *The Puffalumps: A Board Book About Colors: Looking For Green*. New York: Marvel, 1987. ISBN: 0871351978.

In this Puffalumps Board Book of Colors, Puffalump Cow looks for the color green. The book helps children recognize and learn basic colors.

Anastasio, Dina, John Speirs. *Weekly Reader Presents Scooter and Skeeter's Merry-Go-Round Puzzle*. New York: Marvel/Muppet Press, 1986. ISBN: 0871350998.

The last piece of Scooter and Skeeter's merry-go-round puzzle is missing. They try to imagine what animal it might be.

Anstey, David. *Big Book of ABC*. New York: Marvel, 1990. ISBN: 1854000837.

This ABC learning book is based on the Dinosaur Playhouse Series.

Anstey, David. *Big Book of Nursery Rhymes*. New York: Marvel, 1990. ISBN: 1854000713.

In this book, Anstey illustrates a collection of children's rhymes, including "Little Miss Muffett," "Little Jack Horner," and "Old King Cole," among others.

Ballard, S. M., et al. *Cobra Shrinking Ray*. New York: Marvel, 1987. ISBN: 0871352192.

In this coloring book, Cobra develops a special shrinking ray to fight the G.I. Joes.

Ballard, S. M., Jude Kane. *Mighty Mouse: Scrappy's Scrape with Danger*. New York: Marvel, 1988. ISBN: 0871353296.

This is a Mighty Mouse coloring book.

Baum, Max, Brad Joyce, Roberta Edelman, Brad Joyce. *Transformers: Battle for Earth*. New York: Marvel, 1985. ISBN: 0871350 629.

The Decepticons are using the Constructicons to plant bombs all over the Earth. Megatron wants to become ruler of Earth by holding four million hostages. The Autobots go to the Decepticons headquarters and meet with Devastator.

Beach, Lynn. *Earth and the Solar System*. New York: Marvel, 1987. ISBN: 087135120X.

This Young Astronauts coloring book describes Earth and the solar system.

Beach, Lynn. *Secret of Starfish Island*. New York: Marvel, 1987. ISBN: 0871352206.

This is a special G. I. Joe coloring book.

Beach, Lynn, Young Astronauts Council, NASA et al. *Humans in Space*. New York: Marvel, 1987. ISBN: 0871351234.

This Big Looker Storybook provides a brief look at the possibilities of human space travel.

Behling, Steve. *Spider-Man Mysteries*. New York: Marvel, 1998. ISBN: 0785106421.

This book, which stars Spider-Man, is part of the Marvel Kids series. It contains games and interactive adventures for children.

Black, Arlene, et al. *The Puffalumps at Play*. New York: Marvel, 1987. ISBN: 0871352389.

This children's book features those bizarre people, the Puffalumps.

Black, Sonia, Carlos Garzon. *The Magic Gemstone*. New York: Marvel, 1985. ISBN: 087 1350637.

This an adventure story in which a special gemstone is prominently featured.

Black, Sonia, Steven Geiger, Roberta Edelman, et al. *Sectaurs: Secret in the Valley of Meander*. New York: Marvel, 1985. ISBN: 0871 350645.

Large quantities of the crop Skall have been stolen by raiders. Sectaurs of the Shining Realm set up a trap for the thieves. Several Sectaurs, including Dargon, follow the thieves into the Dark Realm and uncover a plan by Empress Devora to destroy those in the Shining Realm.

Bligh, Fenson, Herb Trimpe, Fred Ottenheimer. *G. I. Joe: A Real American Hero: The Spy Eye*. New York: Marvel, 1983. ISBN: 0939766 515.

In this "easy reader" picture novel, Cobra has kidnapped a famous scientist and stolen his Big Eye Satellite. The Joes rescue the scientist and take back the satellite from Cobra.

Brown, Nancy Leigh, Earl Norem. *Mission of Friendship*. New York: Marvel, 1985. ISBN: 0871350580.

This book features the Sectaurs, Warriors of Symbion.

Calder, Lyn, Terry Kovalcik. *I Can Learn Beginner Sounds*. New York: Marvel, 1987. ISBN: 0871351927.

This is a Little People phonetics book for young children.

Calmenson, Stephanie, Cathy Beylon. *A Visit to the Firehouse*. New York: Marvel/Fisher-Price, 1986. ISBN 087135148X.

The Little People go to a visit a firehouse.

Calmenson, Stephanie, Carolyn Bracken. *Meet Baby*. New York: Marvel/Fisher-Price, 1987. ISBN: 087135179X.

Meet the new baby in this Fischer Price Little People book.

Calmenson, Stephanie, Carolyn Bracken. *Meet Lucky*. New York: Marvel/Fisher-Price, 1987. ISBN: 0871351781.

This is a Little People book in which the puppy Lucky is introduced.

Calmenson, Stephanie, Carolyn Bracken. *Meet Penny*. New York: Marvel/Fisher-Price, 1986. ISBN: 0871351528.

Penny, a preschooler, is introduced in this Little People book.

Calmenson, Stephanie, Carolyn Bracken. *Meet Timmy*. New York: Marvel/Fisher-Price, 1986. ISBN: 087135151X.

This is a Little People book about a boy named Timmy.

Carnell, John. *The Demon Baby*. London: Marvel, 1989. ISBN: 1854000756.

This children's book features the *Real Ghostbusters* characters.

Carnell, John, *The Ghostly Shark*. London: Marvel, 1989. ISBN: 1854000608.

This book features the *Real Ghostbusters* characters.

Carnell, John, Andy Lanning. *The Real Ghostbusters and Egon's New Invention*. London: Marvel, 1990.
ISBN: 1854001833.

This book features the *Real Ghostbusters* characters.

Carnell John, Brian Williamson. *The Ghostly Brothers Grimm*. London: Marvel, 1990. ISBN: 1854001787.

This book features the *Real Ghostbusters* characters.

Carnell, John, Brian Williamson. *The Return of Mr. Stay Puff*. London: Marvel, 1989. ISBN: 1854000500.

This book features the *Real Ghostbusters* characters.

Cavalieri, Joey, Hyperdesign, Suzzane Gaffney, et al. *Marvel Chillers featuring the Fantastic Four: Frightful Four*. New York: Marvel, 1996.

In this easy reader based on *Fantastic Four 94 & 126*, the Fantastic Four battle the Frightful Four, which consists of Medusa, Trapster, Sandman, and the Wizard. This book includes parts of the original comics.

Chardiet Jon. *Surprise Saturday*. New York: Marvel, 1987. ISBN: 0871351854.

This is a Little People sticker adventure.

Chardiet, Jon, Manny Campana. *Lucky and the Dog Show*. New York: Marvel/Fisher-Price, 1987. ISBN: 0871351900.

In this book and tape set, Penny and Timmy enter their dog Lucky in a dog show.

Chardiet, Jon. Barbara Lanza. *The Puffalumps and the Big Scare*. New York: Marvel, 1987. ISBN: 0871352451.

Several Puffalumps disguise themselves as monsters and scare a camping group.

Chardiet, Jon, Jon Spiers. *Lucky's Kitten*. New York: Marvel, 1988. ISBN: 0871351102.

A lost kitten comes to Lucky's house.

Chichester, D. G. *An American Tale: Fievel Goes West*. New York: Marvel, 1991. ISBN: 0871 357585.

This is a jumbo-sized adaptation of the hit animated movie.

Cohen, Della. *I Can Learn About Animals*. New York: Marvel/Fisher-Price, 1987. ISBN: 0871351951.

This is a Little People book that teaches toddlers about different animals.

Cohen Della. *I Can Learn About Beginner Math*. New York: Marvel/Fisher-Price, 1987. ISBN: 0871351935.

This Little People book teaches children about math.

Connellan, Maureen, Dawson Hearn. *The Fox Family Feud*. New York: Marvel, 1988. ISBN: 0871353733.

Brother and Sister Fox quarrel while playing.

Corvese, Kelly, Gary Fields. *X-Men: Mutant Search RU1?* New York: Marvel, 1998. ISBN: 0785106448.

The X-Men put out a press release, searching for mutants RU1. A young mutant, Melody, discovers she has the power to make plants grow. She contacts the X-Men through email, and Wolverine and Storm come to help her learn how to control her powers.

This is part of the Marvel Kids imprint. Each book contains a comic story, games, word puzzles, and interactive adventures.

Cray, Daphne. *Rainy Day/Sunny Day*. New York: Marvel/Fisher-Price, 1986. ISBN: 0871351412; 0948936770.

This is a Fisher-Price coloring book.

Daly, James, Chris Claremont, Bill Sienkiewicz, et al. *Marvel Chillers: Blood Storm*. New York: Marvel, 1997. ISBN: 0785102678. Reprints *X-Men Classic 63* (*Uncanny X-Men 159*); *X-Men Annual 6*.

A distant relative of Rachel Van Helsing has a teacher whose son is a vampire. With the help of the X-Men Psylocke, Cannonball, and Wolverine, they stop the vampire from turning the schoolkids into vampires.

This book reprints the complete comic in which Dracula tries to turn Storm into a vampire, and it also has snippets from the story in which Wolverine kills Rachel Van Helsing. This easy reader also contains an original story that is not based on any previous comic, and includes a poster.

DeMauro, Lisa, Chi Chung. *Sam Learns to Cook*. New York: Marvel, 1988. ISBN: 0871353725.

Sam cooks for his aunt, but without much success.

DeMauro, Lisa. Dick Codor. *The Fisher-Price Fun with Food All Year Round Cookbook*. New York: Marvel/Fisher-Price, 1988. ISBN: 087135442X.

This book contains recipes for children, including one for gumdrop Christmas trees and New Year cookies.

DeMauro, Lisa, Dick Codor, Jose R. Pacheco. *The Fisher-Price Fun with Food Cookbook.* New York: Marvel/Fisher Price, 1988. ISBN: 0871351633.

This is an illustrated cookbook for young children, which includes a note to parents on how to use the book with their children. Some of the recipes include: Cookie-Cutter Sandwich, Banana Velvet, and Blue Lemon Fizz, among many others.

DeMauro, Lisa, Dennis Hockerman. *Emma's Sleepover Party.* New York: Marvel, 1988. ISBN: 0871354500.

Emma, a baby bunny, invites several of her animal friends to a sleepover party to see the sunrise. So many come over, and stay up so late, that Emma almost misses her sunrise.

This story also was reprinted, by Playmore, in 1991 in Creative Child Press tales: 229–7.

Dubowski, Cathy East, Yvette Santiago Banek. *Charlie Can't Sleep.* New York: Marvel, 1988. ISBN: 0871353695.

Charlie the chipmunk has trouble sleeping.

Favorite Mother Goose Rhymes. New York: Marvel, 1988. ISBN: 0871353903.

This is a book and tape set with some of the best of the Mother Goose rhymes.

Freed, Carol. *Best Present Ever.* New York: Marvel/Fisher-Price, 1987. ISBN: 0871351757.

This is a Little People coloring book.

Ganeri, A. *Natural World Fact Finder.* New York: Marvel, 1979. ISBN: 1854000772.

This is a mini-almanac for young children.

Gari, Janet. *Scooby Doo: The Mystery of the Ghost in the Doghouse.* New York: Marvel, 1988. ISBN: 0871354861.

Scooby investigates a supposed ghost in a doghouse.

Gatehouse, John, Barrie Appleby. *Dino Goes to Hollyrock.* New York: Marvel, 1990. ISBN: 1854001671.

This story is based on Dino, the Flintstones' televisions character.

Gately, George, Stan Goldberg. *Heathcliff: A Jumbo Coloring and Activity Book.* New York: Marvel, 1987. ISBN: 0871352869.

This is an activity book for young children, starring Heathcliff the cat.

Gautier, Teddy. *Mrs. Bunny's Day Off.* New York: Marvel, 1988. ISBN: 0700970022.

Mrs. Bunny takes a day off from her busy schedule.

Gautier, Teddy, Dennis Hockerman. *Sadie's Bed.* New York: Marvel, 1988. ISBN: 0871353 75X.

Sadie the mouse has an adventure in a pink shoe.

Gelman, Rita Golden, Cathy Beylon. *Care and Share: A Book About Manners.* New York: Marvel/Fisher-Price, 1986. ISBN: 08713 51501.

This easy reader book teaches children fundamental etiquette and manners, such as saying "please" and "thank you."

Gelman, Rita Golden, Cathy Beylon. *Listen and Look: A Safety Book.* New York: Marvel/ Fisher-Price, 1986. ISBN: 0871351498.

This easy reader book teaches children basic safety rules, such as looking both ways before crossing the street.

Geoffrey, Alan, Rob Lee. *SuperTed in Cookie Capers.* New York: Marvel/Redan, 1990. ISBN: 1854001779.

This children's book is based on a popular animated character.

George, Emily, Kristin Johnson. *The Puffalumps: Pillow Poems.* New York: Marvel/Fisher-Price, 1987. ISBN: 0871352427.

This is a collection of poems for bedtime, including "Child's Evening Hymn," "Willie Winkie," and "All the Pretty Horses," among others.

George, Emily, Marja St. John. *Dream Boat.* New York: Marvel/Quaker Oats, 1987. ISBN: 0871352044.

This is an illustrated bedtime story to share with your child.

George, Emily, Marja St. John. *Good Night Sleep Tight.* New York: Marvel/Quaker Oats, 1987. ISBN: 0871352036.

This is a bedtime verse about a young boy who plays, gets his bath, has a bedtime snack, and goes to bed.

Gilkow, Louise, Lauren Attinello. *Weekly Reader Presents: Meet the Muppet Babies.* New York: Muppet Press/Marvel, 1987. ISBN: 08713 50939.

In this easy reader book, the Muppet Babies create a small hole in a cardboard box, and are transported to lands of imagination.

Gilkow, Louise, Tom Brannon. *Weekly Reader Presents Animal Go Bye Bye.* New York: Marvel/Muppet Press, 1986. ISBN: 08713 50971.

Baby Animal from the Muppet Babies imagines that he goes on adventures to an amusement park, a desert island, and an airport.

Gilkow, Louise, Sue Venning. *Weekly Reader Presents Gonzo Saves London Bridge*. New York: Marvel/Muppet Press, 1986. ISBN: 0871350947.
Gonzo and the Muppet Babies come up with a plan to stop the London Bridge from falling down.

Gilmour, H.B. Mary Bausman. *Weekly Reader Presents: If I Were Just Like Kermit*. New York: Muppet Press/Marvel, 1986. ISBN: 0871351005.
Kermit has a cold and his best friend Fozzie tries to cheer him up.

Goldberg, Stan, Gary Brodsky, Susan Weyn. *Heathcliff: The Haunted House*. New York: Marvel, 1983. ISBN: 0939766736.
Heathcliff goes to a haunted house in this delightful coloring book.

Gridley, Laura, Muriel Fahrion. *Smooshees: Squish Fish's Forest Adventure*. New York: Marvel, 1988. ISBN: 0871353814.
A fish who is lonely travels to find friends throughout the pond, encountering many obstacles along the way.

Gruenwald, Mark, Peter Cooper, Suzanne Gaffney Beason, et al. *Marvel Chillers: Shades of Green Monsters*. New York: Marvel, 1997. ISBN: 0785106219. Based on *Hulk 431–432*.
This is an easy reader in which the Hulk fights the Abomination underneath New York streets. The book comes with a poster.

Hall, Willhemina, Steve Smallwood. *Heathcliff, Olympic Champ*. New York: Marvel, 1985. ISBN: 0871353407.
Heathcliff and his family visit the Winter Olympics where Heathcliff gets into all sorts of trouble.

Hama, Larry, Pat Chua, Mark Pennington, et al. *Marvel Chillers: Thing in the Glass Case*. New York: Marvel, 1997. ISBN: 0785106219.
Wolverine and Jubilee, along with the help of several teenagers, fight a mummy and a demented scientist.
This is an easy reader.

Harris, Jack. *History of Space Travel*. New York: Marvel, 1987. ISBN: 0871351188.
This is a Young Astronauts Council coloring book that looks at the history of space travel.

Harris, Jack, William Low. *Caverns of Darkness*. New York: Marvel, 1986. ISBN: 0871351331.
This Big Looker storybook features Chuck Norris and the Karate Kommandos.

Harris, Jack, William Low. *Chuck Norris and the Karate Kommandos: The Caverns of Darkness*. New York: Marvel, 1986. ISBN: 087 51351331.
Members of the Karate Kommandos explore a cave, only to find Super Ninja and his minions of the Cult of the Klaw. Chuck comes out of the cave and fights them.

Harris, Jack, William Low. *Chuck Norris and the Karate Kommandos: Skyscraper Assault*. New York: Marvel, 1986. ISBN: 0871351323.
The Super Ninja and the cult of the Klaw terrorize a skyscraper in D.C. Chuck Norris and his Karate Kommandos defeat them.
The artwork, done in watercolor, is quite good. There were also a number of Chuck Norris sticker adventures and coloring books published by Marvel.

Harris, Jack, William Low. *Skyscraper Assault*. New York: Marvel, 1986. ISBN: 0871351 323.
This is a Chuck Norris Karate Kommandos storybook.

Hartelius, Margaret. *The Great Big Word Book*. New York: Marvel/Fisher-Price, 1985. ISBN: 0871351382.
This book, which is in color, features the Little People. It is a picture and word association book for young children, designed to help them develop language skills. Examples include "bathroom," "cat," and "tea set."

Hovanec, Helene. *G.I. Joe Puzzle and Game Book*. New York: Marvel, 1987. ISBN: 087 1352257.
This book contains puzzles and games featuring the G.I. Joe characters.

Hovanec, Helene, Stan Lee, et al. *Stan Lee Presents Marvel Word Games*. New York: Marvel, 1979. ISBN: 0671248081.
This book contains word games based on characters like Spider-Man, the Hulk, and Captain America.

Howe, James, Kathy Spahr. *Weekly Reader Presents: A Love Note for Baby Piggy*. New York: Marvel/Muppet Press, 1987. ISBN: 087135 098X.
Baby Miss Piggy imagines that Baby Kermit wrote a love note, and asked her to marry him.

Jacobson, Suzyn, Warren Kremer, Roberta Edelman. *Size and Shapes with Heathcliff*. New York: Marvel, 1985. ISBN: 0871350 408.

This book helps children learn various shapes and sizes, and teaches them various activities.

Jay, Shirley, John Constanza. *Heathcliff: The Fish Bandit*. New York: Marvel, 1983. ISBN: 0939766523.

Heathcliff outwits some fishers, and takes their catch. The milkman, from who he steals fish, ends up coming over for a fish dinner at Heathcliff's house.

Jay, Shirley, John Constanza. *Heathcliff: Trickiest Cat in Town*. New York: Marvel, 1983. ISBN: 0939766531.

Spike and Muggsy try to get Heathcliff into trouble, but he turns the tables on them.

Jensen, Kathryn. *The Kung Fu Solution*. New York: Marvel, 1986. ISBN: 0871352273.

This is a Foofur coloring book.

Keating, Barry, Tom Cook. *Weekly Reader Presents Kermit the Hermit*. New York: Marvel/ Muppet Press, 1986. ISBN: 0871350955.

Baby Kermit decides that the nursery is too noisy, so he goes off to be a hermit.

Keating, Helane. *Foofur Plays It Cool*. New York: Marvel, 1987. ISBN: 0871352362.

In this special storybook, Foofur keeps a cool head amidst a crisis.

Keating, Helane. *Foofur's Escape*. New York: Marvel, 1987. ISBN: 0871352354.

Foofur makes a run for it.

Keating, Helane. *I Smell a Rat*. New York: Marvel, 1987. ISBN: 0871352265.

This is a Foofur coloring book.

Ketcham, Hank. *Tiger on the Loose and Other Stories*. London: Marvel, 1990. ISBN: 185 4001485.

This book features Dennis the Menace comic stories.

Koenigsburg, Patricia. *From Pumpkins to Posies*. New York: Marvel, 1987. ISBN: 0871352 397.

This is a coloring book about the seasons of the year.

Koenigsburg, Patricia. *New Surprises in Town*. New York: Marvel/Fisher-Price, 1987. ISBN: 0871351773.

This is a Fisher-Price Little People coloring book.

Kovacs, Deborah, Grace Goldburg. *A Whale's Tale*. New York: Marvel, 1988. ISBN: 0871 354519.

A whale dreams about what it would be like to be another animal, but eventually learns to like herself as she is.

This book was also published by Playmore Press in 1991.

Kraft, David Anthony. *Heathcliff: #1 Cat at the Show*. New York: Marvel, 1983. ISBN: 0939766310.

This is an activity book featuring Heathcliff the cat.

Kraft, David Anthony, Carlos Garzon, John Tartaglione, et al. *Marvel Super Heroes Secret Wars: Amazing Spider-Man and Wolverine in the Crime of the Centuries*. New York: Marvel, 1984. ISBN: 0939766906.

Doctor Octopus and Kang team up, and use a time machine to change the past to their advantage. Wolverine and Spider-Man have to follow them through various mazes to defeat their evil schemes.

This book includes activities and games.

Kraft, David Anthony, Stan Goldberg, Gary Brodsky. *Heathcliff at the Circus*. New York: Marvel, 1983. ISBN: 0939766299.

Heathcliff goes to the circus.

Kraft, David Anthony, Edward Hannigan, Chic Stone. *The Fantastic Four vs. the Frightful Four*. New York: Marvel, 1984. ISBN: 093 9766388.

The Fantastic Four go up against those evil minions the Frightful Four in this delightful coloring book.

Kraft, David Anthony, Stan Lee, et al. *Stan Lee Presents The Incredible Hulk: Trapped*. New York: Marvel, 1982. ISBN: 093976606X.

Greedy men trap miners inside a mine so they can keep all the gold. The Hulk frees the miners and goes after the greedy men.

Kraft, David Anthony, Tor Lokvig, John Strejan, et al. *Stan Lee Presents the Incredible Hulk*. New York: Marvel, 1980. ISBN: 0960414630.

This special activity book for kids features the Hulk.

Kraft, David Anthony, Marie Severin, Earl Norman, et al. *The Amazing Spider-Man: The Big Top Mystery*. New York: Marvel, 1984. ISBN: 093976654X.

Peter Parker goes to the circus with his Aunt May. Spider-Man catches a clown who tries to make the circus a mess when he hears that the owner was going to sell it.

This is a book and tape set.

Kraft, David Anthony, Jane Stine, Marie Severin. *Treasure of Time: Advanced Dungeons & Dragons.* New York: Marvel, 1983. ISBN: 0939766701.

This is a children's Dungeons & Dragons book about an evil wizard, Kelek, who is searching for the Treasure of Time which he thinks will make him invincible.

Krueger, Jim, Dak. *Fantastic Four: Franklin's Adventures.* New York: Marvel, 1998. ISBN: 078510643X.

Franklin sneaks aboard a rocket ship to Mars with the rest of the Fantastic Four. He almost gets left on Mars. He takes a photograph of some Martians to prove there is life on Mars.

This book, which is part of the Marvel Kids imprint, includes puzzles, mazes, and other activities for kids.

Krulik, Nancy, Brad Joyce. *Transformers: Battle for Junk Planet.* New York: Marvel, 1986. ISBN: 0871351161.

The Junkicons fight the Autobots who have to make an emergency landing on Junk.

Krulik, Nancy, Charles Nicholas, Roberta Edelman. *Transformers: Autobot's Secret Weapon.* New York: Marvel, 1985. ISBN: 0871350610.

The Autobots go up against Devastator which is made up of several Constructicons. Optimus Prime comes up with the idea of a Trojan robot for Megatron and the Decepticons. The Autobots hide inside the robot, and are able to defeat Megatron and Devastator inside the Decepticons camp.

Langley, Andrew, Moria Butterfield, Norman Young, et al. *People.* London: Marvel Books, 1980. ISBN: 1854000926.

This children's book describes how people live throughout the world.

Laskin, Darnela. *Freddy's Foiled Treasure Hunt.* New York: Marvel, 1987. ISBN: 0871352524.

This is a *Flintstone Kids* coloring book.

Laskin, Pamela, et al. *A Little Off the Top.* New York: Marvel, 1988. ISBN: 087135232X.

This is a Foofur storybook.

Lawrence, Robb, Frank Hill, Roberta Edelman, Steve Smallwood. *Mighty Mouse: A Big Day in Mouseville.* New York: Marvel, 1988. ISBN: 0871353318.

This is coloring book featuring Mighty Mouse.

Lawrence, Robb, Steve Smallwood. *Heathcliff: Summer Carnival.* New York: Marvel, 1989. ISBN: 0816716633.

Heathcliff and his pals go to the carnival and have a blast riding all the rides.

Lawrence, Robb, Steve Smallwood, George Gately. *Gotta Get a Fish.* New York: Marvel, 1989. ISBN: 0816716641.

Heathcliff does everything possible to get a fish dinner.

Lee, Stan, et al. *Attack of the Tarantula.* New York: Marvel, 1982. ISBN: 0393766043.

The Tarantula attacks Spider-Man.

Lerangis, Peter. *I Can Learn About the Neighborhood.* New York: Marvel/Fisher-Price, 1987. ISBN: 0871351943.

This Little People storybook teaches children about neighborhoods.

Lewison, Wendy Chevette, Vickie Learner Adams. *Raccoon's Messy Birthday Party.* New York: Marvel, 1988. ISBN: 0871353563.

The birthday party at Raccoon's house undoes all the cleaning he did before his guests arrived.

Lewison, Wendy Cheyette, Roz Schanzer. *When An Elephant Goes Shopping.* New York: Marvel, 1988. ISBN: 0871354551.

This book describes what happens when an elephant goes on a shopping spree.

Lord, Suzanne, Ernie Colon, Rick Bryant. *Sectaurs: Secrets of the Dark Domain.* New York: Marvel, 1985. ISBN: 0871350511.

Dargon gets lured to the Dark Domain by General Spidrax.

Lord, Suzanne, Carlos Garzon. *Transformers: Summertime Coloring Book.* New York: Marvel, 1985. ISBN: 0871350335.

The Autobots have to stop the Decepticons and their use of a "molecular transfer device" which transfers fuel directly into their tanks.

Lord, Suzanne, Carlos Garzon, Phil Lord. *The World of the Sectaurs.* New York: Marvel, 1985. ISBN: 0871350491.

This book explains the life and world of the Sectaurs, Warriors of Symbion. It includes major characters and terms.

Lord, Suzanne, Jim Massara. *Heathcliff Has a Birthday.* New York: Marvel, 1985. ISBN: 0871350424.

Heathcliff and his family have a special birthday.

Lord, Suzanne, Frank Springer, Michael Esposito. *Quest for the Shining Realm.* New York: Marvel, 1986. ISBN: 0871350505.

This is a Sectaurs, Warriors of Symbion, storybook.

Low, Alice, Rowan Barnes-Murphy. *Who Lives in the Sea.* New York: Marvel, 1987. ISBN: 087135182X.

This is a riddle game book in which youngsters name various sea animals.

Maccarone, Grace, Manny Campana. *Penny and Timmy Go to School.* New York: Marvel/Fisher-Price, 1987. ISBN: 0871351862.

This is a sticker book in which Penny and Timmy start school.

Maccarone, Grace, Joe Messerli. *Clyde's Storyland Adventure.* New York: Marvel, 1988. ISBN: 0871350718.

Clyde falls asleep and dreams he meets characters from various stories, including Hansel and Gretel, Sleeping Beauty, and Little Red Riding Hood.

Macchio, Ralph, Hyperdesign, Suzanne Gaffney, et al. *Marvel Chillers: The Pryde and Terror of the X-Men.* New York: Marvel, 1996. Based on *X-Men 143.*

The X-Men leave Kitty Pryde alone on New Year's Eve An N'Garai demon decides to terrorize Kitty, but she eventually destroys it using the Blackbird.

This is an easy reader book that came with a poster.

Marvel Chillers, Featuring Spider-Man: Saga of the Alien Costume. New York: Marvel, 1996. ISBN: 0785102701.

At first Spider-Man's new black costume seems like a blessing, but it quickly becomes apparent that the costume is more trouble than it is worth. Spider-Man learns from Reed Richards that the costume is alive and sucking the life out of Peter Parker. It is separated, but feels betrayed and bonds with Eddie Brock to become Venom who has a very big grudge against Spider-Man.

This "easy reader" book is based on *Amazing Spider-Man 252–259; 298–300.* It features selections from the original comic as well as a poster featuring Marvel Vision card art. There is no author is listed for this edition.

Marvel Editors, et al. *Great Monkey Chase.* New York: Marvel/Fisher-Price, 1986. ISBN: 0871351420.

This is a Fisher-Price coloring book.

Marvel Editors, et al. *I Can Learn Letters.* New York: Marvel, 1986. ISBN: 0871351463.

This is a Fisher-Price workbook for young children.

Marvel Editors, et al. *I Can Learn Numbers.* New York: Marvel/Fisher-Price, 1986. ISBN: 0871351455.

This is a Fisher-Price workbook for young children.

Marvel Editors, et al. *I Can Learn Numbers.* New York: Marvel/ Fisher-Price, 1986. ISBN: 0871351447.

This is a Fisher-Price workbook for toddlers.

Marvel Editors, et al. *I Can Learn Opposites.* New York: Marvel/Fisher-Price, 1986. ISBN: 0871351445.

This is a Fisher-Price workbook for toddlers.

Marvel Editors, et al. *I Can Learn Shapes.* New York: Marvel/Fisher-Price, 1986. ISBN: 0871351439.

This is a Fisher-Price workbook for toddlers.

Marvel Editors, et al. *Little People's Farm Adventure.* New York: Marvel/Fisher-Price, 1986. ISBN: 0871351390.

This is a coloring book.

Marvel Editors, et al. *Little People's Moving Day.* New York: Marvel/Fisher-Price, 1986. ISBN: 0871351404.

This is a Little People coloring book.

Marvel Editors. *Revenge of the Decepticons.* New York: Marvel, 1985. ISBN: 0871350246.

This is a Transformer sticker adventure book featuring the Decepticons. There were other sticker adventure and coloring books published by Marvel that relate to the Transformers.

Marvel Editors, et al. *Secret of the Dark Domain.* New York: Marvel, 1986. ISBN: 0517562073.

This is a book for preschool children.

Marvel Editors, et al. *Sectaurs: The Mantor Trap.* New York: Marvel, 1987. ISBN: 0871350548.

This is a Sectaurs, Warriors of Symbion, storybook.

Marvel Editors, et al. *Stamp Fun with the Sectaurs.* New York: Marvel, 1986. ISBN: 0871350564.

This special stamp book features the Sectaur characters.

Marvel Editors, et al. *Transformers Deadly Fuel Shortage*. New York: Marvel, 1984. ISBN: 0871350122.

Some humans, including Sparkplug and Buster Witwicky, are taken captive by the Decepticons.

Marvel Editors, et al. *Transformers Punch-Out Book*. New York: Marvel, 1985. ISBN: 0871350777.

This special activity book features the Transformers.

Marvel Super Heroes Secret Wars: The Secret of Spider-Man's Shield. New York: Marvel, 1984. ISBN: 0939766949.

This is an activity book featuring Spider-Man, who teams up with Captain America, Iron Man, and Wolverine, while trapped in another dimension. Spider-Man uses his magic web shield to help protect his friends.

McGill, Marci, John Speirs. *The Puffalumps Christmas Poems*. New York: Marvel, ISBN: 087135313X.

The Puffalumps get very excited preparing for Christmas. They are mailing cards, baking cookies, and wrapping presents.

McKie, Anne, Ken McKie. *The Emperor's New Clothes; Rumplestiltskin*. New York: Marvel, 1988. ISBN: 0871354764.

These two traditional children's tales are retold.

McKie, Anne, Ken McKie. *Hansel and Gretel; The Pied Piper of Hamelin*. New York: Marvel, 1987. ISBN: 0871354705.

This book contains two popular, illustrated children's tales.

McKie, Anne, Ken McKie, H. C. Anderson. *Jack and the Beanstalk ; The Princess and the Pea : Two Favorite Tales in One Book*. New York: Marvel, 1987. ISBN: 087135473X.

This book contains two classic fantasy tales.

McKie, Anne, Ken McKie, H. C. Anderson. *The Little Tin Soldier: Thumbelina*. New York: Marvel, 1988. ISBN: 0871354756.

These are children's adaptations of these two stories.

McKie, Anne, Ken McKie, Jonathan Swift. *Gulliver's Travels; Frog Prince*. New York: Marvel, 1988. ISBN: 0871354772.

There are two stories in this book.

Mednick, Blanche, Earl Norem. *The Mystical Mirror of Prysmos*. New York: Marvel, 1987. ISBN: 0871351692.

This storybook features the Visionaries, Knights of the Magical Light.

Monfried, Lucia, et al. *Timmy's Birthday Party*. New York: Marvel/Fisher-Price, 1987. ISBN: 0871351870.

Timmy has a birthday party with many friends. This is a Little People book.

Moore, Clement C., Monica Loomis. *The Night Before Christmas*. New York: Marvel, 1988. ISBN: 0871353334.

This is a retelling of the Santa Claus rhyme in which the children's father catches a glimpse of Santa leaving presents. There is also a book and tape set of this traditional story.

Morley, Evan. *Stan Lee Presents Marvel's Mysterious Secret Messages*. New York: Grosset & Dunlap, 1977. ISBN: 0448127458.

This book contains cipher games illustrated with Marvel superheroes.

Moss, David. *Shapes*. London: Marvel UK, 1989. ISBN: 185400008X.

This is a children's guide to geometry.

Nez, John A., Irwin Rabinowitz. *Favorite Christmas Carols*. New York: Marvel, 1988. ISBN: 0871354969.

This book of Christmas carols contains favorites, such as, "We Wish You A Merry Christmas"; "Deck The Halls"; "O Come, All Ye Faithful"; "Fum, Fum, Fum"; "Silent Night"; "Ring, Little Bells"; "The First Noel"; "Up On The Housetop"; and "The Twelve Days Of Christmas." It includes a cassette tape to sing along with.

Pini, Wendy. *Beauty and the Beast: Portrait of Love*. London: Marvel, 1989. ISBN: 185400 1620.

This is a retelling of the classic story.

Randall, Katherine A., Steve Smallwood. *Hanna-Barbera Presents Scooby-Doo: The Gumbo Ghoul*. New York: Marvel, 1988. ISBN: 0871354160.

Scooby investigates the appearance of a ghoul.

Razzi, Jim, Paul Richer. *Follow That Boat: A Story Book*. New York: Fisher-Price/Marvel, 1987. ISBN: 0871352028.

In this book, the reader follows different boats to eventually find the way home.

Razzi, Jim, Paul Richer. *Follow That Truck: A Storybook*. New York: Marvel/Fisher-Price, 1987. ISBN: 087135201X.

This Little People book gives the child a look at the different kinds of trucks, and the types of cargo they carry. It includes a lumber truck, a furniture truck, and a milk truck.

The Real Ghostbusters: Ghostnappers and Other Stories. London: Marvel, 1989. ISBN: 1854 001418.

The contents of this book were taken from British comic strips.

Rimmer, Ian, Paul Harder. *Goodbye to Slimer.* London: Marvel, 1989. ISBN: 1854000551.

This is a children's book that features the *Real Ghostbusters* characters.

Rimmer, Ian, Terry Rogers. *The Forever Fair.* London: Marvel, 1989. ISBN: 1854000659.

This is a children's book that features the *Real Ghostbusters* characters.

Rimmer, Ian, Brian Williamson. *The Phantom Pharaoh.* London: Marvel, 1989. ISBN: 1854000802.

This is a children's book that features the *Real Ghostbusters* characters.

Rose, Laura, Dean Yeagle *Heathcliff in Outer Space.* New York: Marvel, 1985. ISBN: 087 1350866.

Heathcliff and his pal Sonja go to outer space and visit Mars.
This book was also published by Watermill Press (ISBN: 08167126446).

Rosenfeld, Dana, Earl Norem. *Transformers: Car Show Blow Up.* New York: Marvel, 1986. ISBN: 0871351072.

The Decepticons crash a car race, and the Autobots stop them from doing too much damage. Kup is taken hostage by the Decepticons.

Rosenfeld, Dana, John Speirs. *Transformers: Insecticon Attack.* New York: Marvel, 1985. ISBN: 0871350785; 0517559587.

The Decepticon insect hybrids capture the Autobot Grapple.

St. Pierre, Stephanie. *Undersea Mission.* New York: Marvel, 1987. ISBN: 0871352176.

This is a special G.I. Joe coloring book depicting a mission which takes place in the ocean.

St. Pierre, Stephanie, et al. *On Puffalump Hill.* New York: Marvel, 1987. ISBN: 0871352 060.

St. Pierre, Stephanie, et al. *Puffalump's Garden.* New York: Marvel, 1987. ISBN: 0871352 052.

This is a Paint with Water book.

St. Pierre, Stephanie, et al. *Puffalumps's Picnic.* New York: Marvel, 1987. ISBN: 0871352 370.

The Puffalumps go on a picnic.

St. Pierre, Stephanie, Joe Messerli. *A Foofur Goodnight.* New York: Marvel, 1987. ISBN: 0871352346.

This is a special board book which features the cartoon character Foofur and all his friends.

St. Pierre, Stephanie, Joe Messerili. *Foofur: Secrets and Surprises.* New York: Marvel, 1987. ISBN: 0871352338.

This book contains funny animal stories.

St. Pierre, Stephanie, Jody Wheeler. *Mystery in the Woods.* New York: Marvel, 1988. ISBN: 0871353563.

Five animals search for a thief who has apparently taken their possessions.

Salicrup, Jim. *Puzzles of Krull.* New York: Marvel, 1983. ISBN: 0393766280.

This activity book for children's based on the *Krull* movie.

The Search for the Hulk. New York: Marvel, 1990. ISBN: 1854001825.

This children's book is based on the television series.

Sherman, Josepha, Brad Joyce. *Transformers: Battle at Oil Valley.* New York: Marvel, 1986. ISBN: 0871351013.

Galvatron and Grimlock battle in the Oil Valley.

Siegel, Scott K., Earl Norem. *The Transformers: Battle for Cybertron.* New York: Marvel, 1984. ISBN: 0871350165.

This easy reader book describes the Transformers' crash to Earth, and their first meetings with Spike and Sparkplug. This book explains the origin of the war between the Decepticons and Autobots on Cybertron.

Siegel, Barbara, Earl Norem, Scott Siegel. *Operation Raging River.* New York: Marvel, 1987. ISBN: 0871352230.

This is a Big Looker Storybook featuring G.I. Joe.

Siegel, Scott, Barbara Siegel. *Operation Star Fight.* New York: Marvel, 1987. ISBN: 0871352222.

This is a G.I. Joe Big Looker storybook.

Smith, Nora, Gary Albright. *A Dinosaur Lives in My House.* New York: Marvel, 1988. ISBN: 0871353717.

A toy dinosaur changes into whatever type of dinosaur he wishes.

Smith, Nora, Kristin Johnson. *The Puffalumps: Pillow Tales*. New York: Marvel/Fisher-Price, 1987. ISBN: 0871352435.

This Puffalumps book contains various tales to tell your child at bedtime. It includes the story, "How to Carry An Egg."

Sommers, Kevin. *Incredible Hulk: Project H.I.D.E.* New York: Marvel, 1998.

In this easy reader book, a group of young kids help the Hulk hide until he can find a way to become human again. This interactive book includes games and puzzles. This book was part of the Marvel Kids imprint.

Stine, Bob, Marie Severin, Earl Norem. *The Forest of Enchantment: Advanced Dungeons & Dragons*. New York: Marvel, 1983. ISBN: 0939766698.

A young minstrel elf encounters the enchanted forest and the forces for good and evil that are in it. This book includes an appearance by an army of Lizard Men.

Stine, Jovial Bob, Jerry Zimmerman, Skull Face, et al. *The Madballs Gross-Out Book*. New York: Marvel, 1986. ISBN: 0871350467.

This is a collection of gross things one can do with Madballs. It includes a "Meet the Madballs" glossary. Other Madballs books published by Marvel include *Madballs Book of Jokes and Riddles* (ISBN: 0871 350440); *Madballs Handbook* (ISBN: 0871350459); *Madballs Punchline Puzzles* (ISBN: 0871350432); *Madballs History of the World* (ISBN: 0871350475); and *Madballs Alamanac* (ISBN: 0871350483).

Stine, Megan, William Stine. *Amazing Facts About Space*. New York: Marvel, 1987. ISBN: 0871351218.

This is a Young Astronauts Council coloring book which gives facts about comets, light speed, and other interesting space tidbits.

Strejan, John, Chuck Murphy, Tor Lokvig, et al. *Stan Lee Presents Spider-Man*. New York: Marvel, 1980.

This special activity book for kids features Spider-Man.

Teitelbaum, Michael, et al. *The Haunted House*. New York: Marvel, 1987. ISBN: 0871352 29X.

This is a Foofur book.

Teitelbaum, Michael, et al. *Holiday Fun Throughout the Year*. New York: Marvel/Fisher-Price, 1987. ISBN: 0871351749.

This is a Little People cookbook for young children.

Teitelbaum, Michael, et al. *Meet the Puffalumps*. New York: Marvel, 1987. ISBN: 0871352 400.

The Puffalumps are introduced.

Teitelbaum, Michael, Nate Butler, Doug Cushman, et al. *Mighty Mouse: Pearl Pureheart's Problem*. New York: Marvel, 1988. ISBN: 087135330X.

This is a Mighty Mouse coloring book.

Teitelbaum, Michael, Mark Cassutt, et al. *A Clean Sweep*. New York: Marvel, 1986. ISBN: 0871352311.

Foofur and his friends clean their home, but have second thoughts when they find out the house is to be sold.

Thundercats in Astral Prison and Other Stories. London: Marvel, 1989. ISBN: 1854001086.

This is a children's book featuring the Thundercats.

Trimpe, Herb, Stan Lee, et al. *Stan Lee Presents the Incredible Hulk: Ringmaster and His Circus of Crime*. New York: Marvel, 1982. ISBN: 0939766051.

The Ringmaster uses hypnosis to steal from his audience, and the Hulk stops him.

Trimpe, Herb, Guillermo Rozo, Stan Lee. *Stan Lee Presents Spider Man: The Schemer Strikes*. New York: Marvel, 1982. ISBN: 0939766035.

This is an Amazing Spider-Man pop-up book.

Waricha, Jean. *The Big Show*. New York: Marvel/Fisher-Price, 1987. ISBN: 0871351765.

This is a Little People coloring book.

Waricha, Jean, et al. *Foofur and His Friends*. New York: Marvel, 1987. ISBN: 0871352281.

This is a storybook featuring the cast of the cartoon television show of the same name.

Waricha, Jean, et al. *Meet the Flintstone Kids*. New York: Marvel, 1987. ISBN: 0871352 508.

This coloring book introduces the Flintstone children.

Waricha, Jean, Jude Kane. *Christmas Costume Party*. New York: Marvel, 1988. ISBN: 0871353105.

Everyone dresses as an angel for a Christmas party, and Penny is upset because she also wanted to be an angel.

Waricha, Jean, Rosalyn Schanezer. *Ben's Three Wishes*. New York: Marvel, 1988. ISBN: 0871353741.

A young rhino wants to be like the other animals, and ends up with pink skin and spots.

Waricha, Jean, Steve Smallwood. *California Raisins on Tour*. New York: Marvel, 1988. ISBN: 0871354128.

The California Raisins go out on tour. This is a coloring book.

Watson, B. S. *Operation Disappearance*. New York: Marvel, 1983. ISBN: 0939766507.

This book features the G.I. Joe team.

Wenk, Laurie, Kristine Bollinger. *The Big Kitchen Mess*. New York: Marvel/Fisher-Price, 1987. ISBN: 0871351919.

This is a book and tape set in which Penny and Timmy make a huge mess in the kitchen when they bake a birthday cake for their dog.

Weiss, Ellen, Kristine Bollinger. *A Day at the Dentist's*. New York: Marvel/Fisher Price, 1988. ISBN: 0871351056.

A group of young children spend Saturday at the dentist's office, and decide it's not so bad.

Weyn, Suzanne, et al. *Solaris Project*. New York: Marvel, 1987. ISBN: 0871352184.

This is a G.I. Joe coloring book.

Weyn, Suzanne, Nancy Beiman. *Heathcliff Goes to Hollywood*. New York: Marvel, 1985. ISBN: 0871350874.

Heathcliff wins a trip to Hollywood to star in the Little Whiskers Cat Crunchies commercial.

Weyn, Suzanne, Paty Cockrum, Marie Severin, et al. *Dragon's Lair Presents Dirk the Daring in The Quest for the Stolen Fortune*. New York: Marvel, 1984. ISBN: 0871350181.

Dirk tries to find the stolen fortune in the Lizard King's castle. This book includes various games.

Weyn, Suzanne, John Costanza. *Counting and Numbers with Heathcliff*. New York: Marvel, 1985. ISBN: 0871350416.

This book uses Heathcliff to teach children how to count and use numbers effectively.

Weyn, Suzanne, Steven Geiger, Phil Lord, et al. *Summer Fun with Marvel Super Heroes: A Marvel Super Activity Book*. New York: Marvel, 1985. ISBN: 0871350353.

This is a guide to summer activities with the Marvel heroes.

Weyn, Suzanne, Elizabeth Miles. *The Little People and the Big Fib*. New York: Fisher Price/Marvel, 1987. ISBN: 0871351897.

This Little People book includes a lesson about lying, called a "humorous value tale."

Weyn, Suzanne, John Nez. *Frog's Snowy Day*. New York: Marvel, 1988. ISBN: 0871354470.

Frog has fun out in the snow.

Weyn, Suzanne, Charles Nicholas. *Transformers: Return to Cybertron*. New York: Marvel, 1985. ISBN: 0871350254.

This is a stickers book of Transformers adventures.

Weyn, Suzanne, Charles Nicholas. *Transformers: Revenge of Decepticons*. New York: Marvel, 1984. ISBN: 0871350246.

The Decepticons try to strike before the Autobots have a chance to refuel.

Weyn, Suzanne, Cathy Pavia. *The Tiny Trapeze Artist*. New York: Marvel, 1988. ISBN: 0871353709.

Meep the Mouse rescues his adoptive monkey family from captivity by an evil king.

Weyn, Suzanne, John Speirs. *The Day the Frogs Came to Lunch*. New York: Marvel, 1988. ISBN: 0871351099.

Two boys bring fifteen frogs to their mother's luncheon.

Weyn, Regina, John Speirs. *Transformers: Decepticon Hijack*. New York: Marvel, 1985. ISBN: 0871350793.

The Decepticons try to hijack an oil tanker, but the Autobots thwart their plans.

Weyn, Suzanne, Frank Springer, Michael Esposito. *The Choice*. New York: Marvel, 1985. ISBN: 0871350521.

This is a coloring book that features the Sectaurs, Warriors of Symbion.

Wilton, Toby. *Who Lives in the Jungle*. New York: Marvel/Fisher-Price, 1987. ISBN: 0871351838.

This is a preschool riddle book for youngsters to use to learn about various animals who live in the jungle.

Woods, Sonia Black, Ron Friedman, Earl Norem. *The Story of Wheelie, the Wild Boy of Quintesson*. New York: Marvel, 1986. ISBN: 0871351080.

The young Autobot Wheelie crashes on the planet Quintesson, and is taken prisoner as a spy. He escapes and a chase is on, but the Autobots intervene.

Woods, Sonia Black, Frank Springer, Phil Lords. *Transformers: The Lost Treasure of Cybertron.* New York: Marvel, 1986. ISBN: 087135103X.

Kup tells the story of the lost treasure from Cybertron.

Zimmerman, Dwight Jon, Steve Ditko. *Transformers: Autobot Smasher.* New York: Marvel, 1985. ISBN: 0871350394.

A car smasher is disguised as an Autobot rest stop.

Zimmerman, Dwight, Steve Ditko, John Tartaglione, et al. *Transformers: Bumblebee to the Rescue.* New York: Marvel, 1984. ISBN: 0871350106.

Bumblebee frees the Autobots from the Decepticon prison.

This book includes a guide to the Transformers and connect-the-dots activities.

Zimmerman, Dwight Jon, Carlos Garzon, Joe Giello. *Transformers: Search for Treasure Under the Sea.* New York: Marvel, 1984. ISBN: 0871350092.

Megatron plans to salvage gold from a sunken ship in order to buy factories where he can produce his army of Decepticons.

Zimmerman, Dwight Jon, Brad Joyce. *Transformers: Forest Rescue Mission.* New York: Marvel, 1985. ISBN: 0871350378.

Megatron wants to tear up a forest to build a factory.

Zimmerman, Dwight, Phil Lord, Charles Nicholas, et al. *Transformers: Decepticon Patrol.* New York: Marvel, 1984. ISBN: 0871350 378.

Megatron sends his troops to find a factory where he can build more Decepticons.

According to one Transformers expert, Steve Stonebraker, this is one of the more bizarre Transformers books.

Zimmerman, Dwight J., Earl Norem. *Transformers: Great Car Rally.* New York: Marvel, 1984. ISBN: 0871350157.

The Autobots race in a car rally for a prize of free gas and oil for one year. The Decepticons try to keep the Autobots from winning.

Zimmerman, Dwight Jon, Earl Norem, et al. *Sectaurs: Forbidden Quest.* New York: Marvel, 1985. ISBN: 0517559935.

This is a special Sectaurs book in which they go on a "mysterious" journey.

Zimmerman, Dwight J., Paul Richer. *Transformers: Super Activity Book.* New York: Marvel, 1986.

This book features puzzles, mazes, and number activities for young children.

11

Movies and Television

Long live the fighters.—Paul Atreides

Chichester, Dan G. *An American Tail: Fievel Goes West.* New York: Marvel, 1991. ISBN: 0871357585.

This is the "Spectacular jumbo-sized adaptation of the hit movie," which features talking furry critters.

Chichester, Dan, Mike McKone, Bill Reinhold, et al. *Strange Days: The Official Movie Adaptation.* New York: Marvel, 1995. ISBN: 0785101837.

Lenny, a former vice cop now dealing in virtual chips, obtains a disk which contains documentation of the brutal murder of a prostitute friend of his. As he investigates, he goes deeper into the dirty underworld of blackmail, murder, and rape. He tries to protect his ex-girlfriend Faith, who is now a rock singer, from her manager and boyfriend who plans to murder her. Lenny's partner Mace is in love with him. Lenny also uncovers how certain corrupt police are involved.

This is the comic adaptation of the movie by 20th Century-Fox. The movie takes place in 1999, in a future in which virtual chips and data disks which contain recorded memories and emotions are traded, bought and stolen.

Claremont, Chris, David Michelinie, Walt Simonson, et al. *Star Wars: A Long Time Ago Vol. 4: Screams in the Void.* Milwaukie, OR: Dark Horse, 2003. ISBN: 1569717877. Reprints Marvel's *Star Wars 54–67; Star Wars Annual 2.*

The Rebels set up a base on the planet Arbra, and make unusual allies of the telepathic, rabbit-like Hoojibs. Lando goes back to his world Cloud City to find it almost deserted. The Empire has commandeered it, and is trying to disarm several bombs which have been strategically placed throughout the city by the planet's bottom dwellers, the Ugnaughts. Lando makes an uneasy alliance with an imperial commander in order to disarm the bombs, but ends up being betrayed. Lobot saves Lando's life. Luke kills Shira who had become his girlfriend in the Rebels but was actually a mole for the Empire. Luke is considered a traitor to the Rebels and asked to leave before it is brought to light that Shira is a spy. Luke meets a hologram of Darth Vader. Luke, Lando, and C-3PO learn of how Han Solo became a hero on the world of Ventooine.

This story takes place after *Empire Strikes Back* and before *Return of the Jedi.*

Dorkin, Evan, Marie Severin, Stephen Destefano, et al. *Bill and Ted's Most Excellent Adventures Vol. 1.* San Jose: Amaze Ink, 2004. ISBN: 0943151988. Reprints Marvel's *Bill and Ted Most Excellent Comic Book 1–4; Bill and Ted's Bogus Journey.*

Evil robots from the future end up killing Bill and Ted. But our heroes make a pact with death, and are able to return to right the wrongs done by the robots. Bill and Ted get married, and two boyfriends from the girl's past try to stop the wedding. When Death gets drunk, he decides to quit his job, and take a holiday, which causes the world to be overrun with smelly zombies. Bill and Ted search for Death, and try to convince him to get back on the job. They are sued, when a Wyld Stallyns performance is done by Robots, but it was the money hungry record men, who were the culprits. Time Thumb is asked to stop Bill and Ted for all the problems they have caused in the Time Stream. A bass player, Phil, is hired for the Wyld Stallyns, and, after The Station sneezes, they start reproducing, causing all sorts of mayhem.

This volume reprints the official movie adaptation of *Bill and Ted's Bogus Journey,* in which evil robots from the future impersonate Bill and Ted, and cause havoc.

Dorkin, Evan, Marie Severin, Fabian Nicieza, et al. *Bill and Ted's Bogus Journey.* New York: Marvel, 1991. ISBN: 0871357593.

This is the official comic adaptation of the hit comedy movie with the same name. Evil doppelganger robots are sent back through time, to do away with Bill and Ted, and take their places.

Duffy, Jo, Sal Buscema, Randy Stradley, et al. *Star Wars: A Long Time Ago Vol. 6: Wookie World*. Milwaukie, OR: Dark Horse, 2003. ISBN: 1569719071. Reprints Marvel Comics *Star Wars 82–95*.

Luke goes on a diplomatic mission to Iskalon, but the inhabitants do not want to be part of the Alliance. Kiro joins Luke, and leaves with him. Lando is betrayed by a woman with whom he once had an affair. General Drebble finally gets to capture Lando, only to find out that he gets a commendation and decoration for bravery from the Alliance. Princess Leia meets an Imperial guard from her planet, who almost kills her. There are still Imperial forces in the Universe, despite the Empire's defeat, and Leia meets with a cyborg, Dark Lord Lumiya. Luke refuses to train any more Jedi. Chewbacca goes back to his home world, only to find out that slavers are, once again, trying to enslave the Wookie race. He gets reunited with his wife and his son, Lumpy. Luke keeps having nightmares about Darth Vader. The Ewoks declare war on the Lahsbees, and Lumiya does battle with Luke.

Duffy, Jo, Bob Hall, Romeo Tanghal, et al. *Willow: The Official Adaptation of the Hit Movie*. New York: Marvel, 1988. ISBN: 0871353679. Reprints *Willow 1–3*.

A humble farmer, Willow, is entrusted with the care of an infant, prophesied to be a good, and powerful, queen, who will bring about the ruin of the current queen, an evil sorceress. (*Marvel Graphic Novel 38*.)

Duffy, Jo, Al Williamson, Archie Goodwin, et al. *Star Wars: A Long Time Ago Vol. 7: Far Far Away*. Milwaukie, OR: Dark Horse, 2003. ISBN: 156971908X; 1840236205. Reprints Marvel's *Star Wars 97–107*.

Luke is beaten by the Sith Lumiya. The Nagai are trying to destroy the free Alliance of Planets, by taking over the galaxy. Dani is taken captive, and tortured by a Nagi officer. Kiro is supposedly killed. Nien Numb and Han Solo pilot the Millennium Falcon, on a diplomatic mission. Kiro goes back to his home world, Iskolonian, which is being invaded by the Nagi. Princess Leia shows mercy to a captured Nagi, and she has her own group of male Zeltrons, who look out for her. Kiro becomes the Jedi hero of his world. Han Solo's childhood friend, Bey, betrays the Alliance to the Nagi, but later becomes the hero of the Alliance, against the Tofs. The Nagi and Hiromi try to stage an invasion of Zeltron, but are upstaged by the Tofs. The Nagi decide to join the free Alliance rather than fight them. This book includes a pinup of Yoda, by Marie Severin. This is the last book in Dark Horse's complete reprint of the Marvel Comics *Star Wars* series.

Foster, Bob, John Costanza, Sheryl O'Connell, et al. *Disney's Toy Story*. New York: Marvel, 1995. ISBN: 078510187X.

This adaptation of the hit Disney movie tells the story of a group of Toys, which magically come alive, when humans are not looking. It featuring the popular Buzz Lightyear. The toys have to contend with an evil kid, who likes to do experiments on his toys. This book features computer images from the movie.

Foster, Bob, Dan Spiegle, Todd Kurosawa, et al. *Roger Rabbit: Resurrection of Doom*. New York: Marvel, 1989. ISBN: 0871355930.

Roger Rabbit's arch nemesis Judge Doom is brought back to life using an old model sheet and a multiplane camera. Doom plans his revenge on Roger Rabbit by discrediting him so no one will want to see his movies. Eddie Valiant figures out the plan, and finds out that Doom has taken over Maroon Cartoons, and has stolen the real model behind the studio. Valiant destroys Doom by using a gun filled with dip.

This volume also includes a comic adaptation of the cartoon *Tummy Trouble*. (*Marvel Graphic Novel 54*)

Foster, Bob, Dan Spiegle, Carrie Spiegle, et al. *Pocahontas*. New York: Marvel, 1995. ISBN: 078510108X.

This is the graphic novel adaptation of the Disney movie based loosely on historical characters. The tragic love story of Captain John Smith, an Englishman, and the Native American princess Pocahontas entails both being asked to choose sides between their races. The story nicely illustrates the turmoil between the English settlers and the Native Americans who live on the land.

Gallagher, Michael, Dave Manak, Marie Severin, et al. *Alf Vol 1*. New York: Marvel, 1990. ISBN: 0871356554. Reprints *Alf 1–3*.

The alien Alf, who lives with an American family, causes much mischief and mayhem for the family, but they love him anyway. Alf's space ship is taken to the junkyard. The Evil Fogg, from Alf's planet, is defeated by the Loan Officers. Brian takes Alf's antigravity belt for his science project, but the evil teacher wants to use it for his own purposes. Willie Tanner takes an adventure to Alf's planet.

This volume contains "Alf Carrot Cards," and other stories. This comic series was based on the television series by the same name.

Goodwin, Archie, Carmine Infantino, Chris Claremont, et al. *Star Wars: A Long Time Ago Vol. 2: Dark Encounters*. Milwaukie, OR: Dark Horse, 2002. ISBN: 1569717850. Reprints Marvel's *Star Wars 21–38*; *King Sized Star Wars Annual 1*.

Luke, Han, Chewie, and Leia are held captive on the gambling station, the Wheel. Its commander, Senator Greyshade, wants to have Leia for himself.

Chewie and Han have to fight one another in the arena. Darth Vader continues his search to find out who was responsible for the destruction of the Death Star. Leia tells an old story about Obi Wan when he saved a pleasure cruiser from the clutches of the Merson slavers. Luke foils Baron Tagge's plans on Yavin. The bounty-hunter cyborg Valance continues to search for Luke and his droids. The humanoid version of Jabba the Hutt catches Han Solo on the planet Orleon, only to be foiled by Stone Mites. Darth Vader destroys Valance. Princess Leia goes undercover to the Empire satellite Metalorn. An old enemy of Han's, the Majestrix of Skye, comes to torment him and his friends. Luke goes back to Tatooine, and discovers Baron Tagge's plans to destroy the rebels and gain the Emperor's favor over Vader. Han and Luke end up asking the Jawas for help. For the first time, Luke battles Darth Vader, who turns out to be Baron Tagge, not Vader. Leia and Luke end up on a living spaceship.

Goodwin, Archie, All Williamson, Carlos Garzon, et al. *The Empire Strikes Back*. Milwaukie, OR: Dark Horse, 1997. ISBN: 1569710880; 1596712344 (sp ed.). Reprints Marvel's *Star Wars 39–44*.

This special edition includes reprints from the movie adaptation of *The Empire Strikes Back*, long considered the best *Star Wars* movie. It includes painted scenes from the special-edition movie.

Goodwin, Archie, Al Williamson, Carlos Garzo, et al. *Star Wars: Return of the Jedi*. New York: Marvel, 1983. ISBN: 0517551 578. Reprints *Return of the Jedi 1–4*.

Han Solo is frozen in carbonate by the gangster Jabba the Hutt. Luke, Leia, Lando, Chewbacca, C-3PO, and R2-D2 all come to his rescue, but are found out by Jabba and sentenced to a life of servitude. They end up getting out of their predicament, with Luke Skywalker leading the way. Luke visits Yoda, and learns the truth of his father, Darth Vader. Yoda dies. Luke and Leia lead a small band of rebels to the moon of Endor, to try to bring down the shield that is protecting the new Death Star. They make friends with the cute, fuzzy Ewoks who believe C-3PO is a god. Luke fights with Darth Vader and the Emperor. Luke believes that some good still resides in Vader. When the Emperor is about to destroy Luke, the good part of Anakin Skywalker intervenes, and destroys the Emperor. After the shield is down, the Rebel Force, led by Lando, manages to destroy the Death Star and the Imperial forces.

Goodwin, Archie, Al Williamson, Carlos Garzon, et al. *Star Wars: Return of the Jedi*. Milwaukie, OR: Dark Horse, 1997. ISBN: 1569710872; 1569712352 (sp ed.); 1569710899 (box set); 1569712573 (sp ed., box set). Reprints Marvel Comics *Star Wars: Return of the Jedi 1–4*.

This is the official adaptation of *Return of the Jedi*, originally published by Marvel. It is reprinted in this collection with production sketches from all three *Star Wars* movies. There also are still drawings from the extra scenes in the special edition of the movie.

Goodwin, Archie, Al Williamson, Carmine Infantino, et al. *Star Wars: A Long Time Ago Vol. 3: Resurrection of Evil*. Milwaukie, OR: Dark Horse 2002. ISBN: 1569717869. Reprints Marvel's *Star Wars 39–53*.

Luke has to figure out how to circumvent an Imperial probe droid with Artoo's help. Lando and Chewie end up on a bizarre world run by the mental powers of former warrior Sunn-Childe. Childe tries to subdue his past fighting ways. C-3PO and Artoo end up on Droid World, and help stop an Imperial droid takeover. Darth Vader and Princess Leia spar with each other on the planet Aargau, with Vader ultimately getting the upper hand. Luke learns a lesson in humility when an old Jedi who lost his mind sacrifices himself. Luke contracts the disease known as Crimson Forever. A new Death Star–like weapon known as the Tarkin worries the Rebels. A mutiny against Vader is brewing. Leia reminisces about her life on Alderaan.

This volume contains the complete movie adaptation of *The Empire Strikes Back* and continuation of the story.

Goodwin, Archie, Al Williamson, Allen Nunis, et al. *Classic Star Wars Vol. 1–5*: Milwaukie, OR: Dark Horse, 1994–1997. ISBN: 15697 11097 (1); 1569711062 (2); 159710937 (3); 156971178X (4); 1569712549 (5).

This is a reprinted collection, of the *Star Wars* newspaper strips associated with Marvel, and written and drawn by Marvel scribes and artists. The titles include "In Deadly Pursuit"; "The Rebel Storm"; "Escape to Hoth"; "The Early Adventures"; and "Han Solo at Stars' End." These collections have been colored, and provide a nice glimpse into the early world of *Star Wars* comics. They were also published as limited edition hardcovers.

Grant, Alan, Mark Begley, Tony Dezuniga, et al. *Robocop II*. New York: Marvel, 1990. ISBN: 087135666X.

A designer drug called Nuke is being sold on the streets, and Robocop, Alex Murphy, wants to put the pushers and makers out of business. When he goes after Cain, the main supplier, he is torn into pieces and left for dead. He is given new programming to take out all of his negative, violent behavior. Robocop then tries to talk with criminals, rather than kill or arrest them. After Cain is finally left for dead, the corporation O.C.P. takes his brain and makes Robocop 2 who is addicted to Nuke. Murphy defeats him, and regains his harder edge.

This adaptation of the second *Robocop* film is based upon Frank Miller and Wilson Green's screenplay.

Harras, Bob, Javier Saltarest, Alan Kupperberg, et al. *Robocop: Official Adaptation of the Hit Film.* New York: Marvel, 1990. Reprints *Robocop 1.*

A wealthy corporation creates a human/machine cyborg to police the city of Detroit. The cyborg starts asking questions about his previous life as a human being, and exposes the corrupt corporation.

Jippes, Daan, Don Ferguson, Dan Spiegle, et al. *Who Framed Roger Rabbit: The Official Comics Adaptation.* New York: Marvel, 1988. ISBN: 0871354640.

Roger Rabbit is framed for the death of Marvin, the Gag King. Private investigator Eddie Valiant tries to find the killers and clear Roger's name. Judge Doom wants to destroy Toontown.

This is a good adaptation of the film. (*Marvel Graphic Novel 41*)

Johnson, Sam, Rick Parker, Chris Marcil, et al. *MTV's Beavis and Butt-Head: Wanted.* New York: Marvel, 1995. ISBN: 0785101705. Reprints *Beavis and Butt-Head 15–18.*

Beavis and Butt-Head go to Harvard, and try out for a fraternity. They go camping with their teacher, and end up stranded due to a snow storm. They play April Fools jokes on their schoolmates, and go to a hip party, which of course leads to disaster. They try their hands at drawing their own X-rated comic strip. Cable, Dr. Strange, Guido, Brother Voodoo, and Two-Gun Kid, among others, make appearances.

This work also was published by Titan books (ISBN: 1852866969).

Kraft, David Anthony, Brett Blevins, Vince Colletta, et al. *The Dark Crystal.* New York: Marvel, 1982. ISBN: 093976623X. Reprints *Dark Crystal 1–2.*

This is a comic adaptation of the Jim Henson movie about a young Gefling who is on a quest to heal the Dark Crystal, and give balance to the universe. It includes photo stills from the film.

Kraft, David Anthony, Stanford Sherman, et al. *Krull: The Storybook Based on the Film.* New York: Marvel, 1983. ISBN: 0939766793.

The planet Krull is attacked by an alien race known as Slayers. They kidnap Krull's Princess Lyssa on her wedding day. Prince Colwyn, Lyssa's betrothed, is persuaded to track down a magical, five-bladed sword to use against the Slayers.

This young adult novelization of the fantasy movie *Krull* combines full narrative text, with pictures from the film.

Lackey, Mike, Rick Parker, Bob Sharen, et al. *Beavis and Butthead's Greatest Hits.* New York: Marvel, 1994. ISBN: 078510030X. Reprints *Beavis and Butthead 1–4.*

Beavis and Butthead go to a store full of yams, and Butthead's teeth get stuck together while eating a chocolate bar. The boys raid a funeral in a search of zombies. They learn about Anderson's battles during World War II. They go to work at Burger World, and attempt to make fudge brownies at school; both ventures have disastrous results. The boys mud wrestle with large women, and become strippers in a night club. Devil Dinosaur, Silver Surfer, Wolverine, Man Thing, She Hulk, Mary Jane, and the Fantastic Four make appearances, among others.

Each issue has a Beavis and Butthead activity page. This collection also was published by Titan Books (ISBN: 1852865911).

Lackey, Mike, Chris Marcil, Guy Maxtone-Graham, et al. *Beavis and Butthead: Trashcan Edition.* New York: Marvel, 1994. ISBN: 0785100482. Reprints *Beavis and Butthead 5–8.*

Beavis and Butthead become towel boys in a spa, and try to score with Anderson's niece. They go to an Indian camp, and become their own versions of superheroes Doctor Weird and Coolman. The Hulk, Sub-Mariner, Quasar, Darkhawk, and Ghost Rider make appearances, among others.

This book also was published by Titan Books (ISBN: 1852865997 [pbk]).

Macchio, Ralph, Dean Devlin, Roland Emmerich, et al. *Independence Day.* New York: Marvel, 1996. ISBN: 0785102264. Reprints *Independence Day 0–2.*

This is an adaptation of the hit movie *Independence Day.* It is a *War of the Worlds* type of story in which aliens who landed in Roswell, New Mexico, in 1947, come back on July 4, 1996, to take over the Earth. Humanity strikes back by planting a computer virus in the aliens' mother ship.

Macchio, Ralph, Bill Sienkiewicz, Bob Budiansky, et al. *Dune.* New York: Marvel, 1984. ISBN: 0425076326. Reprints *Dune 1–3*; *Marvel Super Special 36.*

The Duke's son, Paul Maud'Dib, becomes an unlikely hero in the world of Dune, which is the source of a much-coveted spice, melange. Both the Emperor and the Baron Harkonnen seek to rule the planet and control the spice. Paul becomes the messiah for whom the planet Dune has been waiting.

This is a nice comic adaptation of the David Lynch epic film, which was based on the works of Frank Herbert.

Manak, David, Ernie Colon, Jacqueline Roettcher, et al. *Bullwinkle and Rocky: Marvel Moosterworks.* New York: Marvel, 1992. ISBN: 087135876X. Reprints *Bullwinkle and Rocky 1–4.*

This book contains stories about Rocky and Bullwinkle, Peabody and Sherman, and Dudley Do-

Right, plus "Fractured Fairly Tales." In the book, Peabody and Sherman visit the Wright Brothers and Alexander the Great, and Bullwinkle becomes *Thyme* magazine's "Moose of the Year."

McKenzie, Roger, Walt Simonson, Ernie Colon, et al. *Battlestar Galactica: Saga of a Star World*. London: Titan, 2004. ISBN: 1840239031. Reprints Marvel's *Battlestar Galactia 1–5, 15–16; Marvel Super Special 8*.

A group of lone human survivors search for a new world where they can live in peace, while the alien Cylons are seeking the death of all humans. The Cylons despise humanity's independent spirit, and seek to crush any life form that will not conform to Cylon ways and lifestyles. The crew of *Battlestar Galactica* learns how humans are being processed for food by the Ovions. The crew goes to the planet Kobol to learn about their history, and to find out about a planet called Earth. Apollo's wife Sernia is killed, and there are some dirty political dealings behind Commander Adama's back. Adama seeks to learn hidden knowledge by using the memory machine. Boomer goes to an old Caprican battle cruiser, and finds it overrun by deadly space vermin. A plague killed the crew, including Adama's wife and the mother of Apollo. The ship passes an uncharted world where the crew goes in search of fuel. Apollo ends up fighting a Cylon berserker known as the MARK III Imperator. Apollo has to use his brains, rather than his brawn to defeat the soldier.

This volume contains an introduction by actor Richard Hatch; histories of the television show, the comics, and novels; and a look at Galactica toys and other merchandise. This is the direct adaptation and continuation of the original television movie *Battlestar Galactica*.

Michelinie, David, Jo Duffy, Gene Day, et al. *Star Wars: A Long Time Ago Vol. 5: Fool's Bounty*. Milwaukie, OR: Dark Horse, 2003. ISBN: 1569719063. Reprints *Star Wars 68–81; Star Wars Annual 3*.

Leia, Chewbaccca, Luke, and Lando are searching for Han Solo who was put into carbonite and taken to Jabba the Hutt by Boba Fett. Luke and Leia also search for captured rebel leader Tay Vanis, only to find out that Darth Vader has captured him. C-3PO falls in love with Vanis's droid, Ellie. The group goes to Iskalon to visit a friend, and are betrayed. Lando and Chewbacca track down some of Solo's former space-pirate friends, to get information about Solo's whereabouts. Luke tries to rescue his best friend from the planet Arbra. Han Solo and princess Leia go back to Tatooinie to try to recover some of Han's money. Evil Jawas capture R2-D2, and during the rescue Boba Fett is found to be alive. Han tries to save him from going into the Sarlaac. To everyone's surprise, Chewbacca takes a nap and becomes close friends with the Ewoks.

The episodes in this volume take place between the *Empire Strikes Back* and one issue shortly after *Return of the Jedi*.

Moore, Steve, Steve Dillon, Dez Skinn, et al. *Absolom Daak: Dalek Killer*. London: Marvel, 1990. ISBN: 1854001132. Reprints *Doctor Who Weekly 17–20, 27–30; Doctor Who Monthly 44–46; Doctor Who Magazine 152–155*.

Absalom Daak, a murderer, is sentenced to "exile D-K," Dalek Killing. Daleks are a violent breed of aliens who wish to subjugate the entire universe. Daak's girlfriend is killed by Daleks, and Absalom swears to destroy them all. With the help of Doctor Who, he destroys the Daleks' death wheel.

This book includes the short story, "Between the Wars."

Parkhouse, Steve, John Ridgway, Gina Hart, et al. *Voyager: A Doctor Who Adventure*. London: Marvel, 1985. ISBN: 1854000454. Reprints *The Doctor Who Magazine 89–99*.

The Doctor becomes traveling partners with a shape-changing Whifferdill. They come in contact with the reality-bending trickster Astrolablus, who eventually meets the Voyager ship and dies. The Doctor also helps to free a young Zyglot from a zoo.

Salicrup, Jim, Marie Severin, Chic Stone, et al. *The A-Team: Storybook Comics Illustrated*. New York: Marvel, 1983. ISBN: 0939766 787. Reprints *A-Team 1–3*.

The A-Team investigates a diamond thief from a prominent diamond company. They interfere with an undercover FBI infiltration of smugglers, and destroy a special enemy aircraft, the Redbird. Japanese brothers hire the A-Team to investigate the kidnapping of their father.

Schultz, Mark, All Williamson, Tom Roberts, et al. *Flash Gordon 1–2*. New York: Marvel, 1995.

Once again, Flash Gordon has to pit his wits against Ming to save Mongo. Ming has threatened Azura's subjects if she does not do his bidding.

Gordon's origin is revealed in a retelling of the original story. This book is part of the Marvel Select series, and is a nice tribute to both Alex Raymond's original character and Buster Crabbe, who played Flash on the screen.

Slott, Dan, Mike Kazaleh, Brad K. Joyce, et al. *Ren and Stimpy Show: Pick of Litter*. New York: Marvel, 1993. ISBN: 0871359707. Reprints *Ren and Stimpy Show 1–4*.

In this collection of the first hilarious issues of *Ren and Stimpy Show* which was published by Marvel, Ren and Stimpy become crooks, and Powdered Toast Man tries to apprehend them. Other stories feature

Frankenstein, Ren and Stimpy becoming beatniks, Ren getting a log for Stimpy, and Powdered Toast Man trying to get away from some kids.

Slott, Dan, Mike Kazaleh, Ed Lazellari, et al. *The Ren and Stimpy Show: Seeck Leetle Monkeys.* New York: Marvel, 1994. ISBN: 0785100644. Reprints *Ren and Stimpy Show 17–20.*

Ren and Stimpy join the army and are guests on the Muddy Mudskipper show.

This book includes such tales as "Poachman Always Rings Twice" and "Bread Over Heels."

Slott, Dan, Mike Kazaleh, Ed Lazellari, et al. *The Ren and Stimpy Show: Your Pals.* New York: Marvel, 1994. ISBN: 0785100377. Reprints *Ren and Stimpy Show 13–16.*

Ren tells Stimpy a Halloween story about a giant piece of bubble gum known as GOO-GUM that terrorizes the world. Ren and Stimpy steal Santa's "who's been naughty or nice" list. Stimpy becomes an Elvis impersonator, and Ren and Stimpy invite the reader into their home.

Slott, Dan, Mike Kazaleh, Ken Mitchroney, et al. *The Ren and Stimpy Show: Don't Try This at Home.* New York: Marvel, 1994. ISBN: 0785100237. Reprints *Ren and Stimpy Show 9–12.*

Ren and Stimpy are bug exterminators, and they sell the squashed bug juice as a soft drink. Stimpy defaces Ren's family crest, and Ren and Stimpy clone themselves on a space ship. Ren designs a Pez dispenser in Stimpy's image for some tribesmen who worship Stimpy.

The book includes an appearance by Spike Jones.

Slott, Dan, Mike Kazaleh, Ken Mitchroney, et al. *The Ren and Stimpy Show: Tastes Like Chicken.* New York: Marvel, 1993. ISBN: 0871359820. Reprints *Ren and Stimpy Show 5–8.*

Ren and Stimpy go as undercover space agents to planet Zed, home of the Croco-Men. Spider-Man gets stuck by Powdered Toast Man's snot while trying to find the real culprit, Dr. Dough-Naught. Kid Stimpy boxes, and both Ren and Stimpy participate in the *Maltese Stimpy.*

Steiner, T. Jeanette, Orlando de la Paz, Brian Mon, et al. *Disney's the Hunchback of Notre Dame.* New York: Marvel, 1996. ISBN: 0785102256.

A disfigured bell ringer, Quasimodo, becomes the hero of the city by saving the life of a young gypsy girl, and saving the city from tyranny.

This is a comic adaptation of the Victor Hugo novel as interpreted by Walt Disney Movies.

Thomas, Roy, Howard Chaykin, Jim Novak, et al. *Star Wars: Doomworld: A Long Time Ago Vol. 1.* Milwaukie, OR: Dark Horse Comics; New York: Marvel, 2002. ISBN: 1569 717540. Reprints *Star Wars 1–20.*

After Han gets the reward from the Rebels, his ship is boarded by Crimson Jack, and all the treasure is taken. On Aduba-3, Han and Chewbacca bring together a team to stop raids on a small farm community. Crimson Jack kidnaps Princess Leia. He finds Solo again, and takes him prisoner. They strike up a loose truce and go to the Doomworld of Drexel where Luke is. Luke is taken prisoner by the inhabitants, and is caught in a civil war. Han and Leia manage to escape from Jack, and take the Millennium Falcon. Chewbacca, who thinks Luke and droids tried to kill Solo, goes on a rampage. Luke reminisces about an experience from his youth in which he saved the life of his best friend from Tusken Raiders who were on a rampage. Han, Luke, the Princess, the droids, and Chewbacca are taken prisoner on the Wheel.

Dark Horse Comics reprinted the original *Star Wars* comics that Marvel published in 1977. Many fans have been clamoring for a collection like this for a long time. It includes the adaptation of the *Star Wars* movie in the first six issues.

Thomas, Roy, Howard Chaykin, Jim Novak, et al. *Star Wars: A New Hope.* Milwaukie, OR: Dark Horse, 1997. ISBN: 1569710864; 1569 712131 (sp ed.). Reprints *Marvel's Star Wars 1–6.*

Published in 1997, this is the beginning of the Star Wars saga, and the first comic series to be associated with *Star Wars.* It is the story of Luke Skywalker, Obi Wan, Han Solo, R2-D2, C-3P0, and Princess Leia, in the fight against Darth Vader and the Empire. This special edition contains scenes from the movie and special artwork.

Vess, Charles, John Ridgway, Demis Rodier, et al. *Hook: Official Movie Adaptation.* New York: Marvel, 1991. ISBN: 087135800X. Reprints *Hook 1–4.*

Peter Pan has grown up and is a successful businessman who cares more about making money than anything else. Captain Hook kidnaps Pan's children and takes them to Never-Never Land. Tinkerbell has to recondition Pan to his former life in order for him to rescue his children and defeat Hook.

This is the comic adaptation of the Tri-Star film *Hook.*

Vornholt, John, Rick Berman, Terry Pallot et al. *Star Trek: First Contact.* New York: Marvel, 1996. ISBN: 0785102957.

The Borg goes back in time to the twenty-first century, to assimilate Earth and be able to take over the galaxy. Picard and his crew follow the Borg back through time, to try to stop them. They meet the legendary pilot Zefram Cochrane who created warp drive. The *Enterprise* is overrun with Borg in an attempt to take the ship. The Borg Queen tries to assimilate Data into the collective, as her king. The first contact is made with the Vulcans, and history goes on as it should.

This is a comic adaptation of the eighth *Star Trek* film. It is based on the Next Generation crew.

Wright, Gregory, Klaus Janson, Jim Nova, et al. *Terminator 2: Judgment Day.* New York: Marvel, 1991. ISBN: 0871357569. Reprints *Terminator 2: Judgment Day 1–3; Terminator 2: Judgment Day Magazine.*

This is the official comic adaptation of the hit movie *Terminator 2*, starring Arnold Schwarzenegger. In this movie, a cybernetic organism known as a Terminator comes from the future to destroy John Connor. However, a second Terminator, Terminator 2, also comes to try to save Connor. The book is based on the screenplay by James Cameron and William Wisher.

Yomtov, Nel, Ron Lim, Carl Potts, et al. *Mighty Morphin Power Rangers: The Movie.* New York: Marvel, 1995.

Zordon is nearly killed by Ivan Ooze. The Power Rangers lose their powers, and have to travel to a distant planet to reclaim them, and save the life of their mentor, Zordon. Ivan Ooze turns humans into zombies to do his bidding, and the Power Rangers have to stop him before he does too much damage.

This is the cardstock-cover adaptation of the *Power Rangers* feature film.

12

Classical, Esoteric, Historical, Music-Related, and Religious Works

Superman, eat your heart out.... The Lord kept me busy tonight.—*Illuminator*

Lots of kids out causing trouble ... nothing too serious....—*Illuminator*

No one has ever dared call me a coward.—*Robin Hood*

Lay me in a grave of green where the arrow falls.—*Robin Hood*

Bank, Lou, Terry Stewart, Marvel Enterprises, et al. *Marvel Comics 93: Direct Distributors Meeting: Presenting Marvel Comics for the First Trimester of 1993*. New York: Marvel, 1993.

Marvel published this special volume to entice distributors with their product for the first part of 1993. There are sections for various Marvel imprints/titles including: *Marvel UK*; *2099*; *Spider-Man*; *Epic Comics*; *Horror*; *Heavy Hitters*; *Humor*; *Science Fiction*; *Barbie*; *Avengers*; *X-Men*; *Marvel Universe*; *Force of Arms* and *Tougher Than Nails*.

Bollers, Karl, Larry Lee, Richard Starkings, et al. *Onyx: Fight*. New York: Marvel, 1995. ISBN: 0785100857.

In this work, which is part of the Marvel Music imprint, the rap group Onyx faces an alien invasion of postnuclear New York City. The artwork in this volume is terrific. A comic and tape, *Break The Chain*, based on the life of KRS-One, was also published, and it included a rap music reading of the comic. In addition, a *Public Enemy* graphic novel was supposed to be published, as were two other rap-related Marvel Music volumes, but I have not been able to find evidence that they were. These include: Fuze, et al. *Snoop Doggy Dogg: Unleashed* (New York: Marvel, 1995), in which the rapper Snoop Doggy Dogg tries

to stop a worldwide conspiracy to cause riots, and Rahsaan, Tim Fielder, et al. *Dr. Dre: Man With a Cold Cold Heart* (New York: Marvel, 1995), in which Dr. Dre and some of his South Central Warriors are dropped into a radioactive battlefield to fight for the future of the world.

Cooper, Alice, Neil Gaimen, Dave McKean, et al. *The Compleat Alice Cooper: Incorporating the Three Acts of Alice Cooper: The Last Temptation*. New York: Marvel, 1995. ISBN: 0785101195. Reprints *Last Temptation Books I–III*.

On the day before Halloween, a young man, Stephen, encounters a bizarre man who has abducted children for a hundred years. He offers Stephen a ticket to the Grand Guignol Theater of the Real. Stephen ends up in a strange world of torture and ghouls.

This comic story, which is part of the Marvel Music imprint, is based on Cooper's album *The Last Temptation*. This fantastic Halloween tale was reprinted by Dark Horse Comics, in 2001 (ISBN: 156971455X).

Edelman, Scott, *Ovaltine Presents the Captain Midnight Action Book for Sports, Fitness, & Nutrition*. New York: Marvel, 1977. ISBN: 0916752240.

This is a fitness and exercise book for adults and kids, which uses the Golden-Age character Captain Midnight as a guide. It includes sections on football, basketball, disco dancing, judo, brushing your teeth, Ovaltine recipes, golf, and tennis. It is perhaps the most bizarre book Marvel ever published.

Ertegun, Ahmet, Gerald Calabrese, et al. *Rock and Roll Hall of Fame and Museum.* New York: Marvel, 1995.

This is the only book published under the Marvel Family Publishing imprint. It gives a brief history of the Rock and Roll Hall of Fame, and is profusely illustrated reproductions of with posters, and photos of memorabilia and musicians. There are separate sections on Elvis, the Beatles, Parliament/Funkadelic, U2, and the Who, among others. Names and photos of the inductees from 1986 through 1995 are included.

Ford, John, William Messner-Loebs, Gray Morrow, et al. *Historical Comics: Epic Battles of the Civil War: Volume 1: First Bull Run.* New York/Philadelphia: Marvel/Historical Souvenir, 1998. ISBN: 1892234009.

This volume tells the story of the first Civil War battle at Manassas, Virginia, the Battle of Bull Run, which took place on July 21, 1861. The Union army expected the war to be over within a few days, but was defeated at Bull Run by the Confederacy. After the battle, the Confederates had a new hero, General T. J. "Stonewall" Jackson. This volume also includes a historical essay, and biographies of P. G. T. Beauregard, Irvin McDowell, and Stonewall Jackson.

Ford, John, William Messner-Loebs, Gray Morrow, et al. *Historical Comics: Epic Battles of the Civil War: Volume 2: Shiloh.* New York/Philadelphia: Marvel/Historical Souvenir, 1998. ISBN: 1892234017.

This volume tells the story of the April 6–7, 1862, battle of Shiloh, near the Mississippi-Tennessee border. The Confederate army took over the Shiloh church from the Union, and thought they had won the battle, but the Union ended up overpowering them. General Albert Sidney Johnston died, which was a great blow to the Confederates. This volume contains a historical essay and biographies of generals William T. Sherman, Ulysses S. Grant, and Albert Sidney Johnston.

Ford, John, Angelo Torres, Curtis Woodbridge, et al. *Historical Comics: Epic Battles of the Civil War: Volume 3: Antietam.* New York/Philadelphia: Marvel/Historical Souvenir, 1998. ISBN: 1892234025.

This volume relates the battle at Antietam, at Sharpsburg, Maryland, September 17, 1862. This battle was a major turning point in the war, and ended the Confederate invasion of the North. The Confederates become too confident in their abilities to overtake the Union, which led to their downfall at this battle. It was the single bloodiest day in the history of the United States. More American lives were lost than at any other time; over 22,000 men died. This volume includes a historical essay and biographies of Generals Ambrose Burnside, George McClellan, and Robert E. Lee.

Gerber, Steve, Ralph Macchio, Alan Weist, et al. *Kiss Classics.* New York: Marvel, 1995. Reprints *Marvel Super Special 1, 5.*

Kiss finds a talisman and become the super-powered Kiss. Dr. Doom also wants the talisman, and seeks to destroy Kiss. Kiss also battles the Dark Lord who seeks to feed off the emotions of others to gain mastery of the world.

The volume includes an essay describing the history of Kiss comics, and a reprint of the original article about Kiss giving their blood. This is part of the Marvel Music series. It reprints the original Kiss comic, and its sequel from the 1970s. The original book had Kiss's blood mixed in with the ink.

Ghiraldi, Jerry, Steve Spratt, Peter Sanderson, et al. *Ultimate Marvel Super Hero Toy Collector's Guide, Year 1–4.* New York: Marvel, 1995. Reprints *Marvel Age 16.*

This series of Prestige books covers the action figures made during the years 1991–1994. Each entry contains a photograph, name, allies, enemies, team affiliation, powers, first appearance, and unique facts about the figure. Year One contains an article about Toy Biz and Marvel, reprinted from *Marvel Age.* Year Two contains pencil sketches, and other volumes have photo layouts of sets, talking figures, and more. Traditional Marvel characters, including Spider-Man, Wolverine, and the Thing, appear along with second-tier characters such as Gideon, Tusk, and Kane.

Hall, Charles, Mort Todd, Gene Colan, et al. *Bob Marley: Tale of Tuff Gong 1–3: Iron; Lion; Zion.* New York: Marvel, 1994–1995. ISBN: 0785100768 (*Iron*); 0785100776 (*Lion*).

This Marvel Music series was intended as a three-part series documenting the life of the great Bob Marley. However, part three, *Zion*, was never published, and the second volume, *Lion*, is quite rare; only a few were published. The story follows Marley's life, from birth all the way up to the shooting at Hope Road, in 1979. Marley's early life and the beginnings of the Wailers, with Bunny and Tosh, are examined in detail. The volumes include a discography of Bob Marley on Tuff Gong records, and the "Dread I-Story: The Roots of Rasta in Jamaica," which gives a detailed history and explanation of Rastafarianism. This fascinating discussion is illustrated, and it explains how slavery, exploitation, Marcus Garvey, and Haile Selassie all became lasting influences on the faith of Jah. The introduction was taken from the speech given by U2's Bono at the Rock and Roll Hall of Fame during Marley's induction.

Herdling, Glen, Craig Brasfield, Frank Turner, et al. *Illuminator*. New York: Marvel/Nelson, 1993–1994. ISBN: 0840769792 (1); 0840778074 (2); 0840762534 (3) 0840762 550 (4); 0840762577 (5); 0849762553 (6).

With the help of Jesus Christ, a young boy, Andy Prentiss, is transformed into the power of light. He battles a Skull-like villain who is feeding off the energy of others. His faith in God helps him beat various villains with whom he comes in contact, including the Channel Master, Metatron.

Hernon, Terry, Skip Dietz, John Marlin, et al. *Marvel Comics Publishing Plan 1994*. New York: Marvel, 1993. Reprints *1994 Marvel Comics Publishing Plan Vol 1: 1 October 1993*.

This is the first Marvel publishing plan for prospective investors, for January–June, 1994. Sections include Avengers, Cosmic Powers, Epic, Force Works, Licensed, Marvel Universe, Midnight Sons, New Warriors, Punisher, Razorline, Spider-Man, 2099 and X-Men. Each section gives basic information on specific titles, and tells how Marvel plans on marketing them. The book provides a fascinating look into the promotion that went into various titles.

Howgate, Mike, Steve White, Una Fricker, et al. *Dinosaurs: A Celebration*. New York: Marvel, 1997. ISBN: 078510562X. Reprints Epic/Marvel's *Dinosaurs: A Celebration 1–4*.

This material was originally published in 1992 as four separate Prestige issues by Epic Comics. Informative narrative text and graphic art were put together to make this an excellent book. Chapters include: "Claws and Tyrants," "Egg Stealers and Earth Shakers," "Bone-Heads and Duck Bills," and "Horns and Heavy Armor." The book includes scientific names, history, and geographic information on the different types of dinosaurs.

Lee, Stan, Mort Todd, Gene Simmons, et al. *Kissnation 1*. New York: Marvel, 1996. ISBN: 0785102728.

Kiss, with superhero powers, fights bizarre monsters and eventually gets help from X-Men, Wolverine and Psylocke. Gene "the Demon" Simmons makes the moves on Psylocke. Meanwhile, in the offices of Marvel comics, Stan Lee and the members of the Kiss band—Paul Stanley, Bruce Kulick, Gene Simmons, and Eric Singer—are going over ideas for a Kiss comic. Eventually the superheroes, who are from an alternate universe, meet the band and get to see them in concert. In the end, however, a question remains: Are both Kisses being controlled by an unseen force?

This was supposed to be a series devoted to Kiss, the band, but this is the only issue that was ever published, and today it is highly collectible. The collection also contains; "Kiss Manifesto," "Kissnation notes," "Kiss Cartoons," "Kiss in Japan," "Kiss reunite," "Kiss

Boots," "Kiss video bootlegging," a fan art gallery, and an article on the tribute bands Cold Gin and Alive.

Lewandowski, John et al. *The New Official Marvel Try-Out Book*. New York: Marvel, 1996. ISBN: 0785102744.

This book was described as "the definitive guide to submitting material to Marvel." It is a newer version of the original *Official Marvel Try-Out Book*.

Lewis, C. S., Charles Hall, E. Pat Redding, et al. *C. S. Lewis: The Screwtape Letters (Christian Classic Series)*. New York: Marvel 1994. ISBN: 0840762615.

This is a graphic adaptation of Lewis's famous book, written as a series of letters from Screwtape to his disciple Wormwood. Each letter contains reverse theology on temptations which lure one into hell. It is beautifully illustrated.

Mantlo, Bill, Dino Castrillo, Robert Lewis Stevenson, et al. *Treasure Island*. New York: Marvel/Fisher-Price, 1984. Reprints *Marvel Classic Comics 15*.

This is a book and audio tape based on the classic Robert Louis Stevenson story about a young boy, Jim, and his sea adventure searching for lost treasure. Long John Silver and his band of pirates, posing as shipmates, take over and eventually Jim teams up with Silver against the other pirates.

McKean, Dave, Mick Jagger, Keith Richards, et al. *Rolling Stones: Voodoo Lounge*. New York: Marvel, 1995. ISBN: 0785100814.

This book was published as part of the Marvel Music imprint. It features the collage art of Dave McKean, and the lyrics from the Stones' *Voodoo Lounge*, interspersed with images, including pictures of the Stones. This book also was packaged with interactive software on a floppy computer disk, and a poster.

Moench, Doug, Frank W. Bolle, Lewis Carroll, et al. *Alice in Wonderland*. New York: Marvel/Fisher Price, 1984. Reprints *Marvel Classic Comics 35*, 1978. Marvel Limited European version. ISBN: 094893607X.

This work is based on Lewis Carroll's classic story about a young girl who goes to a magical place and meets all sorts of interesting characters, including the Mad Hatter, Cheshire Cat, baby pigs, and talking frogs. The Fisher Price version is a book and tape set.

Moench, Doug, Diverse Hands, Charles Dickens, et al. *Christmas Carol*. New York: Marvel, 1987. ISBN: 1854002376. Reprints *Marvel Classic Comics 36*.

This is a comic adaptation of Charles Dickens's timeless holiday favorite about Ebenezer Scrooge, the man who hates Christmas. In it, the three spirits—Ghost of Christmas Past, Ghost of Christmas Present, and the Ghost of Christmas Future—visit Scrooge and show him the error of his selfish ways. Scrooge redeems himself, and learns the true meaning and spirit of Christmas: charity.

Moench, Doug, Rudy Messina, Alfredo Alcala, et al. *Robin Hood.* New York: Fisher-Price/Marvel, 1984. Reprints *Marvel Classics 34.*

This comic book and tape tell the tale of the famous archer who robbed from the rich and gave to the poor. It covers Robin Hood's first meetings with Friar Tuck, Little John, Maid Marian, and King Richard.

Moench, Doug, Yong Monano, George Roussos, et al. *Arabian Nights.* New York: Fisher-Price/Marvel, 1994. Reprints *Marvel Classics Comics 30.*

This was one of the six book and tape sets that Marvel put together in conjunction with Fisher-Price to help young people read the classics. In the book, Sharhryar, the sultan, takes a different wife every night, and then kills her the next day, until he meets Scheherazade, who tells him amazing yarns that keep him captivated. Other stories in this volume include "Ali Baba and the Forty Thieves," the story about a poor merchant who happens to come across the thieves' bounty; "Aladdin and the Magic Lamp," the story about the young boy who by chance comes across a magic ring and lamp, and helpful genies; and "Sinbad the Sailor," the story in which Sinbad tells about the trials and tribulations he went through to gain his amazing wealth. This volume includes a note to parents and a glossary.

Moench, Doug, The Tribe, Sal Buscema, Daniel Defoe, et al. *Robinson Crusoe.* New York: Fisher-Price/Marvel, 1984. Reprints *Marvel Classics 19.*

This comic/tape set tells the tale of a young man shipwrecked on a strange island. He saves the life of a native, Friday, from cannibals. Robinson Crusoe helps to stop a pirate-style mutiny on a passing ship, and goes back to civilization. This book includes a glossary of special seafaring terms.

Newman, Paul S, Dan Barry, Gail Becket, et al. *Billy Ray Cyrus.* New York: Marvel, 1995. ISBN: 0785100865.

Country singer Billy Ray Cyrus is a superhero who helps a couple of scared fans stay at a haunted Indian fort at the site of a colonial battlefield. Billy Ray and company go back to the thirteenth century where he is to fight a dragon or die. They use their laser gun to help a King against his enemies.

The authors do their best to create a fast-paced action story with an uninteresting character. This book, one of the most bizarre and worst books that Marvel

ever published, was published under the Marvel Music imprint.

Niceieza, Fabian, Jose Delbo, Bob Hall, et al. *NFL SuperPro: Forth and Goal to Go.* New York: Marvel, 1991. ISBN: 0871351534.

The first NFL superhero, Phil Grayfield, had to quit profootball because of several recurring leg injuries. He becomes a reporter for an investigative television sports show, *Sports Inside,* and ends up in a freak accident involving experimental plastics. Grayfield is transformed, with the help of a specially designed football suit, and starts fighting crime in the sports world. He cracks an illegal steroid operation which involves a chemistry professor, and a pharmaceutical company.

The volume includes an origin story.

Powell, Martin, Fred Carrillo, Sergio Cariello, et al. *In His Steps (Christian Classic Series).* New York: Marvel/Nelson, 1994. ISBN: 0840769784.

An ill homeless man confronts church members, admonishing them to ask the question, "What would Jesus do?" in any given situation. The man dies, and the pastor challenges members of the church to take up the call. As a result, members of the parish become spiritually rich, while having to deal with the trials that worldly society throw at them.

This is a graphic adaptation of the Christian novel *In His Steps,* by Charles M. Sheldon.

Powell, Martin, Seppo Makinen, John Bunyan, et al. *The Pilgrim's Progress (Christian Classics Series).* New York: Marvel/Nelson, 1992. ISBN: 0840769784.

Christian leaves his family to follow God's teachings which are brought to him through the Bible and a mysterious evangelist. He encounters various evil demons who seek to imprison him, kill him, and test his faith. His companions, Faithful and Hopeful, help Christian along the way.

This is a modern retelling of preacher John Bunyan's famous religious novel. It tells the story of Christian's trials and troubles while searching for the celestial city of God. This version of *the Pilgrim's Progress* includes the brief "Christina's Progress" story, about Christian's wife and her journey to meet with her husband in the celestial city. It is one of the better comic adaptations of a novel.

Salicrup, Jim, Barry Dutter, Stan Lee, et al. *Nightcat.* New York: Marvel, 1991. ISBN: 0871357550.

In this book, a young, sexy lady becomes a singing star turned superhero, and avenges the death of her father at the hands of the wealthy Amanda Gideon. This is one of the silliest stories Marvel ever published. In the story, Nightcat is the real life singer Jacqueline Tavarez who released an album based on that character.

Simonson, Louise, Mary Wilshire, Bill Anderson, et al. *The Easter Story*. New York: Marvel/Nelson, 1993. ISBN: 0840778066.

This story of Jesus Christ's crucifixion, death, resurrection, and ascension into heaven, begins at the Last Supper.

Simonson, Louise, Mary Wilshire, Bill Anderson, et al. *The Life of Christ: The Christmas Story*. New York: Marvel/Nelson, 1993. ISBN: 0840769768.

This book uses the gospels of *Mathew* and *Luke* to tell the story of the birth of Jesus Christ. It includes material related to the shepherds in the fields, the wise men, King Herod, and the birth of Jesus's cousin, John the Baptist.

Stuart, Marty, Paul S. Newman, Pat Boyette, et al. *Marty Stuart: Marty Party in Space*. New York: Marvel, 1995. ISBN: 0785100865.

Marty Stuart is taken hostage by aliens and asked to give them a special magic ring which he hides in his dog's collar. The aliens, from the planet Bluegrass, are at war with aliens from the Hip-Hop planet. Stuart is asked to judge a singing concert from both groups of aliens, to find which group is better. He finds them equally good, and sings a concert, thus ending the bad blood. Both alien groups love Stuart's music, and before returning to Earth, he uses his ring to stop a fast-moving asteroid from smashing into the spaceship.

This book, published as part of the Marvel Music imprint, features country star Marty Stuart. It is one of the weirdest books ever published by Marvel.

Todd, Mort, Charles Schneider, Pat Redding, et al. *Woodstock: The Comic*. New York: Marvel, 1994. ISBN: 078510075X.

This book is part of the Marvel Music series. It features a group of aliens and humans from the future who time travel to the original, 1969 Woodstock, and then travel to the 1994 Woodstock. It includes an essay by Lee Ann Stiff about the history of the Woodstock festivals.

Warner, John, Dino Castrillo, Mary Shelly, et al. *Frankenstein*. New York: Fisher-Price/Marvel, 1984. Reprints *Marvel Classics Comics 20*.

This book/tape set of Mary Shelley's *Frankenstein* tells the tale of Dr. Frankenstein and the monster he reanimated from the dead.

Woodbridge, George, Will Shetterly, John Tartaglione, et al. *Epic Battles of the Civil War: Volume 4: Gettysburg*. New York/Philadelphia: Historical Souvenir/Marvel, 1998. ISBN: 1892234033.

The last major battle of the Civil War took place at Gettysburg, Pennsylvania, July 1–3, 1883. The Confederate Army was forced to retreat, and never again mounted a major offensive. Over 50,000 Americans died during this battle. The authors point out that General Grant did not command the Union Army at Gettysburg, even though most Americans think he did. This book includes the story of Pickett's Charge, historical essays, and biographies of generals Robert E. Lee, George Gordon Meade, and George Pickett.

13

Prose Novels

I may look like the offspring of a blueberry and an orangutan but I'm
every bit as qualified a lexicographer as Noah Webster. — *The Beast*

Avengers

Binder, Otto. *The Avengers Battle the Earth
Wrecker.* New York: Bantam, 1967.

The Avengers battle an alien menace from the sev-
entieth century who is bent on destroying the past, to
ensure his victory in the future. Karazz has brought
about four dooms for the Earth that could completely
destroy it. The Avengers have to fight against Karazz
and his advanced science. In one scene, the Wasp and
Goliath end up fighting a mechanical bug.

This is the first novel published using Marvel characters. The introduction is by Stan Lee. The cover
shows Quicksilver and the Scarlet Witch as Avengers,
but they don't appear in the story.

Michelinie, David, Len Wein, Marv Wolfman.
Avengers: Man Who Stole Tomorrow. New
York: Pocket Books, 1979. ISBN: 0671820
931.

An old Eskimo shaman who believes that Captain
America is a god, kidnaps him and once again en-
cases him in a block of ice. The shaman and his Bantu
tribe had worshipped Captain America in the past,
when he was frozen in a block of ice, and before the
Avengers rescued him. The Eskimo uses his magic
and his creation, Brother Bear, to defeat the Avengers. The Vision and Iron Man seek aid from the Sub-
Mariner to help defeat the Eskimo and rescue Captain America. When the Avengers learn that it was
Kang who gave the Eskimo his "supernatural" powers, they travel, by using Thor's hammer, to the for-
tieth century, to find Kang and seek his aid in freeing the Captain. They encounter all kinds of weird
obstacles in Kang's castle. Despite the awful things
he says about the Vision's status as an android, the
Vision saves Quicksilver's life. The Avengers learn
that Kang plans to go through and conquer every century.

There is one particularly funny moment in the
book when Quicksilver berates the Beast for listening
to Devo in the Avenger's plane. This book is a loose
sequel to *Avengers 4 (Marvel Novel Series 10).* It features the Beast, Scarlet Witch, Thor, Iron Man,
Quicksilver, and Captain America as the Avengers.

Blade

Odom, Mel. *Blade.* New York: Harper, 1998.
ISBN: 0061059137.

Blade, who is half-human and half-vampire, wants
to kill all vampires in revenge for the death of his
mother. Blade and his mentor Whistler have set up
an underground vampire-hunting operation. A
human doctor becomes entangled in Blade's war.
Blade stops the vampire overlord Deacon Frost, who
is actually his father, from calling forth the vampire
Blood God for the apocalypse, known as Blood Tide.
When Blade finally finds his mother, he learns she
has become a vampire, and he is forced to kill her.

This novel is an adaptation of the hit movie *Blade.*

Both the movie and the novel are direct sequels to the graphic novel *Blade: Sins of the Father*. The book is well written and an excellent page-turner.

Rhodes, Natasha. *Blade Trinity*. New York: Black Flame, 2004. ISBN: 1844161064.

The vampires are planning a "final solution," and have resurrected the first vampire, Dracula. They have started human-blood farms, in which the homeless and alive but brain-dead are being drained of their blood. After Blade is framed by the vampires who have a video tape, the FBI chases Blade and Whistler for killing a human. Whistler is killed, but Blade hooks up with his daughter and the vampire hunters, the Nightstalkers. Blade and the Nightstalkers have to stop Dracula from giving the vampires his secret to walking in the daylight hours. The Nightstalkers design a blood virus which will kill vampires all over the Earth instantly. There are cryptic comments about other Marvel characters, including Spider-Man and the comic *Tomb of Dracula*.

This novel is based on the screenplay for the third *Blade* movie, by David S. Goyer. The author tells the story behind the pure-blood vampires and Dracula, and relates more about Blade's relationship to Deacon Frost. As in one of the alternate endings to the movie, this novel ends with the Nightstalkers battling a werewolf. In the Marvel comics, the Nightstalkers are monster hunters.

Captain America

Isabella, Tony, Bob Ingersoll. *Captain America: Liberty's Torch*. New York: Berkley Books, 1998. ISBN: 0425166198.

Captain America befriends a writer of hardboiled mysteries, and reveals his secret identity to him. The novelist is killed by the American militia group Liberty's Torch which he was researching for his next book. When Liberty's Torch blows up various free clinics and housing developments in the black neighborhoods of New York, Captain America and the Falcon investigate, and try to help survivors of the bomb blasts. When Captain America foils one their hate crimes, Liberty's Torch declares him Enemy Number One. They capture Cap and force him to defend himself in a kangaroo court, where he is tried for treason. They compare Captain America to Benedict Arnold, and broadcast his trial on the show *Coast to Coast*. With the help of the Falcon, and a civilian trained in dealing with militia groups, Captain America is able to defeat Liberty's Torch and stop their bombing plans.

Since one of the coauthors of this novel is an attorney, a great deal of the plot takes place in the courtroom. The book also provides detailed looks at how Sam Wilson became the Falcon and of the role of the Red Skull. This is a very well-written novel.

Silva, Joseph, Len Wein, Marv Wolfman. *Captain America: Holocaust for Hire*. New York: Pocket Books, 1979. ISBN: 0671820869.

The Red Skull captures a prominent scientist and his daughter. The Skull wants the scientist to create a super-powered, sonic gun that will destroy whole cities. He wants to usher in a glorious Fourth Reich in which he is the Fuehrer. A young Nazi porter brings the Skull corned beef on pumpernickel, instead of on rye, and the Skull bashes his head in. The Skull has left a trail and a trap for Captain America to follow. Nick Fury and S.H.I.E.L.D. also are doing their best to stop the Skull. The Red Skull is seemingly drowned, but, as is always the case, no body is found.

This novel contains a great deal of background information on both the origins of Captain America and the Red Skull. (*Marvel Novel Series 4*)

White, Ted. *Captain America: The Great Gold Steal*. New York: Bantam, 1968.

Captain America foils plans by the Red Skull to steal a billion dollars worth of gold from a New York bank, and thus upset the economy of the United States and many of its allies who store gold in the U.S. Bank. The Red Skull is wounded but gets away.

This was the second novel that was published using a Marvel character. It contains a detailed retelling of Captain America's origin, and how, after being suspended in ice for twenty years, he was rescued by the Avengers. There are references to comic issues for various events in the plot, and the novel is fun to read. Stan Lee wrote the introduction.

Daredevil and Elektra

Cox, Greg. *Daredevil: A Novel*. New York: Onyx, 2003. ISBN: 0451410807.

Due to an accident, young Matt Murdock is blinded, but gains enhanced senses. When his father is killed by thugs, Murdock decides to begin his quest for justice, which ultimately leads to his becoming the vigilante Daredevil. He becomes involved with the martial arts expert Elektra whose father is killed by the Kingpin's hired assassin Bullseye. Murdock also uncovers a policeman who is in the employ of the Kingpin.

This is a novelization of the hit movie *Daredevil* which is based on the screenplay by Mark Steven Johnson. However, in addition to the main themes in the movie, it contains material outlining how reporter Ben Ulrich deduced that Matt Murdock is Daredevil, and a back story related to a murder case that Matt Murdock and Foggy Nelson take on. The murder involves the Kingpin's lawyer and confidant.

Golden, Christopher, Bill Reinhold. *Daredevil: Predator's Smile*. New York: Boulevard, 1996. ISBN: 1572970103.

Daredevil is forced to consult with his arch enemy, Wilson Fisk, the Kingpin, to stop another crime boss, Gary Wiezak, who is out to take over New York. This pretender to the throne of crime is causing arson and chaos throughout New York. He hires Bullseye to destroy Fisk and Daredevil. Bullseye kidnaps Karen Page from Matt Murdock's apartment, and puts the Black Widow in the hospital. Melvin Potter, formally the Gladiator, also is kidnapped by Wiezak, who wants him to become the Gladiator again. Daredevil and Matt Murdock help Potter find his wife. Potter unwilling dons the Gladiator uniform, and takes a bloody Daredevil mannequin to Wiezak.

There are cameo appearances by Yukio and Ben Ulrich. This high-octane novel is recommended.

Robins, Madeleine E. and Max Douglas. *Daredevil: The Cutting Edge*. New York: Berkley Boulevard Books, 1999. ISBN: 0425169 383.

Daredevil has to face an insane serial murderer, the Cutter, who is killing people in Hell's Kitchen. As lawyer Matt Murdock, he has to confront a greedy corporation, Renen Tech, that is moving into Hell's Kitchen and trampling the rights of residents. After she speaks out against Renen Tech on Karen Page's radio show, one of the residents almost gets killed by the Cutter. It turns out that the Cutter, who also kidnaps Karen Page, may have a connection to the corporation. Matt Murdock agrees to defend a man, who he knows is innocent, but who is accused of causing violent problems at Renen.

The *Cutting Edge* is as good a legal thriller as any by John Grisham or others. This is one of the best Marvel-related novels.

Sullivan, Stephen, Zak Penn, Stu Zicherman, et al. *Elektra: The Junior Novel*. New York: Harper Collins, 2004. ISBN: 0060787066.

Elektra becomes a very powerful ninja, but because her heart is bitter, Stick tells her to leave his school. She becomes a well-paid assassin, but when she is asked to kill a father and child, she saves their lives. An evil ninja group, the Hand, seeks to find the child, who is a martial arts prodigy, to use for itself. Stick's ultimate goal is to train Elektra to learn the meaning of acting selflessly, of letting go of the hate and bitterness. When Elektra has to fight the man who killed her mother, bits and pieces about her childhood are revealed. Other villains include Typhoid Mary and Tattoo.

This young-adult novel is based on the movie *Elektra*, which came out in 2005. Although Elektra was killed in the movie *Daredevil*, she was raised from the dead by sensei Stick. The book contains photos from the *Elektra* movie.

Fantastic Four

Askegren, Pierce, Paul Ryan and Jeff Albrecht, *Fantastic Four: Countdown to Chaos*. New York: Berkley Boulevard 1998. ISBN: 042 5163733.

The Mad Thinker and the Red Ghost team up to gradually disorient the entire world, to disrupt economies and political situations. The Thinker kidnaps a number of prominent individuals, including Reed Richards and the Human Torch, and replaces them with his android agents. One of the young Inhumans becomes enamored with the Kree and seeks to advance the race by using the Terrigen mists. He uses the mists inappropriately, and kills himself, his teacher, and a number of his classmates. Those classmates who do not die immediately will die if the Inhumans cannot find one of their members, who previously went off to become a hermit. However, this Inhuman has been captured by the Thinker, who is trying to learn the secret of the Terrigen mists. The Fantastic Four and the Inhumans team up to find the real Reed Richards, and stop the Thinker. One of the Thinker's prison camps, which is run by robots, is inside Mt. Rushmore.

Collins, Nancy, and Paul Ryan, *Fantastic Four: To Free Atlantis*. New York: Berkley Boulevard, 1995. ISBN: 1572970545.

The Sub-Mariner's cousin, Prince Byrrah, conducts a coup against Prince Namor, and takes over his kingdom of Atlantis. Dr. Doom, who is working with the warlord Kreeg, develops a virus that will kill the Sub-Mariner. He desires several powerful Atlantean artifacts that yield great power. After Namor beaches himself, he is found by a carnie who puts him in a tank, displayed as a freak. While visiting the circus, the Thing recognizes Namor in the tank and frees him. Reed Richards saves the Sub-Mariner's life and reverses the affects of the virus. On behalf of Namor, Reed pleads for aid from the United Nations against Namor's cousin, whose warlord Kreeg plans to start a full-scale war against the surface world. The United Nations rejects Namor's plea, which makes him very upset. With the help of the Fantastic Four, Namor and a band of anti–Byrrah rebels engage Kreeg's forces and defeat them. Doom finds the relics he wants, but unknowingly he rouses the Great Leviathan out of his slumber. Namor is restored to his rightful place as ruler of Atlantis, and the Fantastic Four are honored.

One of the funniest moments in the book is when Johnny Storm is rejected by an Atlantean woman. This book gives a welcome glimpse into the world of the Sub-Mariner and Atlantis. It is highly recommended.

Johnston, William, *Fantastic Four: House of Horrors*: Racine, Wisconsin: Whitman, 1968.

The Fantastic Four go up against a bizarre scientist known as Dr. Weird, who seeks to rule the world. He invites the Fantastic Four to his house of horrors in which each member has to fight Dr. Weird individually. The Fantastic Four, except for the Invisible Woman, are defeated by Dr. Weird. Mr. Fantastic literally gets tied up in knots, and the Human Torch is doused. Eventually the Fantastic Four work together as a team to defeat Dr. Weird, and he perishes.

This easy reader is part of the Big Little Book series. It is nicely illustrated, with drawings that look like they were done by Jack Kirby, but he is not credited.

Wolfman, Marv, and Len Wein, *Fantastic Four: Doomsday*. New York: Pocket Books, 1979. ISBN: 0671820877.

Victor Von Doom and the Fantastic Four attend a college reunion. Doom invites various alumni to Latveria, including the Fantastic Four. The Fantastic Four suspect that Doom has a more sinister purpose for his invitation, and while Doom shows the Americans how wonderful Latveria is, the Fantastic Four end up in several of Doom's traps that were designed to kill them. Doom takes a jet to New York, and goes to the Baxter Building, in order to access the Negative Zone. The Fantastic Four make it back just as Doom goes into the Negative Zone. He wants to find his parents in the world of the Dead so that he can learn Black Magic secrets from his mother. Knowing what a tyrant he is, the spirits of both his mother and father reject Doom's pleas for the forbidden knowledge.

This novel covers the origin and early life of Victor Von Doom. (*Marvel Novel Series 5*).

Hulk

Banner, Bruce, Peter David, and James Schamus, *Hulk: The Junior Novel: Based on the Diaries of Bruce Banner*. New York: Harper Festival, 2003. ISBN: 006051907X.

This book is the fictional diary of Bruce Banner. Each chapter is dated and contains all the key events from the *Hulk* movie. It includes photographic stills from the movie, and is written in a style geared toward young adults.

David, Peter, and George Perez, *Incredible Hulk: What Savage Beast*. New York: Boulevard Books, 1995. ISBN: 0756759676; 0399141 049 (trd); 1572971355 (pbk).

Doc Samson tells William, the nephew of the original Major Glen Talbot and also a major, that Bruce Banner has Multiple Personality Disorder, MPD. Bruce meets Dr. Trotter who has perfected a way to rid Banner of the Hulk forever which would be a great boon to his marriage to Betty who is pregnant. The Hulk reverts to the "savage" Banner while Betty is trying to keep him from being arrested. Dr. Trotter inserts a bio-chip into Banner to stop him from changing into the Hulk. Bruce takes a job as a college physics professor, calling himself Lee Kirby, and for a short while he and Betty try to live a normal life. However, Betty gives birth to conjoined twins, one of

them a white baby who dies, and the other a gray, Hulk-like baby. Special surgery follows. In a panic, Bruce Banner reverts back to the Hulk and tries to siphon the gamma energy to save his children. The Maestro, who is from an alternate future, kidnaps Banner's gray child and takes him to the future. With the help of Dr. Strange, the Hulk follows the Maestro, and ends up twenty years in the future where he tries make his son Brett understand that the Maestro's goal of total conquest is barbaric and evil. The Maestro plans to go to Earth's various dimensions, and start conquering with an army of Hulks which he calls the Hulkbusters. In an act of selflessness, Brett saves Banner but sacrifices his own life.

This is a sequel of sorts to the graphic novel *Future Imperfect*.

David, Peter, James Shamus. *Hulk: Official Novelization of the Film*. New York: Ballantine Books, 2003. ISBN: 0345459679.

David Banner experiments on himself and passes the results on to his son Bruce. Bruce Banner is exposed to gamma radiation while trying to save a colleague. When Bruce becomes angry, he becomes the giant, green behemoth, the Hulk. Banner becomes romantically involved with General Thunderbolt Ross's daughter Betty, who is trying to contain Banner and the Hulk. There is a brief appearance by Henry Pym,

Ant/Giant Man, and it is revealed that David Banner is living as the janitor in Benny Goodman's old house. Glen Talbot is responsible for bringing out the Hulk, and for putting Betty and Bruce together, among other things. It is revealed that Bruce's foster mother is actually an agent of the government, and there is a reference to *Willard*, the movie, in the mention of a giant rat that David Banner created. David Banner becomes the Absorbing Man and fights his son to the death.

Peter David writes an excellent adaptation of the movie and even throws in traditional Hulk thoughts like, "Hulk is the strongest there is," and "Hulk smash." This novelization is based on the screenplay by James Shamus, which itself was based on the writings of David, a longtime Hulk scribe. This novel provides a more detailed view of Bruce Banner and the Hulk than the movie does; the author gets into Banner's head and provides details that were not in the movie.

Glut, Don, et al. *The Incredible Hulk: Lost in Time*. Racine, Wisconsin: Whitman, 1980.

The Hulk goes back in time to follow Tymok who intends to conquer all the time periods just as he has conquered prehistoric humanity. After he saves a young girl from a dinosaur, the Hulk/Banner finds the prehistoric folks are friendly and view him as part of their tribe. Tymok has enslaved the prehistoric people to mine the element chronite which allows him to travel through time. The Hulk gets the people to stop being his slaves, and as retribution Tymok sends a bunch of dinosaurs to the twentieth century where the Hulk has to save New York. The Hulk eventually destroys Tymok's time-traveling glove.

This easy reader book, published as an illustrated novel, belongs to the Little Big Book series.

Henderson, Jason, and James W. Fry. *The Incredible Hulk: Abominations*. New York: Berkley Boulevard, 1997. ISBN: 1572972 734.

There is a mole in the agency S.A.F.E. The head of S.A.F.E. is Sean Morgan, whose son was killed in a car wreck that the Hulk was powerless to stop. Betty asks Banner to tell her about the car wreck, and make her his partner. A dissident group makes an attempt on Blonsky's ex-wife Nadia. Emil Blonsky, the Abomination, whose niece is a member, allies himself with the URSA organization, which is dedicated to restoring the old guard in the Soviet Union. They plan to bomb the Russian Embassy, and blame S.A.F.E. The Abomination and the group take over S.A.F.E.'s Helicarrier, and the Abomination uses the Bible to justify or explain his actions. Betty Banner and Nadia have a personal, heart-to-heart talk, and are taken prisoners when URSA overtakes the Russian Embassy. The Abomination tries to explain various philosophical points of view to the Hulk, about how they are same, that the general public sees them both as monsters, not as human beings.

This is a very good novel filled with suspense and great battle scenes.

Lee, Stan, Peter David, eds., *The Ultimate Hulk*. Berkley Boulevard Books: New York, 1998. ISBN: 0425165132.

Rick Jones relates his initial impressions of the Hulk. Bruce Banner's father Brian is court-martialed. When Bruce is born, his father starts to beat his wife and child. Magneto encounters the Hulk for the first time, and tries to get him to join the Brotherhood of Evil Mutants. In an early Avengers tale, the Hulk is a member of the Avengers, and the Avengers' mansion is attacked by a robot. Bruce Banner and another scientist find a cure for the Hulk, but the scientist has other uses for the Hulk's gamma energy. In a story featuring the Defenders, Bruce Banner gets a glimpse of what a normal life might be like. The Hulk has to fight a dragon for the love of Jarella in the subatomic world. Joe Fixit works with the Rhino to get a score of cash. Doc Samson publishes his journal discussions with Banner, the Hulk, and Joe Fixit.

This is a collection of short stories about the Hulk, from all periods in his life, from his beginnings, to his end. The story "The Beast with Nine Bands" is a sequel of sorts to the graphic novel *Ground Zero*, and "The Last Titan," by Peter David, is an early version of *Hulk: The End*. Each story has a companion illustration.

Myers, Richard. *Incredible Hulk: Cry of the Beast*. New York: Pocket Books, 1979. ISBN: 067 1820850.

A general who wants to harness the radiation in his conquest of the world captures a famous gamma radiation scientist from a small African nation. Bruce Banner and the scientist's daughter are also kidnapped. The daughter falls in love with Banner and his alter ego, the Hulk. In the African wilderness they encounter hostile Pygmies and a band of rhinos which the Hulk destroys. While in prison, Banner transforms into the Hulk and destroys the general's aircraft as he is trying to escape. (*Marvel Novel Series 3*)

Wein, Len, Marv Wolfman, Joseph Silva, et al. *Stalker from the Stars*. New York: Pocket Books, 1978. ISBN: 0671820842.

Rick Jones goes to the community of Crater Falls to find Dr. Stern who he thinks will be able to help Bruce Banner with his Hulk problems. Rick discovers that there are bizarre nighttime rituals occurring in Crater Falls, and that the people of the city are being controlled by an otherworldly intelligence that puts them into a zombie-like trance. Many years ago, the alien life form Sh'mballah crashed on Earth and was buried alive. With the power to control the minds of humans, Sh'mballah has slowly been getting the townspeople of Crater Falls to free him. When Banner finds out Rick is in Crater Falls, he goes in pursuit with General Ross and Clay Quaterman. The Hulk and the alien have a number of intense battles, and the Hulk eventually destroys Sh'mballah.

This was the first novel to feature the Hulk. The introduction was written by Stan Lee. (*Marvel Novel Series 2*)

Iron Man

Cox, Greg, and Gabriel Gecko. *Iron Man: The Armor Trap*. New York: Berkley Boulevard Books, 1995. ISBN: 1572970081.

Tony Stark is kidnapped and taken to an unknown place where he is asked to build the Iron Man armor. Madame Masque takes responsibility for the kidnapping, and requests that Iron Man steal a very powerful energy chip from A.I.M., in exchange for Stark's life. War Machine is asked to fulfill the ransom, and after numerous battles is able to steal the chip from A.I.M.'s underwater headquarters. It turns out, however, that it was a fake Madame Masque who sent the transmission to Stark Enterprises. Meanwhile, Tony Stark realizes that he is in a virtual reality world, but figures out a way to circumvent the program which results in several mind-boggling descriptive sequences. War Machine learns from the real Madame Masque that the transmission sent to Stark Enterprises was bogus, and that there may be something related to it in New Orleans. When War Machine frees Stark, they figure out that there may be a link to Tony's kidnappers somewhere in England. They find Baron Strucker and Hydra headquarters, and a great battle ensues. Iron Man fights Strucker and his hordes, and in the end their castle is destroyed, and Strucker and Iron Man are pulled under the rubble.

This novel contains a brief retelling of Iron Man's origins in Vietnam, and the use of his original gray armor. It also details the turbulent relationship over the years between Jim Rhodes and Tony Stark.

Cox, Greg, Tom Morgan. *Iron Man: Operation A.I.M.* New York: Boulevard Books, 1996. ISBN: 1572971959.

The Spymaster invades Stark Enterprises, and when Iron Man goes to investigate the undersea A.I.M. lab, he encounters a mechanoid octopus and finds the lab totally demolished. He finds one survivor, a female scientist. The original Modok has been killed, but a newer, more deadly version, Modok 1.5, exists, and A.I.M. has been split into two groups. This newer version of Modok has destroyed the lab and plans to create an energy chip that can demolish the world and everyone in it. Iron Man enlists the help of Captain America, the Black Panther, and War Machine. Captain America goes to Wakanda to meet with the Black Panther, and has a close call with death while fighting a feline adversary. Modok sends Mr.

Hyde and the Cobra to face off against Captain America and the Panther. War Machine fights against an evil version of Deathlok and the Cold Warrior, and Iron Man contends with the Mandarian in space. Modok has taken over Stark Enterprises, including the programming of Stark's pet computer HOMER. He wants to build a world where there is no trace of humanity left, and populate it with artificial humans. When Iron Man gets to Stark Enterprises, he has to fight against his old friends Captain America, the Black Panther, and War Machine, but things are not what they seem to be.

The book also contains some history of Ms. America and High Evolutionary.

Rotsler, William. *Iron Man: And Call My Killer Modok*. New York: Pocket Books, 1979. ISBN: 0671820893.

Advanced Idea Mechanics, A.I.M., attempts to kidnap Tony Stark from a high-school assembly where he is speaking. A mole in Stark Enterprises steals a bogus set of Iron Man plans, and Tony Stark puts the plans for the Iron suit up for auction in an attempt to find A.I.M.'s headquarters. A.I.M.'s supreme scientist, Modok, Mental Organism Designed Only for Killing, kidnaps Happy Hogan and Tony Stark. Modok learns that Tony Stark is Iron Man, and forces him to build an Iron Man suit. Pepper Potts arranges a blind date for Stark with a woman who is a belly dancer, car mechanic, model, and actress, but all she wants to talk about is Iron Man. Nick Fury makes an appearance.

This novel includes a detailed explanation of Modok's origin, Iron Man's beginnings, and how Happy Hogan came to be employed by Tony Stark. (*Marvel Novel Series 6*)

Smith, Dean Wesley, Tom Morgan. *Iron Man Super Thriller: Steel Terror*. New York: Pocket Books, 1996. ISBN: 0671003216.

Iron Man and the Avengers go up against Tess-One, Ultron, and his army of androids. Using neutron bombs, Ultron wants to destroy the human race by Christmas. When Iron Man shoots Ultron in the mouth, Ultron's head explodes. The Avengers include Quicksilver, Black Widow, the Vision, Crystal, and Hank Pym.

Spider-Man

Barrett, Neal, Jr., James Fry. *Spider-Man Super Thriller: Warrior's Revenge*. New York: Pocket Books/BPMC, 1997. ISBN: 0671 008005.

The Super Skrull is trying to kill one of Bruce Banner's personal friends, which causes the Hulk to create chaos in New York. The person the Super Skrull is trying to kill is a human rights activist and science fiction writer who the Skrull Empire has declared a traitor. Spidey, the Hulk, and S.A.F.E. team up to track down the Super Skrull, but they also find another Skrull spy lurking about. The Hulk nearly kills the Super Skrull in a moment of rage.

Barrett, Neal, Jr., Louis Small, Jr., Ralph Reese. *Spiderman—Super Thriller: Lizard's Rage.* New York: Pocket Books/BPMC, 1997. ISBN: 067100798X.

The Lizard goes on a rampage. He kidnaps scientist Eileen McKay whom he believes can help him design a whole army of reptilian creatures that can exterminate the human race. Spider-Man teams up with Morbius, the living vampire, to find McKay and defeat the Lizard. Morbius believes that McKay can find him a cure for his vampirism.

Busiek, Kurt, Nathan Archer, Al Milgrom et al. *Spider-Man: Goblin Moon.* New York: Byron Preiss, 2000. ISBN: 0613918649 (trd) 0425174034 (pbk) 0739413899 (Book Club).

Norman Osborn is once again a respectable part of New York society and business. Osborn is outspoken against a group of hired thugs known as the Rat Pack who are breaking into vacuities all over New York. Osborn, who is part owner of the *Daily Bugle* where Peter Parker works, offers Parker a job in Paris as a European correspondent. When the public advocate is found murdered, Osborn, who has his heart set on becoming mayor, steps in to take over. He poisons Mary Jane, and a very angry Spidey takes her to the hospital. As Mr. Green, Osborn controls the Rat Pack who have kidnapped the mayor of New York. As the Green Goblin, his plan is to frame Spidey for the mayor's death. The Goblin and Spidey duke it out while having a discussion about chemistry, and the Goblin's glider is broken over Spider-Man's knee. Boomerang also makes an appearance.

Goblin Moon is one of the best of all the Spider-Man novels. The index includes a chronology of Marvel-related novels.

Castro, Adam-Troy, Mike Zeck. *Spider-Man: The Gathering of the Sinister Six.* New York: Berkley Boulevard, 1999. ISBN: 0425167 747

A famous actor dies of fear, claiming to see monsters everywhere. Because he was a friend of Mary Jane, Spidey is investigating his death. At the actor's funeral, the minister is Mysterio who tries to kill everyone there. Mysterio had written and directed a film called *The Devil's Moon*, and Quentin Beck is taking revenge on everyone who he believes destroyed his movie. Mysterio crashes a Broadway play, and uses mechanical sharks to cause chaos and pain. Jonah Jameson's wife has a run in with one of the sharks. While dining at the Parkers, Betty Brant dumps a plate of lasagna on Flash Thompson's head, in a fit of anger. The Chameleon frees Electro from prison. Mary Jane is asked to reprise her previous role for

Fatal Action 4. Fearing Mysterio, Flash Thompson goes with her as her body guard, and the movie company hires Razorback as security. He does indeed terrorize the set, and Mary Jane is almost killed by him. Spidey saves her at the last moment. Mary Jane finds some old photos of Parker's parents holding a mysterious baby.

This is the first part in a trilogy that brings together a new version of the Sinister Six. The Gentleman reforms the Sinister Six with Pity, who may be Spider-Man's long lost sister, Doc Ock, Electro, Vulture, Mysterio and the Chameleon. This book is a nice beginning for a fantastic trilogy.

Castro, Adam-Troy, Mike Zeck. *Spider-Man: Revenge of the Sinister Six.* New York: iBooks, 2001. ISBN: 0743434668 (trd); 0743444639 (pbk).

The Sinister Six, under the leadership of the mysterious Gentleman, try to destroy Spider-Man. They threaten to destroy thousands of lives at various places where Spidey made mistakes and people died. The bridge where Gwen Stacy died, the building where Captain Stacy died, and other New York places where people lost their lives are possible targets. Peter Parker finds out that he did have a sister, and that his parents were officially declared traitors by the U.S. government. As Spider-Man, he tries to find more information about his parents, but can not do so without revealing his identity. Captain America wants to help, but Parker refuses to disclose his identity. Spidey tries to help the elusive Pity, who may be his sister Carla May. Spider-Man learns a great deal about his past from the Gentleman, who masterminded the death of Peter Parker's parents and had a hand in the destruction of both the *Titanic* and the *Hindenburg.* Mary Jane beats up on the Chameleon.

In this book, the author gives insight into Spider-Man's psyche, and provides interesting background information about several other characters, including clues as to why Jonah Jameson obsesses over Spider-Man; a great deal of background information on the Red Skull and the fake Red Skull, Alfred Malik; and how Timely Underwriters sell insurance to folks who are afraid that supervillains will destroy their property.

Castro, Adam-Troy, Mike Zeck. *Spider-Man: Secret of the Sinister Six.* New York: iBooks, 2002. ISBN: 0743444647. (trd); 0743458 32X. (pbk).

The Gentleman has gotten the Sinister Six to battle Spider-Man. Spidey thinks that Pity, who is one of the Sinister Six and has the power of darkness, may actually be his sister, but he finds out later that she is not. Spidey eventually gets Pity to help him battle the Gentleman and the rest of the Sinister Six. Dr. Octopus captures the Gentleman and attempts to get him to do his bidding. The Gentleman—who, with a version of the Red Skull, was behind the death of Peter Parker's parents—is eventually killed. Mysterio, who is a great silent film fan, has a mysterious illness. The Gentleman plans to use the Sinister Six to cut off power from all computers related to financial institutions, which will send the stock market and the entire financial world into chaos. Electro falls in love with Pity, and Dr. Octopus tries to usurp the Gentleman's authority. Wolverine, Logan, who knew Parker's parents, tells Mary Jane and Peter the truth about his folks and the sister he might have. He also defuses a bomb in their residence. Several low-rent villains, including the Red Bear and the Disc Jockey, make appearances.

This is the final installment of the Sinister Six trilogy. It contains tributes or obscure references to several characters from popular culture, including the sheriff from *Fargo*, Erich Von Stroheim, Marilyn Manson, and Scooby Doo.

Castro, Adam-Troy. Mike Zeck. *Spider-Man: The Sinister Six Combo*. New York: iBooks, 2004. ISBN: 074348715X.

This book is a paperback combo of the two previous Sinister Six novels, *Revenge of the Sinister Six* and *Secret of the Sinister Six*. It contains positive comments from both the *School Library Journal*, which states that the author does an "excellent job," and *Publishers Weekly*, which says that these novels "uphold the Marvel tradition."

Chevat, Richie, Ernie Colon. *You Are Spider-Man vs. Incredible Hulk*. New York: Pocket Books, 1997. ISBN: 0671007971.

Peter Parker attends a lecture by Bruce Banner who helped create the world's first radiation-absorbing decelerator. Banner is kidnapped from the lecture by robots, and Spider-Man tracks him to Dr. Doom's lair.

There is a very funny sequence in which the Hulk has to fight the Doombots. The reader is invited to play a game in which he/she is Spider-Man, and has to win the Hulk to his/her side. Each chapter gives the reader a choice as to where the story will go next. The book also has an appearance by Walker Langkowski, aka Sasquatch.

Chevat, Richie, Neil Vokes, Michael Avon Oeming. *You Are Spider-Man vs. the Sinister Six*. New York: Pocket Books, 1996. ISBN: 0671003194.

Mary Jane is working on the set of *Fatal Action 3*. A stunt that goes wrong starts a battle between Spider-Man and the Sinister Six, who are led by Doc Ock. Ock knows there is a connection between Peter Parker and Spider-Man, and uses the Hobgoblin, Chameleon, Shocker, Mysterio, and the Vulture to fight Spider-Man.

The reader is invited to play a game in which he/she is Spider-Man and makes choices as to what will happen next. Each choice leads to a different result.

David, Peter. *Spider-Man*. New York: Ballantine Books, 2002. ISBN: 0345450051.

Parker is bitten by a genetically altered spider, and discovers he has special powers. He fights his best friend's father, Norman Osborn, as the Green Goblin. They learn each other's identities, and Osborn offers to let Spider-Man join him in his power-hungry crusade. Uncle Ben gets killed. Peter Parker writes diary entries to his dead parents, about his day-to-day activities. Battlin' Jack Murdock fights Bone-Crusher before Parker gets in the boxing ring.

This book is based on the David Koepp's screenplay for the film story of Peter Parker's origins as Spider-Man. The novel gives great insight into Peter Parker's background, including the time when his parents died and he came to live with Uncle Ben and Aunt May. This novel makes an excellent complement to the first Spider-Man movie.

David, Peter. *Spider-Man 2*. New York: Ballantine Books, 2004. ISBN: 0345470540.

Peter Parker's personal life is a wreck. He misses classes, and his friends feel alienated from him. Spider-Man is getting in the way of Parker's personal life. After Parker goes to see a doctor—who happens to be wearing a Grateful Dead shirt—and gets a clean bill of health, he decides to quit being Spider-Man, and try to live a normal life. His costume ends up in Jonah Jameson's office. Dr. Otto Octavius's wife dies in an accident that happens when an experiment with a highly dangerous substance, tritium, goes bad. As a result of the accident, Dock Ock's metal arms merge with him, and start taking control of his psyche. When Doc Ock decides to kidnap Mary Jane, Spider-Man goes back into action, but he is defeated by Ock and given to Harry Osborn who wants to kill him. When Osborn finds out Parker is Spidey, he lets him go, and Spider-Man eventually finds a way to defeat Ock and save Mary Jane. Many people, including Doc Ock and Mary Jane, find out that Parker is Spider-Man. Hank Pym makes a cameo appearance, and throughout the book Peter has imaginary debates with his late uncle, Ben Parker.

This is the official novel for the hit movie *Spider-Man 2*, based on the screenplay by Alvin Sargent. It also is available on audio tape and CD: ISBN: 0739312359; 0739312332.

DeCandido, Keith R.A., Jose R. Nieto, Joe St. Pierre. *Spider-Man: Venom's Wrath*. New York: Berkley Boulevard Books, 1998. ISBN: 0425165744.

A radical Puerto Rican political group called the Cane Cutters kidnaps three people: a lawyer, who is Venom's ex-wife; a journalist, staff writer Robbie Robertson of the *Daily Bugle*; and a police officer, who has a brother in their movement. The most evil of the Cane Cutters is a ruthless, shape-changing mutant named Sombra. Because Spider-Man's advocate and friend Robbie has been taken, and because it is inevitable that Venom will be involved, Spider-Man is especially interested in making sure that as few people as possible get hurt. He has a bizarre encounter with a villain wannabe called the Iron Monger, and he has a loose association with the NYPD, as they work together on this case.

This novel contains some great character development, particularly with Betty Brant. We also learn a great deal about Venom's and Robertson's backgrounds. There are some excellent battle scenes between Spidey, who is called a "bug man," and Venom. Much of this novel reads like a mystery, and it keeps the reader on the edge of the seat.

Delrio, Martin, Neil Vokes, Michael Avon Oeming. *Spider-Man Super Thriller: Midnight Justice.* New York: Pocket Books, 1996. ISBN: 0671568515.

Venom is very upset when he sees that Peter Parker, Spider-Man, and the Human Torch win citizen awards from the mayor of New York, and he sets out on a plan to discredit Parker's journalistic credentials and Spider-Man's moral standing. He tries to make Spider-Man look like a crook and killer. Eddie Brock/Venom, who can change shapes, impersonates Spidey. In doing so, he attempts to have himself filmed while he is beating up a police officer. However, Spidey makes Venom so mad that he reverts back to his true form. Brock even breaks into the Fantastic Four's headquarters. Throughout the story, the Human Torch helps Spidey foil Venom's plots.

This is one of the better novels in the Super Thriller series.

Duane, Diane, Ron Lim. *Spider-Man: Venom Factor.* New York: G.P. Putnam/Byron Preiss, 1994. ISBN: 0399140026, 1572970383 (trds); 0425169782 (pbk).

Homeless people are being killed, and radioactive products are being stolen and eaten. It is reported that the culprit looks like Venom who shows up and wants to find out who is impersonating him. There are numerous battles between Hobgoblin, Venom, and Spider-Man. Hobgoblin threatens to blow up Manhattan with a nuclear bomb unless he is paid an exorbitant amount of money. The Venom look-alike eats radioactive material, and has tremendous strength; he even over turns a train. Mary Jane, who finally gets a decent acting part, turns it down because of Hobgoblin's threat, and because she does not want to leave New York. Venom and Spider-Man get into a funny argument about what a spleen is. The Venom-like creature is blown into tiny, bipedal creatures, which Spider-Man is able to capture more easily.

Duane, Diane, Darich Robertson, Jeff Albrecht. *Spider-Man: The Octopus Agenda.* New York: Boulevard/Putnam, 1997. ISBN: 0399142118 (trd); 1572972793 (pbk).

A nuclear explosion happens in Dolgeville, New York, and other places around the United States. Mary Jane's phone was cloned, and their bill was over $4,000. While Peter is investigating this, he also finds some details about Russian mobsters who have come to America to make their fortune. One such group has been stockpiling weapons, and plans to destroy a number of key cities. An old enemy, the Master Planner, Doc Ock, is behind this plan. Spidey is curious about a new crime technique known as "ram raiding." Mary Jane starts hand modeling, but injuries her hand. Then she tries to model her face, but walks off the set when the director calls her "a useless, red-headed bimbo, with the brains of a duck." Mary Jane tells him off, and ends up getting a voice job for a superhero cartoon. Venom, who is also after the Master Planner joins Spider-Man as both put aside their differences to stop Doc Ock, who plans to bomb the World Trade Center. Peter Parker helps a reporter who is doing a story on the Russian mob. When Venom and Spider-Man are captured by Doc Ock, they fight each other to get his attention.

Duane, Diane, Darich Robertson, Scott Hoblish, *Spider-Man: The Lizard Sanction.* New York: Berkley Boulevard, 1995. ISBN: 0399141057 (trd); 042517865X, 1572971487 (pbks); 0671044192, 0671569139 (aud).

Spider-Man goes to the Florida Everglades to stop the Lizard who is searching for a cure for his horrible condition. Venom is also hunting the Lizard, which makes Spider-Man's job all the more difficult. Mary Jane is working in Florida. When Peter Parker goes with a reporter from the *Daily Bugle* to get the scoop on a shuttle launch, he finds out that there are saboteurs who plan to bomb the shuttle. A new substance, similar to smoke, called Hydrogel, plays a big part in the plot. Spidey and Venom form a loose alliance to find out what exactly is going on in the Everglades. The Lizard, with the conscience of Curt Connors, actually saves Spider-Man and Venom from being blown up.

This book has been released in a number of editions, including audio. It has proved to be one of the most popular Spider-Man novels ever published.

Elrick, George S. *Spider-Man Zaps Mr. Zodiac.* Racine, Wis: Whitman, 1976.

A new astrologist columnist, Jane Virgo, comes to work at the *Daily Bugle.* She befriends Peter Parker and they start going out to lunch together. At night, Spider-Man goes after Mr. Zodiac, who is Jane Virgo and who has lived for thousands of years and can change into any of the Zodiac signs. Eventually, Jane realizes that Parker is Spider-Man, and she tries to thwart his plans to stop Zodiac. Parker realizes that Jane is Mr. Zodiac, and when Mr. Zodiac threatens his friends, Spider-Man defeats him. Zodiac crumbles into parchment dust and is blown away by the subway.

This novel with illustrations is the only Spider-Man Big Little Books published by Whitman in 1976. Originally published in 1968, it was reprinted in 1978 and 1980.

Gardner, Craig Shaw, Bob Hall. *Spider-Man: Wanted Dead or Alive.* New York: BP books,

1998. ISBN: 0399143858 (trd); 0425169 308 (pbk).

Spider-Man is blamed for the accidental shooting of an innocent bystander. The press and mayoral candidate Brian Timilty have a field day slandering Spider-Man as a public enemy. When Timilty's campaign manager is killed, a picture of Spider-Man holding a knife is leaked to the press. Spider-Man must try to clear his name without being shot on sight. In one instance he is surrounded. Apparently Timilty is being controlled, behind the scene by a wealthy industrialist. Electro tries to take control of the New York water supply. The Rhino actually gives himself up to Spider-Man, and is shocked that Spider-Man is speechless, for once.

Jameson, Jonah, Jacob Ben Gunter, Ben Urich, et al. *Spider-Man 2: The Daily Bugle Stories*. New York: HarperFestival, 2004. ISBN: 0060571322.

Jonah Jameson rants about what a menace Spider-Man is, while Mary Jane gets accolades for her performance in Oscar Wilde's *The Importance of Being Earnest*. Among many other Spidey scoops, it is revealed that Parker writes to "Dear Lotta" about his problems.

This young-adult novel is based on the movie, *Spider-Man 2*. It includes editorials, articles, and various stories from the *Daily Bugle* newspaper.

Kupperberg, Paul, Len Wein, Marv Wolfman. *Crime Campaign*. New York: Pocket Books, 1979. ISBN: 0671820907.

The Kingpin puts one of his cronies, Ian Foster, in the campaign for mayor of New York. Spider-Man is being hunted by authorities for a crime he did not commit, and. a fake Spider-Man threatens to kill Ian Foster if he wins. Peter Parker meets Jonah Jameson's niece who is hired to work with him, taking photographs, but she actually is a private investigator hired to find out how Parker takes pictures of Spider-Man. The Kingpin enlists the help of all the mob bosses to back Ian Foster. When Kingpin kidnaps Foster's daughter, Foster asks crime boss Silvermane for help in rescuing her. Kingpin and Spidey fight in a posh restaurant, and Fisk throws Spidey out of a window. Wilson Fisk's wife Vanessa takes Spider-Man to the hospital, and saves his life. In the climax, Kingpin and Silvermane have a showdown in which Silvermane is killed by Fisk, and Vanessa leaves Fisk. Jonah Jameson also runs for the mayor of New York. (*Marvel Pocket Novel 8*)

Lee, Stan, Kurt Busiek eds., *Untold Tales of Spider-Man*. New York: Boulevard Books, 1997. ISBN: 1572972947.

Spidey meets Ant-Man for the first time, and goes up against Egghead. When the Sandman breaks up the Human Torch's date at a posh restaurant, Spider-Man is close by. Spider-Man takes on the Looter, and the Green Goblin terrorizes the *Daily Bugle*. The Parker family doctor tries to give Peter Parker a job in the lab, a job that would be safer than going around shooting pictures of Spider-Man. Spider-Man goes up against a Jack the Ripper wannabe who is killing Gwen Stacy look-alikes and calls himself the Ripper. Parker helps Enforcer Fancy Dan save his son from a kidnapping, and saves Jonah Jameson's life from the Scorpion and the Spider Slayers. Peter Parker, who has gone insane, ends up in an asylum while waiting for Kraven to find him. The Shocker is very upset because his brother has committed suicide.

This collection of short stories covers Spider-Man's career, from shortly after he became Spider-Man, to the present day. There is a continuity guide.

Lee, Stan, Jack Kirby, Steve Ditko, et al. *The Ultimate Spider-Man*. New York: Berkley Boulevard, 1996. ISBN: 1572971037 (trd); 0425170004 (pbk).

This is a collection of short stories that show the various aspects of Spider-Man's life, including his early career. One story tells about Spider-Man going to Brooklyn to help save a girl who needs a liver transplant. The book is highly recommended.

McCay, Bill, John Nyberg. *Spider-Man Super Thriller: Deadly Cure*. New York: Pocket Books, 1996. ISBN: 0671003208.

A scientist finds a way to create the perfect human from what seems to be a variation of the Super Soldier Formula. When some thugs try to take it away from him, the scientist inadvertently absorbs the formula. The Kingpin has been financing the scientist, and wants the formula to help heal his wife. After his thugs fail to find and capture the scientist, Wilson Fisk hires the Hobgoblin to try to capture the renegade scientist, who has since gone into hiding. The Hobgoblin has plans to use the formula on himself. Both Spider-Man and Daredevil try to stop the formula from falling into the hands of either the Kingpin or Goblin. It turns out that the formula has turned the scientist into a monster, and it will eventually kill whoever absorbs it. Aunt May also is sick.

Michelinie, David, Dean Wesley Smith, James Fry, et al. *Spider-Man: Carnage in New York*. New York: Berkley Boulevard, 1995. ISBN: 1572970197 (trd); 0425167038 (pbk).

Scientists, believing they can separate and kill Cletus Kasady's symbiote, move Carnage from the Vault to New York. Spider-Man helps a scientist who has created a formula called a "trigger," that fills people with rage; it makes people go crazy and want to kill one another. In attempting to destroy the serum, the scientist inadvertently lets Carnage out of police custody, and gives Carnage the serum. The *Daily Bugle* sponsors a "feed the homeless" event that Carnage terrorizes. He plans to put the "trigger" into the soup that was made to feed the homeless, but Spider-Man stops him, and gives the serum to Reed Richards for safekeeping. Aunt May is being evicted from her home by the mortgage company.

O'Brien, Judith, Mike Mayhew. *Mary Jane.* New York: Marvel, 2003. ISBN: 0785113 088 (trd); 0785114408 (pbk. 2004).

This was the first young-adult novel published and marketed by Marvel. It is set in the Ultimate Spider-Man Universe and reveals events in Mary Jane's life from her perspective. Mary Jane comes from a broken home; her mother's boyfriend was a loser, and she and Peter Parker were childhood friends. Stories about Peter's spider bite, his winning a wrestling match, their high school romance, and Uncle Ben's murder also are included in the book. There is information about Mary Jane becoming anorexic; receiving a scholarship to a prestigious ballet school; and discovering that a new sports drink, Oz, contains harmful chemicals. Oz was made by Norman Osborn's company, and this information is given to the press. The novel also reveals that after Harry Osborn tried unsuccessfully to make the moves on Mary Jane, she realized that she was in love with Peter Parker. Everything in the Spider-Man mythos is included in this novel. It is well-written and well-paced, throughout. It belongs in every public library.

O'Brien, Judith, Mike Mayhew *Mary Jane 2.* New York: Marvel, 2004. ISBN: 0785114 335.

Mary Jane guesses that Peter might be Spider-Man. After borrowing money to pay for a $400 dinner date, Mary Jane has to get a job at a local store. Her friend Wendy gets a big part in the musical *My Fair Lady,* and Mary Jane becomes the choreographer. Harry Osborn hangs out with freshmen, and starts helping them steal cars. Peter hangs out with Gwen Stacy, which makes Mary Jane jealous. Mary Jane's mother starts dating Gwen Stacy's father. Spider-Man saves Mary Jane from being mugged, and has a talk with Harry Osborn about Harry's unsavory company and activities. Peter and Mary Jane go to the winter formal.

This second Mary Jane novel contains tales of her life in high school and her relationship with Peter Parker. This sequel is actually better than the first Mary Jane novel.

Smith, Dean Wesley, James W. Fry *Spider-Man: Goblin's Revenge.* New York: Berkley Boulevard, 1996. ISBN: 157297172X.

Carnage has escaped from prison with the help of an unnamed benefactor. A deadly serum that causes anyone who touches it to go insane has been stolen. Spider-Man must deal try to stop Carnage, and catch the thief who stole the serum. The Green Goblin, a foe who Spider-Man thought was dead, has returned. Is it Norman Osborn, the original Goblin, or an impostor? Mary Jane, Flash Thompson, and Liz Allen are ambushed, and Mary Jane is taken to the same place where the Goblin killed Gwen Stacy. Carnage,

who is trying to kill Spider-Man, is on a rampage, and takes a plane hostage. Carnage kills many people in very gruesome ways.

If this were a movie, it would be R-rated.

Smith, Dean Wesley, Bob Hall. *Spider-Man: Emerald Mystery.* New York: Berkley Boulevard. 2000. ISBN: 0425170373.

Spider-Man is helping a private investigator find her partner's murderer. Ordinary people are suddenly transformed into zombies, and are committing crimes of which they have no memory. A mysterious figure known as the Jewel takes credit for turning people into zombies and for the crimes. He threatens that things will turn more violent if his warnings are not heeded. Peter Parker and the *Daily Bugle* staff begin to find clues as to the Jewel's identity. The criminal has been sending threatening messages outlining his plans to the *Bugle.* It turns out that the Jewel is nothing more than a small-time hood who came across some radioactive material from the same jewels that turned Cain Marko into the Juggernaut.

This book is a sequel to the X-Men novel *Jewels of Cyttorak.* It takes placed over a period of two weeks, and reads more like a traditional mystery novel than a superhero story.

Teitelbaum, Michael, David Koepp, Zade Rosenthal, et al. *The Adventures of Spider-Man.* New York: Avon Books, 2002. ISBN: 0064410730.

This young-adult novel is based on the hit movie *Spider-Man.* It includes the origin story of Spider-Man and his battles with the Green Goblin.

Vornholt, John, Ed Hannigan & Al Milgrom. *Spider-Man: Valley of the Lizard.* New York: Boulevard Books, 1998. ISBN: 1572973 331.

Several pieces of pre–Columbian art are stolen in New York and several other places around the world, by a woman and her gargoyle followers. The Lizard shows up at one of these thefts. Curt Connors, the Lizard, keeps a journal about his travels in Mexico where he went to escape his life as the Lizard. Connors's wife Martha goes to Peter and Mary Jane's house, and gives Connors journal to Peter. While near the Mexican border, Connors encounters the Chupacabras, creatures of legend known as the goatsuckers. Connors is fascinated by these reptilian creatures. He goes to the Valle del Lagarto, the Valley of the Lizard, deep within the mountains, to seek them and possibly find a cure for himself. He finds an ancient race of creatures who are seeking to replenish their species by hatching millions of eggs. Connors agrees to help them, but the Lizard intervenes and becomes their messiah. The Lizard wants to use the Chupacabras as an army to wipe out all humans. Needless to say, Spider-Man goes to Mexico to try and stop him.

Connors's journal, which is reprinted in this novel,

is the most interesting part of the novel. This is one of the most creative and satisfying Marvel-related novels.

Wein, Len, Marv Wolfman. *Amazing Spider-Man: Mayhem in Manhattan*. New York: Pocket Books, 1978. ISBN: 0671820443.

Spider-Man is wanted for a murder he did not commit, and he is trying to clear his name. Doctor Octopus is blackmailing a group of the world's biggest oil companies. Peter Parker gets fired because he won't go on an assignment with J. J. Jameson's niece.

This was the first in a series of ten novels based on Marvel characters. It has an introduction written by Stan Lee. (*Marvel Novel Series 1*)

X-Men/Wolverine and Related

Bergen, Lara. *X-Men*. New York: Dell Publishing, 2000. ISBN: 0440417120.

This is a young-adult novelization of the *X-Men* movie, in which the X-Men stop Magneto from his terrorist strike against humankind. It is based on the screenplay by Christopher McQuarrie and Ed Solomon, and includes stills from the movie.

Byers, Richard Lee, Leonard Manco. *X-Men: Soul Killer*. Byron Preiss: New York, 1999. ISBN: 0425167372.

The X-Men/Excalibur team up with Dracula to fight the demon Belasco. Rogue ends up absorbing the power of Vampire, and tries to absorb Storm's essence. A fake version of Rogue is killing people, and is claiming that the X-Men are going to conquer humanity. Belasco wants to let the Dark Ones from the Elder Gods loose on the world, but he needs Rogue's powers to help him do so. Dracula possesses Nightcrawler's sorcerer girlfriend Amanda. Belasco lets loose a tentacle reminiscent of Cthulu on Excalibur's ship, but Dracula, Colossus and Nightcrawler eventually destroy it. Dracula confesses his love for Storm and tries to win her to his side as his queen. After Belasco is defeated, Dracula and Wolverine have a very heated battle, and Amanda transports Dracula across the world. The essences of those that Rogue had previously absorbed, including those of Captain America and Magus, come to life and fight the demons.

This novel is filled with Lovecraftian imagery. All in all, it is one of the most creatively written of the Marvel-related novels.

Cerasini, Marc. *Wolverine: Weapon X: Limited Edition*. New York: Marvel, 2004. ISBN: 0785116052.

Logan is captured for use in the Weapon X project where he undergoes the bonding of metal adamantium to his skeleton and is turned into the ultimate weapon. Logan has flashbacks to a covert operation in North Korea, and—in a virtual reality sequence— Subject X, Logan, goes into a rage and kills all the scientists and staff in the Weapon X complex. The scientists force Logan to battle and kill wolves, a bear, and a tiger, and one scientist wants to use Logan's blood in immunology experiments, in attempts to find cures for various diseases. The Professor, who is the leader of the Weapon X project, wants to brainwash Logan to serve his commands, and make Logan into the perfect killing machine.

This book is Marvel's first jump into fully adult-oriented novels. It is based on Marvel characters and Barry Windsor-Smith's Weapon X storyline that was originally presented in *Marvel Comics Presents 80*. This novel contains three very gory stories that run concurrently, and there are references to psychological and scientific theory throughout. This book is definitely not for kids. Published in 2005 as a paperback (ISBN: 141652164X).

Claremont, Chris. *X-Men 2: A Novelization*. New York: Ballantine, 2002. ISBN: 034 5461967.

In retaliation for Xavier's failure to cure his mutant son, mutant-hater William Stryker plans to destroy all mutants through mutanticide. He learns all about the X-Men from Magneto who is under mind control. Storm gives Jean Grey a hard time about her feelings toward Logan who captures Xavier and Cyclops. Stryker plans to use his son, Mutant 143, Professor X, and the mutant-finding machine Cerebro, to slaughter the entire mutant population of the world. Magneto and Mystique temporarily form a loose alliance with the X-Men to stop Stryker's death plans. Rogue and Iceman form a romantic relationship. Wolverine fights Stryker's mutant puppet Lady Deathstrike, and defeats her by pushing liquid adamantium into her body. Pyro leaves Xavier's school and joins Magneto. Mutants Jubilee, Artie, Hank McCoy, the Beast, Psylocke, and Gambit make cameo appearances, and Nightcrawler, Colossus, and Kitty Pryde are introduced.

This is a very detailed novelization of the hit movie *X-Men United*, by longtime X-Men scribe Chris Claremont. In the movie, Jean Grey dies or disappears after saving the X-Men, but in this novel she is just blinded. The novel fleshes out the characters and the movie by providing a little more detail. It makes a nice companion to the movie. Claremont also wrote the *X3* novel which was published in 2006 (ISBN: 034 5492110).

Clark, Catherine, et al. *Upstarts Uprising*. New York: Bullseye, 1996. ISBN: 067987660X.

This is a novel in which the X-Men fight the Upstarts. The Upstarts are a gang of evil mutants who are holding other young mutants as hostages, frozen in space. (Never Published)

Conner, Ted. *X-2*. New York: Bantam, 2003. ISBN: 0553487760.

This young-adult novel is based on the hit movie *X-Men 2*, in which Magneto and the X-Men form a loose alliance to stop William Stryker from killing all mutants. In the book, Pyro leaves the X-Men to join up with Magneto.

Duane, Diane, Ron Lim, Bob McLeod. *X-Men: Empire's End*. New York: Boulevard: Putnam, 1997. ISBN: 0399143343 (trd): 042 5164489 (pbk).

Professor X and his alien love Empress Lilandara, who is from the Shi'ar empire, team up to stop an alien who devours stars and is headed toward Shi'ar space. They enlist the aid of the X-Men to help stop this creature, and use a device, the Noumenoextensor, that increases the X-Men members' strength, but also has an addictive power. There are several attempts on the life of Professor X, and Xavier learns that at one time Lilandara and the Shi'ar Empire considered conquering Earth. Many within the Empire are not happy that Lilandara and Xavier are lovers. The X-Men team includes Storm, Cyclops, Wolverine, Jean Grey, Beast, Gambit and Iceman. There is a brief cameo of the Imperial Guard.

This was the first X-Men novel published in hardback.

Dutter, Barry, et al. *Storm*. New York: Random House, 1994. ISBN: 9994696378.

This novel focuses on the X-Man Ororo Munroe/ Storm. (Never Published)

Friedman, Michael Jan, Jose Ladronn. *X-Men: Shadows of the Past*. New York: BP books, 2001. ISBN: 0743400186 (trd); 0743423 78X (pbk).

Lucifer, who is responsible for crushing the spine of wheelchair user Xavier, replaces Xavier with an impostor made of ionic energy. He also makes an impostor version of the Angel. Professor X is kidnapped into the Nameless Zone, and is forced to watch helplessly as the impostor carries out Lucifer's plan. The fake Xavier seeks technology from various abandoned Quistalian bases, and dispatches the original five X-Men to retrieve it. Xavier finds hope in the friendship of a mentally challenged teenager, Jeffery Saunders, with whom he mind-melds. It is almost too late by the time the X-Men realize that they have been duped. At every opportunity, Lucifer tries to thwart them, but in the end the X-Men manage to free Xavier before Lucifer is let loose from the Nameless Dimension.

This novel is a very loose sequel to the comic book *Uncanny X-Men 20*, in which Professor X and the X-Men battle Lucifer, the alien Quistalian. This novel is indispensable for fans of the original team of X-Men.

Golden, Christopher, Rick Leonardi, Terry Austin. *X-Men: Mutant Empire*. New York. Guild America Books, 1997. ISBN: 1568 655436.

Magneto takes over New York for a mutant haven, and the X-Men have to intervene to stop his plans of becoming the dictator of Haven.

This special hardback edition combines all three parts of the *Mutant Empire* saga: *Siege, Sanctuary, and Salvation*.

Golden, Christopher, Rick Leonardi, Terry Austin. *X-Men: Mutant Empire Book 1: Siege*. New York: Berkley Boulevard, 1996. ISBN: 1572971142.

Magneto takes over a covert government installation which is secretly producing mutant-hunting robots, the Sentinels. The X-Men intervene, and are held responsible for the takeover of the installation by the United States. Half of the X-Men team goes into space to save Cyclops's father Corsair. Magneto and his Acolytes—who believe he is their god and savior, and call him Lord Magneto—take over a secret government installation of Sentinels known as Operation Wideawake. Deathbird and Henry Peter Gyrich are the other main villains. Through a back door installed by the Hellfire Club's Black Knight, Magneto, who was once a White Knight in the Hellfire Club, is able to evade the Sentinels' anti-mutant programming, and control them. The Iceman, Storm, Wolverine, Beast, and Bishop are sent to deal with Magneto, and have to fight the U.S. Army as well. Bishop is particularly upset at having to deal with Sentinels in any form, and fears the worst, and Iceman nearly kills the Acolyte Unuscione. Magneto plans to make his own mutant utopia by using the Sentinels to take Manhattan Island. Xavier does some damage control on television by debating Greydon Creed and Senator Kelly on the mutant issue. A subplot has the ship *Starjammer* crashing into a lake. Cyclops's father Corsair and his girlfriend are taken captive by Deathbird, and are to be put to death for treason against the Shi'ar Empire. The remaining Starjammers seek help from X-Men, and a team featuring Archangel, Rogue, Gambit, Jean Grey, and Cyclops is sent into space to rescue Corsair and the other captives. The X-Men and the Starjammers have to fight the Gladiator and the Imperial Guard, who have to obey Deathbird despite the fact that she is insane. Cyclops is taken captive. There are several great battle sequences, including one in which Archangel fights Deathbird. They manage to rescue Corsair, but lose a comrade, and their ship ends up drifting in space.

Golden, Christopher, Rick Leonardi, Terry Austin. *X-Men: Mutant Empire Book 2: Sanctuary*. New York: Boulevard Books, 1996. ISBN: 1572971800.

Magneto has taken over Manhattan Island as his Mutant Empire, and has renamed it Haven. The Sentinels guard the island, only allowing mutants to pass through. No humans are allowed to enter except for Trish Tiby who is allowed access to Magneto for news broadcasts. Magneto adds Toad, the Blob, and Pyro to his team. The *Starjammer* still drifts in space, while they attempt to repair the ship. Archangel is in charge of watching over Gambit who is very ill from a previous battle with Warstar of the Imperial Guard, and when he finally awakens, Gambit thinks the warden is Mr. Sinister. The X-Men infiltrate New York, and fight several former Marauders who decide to band together. Iceman goes off by himself, and gets left for dead by the Acolytes. Professor X is forced to breach his ethics, and infiltrates Henry Gyrich's mind to get the access codes to stop the Sentinels. During a fight with Magneto's cronies, the X-Men inadvertently learn from the Blob where Magneto's headquarters are. When the X-Men minus Wolverine are taken captive, Bishop tries to reason with them by telling them tales of a doomed future to come, by using the Sentinels. The *Starjammer* overcomes faulty equipment, blowups, and problems in space to make it back to Earth, and Iceman is found by a group of anti-mutant humans.

Golden, Christopher, Rick Leonardi, Terry Austin. *X-Men Mutant Empire Book 3: Salvation*. New York: Berkley Boulevard, 1997. ISBN: 0425166406.

Iceman helps free the X-Men from captivity by Magneto. Val Cooper, Gambit, and Archangel reprogram the Alpha Sentinel to attack Magneto. Juggernaut, who is not a mutant but is a career criminal, decides that he is better off siding with the X-Men against Magneto and his Acolytes. The Blob and Juggernaut fight, and Xavier debates Senator Kelly on live television. In addition to talking with Magneto, and trying to convince him of the futility of Haven, Xavier deceives Magneto on the astral plane. Magneto's maxim is that mutants shall control the world "by any means necessary." He sees himself as a savior. The Juggernaut leaves the X-Men to do the fighting against Magneto himself. Magneto defeats all the X-Men except for the original five, and they also are almost killed. Wolverine tries to kill Magneto, and the military attacks Haven. There are many battle sequences in which the X-Men take on Magneto's Acolytes and the mutants who have come to Haven looking for a place to live.

Golden, Christopher, Darich Robertson, *Codename Wolverine*. New York: Berkley Boulevard, 2000. ISBN: 0399144501 (trd). 042 5171116 (pbk).

Members of the former covert-ops group Team X are being kidnapped. It goes back to a certain mission during the Cold War which involved the Black Widow working for the Soviets and in possession of a disk vital to western security. Banshee works for Interpol and has a vendetta against the Widow. Wolverine, Sabretooth, Silver Fox, John Wraith, and Maverick, members of Team X, and Mystique, who is working for Mossad, all are trying to get the disk. Wolverine and Mystique break into S.H.I.E.L.D. and learn that the kidnappings point in the direction of Logan's old associate John Wraith. Mystique and Logan also break into CIA headquarters. The kidnappings involve a government official who has an old vendetta against everyone involved in that particular Cold War op.

This book is written in a then-and-now, past-and-present style, and is more of an espionage thriller than a traditional superhero story. It reveals some surprising personal information about the relationship between Victor Creed and Raven Darkholme and also includes a chronology.

Hughes, Francine, Dana Thompson, Aristides Ruiz, et al. *X-Men: Wolverine Top Secret*. New York: Random House, 1994. ISBN: 0679860045.

When he meets Professor X, Wolverine leaves the Canadian service, and joins the X-Men. Jean Grey becomes the first object of his affections, and he battles Sabretooth on top of the Empire State Building.

This book is based on *Wolverine 47, 49–50*; *Classic X-Men 1*; *Marvel Comics Presents 72–84*; *Giant Size X-Men 1*; *Incredible Hulk 181–182*. It is a young-adult novel that focuses on Wolverine's past, including his years in high school when he takes Silver Fox to the prom, much to the chagrin of his racist classmates. This novel also describes the Weapon X program and Wolverine's first meeting with the Hulk as a Canadian agent.

Hughes, Francine, Dana Thompson, Del Thompson, et al. *X-Men: Wolverine Duty and Honor*. New York: Random House, 1994. ISBN: 0679861548.

Wolverine/Logan goes to Japan and falls in love with Mariko whose father has strong ties to the Japanese crime syndicate. He kills Mariko's father in a duel for honor, and then asks her to marry him, but she calls off the wedding at the last minute. He has a short, romantic tryst with an assassin named Yukio. Mariko unwillingly gets involved with the underworld, and, in an intense climax, Mariko is poisoned by blowfish toxin and asks Logan to kill her.

This is a very tragic love story based on *Classic X-Men 24*; *Wolverine 1–4*; *Uncanny X-Men 172–174*; and *Wolverine 57*.

Kamida, Vicki, Chris Claremont, Louise Simonson, et al. *X-Men: X-Tinction Agenda*. New York: Random House, 1992. ISBN: 0679865675.

Storm, Havok, and Rahne are captured by Cameron Hodge and taken to Genosha. They are turned into mutant slaves for Hodge whose purpose is to defeat the X-Men. The X-Men team, including Cable, goes to rescue their teammates, and they are almost defeated and killed. Havok and Cyclops end up battling each other, brother against brother. Hodge is defeated with the help of the Genegineer, who turns against him.

This young adult novel is based on *X-Men 270–272*; *New Mutants 95–97*; *X-Factor 60–62*; and *X-Men: X-Tinction Agenda*.

Kamida, Vicki, Larry Hama, Fabian Nicieza, et al. *X-Men: Sabretooth Unleashed*. New York: Random House, 1995. ISBN:0679876618.

Sabretooth, who is kidnapped by the Tribune and has a bomb placed inside him, is asked to assassinate Mystique. He searches for Mystique, and finds her and Wolverine in Paris where they demolish a restaurant while having dinner. Sabretooth finds out that his own mutant-hating son Grayson hired him to wipe out his mother, Mystique. When Sabretooth's partner Birdy is killed, he goes in search of mental peace, which leads him to Charles Xavier and the X-Men. There are glimpses of Victor Creed's past and childhood throughout the novel.

This pre-adolescent novel is based on the comics *X-Men Unlimited 3* and *Sabretooth: Death Hunt 1–4*.

Kamida, Vicki, Aristides Ruiz, Dana Thompson, et al. *X-Men: Days of Future Past*. New York: Random House, 1994. ISBN: 0679 861815.

Kitty Pryde of 2026 goes back in time to stop the assassinations of Senator Kelly and Professor X by the Brotherhood of Evil Mutants. With the help of the X-Men, they defeat Mystique, the Blob and the rest of the evil mutants. In 2026, Sentinels rule the Earth and most mutants have been exterminated. Wolverine dies, as does Franklin Richards, Storm, and Colossus.

This young-adult novel is based on Chris Claremont's original story in *Uncanny X-Men 141–142*.

Kamida, Vicki, Dana and Del Thompson, Jeff Parker. *X-Men: Dark Phoenix*. New York: Random House, 1995. ISBN: 0679870725.

Mastermind transforms Jean Grey into Black Queen of the Hellfire Club. After she realizes the Mastermind's deception, she goes berserk, and the Dark Phoenix power is awakened. Eventually, Xavier is able to temporarily control the Phoenix power, but that is only after damage has been done. The X-Men go up against the Imperial Guard to save Jean Grey's life.

This young adult novel is based on *X-Men 100–101*;*Uncanny X-Men 129–137*; and *X-Men: Dark Phoenix Saga*.

Korman, Justine, Dana and Del Thompson, Aristides Ruiz. *X-Men: the Xavier Files*. New York: Random House, 1994. ISBN: 0679861777.

Professor Xavier's personal files on the most famous X-Men, including Beast, Jubilee, Storm, Cyclops, Rogue, Jean Grey, Gambit, and Wolverine, are printed in this young-adult novel.

Lee, Stan, John J. Ordover, Susan Wright, et al. *Five Decades of the X-Men*. New York: iBooks/BP Books, 2002. ISBN: 0743475 011; 0743435001.

This book contains five novellas which cover the X-Men over five decades, starting in the 1960s. The first story is basically a prose reprint of *X-Men 1*. It includes material in which Iceman has a date and reveals his mutant powers to his companion. The second story deals with a scientist who is part of the Secret Empire and is working for a company that is experimenting illegally on mutants. The X-Men are brought in to stop the experimentation, and save the scientist's life. In the third story, Banshee, with the help of Callisto, is on Muir Island, training Havok, Psylocke, Rogue, Dazzler, and Longshot. This story takes place right after the Mutant Massacre storyline, and in it the X-Men have to go up against the demon N'-gari. In the fourth story, a loose sequel to "God Loves Man Kills," Stryker is released from prison, and the Stryker crusade cronies briefly join another anti-mutant group, the Purifiers. The leader of Stryker's group, who fears that his leadership will be usurped now that Stryker is out of jail, wants to make Stryker a martyr. In an ironic twist, Wolverine ends up saving Stryker's life. In the fifth and last story, the X-Men help both a high school teacher and a student come to grips with their emerging mutant powers. All the novellas are quite good, but the book was poorly edited.

Lee, Stan, Joe St. Pierre, Eluki Bes Shahar, et al. *The Ultimate X-Men*. New York: Byron Preiss Multimedia Boulevard Books, 1996. ISBN: 1572972173.

Warren "Angel" Worthington III gives an interview for the show *Viewpoints* in which he discusses everything from being in the Champions and X-factor, to the violent injury he received on his wings. The original X-Men team helps a mutant on the run. Wolverine meets a lady in the woods. Gambit goes back to New Orleans where someone is killing children and turning them into zombies. Iceman gets picked for jury duty on a case involving a mutant and the Friends of Humanity. Rogue has a fantasy about being without her powers. The Acolytes threaten to use a very powerful bomb against the United States, and Storm, Logan, and the Beast have to find the bomb before it is detonated. Logan and Jean Grey go up against a serial killer who is holding a symbiotic mutant hostage. Jubilee and Storm have to fight a dangerous, mathemagical creature.

This is a collection of short stories detailing the day-to-day life of the X-Men.

Lee, Stan, Mike Zeck, Brian K. Vaughn, et al. *X-Men: Legends*. New York: Berkley Boulevard, 2000. ISBN: 0425170829.

Warren Worthington, the Angel, is in high school when his mutant powers first appear. His best friend, who is also a mutant, is bloodthirsty and must eat human flesh (this takes place before *X-Men 1*). Carol Danvers interviews the Beast, Hank McCoy, for *Now* magazine, while he is still a member of the Avengers. After his death, Jean Grey reads the Changling's diary, written when he was posing as Professor X. Jamie Madrox, the Multiple Man, briefly lives with the X-Men, but refuses to accept Professor X's invitation to join. (This takes place between *Giant Size Fantastic Four 4* and *Giant Size X-Men 1*.) Wolverine breaks into Misty Knight and Jean Grey's apartment (after *Iron Fist 15*). Kitty Pryde falls for an ice-skating professional who gets booted out of the league for being a mutant, and saves his life (shortly after *X-Men Vol. 2: 3*). Other characters featured include Banshee, Gambit, Rogue, Callisto, Colossus, and Nightcrawler.

This book contains thirteen short stories that take place during various periods of X-Men history, from the earliest years up to the present. The story about Changling's diary occurs between *X-Men 43* and *X-Men 66*. The book also contains a continuity guide.

Lobdell, Scott, Elliot S. Maggin, Tom Grummett, et al. *Generation X*. New York: Boulevard, 1997. ISBN: 1572972238.

Emma "White Queen" Frost feels guilt over the massacre of teenage mutants who were under her supervision. She thinks the guilt is manifesting itself as ghosts of her former students who threaten the current team. The new mutant team member Statis is dying from the Legacy virus, and Dr. Henry McCoy, the Beast, is brought in to treat him. The demon, D'Spayre, who is the cause of the strange manifestations of the past, takes over the minds of the students and headmasters, and Chamber plays a central role in defeating him. Skin and Synch go into Boston in search of girls and good times, and end up at a Friends of Humanity meeting. Penance makes brief appearances throughout.

This, the first of the Generation X novels by Scott Lobdell, is highly recommended.

Lyons, Steve, Nick Choles. *X-Men: Legacy Quest Book 2*. New York: BP Books, 2003. ISBN: 0743474449; 0743452437.

The Black Queen, Selene, casts a spell that puts the X-Men a year into the future. She has the Legacy Virus cure taken from Hank McCoy's blood. Sebastian Shaw asks Storm to become a member of Hellfire Club. Shaw kills a future version of himself, and Selene captures New York. She aligns herself with the demon Blackheart, and gives the Legacy Virus cure to those she has enslaved. The X-Men eventually prevail against Selene, and Wolverine kills her. That makes that future irrelevant, and the X-Men are transported back to the present, where they defeat Selene and save McCoy's life.

The narrative goes from the future to the present, alternating between chapters, which makes the book

very interesting, but also hard to follow at times. *Publishers Weekly* called the book a "solid cliffhanger."

Lyons, Steve, Nick Choles. *X-Men: Legacy Quest Book 3*. New York: BP Books, 2003. ISBN: 0743475194; 0743452666.

Both Sebastian Shaw and Magneto are planning something sinister for the Winter Solstice. Magneto plans to have the Hellfire Club release the Legacy Virus into the air, thus infecting the whole world. Iceman, Rogue, Nightcrawler, and Wolverine infiltrate Genosha, but are captured. Magneto is considered a savior and deity, and a religion springs up around him. When Storm, Beast, Phoenix and Cyclops go to the Australian branch of the Hellfire Club to find out what Shaw is planning, they also are captured. Eventually, after several battles, both X-Men teams, with Shaw in tow, confront Magneto in Genosha. Shaw eventually gets his hands on the cure for the Legacy virus, and it is destroyed. Iceman makes friends with a human, and takes part in a violent raid on mutants. There also are appearances by Emma Frost and Hellstrom.

Lyons, Steve, Nick Choles. *X-Men: Legacy Quest Trilogy*. New York: iBooks, 2003. ISBN: 0739437356.

This hardback book contains more than six hundred pages of reprints from the three-volume *Legacy Quest* story. The author notes that this storyline takes place after events recounted in the *New-Men 87* comic book.

Lyons, Steve, Jordan Raskin. *X-Men Legacy Quest Book 1*. New York: BP Books, 2003. ISBN: 0743458486; 074344468X.

Henry McCoy, the Beast, is working on a cure for the Legacy Virus, the mutant-killing disease. He surrenders himself to the Hellfire Club, and finds out that Sebastian Shaw, the mutant Black King, has kidnapped Moria McTaggert and several scientists whom Shaw infected with the Legacy virus. McCoy infects himself with the virus in order to test the cure. When the X-Men break into the Hellfire Club's island, they are taken prisoner. Jean Grey has an intense mind battle with Cyclops's ex-wife, Madeline Pryor. Cyclops is almost killed by Fitzroy. Shaw and the X-Men finally come to an uneasy truce, and work together to find the cure.

Mantell, Paul, Avery Hart, Chris Claremont, et al. *X-Men: The Brood*. New York: Random House, 1994. ISBN: 0679865683.

The X-Men battle the alien Brood who implants Brood embryos inside the X-Men's bodies. Wolverine's healing factor destroys the embryo, but the other X-Men are not so lucky. The White Queen, Wolverine, and Storm help destroy the Brood Queen, and free the Brood's captive, the Acanti.

This young-adult novel is based on *Uncanny X-Men 154–157, 162–166*.

Mantell, Paul, Avery Hart, Steve Lightle, et al. *X-Men: Cyclops and Phoenix*. New York: Random House, 1995. ISBN: 0679876596.

Mother Askani brings Jean Grey and Scott Summers two thousand years into the future. Askani, actually their daughter Rachel Summers, brings them forward to take care of Nathan Dayspring who is actually Cyclops's son. Nathan will eventually grow up to be Cable. In this future, Apocalypse has become the dictator who enslaves and destroys, while mutants are at the top of the social and political chain. Nathan's clone Stryfe, whose evil nature is apparent, is being groomed by Apocalypse to be used as his vessel. Apocalypse is burning out the body in which he currently resides. Nathan, Cyclops, and the Phoenix, Jean Grey, help overthrow and destroy Apocalypse.

This young-adult novel is based on *The Adventures of Cyclops and Phoenix 1–4*.

Mantell, Paul, Avery Hart, Steve Lightle, et al. *X-Men: Phalanx Covenant*. New York: Random House, 1995. ISBN: 0679871608.

The X-Men and the New Mutants tangle with the techno-organic alien Phalanx. Phalanx is trying to learn how to assimilate mutants like it does non-mutant humans. When numerous X-Men are captured, Banshee, the White Queen, and Sabretooth form an uneasy alliance to find and save the X-Men. Cyclops, Cable, Jean Grey, and Wolverine are left to destroy the Phalanx, and rescue their teammates. Numerous New Mutants also are kidnapped, and Muir Island is blown up.

This novel is based on *Uncanny X-Men 312–313, 316–317*; *X-Men 36–38*; *X-Factor 106*; *Excalibur 82*; *Cable 16*; and *Wolverine 85*.

Mantell, Paul, Avery Hart, Jeff Parker, et al. *X-Men Kidnapped in the Catacombs*. New York: Random House, 1995. ISBN: 0679870717.

Kitty Pryde asks Professor Xavier to allow her to stay in the X-Men, rather than be on the New Mutants team. Storm's old nemesis Callisto kidnaps Colossus. Callisto lures Storm and the X-Men to the Morlocks, so there can be a rematch between Callisto and Storm for control of the Morlocks. Kitty Pryde is touched by plague and almost dies. Her new pet, Lockheed, a small dragon, becomes a valued member of the group.

This young-adult novel is based on *Uncanny X-Men 168–176*; *Uncanny X-Men 260–263*; and *X-Men From the Ashes*.

Mantell, Paul, Avery Hart, Dana Thompson, et al. *X-Men in the Savage Land*. New York: Bullseye/Random House, 1994. ISBN: 0679867007.

The X-Men go to the Savage Land and help Ka-Zar defeat Sauron and his followers. Karl Lykos's girlfriend enlists the aid of Archangel to help find Lykos, who is Sauron. Brainchild develops a machine that can devolve mutants into lower life forms. The Archangel gets turned into an amphibious monster, as do some of the other X-Men.

This young-adult novel is adapted from a story by Chris Claremont in *Marvel Fanfare 1–4* and *X-Men in the Savage Land*.

Mantell, Paul, Avery Hart, Dana Thompson, et al. *X-Men: Second Genesis*. New York: Random House, 1994. ISBN: 0679860126.

The original X-Men are prisoners on a mutant island, and Professor X puts together a new team of X-Men with Wolverine, Nightcrawler, Storm, Thunderbird, Colossus, Banshee, and Sunfire. Cyclops goes with the new X-Men to the island of Krakoa, to help rescue his teammates. The island itself is alive and wants them all as prisoners.

This short novel is based on *Giant Sized X-Men 1*, by Len Wein. It is a nice adaptation of the original comic, and is a real page-turner.

Mantell, Paul, Avery Hart, John Synder. *X-Men: Gambit: Unfinished Business*. New York: Random House, 1996. ISBN: 0679873198.

Apparently this novel, which features Gambit's quest to save his wife's life, was never published. However the publisher went so far as to give the title an ISBN and a color cover.

Nocenti, Ann, Leonardo Manco. *X-Men: Prisoner X*. New York: Berkley Boulevard, 1998. ISBN: 0425164934.

Longshot is unjustly imprisoned in an orbiting facility known as Ultramax, and Rogue goes undercover to try to liberate him. The Beast and Wolverine discover that a new virtual-reality game is linked to the disappearance of teenagers, and that the other-dimensional psycho Mojo is behind both the game and the prison. The X-Men have to stop him in his quest for unorthodox entertainment. When Longshot is scheduled to be executed on live television, Gambit gets himself arrested so that he can be with Rogue who used to be in love with Longshot; Gambit and Longshot get into a fight. This virtual-reality game, which has Spiral's insignia on it, is causing kids to commit suicide. When Jean Grey also appears in the prison after playing the game, Mojo tries to get her to go along with his plans, almost to the point of flirting with her. The Warden of Ultramax is a robot that was created by Mojo. All the while, a group of prisoners, including Longshot's old lover Ricochet Rita, plan a prison revolt and break out. The X-Men help free the prisoners and expose the abuses.

Roman, Steven A., Mark Buckingham. *X-Men: The Chaos Engine Trilogy*. New York: BP books, 2004. ISBN: 0743497740. Reprints *X-Men: The Chaos Engine Trilogy 1–3*.

This is a paperback collection of the three *Chaos Engine* books: *Doom, Magneto,* and *Red Skull.*

Roman, Steven A., Mark Buckingham. *X-Men: Dr. Doom: Chaos Engine Trilogy, Book 1.* New York: Berkley Boulevard, 2000. ISBN: 0743400194 (trd); 0743434838 (pbk).

After helping save the Omniverse, the X-Men return to Earth and find that Dr. Doom is ruling as a tyrant. Many of the X-Men's super-powered friends have even aligned themselves with Doom who is using the Cosmic Cube to reshape reality so that he is the sole sovereign. Storm is Doom's wife. The X-Men free Carol Danvers from a concentration camp, but are taken captive. The Gambit is infected with a techno-organic virus and dies. Magneto seeks to overthrow the tyrant and shape the world for Homo Superior. Magneto's minions help free the X-Men, who then align themselves with Magneto, and attempt to oust Doom. Psylocke sings at a huge ball given in honor of Victor Von Doom which the X-Men and Magneto's brotherhood crash. The Angel is killed, and Psylocke is swept away. The X-Men destroy Doom, who turns out to be a Doombot. The real Doom is an old man who needs Psylocke to help put the rest of his plans in motion. In an attempt to stop Doom from doing more damage, the X-Men try to get the Cosmic Cube, which drains the life force from anyone who uses it, and try to set the Universe right. However, they are too late, and Magneto gets the Cube.

Roman, Steven A., Mark Buckingham. *X-Men: Magneto: The Chaos Engine Trilogy Book 2.* New York: BP Books, 2002. ISBN: 074340 0232.

Magneto, who has the Cosmic Cube, reshapes the Earth with Homo Superior as the masters, and with mutants living side by side with humans. His version of the world is similar to the one for which Professor X had always hoped. Professor Xavier and Psylocke are not affected by the reality-shifting powers of the Cube, and when they come to Earth to try and stop Magneto, the X-Men are against them. Professor X is taken captive by Magneto. The Cube's powers are draining the life out of Magneto, and he agrees to give it to the Professor if the Professor will agree to save the life of Magneto's daughter. In the Omniverse, Dr. Doom is taken captive and split into two versions. The younger version escapes, kills the older version, and helps free the evil Satyrnin. Both of them seek to overthrow Roma the Controller who turns out to be the Red Skull and continues to keep a watchful eye on the Cube and those who are trying to master it, and takes the Cube away from Professor X. Psylocke rekindles a romance with the fake Warren Worthington. While on television, the Angel and Jean Grey discuss Magneto's roots as a Jewish survivor of the Auschwitz camp during World War II.

Roman, Stephen A., Mark Buckingham. *X-Men: Red Skull: The Chaos Engine Trilogy, Book 3.* New York: BP Books, 2003. ISBN: 0743452801 (trd); 0743479580 (pbk).

Dr. Doom has taken over Omniverse, and it is up to Psylocke and Angel to help Roma get her throne back. The Red Skull continues Hitler's "Thousand-Year Reich" paradise, in which he is in complete command, and mutants, Jews and others are put into concentration camps. Steve Rogers, Captain America, works at one. Magneto, who is imprisoned in a camp, is saved by Wolverine. When the Red Skull took the Cube from Magneto, he was very distressed that a Jew should have such power. Jean Grey starts to see beyond the Skull's facade, and is captured. The Skull is told about a so-called mutant conspiracy to oust him. It turns out that each world created by the Cube actually has a parallel universe. When the Red Skull gets greedy and wants the power of the Omniverse, he ends up being thrown into a vortex and Psylocke gets the Cube. The Red Skull's assistant sacrifices himself in order to bring reality back. Professor X asks Roma to spare Dr. Doom's life.

This is the final part of the *Chaos Engine* story in which the Red Skull took control of the Cosmic Cube and reshaped the world in his image. The book contains a detailed origin story of the Red Skull, and is the best of the three novels in the trilogy.

Rusch, Kristine Kathryn, Dean Wesley Smith, et al. *X-Men.* New York: Del Rey, 2000. ISBN: 0345440951.

Magneto seeks to turn all humans into mutants by using a machine. The mutant he wants is Rogue, but at first everyone thinks he wants Logan, Wolverine. When Wolverine meets the X-Men, he is less than impressed, but eventually he succumbs to being a team player. At an event of world leaders, Magneto seeks to unleash the mutant change above the Statue of Liberty. The X-Men have to stop Mystique, Toad, and Sabretooth from allowing Magneto's plan to come to fruition. Logan calls Professor X, Chuck, and the Senate's proposed Mutant Registration Act is defeated. Professor X tells Logan a story about a teacher who was going to fail him, just because the teacher did not like him. Eric Lehnsherr, Magneto, was the first mutant Professor X met.

This book is based on the movie that was written by Christopher McQuarrie and Ed Soloman. It is the novelization of the hit movie that set the stage for the X-Men on film. There is a great deal more character development in this novel than in the film, including information about Magneto's time in the death camps; Rogue's problems at school once her power develops; the first time Cyclops loses control of his eyes; and Storm's problems when her power manifests itself, and she taunts children. The book also has bit parts for Kitty Pryde and Jubilee.

Shahar, Eluki Bes, Roger Cruz, *X-Men: Smoke and Mirrors.* New York: Boulevard Books, 1997. ISBN: 1572972912 (trd); 0425171256 (pbk).

The X-Men try to stop the Emergency Intervention Bill which would require all mutants to be "cured" of their mutant DNA and powers by the Center for

Genetic Improvement (CGI). Mister Sinister poses as the scientist who created this miracle cure which has a 50% fatality rate. Several teenage mutants are kidnapped by the Ohio Mutant Conspiracy, and are taken to the CGI. Wolverine finds out about Project Trapdoor, which turns ordinary humans into mutant-fighting machines. Mantrap, who makes Wolverine seem tame, was created by this group. Because she was created to be the "perfect predator," Mantrap's bloodlust is extreme. Professor X goes to Washington to try to convince the senator who sponsored the bill to reconsider the consequences. Gambit is the first X-Man to realize that Sinister is behind this project. Rogue allows herself to be taken captive by Sinister's henchmen, and when she goes to the one of the work sites, it reminds her of the *Lord of the Rings'* land of Mordor. The X-Men finally engage Sinister, but he gets away and kills Mantrap. However, they do stop the Emergency Intervention Bill from passing.

This novel reads more like a traditional thriller.

Smeds, David, Max Douglas, *X-Men: Law of the Jungle*. New York: Berkley Boulevard, 1998. ISBN: 0425164861.

Sauron and his mutants are causing all kinds of problems for Ka-Zar, Shanna, and the people of the Savage Land. Sauron is more powerful and less human than in times past. Wolverine wants to kill Sauron, much to Storm's dismay. The X-Men team of Storm, Cannonball, Archangel, Wolverine, the Beast, Iceman, and Psylocke go to help Ka-Zar; Ka-Zar and Psylocke flirt with each other, much to Shanna's disapproval. Lupo, the mutant, is captured. Sauron captures Ka-Zar and all of the X-Men except for the Beast, and is using their life energies to feed himself. Several of the X-Men, including Wolverine and Archangel, have to go through several humbling experiences at Sauron's hands. With the help of Zabu, the Beast is able to break into Sauron's stronghold using mammoths. When Sauron lands in a pool of water, he is ripped apart by carnivorous animals, and is seemingly killed.

This novel contains material related to the history of Sauron and various dealings that the X-Men, including the original X-Men, have had with him over the years. Through Psylocke, we also learn a great deal about Lupo's past.

Smith, Dean Wesley, Chuck Wojtkiewicz. *X-Men: Jewels of Cyttorak*. New York: Boulevard, 1997. ISBN: 1572973293.

Another gem, an emerald that contains the power of Cyttorak, is discovered. This gem has been split into three parts. One person is using the first part to live for a hundred years; another person is using the second part to become a crime lord in New Orleans; and a third individual wants the third part so that he can be like the Juggernaut, Cain Marko. When Robert Service taps into the power of the emerald, the Juggernaut starts to feel pain. Theoretically, if Cain's ruby of Cyttorak is combined with the complete emerald, the individual who has the combined gem will become even more powerful, and the demon Cyttorak could actually inhabit that individual. Because Juggernaut starts to feel the draw of the other stones, thus the pain, he is drawn to where the three pieces are. Robert Service starts on his journey as well, and he kills the hundred-year-old man. Professor X sends the X-Men to help Cain get to his destinations, so that he will stop tearing up the countryside. Gambit sees his wife Bella Donna kill the New Orleans crime lord, who attempts to make a truce with the Assassins' Guild. When Service ends up with all three parts, and becomes like the Juggernaut, he defeats the X-Men. But when he fights Juggernaut, they are at a standstill. The powers of the stones cancel each other out, and, eventually, Bishop uses his energy powers to destroy the emerald.

This is a fun, fast read. This book leads right into the novel *Spider-Man Emerald Mystery* in which one of the stones is sent to a New York alley.

York, J. Steven, Mark Buckingham, *Generation X: Crossroads*. New York: Berkley Boulevard, 1998. ISBN: 0425166317.

Banshee, White Queen, Husk, Chamber, Jubilee, Skin, Synch, and M go on a cross-country trip in Winnebagos. The Gen X teens go on a road trip with Emma Frost, the White Queen, and Sean Cassidy, the Banshee. They encounter all kinds of terrorist activity and anti-mutant sentiment throughout their journey. The kids foil the first attack, which is in the Seattle airport. They meet up with another group of mutant teens who are part of the M.O.N.S.T.E.R., Mutants Only Need Sympathy Tolerance and Equal Rights, group, which Henry McCoy, the Beast, helped start. The former Extripate for Genosha has one of his cronies spy on the mutant teens, and is supplying the terrorists with weapons. He is a program director for an anti-mutant radio show: *The Walt Norman Show*. When Page Guthrie, Husk, calls in to the show, its ratings go through the roof. The Extripate plans to frame Page when she comes to the show, to pin on her the death of Walt Norman, and he plans to use Mandroids to carry out his plan. At Mount Rushmore, Generation X foils another terrorist plot. Although they try to keep their mutant profile low, along the way they do expose themselves as mutants to the public. They meet the mutant-loving Genogoths for the first time. Synch admits he is an Oprah fan.

This book leads right into the *Generation X: Genogoths* novel (see below). It contains a novel chronology and sound bites from radio news. It is highly recommended.

York, J. Steven, Mark Buckingham. *Generation X: Genogoths*. New York: Berkley Boulevard, 2000. ISBN: 0425171434.

Young mutants are kidnapped by a secret government agency to be brainwashed and turned into mutant-hunting trackers. Generation X tries to find them and rescue them. The Genogoths, a secret group of regular humans dedicated to protecting mutants, tries to foil Generation X's rescue attempts in order to keep their group a secret. When one their charges, Catfish, is kidnapped, they team up with Generation X to rescue the captured mutants. Chamber also is kidnapped for a short time.

Preceding each chapter of this novel is a quote from Charles Darwin on some facet of evolution. The book also contains a Marvel novel chronology. This is the sequel to the *Crossroads* novel, and it is one of the more interesting Marvel novels.

Team-Ups

Askegren Pierce, Mark Bagley, Jeff Albrecht. *The Avengers and the Thunderbolts*. New York: Berkley Boulevard, 1999. ISBN: 042 5166759.

Baron Zemo forms an alliance with Hydra's Baron Strucker, and the Avengers and Thunderbolts must stop them from unleashing a terrible bomb. Vision and Atlas are taken prisoner, and are studied by Techno who also captures Wonder Man for a brief period of time. Hawkeye is now the leader of the Thunderbolts. Captain America agrees to become a prisoner in place of Atlas and the Vision, but Zemo betrays them. While working for Hydra, Techno creates an elite force of fighting soldiers known as the Blitz. Zemo and Strucker sever their alliance, and Zemo supposedly kills Strucker.

This book has a detailed chronology of all the Marvel novels and short stories.

Askegren, Pierce, Eric Fein, Steven Butler. *Spider-Man & Fantastic Four: Wreckage (Doom's Day Book 3)*. New York: Boulevard Books, 1997. ISBN: 1572973110.

Dr. Doom kidnaps Dr. Octopus to help him design his Doom's Day device. By using power taken from the Negative Zone, Doom plans to usher in his idea of utopia, with him as leader. Spider-Man, the Fantastic Four, and S.A.F.E. band together to stop him. Doom scares Doc Ock by giving him one of the bombs that Ock was going to use to destroy Latveria. Then Doom sends his robots out to cause havoc so that the Fantastic Four will leave their headquarters, and Doom and Ock can break into it. Ock betrays Doom by sending him to the Negative Zone, but Doom breaks free and is angry with Ock. The New York police are upset with Sean Morgan and S.A.F.E., because Morgan uses the police as "Spidey's answering service" when he is looking for Spider-Man. Doom takes over the World Trade Center, and captures and tortures Reed Richards who tries to appeal to Doom's ego by pointing out that Doom's accomplishments are built upon the work of others, that there are no original thoughts in his scientific devices. The Thing clobbers Doom, and Mary Jane gives Spidey an "I survived Doom's Day" shirt.

See the novel *Octopus Agenda*, by Diane Duane, et al. for more information about Dr. Ock's plans to destroy Latveria. This book includes a chronology.

Askegren, Pierce, Danny Fingeroth, Steven Butler. *Spider-Man & Iron Man: Sabotage (Doom's Day Book 2)*. New York: Berkley Boulevard/BPMC, 1997. ISBN: 0425169 073.

Tony Stark and his scientists have created a potentially unlimited source of cheap energy called the Infinity Engine. The Infinity Engine is hailed as proof of Albert Einstein's unified field theory. Stark hires Peter Parker to help the scientists who worked on the Infinity Engine, because Hydra and A.I.M. both want to commandeer the engine and turn it into a weapon. Stark sends the Infinity Engine to his orbiting space station Ad Astra, and Baron Strucker sends his Hydra agents to kill the scientists and steal the schematics for the engine. Baron Strucker televises demands for money and to be made emperor of the world. When Hydra takes over the space station and a Dreadnought destroys a version of Iron Man, Spider-Man and Iron Man team up with S.A.F.E. to take the station back. Meanwhile, Dr. Doom had unknowingly placed agents in both Hydra and A.I.M. the latter also tries to take over the station. Dr. Doom wants the Engine for his own nefarious purposes.

This is the second volume in the Spider-Man Team-Up Doom's Day series.

Cox, Greg, George Perez, Julie Bell. *X-Men and Avengers: Lost and Found (Gamma Quest Book 1)*. New York: Berkley Boulevard, 1999. ISBN: 0425169731.

The Scarlet Witch, Wolverine, and Rogue are kidnapped. A bizarre version of the X-Men attack S.H.I.E.L.D.'s Helicarrier, and, at the sites of all the disappearances, traces of gamma radiation is found. The X-Men and the Avengers look for Bruce Banner to help them in the search for their comrades. However, before they can get to Banner, they have to deal with the Hulk who will have none of it, and fights both the X-Men and the Avengers in a pulse-pounding battle at the Canadian border. The Hulk tears an arm off of the Vision. Meanwhile, in captivity, Rogue, Wolverine, and the Scarlet Witch undergo terrible torture, and Rogue is forced to absorb Wolverine, almost to the point of death. The Beast infiltrates the New York Police Department to get evidence about Rogue's kidnapping. Iron Man ends up falling down the Niagara Falls, and Storm, Beast, and Cyclops are defeated by the Brood. Because the Scarlet Witch is taken prisoner by puppets, the Puppet Master is implicated in her kidnapping.

Cox, Greg, George Perez, Julie Bell. *X-Men and Avengers: Search and Rescue (Gamma Quest Book 2).* New York: Berkley Boulevard, 1999. ISBN: 0425169898.

The Beast irons out a truce with the X-Men, Avengers, and the Hulk. The X-Men and Avengers team up to rescue Rogue and the Scarlet Witch. With the Hulk's help, they learn that their foe is the Leader, who has kidnapped their colleagues. The Leader is using the gamma Sentinels in the form of Hulk, Abomination, Harpy, and Doc Samson, with whom the heroes have to contend. The Hulk goes to Muir Island with Iron Man, Storm, and a fake Wolverine, to rescue Moria, Iceman and Nightcrawler; Captain America and Cyclops go to the Leader's underground society. Wolverine, Scarlet Witch, and Rogue manage to escape the Leader, only to be beaten by his robotic humanoids. The captives find that they are not on Earth. After a brawl, Wolverine lets the fake Hulk go.

Cox, Greg, George Perez, Julie Bell. *X-Men and the Avengers: Friend or Foe? (Gamma Quest Book 3).* New York: Berkley Boulevard, 2000. ISBN: 0425170381.

The Avengers, X-Men, and the Hulk join forces against the Leader, and trace him to his base on the moon. Captain America gets the Hulk to change back into Banner, in order to fit into the quinjet carrying the X-Men and the Avengers to the moon. The Leader brainwashes Rogue, Wolverine, and the Scarlet Witch into fighting for him. The Leader is able to harness the powers of the other superheroes, giving the Skrull, who is posing as Wolverine, temporary additional powers. Hank McCoy, the Beast, tries to defeat the Super Skrull by baiting him with "Kree propaganda," and the Super Skrull turns on the Leader in an unsuccessful attempt to kill him. Wolverine is ordered to kill Banner, but something within him stops him from doing it, and he finally breaks free from the Leader's control. The Leader was able to control Rogue's parasitic powers, but once freed from his control, she cannot remember how he did it.

DeFalco, Tom, Adam-Troy Castro, Tom Grummett, et al. *X-Men and Spider-Man: Time's Arrow Book Two: The Present.* New York: Berkley Boulevard, 1998. ISBN: 0425164152.

Bishop and Spider-Man are trapped in the present time stream in an alternative world. In this world, the X-Men are the police who bring down and arrest people with super powers, Sponkies. In this "mirror Universe," Uncle Ben is still alive and well, and Peter Parker confronts another version of himself. Bishop finally begins to understand Spider-Man's motivations, and Magneto is one of the good guys, leading a breakout of this world's superpower against the

X-Men, with Cable's alternative wife in tow. Kang has sent out several more time arrows to wreak havoc on present reality, and various X-Men are sent out to destroy the time arrows in the present. Actually, Kang wants the X-Men to destroy the arrows. The Beast and Rhino have words, and the Beast suggests that the Rhino call himself the "Hippo," and the Wrecking Crew actually turn out to be wimps. Wolverine gets fried by Electro.

Some of the other characters featured in this novel include Titana, Razorback, and Speedball. There are so many different versions of the same characters in this book that it is sometimes hard to keep everyone straight.

DeFalco, Tom, Jason Henderson, Tom Grummett, et al. *X-Men and Spider-Man: Time's Arrow Book One: The Past.* New York: Berkely Boulevard, 1998. ISBN: 0425164527.

Spider-Man finds an old picture of himself, Bishop, and the Two-Gun Kid at an exhibit, and goes to the X-Men to investigate. Cable makes the unsettling discovery that at the influential Time Displacement Core, Kang has shot four "time arrows" into the past, an event that could destroy dozens of timelines. Spider-Man teams up with Bishop to go back to the old West where they meet Two-Gun Kid who initially thinks they are criminals; Gambit and Iceman go back to the 1940s, and meet the Human Torch and Toro. Cable and Storm go back to medieval times, and meet with the original Black Knight. Beast and Wolverine go so far back in time that they encounter Moon Boy and Devil Dinosaur. Cable also encounters a living version of his wife Aliya from a different time stream. By destroying all the time arrows, they actually are doing what Kang wants. Kang is still searching for a different version of his love that is still alive in another time stream.

DeFalco, Tom, Eluki Bes Shahar, Tom Grummett, et al. *X-Men and Spider-Man: Time's Arrow Book Three: The Future.* New York: Berkley Boulevard, 1998. ISBN: 0425165000.

In order to confront Kang, the X-Men and Spider-Man must travel to alternate futures. In 2020, Spider-Man does battle with his grown-up daughter May Parker/Spider-Girl, and eventually reveals to her that he is her father from an alternate timeline. The X-Men of 1998 fight the X-Men of 2099, and Cyclops and Jean Grey meet the granddaughter they never had. Wolverine, Bishop, and Iceman fight against Guardians of the Galaxy, and then team up against bizarre, alien parasites that have acid blood. Spidey and Cable team up with the 2020 Midnight Wreckers. Machine Man fights against Iron Man 2020 and Spider-Girl, and as he encounters the former Avenger, the Beast, Kang laments the fact that he is always foiled by the Avengers. He finally finds the only version of his love Ravonna in the universe, but as though one cannot fight the fates, he inadvertently kills her for the second time, and is put in jail. The X-Men end up in Kang's limbo. Cable's love, Aliya, sacrifices herself to save the universe. There is an obscure mention of Batman.

Fingeroth, Danny, Eric Fein, Steven Butler. *Spider-Man and the Incredible Hulk: Rampage (Doom's Day Book 1)*. New York: Berkley Boulevard, 1996. ISBN: 0425170608, 1572 971649.

Secret agent Burton Hildebrandt, who wants to create an army of Hulk clones, kidnaps Bruce Banner and his wife. When his proto–Hulks are released in New York, Spider-Man is horrified to find out that his friend Flash Thompson is one of the Hulk clones. Dr. Doom and the Black Cat also play a role in the drama. Using a gamma amplifier, Dr. Doom conducts experiments on gamma radiation to create his own version of the Hulk, and almost kills Hildebrandt, his scientist. Hildebrandt joins the ranks of Hydra; Hydra and A.I.M. work together to create their own version of the Hulk. They kidnap Bruce Banner, his wife Betty, and fourteen humans to use as guinea pigs, one of whom is Flash Thompson. While keeping the real Hulk in a coma, they drain the radiation from Banner and transfer it to the human subjects. The fake Hulks become filled with burning, green rage, and spontaneously combust—the experiment is not successful. Hydra invades Doom's Latveria, and because Flash Thompson is involved, both Spider-Man and the Black Cat get involved. They end up working with S.A.F.E. to find Hydra's experimental installation. The Hulk is obviously very upset that his wife was taken hostage, and goes on a rampage. He agrees to work with Spider-Man and S.A.F.E. to track down the other fake Hulks and find his wife. In one bizarre instance, the Hulk reverts back to Bruce Banner, but retains the mindless Hulk's personality. Dr. Doom actually takes off his mask, and reveals his face to Hildebrandt, whom he then kills.

Freidman, Michael Jan. *X-Men and Star Trek: The Next Generation: Planet X*. New York: Pocket Books, 1998. ISBN: 0671019163.

The *Enterprise* is dispatched to the planet Xhaldia. The inhabitants of Xhaldia are mutating into strange creatures with amazing powers. The X-Men, featuring Storm, Wolverine, Colossus, Nightcrawler, Archangel, Shadowcat, and Banshee, come from another reality to help stop hostile aliens, Draa'kon, from kidnapping the people of Xhaldia. The Draa'kon plan to put the people of Zhaldia into an army to fight against the Federation. Worf comes back from DS9, and is congratulated on his marriage. On the starbase where the X-Men first materialize, Wolverine gets into trouble and is thrown in the brig. Wolverine and Worf form a special friendship and go to the holodeck to do battle against the aliens and the X-Men's enemies, including the Blob, Unus, Sabretooth, and Juggernaut. On a challenge from Guinan, Wolverine drinks prune juice for the first time. Captain Picard is angry at Archangel for flying around the *Enterprise*, and when Picard meets a holodeck version of Professor X, they have a nice, philosophical conversation.

This novel is a sequel to the comic book *Star Trek/X-Men Second Contact*, and is an interesting combination of two pop culture icons. It also is available as an e-book.

Friedman, Michael Jan, and George Perez. *Fantastic Four: Redemption of the Silver Surfer*. New York: Boulevard Books, 1998. ISBN: ISBN: 039914269X (trd); 0425164896 (pbk).

Mr. Fantastic, the Thing, and the Human Torch are tricked by their nemesis Blastaar into going into the Negative Zone. Blastaar takes the heroes to his home planet, and asks for their help to fight the destroyer of worlds, Prodigion. Prodigion is the opposite of Galactus who drains worlds of life; he puts *too much* life into a planet. The planets that get his seed become overpopulated and overrun with life. The Invisible Girl enlists the aid of the Silver Surfer to find and rescue her teammates, and the Surfer goes into the Negative Zone for the first time, where he falls in love with one of Prodigion's heralds. He is tricked into helping Prodigion find a planet. Eventually the Fantastic Four, the Surfer, and Blastaar make a loose alliance to stop Prodigion from doing any more damage. Annihilus makes a cameo appearance.

This is a nice story that utilizes one of Marvel's underrated heroes, the Silver Surfer.

Kupperberg, Paul, Len Wein, Marv Wolfman. *Hulk & Spider-Man: Murdermoon*. New York: Pocket Books, 1979. ISBN: 0671820 94X.

America's "spy in the sky" satellite has fallen out of orbit, and is headed toward Earth. An underground criminal intelligence organization has commandeered the satellite with the help of the Hulk, who is under mind control. The group wants to use this satellite's technology to put another satellite into orbit, in order to monitor all intelligence information across the globe. They plan to sell the information to the highest bidder, and it is up to Spider-Man and the Hulk to foil their plans. The Hulk is controlled through a small receiver that the greedy scientists created, and which is in his ear. Spidey inadvertently gets involved when he tries to stop a robbery, and in a bizarre turn of events, Bruce Banner becomes a soda jerk for a day.

This novel reads more like a spy thriller than a superhero action story. It was the last novel produced in the Marvel Novel series (*Marvel Novel Series 11*)

Rucka, Greg, Yoshitaka Amano. *Elektra and Wolverine: The Redeemer*. New York: Marvel, 2002. ISBN: 0785109110. Reprints *Elektra and Wolverine: The Redeemer 1–3*.

Elektra is hired to kill a scientist. The scientist's daughter Avery witnesses the murder, and a former Weapon X boss hires Wolverine as Avery's bodyguard.

However, Elektra ends up kidnapping Avery from him, and puts two *sais* straight through Wolverine's chest. Avery has a power-healing factor similar to Wolverine's, and the government wants her for experiments. Elektra and Avery form a unique bond and friendship, and Wolverine and Elektra eventually team up to thwart the plans of the secret government men.

The book includes an interview with Greg Rucka and an endorsement by author Brad Meltzer. This is a beautiful, deluxe, hardcover novel, wonderfully written, and illustrated by the famous Japanese artist Yoshitaka Amano.

Other Characters and Novels

Byrd, Bob, J.W. Scott, L. F. Bjorklund. *Ka-Zar: King of Fang and Claw.* California: Eberville Press, 2004. ISBN: OL371191. Reprints Timely/Manvis/Marvel's *Ka-Zar: Adventures of Ka-Zar the Great 1.*

After their plane crashes in the jungles of the Congo, David Rand loses both his parents. His father is murdered by a greedy emerald prospector, and his mother dies from disease. After David saves a lion from death in quicksand, they become partners and David adopts the name Ka-Zar, "Brother of the Lion." Ka-Zar, who is somewhat of a Tarzan clone, becomes king of the jungle. He is able to communicate with all the animals, and even has fights with a gorilla and a leopard for dominance of the jungle. When a prospector shows up with several guides and another white man, Ka-Zar recognizes him as the man who killed his father, and takes his revenge.

This book reprints the first issue of the pulp magazine *Ka-Zar*, originally published in 1936 by Manvis Publishing Company, owned by Martin Goodman. It features the first appearance of the Golden-Age Ka-Zar who later appeared in *Marvel Comics 1* (Timely/Marvel Comics). In 1976, Odyssey Publications reprinted the issue as a book, *Ka-Zar: Adventures of Ka-Zar the Great*, in which W. H. Desmond wrote the introduction. In London in 1937, Wright and Brown also published this book. There is no introductory material in the current edition, but it is highly recommended.

Keller, David Henry. "The Thirty and One," in *Life Everlasting and Other Tales of Science Fantasy and Horror.* Editor: Sam Moskowitz. Westport, Co: Hyperion Press, 1974. ISBN: 088355111X (trd); 0883551403 (pbk). Reprints *Marvel Science Stories 2*, November 1938, Postal/Manvis Publications.

This book, originally published in 1947, features a story that was published in Marvel/Timely's pre-comic pulp magazine, *Marvel Science Stories.* The story deals with a lovely lady who synthesizes thirty men into her body to stop a giant who is blocking a trade route for her kingdom. The men burst out of her and kill the giant. This bizarre story also features the human-made Homunculus, who wishes for nothing more than to be put back into the bottle of his creation. Keller also published several stories in the earlier pulp *Marvel Tales.*

Kuttner, Henry. "Avengers of Space," "Dictator of Americas," and "Time Trap" in *Girls for the Slime God.* Editor: Mike Resnick. United States: Obscura Press, 1997. ISBN: 0965956903. *Reprints Marvel Science Stories 1, August 1938; Marvel Science Stories 2,* November 1938, Postal/Manvis Publications.

This collection contains three science fiction stories that were originally published in Marvel/Timely's pre-comic pulp magazine *Marvel Science Stories.* All the stories feature bug-eyed monsters and scantly clad women who get caught and subsequently have their clothes ripped off by the aliens. The protagonist always rescues the girl in time. "The Time Trap" is a cross between H. G. Wells's *The War of the Worlds* and *The Time Machine.* This collection features articles by William Knoles, Barry N. Malzberg, and Isaac Asimov. Carol Resnick's play adaptation of "Avengers of Space" is also included. These stories read like versions of old movie serials.

Lee, Stan, Dave Gibbons, Tom DeFalco, et al. *Ultimate Silver Surfer.* New York: Berkley Boulevard, 1997. ISBN: 1572970294 (trd); 1572972998 pbk.

The Silver Surfer helps a Red Cross volunteer in a war-torn country, and learns the meaning of giving for others. He helps the NYPD get guns off the streets, and stops a young girl from committing suicide. Mephisto tries to trick the Surfer into harming someone whose planet had been ravaged by Galactus. A group of Silver Surfer female fanatics are on an Oprah-like television program, and the Silver Surfer goes to the apartment of one of them. The Surfer goes to a planet, the mythical Sambatyon, which is actually run by one of the twelve lost tribes of Israel. He saves the planet from attack, and cleanses his soul. He meets the three fates, and stops Morg, Galactus's herald, from allowing Galactus to eat a planet. Thanos gets caught in a never-ending loop, battling Morg and the Silver Surfer.

The collection is divided into three parts: Origin, Exile on Earth, and Freedom. Tom DeFalco retells the Silver Surfer's origin in prose form, and Stan Lee provides the introduction.

Lee, Stan, Mike Zeck, Richard Lee Byers, et al. *The Ultimate Super Villains*. New York: Byron Preiss Multimedia/Boulevard Books, 1996. ISBN: 1572971134.

Kang has taken over the Earth and uses Baron Mordo, the Abomination, and Cobra as his lieutenants. They of course try to deceive him and take power. Magneto and Professor X fight against a mutant who is connecting a whole town full of people. The Ringmaster reminisces about his childhood days in his family's carnival. Mephisto promises to heal a young boy's older brother if he will destroy Ghost Rider. Ultron kidnaps a new android prototype, but finds out it is a human in an android's body. Iron Man and Giant Man save her from Ultron. Venom and the Absorbing Man break out of jail together. Carnage tries a new serum that is supposed to stop his urge to kill. The Sandman tries to save Silver Sable from the Wizard. The Trapster, who goes straight and goes to work for a TV company, is a big hit when the CEO has him appear on a television program. The Wizard recognizes the Trapster, and tries to get him back into crime as Paste-Pot Pete. Loki actually saves Thor so that he can defeat him at a later time. Other villains include Nightmare, Dr. Doom, Typhoid Mary, and Super-Skrull.

This book features a collection of short stories that highlight Marvel villains.

Murray, Will, Jim Steranko, Joe Jusko. *Nick Fury: Agent of S.H.I.E.L.D.: Empyre*. New York: Berkley Boulevard, 2000. ISBN: 0425168166.

A madman from the Middle East, Nadir al-Bazinda, who has aligned himself with Hydra, causes several planes to crash. They try to assassinate Nick Fury and send a plane to crash into the Helicarrier. Nick Fury and his sidekick "Dum Dum" Dugan enlist the help of psychic Starla Spacek to use her remote-viewing techniques to pinpoint which planes have a bomb onboard. S.H.I.E.L.D. reopens their special powers unit. Fury, Spacek and a high-ranking, Middle-East Hydra agent are captured by Bazinda. He betrays Hydra, and attempts to bomb the rest of the world on Christmas Eve. Fury and his team work fast to stop the bombs from going off.

This is a fun book, a page turner in the vein of the best of spy/espionage literature. Steranko returned to do the illustrations.

Rotsler, William. *Dr. Strange: Nightmare*. New York: Pocket Books, 1979. ISBN: 0671820885.

Nightmare, one of Stephen Strange's old nemeses, is trying to come out of the dream world into the real world by using an assassin, a movie star, a boxer, and a televangelist, Reverend Jacks. Nightmare is using Jacks, one of the most popular preachers, to influence thousands of people during his worldwide Crusade for Change. The Reverend's wife seeks help for his bizarre behavior from Dr. Strange. The parson views Strange as a charlatan and an imp from Satan. The dream world begins to reject Nightmare, who is seeking the natural world for solace and self-reaffirmation.

This book includes a detailed explanation of Dr. Strange's origin and his first encounter with the dreaded Dormammu. It is filled with Lovecraftian imagery, and the author peppers the story with many little comments about the history of Hollywood. The book deserves to be republished. (*Marvel Novel Series 7*)

Shelley, Mary Wollstonecraft, Berni Wrightson, Stephen King, et al. *Frankenstein; or the Modern Prometheus*. New York: Marvel, 1983. ISBN: 0939766752.

This illustrated novel is an edition of the famous novel that was first published in 1818. It has long been considered to be one of the very science fiction and horror novels, and has been made into countless films. It is a staple of popular culture. It is the story of Victor Von Frankenstein and the undead creation he brings to life. He abandons his creation, which he calls "the monster," and leaves the creation to fend for himself. As revenge for his cruelty, the monster stalks Frankenstein and kills his brother, best friend, and wife. The monster asks Frankenstein to create him a mate, which is started and then destroyed. This version combines the original text with Wrightson's art, to make a unique version of the tale. Stephen King wrote the introduction in which he discusses both the importance of the novel to horror, and Wrightson's wonderful artwork.

Stern, D.A. Jonathan Hensleigh. *The Punisher: Official Novelization*. New York: Del Ray, 2004. ISBN: 0345475569.

FBI agent Frank Castle is involved in a botched arms sale in which the son of Howard Saint is inadvertently killed. Saint, a prominent businessman and a candidate for governor of Florida, finds out that Castle was involved in his son's death. Castle's FBI partner and best friend, Jimmy Weeks, betrays Castle to Saint, and Livia, Saint's wife, asks that Castle's whole family be gunned down while they are vacationing in Puerto Rico. Saint's other son and henchmen shoot Castle's wife, kid, mother, father, and many of his other relatives. Although near death, Castle manages to stay alive. He then sets out to get Saint and his family. Castle ends up destroying Saint, his wife, his kids, and his most trusted advisors. Castle almost commits suicide, but instead decides to start his own private war against rapists, drug dealers and murders, who always manage to get away with their evil deeds.

This novelization is based on Jonathan Hensleigh's screenplay for the feature film *Punisher*. It. is well written, and provides greater insight to the Castle character. While it stays true to the spirit of the *Punisher*, it also updates it.

Wein, Len, Marv Wolfman, et al. *The Marvel Superheroes*. New York: Pocket Books, 1979. ISBN: 0671820915.

The Avengers go up against Ultron who has captured the Scarlet Witch, and Iron Man becomes Ultron's slave. The X-Men stop Magneto from detonating nuclear bombs. Daredevil, who tangles with the Owl, learns that the woman with whom he is in love is one of the Owl's cronies. The Hulk, Man-Thing, and the Golem become the Collector's exhibits.

This book is a collection of four novelettes featuring the Avengers, Daredevil, the X-Men, and the Hulk. (*Marvel Novel Series 9*)

Weiner, Ellis. *Howard the Duck*. New York: Berkley Books, 1986. ISBN: 0425092755.

Howard the Duck is magically transported from Duck World to Earth, where he is stuck in a world he never made. He makes friends with a human, Beverly. Howard eventually saves the world from the Dark Overlord, who wants to bring more of his kind to Earth and take it over.

This novelization of the movie *Howard the Duck* is based on the screenplay by Willard Huyck & Gloria Katz. While many feel the movie was just plain awful, the novel is a wonderful read, much better than the movie. The author writes in a humorous, satirical style that provides an interesting analysis of 1980s culture. The book contains several in-depth inserts which cover items not discussed in the movie, including Howard's psychological profile; a comparison between the leisure chairs on Duck World and on Earth; and a look at the Nexus of Sominus.

14

Articles, Books, Guides, and Indexes

For a hero lacking super-powers, Marvel Comics' Nick Fury
has enjoyed an impressive history.—*Michael Eury*

Articles and Books

Adams, Neal, Arlen Schumer J. David Spurlock. *Neal Adams Sketchbook*. Lebanon, NJ: Vanguard Productions, 1999. ISBN: 1887 591052 (trd); 1887591060 (pbk).

This is a nice collection of rare and unpublished sketches from artist Neal Adams, which includes several Marvel characters: Thor, Avengers, Conan, Dracula, the X-Men and the Inhumans. Adams gives his commentaries throughout the book. The Introduction is by filmmaker Stuart Gordon.

Behling, Steve, Bob McLeod. *How to Draw Ghost Rider*. Laguna Hills, CA: Walter Foster Publishing, 1996. ISBN: 1560102 047.

This is a step-by-step guide to drawing Ghost Rider, his enemies, and his allies.

Behling, Steve, Bob McLeod, Alex Saviuk, et al. *How to Draw Spider-Man*. New York: Troll Communications, 2002. ISBN: 0816 774471.

This is a step-by-step guide to drawing Spider-Man and his villains, including Vulture, Mystero, Lizard, Dr. Ock, and Venom, among others.

Behling, Steve, Paul Ryan, Bob McLeod, et al. *How to Draw Iron Man*. Laguna Hills, CA: Walter Foster, 1997. ISBN: 1560102071.

This work contains text and graphics that detail how to draw Iron Man effectively. It shows different armor styles, and various Iron Man associates and villains, including War Machine, Scarlet Witch, Hawkeye, U.S. Agent, Spider-Woman, Century, Mandarin, Fin Fang Foom, and Modok.

Behling, Steve, Paul Ryan, Bob McLeod, et al. *How to Draw the X-Men*. New York: Troll, 2003. ISBN: 081677577X; 1560102063 (1997).

This is a step-by-step guide to drawing the X-Men and their foes, including Wolverine, Beast, Gambit, Magneto, Storm, and Mr. Sinister, plus the X-Men's ship, the *Blackbird*.

Behling, Steve, Paul Ryan, Al Milgraom, et al. *How to Draw the Silver Surfer*. Laguna Hills, CA: Walter Foster, 1998. ISBN: 1560 102071.

This is a step-by-step guide to drawing the Silver Surfer and his associates, including Thanos, Skrull Warrior, Kree Warrior, Galactus, Shalla Bal, Nova, and Destroyer, plus alien landscapes.

Benton Mike. *The Comic Book in America: An Illustrated History*. Dallas, TX: Taylor, 1993. ISBN: 0878338357.

This is a well-written detailed history of comics from 1896 to 1989, with year-by-year breakdowns. It has sections titled "Mighty Marvel," "Captain America Returns," "The Marvel Explosion," and "Marvel's Silver Anniversary," among others. There also are histories of different comic book companies, including Marvel, as well as less well known companies like Gilberton/Holyoke publishing. Benton has section in which he details various comic genres, such as crime, horror, romance, funny animals and educational comics. The volume contains plenty of reprints of rare Marvel-related covers, including *Millie the Model 2*; *All Select 8*; *Combat 1*; *Sub-Mariner 42*; and *Tales to Astonish 1*.

Benton Mike. *The Illustrated History of Horror Comics*. Dallas, TX: Taylor, 1991. ISBN: 0878336613.

This volume contains a detailed history of horror comics, from the beginnings of comics to the early 1980s. There are details about Marvel's venture into horror comics, from the Atlas days to their Epic imprint. There are many color cover reproductions, and there is a guide and a checklist to individual titles from Marvel and other comic companies, including *Tomb of Dracula*, *Werewolf by Night*, *Adventures into Weird Worlds*, *Nightmare on Elm Street* and *Legion of Monsters*, *Men's Adventures*, *Man Thing*, and many others.

Benton Mike. *The Illustrated History of Science Fiction Comics*. Dallas, TX: Taylor, 1992. ISBN: 087833789X.

This is a detailed history of science fiction comics, from the early pulps to the early 1990s. There are details about the early ventures of Martin Goodman with *Marvel Science Stories* and the early Atlas sci fi comics. Benton has a chapter in which he discusses the early Marvel *Star Trek* comics, and how Marvel published the earliest *Star Wars* comics a few weeks before the movie came out. The comic's checklist includes various Marvel/Epic titles, including *Alien Legion*, *Battlestar Galactica*, *Unknown Worlds of Science Fiction*, *Weird Wonder Tales*, *Journey Into Mystery*, *Marvel Classic Comics*, and *Planet of the Apes*, among many others.

Benton Mike. *The Illustrated History of Superhero Comics of the Golden Age*. Dallas, TX: Taylor, 1992. ISBN: 087833808X.

This is a detailed history of comics from the Golden Age, including material on Timely Comics and its characters, including Captain America, Young Allies, Ms. America, and Human Torch, among many others. It is profusely illustrated, and has a checklist.

Benton Mike. *The Illustrated History of Superhero Comics of the Silver Age*. Dallas, TX: Taylor Publishing, 1991. ISBN: 0878337466.

This volume includes a short chapter on the history of the Marvel Universe (pp. 17–28). There are entries for various Marvel heroes, such as Thor, Iron Man, and the Hulk, and for the artists, like Sterenko and Kirby, who created the characters. The volume contains many illustrations, and a checklist for the most important comics of the Silver Age.

Benton Mike. *Masters of Imagination: The Comic Book Artists Hall of Fame*. Dallas, TX: Taylor Publishing, 1994. ISBN: 0878338594.

This volume is a collection of essays paying tribute to important artists in the history of comics, including those who have produced substantial Marvel content, such as Jack Kirby and Steve Ditko. Other artists include Will Eisner, Joe Shuster, C. C. Beck, Jack Cole, Carl Banks, Walt Kelly, Basil Wolverton, Harvey Kurtzman, Wally Wood, Bernard Krigstien, and Alex Toth. There is also an artist's guide and checklist, and an essay on the art of the comic book. The volume is profusely illustrated with reprints of covers from *Fantastic Four 82*, *X-Men 7*, *Captain America 102*, and *Incredible Hulk 6*, among others.

Bizony, Piers, *Digital Domain: The Leading Edge of Visual Effects*. London: Aurum, 2001. ISBN: 1854107070.

This volume contains a section on the special effects in the first *X-Men* movie and other films, such as *Fight Club*, *Titanic*, and *Apollo 13*.

Blumberg, Arnold T. "Going Green: the Best of the Hulk," pp. 956–959, in Robert Overstreet, et al. *Overstreet Comic Book Price Guide 34th edition*." New York: Gemstone/House of Collectables, 2004. ISBN: 1400 046696.

This is a brief overview of the history of the Hulk. It covers the *Tales to Astonish* years, Sal Buscema, Herb Trimple, Peter David, and the Bruce Jones years.

Blumberg, Arnold T. "Spider-Man Goes to Hollywood," pp. 44–46, in Robert Overstreet, et al. *Overstreet Comic Book Price Guide 32nd Edition*. New York: Gemstone, 2002. ISBN:0609808214.

This is a brief look at Spider-Man's visits to Hollywood, and on the silver screen in the early issues.

Blumberg, Arnold T. "The World's Greatest Family: Why the Fantastic Four Made It to Forty," pp. 20–24, in Robert Overstreet ed., *Official Overstreet Comic Book Price Guide 31st Edition*. New York: Gemstone, 2001. ISBN: 0609808206.

The author gives forty reasons why the first family of comics is perennially popular.

Bly, Robert, *Comic Book Heroes: 1001 Trivia Questions About America's Favorite Superheroes From the Atom to the X-Men*. New York: Citadel, 1996. ISBN: 0806515716.

This is a trivia-game book covering different comic superheroes, including full chapters on Spider-Man,

Hulk, Spider-Woman, Iron Man, X-Men, Captain America, Daredevil and the Fantastic Four. It includes questions about Stan Lee, Jack Kirby, and Marvel characters, such as the Avengers, Captain Marvel, Bishop, and others.

Brewer, H. Michael. *Who Needs a Superhero? Finding Virtue, Vice and What's Holy in Comics*. Grand Rapids, MI: Baker Books, 2004. ISBN: 0801065100.

This is a Presbyterian minister's detailed look at superheroes from a Christian perspective. Each chapter is presented as a homily. There are chapters that look at the Hulk, Iron Man, Thor, Spider-Man, Daredevil, the Fantastic Four, the Punisher and Galactus, and Captain America. The author tries to show what biblical lessons can be learned by looking at the stories of these heroes. Superman, Batman, the Spirit, and Wonder Woman are also in the work. It includes a superhero self-quiz one can use to identify one's personal superhero type, and biblical study questions.

Bruegman, Bill, Joanne M. Bruegman, Ken Fromm, et al. *Superhero Collectibles: A Pictorial Guide*. Akron, OH: Toy Scouts Inc, 1996. ISBN: 0963263757.

This volume includes two essays which deal with Marvel: "Marvel Cartoons of the 1960s" (pp. 27–30) and "When Captain America Throws His Mighty Shield" (pp. 34–35). The latter essay looks at the items people sent when they joined Captain America's Sentinels of Liberty during the 1940s. There also is a chapter devoted to Marvel Collectables (pp. 112–141) which contains such items as the Captain America Rocket Car, a Daredevil greeting card, a Spider-Man toothbrush holder and bubblebath, "The Thing" bike plate, a Mr. Fantastic costume, and many other odd Marvel-related collectibles.

Bryne, John. *Art of John Byrne*. New York: S. Q. Productions, 1980. ISBN: 0865620008.

This is an excellent but hard to find tribute to John Byrne and his career. It contains interviews and sketches of his work, including Marvel characters such as the X-Men, Alpha Flight, and the Black Widow.

Buscema, John, Sal Quartuccio, Bob Keenan. *Art of John Buscema*. Brooklyn, NY: S. Quaruccio, 1978.

This book contains a detailed interview with Buscema which focuses on his work with Marvel and with Stan Lee. It features Buscema's interpretations of Conan, Silver Surfer, and many others in the Marvel Universe.

Buscema, John, J. David Spurlock, Jim Steranko. *John Buscema Sketchbook*. Lebanon NJ: Vanguard, 2001. ISBN: 1887591176 (trd); 1887591192 (pbk).

This volume contains a collection of sketches and interviews with artist John Buscema. Buscema reminisces about working for Timely and Marvel. The book includes cover reproductions of numerous Marvel comics, as well as a discussion of Buscema's work on Conan.

Callahan, Bob, ed. *The New Smithsonian Book of Comic-Book Stories: From Crumb to Clowes*. Washington DC: Smithsonian Books, 2004. ISBN: 1588341836. Reprints Marvel's *Captain America 113*; *Fantastic Four 21*; *Amazing Spider-Man 33*.

This collection reprints modern comic stories, from the underground Silver Age, to modern contemporary works, including several Marvel stories by Stan Lee, Jim Steranko, and Steve Ditko. In these stories, the Fantastic Four go up against the Hate Monger; Captain America fakes his own death; and Spider-Man deals with Aunt May's illness in the hospital. The black-and-white collection includes an appearance by Nick Fury and the Avengers. Other authors represented include Robert Crumb, Frank Miller, Rick Geary, Eddie Campbell, Daniel Clowes, and Chris Ware.

Cannon, Martin, Steve Gerber, James Van Hise, et al. *Howard the Duck Files*. San Bernardino, CA: Borgo Press, 1987. ISBN: 0809 58123X; 1556980051 (1986).

This is a profile of Howard the Duck's creator, Steve Gerber. It describes the character's origin, and includes stories related to the comic book and feature film.

Carter, Gary M., Pat S. Calhoun. "Journey into Unknown Worlds of Atlas Fantasy," in Robert M. Overstreet, ed., *Overstreet Comic Book Price Guide 22nd Edition*. New York: Avon Books, 1992. ISBN: 0380769123.

This wonderful essay looks at the elusive world of Marvel during the Atlas years of the 1950s. This is one of the first articles to really go into that mystery-engulfed period in depth, examining an era that produced some of the most interesting comics in Marvel's history. The authors list three major divisions of the Atlas period: pre–Comics Code, May 1949–1955; April 1955–October 1957; and the Atlas implosion, October 1957–November 1961, with subsequent publication of *The Fantastic Four*. The authors divide these three periods into detailed chunks of time, and discuss what was published during these years. This article is illustrated with amazing reprints of covers, including first issues of titles such as *Strange Tales* and *Journey Into Mystery*. The authors include several charts and a general timeline for pivotal events during this period.

Chabot, Bart, Anton Corbijn. *Captain America*. Utgeverij De Bezige BIJ: Amsterdam, 1982. ISBN: 902344580.

This is a very bizarre book which combines photography and poetry which is written in Dutch. The poem deals with Captain America and his fight against the Nazis.

Conroy, Mike. *500 Comic Book Villains*. Hauppauge, NY: Barron's, 2004. ISBN: 076412 9082.

This is a companion volume to *500 Comic Book Heroes*. It is a profusely illustrated collection that has many entries related to Marvel characters, including Dr. Doom, Red Skull, Magneto, Mephisto, Baron Blood, Dormammu, Kang, and Galactus. The chapter titles are "Male Villains," "Female Villains," "Villainous Teams," "Enemies of the People," "Monsters and Machines," and "Sorcerers and Space Invaders." The book includes detailed essays describing supervillains, secret societies, Hitler, and the Yellow Peril. It also has a detailed index, and an introduction by Roy Thomas.

Cooke, Jon B., ed. *Comic Book Artist Collected Edition Vol. 1*. Raleigh, NC: TwoMorrows Press, 2000. ISBN: 1893905039. Reprints *Comic Book Artist 1–3*.

This volume contains several interviews with Marvel Comics writers/artists, including Stan Lee, Roy Thomas, with discussion of Conan and New X-Men; Bill Everett's daughter; Mike Friedrich, on Bill Everett; Gil Kane on Marvel cover work; Barry Windsor-Smith, on Marvel topics; Mike Ploog, on Marvel Horror; Jim Starlin; Steve Englehart; Alan Weiss; and Neal Adams including unpublished pages from an X-Men graphic novel and a Marvel checklist.

Cooke, Jon B., ed. *Comic Book Artist Collection Vol. 2*. Raleigh, NC: TwoMorrows, 2002. ISBN: 1893905136. Reprints *Comic Book Artist 5–6*.

This volume contains interviews with artists and writers, some of whom detail their years at Marvel: John Romita Sr., Marie Severin, Dave Cockrum, Frank Miller, Craig Russell, and Don McGregor, Marvel's *Planet of the Apes*, and Marvel's aborted attempt at adapting the television series *The Prisoner* are also covered. The book contains interesting tidbits related to Spider-Man, the Black Panther, Killraven, Howard the Duck, and Nightcrawler.

Crawford, Hubert H. *Crawford's Encyclopedia of Comic Books*. Middle Village, NY: Jonathyan David Publishers, 1978. ISBN: 082 4602218.

This book contains a chapter which outlines the history of Timely/Marvel (pp. 337–348), with reproductions of various Captain America covers and information about the original Captain America motion picture serial. It also includes an alphabetical listing of nearly all Marvel/Timely titles from 1940 to 1978.

Daniels, Les. *Comix: A History of Comic Books in America*. New York: Bonanza, 1971. ISBN: 0876900341.

This is history of comics contains a chapter on the mighty Marvel. It includes comic strips from *Not Brand Echh*, *Sub-Mariner 40*, *Captain America 146*, 150 (1942), *Fantastic Four 11*, *Strange Tales 110*, and *Tower of Shadows 1*.

Daniels, Les. *Marvel: Five Fabulous Decades of World's Greatest Comics*. New York: Henry N. Abrams, 1993. ISBN: 0810938219 (trd); 0810925664 (pbk).

Originally published in 1991, this book contains the complete history of Marvel comics, from Timely's pulp publishing, through 1990. This book is still essential reading for anyone who wants to learn about Marvel. It is beautifully illustrated and thoroughly documented, with many rare photos and interviews with Marvel editors and employees. The book includes profiles of characters such as the original X-Men, Captain America, and Captain Marvel. It also includes reprints of classic Marvel stories from *Sub-Mariner 35*, *Amazing Spider-Man 2*, *Fantastic Four 51*, and the unpublished "Wolverine: The Hunter" story by Chris Claremont. Stan Lee wrote the introduction. All libraries should own this book.

DeFalco, Tom. *Comic Creators on Spider-Man*. London: Titan, 2004. ISBN: 1840234229.

This book interviews writers and artists who have had a role in creating the Spider-Man mythos: Stan Lee, John Romita, Gerry Conway, Len Wein, Marv Wolfman, Sal Buscema, Roger Stern, Ron Frenz, David Michelinie, Todd McFarlane, J.M. DeMatteis, Mark Bagley, Howard Mackie, Paul Jenkins, Mark Buckingham, Brian Michael Bendis, and Axel Alonso. The book is illustrated with unused art, covers, and script samples, and contains mini-essays that deal with Spider-Man villains, famous story sagas, Marvel Knights, Ultimate Spidey, the first movie, and a breakdown of all the different *Spider-Man* titles. It is highly recommended for those wanting to know more about the most popular comic character of all time.

DeFalco, Tom. *Hulk: Incredible Guide*. New York: D.K. Publishing, 2003. ISBN: 0789 492601.

This hardcover book details the history of the Hulk and various people in the Hulk's life in the comics. The book has entries for the various incarnations of the Hulk, and his adversaries, like General Ross, the Glob, Ringmaster, U-Foes, and Soviet Super Soldiers, among others. It also contains a history of the Hulk by the decades, starting in the sixties, and going through the 2000s; material on Ultimate Universe Hulk, the Hulk's end, and Hulk around the world; a gazetteer of comics; and an introduction by Stan Lee. This is an excellent source for those wanting the whole scoop on the Hulk in the comics.

DeFalco, Tom. *Spider-Man: The Ultimate Guide*. New York: DK Books, 2001. ISBN: 0789 47946X.

This is an oversize hardcover which details the world of Spider-Man. It includes a history of the character, from the sixties to the nineties, and has sections on villains, girl friends, parents, super powers, Spider-Man 2099, the clone saga and other famous storylines, Spider-Girl, and Spider-Woman, among other things. It is a fantastic guide to all things Spider-Man. The introduction is by Stan Lee.

Duey, Kathleen, Eugene Epstein, Robert Gould, et al. *Ultimate Super Hero: Spider-Man/X-Men*. Carlsbad, CA: Big Guy Books, 2003. ISBN: 1929945388.

This is a slipcase special edition version of the Spider-Man and X-Men picture books. It is a good gift for children superhero fans, and a nice collectible for adults. It was dedicated to Stan Lee.

Duey, Kathleen, Robert Gould, Eugene Epstein, et al. *Spider-Man: The Ultimate Picture Book 1*. Carlsbad, CA: Big Guy Books, 2003. ISBN: 1929945221 (trd); 1929945 256 (pbk).

This beautiful picture book is set in the Ultimate Universe. It tells the story of Spider-Man using pictures of real people and photo-animation. In the book, Peter Parker fights with Norman Osborn who transforms into the Green Goblin. Mary Jane, Uncle Ben, and even Stan Lee are characters in the book, which was dedicated to Lee.

Duey, Kathleen, Robert Gould, Eugene Epstein, et al. *X-Men: The Ultimate Picture Book*. Carlsbad, CA: Big Guy Books, 2003. ISBN: 1929945248 (trd); 1929945264 (pbk).

Magneto is professor X's brother, and Cyclops leaves the X-Men to join Magneto's Brotherhood of Mutants. Quicksilver has doubts about his father's intentions toward the world, and attempts to dismantle nuclear weapons which Magneto intends to launch against humanity. The Sentinels terrorize mutants, including a young Bobby Drake, Iceman.

This is a high-tech picture book which combines computer animation and live action photos. It contains information about the X-Men and other characters, including the Blob, Scarlet Witch, Toad, Jean Grey, Storm, Beast and Wolverine. This book contains numerous editing mistakes and typos, and it portrays Professor X and Magneto as being far too young, but the graphics are cool.

Eisner, Will. *Shop Talk*. Milwaukie, OR: Dark Horse, 2002. ISBN: 156971536X.

This book contains interviews with such great artists and writers in the history of comics as Neal Adams, Joe Simon, Jack Kirby, C. C. Beck, Gil Kane, Joe Kubert, and Phil Seuling. There are Marvel references in some of the interviews, including Jack Kirby's claim to have created Spider-Man.

Eury, Michael. *Captain Action: The Original Super Hero Action Figure*. Raleigh, NC: TwoMorrows Publishing, 2002. ISBN: 1893905179

This profusely illustrated book tells the history of the first action figure, Captain Action. There were a number of superhero characters that were made under the Captain Action banner, including Batman, Superman, Robin, Lone Ranger, and the Phantom. This book also includes Marvel characters Sgt. Fury, Captain America, and Spider-Man. Each section includes a history of the featured character, as well as of Captain Action as that character. The book includes a detailed listing of parts included with the action figure.

FantaCo editors. *The Fantastic Four Chronicles*. Albany NY: FantaCo Enterprises, 1982. ISBN: 0939766507

This volume relates the life and times of the Fantastic Four, including discussions with writers and artists who worked with the Fantastic Four throughout the years.

Gertler, Nat, ed. *Panel One: Comic Book Scripts By Top Writers*. Thousand Oaks, CA: About Comics, 2002. ISBN: 0971633800. Reprints Marvel Comics' *Deathlok 5*.

This collection of comic scripts includes Dwayne McDuffie's complete script for *Deathlok 5*, in which the Fantastic Four, the X-Men, and Deathlok go up against the cyborg Ultron, various Doombots, and Mechadoom. The volume includes an introduction by the author.

Goulart, Ron. *Great History of the Comic Books*. New York: Contemporary Books, 1986. ISBN: 0809250454.

This is a complete history of comic books, from the beginnings to the 1980s. Timely Comics is featured in "Mighty Marvel" (pp. 145–158). This chapter gives a detailed account of the comics that Timely published during the 1940s. Marvel is also discussed in "Coming of the Silver Age" (pp. 275–292). Numerous illustrations from various Marvel books are reprinted in this book, including color reproductions of *Where Monsters Dwell 20*; *Sub-Mariner 57*; *Kid Colt Outlaw 206*; and *Red Sonja 3*. It also includes page reprints from *Elfquest*, *Thor*, and *Spider-Man*.

Gross, Edward, ed. *Superheroes on Screen Files: Superman and Spider-Man 1 & 2*. San Bernardino, CA: Borgo Press, 1986. ISBN: 0809580888 (Vol. 1); 080958087X (Vol. 2).

This book contains material on the ill-fated first attempt at a Spider-Man movie, along with information about Marvel Productions. It also contains articles about the Spider-Man television program.

Gross, Edward. *Spider-Man Confidential*. New York: Hyperion, 2002. ISBN: 0786887222.

This history of Spider-Man includes an episode list for the five television series; a comic-book checklist; material on the development of the Spider-Man feature film; and a guide to villains. It is an encyclopedic guide to everything Spider-Man.

Gruenwald, Mark, Kim Thompson. *A Treatise on Reality in Comic Literature*. Oshkosh, WI: Alternity Enterprises, 1976.

This is a philosophical look at how comic books present reality. It looks at reality in books like Marvel's *Fantastic Four* and *Spider-Man*. This book was privately published.

Hofstede, David. *Hollywood and the Comics*. New York: Zanne-3, 1991. ISBN: 0962917 648.

This book covers selected comic book–related movies, television shows, and serials up to 1991. Marvel-related chapters include ones on Spider-Man, Captain America, Dr. Strange, Howard the Duck, and the Incredible Hulk. The book is well written and informative.

Howe, Sean, ed. *Give Our Regards to the Atom Smashers! Writers on Comics*. New York: Pantheon Books, 2004. ISBN: 0375422 560.

In this book, various mainstream writers, like Greil Marcus, Brad Meltzer, and Steve Erickson, give their views on comics and characters. Marvel-related chapters include ones on Marvel and Jack Kirby, Spider-Man, Marvel and DC, Nick Fury, Warlock and collecting, and Steve Ditko's work on Dr. Strange, This is a very good collection of essays and articles.

Johnson, Robert K., Catherine M. Barsottie. *Finding God in the Movies: 33 Films of Reel Faith*. Grand Rapids, MI: Baker Books, 2004. ISBN: 0801064813.

This book contains a section on the first *X-Men* film, and describes how Christians can find biblical ideas in this film, and many other contemporary films. The authors look at both Xavier's and Magneto's ideas throughout the movie. They address issues of racism, and affirm the human spirit and personal transformation in the film. They suggest certain films that the Christian viewer should watch, ask questions about, and think about. They also suggest Bible verses to contemplate while watching films.

Khoury, George, ed. *True Brit: A Celebration of the Great Comic Book Artists of the UK*. Raleigh, NC: TwoMorrows, 2004. ISBN: 1893905330.

This book contains interviews with several artists who have worked for Marvel UK and USA, including Alan Davis, Bryan Hitch, Dave McKean, Frank Quitely and Barry Windsor-Smith. There is a great deal of material in the interviews about Marvel UK, and its early history. This book is a detailed history of British comic books, which includes interviews with Hunt Emerson, Brian Bolland, Bryan Talbot, and others.

Kirby, Jack, Steve Bissette, Jim Amash, et al. *The Collected Jack Kirby Collector, Volume Three*. Raleigh, NC, TwoMorrows, 1999. ISBN: 1893905020. Reprints *Jack Kirby Collector 13–15*.

This volume contains previously unpublished artwork related to Kirby and Marvel. There are articles on the Golden-Age Vision; Kirby's early Marvel monsters like Diablo, Sporr, and others, from *Tales of Suspense*; a Spider-Man prototype; *Devil Dinosaur*; a special issue devoted to the *Mighty Thor*; Kirby science fiction concepts, including Inhumans, Galactus, and the Celestials; an Al Williamson interview with Marvel content; Silver Surfer; *The Eternals*; *Machine Man*; and *2001 A Space Oddity*. This volume also reprints some old interviews with Kirby.

Kirby, Jack, Mark Evanier, Steve Sherman. *Kirby Unleashed: A Collection of the Artistry of Jack Kirby*. Newbury Park, CA: Communicators Unlimited, 1971.

This is one of the first books published as a tribute to Jack Kirby. It includes information about his Marvel years, and several drawings of Marvel characters, including: the Watcher, Thor, Crystal, Fantastic Four, and the Fighting American, among others. It also contains his then new DC work.

Kirby, Jack, Gary Goth, Earl Wells, et al. *Comics Journal Library Vol. 1: Jack Kirby*. Seattle: Fantagraphics, 2002. ISBN: 1560974664.

This monograph celebrates the life and legacy of Jack Kirby throughout his years. There are reprints of *Comics Journal* interviews with Kirby from 1969, 1971, 1985, and 1989, in which Kirby discusses in detail his time at Marvel, and how he created many of the Marvel characters we know and love. There is also a section on Kirby's lawsuit against Marvel, and the fight to get back his art. Earl Wells wrote the essay, "Once and For All, Who Was the Author of Marvel?" which details Kirby's time at Marvel with Stan Lee. Much of the artwork in this volume features the Fantastic Four, but there is also art from *Fighting American*, *Boy's Ranch*, *Popeye*, *The Blue Beetle*, *Young Romance*, *Thor*, *Eternals*, *2001 Space Odyssey*, *New Gods*, *Captain America*, and many others. Barry Windsor-Smith wrote the introduction.

Kirby, Jack, John Morrow, Mark Evanier, et al. *The Collected Jack Kirby Collector, Volume One*. Raleigh, NC: TwoMorrows, 2004. ISBN: 1893905004. Reprints *Jack Kirby Collector 1–9*.

This volume contains the first nine issues of *Jack Kirby Collector*, the award-winning magazine devoted to the work of Kirby. The volume also contains an interview with Joe Simon; material on the creation of Captain America; material on Kirby's work on monsters, like Fing Fang Foom and Googam; unpublished art for the *Fantastic Four*; a "Marvelmania" portfolio; Kirby on Captain America and other Marvel characters; material on *Young Allies* and war comics; *Boys Ranch*; a Steranko-Kirby interview, with sketches of Captain America and Eternals; and a *Fantastic Four* special issue.

Kirby, Jack, Pamela Morrow, Glen B. Fleming, et al. *The Collected Jack Kirby Collector, Volume Two*. Raleigh NC: TwoMorrows Publishing, 2004. ISBN: 1893905012. Reprints *Jack Kirby Collector 10–12*.

In this volume, Fleming describes his visit to Kirby's home, and talks about Kirby's work at Marvel. This section includes some information about the Eternals, Thor, Hulk, Nick Fury, and the Prisoner. The book also contains an interview with Jack's wife Roz, a *Fighting American* article, *Not Brand Echh*, Kirby's work on *2001* and the *Prisoner*, Kirby's work on the *Fantastic Four* cartoon, Kirby in England with a picture of Captain Britain and Captain America together, a Captain America and Jack Kirby interview, and Marvel-related work from a September 1966 *Esquire* article. Sketches of Captain America are scattered throughout this volume.

Kirby, Jack, John Morrow, Tom Ziuko. *The Collected Jack Kirby Collector, Volume Four*. Raleigh, NC: TwoMorrows, 2004. ISBN: 1893905322. Reprints *Jack Kirby Collector 16–19*.

The fourth volume of this collection contains articles on Kirby's Marvel westerns, Rawhide Kid, Sgt Fury and others, the Atlas implosion, Captain America, Ant-Man, Marvel superheroes, The Lee-Kirby debate, the Eternals, Black Panther, Silver Surfer, and the price list for original Thor art. This collection contains interviews with Roy Thomas, Stan Lee, Jack Kirby, Joe Kubert, John Buscema, and Marie Severin. Many of the interviews contain insights into Kirby's work for Marvel and beyond. As in the previous volumes, there is a wealth of artwork from Kirby's career, including many Marvel characters.

Kirby, Jack, Greg Theakston, Richard Howell, et al. *The Complete Jack Kirby Volume 1: 1917–1940*. New York: Pure Imagination, 1997. ISBN: 1566850061. Reprints *Daring Mystery Comics 1*; *Red Raven Comics 1*.

This tribute to Jack Kirby reproduces many of his earliest, and consequently rarest stories, along with commentary. The authors also provide insight and history about periods of Kirby's life. The "Fiery Mask" story, from *Daring Mystery Comics*, is reprinted, as is

the Mercury space adventure, "Comet Pierce," from *Red Raven* comics. This black-and-white series is essential for any fan of Kirby's.

Kirby, Jack, Greg Theakston, Joe Simon, et al. *The Complete Jack Kirby Volume 2: 1940–1941*. Atlanta, GA: Pure Imagination, 1997. ISBN: 156685007X. Reprints *Daring Mystery Comics 6*.

This collection of reprints features work done by Jack Kirby during the early forties, and includes much historical information about Kirby's days at Timely comics, as well as his work for other companies. Some of the information includes material related to the origin of Captain America and the original Vision, plus such characters as the Black Owl; Blue Bolt; the original Captain Marvel, Shazam; Lightnin's; and the Lone Rider. The origins of the original Marvel Boy are shown, fighting, against the Nazis, the Fiery Mask, the devil and his demons.

Kirby, Jack, Greg Theakston, Jim Steranko, et al. *Jack Kirby's Heroes and Villains*. New York: Pure Imagination, 1994. ISBN: 1566850029.

This special volume contains drawings of characters that Kirby worked on. This was originally a book given to his wife Roz. This version, known as the Black Magic Edition, includes over 125 artists who ink and color Kirby's original drawings. There were several hardcover printings of this book, including one of which only 333 were bound, making them very hard to find. Some of the characters featured in this volume include the original monster Hulk; the Incredible Hulk; Sgt. Fury; Odin; members of the Fantastic Four; Wabash; Yellow Claw; Inhumans; Red Skull; Rawhide Kid; Fun Commies; Princess Python; Moleman; the Eternals; Spragg, the Living Hill; Devil Dinosaur; and Moon Boy. Steranko wrote the introduction.

Klutz, editors. *Draw the Marvel Comics Super Heroes*. Palo Alto, CA: Klutz, 1995. ISBN: 1570540004.

This is a spiral-bound, step-by-step guide to drawing Marvel heroes, including Captain America, Cyclops, Namor and Magneto. There are tracing pages, crib sheets, and examples of drawing feet, hands, and action. This is an excellent starting guide, recommended for ages 6 and up.

Krigstein, Bernie, Greg Sadowski, Marie Severin, et al. *B. Krigstein: Comics*. Seattle, WA: Fantagraphics, 2004. ISBN: 1560975733.

This deluxe hardcover volume contains restored reprints of Bernie Krigstein's comic stories, 1948–1957. The stories cover a wide variety of categories, including westerns, romances, crime, science fiction, and horror. Stories from Marvel/Atlas magazines include work from *Astonishing, Mystic, Battleground, Navy*

Tales, Marvel Tales, and *All True Crime.* There are many other fan favorites, such as EC's *Tales from the Crypt* and DC's *Our Army At War.* This book is highly recommended.

Lee, Stan, John Buscema. *How to Draw Comics the Marvel Way.* New York: Simon and Schuster, 1978. ISBN: 0671225480

This is the first edition of the perennially popular Marvel drawing book. It includes step-by-step text and graphics that teach the would-be artist to draw in the Marvel style. There are many illustrations from actual comic books, as well as sketches.

Lee, Stan, John Buscema. *How to Draw Comics the Marvel Way.* New York: Fireside, 1984. ISBN: 0671530771.

This is a revised edition of this title. It is a page-by-page guidebook on how to draw and plot using Marvel characters.

Lee, Stan, George Mair. *Excelsior: The Amazing Life of Stan Lee.* New York: Simon and Schuster, 2002. ISBN: 0743228006 (trd); 0684873052 (pbk).

In this volume, Mr. Marvel, Stan Lee, describes his early life and his years in the comic business. He recounts the stories behind the creation of Spider-Man, Hulk, X-Men, Dr. Doom, and many other Marvel Universe characters. Lee writes with flair, in a conversational style that makes this book a joy to read. This is Lee's autobiography, outlining his life from his beginnings at Timely Comics, throughout his days at Marvel and beyond. Lee writes in a personal style, with Mair using the third person to describe certain pivotal events. During Lee's time in the army, he wrote a comic strip warning GIs of the dangers of VD. This book includes the stories behind the creation of most of Marvel's major characters, like Spider-Man and the Fantastic Four, and gives a detailed account of the company's history, and Lee's role in it. The fall of Stan Lee Media is included. This volume is essential for all libraries.

Lee, Jim, Wizard editors, Richard Ho, et al. *The Wizard: Jim Lee Millennium Edition.* Congers, NY: Wizard Press, 2004. ISBN: 0974325333.

This special hardback book spotlights the work of artist Jim Lee. It includes interviews, profiles, a checklist, and a story on Lee's work on Superman. It also includes the history of Image Comics, with profiles of the creators, a sketchbook, and reproductions of covers from such Marvel titles as *Avengers, X-Men, X-Factor, Captain America, Wolverine, Conan, Transformers,* and many others from Lee's career.

McCallum, Pat, Tom Root, Douglas Goldstine, et al. *Twisted Toyfare Theatre Volume 1.* Yorktown Heights, New York: Wizard Press, 2003. ISBN: 0967248922. Reprints *Toyfare 2, 8–9, 12, 14, 17, 27–28, 31, 34–35, 39–40, 45–46.*

From the pages of *Toyfare* magazine comes *Twisted Toyfare Theatre,* which uses Marvel Mego toys in humorous situations. In this volume Thor and Spider-Man crush helpless Jawwas; the Punisher blows up Kang for robbing the piggybank of a small child; Reed Richards finds out they are only toys; Venom pulls the head off of Bill Gates and Iron Man; the Thing gets toasted; and Thor, Spider-Man, and the Hulk go to a comic convention where they get lost overnight, in "The Mego Witch Project." This volume is absolutely hilarious. The introduction is by filmmaker Kevin Smith.

McCallum, Pat, Tom Root, Douglas Goldstine, et al. *Twisted Toyfare Theatre Volume 2.* Yorktown Heights, NY: Wizard Press, 2003. ISBN: 096724851. Reprints *Toyfare 3–4, 21, 26, 30–31, 36–37, 43–44, 48, 52.*

Charlie Brown gets smashed while Hulk is opening the door. The Hulk farts, to the horror of the other Marvel Meggs. The Green Goblin goes hot tubbing with some Barbie babes. Hulk goes to meet the Autobots, but runs afoul of Megatron after he shows off the Cher autograph on his tush. Hulk accidentally kills an Ewok, and they are out for his blood. The Thing becomes a panty bandit, and Spider-Man gets caught parking in a handicapped zone. The Hulk takes a dump inside a street pothole in which some Morlocks are lounging.

This is the second collection in which Marvel Mego figures are doing strange things, and there are more laughs in this volume than in the first one. This volume includes a section on *Twisted Toyfare* ideas that were too risqué, and a tour of the room where the action figures come to life. Spider-Man also gives readers a lesson in grading your action figures. The introduction is by Seth Green.

McCallum, Pat, Tom Root, Douglas Goldstein et al. *Twisted Toyfare Theatre Vol. 3.* Yorktown Heights, NY: Wizard Press, 2004. ISBN: 0974325309. Reprints *Toyfare 6, 10, 33, 47, 49, 54, 55, 57, 58, 59, 60, 65; X-Men Special.*

Dr. Doom steals Christmas and becomes the Kool-Aid Man. Some farmworkers use the Watcher's head as a Piñata. Spider-Man gets an invitation to become part of the Defenders. Bucky is killed by the Red Skull, after he surrenders to Captain America. The Hulk tells a bedtime story. Spider-Man poses as Harry Potter. Sue Richards has been had by Power Man, Mr. T, and the Falcon, while Reed tries to figure out what to with the Thing's bachelor party gift. Thor buys an X box on which to watch DVDs, but his choice in DVDs is terrible. While Thor and Spider-Man watch *Star Trek the Motion Picture,* Thor falls asleep. The original Star Trek crew goes back in time, and they meet Spider-Man. Spider-Man has the anti–G.I. Joe terrorist group, COBRA, living in a mouse hole in his home.

This volume also contains Mego super heroes, "The Secret Wars," and "Handbook of Twisted Toyfare Theatre Universe Vol. 1." The introduction was written by *Star Wars* star Mark Hamill, and "the Pope."

McCallum, Pat, Tom Root, Douglas Goldstein et al. *Twisted Toyfare Theatre Vol. 4.* Yorktown Heights NY: Wizard Press, 2004. ISBN: 0974325341. Reprints *Toyfare 22, 24, 29, 63, 70, 73, 75–76, 78–79; Inquest 87.*

The cops from *CHiPS* start on a rampage. Some Mexican wrestlers become substitute officers in Megoville. The Hulk throws the Sandman into Bucky's face, and falls in love with Daisy Duke. Iron Man gets sloshed, and the cat, Mr. Buttons, takes over his armor. The Thing takes Franklin to the fair, while his mom is having fun with Sub-Mariner. William Shatner gets his own *Ultimate* series, the *Ultimate Kirk*, after singing Mr. Tambourine Man on *American Idol*. H.E.R.B.I.E. gets on Battle Bots, and beats everyone, much to the Human Torch's dismay. The Smurfs are turned into Zombies. George W. Bush becomes mayor of Megoville, Northstar advertises mints, and Doc Ock gets Aunt May pregnant.

In this volume, we learn the origin of Bat-Hulk and the Thing. The volume also contains "Handbook of the Twisted Toyfare Theatre Universe Vol. 2" and "Hall of Shame." Newer releases include Volumes 5–7. ISBN: 0974325384 (5); 0976287463 (6); 0977861325 (7).

McCarron, Owen, Stan Lee, et al. *Stan Lee Presents The Mighty Marvel Superheroes Fun Book.* New York: Simon and Schuster, 1976. ISBN: 0671223100 (1); 0671227580 (2); 0671242237 (3); 0671243896 (4); 0671248 103 (1–3, *Jumbo Fun Book*).

This book is a collection of games and puzzles related to Marvel characters. It includes word games, mazes, and crossword puzzles.

Malis, Gene, Jody Cameron Malis, Joe Giella, et al. *Stan Lee Presents the Mighty Marvel Superheroes' Cookbook.* New York: Marvel, 1977. ISBN: 0671225596.

This profusely illustrated cookbook contains fun recipes for "Captain America Day Starters," "Hawkeye's Corned Beef Hash," "The Thing's Clobbered Omelet," "Hulk's Sloppy Joes," "Thor's Asgardian Vegetable Soup," "Sub-Mariner's Magnificent Tuna Bake," "Powerman's Fillet of Sole," "Hulk's Applesauce Cake," "Daredevil's Food Cake," and "Captain America's American Pie," among others.

Mallory, Michael. *Marvel: The Characters and Their Universe.* New York: Hugh Lauter

Levin Associates, 2002. ISBN: 0883631 105; 0883631091 (2001).

This is a massive, leather-bound, hardback collector's book that details the history of various Marvel characters. It contains chapters on Captain America, the X-Men, Spider-Man, Hulk, and the world of Marvel. It also has a section on Marvel superheroes. While this book is not as detailed as the Daniels and Sanderson Marvel books, it does provide in-depth insight into all the various Marvel-related media projects, such as cartoons and full-length films that feature Marvel characters. Mallory details the history behind the Japanese movie, *Tomb of Dracula*; the *Spider-Man* series; the *Generation X* movie; the unreleased Fantastic Four movie; the Captain America serial, film, television show, and cartoons; *Blade*; the never-made Sub-Mariner television series; and the nineties Marvel cartoon series. The work has been updated to include the first Spider-Man movie and *X-Men: Evolution*. It is profusely illustrated and belongs in every library.

Mallory, Rik, Steve Webb, Roger Green, et al. *X-Men Chronicles.* Albany, NY: FantaCo Enterprises, 1981.

This special book contains a look at the history of the X-Men. It also contains an analysis of the Roy Thomas years, a Jim Shooter interview, an X-Men checklist, and a look at the new X-Men, including the special issue published with Teen Titans.

Marshall, John. *Comic Book Hero Toys.* Atglen, PA: Schiffer Publishing Ltd, 1999. ISBN: 0764309226.

This full-color illustrated book of various superhero toys includes chapters on Spider-Man, Hulk, and Marvel superhero figures. Some of the items pictured are Spider-Man web-shooters, Hulk soap and helicopter, a Captain America game, Captain Marvel and Dr. Doom cars, and a "Scream Along with Marvel" record. There are many other unique toys shown. This book is recommended.

Martone, Michael. *The Sex Life of the Fantastic Four.* Tuscaloosa, AL: Strode Cabin Press, 1998.

This poetry book contains sections on Invisible Girl, Human Torch, Mister Fantastic, and The Thing.

Marvel Entertainment Group. *Prospectus: 35,000 Shares of Common Stock.* New York: Merrill Lynch Co/First Boston Corp, 1991.

This is a detailed look at Marvel for the stockholders. It includes selected financial data and Marvel's publishing schemata, including Spider-Man, Epic comics, trade paperbacks, graphic novels, and the Masterworks series.

Miller, Frank, Hal Schuster, Jim Keegan, et al. *Frank Miller: A Work in Progress: Great*

Comics Artists File. San Bernardino, CA: Heroes Publications, 1986.

This volume offers a look at the history of Frank Miller's artistic works, focusing on his work for Marvel, which includes *Daredevil, Spider-Man, Elektra,* and *Wolverine,* among others. It leads into his work on *Ronin* and *Batman,* and contains detailed interviews with Miller in which he discusses his work with Marvel. This volume is illustrated with many Marvel characters.

Misiroglu, Gina Renée, David A Roach. *The Superhero Book: The Ultimate Encyclopedia of Comic-Book Icons and Hollywood Heroes.* Canton, MI: Visible Ink Press, 2004. ISBN: 0780807723 (trd) 1578591546 (pbk).

This exhaustive, 700-page, A–Z collection covers the whole world of superheroes, from comics to radio and film. Some of the Marvel characters included are Ant-Man, Marvel Boy, the Cat, Defenders, Northstar, Power Man, Silver Surfer, Ghost Rider, and the Avengers, among many others. Essays cover Daredevil, the Fantastic Four, X-Men in the media, World War II and superheroes, love interests, and multiculturalism in comics. The work includes an index and illustrations.

Muir, John Kenneth. *The Encyclopedia of Superheroes on Film and Television.* Jefferson, NC: McFarland, 2004. ISBN: 0786417234.

This beautiful volume provides a detailed look at various celluloid and small-screen versions of superheroes. The Marvel characters include Spider-Man, Blade, Captain America, Daredevil, Doctor Strange, Fantastic Four, Thor, Generation X, Hulk, Iron Man, Mutant X, Nick Fury, Silver Surfer, and X-Men. This volume covers feature films, television series, television movies, animated films, and serials. Nearly ever superhero that graced the screen is listed, from Batman and Buffy, to the Shadow and Captain Nice. There is even an entry for the groundbreaking film *Unbreakable.* It is highly recommended.

Nolen-Weathington, Eric. *Modern Masters Volume 1: Alan Davis.* Raleigh, NC: TwoMorrows, Publishing, 2003. ISBN: 189390 5195.

This volume is dedicated to the work of Alan Davis. who discusses how he first came to Marvel UK, and his groundbreaking work on Captain Britain. It includes many sketches of various Marvel heroes including Spider-Man, X-Men, and the Avengers.

Nowlan, Kevin, Eric Nolen-Weathington, eds. *Modern Masters Volume 4: Kevin Nowlan.* Raleigh, NC: TwoMorrows, 2004. ISBN: 1893905381.

This volume is a tribute to artist Kevin Nowlan. It includes detailed interviews, divided into various parts. One of these, "Marvel Comics and a Baptism of Fire," details Nowlan's first work for Marvel which was on *Dr. Strange* and *Moon Knight.* Nowlan also discusses his work on *Batman* and others, for DC. There are sketches of Marvel characters throughout the volume, depicting Scarlet Witch, Dr. Strange, Moon Knight, Man Thing, and others.

Olshevsky, George. "The Origin of Marvel Comics," in *The Comic Book Price Guide 1980–1981 10th Edition,* by Robert M. Overstreet. Cleveland, TN: Overstreet Publications, 1980. ISBN: 0517540215.

This is a well-written, detailed account of the origin of Marvel comics, by Marvel indexer George Olshevsky. Olshevsky covers all the early creators and characters, and the history of Marvel/Timely Comics, through the Golden Age, up to 1950. This issue of the price guide also has a section featuring color reproductions of Timely Comics, including the six most sought issues.

Perez, George, Eric Nolen-Weathington, Marv Wolfman, et al. *Modern Masters Volume 2: George Perez.* Raleigh, NC: TwoMorrows Press, 2003. ISBN: 189390525X.

This collection contains a detailed look at artist George Perez's career. The volume includes a chapter on his work at Marvel in which he discusses in detail his work on the Avengers and other Marvel titles. There is an art gallery which includes Marvel characters like the Thing, Captain America, Black Widow, and Spider-Man.

Picardo, Ann, Joe Giella. *Stan Lee Presents the Mighty Marvel Strength and Fitness Book.* New York: Simon and Schuster, 1976. ISBN: 0671223127.

This is a collection of exercises using illustrations of Marvel characters. It includes such techniques as the Jameson Roar, the Torchie Twist, Silver Surfer's Heralded Highways, Ghost Rider's Bizarre Bicycles, and the Patriotic Pull, among others. This is a fun book, full of nostalgia.

Raphael, Jordan, Tom Spurgeon. *Stan Lee and the Rise and Fall of the American Comic Book.* Chicago: Chicago Review Press, 2003. ISBN: 1556525060.

This was the first full-length biography and study of Stan Lee, his role in the creation of Marvel, and key changes in the comic book industry. The authors describe in detail Lee's Timely/Atlas experience and how he rose to prominence within the company. This is a very good history of Marvel, relating how many of the characters were created. It also has details about folks like Jim Shooter, Jack Kirby, Steve Ditko, and others who have gone through the Marvel bullpen. Lee became a head of Marvel, and lectured at universities. There is a detailed description of Marvel's failed attempt to produce underground comics with Denis

Kitchen. Lee moved out to California to try to get Hollywood interested in Marvel's characters. It documents the ups and downs of the nineties when Marvel almost went bankrupt, and the turbulent fall of Stan Lee Media. The volume also includes a detailed look at Martin Goodman's role, and his subsequent comic book fight with Marvel in the early seventies. This is a well-written account which has a scholarly flair and is much more detailed than Lee's autobiography. There are rare photographs of Steve Ditko, Lee and his family, an old Timely Comics Christmas card, and photos from a Stan Lee commercial for razor blades. This volume is highly recommended.

Ravi, Dan. *Comic Wars: How Two Tycoons Battled Over the Marvel Comics Empire and Both Lost*. New York: Broadway Books, 2002. ISBN: 0767908309.

This is a fascinating story about how millionaires Ron Pearlman and Carl Icahn fought over Marvel during the harrowing bankruptcy proceedings of the mid-nineties. Both men lost to Toz Biz, Avi Arad, and Ike Perlmutter. This detailed book goes a long way in showing how lawyers, banks, and the very rich try to manipulate the system for their personal gain. It is a behind-the-scenes look at how financial giants and their lawyers operate. This book belongs in every library.

Ro, Ronin. *Tales to Astonish: Jack Kirby, Stan Lee, and the American Comic Book Revolution*. New York: Bloomsbury, 2004. ISBN: 1582343454.

This is not a biography per se, but a novel-like tribute to Jack Kirby and his role in influencing comic book history. Although Stan Lee, Joe Simon, and Steve Ditko are discussed, they are not the focus of this work. The volume contains information about; Kirby's early role at Marvel; his time overseas, during World War II; his role in the Marvel Age of the 1960s; his defection to DC in the early seventies; his return to Marvel in the late seventies, and his subsequent departure. Ro gives many details about Kirby's attempts to get his original artwork back from Marvel, during the 1980s, his fallout with Stan Lee, and the controversy concerning the creation of Spider-Man. This book is well written and well researched, and is a must for anybody interested in the history of comics.

Robbins, Trina. *The Great Women Superheroes*. Northampton, MA: Kitchen Sink Press, 1996. ISBN: 0878164820 (trd); 0878164812 (pbk).

This volume contains an excellent survey and history of women superbeings. It includes some material on Marvel heroines like Ms. Marvel, Elektra, the Cat, Black Widow, and Valkyrie, among others.

Romita, John Sr., David Spurlock. *John Romita Sketchbook*. Lebanon, NJ: Vanguard Pro-

ductions, 2002. ISBN: 1887591273 (trd); 1887591821 (limited hdc); 188759129X (pbk).

This is a showcase for John Romita Sr.'s art and sketches. It contains a very detailed interview in which Romita discusses his years at Marvel, from the Timely period to the present day. There is a lot of Spider-Man artwork as well as artwork featuring the Beast, the Thing, Ms. Marvel, Mary Jane, Nova, Omega, Wolverine, and Captain America. Romita describes his idea for the defunct Femizons, who originally appeared in *Savage Tales 1*. Stan Lee wrote the introduction.

Root, Tom. Andrew Kardon, *Writers on Comic Scriptwriting 2*. London: Titan, 2004. ISBN: 1840238089.

This volume contains interviews with the crème de la crème of comic writing. It includes Marvel authors Brian Vaughn, Peter Milligan, Kevin Smith, Brian Michael Bendis, Bruce Jones, and Mark Millar. Other writers interviewed include Paul Dini, Brian Azzarello, Andy Diggle, Jill Thompson, and Mike Mignola. The volume has sample script pages from *Wolverine 20*, *Spider-Man 6*, *X-Statix 26*, *Runaways 1*, and others. All the authors interviewed discuss their Marvel work.

Ross, Alex, Christopher, Lawrence, Scott Brick, et al. *Wizard: The Alex Ross Special Millennium Edition*. Cangers, NY: Wizard, 2003. ISBN: 0967248973; 0967248906 (1999).

This is a special hardback book that commemorates the art and work of Alex Ross. It contains interviews with Ross, photos of his superhero figure collection, and a detailed look at his work for Marvel and DC Comics, including *Marvels* and *Earth X*, plus many reproductions of Marvel artwork and a complete checklist for the works of Ross. It also includes his drawing of Danny DeVito as Wolverine.

Rovin, Jeff. *Encyclopedia of Superheroes*. New York: Facts on File, 1985. ISBN: 0816011 680.

This A–Z of superheroes includes many Marvel characters. Each entry includes a biography, and information about alter ego, first appearance, occupation, tools, and costume. It contains entries for many Golden-Age Marvel characters, such as the first Angel, Black Marvel, and Citizen V.

Sadowksi, Greg B. *Krigstein Volume 1*. Seattle, WA: Fantagraphics, 2002. ISBN: 1560974 664.

This volume documents the life, career, and art of Krigstein, including a short section on his years at Timely and Atlas.

Saffel, Steve. "Spider-Man: An Amazing Success Story" in Robert M. Overstreet ed.,

Overstreet Comic Book Price Guide 22nd ed. New York: Avon Books, 1992. ISBN: 0380 769123.

In this well-written piece, the author looks at the history of Spider-Man. He starts by looking at the first Spider-Man, created by Joe Simon, and later the Silver Spider. This work was shown to Stan Lee who improved on the author's concept and then came up with his own version of Spider-Man. The "secret origin," in *Amazing Fantasy*, is discussed in detail, as are pivotal moments in the character's history, e.g., "Death of Gwen Stacy," "Death of Jean DeWolf," "Peter Parker's Graduation from High School," "The Saga of the Black Costume," and "The Kid Who Collects Spider-Man," among several others. There is also a discussion of *Spider-Man*'s cast of characters" and how the comic's supporting cast helped make Spidey the success he is today.

Salisbury, Mark. *Artists on Comic Art.* London: Titan, 2000. ISBN: 1840231866.

This is a collection of interviews with famous artists, including Frank Miller, Jim Lee, Alex Ross, Steve Dillon, Dave Gibbons, J. Scott Campbell, Brian Bollard, Bryan Hitch, and Dave McKean, among others. Joe Quesada discusses his work on *Daredevil* and the Marvel Knights imprint, and John Romita Jr. discusses his work on *Spider-Man* and other Marvel characters. The volume includes some of Alex Ross's art on *Earth X, Captain America,* and Jim Lee's *X-Men.* Ross briefly discusses *Marvels.*

Salisbury, Mark. *Writers on Comic Scriptwriting Vol. 1.* London: Titan, 1999. ISBN: 18402 3069X.

This collection includes interviews with Marvel writers Peter David (*Hulk*), Joe Kelly (*Deadpool*), Dan Jurgans (*Thor*), Kurt Busiek (*Marvels*), and Jeph Loeb (*X-Men*). Other writers included are: Devin Grayson, Garth Ennis, Neal Gaiman, Todd McFarlane, Grant Morrison, Frank Miller, Mark Waid, and Chuck Dixon, among others. This book also contains script samples from *Incredible Hulk 467; Punisher Condemned;* and *Captain America 4* and *14.* This book represents an excellent job of research, in which the writers talk about their work for Marvel, DC, and other companies.

Sanderson, Peter. *Marvel Universe.* New York: H.N. Abrams, 1996. ISBN: 0810942852; 0810981718 (1998, Abradale Press).

This is a wonderful illustrated history of the Marvel characters, and the universe they inhabit. Chapters include "The Fantastic Four; X-Men and Mutants"; "Spider-Man"; "Antiheroes—Human Torch, Hulk, Sub-Mariner"; "Avengers"; "Heroes of the Supernatural—Dracula, Ghost Rider, Son of Satan"; "Protectors of the Universe—Silver Surfer, Captain Marvel, Warlock"; and "Vigilantes and Lawmen—Daredevil, Moon Knight, Elektra, and Punisher." Anybody interested in Marvel should read this book. It is beautifully written and is essential for libraries.

Sanderson, Peter, Peppy White, Chris Claremont, et al. *The X-Men Companion II.* Stamford CT: Fantagraphics Books, 1982.

This 100+ page book has detailed interviews of X-Men writers and artists, including the second part of Chris Claremont's interview in which he discusses his favorite science fiction authors, his influences, and his work on the X-Men. Others here include John Byrne, Terry Austin, and Louise Jones. Claremont and Louise Jones are interviewed together, discussing the second *X-Men* series, and the *X-Men Teen Titans* crossover. Terry Austin and John Byrne discuss their artistic work on the X-Men. Sanderson writes a detailed essay on why the X-Men have a wider appeal than other Marvel and DC superheroes. This volume includes artwork by Gil Kane and Fred Hembeck.

Sanderson, Peter, Peppy White, Michael Golden, et al. *X-Men: Companion I.* Stamford, CT: Fantagraphics Books, 1982.

This well-illustrated guide to all things X-Men contains a detailed history of the group, from their beginnings to 1982. Sanderson provides-an-issue by issue commentary on the early years. Roy Thomas is interviewed about his views on the new X-Men, and his tenure on the title during the 1960s. Len Wein is interviewed about putting together the new X-Men, and his work on the title, as is Dave Cockrum. Chris Claremont is interviewed, a conversation that continues in the book's second volume. He discusses his views on the early X-Men, his early work at Marvel, and his views on the Phoenix.

Schamus, James, John Thurman, Michael France, et al. *Hulk: Illustrated Screenplay.* New York: New Market, 2003. ISBN: 1557045976 (trd); 15557045852 (pbk).

This is the complete screenplay for the hit movie *Hulk,* with a foreword by director Ang Lee. The book is profusely illustrated and contains storyboards and sections on the comic, the television Hulk, the special effects used for the movie, the main characters, and the actors involved. It is highly recommended.

Schelly, Bill, ed. *The Golden Age of Comic Fandom.* Seattle, WA: Hamster Press, 1999. ISBN: 096456694X.

This is a collection of wonderful articles covering the 1960s era, the Golden Age of comic fandom. In chapter 7, there is a discussion about 1965, a watershed year when fan Roy Thomas was about to become a famous writer for Marvel Comics. The volume includes reprints from the Fantastic Four Fan Page, which includes letters from future writers, including Mark Gruenwald, Roy Thomas, Steve Gerber, Dave Cockrum, Paul Gambaceini, G.B. Love and Landon Chesney. The volume is profusely illustrated.

Schoell, William. *Comic Book Heroes on the Screen.* New York: Citadel Press, 1991. ISBN: 0806512520.

This work contains chapters on various Marvel-related heroes, including Captain America, Hulk and Daredevil, Spider-Man, Dr. Strange, Howard the Duck, and Punisher. There is a short section on movies based on characters from Marvel comics, including Conan, Flash Gordon, Robocop, Conan, and Doc Savage. The author discusses the original comics, and then discusses how the films fared next to the comics. The volume is highly recommended.

Schomburg, Alex, Jon Gustafson, Harlan Ellison, et al. *Chroma: The Art of Alex Schomburg*. Poughkeepsie, NY, 1986. ISBN: 0936 861010 (trd); 0936861002 (pbk).

This volume is a tribute to Alex Schomburg, the artist who drew many of the covers for Timely Comics and science fiction magazines. The thrilling art in this volume includes full-color reproductions of *Captain America*, *Marvel Mystery*, *USA*, *All Winners*, *All Select*, and the *Invaders* comic covers. Stan Lee wrote the introduction to the chapter that deals with the early Timely material.

Schumer, Arlen. *The Silver Age of Comic Book Art*. Portland, OR: Collector's Press, 2003. ISBN: 1888054867 (trd); 1888054859 (pbk).

This is a wonderful book that highlights some of the most famous artists from the Silver Age of comics. There are chapters on Jim Steranko, Steve Ditko, Jack Kirby, Gil Kane, Gene Colon, and Neal Adams. Work done for Marvel and DC, as well as work done for other companies, are highlighted throughout the book. The chapter on Ditko, which discusses his work on Spider-Man, is especially good. The author compares the rise of the Beatles to the Fantastic Four. This book goes a long way toward giving comic art the respect and recognition it should have as high art.

Schuster, Hal, ed. *Comics File Magazine Spotlight on Spider-Man*. San Bernardino, CA: Borgo, 1986, ISBN: 0809581035.

This excellent book contains a history of Spider-Man, sections on the Romitas, and a "Talk with Various Spider Writers," including David Michelinie and Tom DeFalco. The book also contains an essay, "The Spider and I," written by Sam Kujava.

Schuster, Hal, Doug Highsmith, et al. *Comics File Spotlight on the Avengers Files*. San Bernardino, CA: Borgo Press, 1987. ISBN: 0809581310.

This is an excellent collection about "Earth's mightiest heroes," the Avengers. The book contains a very detailed history of the various Avenger lineups, and the changes in the group. Jim Shooter's writing on the *Avengers* book is analyzed, and the year 1981 is reviewed in detail. Roger Stern and Steve Englehart are also interviewed in the book.

Schuster, Hal, James Van Hise, John Peel, et al. *Comic Files Magazine Spotlight on G.I. Joe: The 'Nam; Merc; Frontline Combat File*. Canoga Park, CA: MPS, 1986. ISBN: 1556980116; 1556980256.

This tribute book covers Larry Hama's work on Marvel's *G.I. Joe* comic and Steve Gerber's work on the animated series. There is also a detailed analysis and an interview with Doug Murray about his work on *The 'Nam*, and the New Universe character, Mark Hazzard, *Merc*. The book also includes an essay about the classic book *Frontline Combat*, and illustrations and sketches from various comics. This is a very interesting and enlightening look at some of the best-selling, unique comics Marvel published during the 1980s.

Schuster, Hal, James Van Hise, Murry Ward, et al. *Comics File Magazine Spotlight on The X-Men File* and *Sons of the X-Men: Comics File Magazine Spotlight on The X-Men File*. San Bernardino, CA: Borgo Press, 1986–1987. ISBN: 0809580861 (1); 080958106X (2, *Sons of the X-Men*).

These volumes include a nice history of the first X-Men team, an interview with Chris Claremont, and articles on the New Mutants, Alpha Flight, and other X-Men related characters. Both volumes contain useful information for the X-fanatic.

Shaner, Timothy. *The Art of X2: The Making of a Blockbuster Movie*. New York: Newmarket Press, 2003. ISBN: 1557045771 (trd); 1557 045771 (pbk).

This is a photographic look at the creation of the second X-Men movie, *X2*. It contains photographs of characters and scenes, quotes from the cast about the movie, detailed storyboards, illustrations, and a full credits list. This limited edition hardcover also has the complete *X2* script, sections on Nightcrawler posters, and art from the first film, *X-Men*.

Shooter, Jim. "Marvel and Me," in Overstreet, Robert, *The Comic Book Price Guide 1986–1987*. New York: Harmony, 1986. ISBN: 0517561034.

In this article Shooter writes about his experience with Marvel comics from the time he was a young fan to becoming Marvel's editor-in-chief. This work also contains Stan Lee's "Twenty-Five Years—I Don't Believe It!" This was the Marvel 25th anniversary issue.

Shooter, Jim, John S. Romita, Allen Milgrom, et al. *The Official Marvel Comics Try-Out Book 1*. New York: Marvel, 1983. ISBN: 0939766760.

This is an oversized guide to drawing, scripting, lettering, coloring, plotting and correctly producing a Marvel comic.

Shutt, Craig. *Baby Boomer Comics: The Wild Wacky, Wonderful, Comic Books of the 1960s.* Iola, WI: Krause Publications, 2003. ISBN: 087349688X.

This volume provides a detailed look at the Silver Age of comics by the man who calls himself. Mr. Silver Age. While it concentrates on DC and Marvel books, there are sections on other comics. Some of the Marvel chapters include cover Patsy Walker, Karen Page and Daredevil, Nick Fury, Thor and Sif, Marvel characters going to Hollywood. There's even a Spider-Man quiz. There are many tidbits of Silver-Age comic trivia in this volume.

Simmons Market Research. *Characteristics and Advertising Response of Marvel Comics Primary Audience.* New York: Simmons Market Research, 1984.

Marvel Comics commissioned a study to see how well advertising worked for them. Ten thousand questionnaires were prepared and inserted into *Alpha Flight, Peter Parker: Spider-Man,* and *Star Wars.* Readers between the ages of 6 and 18 were encouraged to complete and send back the questionnaires to receive free copies of *Alpha Flight, Fantastic Four,* or *Spider-Man* which contained special advertisements. The readers were then asked to endure a fifteen-minute telephone interview which assessed the effectiveness of the test advertising. Some of the products looked at included Superman peanut butter, Lee jeans, A.I.M. toothpaste, and Pringles potato chips. In general, the results of the study showed that: Marvel readers respond well to promotional offers; they exert considerable influence over purchase of an item; comics generate considerable pass-along readership; advertising in Marvel is read and remembered; and parents look more favorably on their children reading comics, than on television viewing. The volume includes the complete questionnaire, callback interview questions, sample ads, and a detailed explanation of the whole process. This volume was privately published.

Simon, Joe, Jim Simon. *The Comic Book Makers.* New York: Crestwood Publications, 1990. ISBN: 0962685801; 1887591354 (2002).

This volume contains Simon's memoirs of life in the comics industry during the Golden Age. He describes his time as an editor for Timely/ Marvel during the forties. He reminisces about his creation of Captain America along with Jack Kirby, and the copyright problems, labeled "the Captain America Wars," that developed much later. He also recounts the previously untold origin story of Spider-Man, by Jack Kirby and himself.

Steranko, Jim. *Steranko History of Comics Volume 1.* Reading, PA: Supergraphics, 1970.

This is a well-written history of comics in the Golden Age, by Steranko, one of the industry's comics greatest artists. The volume contains chapters on the creation of Captain America, Human Torch, and Sub-Mariner, along with a wealth of information about Marvel's years as Timely Comics. There are many reprints of original covers in black and white. The introduction was written by Italian filmmaker Federico Fellini.

Teitelbaum, Michael, Ron Zalme. *How to Draw Monster Jam.* Mahwah, NJ: Troll, 2003. ISBN: 0816776016 (trd); 0816770158 (pbk); 0816770158 (2001).

This special drawing book for kids is part of the Monster Truck series. It includes special Marvel trucks for Spider-Man, Wolverine, and the Hulk.

Theakston, Greg. "The Road to Spider-Man" in *Steve Ditko Reader Vol. 1.* Brooklyn, NY: Pure Imagination, 2002. ISBN: 155850118.

The "Road to Spider-Man" details how Ditko became involved in helping create the character of Spider-Man, and his early work at Marvel. The author looks at an earlier creation by Joe Simon, the Silver Spider, and its influence on Spider-Man. Most of the book consists of black-and-white reprints of Ditko's science fiction/monster work for companies other than Marvel. The book includes a reprint of Ditko's unused cover for *Amazing Fantasy 15.*

Thomas, Harry, Gary M. Carter. "1941: Comic Books Go to War: Those Fabulous Comics of World War II" in Robert M. Overstreet, *Official Overstreet Comic Book Price Guide 21st Edition.* Cleveland, OH: Overstreet Publications, 1981. ISBN: 0876378599.

This article describes comics produced during the years of World War II. While the article does not focus on Timely per se, there is a considerable section on Timely heroes, such as the Human Torch and Captain America, and on *All Winner's* and *Marvel Mystery Comics.* The article includes DC, Fawcett, and other publishers of war comics.

Thomas, Roy, ed. *Alter Ego: The Comic Book Artist Collection.* Raleigh, NC: TwoMorrows, 2001. ISBN: 1893905063. Reprints *Alter Ego Vol. 2: 1–5.*

This work contains a great deal of Marvel content, including "Fantastic First: The Creation of the Fantastic Four and Beyond" (pp. 32–37); reproductions of original typed plots of *Fantastic Four 1 and 8,* by Stan Lee; Roy Thomas's "OK Axis, Here We Come Again: The Retro Birth of the Invaders" (pp. 42–44); "Art of the Invaders" (pp. 45–50); Steve Ditko's essay in response to Jack Kirby's claim of creating Spider-Man (pp. 56–59); collaboration with Neal Adams on the X-Men, by Roy Thomas (pp. 93–101); a Ditko interview from 1966, discussing Spider-Man (pp. 107–108); an issue-by-issue annotation by Roy Thomas, describing the Kree-Skrull War in the

Avengers (pp. 109–120); and the Roy Thomas and Neal Adams collaboration on *Conan* and *War of the Worlds/Amazing Adventures* (pp. 129–132).

Thomas, Roy, Bill Schelly, eds. *Alter Ego: Best of the Legendary Comics Fanzine.* Seattle, WA: Hamster Press, 1997. ISBN: 0964566923. Reprints *Alter Ego 1–11.*

This volume contains material from the first eleven issues of the comics zine *Alter Ego*, with the following Marvel content: Roy Thomas's review of *Fantastic Four 1* from 1961 (p. 45); Alley Awards for 1962 in which the Fantastic Four got chosen best comic of the year (p. 86); Stan Lee and Steve Ditko write to the mag (p. 87); an interview with Gil Kane (pp. 157–168); and an interview with Bill Everett, focusing on Sub-Mariner (pp. 173–181).

Townsend, John. "Three Uncanny Decades of the X-Men," in Robert Overstreet ed., *Overstreet Comic Book Price Guide 24th Edition.* New York: Avon Books, 1994. ISBN: 0380778548.

This article gives a complete history of the X-Men, from the early team through 1993. The author divides the history into six different eras. The article includes an X-Men timeline, 1963–1993.

U.S. Department of Energy. *Energy Back-grounder for the Captain America Comic Book.* Washington DC: U.S. Department of Energy, 1980. E/.33/3:0054

This government document is an educator's guide for the Captain America comic book which was given to schools to help children learn the importance of energy and its uses.

Vallejo, Boris, Julie Bell, Nigel Suckling, et al. *Superheroes: The Heroic Visions of Boris Vallejo and Julie Bell.* New York: Thunders Mouth Press, 2000. ISBN: 1560252731 (trd); 1560253398 (pbk).

This is a wonderful collection of artwork, mostly Marvel-related, that originally appeared on Fleet trading cards. Chapters cover: Spider-Man, "Marvellous Universes," Marvel Knights, the Avengers, X-Men, X-Woman, and X-Marauders. Obscure characters like Vengeance, Jackyl, Psi-Lord, and the Gray Daredevil are featured throughout the book, alongside mainstream Marvel characters. The book is highly recommended.

Van Hise, James. *Critics Choice Magazine Presents: The Silver Surfer: An Analysis of Issues 1–9.* Canoga Park, CA: Psi Fi Press, 1987.

This is a detailed look at the first nine issues of *The Silver Surfer*, as done by Stan Lee and John Buscema. This critical review includes a look at the Surfer's early history in comics, starting with *Fantastic Four 48*.

Each of the first nine issues is studied in detail, and there are reprints of the covers. These reviews of the comics could be compared to commentaries done on DVDs today. This excellent book should be sought by fans of this character.

Van Hise, James. *Critics Choice Magazine Presents: The X-Men: Issues 129–145.* Canoga Park, CA: Psi Fi Press, 1987. ISBN: 15569 81465.

This is a special book which analyzes the stories in *X-Men 129–145.* These include the Dark Phoenix storyline and Doctor Doom's kidnapping of Storm. Each issue is looked at in detail, and contains a reprint of the cover and information which details the original creators.

Van Hise, James, Hal Schuster, Jim Keegan, et al. *Comics File Spotlight on Fantastic Four Files.* San Bernardino, CA: Borgo Press, 1986. ISBN: 0809580837

This book contains the history of the Fantastic Four and its writers, Jack Kirby, Roy Thomas John Byrne, Mike Carlin, and Roger Stern. It includes chapters on heroes and villains, and a checklist of all *Fantastic Four* issues through November 1986.

Van Hise, James, Al Williamson, William Stout, et al. *The Art of Al Williamson.* San Diego, CA: Blue Dolphin, 1983. ISBN: 0943128048. Reprints *Two-Gun Kid 25; Mystery Tales 5; World of Suspense 9; Kid Slade Gunslinger 7.*

This book is a tribute to artist Al Williamson, with reprints of western and monster short stories published by Atlas/Marvel in the 1950s. It also contains several interviews with Williamson on his career, and tributes from others in the industry, including filmmaker George Lucas. There is a complete Williamson checklist up to 1983, covering various strips. "The Vicious Space Pirates" and "Secret Agent Corrigan," which are from other publishers, and an unused *Star Wars* newspaper strip written by Archie Goodwin, are also included. This was also published in a limited, black-and-white, hardcover edition.

Vaughn, J.C. "Not Just Another Justice League? Earth's Mightiest Heroes Don't Think So," in Robert Overstreet, et al. *The Overstreet Comic Book Price Guide 29th Edition*, pp. 94–100. New York: Gemstone, 1999. ISBN: 0380807807.

The author argues that with thirty-six years of the *Avengers* comics and counting, the Avengers were not rip-offs of DC's *Justice League* comic. The article looks at milestones in the group's history, and has a chart for those milestones. It also looks at the Avengers West Coast, *Avengers* books that are in print, and at mini-series, graphic novels, and one-shots.

Vaz, Mark Cotta. *Caught in the Web: Dreaming Up the World of Spider-Man 2*. New York: Del Ray, 2004. ISBN: 0343470508.

This very detailed guide looks behind the scenes of the *Spider-Man 2* movie. It contains storyboards, designs, and sketches of Doc Ock, and all the little details that went into making the movie great. The comics relating to the battles between Spider-Man and Doc Ock are examined, and there is a lot of detail on how Doc Ock's costume was made. There is also a very detailed guide to Peter Parker's New York, and a cameo appearance by longtime *Spider-Man* artist, John Romita Sr.

Vaz, Mark Cotta, Stan Lee. *Behind the Mask of Spider-Man: The Secrets of the Movie*. New York: Del Ray, 2002. ISBN: 034545605X (trd). 0345450043.

This book contains the complete story of the first Spider-Man movie and the battles to get it to the silver screen. It includes storyboards, anecdotes from the actors and director, and stories about how the special effects were done. The book is profusely illustrated.

Weist, Jerry, Jim Steranko. *100 Greatest Comic Books*. Atlanta, GA: Whitman, 2004. ISBN: 0794817580.

This volume provides a detailed look at the one hundred best comics ever published, including the following Marvel related titles: *Marvel Comics 1*; *Amazing Fantasy 15*; *Captain America 1*; *Motion Picture Funnies Weekly 1*; *Young Allies 1*; *Fantastic Four 1*, *48*; *Amazing Spider-Man 1* and *129*; *Conan the Barbarian 1*; *Uncanny X-Men 1*; *Giant Size X-Men 1*; *Miss Fury 1*; *Journey Into Mystery 83*; *Daredevil 168*; *Avengers 4*; *Strange Tales 1*; *Incredible Hulk 1*, *181*; *Nick Fury: Agent of S.H.I.E.L.D. 1*. Steranko wrote the introduction, "Ten Comics that Rocked the World," and gave his perspective on the history of comics.

Williamson, Al, J. David Spurlock. *Al Williamson Sketchbook*. Lebanon, NJ: Vanguard Productions, 1998. ISBN: 1887591036 (trd); 1887591028 (pbk).

This is a collection of sketches by famed artist Al Williamson, including some of his work done on Marvel characters.

Wood, Wallace, Greg Theakston. *Wallace Wood Treasury*. New York: Pure Imagination, 1980.

This tribute to Wally Wood features various unpublished works of art, as well as some story material. There is a checklist that includes his work for Marvel.

Wood, Wally, J. David Spurlock, Bill Pearson, et al. *Wally Wood Sketchbook*. Lebanon, NJ: Vanguard Productions, 2000. ISBN: 1887 591079 (trd); 1887591087 (pbk).

This is a collection of sketches, interviews, and tributes to comics artist Wally Wood. In the book, there is an essay by Steranko that praises Wood's achievements. The book also includes sketches of Marvel characters Daredevil, Sub-Mariner, and the Cat.

Wyman, Ray Jr., Robert C. Crane, Catherine Hohlfeld. *The Art of Jack Kirby*. Orange, CA: Blue Rose Press, 1992. ISBN: 09634 46703 (trd); 0963446711 (pbk).

This is an official biography and study of the late Jack Kirby's career in comics. This well-written study looks at all of Kirby's work, from the early Timely days, through his last comic work and his last work for Marvel. The volume also recognizes his Atlas work, including the original Hulk from *Journey Into Mystery 62* and *66*. There is a complete chapter discussing the salad days of the 1960s, when he helped create the Marvel Universe with Stan Lee. This is the most in-depth look at the King and his work. It has many full-page, color, cover illustrations, and is highly recommended.

Yaco, Linc, Karen Habor. *Science of the X-Men*. New York: BP Books, 2000. ISBN: 0743 400208 (trd); 0743434781 (pbk).

This is a scientific look at the real-life possibilities of the X-Men's mutations, and of their advanced robotic equipment. Chapters cover: "Psionics"; "Exotic Powers"; "Physical Attributes"; "Technology"; and "Alien Races." Specific X-Men/mutants discussed include Iceman, Jean Grey, Professor X, Nightcrawler, Beast, Wolverine, Magneto, Mastermind, Storm, Unus, Blob, Scarlet Witch, Angel, Sentinels, and Cerebro, among others. This volume is written in a style accessible to the layperson.

Zimmerman, David. *Comic Book Character: Unleashing the Hero in Us All*. Downer's Grove, IL: InterVarsity Press, 2004. ISBN: 0830 832602.

This book contains a look at various superheroes from a Christian theological perspective which is honest and insightful, but not preachy. There are sections on the Spider-Man and the Hulk; Punisher; X-Men, in which the author compares the X-Men's vision to Martin Luther King's vision; Captain America; Avengers; Daredevil; and Magneto and Galactus. This is a warm self-help book that encourages readers to find the hero within.

Guides and Indexes

Adams, Neal. Greg Theakston, *The Neal Adams Treasury*. Detroit, MI: Pure Imagination, 1976.

This volume is a tribute to the work of Neal Adams who have discusses his work for Marvel, including the X-Men. It contains an index which gives information about the covers and issues Adams has worked on, including all those for Marvel through 1976.

Almond, Nick, Lamprey, Frank Plowright., et al. *X-Index*. London. 1980.

This bizarre, privately published X-Men index features a detailed look at Cyclops's life and includes a bibliography of his appearances in other Marvel titles. The volume also contains essays which provide biological information on three dead mutants—the Mimic, Thunderbird, and Changeling—and a profile of Havok.

Bails, Jerry. *Collector's Guide to the First Heroic Age*. Detroit, MI: Panelologist Publications, 1969.

This wonderful book provides an index to Golden Age superheroes, and various comics in which they appeared, including Marvel/Timely Atlas, DC, and Fawcett. The following Timely/Marvel Golden Age heroes are listed: All Winner's Squad; American Avenger; the Angel; Black Avenger; the Black Cat; the Black Marvel; the Black Widow; Blackstone: Magician Detective; the Blazing Skull; Blonde Phantom; Blue Blaze; Blue Diamond; Captain America; Captain Daring; Captain Dish; Captain Wonder; the Challenger; Citizen V; Dakor, the Magician; the Defender; the Destroyer; Dynoman; Dynamic Man; Electro; the Falcon; Fathertime; Fiery Mask; Fighting Yank; the Fin; Flexo the Rubber Man; Fourth Musketeer; Hercules; Human Top; Human Torch; Hurricane; Marvel Boy 1 & 2; Mantor the Magician; Masked Raider; Master Mind Excello; Miss America; Miss Fury; Mr. E; Mr. Liberty; Monako, Prince of Magic; Namora; Moon Man; Phantom Reporter; Purple Mask; Red Raven; Rockman Underground Secret Agent; Secret Stamp; Silver Scorpion; Subbie; Sub-Earth Man; Sub-Mariner; Sun Girl; Super Slave; the Terror; Thin Man; the Thunderer; Tough Kid Squad; Venus; Young Allies; Vagabond; the Whizzer and the Young Avenger.

Beppe, Sabatini. *Neal Adams Reprint Index*. East Lansing, MI, 1979.

This five page book documents and reprints Neal Adams's work. There is a special section on Adams's Marvel work.

Berman, Gary, Dave Hamburg. *The Comic Checklist for Marvel Comics*. Garden City, NY: Creation, 1982.

This work contains a checklist for the following Marvel Comics: *Amazing Spider-Man, Avengers, Captain America, Conan, Daredevil, Dazzler, Defenders, Dr. Strange, Fantastic Four, Hulk, Iron Man, Ka-Zar, King Conan, Marvel Comics Super Special, Marvel Team-Up, Marvel Two-In-One, Master of Kung Fu, Micronauts, Moon Knight, Peter Parker Spectacular Spider-Man, Powerman/Iron Fist, Spider-Woman, Star Wars, Thor, Team America, What IF, X-Men, Crazy, Marvel Fanfare, Epic, Marvel Preview/Bizarre Adventures, Savage Sword, Amazing Adventures, Adventure of Planet of the Apes, Astonishing Tales, Battlestar Galactica, Black Panther, Black Goliath, Captain Marvel, Champions, Eternals, Godzilla, Howard the Duck, Inhumans, Invaders, John Carter, Iron Fist, Ka-Zar* (1st series)*, Kull, Logan's Run, Man-Thing, Marvel Classics, Marvel Collector's Item Classics, Marvel Feature, Marvel's Greatest Comics, Marvel Premiere, Marvel Super Heroes, Marvel Triple Action, Ms. Marvel, Nick Fury, Not Brand Echh, Nova, Red Sonja, Omega, Sgt. Fury, Savage She-Hulk, S.H.I.E.L.D., Shogun Warriors, Silver Surfer, Star Trek, Strange Tales, Sub-Mariner, Super Villain Team Up, Tales of Suspense, Tarzan, Tomb of Dracula, Warlock*, and *Werewolf by Night*. It also has an introduction, a user guide, and notes through 1982.

Dlin, Doug. *Cybertronian: The Unofficial Transformers Recognition Guide 1–6*. San Antonio, TX: Antarctic Press, 2000–2003.

This series details most of the Transformers action figures, but each issue has a guide annotating the related Marvel issues of the *Transformers* comic book.

Flowers, James Jr. *The Incredible Internet Guide to Comic Books and Super Heroes*. Tempe, AZ: Facts on Demand Press, 2000. ISBN: 1999150150.

This guide to comics on the Internet includes sections on Marvel-related characters in various media forms, including Blade and X-Men in movies; Hulk and Spider-Man in television; and Marvel's *Age of Apocalypse*. There is a whole chapter devoted to specific Marvel characters, a Marvel chronology, and an A–Z organizational chart.

Furman, Simon. *Ultimate Guide to the Transformers*. New York: DK Publishing, 2004. ISBN: 1405304618.

In this book, longtime *Transformers* scribe Simon Furman gives the reader a detailed look at the world of the Transformers, including short sections on the Marvel comics published in the United States and Britain. This guide also includes information about Transformers toys, movies, and television appearances, as well as the now defunct Dreamwave comics.

Gerber, Ernst, Mary Gerber, *The Photo-Journal Guide to Comic Books Volume I (A–J)*. Minden, NV: Gerber Publishing, 1989. ISBN: 0962332801; 096233281X (1 & 2).

This is a beautiful, deluxe hardcover that has photographs of nearly every comic cover ever produced, from the beginning of the Golden Age of Comics, through the beginning of the Silver Age. Some of the cover reproductions in this volume are the only ones in existence. In addition, the volume contains a detailed history of the project, revealing its inspiration. The book includes information on how to grade comics, and provides a detailed grading scale. It includes a comic value guide and a scarcity index, for the less than 1 percent of Golden Age comics still in existence today. Other features include a look at special pedigree collections, information on how to preserve and store comics, and a detailed key to the book. Timely/Atlas/Marvel comic covers reproduced here include *Actual Romances; Adventures into Terror; Adventures into Weird Worlds; All Teen; All True Crime Cases; All Winners; Amazing Adventures; Amazing Fantasy; Amazing Comics; Amazing Mystery; Amazing Detective; Apache Kid; Annie Oakley; Amazing Spider-Man (1–20); Astonishing; Avengers (1–9); Battle; Battlefront; Battleground; Blaze Carson; Blaze Wonder Collie; Captain America; Casey—Crime Photographer; Comedy Comics; Combat Kelly; Comic Capers; Crazy; Crime Can't Win; Crime Cases; Crime Exposed, Crime Fighters; Crime Must Lose; Daredevil (1–8); Daring Mystery Comics; Jeanie; Cowgirl Romances; Date With Millie; Date With Patsy; Fantastic Four (1–12); Funny Comics; Gay Comics; Georgie Girl Comics; Hedy Devine; Homer Hooper; Homer the Happy Ghost; Human Torch; Ideal: A Classic Comic; Incredible Hulk (1–6); It's a Duck's Life; Jann of the Jungle; Joker Comics; Journey Into Mystery; Journey Into Unknown Worlds; Jungle Tales; Junior Miss;* and *Justice Comics;* among others. The volume has an index.

Gerber, Ernst, Mary Gerber. *The Photo-Journal Guide to Comic Books Volume II (K–Z).* Minden, NV: Gerber Publishing, 1990. ISBN: 0962332828; 096233281X (1 & 2).

This volume contains introductory essays on comic collecting, buying, and selling, and a detailed look at the historical and social impact of comics from the 1940s through the early 1960s. The latter essays are must reading for any popular culture historian. Marvel/Timely/Atlas Comics covers reproduced in this volume include *Kathy; Kid Colt Outlaw; Kid from Texas; Kid Comics; The Kellys; Krazy Comics; Lana; Lawbreakers Always Lose; Life with Millie; Lorna the Jungle Queen; Love Adventures; Love Secrets; Man; Marines in Battle; Marines in Action; Marvel Mystery Comics; Marvel Boy; Marvel Tales; Matt Slade; Menace; Men in Action; Men's Adventures; Millie the Model; Miss Fury; Miss America; Mitzi; My Friend Irma; Mystery Tales; Mystic; Mystical Tales; Nellie the Nurse; Navy Combat; Official True Crime Cases; Oscar; Our Love; Outlaw Kid; Patsy and Hedy; Patsy Walker; Police Action; Powerhouse Pepper; Quick Trigger Western; Red Raven Comics; Rex Hart; Ringo Kid; Rock Jordan, Private Eye; Romances of Nurse Helen Grant; Rugged Action; Rusty*

Comics; Sergeant Barney Baxter; Silly Seal; Six-Gun Western; Speed Carter, Spaceman; Space Squadron; Spellbound; Sports in Action; Spy Comics; Spy Fighters; Strange Tales; Strange Tales of the Unusual; Strange Worlds; Sub-Mariner; Sun Girl; Super Rabbit; Real Life Tales of Suspense; Tales of Suspense; Tales To Astonish; Tessie the Typist; Real Experiences; Texas Kid; Tex Morgan, Tex Taylor; 3-D Action; Tough Kid Squad; True Western; Two-Gun Kid; Two-Gun Western; Uncanny Tales; USA Comics; Venus; War Adventures; War Combat; War Comics; Western Outlaws; Wild West; Witness; World of Fantasy; Worlds of Suspense; World of Mystery; Yellow Claw; X-Men 1–17; Young Allies; Young Men; and *Zig Pig,* among others. The volume includes an artist index and a character index.

Gerber, Ernst, Mary Gerber, Paul Theiss. *Photo-Journal Guide to Marvel Comics Volume III (A–J).* Minden NV: Gerber Publishing, 1991. ISBN: 0962332844; 0962332 879 (3 & 4); 0962332887 (Deluxe hardcover set, 3 & 4).

This is the third volume in Gerber's Photo-Journal series. It includes reproductions of all the covers of Marvel books published up to 1990, including the Epic imprint. Some of the books included are *Adventures of the Planet of the Apes; Alien Legion; Alpha Flight; Amazing Adventures; Amazing Fantasy; Amazing Spider-Man; Amazing High Adventure; Annie; Astonishing Tales; Arggh; Avengers; Battlestar Galactica; Black Goliath; Blade Runner; Captain America; Captain Marvel; Captain Savage, The Cat; Chamber of Chills; Chamber of Darkness; Champions; Cloak and Dagger; Combat Kelly; Conan the Barbarian; Crash Ryan; Crazy; Creatures on the Loose; Crypt of Shadows; Daredevil; Dazzler; Dead of Night; Defenders; Doc Savage; Doctor Strange; Doctor Who; Dragon's Claws; Dreadstar; Dune; Elektra Saga; Elfquest; The Eternals; Falcon; Fantastic Four; Fantasy Masterpieces; Fear; Further Adventures of Indiana Jones; Ghost Rider 1966; Ghost Rider 1973; Ghost Rider 1990; G.I. Joe: An American Hero; Godzilla King of Monsters; Groo; Gunhawks; Hawkeye; Hercules; Hero for Hire; Howard the Duck; Human Fly; Human Torch; Iceman; Incredible Hulk; Inhumans; Invaders; Iron Fist; Iron Man; John Carter, Warlord of Mars; Journey Into Mystery;* and *Jungle Action.* The introduction is by Stan Lee.

Gerber, Ernest, Paul Theiss, Stan Lee, et al. *The Photo-Journal Guide to Marvel Comics Volume IV (K–Z).* Minden, NV: Gerber Publishing, 1991. ISBN: 0962332852; 0962332 879 (3 & 4); 0962332887 (Deluxe hardcover set, 3 & 4).

This is the fourth volume in the Photo-Journal series. Its beautiful photographs of the cover of each comic covers the second half of Marvel's output, from 1961 to 1991. There are short introductory essays on collecting, grading, buying, selling, and investing in Marvel Comics, and comics in general. The volume also includes a key to using the book, a short essay on storage, preservation and restoration, and a short historical look at "Marvel fever." Books that appear include *Ka-Zar*; *Kid Kolt Outlaw*; *King Conan*; *Kitty Pryde and Wolverine*; *Kull*; *Life of Captain Marvel*; *Logan's Run*; *Longshot*; *Machine Man*; *Madballs*; *Magik*; *Man Called Nova*; *Man from Atlantis*; *Man-Thing*; *Marvel Adventures*; *Marvel Classics*; *Marvel Collector's Item*; *Marvel's Greatest Comics*; *Marvel Double Feature*; *Marvel Fanfare*; *Marvel Feature*; *Marvel Premiere*; *Marvel Presents*; *Marvel Secret Wars*; *Marvel Spotlight*; *Marvel Super Action*; *Marvel Super Heroes*; *Marvel Tales*; *Marvel Team-Up*; *Marvel Treasury Edition*; *Marvel Triple Action*; *Marvel Two-In-One*; *Micronauts*; *Mighty Marvel Western*; *Mighty Thor*; *Millie the Model*; *Monster of Frankenstein*; *Monsters on the Prowl*; *Moon Knight*; *Mother Teresa*; *Ms. Marvel*; *'Nam*; *New Mutants*; *Official Handbook of the Marvel Universe*; *Omega the Unknown*; *Outlaw Kid*; *Patsy Walker*; *Power Man*; *Power Pack*; *Punisher*; *Rawhide Kid*; *Red Sonja*; *Red Wolf*; *Ringo Kid*; *ROM*; *Saga of Crystar*; *She-Hulk*; *Sgt. Fury*; *Shogun Warriors*; *Silver Surfer*; *Six From Sirius*; *Skull the Slayer*; *Smurfs*; *Son of Satan*; *Special Marvel Edition*; *Spectacular Spider-Man*; *Spider-Woman*; *Spidey Super Stories*; *Squadron Supreme*; *Star Lord*; *Star Trek*; *Star Wars*; *Strange Tales*; *Sub-Mariner*; *Supernatural Thrillers*; *Super-Villain Team-Up*; *Tales of Suspense*; *Tales to Astonish*; *Tarzan*; *Team America*; *Thing*; *Thongor*; *Tomb of Dracula*; *Tower of Shadows*; *Transformers*; *Two-Gun Kid*; *2001 Space Odyssey*; *U.S. 1*; *Uncanny Tales*; *Vault of Evil*; *Vision and Scarlet Witch*; *War is Hell*; *Warlock*; *Web of Spider-Man*; *Weird Wonder Tales*; *Werewolf by Night*; *West Coast Avengers*; *Western Gunfighters*; *What If*; *Where Monsters Dwell*; *Wolverine*; *World's Unknown*; *X-Men*; *X-Men and Avengers*; *X-Men and Micronauts*; *Classic X-Men*; and *X-Terminators*, among others.

Giolitto, Bob, Pete Giolitto, Dan Kelch, et al. *Marvel Index*. Midland, MI: B&P Giolitto, 1967.

This index includes issue number, date, title of story, credits, and main villains for the following comics up to 1967: *The Avengers*; *Daredevil*; *Spider-Man*; *Fantastic Four*; *Journey Into Mystery*; *Sgt. Fury*; *Tales of Suspense*; *X-Men*; *Tales to Astonish*; and *Strange Tales*.

Gohn, Roz Q. *This Is the Complete Marvel Comics Checklist, Everything Up to 1973*. San Francisco, CA: 1973.

This is an index to Silver Age Marvel comics, starting with *Fantastic Four 1*, through 1973. It includes characters, artists, villains, reprints, etc., all categorized into various sections.

Goulart, Ron. *The Comic Book Reader's Companion: An A-to-Z Guide to Everyone's Favorite Art Form*. New York: Harper/Perennial, 1993. ISBN: 0062731173.

This encyclopedic look at the comics genre, contains many entries for Marvel, including comics from the Golden, Silver, and Bronze Ages, e.g., *All Winners Comics*, *Marvel Mystery Comics*, and the *Tomb of Dracula*.

Green, Paul, Laura Taylor. *Green's Guide to Collecting TV, Music & Comic Book Annuals Price Guide 1950–2001*. Norfolk, UK: GT Publications, 2000. ISBN: 0953876802.

This guide to UK annuals provides detailed information about all kinds of annuals, including those published by Marvel and those that use Marvel characters. The entries date from the very first Marvel-related annual in 1968, *Marvel Storybook Annual*, which was an all-prose book, to 2001. The guide includes an essay about the American collecting market by comics historian and seller extraordinaire Doug Sulipa.

Hake, Ted. *Official Hake's Price Guide to Character Toys, Edition 5*. New York: Gemstone Publishing, 2004. ISBN: 140004667X.

This book is a price guide to many different types of toys, including Batman, Captain Marvel, Crunch, and Star Wars figures among others. Marvel-related sections include ones on Captain America, Marvel Comics itself, X-Men, and Spider-Man. The book is profusely illustrated.

Hill, Michael. *The Timely Index*. London, UK: M Hill, 1983.

This is a privately published index to the Golden Age of Marvel's Timely characters. In it, Hill explains why and how he attempted to document the artists and writers who worked on these early Marvel comics. He also gives issue-by-issue commentaries on early Timely characters. Some of the books documented include *All Select*, *All Winners*, *Amazing*, *Blonde Phantom*, *Captain America*, and *Blackstone the Magician*.

Keltner, Howard, Jerry Bails. *Index to Golden Age Comic Books*. Detroit: [Privately published], 1976.

This is a rare, in-depth index that includes many of Timely's Golden Age titles, e.g., *Miss America Comics*, *All Winners Comics*, and *Captain America Comics*.

Kirby, Jack. *Jack Kirby Checklist*. Raleigh, NC: TwoMorrows, 1998.

This volume contains a complete listing of nearly everything produced by Jack Kirby, including artwork, stories, covers, articles, books, videos, CD-ROMs, and more. It is the most complete guide to Kirby's works ever published. It includes listings from all of his Marvel works, including material from the Golden Age of Comics.

Mahony, Jeff, Mellissa A. Bennett, Jan Cronan, et al. *X-Men: Collector's Value Guide*. Middletown, CT: Checkerbee Publishing, 2000. ISBN: 1585980684.

This beautifully illustrated book lists values for all the *X-Men* comics and related titles, including *Generation X, Excalibur, Cable, Bishop*, and others. It contains a price guide for X-Men action figures and cards, and information about other X-Men merchandise. There are brief histories of the comic medium and the X-Men.

Malloy, Alex, Stuart W. Wells III, Robert J. Sodora, et al. *Comics Values Annual 2004.* Iola, WA: Krause Publications, 2004. ISBN: 087349802X.

This comic guide has chapters devoted to Marvel, DC, Dark Horse, Amalgam, Image, and various Golden Age comics. This sets it apart from other guides which put all comics together in one listing. Previous editions also followed this format.

Marvel Entertainment Group. *Carrying Marvel Comics.* New York: Marvel, 1987.

This is a special guide for bookstore owners who sell Marvel comics in their stores.

Merker, Dan, Kerry Gordon. *The Illustrated Marvel Handbook and Checklist.* Toronto: 1967.

This privately published guide features a checklist which includes credit information for writers and artists who contributed to *Amazing Spider-Man, Avengers, Daredevil, Fantastic Four, Incredible Hulk, Mighty Thor, Sgt. Fury, Strange Tales, Tales to Astonish, Tales of Suspense*, and the *X-Men.* For each series, the authors provide a synopsis and background.

Mougin, Lou. *Marvel War Comics Personnel Cross-Index.* L. Mougin, 1985.

This volume is an index to writers and artists who worked on *Sgt. Fury, Captain Savage, War Is Hell, Sgt. Fury Annual*, and *Combat Kelly.* It contains a cross index of guest stars, supporting characters, and major characters for the above titles.

Mullaney, Dean. *Gene Colan Marvel Checklist.* Philadelphia, PA: Mullaney, APA-I, 1978.

This is an index of Gene Colan's work for Marvel, dating from 1965. It is divided into three sections: books by Colan, indexed alphabetically with date of issue, pages, inker, and writer; Gene Colan checklist by inker; and a checklist by writer. Some of the titles indexed include *Tomb of Dracula, Iron Man, Haunt of Horror*, and *Marvel Spotlight.*

Mullaney, Dean. *The Steve Gerber Index.* Philadelphia, PA: Mullaney, 1978.

This volume indexes the work of Steve Gerber, focusing on his Marvel work, but also his DC work. Some of the titles indexed include *Adventures into Fear, Man-Thing, Creatures on the Loose, Defenders, Howard the Duck, Dracula Lives, Marvel Spotlight, Son of Satan, Tales of the Zombie*, and *Omega.* The volume includes an artist team-up checklist.

Nolan, Mike. *Timely Comic Index.* San Jose, CA: M. Nolan, 1969.

This volume indexes nearly 400 comics from the Timely period, and it has special sections on superheroes and collecting Timely Comics. The titles indexed include *Captain America, Tough Kid Squad, Red Raven, Human Torch, Kid Komix, Marvel Boy, USA Comics, Astonishing, Marvel Mystery, Young Allies, Mystic, Second Mystic, Amazing/Complete, Miss America, All Winners, Second All Winners, Young Men, All Select, Blonde Phantom, Sun Girl, Namora, Daring Mystery, Comedy, Sub-Mariner, Men's Adventures*, and *Second Daring Mystery.*

Olshevsky, George. *Marvel Superheroes Comic Checklist Through September 1971.* Toronto, Canada: University of Toronto, 1971.

This is a privately published, complete checklist of Marvel comics through 1971. It includes a brief history of Marvel and a synopsis for each series, in a 300+ page computer printout. It was a precursor to Olshevsky's character indexes.

Olshevsky, George, Tony Frutti. *The Marvel Comics Index: Daredevil 9B.* San Diego, CA: Pacific Comics Distributors, 1982. ISBN: 0943348536; 0943348501 (Marvel Index Set).

This volume contains an annotated index for *Daredevil 1–181*, along with various specials and annuals. Each entry has artist and writing credits, and a brief statement about the content. Other comics indexed include *Jungle Action*, featuring the Black Panther; *Shanna the She Devil; Black Goliath; The Human Fly;* and *Dazzler.* The volume has a personnel cross-index and a major characters cross-index. For each character there is a historical synopsis and some interesting facts. For example, the Human Fly was based on an actual person.

Olshevsky, George, Tony Frutti, Neal Adams, et al. *The Marvel Comics Index: Avengers 3.* Ontario: G&T Enterprises, 1976. ISBN: 0943348501 (Marvel Index Set).

This is an index and history of the *Avengers, Avengers Annual*, and *Giant Size Avengers*, up to 1976. It contains indexes to the original, fifties, *Black Knight, Captain Marvel*, and *The Defenders*, and it has cross-indexes to major characters. There are also Avengers lineups and storylines, as well as a history of Marvel superhero teams, including the All Winners Squad from Marvel's Timely years.

Olshevsky, George, Tony Frutti, Brent Anderson, et al. *The Marvel Comics Index: Heroes from Strange Tales 6.* San Diego, CA: G&T Enterprises, 1977.

This is an index and history of Dr. Strange, Nick Fury, and Adam Warlock. Comics indexed include: *Strange Tales, Strange Tales Annual, Doctor Strange 1*

& 2 Series, Giant Size Doctor Strange, Doctor Strange Annual, Nick Fury: Agent of S.h.i.e.l.d., Nick Fury and His Agents of S.h.i.e.l.d., Power of Warlock, and *Warlock.* It includes a synopsis, and personnel and major characters indexes.

Olshevsky, George, Tony Frutti, Brent Anderson, et al. *The Marvel Comics Index: X-Men 9A.* San Diego, CA: G&T Enterprises, 1981. ISBN: 0943348501 (Marvel Index Set).

This index and history of the X-Men through 1981 indexes *X-Men, X-Men Annual, Giant Size X-Men, Amazing Adventures, Ghost Rider,* and *Champions.* It includes a synopsis, personnel and major character cross indexes, and a Golden-Age cover gallery.

Olshevsky, George, Tony Frutti, Tim Conrad, et al. *The Marvel Comics Index: Conan 2.* Ontario: G&T Enterprises, 1976. ISBN: 0943348501 (Marvel Index Set).

This volume includes the histories of Conan, Ka-Zar, and Kull. Publications indexed include *Conan the Barbarian, King Size Conan, Savage Sword of Conan, Savage Sword of Conan Annual, Ka-Zar: Lord of the Jungle, Kull the Conqueror, Kull the Destroyer, Kull and the Barbarians, Savage Tales, Chamber of Chills, Chamber of Darkness, Monsters on the Prowl, Tower of Shadows, Creatures on the Loose,* and *Worlds Unknown.* It includes cross-indexes for personnel and characters, as well as cover galleries.

Olshevsky, George, Tony Frutti, Tim Conrad, et al. *The Marvel Comics Index: The Mighty Thor 5.* Ontario: G&T Enterprises 1977. ISBN: 0943348501 (Marvel Index Set).

This index and history of Thor up to 1977, contains all of the Thor issues of *Journey Into Mystery* and all of the Thor annuals. Other titles indexed include *Mighty Thor, Tales of Asgard,* and *Giant-Size Thor.* It also includes a detailed history and cross index of the titles, and a Marvel characters cross index.

Olshevsky, George, Tony Frutti, Bill Everett, et al. *The Marvel Comics Index: Tales to Astonish: Book Two: The Sub-Mariner and Others 7B.* Ontario: G&T Enterprises, 1978. ISBN: 0943348501 (Marvel Index Set).

This volume contains the history of the Sub-Mariner and a Golden-Age Sub-Mariner cover guide. Publications indexed include *Sub-Mariner, Sub-Mariner Annual, Astonishing Tales, Giant Size Super Villain Team Up, Giant Size Invaders, Invaders Annual,* and *Invaders.* It also has personnel and major characters cross-indexes.

Olshevsky, George, Tony Frutti, Ken Steacy, et al. *Marvel Comics Index: Heroes from Tales of Suspense Book 2: Iron Man 8B.* Ontario:

G&T Enterprises, 1978. ISBN: 0943348 501 (Marvel Index Set).

This volume contains a synopsis and history of Iron Man through 1978. Titles indexed include *Invincible Iron Man, Iron Man and Sub-Mariner, Iron Man Annual, Giant Size Iron Man, The Cat, Nova, Omega: The Unknown, Ms. Marvel, Skull the Slayer, Inhumans,* and *Amazing Adventures.* There is also a personnel cross-index and a major characters index.

Olshevsky, George, Tony Frutti, Ken Steacy, et al. *The Marvel Comics Index 7A: Tales to Astonish: Book One: The Incredible Hulk.* Ontario: G&T Enterprises, 1978. ISBN: 0943348501 (Marvel Index Set).

This volume gives a synopsis and history of the Hulk, Wasp, and Henry Pym. It indexes *Tales to Astonish, Incredible Hulk 2nd series, Hulk Annuals Giant Size Hulk, Rampaging Hulk,* and *The Hulk!* up to 1978. It also contains a major character and personnel cross-index for the Hulk.

Olshevsky, George, Tony Frutti, Jim Steranko, et al. *The Marvel Comics Index: Fantastic Four 4.* Ontario: G&T Enterprises, 1977. ISBN: 0943348501 (Marvel Index Set).

This is an index and history of the Fantastic Four and the Silver Surfer. It contains cross-indexes of personnel and major characters. Magazines indexed include: *Fantastic Four, Fantastic Four Annual, Giant Size Super Stars, Giant Size Fantastic Four, The Human Torch,* and *The Silver Surfer,* up to 1977. It also has an index and history of Marvel Boy from the 1950s.

Olshevsky, George, Tony Frutti, Jim Steranko, et al. *Marvel Comics Index: Heroes from Tales of Suspense Book 1: Captain America 8A.* Ontario: G&T Enterprises 1979. ISBN: 0943 348501 (Marvel Index Set).

This history and synopsis of Captain America up to 1979, goes back to his beginnings in the 1940s. Titles indexed include *Yellow Claw, Tales of Suspense, Captain America, Captain America Annual, Giant Size Captain America,* and *Marvel Treasury Edition Captain America.* The volume has personnel and major characters cross-indexes.

Olshevsky, George, Tony Frutti, Ron Sutton, et al. *The Marvel Comics Index: Spider-Man 1.* Ontario: G&T Enterprises, 1976. ISBN: 0943348501 (Marvel Index Set).

This is a history and index to Spider-Man. The publications indexed include *Amazing Fantasy, Amazing Spider-Man, Amazing Spider-Man Annual, Spectacular Spider-Man, Amazing Spider-Man Mini-Comic, Giant-Size Super Heroes, Giant Size Spider-Man,* and *Spider-Man Super Stories.* It also contains indexing for the pre–Spider-Man *Amazing Adult Fantasy.* There is cross indexing for personnel and major characters.

Pearson, Lars. *Now You Know: The Unauthorized Guide to G.I. Joe TV & Comics*. New Orleans, LA: Mad Norwegian Press, 2002. ISBN: 1570329028.

This is a complete guide to the world of G. I. Joe which covers the television series. Every comic published by Marvel and Marvel UK is discussed in detail: *G. I. Joe 1–155, Special Missions 1–28, Action Force 1–5*, and *European Missions 1–15*.

Pearson, Lars. *Prime Targets: An Unofficial Story Guide to Transformers, Beast Wars, and Beast Machines*. New Orleans, LA: Mad Norwegian Press, 2001. ISBN: 157032901X.

This is a complete guide to the world of the Transformers, including various television shows, toys, and comics. Every Marvel issue (1–75) and Marvel UK issue (1–289) that was published is discussed in detail, including the *Generation 2, 1–12* series, and guest appearances in the *G.I. Joe, 139–142* series.

Richardson, Mike, Steve Duin, Jackie Estrada, et al. *Comics Between the Panels*. Milwaukie, OR: Dark Horse, 1998. ISBN: 1569713448.

This is the definitive guide to the world of comics, with entries on characters, comic movements, artists, and writers. It is an excellent source for anyone who wants to know the history of this unique art form, or a quick biography of many Marvel writers and artists, including Jack Kirby, Jim Shooter, Wally Wood, Martin Goodman, and many others. It is beautifully illustrated.

Sanderson, Peter. *The X-Men: Ultimate Guide*. New York: DK Books, 2003. ISBN: 07894 9258X; 0789466937 (2000).

This is an oversize hardcover that explores the world of the X-Men. It contains a full history of the X-Men. Each character has a separate chapter, and there are sections on villains, Generation X, Age of Apocalypse, Weapon X, the X-Men movie, animated X-Men, the Danger Room, the Hellfire Club, and Xavier's estate, among other things. The updated 2003 edition includes entries for *X2*; origins; New X-Men; X-Static; X-Treme X-Men; and Ultimate X-Men. The afterword is by Chris Claremont, and the introduction is by Stan Lee.

Scott, Randell. *Citation Index to Marvel Comics 1961–1980: The Avengers 1–100*. East Lansing, MI: R. Scott; APA-I, 1977.

This preliminary index covers issues of the *Avengers* which are footnoted in other *Avengers* issues and other comics, including *Avengers Annual, Giant Size Avengers*, and *Marvel Triple Action*. It also covers issues of *Avengers* that were mentioned in the letters page. For the issues in the index, one will find "titles, numbers, and dates, of those comics which reprint, cite, or discuss the issue in question." This index covers the years 1963–1977, and lists two hundred comics.

Scott, Randell. *Citation Index to Marvel Comics 1961–1980: Incredible Hulk 1–6; 102–200*. East Lansing, MI: R. Scott, APA-I, 1979.

This preliminary index covers issues of *Hulk* that are footnoted in other *Hulk* issues, and other Marvel titles, such as the *Defenders, Marvel Collector's Item Classics, Tales to Astonish* and others related to *Hulk*. This index also contains references to issues mentioned in the letters sections of the comic. It is an amazing resource.

Scott, Randell. *Citation Index to Marvel Comics 1961–1980: Iron Man 1–100*. East Lansing, MI: R. Scott; APA-I, 1978.

This preliminary index covers issues of *Iron Man* footnoted in other *Iron Man* issues and other Marvel titles, including *Avengers* and *Marvel Super Heroes*. It also covers reprints and references to the issues mentioned in the letters section of the comic. This index covers the years 1968–1978, despite its title.

Sinkovec, Jerome, Mike Teifenbacher. *The Complete Marvel Index*. Menomonee Falls, WI: House of Ideas Publications, 1970.

This volume indexes *Avengers, Amazing Fantasy, Captain America, Captain Marvel, Captain Savage, Daredevil, Doctor Strange, Fantastic Four, Fantasy Masterpieces, Hulk, Journey Into Mystery, Marvel Collector's Item Classics, Marvel Tales, Nick Fury, Sgt. Fury, Not Brand Echh, Silver Surfer, Amazing Spider-Man, Spectacular Spider-Man, Strange Tales, Sub-Mariner, Tales of Suspense, Tales to Astonish*, and their respective annuals. Each entry contains date, story are, special features, list of main villains, and information about who did the script, art, inking, and lettering. There are also short sections on the Marvel-related books published by Bantam and Lancer, and on *America's Best TV Comics*, based on the 1960s cartoons. The volume includes a mock cover for *Marvel Man 1*.

Stine, Megan. *The Marvel Super Heroes Guide Book*. New York: Parachute Press, 1991. ISBN: 0938753568.

This is a guide to some of the basic heroes and villains who make up the Marvel Universe. It covers the biggest battles, best weapons, fantastic facts, vehicles, and a list of the ten most valuable Marvel comics. The guide, which was written for young adults, also includes a section on female heroes.

Sundahl, Steve, Ray Walsh, Jerry Bixby, et al. *A New Marvel Super Hero Index Updated To April 1973*. Pontiac, MI: Sundahl, 1973.

This volume indexes the following Marvel magazines: *Fantastic Four, Spider-Man, X-Men, Strange Tales/Dr. Strange, Combat Kelly, Tomb of Dracula, Western Ghost Rider, Shanna the She Devil, War is Hell, Nick Fury, Marvel Premiere, The Cat, Marvel Feature, Iron Man & Sub-Mariner, Ka-Zar, Astonishing Tales, Warlock, Doc Savage, Defenders, Amazing Adventures,*

Marvel Spotlight, Marvel Team Up, Luke Cage, Kull, Jungle Action, Marvel Triple Action, S.H.I.E.L.D., Captain Marvel, Captain Savage, Strange Tales, Silver Surfer, Avengers, Collector's Item Classics, Not Brand Ecch, Journey Into Mystery/Thor, Iron Man, Tales of Suspense/Captain America, Hulk, Marvel Superheroes, Crazy, Special Marvel Edition, Daredevil, Sub-Mariner, Tales to Astonish/Hulk, Spoof, Monsters on the Prowl, Creatures on the Loose, America's Best Comics, and *Sgt. Fury*: Each entry contains title, author, year, issue number, guest appearances, and annuals. There is a special section on artists. This volume was privately published.

Thompson, Don, Maggie Thompson, eds. *Marvel Comics Checklist and Price Guide 1961 to Present*. Iola, WI: Krause Publications, 1993. ISBN: 0873412451.

This is a price guide for Marvel comics from 1961 to 1992. It includes a brief history of Marvel, and price guides for Marvel-related novelties, cards, posters, collectibles, books, and comic books. Although this volume is now quite outdated, it does provide a good listing of the comic books Marvel published, and is es-

sential for any fan of the genre. A nice photo spread is integrated into the book.

Yronwode, Catherine. *An Index to Ritual Power Objects in Dr. Strange's Reality*. Willow Sprints, MO, APA-I, 1978.

This is an index to various tools, amulets, protective shields, and mystic globes, e.g., *Orb of Agamotto*, among other magical items in the pages of *Strange Tales, Marvel Premiere,* and *Dr. Strange*. It contains "Frequency Graph of Rhymed & Unrhymed Spells," by the author. This is a small section of an uncompleted monograph, *The Lesser Book of Vishanti*. This book was privately published.

Zimmerman, Dwight John. *The Marvel X-Men Guidebook*. New York: Parachute Press, 1992. ISBN: 093875396X.

This is a young-adult guide to the world of the X-Men, which includes history, team members, villains, answers to frequently asked questions, a listing of the most valuable comic issues, and other items of X-Men lore.

15

Children's Books

The X-Men were not your typical team of
Super Heroes. — *The Story of the X-Men*

Arkadia, Dana Thompson, and Del Thompson. *X-Men X-Tra Large Coloring and Activity Book*. New York: Random House, 1994. ISBN: 067986864X.

This is an activity book featuring the X-Men.

Bauman, Amy. *Spider-Man 2 Sound Storybook*. Des Moines, IA: Meredith Books, 2004. ISBN: 0696220059.

This is a story book of the movie, with sound.

Bauman, Amy, Alvin Sargent, Stan Lee, *Spiderman 2 Deluxe Sound Story Book*. Des Moines, IA: Meredith Books, 2004. ISBN: 0696220067.

This is a special book with pictures and sounds. Super sounds accompany Spider-Man's battles with Doc Ock.

Brown, Wells, Jacobs. *Spider-Man: Caged Captive*. Burbank: Fun Works, 1996. ISBN: 1570823499.

In this book, Jonah Jameson is kidnapped by Mysterio. The book came with a "Crystal Decoder" to help decode the web-patterned clues on each page.

Buckley, James. *Incredible Hulk's Book of Strength*. New York: DK Books, 2003. ISBN: 0789495430 (trd); 0789492636.

This book provides a look at who the Hulk is, and how he got his powers. It includes an explanation about how to strengthen one's muscles, and how sports make people strong. The book also contains a look at strong animals, like elephants, and animals that transform themselves, like lizards and pufferfish. The volume is profusely illustrated.

Buckley, James. *Spider-Man's Amazing Powers*. New York: DK Books, 2001. ISBN: 07894 79230.

This is an easy reader book. It contains a detailed explanation of Spider-Man's powers, comparing them to the abilities of real spiders. The book is profusely illustrated. It is excellent for young children.

Cinnamon House. *Stan Lee Presents the Incredible Hulk Incredible Crosswords*. New York: Grosset & Dunlap, 1978. ISBN: 0448159 910.

This is a book of Hulk crossword puzzles.

Cinnamon House. *Stan Lee Presents the Incredible Hulk's Smashing Puzzlers*. New York: Grosset & Dunlap, 1978. ISBN: 044815 989.

This is a book of Hulk puzzles and games.

Coll, Shane, David Koepp, Zade Rosenthal, et al. *Spider-Man: The Movie Storybook*. New York: HarperFestival, 2002. ISBN: 069401 6462.

This is an easy reader story of the Spider-Man movie. It contains text and pictures from the movie.

Dahlstrom, Carol Field, ed. *Spider-Man and Friends Party Book*. Des Moines, IA: Meredith Books, 2004. ISBN: 0696219964.

This is a special activity book for children.

Driggs, Scout, James Schamus. *The Hulk: Beast Within*. New York: HarperFestival, 2003. ISBN: 0060519037.

This easy reader is based on the movie, and is filled with pictures from it. It includes Bruce Banner's transformation into the Hulk.

Driscoll, Laura, James Schamus. *The Hulk Movie Storybook*. New York: HarperFestival, 2003. ISBN: 0060519088.

This is another illustrated easy reader book. It is based on the hit movie *Hulk*, in which Bruce Banner becomes the green goliath, Hulk.

Edens, Mark Edward, Marie Severin, Lourdes Sanchez. *X-Men: Enter the X-Men*. New York: Random House, 1993. ISBN: 067985 7079.

In this book, the X-Men save Jubilee from the Sentinels, and destroy the Mutant Control Agency's files on mutants. The book and the tape are based on the *X-Men* television series.

Egan, Kate, Bob Ostrom, Alvin Sargent, et al. *Hurry Up, Spider-Man*. New York: HarperFestival, 2004. ISBN: 0060571373.

In this easy reader book, Spider-Man misses Mary Jane's theater performance because he was out saving the world.

Egan, Kate, Alvin Sargent, David Koepp, et al. *Hands Off Doc Ock*. New York: HarperFestival, 2004. ISBN: 0060571330.

This easy reader book is based on *Spider-Man 2*. In it, Spider-Man fights with Doc Ock.

Egan, Kate, Alvin Sargent, David Koepp, et al. *Spider-Man 2: Movie Storybook*. New York: HarperFestival 2004. ISBN: 0060571365.

This is an easy reader picture book based on the movie *Spider-Man 2*.

Fantastic Four Coloring Book: Meet the Witch. Racine, WI: Western, 1997.

This is a special coloring book featuring the Fantastic Four.

Feldman, Thea. *Spider-Man 2: The Joke Book*. New York: HarperFestival, 2004. ISBN: 0060571357.

This joke book is based on the *Spider-Man 2* movie.

Figueroa, Acton, James Goodridge. *I Am the Hulk*. New York: HarperFestival, 2003. ISBN: 0060519053.

This easy reader book is about Bruce Banner's change to the Hulk.

Figueroa, Acton, David Koepp, Ron Lim. *Spider-Man Saves the Day*. New York: HarperFestival, 2002. ISBN: 0694016454.

In this easy reader book Spider-Man helps people.

Figueroa, Acton, Ron Lim, Emily Y. Kanalz, et al. *I Am Spider-Man*. New York: HarperFestival, 2002. ISBN: 0694016446.

This easy reader book is based on the hit movie *Spider-Man*, adapted from the screenplay.

Figueroa, Acton, Shawn McKelvey. *The Hulk Escapes*. New York: HarperFestival, 2003. ISBN: 0060519061.

In this easy reader book, Bruce Banner is captured and the scientists want to study him, but when he changes into the Hulk and escapes, the soldiers come.

Figueroa, Acton, Alvin Sargent, David Koepp, et al. *Spider-Man 2: Everyday Hero*. New York: HarperFestival, 2004. ISBN: 00605 73635.

In this easy reader book, Spider-Man is an everyday hero for young children.

Figueroa, Acton, Ivan Vasquez, Jesús Redondo, et al. *Spider-Man versus Doc Ock*. New York: HarperFestival, 2004. ISBN: 006057 3643.

In this illustrated easy reader book, Spidey fights Doc Ock.

Fontes, Ron, Justine Korman, Aristides Ruiz, et al. *X-Men: Masquerade*. New York: Random House, 1994. ISBN: 067986430X.

This easy reader book is about Jubilee's birthday, for which the X-Men throw her a masquerade party.

Frantz, Jennifer, Gary Ciccarelli. *The Hulk Activity Book*. New York: HarperFestival, 2003. ISBN: 0060519002.

This book of games, puzzles, and action scenes is based on the *Hulk* movie.

Fujimoto, Michi, Jeff Albrecht, et al. *Hulk Rage: Get Ready for Hulk* (ISBN: 1576578607); *Hulk's Big Mess* (1576578224); *Hulk: Ready or Not* (157657817); *Adopt-a-Hulk* (157657 8194); *Hulk the Hero* (1576578216); *Hulk: Where Is Everybody* (1576578186); *Hulk Rage: The Transformation* (1576578631); *Peek-a-Boo Hulk* (157657816X); *Meet the Incredible Hulk* (1576578569); *Hulk Rage: Follow the Leader* (1576578615); *Hulk Rage: The Strongest of Them All* (1576578623). Wheaton, IL: Paradise Press, 2002.

These easy reader books feature the Hulk in different adventures. They are good for very young children. Some books feature Spider-Man and the Hulk together.

Fujimoto, Michi, Jeff Albrecht, et al. *One for Me, Zoo for You; Camp Spidey; Fun and Games; Farmyard Fun.* Wheaton, IL: Paradise Press, 2002. No ISBNs listed.

These board books belong to the Spider-Man & Friends, Ready for Adventure! series.

Fujimoto, Michi, Jeff Albrecht, et al. *Spider-Man in the City* (ISBN: 1576577759); *Meet Spider-Man* (1576578577); *Meet Spider-Man & Friends* (1576578585); *Spider-Man & Friends: Please and Thank You* (1576578208); *Spider-Man & Friends: The Tree House Lab* (1576578267); *Spider-Man & Friends: Do You See What I See* (1576578151); *Spider-Man & Friends: No Villains Allowed!* (1576578240); *Spider-Man & Friends: Heroes in Training* (No ISBN). Wheaton, IL: Paradise Press, 2002.

These children's books belong to Fujimoto's Spider-Man & Friends series.

Fujimoto, Michi, Jeff Albrecht, et al. *The X-Men: X-Class* (ISBN: 1576578674); *X-Men: The Beast* (157657864X); *Meet the X-Men* (1576578593); *X-Men: Mutant Race* (1576578658); *X-Men: Storm Is Coming* (1576578666); *Children of the Atom* (no ISBN listed). Wheaton, IL: Paradise Press, 2002.

These easy reader X-Men books are printed on card stock.

Fujimoto, Michi, Locke. *Spider-Man and Friends: Power Struggle*; *Lizard Exhibit*; *Spider-Man's Sandtrap*; *Museum Morph*. China: Paradise Press, 2002.

This is a unique collection of children's books that belong to Fujimoto's Spider-Man & Friends: Special Helpers series. They feature Electro, the Lizard, the Sandman, and the Chameleon, and were written to teach young children how to help others.

Fujimoto, Michi, Charles Park. *Spider-Man: Air Rescue Officers; Spider-Man Doctors; Spider-Man: Firefighters; Spider-Man: Police Officers.* New York: Paradise Press; Marvel.com, 2002.

These easy reader books belong to the Spider-Man, Neighborhood Heroes series. Each book highlights Spider-Man's service to the community in helping public servants do their jobs.

Fujimoto, Michi, Long Vo. *Basketball Spider-Man: Slam Dunk; Baseball Spider-Man: Home Run; Football Spider-Man: Touch*

Down; Soccer Spider-Man: Goal. New York: Paradise Press; Marvel.com, 2002.

These sturdy, tabbed, easy reader books belong to the Spider-Man, Sport series. Each book deals with Spider-Man's fine sports talents.

Geary, Rick, Ken Steacy. *Spider-Man: Ghosts, Ghouls and the Hobgoblin.* New York: Fun Works, 1996. ISBN: 1570824436.

In this story, Spider-Man and his wife go to a masquerade party, and his secret identity is almost discovered by the Hobgoblin.

Gerger, Dawn. *Stan Lee Presents Spidey Skill Search-a-Words.* New York: Grosset & Dunlap, 1977. ISBN: 0448127423.

This is a book of Spider-Man games and puzzles.

Golden Books. *Spider-Man: Web of Villains,* New York: Golden Books, 1997. ISBN: 0307036421.

This is a collection of mazes, puzzles, brainteasers, and activities based on Spider-Man and his foes.

Goldman, Leslie, David Koepp, Zade Rosenthal. *Spider Bite.* New York: Avon, 2002. ISBN: 0064421775.

This easy reader has text and pictures from the first *Spider-Man* movie. It tells the story of Spider-Man being bitten by a radioactive spider, and gaining his new powers.

Gregg, Leslie, Jerry Ordway, Wayne Dober, et al. *A Golden Everything Workbook Featuring Captain America and Other Super Heroes Characters.* Racine, WI: Western, 1980. ISBN: 0307064573.

This special children's book has various projects which feature Captain America.

Gregg, Leslie, Jerry Ordway, Wayne Dober, et al. *A Golden Everything Workbook Featuring the Incredible Hulk and Other Super Heroes Characters.* Racine, WI: Western, 1980. ISBN: 0307064557.

This workbook contains games for children which feature the Hulk.

Gregg, Leslie, Jerry Ordway, Wayne Dober, et al. *A Golden Everything Workbook Featuring Spider-Man and Other Super Hero Characters.* Racine: WI: Western, 1980. ISBN: 0307064549.

This is a workbook with games for children that feature Spider-Man.

Gunter, Jacob Ben, Alvin Sargent, David Koepp, et al. *Spider-Man: Doc Around the*

Clock, New York: HarperFestival, 2004. ISBN: 0060571349.

This easy reader is based on the movie *Spider-Man 2* in which Doc Ock is created and becomes a criminal. It contains pictures from the movie.

Hamilton, Tisha, David Koepp, Alvin Sargent, et al. *Spider-Man 2: Behind The Mask*. New York: Scholastic, 2004. ISBN: 0439444 39X.

This is a young-adult look at the movie *Spider-Man 2*.

Hautzig, Deborah, Mark Edward Edens, Aristides Ruiz, et al. *X-Men: Battle of the Sentinels*. New York: Random House, 1994. ISBN: 0679860290; 0679960295.

In this story, Jubilee meets the X-Men for the first time when the robot police, the Sentinels, try to take her down. This story also came in a book and tape set.

Herdling, Glenn, Ben Herrera, Jeff Albrecht, et al. *X-Men in SFX: Play a Sound*. Lincolnwood, IL: Publications International Ltd., 1996. ISBN: 0785316248.

This book is a combination of text and soundboard. In it, Sam Greenhorn, a mutant who controls soundwaves, leads the X-Men into Magneto's hands.

Hughes, Francine, Chris Claremont, Aristides Ruiz, et al. *X-Men: Gambit and the Shadow King*. New York: Random House, 1994. ISBN: 0679861920.

In this story, Storm meets Gambit for the first time, and they team up together to defeat the Shadow King.

Hughes, Francine, Roy Thomas, Arnold Drake. *Havok: Secret of Cyclops' Brother*. New York: Random House, 1994. ISBN: 0679861890.

In this children's picture book, Alex Summers, Havok, is introduced as Cyclops's brother. He and the X-Men go up against the Pharaoh, and Havok learns the extent of his superpowers. The book is based on *Uncanny X-Men 54–55*.

Janes, James, Dave Simons, Janice Parker, et al. *Look and Find the X-Men*. Lincolnwood, IL: Publications International, 1992. ISBN: 1561737038.

This book allows the reader to search each picture to find the tools that enable the X-Men to complete their mission. Locales include the Danger Room, Genosha, the Sentinel's Base, and the Savage Land. The book includes a short quiz about each mission.

Jones, Jasmine, James Schamus. *Hulk Fights Back*. New York: HarperFestival, 2003. ISBN: 0060519045.

This is an easy reader based on the movie in which the Hulk escapes from a science lab where he is a prisoner, and is pursued by soldiers. His father becomes the Absorbing Man, and takes the Hulk's rage. The novel is filled with many pictures from the movie.

Klemm, Julianne, Gray Morrow. *X-Men: To Stop a Juggernaut*. New York: Random House, 1993. ISBN: 0679857095.

In this book, Xavier's half brother Juggernaut destroys the X-Mansion, and starts to rob banks. He is causing havoc in the city, and Colossus is falsely blamed. The X-Men come out in full force to stop him. The book is based on the television show.

Koziakin, Vladimir. *Stan Lee Presents Revenge of Mighty Marvel Mazes*. New York: Grosset & Dunlap, 1977. ISBN: 0448127482.

This is another maze book that uses Marvel characters.

Kraft, David Anthony, Jack Kirby, Stan Lee, et al. *The Fantastic Four: The Secret Story of Marvel's Cosmic Quartet*. Chicago: Children's Press, 1981. ISBN: 0516024124.

This combination of graphic and narrative text tells the origin story of the Fantastic Four. It includes a story that features the Inhumans, and information about the allies and villains encountered by the Fantastic Four.

Kraft, David Anthony, Stan Lee, Jack Kirby, et al. *Captain America: The Secret Story of Marvel's Star-Spangled Super Hero*. Chicago: Children's Press, 1981. ISBN: 0516024116.

This combination of narrative and graphic text tells the history of Captain America. It covers his origin, his joining the Avengers, and the "Red Skull Supreme" stories. It also contains a list of the allies and villains he has encountered, and a picture of him in front of the Declaration of Independence.

Kraft, David Anthony, Stan Lee, Jack Kirby, et al. *The Incredible Hulk: The Secret Story of Marvel's Gamma-Powered Goliath*. Chicago: Children's Press, 1981. ISBN: 05162 24131.

This book, which combines narrative and graphic text, recounts the origin story of the Hulk.

Kraft, David Anthony, Marie Severin, Earl Norem. *The Fantastic Four: The Island of Danger*. New York: Marvel Books, 1984. ISBN: 0939766558.

In this story, the Fantastic Four go on an island vacation, and end up battling a giant octopus.

Lukas, Noah, Aristides Ruiz, Thompson Brothers. *X-Men: Ambush: Featuring a Sudden*

Offense from Omega Red. New York: Random House, 1995. ISBN: 0679870253.

This is a special pop-up book in which the X-Men fight the Russian mutant Omega Red.

Magic Eye. *Spider-Man: 3-D Illusions by Magic Eye*. Kansas City: Andrews and McMeel, 1996. ISBN: 0836213327.

This is a stunning combination of Magic Eye stereograms linked with Spider-Man. Viewers can find action-packed scenes hidden in each picturesque 3D drawing. The book includes a guide to viewing techniques, and a magic eye key for 3D drawing.

Mantell, Paul, Arkadia, et al. *X-Men: Slaves of Genosha*. New York: Random House, 1994. ISBN: 0679862021.

In this book, the X-Men go to Genosha for a vacation and end up being slaves in a concentration camp for mutants. Cable and Gambit help free them.

Mantell, Paul, Michael Edens. *Experiment on Muir Island*. New York: Random House, 1994. ISBN: 0679862013 (pbk); 0679873 902 (trd).

In this book, Apocalypse lets his Four Horsemen loose.

Mantell, Paul, Avery Hart, Arkadia, et al. *X-Men: Beauty and the Beast*. New York: Random House, 1994. ISBN: 067986931X.

Hank "Beast" McCoy saves a blind girl who is kidnapped by the racist Friends of Humanity. Wolverine goes undercover in the group, and the X-Men break up the group when the leader finds out his father is the mutant Sabretooth.

This easy reader book is based on the television series.

Mantell, Paul, Avery Hart, Arkadia, et al. *X-Men: The Wedding of Jean and Cyclops*. New York: Random House, 1994. ISBN: 0679869328.

In this book, Jean Grey and Scott Summers get married, much to the dislike of Wolverine. Morph and the Friends of Humanity are used by Mr. Sinister to stir up mutant hysteria in the public.

Meiksin. *Golden Sound Story X-Men: Repo Man*. New York: Golden Books, 1995. ISBN: 0307709310.

This is a sound book featuring the X-Men for preschoolers.

Morley, Evan. *Stan Lee Presents Marvel's Mysterious Secret Messages*. New York: Grosset & Dunlap, 1977. ISBN: 0448127458.

This kids' book contains puzzles and games to be searched for secret messages. It is based on Marvel characters.

Richards, Kitty, Zade Rosenthal, Steve Khan. *Your Friendly Neighborhood Spider-Man*. New York: Avon, 2002. ISBN: 0064421 767.

Based on the hit movie, this easy reader contains pictures from the movie in which Peter Parker becomes the *Daily Bugle* photographer by taking his own pictures as Spider-Man. The novel includes some mock stories from the *Daily Bugle* about Spider-Man, and a list of Parker's top ten powers.

Ruiz, Aristides, Dana Thompson, Del Thompson. *X-Men Pop-Up Book*. New York: Random House, 1994. ISBN: 0679863907.

This is a wonderful little pop-up book featuring the X-Men.

Salicrup, Jim, Stan Lee, et al. *Stan Lee Presents the Mighty World of Marvel Pin-Up Book*. New York: Simon and Schuster, 1978. ISBN: 067124390X.

This is a collection of special pin-ups of Marvel characters.

Seidman, David, Louie De Martinis. *Spider-Man. The Super Spider*. Des Moines: Meredith Books, 2004. ISBN: 0696225166.

Peter Parker attends a class about spiders. His professor ends up turning herself into a giant spider and battles Spider-Man, whom she hates.

Severin, Marie, et al. *X-Men: Xavier's School for Gifted Youngsters*. New York: Random House, 1994. ISBN: 0679861882.

This is an easy reader toy and picture book about the X-Men and Xavier's School.

Shea, Christopher, Aristides Ruiz, Thompson Brothers. *X-Men: Heroes*. New York: Random House, 1995. ISBN: 0679871748.

This is an easy reader guidebook to good guys in the X-Men, including Professor X, Jubilee, Strong Man, Gambit, Cable, and Bishop, among others.

Shea, Christopher, Aristides Ruiz, Thompson Brothers. *X-Men: Villains*. New York: Random House, 1995. ISBN: 0679871756.

This is an easy reader guidebook to the bad guys in X-Men stories, including Magneto, Pyro, Mojo, Juggernaut, Sinister, and Avalanche, among others.

Skir, Robert N., Marty Isenberg, Gray Morrow. *X-Men: Morlock Madness*. New York: Random House, 1993. ISBN: 0679857109.

This picture book features the mutant exiles, the Morlocks. It is based on an episode of the television series.

Steele, Michael Anthony. *How to Draw Spider-Man 2*. New York: Scholastic, 2004. ISBN: 0439650801.

This is a special drawing book, based on the *Spider-Man 2* movie.

Stern, Roger, Stan Lee, Steve Ditko, et al. *Spider-Man: The Secret Story of the Marvel's World Famous Wall Crawler*. Chicago: Children's Press, 1981. ISBN: 0516024140.

This book combines narrative and graphics to tell Spider-Man's origin story, and describe his powers, his friends, and his most famous villains. It includes a rare Chameleon story.

Teitelbaum, Michael. *The Story of the Incredible Hulk*. New York: DK Publishing, 2003. ISBN: 0789495449 (trd); 0785492628 (pbk).

This is an easy reader book that tells the history of the Incredible Hulk, from his beginnings forty years ago, to the present day. It has profusely illustrated chapters on Rick Jones, She-Hulk, the Avengers, the Gray and Green Hulks, the Defenders, and Wendigo, among others. This is an excellent introduction to the Marvel character for young children.

Teitelbaum, Michael. *The Story of Spider-Man*. New York: DK Books, 2001. ISBN: 0789 479214.

This is another easy reader book that tells about the Spider-Man's origin, powers, and opponents.

Teitelbaum, Michael. *The Story of the X-Men: How It All Began*. New York: D.K. Publishing, 2000. ISBN: 0789466961 (trd); 078946 697X (pbk).

This easy reader book tells the story of the mutant group from its origins in the comic book series. It is profusely illustrated with both color artwork and photos.

Teitelbaum, Michael, Steven Butler, Jeff Albrect, et al. *Spider-Man: Caught in the Web*. New York: Golden, 1997. ISBN: 0307129 616.

In this book, Spider-Man catches both the Scorpion and the Hobgoblin in his web, for the police.

Teitelbaum, Michael, Kirk Jarvinen. *Meet the Amazing Spider-Man*. New York: Golden, 1996. ISBN: 030710379X.

This is an easy reader book that relates the story of Spider-Man's origin and special powers.

Teitelbaum, Michael, Alvin Sargent, David Koepp, et al. *Spider-Man 2: Friends and Foes*. New York: HarperFestival, 2004. ISBN: 0060571330.

This easy reader book presents pictures of the cast of characters in the *Spider-Man 2* movie. There are pictures of Mary Jane, Professor Connors, J. J. Jameson, Doc Ock, Betty Brant, and John Jameson, among others.

Thomas, Jim, Aristides Ruiz, Isidre Mones, et al. *X-Men: Spellbound*. New York: Random House, 1994. ISBN: 0679864369.

This easy reader book is based on a story by Chris Claremont, in which Jubilee helps save the X-Men from being prisoners in Mesmero's carnival. The book came with X-Men tattoos.

Thompson, Dana. *X-Men: Mask*. New York: Random House, 1994. ISBN: 0679861432.

This is a Jellybean Book for young readers, featuring the X-Men.

Thompson, Dana. *X-Men: Mazes and Puzzles to Collect*. New York: Random House, 1994. ISBN: 0679868674

This activity book features the X-Men.

Weiner, Eric, Mark Edward Edens, Dana Thompson, et al. *Enter Magneto*. New York: Random House, 1994. ISBN: 067986 0436 (pbk); 0679960430 (trd).

In this kids' book, Magneto tries to take over a missile base and a chemical plant.

Williams, Wayne. *Stan Lee Presents Spidey's Wall-Crawler Wordwebs*. New York: Grosset & Dunlap, 1977. ISBN: 0448127377.

This book contains games with words using Spider-Man.

Xyz Group. *X-Men: Beware of the Blob*. Texas: Premier Publishing, 1997. ISBN: 1879332 40X.

This book and toy collection is supposed to be for children ages 4 to 8, but I could not verify that it was actually published.

Zimmerman, Dwight. *Look and Find the Amazing Spider-Man*. Lincolnwood, IL: Publications International, 2002. ISBN: 07853 51841; 0785311718 (1994).

The reader is supposed to find the items Spider-Man needs to complete his mission by searching through each scene in this book.

16

Scholarly Publications

The entries in this chapter refer to scholarly writings. Many of them appear in academic books, chapters or articles taken from academic books, theses, dissertations, or on the Internet. In one way or another, they are all related to Marvel.

Super-heroes ALWAYS begin as weak characters.—*Bernard Beck*

The publications of Marvel Comics Group warrant serious consideration as a legitimate narrative enterprise that is frequently both literate and technically and philosophically sophisticated.—*Donald Palumbo*

Spider-Man, the Hulk, the X-Men, Daredevil ... that's us on the big screen. No wonder we're packing the theaters to watch.—*Nick Gillespie*

Alaniz, Jose. "Supercrip: Disability and the Marvel Silver Age Superhero." *International Journal of Comic Art* 6, no. 2, (Fall 2004): 304–324.

In this article the author looks at the "supercripple" or "supercrip" in Marvel's Silver and Bronze Age. He argues that the disabilities of the Silver Age heroes were an integral part of their make-up. He quotes from those social critics who view the "supercrip" as just another example of the outside, non-disabled world saying that we should pity those who are disabled. The characters discussed include Donald Blake, Thor, who is lame; Tony Stark, Iron Man, who has a bad heart; Stephen Strange, Dr. Strange, whose hands are damaged; Matt Murdock, Daredevil, who is blind; and X-Men, mutants who are just born different. Oddly, the author does not mention that Charles Xavier is without the use of his legs, and uses a wheelchair. One of the characters mentioned is one of my favorites, Roy Thomas's 3D Man. 3D Man can only appear when his polio-stricken brother Hal is unconscious. Alaniz also goes into detail about Dr. Doom's scar. Many villains in literature and popular culture are disfigured, scarred or disabled, and that has somehow become a symbol of the evil lurking within. In some cases, the villains are so evil that something debilitating happens to them, thus their affliction is somehow justified.

Alberich, R., J. Miro-Julia, F. Rossell. "Marvel Universe Looks Almost Like a Real Social Network." (2002). http://xxx.lanl.gov/abs/cond-mat/0202174.

This article looks at the structure of the Marvel Universe and its subsequent networks. By using the massive website Marvel Chronology Project, the authors argue that although the Marvel Universe is fictional and artificial, it has characteristics of real life, collaborative networks. The Marvel Universe creators attempt to make it look like a real Universe, and largely they succeed. The authors look at and use statistical data. There are a number of bipartite graphs they use to argue their points, which include 6,486 characters in 12,942 books. Spider-Man has the most appearances throughout the Marvel Universe. The authors also include a brief history of Marvel.

Barnes, Stephen James. *Marvel Comic Books and the Cold War, 1963–85: The Black Widow and Other Cold War Warriors.* Master's thesis, University of Southampton, 2000.

This thesis looks at various Marvel comics which are related to the Cold War, and feature the Black Widow, Iron Man, and others.

311

Baron, Lawrence. "X-Men as J Men: The Jewish Subtext of a Comic Book Movie." *Shofar: An International Journal of Jewish Studies* 22, no. 1. (2003): 44–52.

The author traces the history of early Jewish comic book writers like Stan Lee and Jack Kirby, and the history of the X-Men comic book. He looks at parallels between racism against Jews and racism against mutants. His focus however is Brian Singer's first *X-Men* movie, and its use of the Auschwitz concentration camp at the beginning of the film as Magneto's justification for his war on humanity. Magneto is not an "innately evil man" seeking to overthrow the world, but rather someone who is a victim of a "previous genocide." The film anticipates that mutants will be persecuted and killed, the way Jews were under Nazi Germany.

Beck, Bernard. "Where's Poppa? Spider-Man, *Six Feet Under*, and Rebuilding Families." *Multicultural Perspectives* 5 (2003): 25–28.

The author looks at how young men are disenchanted when looking for a place they can call home. He analyzes the first *Spider-Man* movie, and compares it to the 2001 film, *Dogtown and Z-Boys*. Spider-Man is considered "an emblem of contemporary young manhood." The author also looks at movies like *My Big Fat Greek Wedding* and the TV series *Six Feet Under*, and contemplates how these can relate to creating a sense of roots and home.

Bell, Elizabeth. "The *Incredible Hulk* as a Modern Grail Quest." *Studies in Popular Culture* 5 (1982): 56–60.

In this work, Bell argues that the *Hulk* television program is a step above most of the television programs which are in a "composite cultural wasteland." She argues that the *Hulk* show is a "direct descendent" of the King Arthur Knights of the Round Table tales, and their quest for Christ's Holy Grail. She sees David Banner as a quester, and finds both Sir Gawain and the Green Knight, within Banner and the Hulk. She points out how technology and science work within the series, and how Banner's quest is never ending.

Berger, Arthur Asa. *The Comic-Stripped American*. New York: Walker, 1973. ISBN: 0802 704301.

This is one of the first scholarly examinations of how comics affect society and popular culture at large. The section on Marvel Comics (pp. 199–207), deals with the role of machines/science in the pages of the *Fantastic Four*. Berger also quotes from D. H. Lawrence, while comparing Cooper's *Deerslayer* to the *Fantastic Four*, regarding the myth of America.

Berger, Arthur Asa. "Marvel Language Comic Book and Reality." *ETC: A Review of General Semantics* 29, no. 2 (June 1972): 169–180.

This author looks at the language used in various *Fantastic Four* and *Spider-Man* comics. He argues that it is Stan Lee's use of irony, self-parody, hyperbole, and alliteration that sets these comics apart from childish trash. He is probably the first to point out that the Silver Surfer is a Christ-like figure, and that his adventures in the *Fantastic Four* and beyond are really epics in a true literary sense. He quotes two pages of dialogue from *Amazing Spider-Man 10*, and points out that it reads just like a play. He also brings out the fact that within the twenty-two page comic there are probably five thousand words, about the same number as in a short story. However, Berger dismisses the Captain America comic as being "childish and uninteresting." The Captain America comic is one of my favorites, and I strongly disagree with Berger's assessment.

Berger, Arthur Asa. *Pop Culture*. Dayton, OH: Pflaum/Standard, 1973. ISBN: 0827800 231.

This book includes "Marvel Comics: Language, Youth, and the Problem of Identity" (pp. 32–43), and essay which looks specifically at Stan Lee's use of language in the pages of the *Fantastic Four* and *Spider-Man*. Berger argues that comics, while not high literature, can be considered epic stories in the tradition of the *Odyssey* or *Beowulf*. According to Berger, comics are actually illustrated plays, and he cites an example from *Spider-Man 10*. In this example, the author presents the text as it would appear in a play. Lee's use of alliteration is also explored in detail.

Blackmore, Tim. "Blind Daring: Vision and Revision of Sophocles' *Oedipus Tyrranus* in Frank Miller's *Daredevil: Born Again*." *Journal of Popular Culture* 27, no. 3 (Winter 1993): 135–162.

This very detailed article compares Sophocles' Oedipus with Daredevil and the Frank Miller storyline "Born Again." Both characters suffer through awful turmoil, and have their worlds turned inside out. Both eventually emerge stronger, and become heroes in the end. By sinking as low as a human can, one can be reborn into something greater, and, in the case of Matt Murdock, become selfless and true. The author sees the city of Sophocles, Athens, as being the equivalent of Frank Miller's New York. He invokes and applies films like *Deathwish* and events like the Bernard Goetz subway incident to Miller's world view. Blackmore finds it simple to "substitute Murdock for Oedipus." Both Sophocles and Miller have created a saga of death and rebirth; they "both criticize and teach the audience what to think and do." This is a very well-illustrated, in-depth piece. It is one of the best pieces of comics scholarship that has been published.

Blackmore, Tim. "Doug Murray's *The 'Nam*, a Comic Battle for Vietnam at Home and Abroad." *LIT: Literature Interpretation Theory* 5 (1995): 213–225.

Blackmore looks at the history of *The 'Nam* comic from its beginnings to its end, issue *84*. He discusses Doug Murray's original vision for the title, and how he was taken off of the title, as was Chuck Dixon. He reveals how the marketing folks at Marvel tried to up the sales by introducing characters like the Punisher, and how subsequent comics were taken out of the true-to-life universe of Doug Murray's vision, and moved into the Marvel Universe. This illustrated article also looks at how the readers, through their letter writing, shaped the title. In a bold political statement, he argues that the Marvel Universe and President Reagan's America are "fantasy islands." I think that *The 'Nam* deserves to be reprinted in its entirety, either as an Essential book or trade paperback title.

Blumberg, Arnold. "The Night Gwen Stacy Died: The End of Innocence and the Birth of the Bronze Age." *Reconstruction: Studies in Contemporary Culture* 3, no. 4 (Fall 2003). *http://reconstruction.eserver.org/034/ blumberg.htm.*

Blumberg looks at the reasoning behind killing Peter Parker's love, Gwen Stacey. Many comics historians view this pivotal moment in comic's history as the real birth of the seventies Bronze Age of comics. The precedent was set by Marvel earlier when they published the codeless Spidey story about drugs. Marvel was responsible for bringing in a "new era in mature storytelling." One of the most controversial words in the Gwen Stacy epic is the word "Snap" when she falls and Spider-Man catches her. Fans, writers, and artists have long debated what this means. Blumberg also provides a brief history of Marvel in the earlier seventies. This foreshadowed the bringing of darker characters, like the Punisher and Wolverine, to the forefront of the Marvel Universe.

Bower, Katharine. "Holocaust Avengers: From 'The Master Race' to Magneto." *International Journal of Comic Art* 6, no. 2 (Fall 2004): 182–194.

Bower looks at vengeance for the crimes of the Holocaust, as portrayed in comics. She starts with a 1945 issue of *Captain America Comics 26*, which portrayed a concentration camp, and moves in to Kriegstein's "The Master Race" and Robin Snyder's *Manimal*. Magneto is the focus of the essay which looks at how his experience at Auschwitz gave him the desire for vengeance against the human race, for their hatred of mutants. The article concludes that acting out retribution leads to a "moral vacuum."

Bukatman, Scott. *Matters of Gravity: Special Effects and Supermen in the 20th Century.* Durham, NC: Duke University Press, 2003. ISBN: 0822331195 (pbk).

This book contains "X-Bodies: The Torment of the Mutant Superhero" (pp. 48–78), which was originally published in 1994. It contains a detailed look at body narratives as they relate to the concept of the mutant in *X-Men* and other comics. Bukatman compares Star Trek's TNG with the X-Men, noting similarities in attitudes toward the body. The book also includes a brief look at Spider-Man in New York (pp. 206–207).

Carter, James Bucky. "There Be Others Converging: Fighting American, the Other, and Governing Bodies." *International Journal of Comic Art* 6, no. 22 (Fall 2004): 364–375.

The Fighting American was Joe Simon and Jack Kirby's answer to the red scare of the 1950s. Although written in satiric style, the Fighting American was a message that the might of United States could overcome all the evil commies. While the bad guys are seen as having some intelligence, it is the brawn and strong body of Johnny Flagg, the Fighting American, that is able to defeat the bad guys at every turn. Carter provides a history of the Fighting American character, and analyzes all seven issues of the 1950s comic. Although the enemies are described as "commies," their nationality as Russian is never stated, but their names (e.g., Poison Ivan and Hotski Trotski) make it obvious that they were from Russia. It is the physique of Flagg that is most important. Kirby and Simon obviously were patriots who created a hero that fitted within the American personality of the 1950s, and integrated "patriotism, nationality, and the masculine body."

Charap, Ross J., Faith Wu. "Whose Right Is It Anyway? Captain America Smashes Through to Preserve an Author's Right to Terminate a Copyright Grant, Notwithstanding a Retroactive Work for Hire Agreement." *NYSBA: Entertainment and Sports Law Journal.* (Spring 2003). *http:// www.mossinger.com/articles/files/Captain America503.pdf.*

Charap and Wu go into detail about Joe Simon's legal woes while trying to reclaim copyright and monetary compensation for the creation of Captain America. He took Marvel to court several times from 1966 to 1969, and most recently in 1999, to assert his rights as the cocreator of Captain America with Jack Kirby. The authors go into detail about various court rulings concerning copyright law, and in Simon's case, "work for hire." After much legal wrangling, Simon was finally awarded the right to his cocreation.

Cremins, Brian. "Why Have You Allowed Me to See You Without Your Mask? *Captain America 133* and the Great American Protest Novel." *International Journal of Comic Art* 4. no. 1 (Spring 2002): 239–247.

Cremins analyzes the story "Madness in the Slums" from *Captain America 133*, in detail. He places this story in the genre of American protest novel, along with Stowe's *Uncle Tom's Cabin*. Although writer James Baldwin was critical of the protest novel, and would not have liked this issue of *Captain America* either, Cremins argues that it can be used as a tool for political and racial awareness. He also discusses, in detail, the ads in the comic book, and what those ads tells us about popular culture. Anyone who is a fan of Captain America should read this article; it provides one of the best individual analyses of a single comic book ever written.

Davies, Paul. *Exactly 12 Cents and Other Convictions: Four Imaginary Letters from Paul Davies*. East Haven, CT: ECW Press, 1994. ISBN: 1550222309.

In this book, are four philosophical letters addressed to Stan Lee and Jack Kirby, describing the author's thoughts on comics in general, and early Marvel comics, specifically. The author describes his love for the character of Iron Man, confessing affinity for the early gray Iron Man costume, from *Tales of Suspense 39*. He describes in detail when he bought that issue. This is a good primer on the philosophy of comics, and also is one of the strangest Marvel-related books published.

Dillard, Brian J. "A Kiss Is Just a Kiss: Portrayals of Women in Marvel Comics *X-Men*." unpublished pages, Michigan State University, 1992.

Dillard examines *X-Men 1–12* to see how women are portrayed in the comic. He concludes that most attitudes are sexist, and that nearly all the women wear sexually provocative suits. Female heroes are unwilling objects of sexual desire, but male heroes are not portrayed as sexual objects. *X-Men* downplays the importance of women, and is full of gender stereotypes. This work was never published.

Dyson, Anne Hass. "The Ninjas, the X-Men and the Ladies: Playing with Power and Identity in an Urban Primary School." *Teacher's College Record* 92, no. 22 (1994): 219–239. Available online: http//www.writingproject.org/cs/nwpp/print/nwpr/691, *National Center for the Study of Writing and Literacy Technical Report #70*.

This article analyzes the gender roles in a second-grade class located in San Francisco, using original "Author's Theater" plays. Dyson did some practical studies on children's play acting and writing, using the Ninja Turtles and, more importantly, the X-Men. From the X-Men cartoon on Fox, most of the children were more inclined to use the X-Men as a form of role playing. The X-Men, by its vary nature, has strong female characters, and the girls were not left out. Most of the girls seemed to identify with Rogue and Storm. Dyson looks at individual girls, and at how this role-playing game, or "Author's Theater," affected

the class as a whole. She includes the stories as the kids wrote them, and adds her "translations" of the language. The author discusses how female characters were used in the children's plays. Some of the characters the girls used included the Blob, Storm, Rogue, and Jean Grey. Having the children write and act out their X-Men plays provided a healthy way of encouraging creativity and interaction among boys and girls. Gambit seemed to be the character the boys liked best for role-playing. This is a fascinating article that should be read by elementary and middle school teachers.

Feiffer, Jules. *The Great Comic Book Heroes*. New York: Bonanza Books, 1977. ISBN: 080373 0454.

First published in 1966 by Dial Press, this is the groundbreaking study of early comics history. It contains reprints from *Marvel Comics 1*; *Marvel Mystery Comics;* and *Captain America 1*, which feature Sub-Mariner, Human Torch and Toro, and Captain America and Bucky. Fantagraphics republished Feiffer's original essay in 2002 (ISBN 1560975016).

Fingeroth, Danny. *Superheroes on the Couch: What Superheroes Really Tell Us about Ourselves and Our Society*. New York: Continuum, 2004. ISBN: 0826415393 (trd); 0826 415407.

This book answers the question, "Why have superheroes become such an important part of modern popular culture?" Superheroes are just a reflection of humanity, and their roots go back to ancient heroes in epic literature, like Gilgamesh and the Bible. There are sections on Spider-Man (pp. 63–78, 139–154), X-Men and Fantastic Four (pp. 98–117), Hulk and Wolverine (pp. 120–137), and Magneto (pp.155–168). Fingeroth also states that a dysfunctional group like the Avengers is the Ozzy Osbornes of the superhero world; DC's Justice League is more like Ozzie and Harriet; and the Fantastic Four would be the Swiss Family Robinson with superpowers. This is a well-written, very readable account of the rise of the superhero. Stan Lee wrote the introduction.

Fischer, Craig. "Fantastic Fascism? Jack Kirby, Nazi Aesthetics and Klaus Theweleit's *Male Fantasies*." *International Journal of Comic Art* 5, no. 1 (Spring 2003): 334–353.

Fischer looks at the history of comics, and views them as a subtle form of fascism. Because superheroes go outside the law, they can be viewed as fascists, even when fighting against fascists. There are those critics, like Klaus Theweleit, in his volume *Male Fantasies*, who saw much in Jack Kirby's work that they deemed to be fascist. There is a section in this article that discusses in detail the origin of Dr. Doom and the Fantastic Four, and discusses how Dr. Doom is a Hitler type. Kirby viewed Doom as being so arrogant that only a little scratch on his face caused him to become a despot. There is much debate about this in the world of comics, but Fischer defends Jack Kirby's work against "explicit and implied charges of Fascism by looking at his work in light of the complex theories of Nazi aesthetics" presented by Theweleit's work.

Franc, Joelle. "X-Men as a Mirror Image of American History During the 1960s through the 1980s." Paper, George Washington University, 2003. *http://www2.gwu. edu/~english/ccsc/2003/papers/franc.pdf* (accessed November 12, 2006; site now discontinued).

Franc argues that one can find civil rights parallels in the *X-Men* comics. Professor X is a Martin Luther King type of character, while Magneto is more akin to Malcolm X. Storm is the bastion of feminism, and Mother Nature as a woman who does not need a man. Although some critics argue that Wolverine is a right-winger, Franc sees him as anti-government because he was exploited and used by the government during the Weapon X project.

Gabillet, Jean Paul. "Cultural and Mythical Aspects of a Superhero: The Silver Surfer 1968–1970." *Journal of Popular Culture* 28, no. 22 (Fall 1994): 203–213.

Gabillet examines how the first *Silver Surfer* series was a step above the typical superhero material of the time, 1968–1970. The first eighteen issues of *Silver Surfer* provide a unique glimpse into mythical stories which have far more meaning than most comics produced at that time. There is a brief discussion and history of the Silver Surfer, before he received his title. According to Gabillet, Stan Lee and John Buscema created a mythical structure not unlike the classic stories and myths that have been told throughout the ages. The Surfer has a definite "messianic quality" that is far removed from most superheroes. The stories deal with ethical dilemmas and the Surfer's selflessness. There is both the messiah and the fallen angel (or fallen human, like Adam) within the Surfer's persona. Like Jesus Christ and other prophets, the Surfer seems always to be rejected by those he saves. The author also looks at how one can apply mythical and historical symbolism to the *Silver Surfer* stories.

Gibson, Mel. "Wham Bam! The X-Men Are Here: The British Broadsheet Press and the X-Men Film and the Comic," *International Journal of Comic Art* 3, no. 2 (Fall 2001): 239–249.

In this article Gibson discusses the reviews of the *X-Men* movie in the British press. Many of the reviewers looked at the comic book rather than the content of the movie. Some of them viewed the film through the eyes of the middle class, as a reflection of lowbrow culture. One reviewer considered the film's opening scene as just plain "crass." Some of the reviewers were dismissive of the film without studying its content, and felt that one of the film's only saving graces was the employment of British actors, including Sir Ian McKellen and Patrick Stewart. Although some British reviewers praised the film, there were others who saw it as a film "that takes itself too seriously for its own good." Gibson discusses the negative view of comics in Britain during the 1950s.

Gillespie, Nick. "Make Mine Mutants: Marvel Comics and Plenitude in Contemporary America." *Reason* 35, no. 1 (May 2003): 64–65.

Gillespie looks at why Marvel comic book films seem to be better than their distinguished competition's films, i.e., *Superman IV* and *Batman and Robin*. *Spider-Man* came in as the fifth biggest movie of all time. The author argues that Marvel's success is due to the fact that it deals with "engaging themes," to which American society, as a whole, can relate. People relate to the Marvel characters in the comic and on the big screen.

Gresh, Lois H. Robert Weinberg. *The Science of Super Heroes.* New York: J. Wiley & Sons, 2002. ISBN: 0471024600 (trd); 0471468 827 (pbk).

In this book, the authors present a scientific look at the possibility of superheroes, told in lay's terms, without sacrificing any scientific detail. The book contains chapters on the Fantastic Four and the Hulk (pp. 19–32), Sub-Mariner (pp. 47–64), Spider-Man (pp. 65–82), Ant-Man (pp. 99–103), and the X-Men (pp. 129–144), as well as DC heroes like the Flash, Batman, Superman, and the Atom, among others. A sequel, *Science of Supervillains*, was published in 2005 (ISBN: 0471482056), and the *Physics of Superheroes* was published in 2006 (ISBN: 1592402429).

Hersey, George L. *The Evolution of Allure: Sexual Selection from the Medici Venus to the Incredible Hulk.* Cambridge: MIT Press, 1996. ISBN: 0262082446 (trd); 0262581647 (pbk).

This scholarly work by George Hersey looks at the history of body types. The Hulk, Killpower, and Motormouth body types are discussed.

Holte, James Craig. "*Blade*: A Return to Revulsion." *Journal of Dracula Studies* 3 (2001). Online, World Wide Web: http://www. blooferland.com/drc/images/03Holte.rtf.

In this article, the author examines the first *Blade* movie and the ten issues of *Blade: The Vampire Hunter*, published by Marvel. Both the movie and the comic hark back to the Golden Age of pulps, the 1950s. The vampires depicted in *Blade* are not the classy, sensuous vampires of modern literature (e.g., Anne Rice's), but vicious and cruel creatures who view humanity as food. Holte argues that Whistler in the movie is a cross between "Willie Nelson and Professor Van Helsing." He also presents a brief discussion of Blade's history in the comics, and examines how Dracula figures into the Blade story. This is an interesting and well-written article.

Hughes, David. *Comic Book Movies*. London: Virgin Books, 2003. ISBN: 073507676.

Hughes presents a critical review of recent comic book–related movies. There are chapters on such Marvel films as *Blade, X-Men, Spider-Man, Hulk* and *Daredevil*, as well as other comic-related properties. Each chapter contains a synopsis plus information about cast, title sequence, origin, development, how the press saw the film, and DVD availability.

Iaccino, James F. *Jungian Reflections Within the Cinema*. Westport, CT: Praeger, 1998. ISBN: 0275950484.

This book contains "The Incredible Hulk: The Search is On for the Misunderstood Beast" (pp. 168–172). In this section, Iaccino looks at the *Hulk* television show, and compares the relationship between Jung's idea of the Shadow Pursuer with reporter Jack McGee's pursuit of the Hulk, throughout the series.

Jacobs, Will, Gerald Jones. *Comic Book Heroes: From the Silver Age to the Present*. New York: Crown Publishers, 1985. ISBN: 0517 554402.

This semi-academic history of comics includes chapters on the Fantastic Four (pp. 48–55); Spider-Man (pp. 62–67); "Marvel Age of Comics" (pp. 87–97); Marvel's hero teams (pp. 107–113); "The Cosmic Saga" (pp. 120–126); Marvel expansion (pp. 140–150); "Marvel Phase 2" (pp. 162–168); Conan and King (pp. 174–178); "Marvel's Monstrous Heroes" (195–203); "Cosmic Zap" (pp. 226–231); "Masters of Kung Fu" (pp. 232–237); New X-Men (pp. 245–258); and New Visions (pp. 264–268). The book also contains a detailed history of DC Comics.

Jewett, Robert, John Shelton Lawrence. *Captain America and the Crusade Against Evil: The Dilemma of Zealous Nationalism*. Grand Rapids, MI: William B. Erdmans, 2003. ISBN: 0802860834.

The authors briefly discuss the origin of Captain America and his relationship to the concept of nationalism, and look at Captain America's history in the comics. The book has a cover reproduction of *Captain America 16*, from 1999.

Johnston, W. Robert. "Splash Panel Adventures." *Smithsonian Studies in American Art* 3, no. 33 (Summer 1989): 38–53.

In this article, Johnston looks at and reproduces a number of comic panels, and argues for their artistic integrity and worth. He spends a great part of the article discussing the Silver Surfer and that character's history. There is also a nice two-page spread of the

Surfer. Other Marvel characters discussed and shown include Captain America, Daredevil, Moon Knight, and the New Mutants. The author also discusses the artists who did Swamp Thing, Watchmen, American Flagg, Batman, Superman, and the Rocketeer, and especially Sienkiewicz's work on Warlock.

Kallis, Leonard. *From Hercules to Captain America: How Comic Books Adapt Mythology*. Master's thesis, University of South Dakota, 1993.

This is a beautifully written Master's thesis which looks at how comics, and particularly Marvel comics, have adapted traditional mythological themes into Superhero stories. The author makes use of Joseph Campbell's ideas, and shows how his concepts are used in comic storylines. The role of mythological ideas in the Avengers and Captain America are discussed in detail. The author argues that comics should not be "designated as mere children's literature ... but studied as a fantasy vehicles, that reflect the society that produces them, and promote values accepted by the society." The thesis includes a glossary of mythological characters and superheroes.

Klock, Geoff. *How to Read Superhero Comics and Why*. London: Continuum, 2002. ISBN: 0826414192.

This literary analysis of graphic novels argues that the future of the superhero narrative lies in books like *Planetary, The Authority*, and *Wildcats*. Klock also looks at the *Dark Knight Returns, Watchmen*, and *Astro City*, in order to detail his arguments. . There is some Marvel content. Klock discusses *Marvels* (pp. 78–87), Mike Allred's *X-Force*, Grant Morrison's *New X-Men*, and *Marvel Boy* (pp. 172–177). Klock places these works published by Marvel in literary context with some of the above-mentioned works. He also looks at how these graphic novels and stories fit into popular culture.

Klock, Geoff. "X-Men, Emerson, Gnosticism." *Reconstruction: Studies in Contemporary Culture* 4, no. 33 (Summer 2004). *http://reconstruction.eserver.org/043/Klock/Klock.html.*

Klock compares the *Ultimate X-Men* and Grant Morrison's *New X-Men* to Ralph Waldo Emerson and the theories of Christian Gnostism. He argues that although Gnosticism is no longer being practiced, one can still find its essence in various literary sources, including the X-Men. He argues that the X-Men comics have a *"Post-Human"* identity which corresponds to the Gnostic "pneuma," or spirit. He goes into detail concerning the basic plots of the *Ultimate X-Men* and the *New X-Men*. While Xavier is honorable at times, he also is a manipulator. In both series the X-Men "lead the fight for their Post-Human brethren." The storyline from Grant Morrison's run, with which Klock is most concerned, is the "Assault on Weapon Plus" story in which Cyclops, Wolverine, and Fantomex must infiltrate a "factory-city connected to the Weapon X program." This is an amazingly detailed essay that reads well and shows a tremendous amount of thought.

Lavin, Michael. "A Librarian's Guide to Marvel Comics." *Serials Review* 24, no. 22 (1998): 47–63.

This essay provides a guide to the world of Marvel Comics for the uninformed librarian, and anyone interested in the world of Marvel in 1998. Lavin describes the history of the company, and the history of the various characters. He discusses various eras, with sections on "Marvel Reborn" and "Marvel's Trouble on Wall Street." The titles he annotates and reviews include *Uncanny X-Men, X-Factor, X-Force,* and *Generation X; Spider-Man, Fantastic Four, Captain America, Avengers, Iron Man, Daredevil, Incredible Hulk, Silver Surfer, Alpha Flight, Deadpool, Thunderbolts, Ka-Zar, Quicksilver, Heroes for Hire, Conan,* and *Marvel Adventures.* This is a well-written article. While it is dated, it is still worth reading.

Lees, Tim, Sue Ralph. "To Others He's Just a Helpless Man in a Wheelchair! But When I See Him Like This: Case Studies of Physical Disability in Marvel Comics, 1961–1970." Washington D.C., 1995.

This essay was originally presented to the Media and Disability Interest Group of the Association for Education in Journalism and Mass Communication, at the Association's national conference, August 10, 1995, but it was also privately published. The authors look at how disabilities are portrayed in Marvel Comics.

Lippert, David. L. *Alienation and Comic Books: The Construction of Good and Evil in the Fantastic Four.* Master's thesis, University of Wyoming, 1991.

By analyzing early issues of the *Fantastic Four,* the author looks at how good and evil are portrayed. Often good and evil are blurred in these early issues. For example, in issue 2, the Fantastic Four are seen as evil because they are impersonated by Skrulls. Yet the Fantastic Four are supposed to be the good guys. Lippert also looks at the Fantastic Four's first meeting with the Hulk, in which he is framed for acts he didn't commit. Even the Fantastic Four's encounter with the Mole Man, in issue 1, is suspect, because the Mole Man is not "truly evil"; he is just a victim of a society that made him an outcast. Good and evil are not always black and white, as Stan Lee's early writings bear out. The author compares the *Fantastic Four* to Milton's *Paradise Lost.* Lippert's thesis includes a copy of a short letter that Stan Lee wrote to him. The thesis is well written and entertaining, and filled with philosophical ideas. It was never printed.

Macdonald, Andrew. Virginia Macdonald. "SOLD AMERICAN: The Metamorphosis of Captain America." *Journal of Popular Culture* 10, no. 1 (Summer 1976): 249–255.

The Macdonalds look at the various changes Captain America has gone through in the decades since his inception in the 1940s, and they argue that Captain America's changes reflect America's changes. In the 1940s he was fighting the Nazis, as the face of America in the World War II. In the 1950s, Captain America was the "Commie Smasher," battling against the red menace. During the 1960s, he was involved in America's racial and domestic strife, and even the Vietnam conflict. And the disillusionment of the 1970s was not lost on Captain America. The authors argue that Captain America represents the typical American success story of "myth and Horatio Alger: poor but deserving kid makes good."

Matton, Annette. "From Realism to Superheroes in Marvel's *The 'Nam.*" In *Comics and Ideology.* Matthew P. McAllister, Edward H. Sewell Jr., and Ian Gordon, eds. New York: Peter Lang, 2001. ISBN: 0820 452491.

This is an analysis of the Vietnam-based comic *The 'Nam.* The author describes the history of the series, from its beginnings to the end of the run. Many fans were upset when Captain America appeared in issue 41, but were pleased when the Punisher appeared, as Frank Castle, in later issues. Matton sees the series as reflecting the conservative view of the Vietnam conflict, without much attention to the negative side, or the protests that occurred because of the war. The ideology reflected in the comic series never really went through any radical changes.

Matton, Annette. "Reader Response to Doug Murray's *The 'Nam.*" *International Journal of Comic Art* 2, no. 1 (Spring 2000): 33–44.

Matton analyzed various fan letters throughout *The 'Nam*'s publication history, from its beginnings through its cancellation. She found that many fans, including Vietnam veterans and young adults, could relate to the realistic storylines and subject matter. When Captain America was introduced into the comic, it garnered a tremendous amount of negative criticism. This did not happen when Frank Castle, the Punisher, was introduced as a sergeant; this was before Castle became the Punisher, in line with the realistic storytelling. The author also looks at letters that lament the title's cancellation.

McCue, Greg S., Clive Bloom. *Dark Knights: The New Comics in Context.* Boulder CO: Pluto Press, 1993. ISBN: 0745306624 (trd); 074530663 (pbk).

This publication contains a scholarly look at the new wave of comics and comic writers. It includes "The Merry Marvel Marching Society" and the "Hero Who Could Be You." The authors briefly discuss the formation of the Marvel Universe, and the creation of the Fantastic Four, the Hulk, and Spider-Man. They go into detail about how early Marvel Comics were aimed not just at kids, but adults as well. The book includes interviews with Stan Lee and Marvel's editor in chief Tom DeFalco.

Meyer, Michaela D.E. "Utilizing Mythic Criticism in Contemporary Narrative Culture: Examining the 'Present Absence' of Shadow Archetypes in *Spider-Man*." *Communication Quarterly* 51, no. 4 (Fall 2003): 518–529.

This article looks at mythical shadow archetypes involved in how the Green Goblin was portrayed in the first *Spider-Man* movie. The Green Goblin has more depth than most villains in typical superhero movies. Norman Osborn's inner dialogues where Osborn and the Goblin have conversations and interact with one another invoke the doppelganger mythos, but with more substance than is usually the case in this type of film or literary narrative. The use of the mirror, which is a common literary device, is also invoked.

Mondello, Salvatore. "Spider-Man Superhero in the Liberal Tradition." *Journal of Popular Culture* 10, no. 1 (Summer 1976): 232–238.

This is a historic survey of American liberalism in the pages of the *Amazing Spider-Man*. *Spider-Man* comic books in the 1960s could serve the same function as the *New England Primer* did for early Americans, in educating America's young people. Spider-Man helped "keep alive American liberalism among the young, a tradition stressing cooperation among individuals and minorities rather than conflict, moderation in politics rather than extremism, and the right of each American to social recognition and economic opportunity." The author also looks at how Spider-Man dealt with American social issues, like pollution, bigotry, drug abuse and organized crime, in the late 1960s and early 1970s. He compares Spider-Man to FDR.

Muir, John Kenneth. *The Unseen Force: The Films of Sam Rami*. New York: Applause, 2004. ISBN: 1557836078.

This book includes a scholarly analysis of all of Sam Rami's films, including *Spider-Man* (pp. 265–285) and *Spider-Man 2* (pp. 287–292). The author looks at how each film was created, and the various steps taken to insure that *Spider-Man* was a quality film.

Murphy, B. Keith. *Revisionist Reality: Alpha Flight 106 and the Marvel Universe*. Journal of the Georgia Association of Historians 20 (1999): 1–24.

This academic paper is illustrated with examples from the comics. It looks at the undercurrents of homosexuality within the *Alpha Flight* comic.

Nelson, Tim. "Even an Android Can Cry." *Journal of Gender Studies* 13, no. 3 (November 2004): 251–257.

Nelson analyzes the panel from *Avengers 58* in which Vision cries when he is accepted into the Avengers. There is a dichotomy between portraying an android with such human emotion, and with muscles fit for a bodybuilder. The author argues that Vision, Spider-Man, and Superman are closeted bodybuilders, who were "just born" that way and don't go to the gym. Bodybuilding has not been seen in the best of lights in American society. The Sylvester Stallone and Arnold Schwarzenegger movie roles, *Rocky* and *Conan*, have done much to enhance the role of male bodybuilding in society. The author discusses, in some detail, both the *Rocky* movie and the Marvel *Conan* comic. Charles Atlas's role is also discussed. Marvel's use of the Vision, and his subsequent crying, is "proof of humanity and authenticity." Nelson also looks at Philip K. Dick's novel *When Androids Dream of Electric Sleep*, and applies its view of masculinity. The Vision may have looked like a muscleman, but he "was really an intellectual."

Palumbo, Donald. "Adam Warlock: Marvel Comics' Cosmic Christ Figure." *Extrapolation* 24, no. 1 (1983): 33–46.

This is a very detailed account of Adam Warlock's appearances in Marvel Comics, up until 1983. Like Christ, Warlock is born pure, in a manager, and becomes savior for Counter-Earth. He fights the Man-Beast (Satan), is crucified and resurrected, ascends to the stars, and later goes to paradise (Heaven) in his soul gem. Warlock goes through a number of births, deaths, rebirths, and resurrections during his tenure in Marvel Comics. The author also compares Warlock's cosmic quest to Dostoyevsky's "Dream of a Ridiculous Man," and *Brothers Karamazov*; Milton's *Paradise Lost*; and Wells's *Island of Dr. Moreau*. Palumbo looks at how Warlock's life was influenced by the roles played by the High Evolutionary, Thanos, Pip, Magus (Warlock's older doppelganger), the In-Betweener, Gamora, and the Avengers.

Palumbo, Donald. "Comics as Literature: Plot Structure, Foreshadowing, and Irony in the Marvel Comics' 'Cosmic Epic.'" *Extrapolation* 22. no. 4 (1981): 309–324.

This article provides a very detailed analysis of the Korvac Saga in the Avengers comic. The author sees this work as an epic, as real literature that should not be dismissed as mere fodder. He calls the Avengers tale a "beautifully orchestrated, skillfully balanced plot structure" and points out just how complicated the Avengers tale actually is. Palumbo looks at how various subplots, and other literary devices like foreshadowing, are used within the tale.

Palumbo, Donald. "The Marvel Comics Group's Spider-Man Is an Existentialist Super Hero; or 'Life Has No Meaning Without

My Latest Marvels!'" *Journal of Popular Culture* 17, no. 2 (Fall 1983): 67–81.

Palumbo looks at Existentialist philosophy throughout the pages of *Spider-Man*, and argues that Spider-Man is the typical Existentialist hero. He quotes from various philosophers and literary figures, such as Sartre, Camus, and Kafka, to argue his point. The author looks at Spider-Man's meeting with Killraven in a future in which the Martians have taken over. Spider-Man asks Killraven what the point of it all is if the future is destined to be so terrible. Palumbo looks at the absurdity, dualism, and irony within Peter Parker's personality, and identity. Since *Spider-Man* is "absurdist fiction," and "art is an ordered restructuring of reality," Spider-Man contains all of the basic elements of Existentialism.

Palumbo, Donald. "Marvel's *Tomb of Dracula*: Case Study in a Scorned Medium." In Lydia Cushman Schurman, and Deidre Johnson, eds., *Scorned Literature.* Westport: Greenwood Press, 2002. ISBN: 0313320 330.

This excellent essay is a survey of how Dracula is portrayed in the complete sets of *Tomb of Dracula* and *Dracula Lives*. The author believes Dracula is portrayed as a being who wrestles with the moral issues of right and wrong. Dracula is not always a villain, but does act heroically on occasion, even saving the lives of his enemies.

Palumbo, Donald. "Metafiction in the Comics: *Sensational She-Hulk.*" *Journal of the Fantastic in the Arts* 8, no. 3 (December 1997): 310–330.

After giving a brief history of the She-Hulk, Palumbo gives a detailed analysis of the *Sensational She-Hulk* comics, by discussing the brilliant writing contained in that book. He discusses how She-Hulk is self-aware all through the sixty-issue run. Jennifer Walters knows that she is in a comic book, and often engages the artists and writers, as well as the readers, in the book. He describes how She-Hulk's partner in adventure is now an aged woman from the Golden Age, who was once the hero Blonde Phantom. Palumbo also discusses the cheesecake factor in portraying a sexually active, scantly clad She-Hulk who almost, but doesn't quite, go beyond the Comics Code which is ridiculed throughout the *Sensational She-Hulk.*

Palumbo, Donald. "Patterns of Allusions in Marvel Comics." *Proteus* 6, no. 1 (Spring 1989): 61–64.

Because of the many allusions they make to literature, films, music, and advertising, Marvel comics serve as a mirror for Western culture. Allusions to the Bible, James Joyce, Shakespeare, Greek and Roman mythology, Arthurian folk legends, and Dante, among many others, are all found in Marvel comics. Even plays, like Arthur Miller's *The Crucible*, and films, like *The Wizard of Oz*, are often referenced in Marvel Comics stories. Palumbo gives a very detailed explanation of how Marvel used common allusions in its stories, from the *Fantastic Four*, to the *Micronauts*, to "unknown" titles like *Night Mask*.

Palumbo, Donald. "The Use of Comics as an Approach to Introducing the Techniques and Terms of Narrative to Novice Readers." ERIC document, 1979: ED190980.

Palumbo looks at how Marvel comics can be used in the classroom. He argues that Marvel comics are literate, that they have a well-balanced narrative structure, and that they should not be dismissed as junk reading.

Pustz, Matthew. *Comic Book Culture: Fanboys and True Believers.* Jackson, MS: University of Mississippi Press, 1999. ISBN: 1578062004 (trd) 1578062012 (pbk).

This is a scholarly look at the culture of fandom in the comic book world. There is a chapter on "Marvel Zombies," people who love Marvel and its characters, and read all or most of the Marvel books. In this chapter, Pustz looks at the early Marvel fan community. He discusses the Merry Marvel Marching Society, and Friends of Marvel, FOOM, in great detail. He argues that one of the reasons that Marvel became so successful was the realism found in characters like the Fantastic Four and Spider-Man. Marvel's comics were more intelligent during the 1960s, and thus they achieved more respect, than those of the distinguished competition. The author talks about various Marvel comics throughout the whole book.

Reynolds, Richard. *Super Heroes: A Modern Mythology.* Jackson: MS: University of Mississippi Press, 1994. ISBN: 0878056 939 (trd); 087056947 (pbk).

In this work, Superheroes are seen as modern myths which affect everyday life. This book includes two sections related to Marvel, "Explicitly Mythology: Thor" (pp. 53–60) and "*X-Men 108–143*" (pp. 84–95). Thor is examined in the context of Norse mythology, and the X-Men's interpersonal relationships are explored.

Richardson, Niall. "The Gospel According to *Spider-Man.*" *Journal of Popular Culture* 37, no. 4 (May 2004): 694–703.

The author looks at Christian parallels in the first *Spider-Man* movie. He argues that Peter Parker is conflicted between his desires of the flesh (Mary Jane), and his acts of selflessness, being Spider-Man. Much like the devil tempted Jesus in the desert, the Green Goblin tempts Spider-Man when the Goblin offers a partnership with him. Like much Christian thought, this film centers on Peter Parker's shame and guilt for allowing his Uncle Ben to die. He felt guilty because he had not stopped the robber previously when he had a chance. It is this pivotal event which makes him see that, "with great power comes great responsibility."

Robbins, Trina. *From Girls to Grrlz: A History of Women Comics from Teen to Zines.* San Francisco: Chronicle Books, 1999. ISBN: 08118219914.

This is a scholarly history of women in comics, from the Golden Age to the present. What makes this book related to Marvel, is its brief discussion of the Timely titles (pp. 22–39). Timely published more women-related and teen comics, than most other publishers. *Miss America, Patsy Walker's Fashion, Girl's Life, Tessie the Typist, Annie Oakley,* and *Millie the Model* were published in this twenty-eight year period.

Robinson, Lillian S. *Wonder Women: Feminisms and Superheroes.* New York: Routledge, 2004. ISBN: 0415966310.

The author looks at the history of female superheroes, trying to discern various feminist aspects in the writing. Marvel characters who are discussed include Invisible Woman (pp. 88–94, 110–114); She-Hulk (pp. 99–110); women in the Avengers (pp. 114–126); and Elektra (p.126).

Rosemont, Franklin. "Introduction to the Incredible Hulk." In Franklin Rosemont, ed., *Dancin' in the Streets!: Anarchists, Iwws, Surrealists, Situationists & Provos in the 1960s as Recorded in the Pages of the Rebel Worker & Heatwave: Critical Theory at Its Bugs Bunnyist Best! Dialectics in the Spirit of the Incredible Hulk.* Chicago: Charles Kerr, 2004. ISBN: 0882863010 (pbk); 0882863029 (trd).

The author argues that the Hulk can been seen as a revolutionary who workers and sixties revolutionaries could relate to. There are references to the Hulk throughout the book, and the Silver Surfer and Plastic Man are mentioned, among others (pp. 319–320).

Savage, William. *Commies, Cowboys, and Jungle Queens.* Hanover, NH: Wesleyan University Press, 1990. ISBN: 0819563382.

This essay concerns the communist "menace," as shown in comics during the fifties. The author uses the reprinted story "Terror in Tibet," from *Kent Blake of the Secret Service* as a comic example.

Schmidt, Peter Allon, Jr. *The History of Atomic Power and the Rise of the American Comic Book Superhero.* Master's thesis, Arizona State University, 2002.

The author looks at the history of atomic power. The relationship of the Fantastic Four, the Hulk, and Spider-Man to all things atomic is discussed in detail. However, the author makes several grave historical errors when he talks about comics featuring the 1940s character of Captain Marvel, Shazam, as being published by Marvel Comics. Actually, they were first published by Fawcett, and later by DC. Marvel does have a Captain Marvel, but it is not the same character. This thesis was never published.

Schweizer, Reinhard. *Ideology and Propaganda in Marvel Superhero Comics.* Frankfurt, Germany: Peter Lang, 1992. ISBN: 36147 44605.

This is a study of the political ideologies in Marvel comics from the 1940s to the early 1970s. The author looks at Nazism and Hitler, Captain America, the rise of the communist "menace" in the 1950s and early 1960s, and the Vietnam conflict, among other issues. There are sections on Silver Surfer, Avengers, Iron Man, Spider-Man, Hulk, Thor, Fantastic Four, and Ant-Man, in German.

Shepard, Lucius. "eXCreMent." In *Projections: Science Fiction in Literature & Film,"* edited by Lou Anders, 241–246. Austin: Monkey Brain Books, 2004: ISBN: 1932265120.

This is a bizarre review of the first X-Men movie, in which the author initially describes the film as a dystopian fantasy, and then goes on to compare it to pizza: "The film is not a top-of-the line pie ... nor is it slimy cardboard."

Silvio, Carl. *Postmodern Fiction and the Marvel Universe: A Performative Study.* Master's thesis, State University of New York, Brockport, 1994.

The author looks at postmodernist philosophy and applies it to comic book narratives, and more specifically to the Marvel Universe. Silvio states that the Marvel Universe challenges "traditional and conventionally held ideas about reading and literature," and therefore can be considered postmodern. He views the Marvel Universe as an example of an "ontologically reconfigured text." This thesis was never published.

Sparks, Glenn G. Joanne Canton, "Developmental Differences in Responses to *The Incredible Hulk*: Using Piaget's Theory of Cognitive Development to Predict Emotional Effects." ERIC Document, 1983, ED236737.

The authors use the *Incredible Hulk* television program to see if young children showed various levels of fear, and at what age fear dissipated. Jean Piaget's preoperational theory was applied to the various transformations of Banner to the Hulk, and vice versa, and the children's understanding of those transformations.

Stephens, C.M. "Spider-Man: An Enduring Legend." In *A Necessary Fantasy? The Heroic Figure in Children's Popular Litera-*

ture, edited by Dudley Jones and Tony Watkins, 251–265. New York: Garland, 2000. ISBN: 0815318448.

Stephens examines why Spider-Man has remained such a popular figure among young people for almost forty years. She points out the similarities and differences between Spider-Man and Batman. Like Bruce Wayne as Batman, Peter Parker as Spider-Man seeks to atone for a personal sin. Unlike Bruce Wayne, he is not rich. Peter Parker is the kind of disenfranchised teenager that youth can relate to. He has to make hard choices, and his life does not necessarily get better after he gets super powers. Spider-Man also continues to be relevant because of the modern-day issues tackled within the comic, such as drug and child abuse, organized crime, and racial issues. Spider-Man comics both relate to and help shape modern popular culture.

Thompson, Don. "OK Axis, Here We Come." In *All in Color for a Dime*, edited by Dick Lupoff and Don Thompson, 110–129. Iola, WI: Krause Publications, 1997. ISBN: 0873414985.

This work contains a history and discussion of the original Human Torch, Sub-Mariner, and Captain America, during the Timely/Atlas years, the forties and early fifties. The author gives a critical analysis of each character's origin story, and a synopsis of important issues. This is one of the best essays written about Marvel's early period.

Tranen, Jan. *Superheroes: A Study of the Significance of Television Superheroes with a Group of Five-Year-Olds*. Master's thesis, Bank Street College of Education, 1982.

Tranen looks at various superhero programs, including the 1960s *Batman, Greatest American Hero, Wonder Woman, Six Million Dollar Man, Superfriends,* and *The Incredible Hulk.* The study looks at how five-year-olds use role-playing based on the characters in the television programs. *The Incredible Hulk* was one of the more popular programs for the kids, and the appendix here includes an explanation as to why a certain child likes the character of the Hulk. This thesis was never published.

Traxler, Joshua William. *Marvel Comics and the 1960s: A Cultural History*. Master's thesis, Winthrop University, 2002.

This history thesis uses Marvel comics, and in particular Stan Lee's writing, to explain Marvel's world view during the turbulent 1960s. Using *Fantastic Four, Captain America, Incredible Hulk, Tales of Suspense, Iron Man, Tales to Astonish, Ant-Man, Strange Tales, Amazing Adult Fantasy,* and *Journey into Mystery* as primary sources, along with appropriate historical secondary sources, the author explains how Marvel tackled political, racial, ideological, and social issues during the sixties. The Vietnam conflict, radical racial groups, and drug use are all topics that were discussed in the comic books.

Trushell, John M. "American Dreams of Mutants: The X-Men: Pulp Fiction, Science Fiction and Superheroes." *Journal of Popular Culture* 38, no. 1 (August 2004): 149–168.

Trushell describes some of the history of the science fiction and pulp literary genres, and places the X-Men in the same category. There are definite literary precedents for "Homo-Superior" mutants before the X-Men, e.g., in the "Children of the Atom" stories by Wilmar Shirars, and in the works of Olaf Stapledon and Stanley Weinbaum, among others. The author believes that in the *X-Men* stories of the 1960s, Xavier could be seen as Martin Luther King, Magneto as Malcom X, and Wolverine as a libertarian. The current crop of *X* titles reflects a "cyberpunk" influence. The X-Men's history is rooted in science fiction and pulp literature of the past, and this author does a good job of proving that.

Vilea, Marco Tulio, Waldomiro Vergueiro. "The Brazilian X-Men: How Brazilian Artists Have Created Stories That Stan Lee Does Not Know About." *International Journal of Comic Art* 6, no. 1 (Spring 2004): 221–235.

After giving a brief history of the X-Men and other Marvel characters, in Brazilian comics, the authors discuss how the small publisher GEP published eight original short stories featuring the X-Men. These stories have never been translated into English and are quite rare. Gedeone Malagola, a policeman and attorney who loved to write comics, plotted the stories. Some of the original villains include *Lahar, Octopus* (different from the Spider-Man nemesis), and, weirdest of all, *Thor o Viking*, who is not Marvel's Thor, but an evil Thor. The authors discuss all eight issues in detail, and provide a synopsis. There are some reprinted pages from the stories, as well. This is one of the most interesting Marvel-related articles ever published. It is simply fascinating, and it would be wonderful if someone would reprint and translate these stories into English.

Warren, Brian Patrick. *An Historical Review of the Black Panther: The First Black Superhero in American Comic Books*. Master's thesis, University of Florida, 1992.

The author gives the reader a detailed look at Marvel's creation and use of the Black Panther. He starts out by looking at the history of blacks in comic strips, and then proceeds to look at how Stan Lee and Jack Kirby created the Panther. Warren focuses on four major Panther stories, all written by Don McGregor: "Panther's Rage," and "The Panther versus the Klan," in the pages of *Jungle Action*; "Panther's Quest," in the pages of *Marvel Comics Presents*; and the four-part graphic novel series, *Panther's Prey*. The differences in

V. Selected Marvel-Related Publications

style between Don McGregor and Jack Kirby are also discussed, as are other minority heroes. Stan Lee was interviewed for this thesis. Warren did an excellent job on an interesting topic. This thesis was never published.

Weinarch, Jeff. "Spider-Man vs. the Incredible Hulk." *Environmental Quality Management* 9, no. 4 (Summer 2000): 95–98.

Weinarch uses Spider-Man's phrase, "With great power, there must come great responsibility," as a motto for environmental health and safety (EHS) training. The story of Spider-Man is the right approach to health and safety. The Incredible Hulk's motto, "Hulk Smash," however is not to be followed. Basically the Hulk and Spider-Man are allegories for what to do and what not to do in EHS.

Williams, David E. "Temper, Temper: Directory of Photography Frederick Elms, ASA lends dramatic moods to the *Hulk*, the Big Screen Debut of a Very Angry Superhero." *American Cinematography* 84, no. 7 (July 2003): 34–45.

This article looks in detail at how the cinematographer for the *Hulk* movie, Frederick Elmes, worked on Ang Lee's picture. There is a tremendous amount of technical information as to how the filming was done. The author also provides a brief history of the Hulk, the character's early television history, and how the *Hulk* film eventually went into production.

Wolf-Meyer, Matthew. "The World of Ozymadias Made: Utopias in the Superhero Comic, Subculture and the Conservation of Difference." *Journal of Popular Culture* 36, no. 3 (Winter 2003): 497–517.

This essay looks at various utopian systems written about in comic series. There is a section on Marvel's Avengers and the Squadron Supreme. The author points out that the Avengers have often "endangered" their status as "America's Superteam" by acting outside of the traditional governmental mold. The story in *Avengers 238–254*, in which the Vision takes it upon himself to set up his own version of a utopia and world dominion, is analyzed in detail. The Squadron Supreme, Marvel's "clone" of the Justice League of America, takes it upon themselves to become the world's protectors, judge, and jury, by attempting to get rid of poverty, crime, and all due process of law. The Squadron sets themselves up as philosopher kings who are the moral arbitrators of the world. The author also looks at pivotal series such as *Watchmen* and *The Authority*.

Wood, Susan. *The Poison Maiden & the Great Bitch: Female Stereotypes in Marvel Superhero Comics: Essays in Fantastic Literature 5*. San Bernardino, CA: Borgo Press, 1989. ISBN: 0893705373.

This work was originally published in 1974 by T.K. Graphics. In this highly negative analysis, Wood argues that Marvel comics have continually stereotyped women as heartbreakers, homemakers, or bitches. The heroes are always lamenting the pain from broken relationships, which hurts them more than any encounter with supervillains. The comics that Wood analyzes include *Hulk, Fantastic Four, Daredevil, Spider-Man, Captain America, Sub-Mariner, Thor, Avengers, Conan,* and *Savage Tales*. She vehemently attacks Marvel staff and Stan Lee, and asks for a "little *less* stereotyping and a little *more* imagination."

Wright, Bradford. *Comic Book Nation*. Baltimore, MD: John Hopkins University Press, 2003. ISBN: 0801874505; 080186514X.

This work was originally published in 2001. The 2003 edition has an extra chapter, "Spider-Man at Ground Zero" (pp. 287–293), relating how the comicbook Spider-Man dealt with the 9/11 tragedy. This scholarly look at how comics have influenced our culture contains many references to the history of Marvel and its impact on the world in general. The author examines other companies, but the emphasis is on Marvel. The work is highly recommended.

Yanes, Nicholas. *X-Men as a Reflection of Civil Rights in America*. Bachelor's thesis: Florida Atlantic University, 2004.

The X-Men have acted as a symbol for civil rights in America. From its beginnings in the 1960s, the X-Men comics have inadvertently dealt with issues related to ostracized groups in America, from women's issues to homosexuality. The comic also has been updated to deal with post–9/11 concerns and politics. This thesis was never published.

Young, Stephen. "Are Comic Book Super-Heroes Sexist?" *Sociology and Social Research: An International Journal* 75 (1991): 218–225.

This article analyzes Marvel Universe Trading Cards, and looks at how superhero women are portrayed. Young argues that the portrayal of women in the Marvel Universe Trading Cards is not only sexist, but underrepresented as well. Women generally do not play a big role in comic book morality tales.

Zenari, Vivian. "Mutant Mutandis: The X-Men's Wolverine and the Construction of Canada." In *Culture the State Vol. 3: Nationalisms*, edited by Gabrielle E. M. Zezulka-Mailloux and James Gifford. Edmonton, CRC Humanities Studio, 2003. ISBN: 1551951479. http://www.arts.ual berta.ca/cms/zenari.pdf.

The author looks at the uniqueness of Wolverine as Canada's premier superhero and most popular X-Man. Zenari looks at the debate which took place during the discussion of the series *Origin*, about whether Logan would be kept a born Canadian, or become a transplanted American. Certainly, Logan has always maintained that he was a Canadian whenever he was accused of being a U.S. citizen. The author discusses pivotal stories in Wolverine's career, including "Bloodlust," "Havok," "Wolverine Meltdown," the X-Men stories, the above-mentioned *Origin*, the Wolverine solo books, and even Logan's work during World War II. She points out that whenever Wolverine wants to "get away from it all," he goes to the untamed Canadian wilderness where his true soul lies. Wolverine stands above all the rest as a mascot for Canada.

Appendix 1:
Marvel and Marvel-Related Publications, 2005

Adventures of Red Sonja. Dynamic Forces, 2005. ISBN: 193330507X. (Reprints original Marvel books)

Alpha Flight Vol. 2: Waxing Poetic. New York: Marvel, 2005. ISBN: 0785115692.

Amazing Spider Man Vol. 8: Sins Past. New York: Marvel, 2005. ISBN: 0785115099.

Amazing Spider-Man Vol. 9: Skin Deep. New York: Marvel, 2005. ISBN: 0785116427.

Amazing Spider Man Vol. 10: New Avengers. New York: Marvel, 2005. ISBN: 0785117644.

Arana Vol. 1: Heart of the Spider. New York: Marvel, 2005. ISBN: 0785115064.

Arana Vol. 2: In the Beginning. New York: Marvel, 2005. ISBN: 0785117199.

Astonishing X-Men Vol. 2: Dangerous. New York: Marvel, 2005. ISBN: 078511677X

Avengers: Above and Beyond. New York: Marvel, 2005. ISBN: 0785118454.

Avengers Assemble, Vol. 2. New York: Marvel, 2005. ISBN: 0785117733 (Hardcover)

Avengers Disassembled. New York: Marvel, 2005. ISBN: 0785114823.

Avengers: Earth's Mightiest Heroes. New York: Marvel, 2005. ISBN: 0785114386. (Hardcover).

Avengers: Kang: Time and Time Again. New York: Marvel, 2005. ISBN: 0785118209.

Avengers: The Serpent Crown. New York: Marvel, 2005. ISBN: 0785117008.

Avengers: Vision and the Scarlet Witch. New York: Marvel, 2005. ISBN: 0785117709.

Avengers the Ultimate Guide. London: DK Books, 2005. ISBN: 0756614619

Avengers West Coast: Vision Quest TPB. New York: Marvel, 2005. ISBN: 0785117741.

Best of Spider Man Vol. 4. New York: Marvel, 2005. ISBN: 0785118276. (Hardcover)

Best of the Fantastic Four Vol. 1. New York: Marvel, 2005. ISBN: 0785117822. (Hardcover)

Black Panther: Who Is the Black Panther. New York: Marvel, 2005. ISBN: 0785117482. (Hardcover)

Black Panther by Jack Kirby Vol. 1. New York: Marvel, 2005. ISBN: 0785116877.

Black Widow: Homecoming. New York: Marvel, 2005. ISBN: 0785114939.

Bullseye: Greatest Hits. New York: Marvel, 2005. ISBN: 0785115129.

Cable/Deadpool Vol. 2: The Burnt Offering. New York: Marvel, 2005. ISBN: 0785115714.

Captain America and the Falcon: Secret Empire. New York: Marvel, 2005. ISBN: 0785118365.

Captain America and the Falcon Vol. 2: Brothers and Keepers. New York: Marvel, 2005. ISBN: 0785115684.

Captain America: Jack Kirby Bicentennial Battles. New York: Marvel, 2005. ISBN: 0785117261.

Captain America: Winter Soldier. New York: Marvel, 2005. ISBN: 0785116516. (Hardcover)

Captain Britain. New York: Marvel, 2005. ISBN: 0785116001. (Reprint)

Captain Universe: Power Unimaginable. New York: Marvel, 2005. ISBN: 0785118918.

Chronicles of Conan Vol. 7: The Dweller in the Pool. Dark Horse, 2005. ISBN: 1593073003. (Reprints original Marvel comics)

Chronicles of Conan Vol. 8: Tower of Blood. Dark Horse, 2005. ISBN: 1593073496. (Reprints original Marvel comics)

Combat Zone: True Tales of GIs in Iraq. New York: Marvel, 2005. ISBN: 0785115161.

Comic Creators on the Fantastic Four. London: Titan, 2005. ISBN: 1845760530.

Comics Go to Hell: A Visual History of the Devil in Comics. Fantagraphics 2005. ISBN: 1560976160.

Daredevil: Father. New York: Marvel, 2005. ISBN: 0785115447. (Hardcover)

Daredevil: Redemption. New York: Marvel, 2005. ISBN: 0785115668.

Daredevil Vol. 4. New York: Marvel, 2004. ISBN: 0785113428. (Hardcover)

Daredevil Vol. 11: Golden Age. New York: Marvel. 2005. ISBN: 0785113959.

Daredevil Vol. 12: Decalogue. New York: Marvel, 2005. ISBN: 0785116443.

Defenders: Indefensible. New York: Marvel, 2005. ISBN: 0785117628.

District X Vol. 1: Mr. M. New York: Marvel, 2005. ISBN: 0785114440.

District X. Vol. 2: Underground. New York: Marvel, 2005. ISBN: 0785116028.

Doctor Spectrum: Full Spectrum. New York: Marvel, 2005. ISBN: 0785115862.

Earth X. New York: Marvel, 2005. ISBN: 0785118756. (Hardcover)

Elektra:The Hand. New York: Marvel, 2005. ISBN: 0785115943.

Elektra: The Movie. New York: Marvel, 2005. ISBN: 078511713X.

Emma Frost Vol. 2: Mind Games. New York: Marvel, 2005. ISBN: 0785114130. (Digest)

Emma Frost Vol. 3: Bloom. New York: Marvel, 2005. ISBN: 0785114734. (Digest)

Essential Avengers Vol. 1. New York: Marvel, 2005. ISBN: 0785118624. (Reprint)

Essential Daredevil Vol. 1. New York: Marvel, 2005. ISBN: 0785118616. (Reprint)

Essential Daredevil Vol. 3. New York: Marvel, 2005. ISBN: 0785117245.

Essential Defenders. Vol. 1. New York: Marvel, 2005. ISBN: 0785115471.

Essential Doctor Strange Vol. 2. New York: Marvel, 2005. ISBN: 0785116680.

Essential Fantastic Four Vol. 1. New York: Marvel, 2005. ISBN: 0785106669. (Reprint)

Essential Fantastic Four Vol. 4. New York: Marvel, 2005. ISBN: 078511484X.

Essential Ghost Rider. New York: Marvel, 2005. ISBN: 0785118381.

Essential Hulk Vol. 3. New York: Marvel, 2005. ISBN: 0785116893.

Essential Iron Man Vol. 1. New York: Marvel, 2005. ISBN: 0785118608. (Reprint)

Essential Killraven Vol. 1: War Of The Worlds. New York: Marvel, 2005. ISBN: 0785117776.

Essential Luke Cage, Power Man Vol. 1. New York: Marvel. 2005. ISBN: 0785116850.

Essential Marvel Team-Up. New York: Marvel, 2005. ISBN: 0785108289 (Reprint)

Essential Marvel Two-in-One. New York: Marvel, 2005. ISBN: 0785117296.

Essential Peter Parker: The Spectacular Spider-Man Vol. 1. New York: Marvel. 2005. ISBN: 0785116826.

Essential Silver Surfer. New York: Marvel, 2005. ISBN: 0785120084 (Reprint)

Essential Spider-Man Vol. 2. New York: Marvel, 2005. ISBN: 0785118632. (Reprint)

Essential Spider-Man Vol. 3. New York: Marvel, 2005. ISBN: 0785106588. (Reprint)

Essential Spider-Man Vol. 4. New York: Marvel, 2005. ISBN: 0785118659. (Reprint)

Essential Spider-Man Vol. 7. New York: Marvel, 2005. ISBN: 0785118799.

Essential Spider-Woman Vol. 1. New York: Marvel, 2005. ISBN: 0785117938.

Essential Tales of the Zombie. New York: Marvel, 2005. ISBN: 0785119167.

Essential Tomb of Dracula Vol. 4. New York: Marvel, ISBN: 0785117091.

Essential Thor Vol. 2. New York: Marvel, 2005. ISBN: 0785115919.

Essential Werewolf by Night Vol. 1. New York: Marvel, 2005. ISBN: 078511839X.

Essential Wolverine Vol. 1. New York: Marvel, 2005. ISBN: 0785118675. (Reprint)

Essential X-Factor. New York: Marvel, 2005. ISBN: 0785118861.

Essential X-Men Vol. 6. New York: Marvel, 2005. ISBN: 078511727X.

The Eternal. New York: Marvel, 2005. ISBN: 0785112340. (Max)

Excalibur: Classic Vol. 1 The Sword is Drawn. New York: Marvel, 2005. ISBN: 0785118888.

Excalibur Vol. 2: Saturday Night Fever. New York: Marvel, 2005. ISBN: 0785114769.

Exiles Vol. 9: Bump in the Night. New York: Marvel, 2005. ISBN: 0785116737.

Exiles Vol. 10: Age of Apocalypse. New York: Marvel, 2005. ISBN: 0785116745.

Exiles Vol. 11: Time Breakers. New York: Marvel, 2005. ISBN: 078511730X.

Fantastic Four: Books of Doom. New York: Marvel, 2005. ISBN: 0785122710.

Fantastic Four Clobberin' Time. New York: Marvel, 2005. ISBN: 0785117385. (Digest)

Fantastic Four: Cosmic Storm. New York: Harper Kids, 2005. ISBN: 0060786175. (Children's book)

Fantastic Four: The Dawn of Doctor Doom. New York: Harper Kids, 2005. ISBN: 0060786213. (Children's book)

Fantastic 4 Sticker Storybook. New York: Harper, 2005. ISBN: 0696225077. (Children's books)

Fantastic Four: Foes New York: Marvel, 2005. ISBN: 0785116621.

Fantastic Four: Invulnerable. New York: Marvel, 2005.

ISBN: 0785117180.

Fantastic Four Jumbo Color and Activity Book. New York: Meredith Books, 2005. ISBN: 0696225123. (Children's book)

Fantastic Four Making of the Movie. London: Titan, 2005. ISBN: 1845760832.

Fantastic Four: Meet the Fantastic Four (Festival Reader). New York: Harper Kids, 2005. ISBN: 0060786116. (Children's)

Fantastic Four: The Movie. New York: Marvel, 2005. ISBN: 0785118098.

Fantastic Four: The Novel. New York: Pocket Star, 2005. ISBN: 1416509801.

Fantastic Four Omnibus Vol. 1. New York: Marvel, 2005. ISBN: 0785118705; 0785117245. (Hardcover)

Fantastic Four Premiere Edition Vol. 1. New York: Marvel, 2005. ISBN: 0785120297. (Hardcover)

Fantastic Four/Spider-Man Classic. New York: Marvel, 2005. ISBN: 0785118039.

Fantastic 4: Deluxe Sound Storybook. New York: Meredith Books, 2005. ISBN: 0696223953. (Children's book)

Fantastic Four: Unstable Molecules. New York: Marvel, 2005. ISBN: 0785111123. (Reprint)

Fantastic Four: Tales Vol. 1. New York: Marvel, 2005. ISBN: 0785117385 (Digest)

Fantastic Four: The Ultimate Guide. London: DK books, 2005. ISBN: 0756611733. (Reference book)

Fantastic Four Visionaries: Jim Lee Vol. 1. New York: Marvel, 2005. ISBN: 0785116354.

Fantastic Four Visionaries: John Byrne, Vol. 4. New York: Marvel, 2005. ISBN: 0785117105.

Fantastic Four Visionaries: John Byrne Vol. 5. New York: Marvel, 2005. ISBN: 0785118446.

Fantastic Four Visionaries: George Perez, Vol. 1. New York: Marvel, 2005. ISBN: 0785117253.

Fantastic Four Vol. 2. New York: Marvel, 2005. ISBN: 078511775X. (Hardcover)

Fantastic Four Vol. 3. New York: Marvel, 2005. ISBN: 0785120114. (Hardcover)

Fantastic Four Vol. 3: Return of Doctor Doom. New York: Marvel, 2005. ISBN: 0785116222. (Digest)

Fantastic Four Vol. 6: Rising Storm. New York: Marvel, 2005. ISBN: 0785115986.

Fantastic Four War Cards. New York: Pocket Star, 2005. ISBN: 1416509658. (Novel)

Fantastic War II. New York: Marvel, 2005. ISBN: 0743493141.

Gambit: Hath No Fury. New York: Marvel, 2005. ISBN: 0785117474.

Gambit: House of Cards. New York: Marvel, 2005. ISBN: 0785115226.

Giant-Size Marvel Vol. 1. New York: Marvel, 2005. ISBN: 0785117849.

GLA: Misassembled Vol. 1. New York: Marvel, 2005. ISBN: 0785116214.

Gospel According to Superheroes. New York: Peter Lang, 2005. ISBN: 0820474223.

Gravity: Big City Super Hero. New York: Marvel, 2005. ISBN: 0785117989. (Digest)

Great Day (Spider Man). New York: Meredith Books, 2005. ISBN: 0696225158. (Children's book)

Guardians Vol. 1. New York: Marvel, 2005. ISBN: 0785115188.

Gun Theory. New York: Marvel, 2005. ISBN: 0785113274. (Max)

Hercules: New Labor of Hercules. New York: Marvel, 2005. ISBN: 0785117520.

Holy Superheroes. Colorado Springs: Piñon Press, 2005. ISBN:0812695739.

House of M: Excalibur—Prelude. New York: Marvel, 2005. ISBN: 0785118128.

House of M: Fantastic Four/Iron Man. New York: Marvel, 2005. ISBN: 078511923X.

House of M: Incredible Hulk. New York: Marvel, 2005. ISBN: 0785118349.

House of M: New X-Men. New York: Marvel, 2005. ISBN: 0785119418.

House of M: Spider Man. New York: Marvel, 2005. ISBN: 0785117539.

House of M: Uncanny X-Men. New York: Marvel, 2005. ISBN: 078511663X.

House of M: World of M. New York: Marvel, 2005. ISBN: 0785119221.

Hulk & Thing: Hard Knocks. New York: Marvel, 2005. ISBN: 0785115765.

Hulk Gray. New York: Marvel, 2005. ISBN: 0785113460. (Paperback)

Hulk: Incredible. New York: Marvel, 2005. ISBN: 0785116168. (Digest)

Hulk: Tempest Fugit. New York: Marvel, 2005. ISBN: 0785115439.

Hulk Visionaries: Peter David Vol. 1. New York: Marvel, 2005. ISBN: 0785115412.

Hulk Visionaries: Peter David Vol. 2. New York: Marvel, 2005. ISBN: 0785118780.

Human Torch Vol. 1: Burn. New York: Marvel, 2005. ISBN: 0785117571. (Digest)

Imagination Trap (Fantastic Four). New York: Meredith Books, 2005. ISBN: 0696225085. (Children's book)

Imagination Ring (Fantastic Four). New York: Meredith Books, 2005. ISBN: 0696225085.

Incal Vols. 1–2. New York: DC Comics, 2005. ISBN: 1401206298 (1); 1401206468 (2); 1930652887. (Reprints original Epic material)

Incredible Hulk. New York: Marvel, 2005. ISBN: 0785112375. (Hardcover)

The Incredible Hulk Big Color & Activity Book with Stickers. New York: Meredith Books, 2005. ISBN: 0696226766.

The Incredible Hulk Jumbo Color & Activity Book. New York: Meredith Books, 2005. ISBN: 0696226545. (Children's book)

Infinity Gauntlet. New York: Marvel, 2005. ISBN: 0785108920. (Reprint)

328   Appendix 1: Marvel and Marvel-Related Publications, 2005

Inhumans Vol. 1: Culture Shock. New York: Marvel, 2005. ISBN: 0785117555. (Digest)

Iron Man Big Color & Activity Book with Stickers. New York: Marvel, 2005. ISBN: 0696226812.

Iron Man Jumbo Color & Activity Book. New York: Marvel, 2005. ISBN: 0696226561.

Jubilee Vol. 1. New York: Marvel, 2005. ISBN: 0785115218. (Never Published)

Last Hero Standing. New York: Marvel, 2005. ISBN: 0785118233.

Livewires: Clockwork Thugs. New York: Marvel, 2005. ISBN: 0785115196. (Digest)

Loki. New York: Marvel, 2005. ISBN: 0785116524. (Hardcover)

Machine Teen: History 101001. New York: Marvel, 2005. ISBN: : 0785117997. (Digest)

Madrox: Multiple Choice. New York: Marvel, 2005. ISBN: 0785115005.

Man Thing: Whatever Knows Fear. New York: Marvel, 2005. ISBN: 0785114882.

Marvel Adventures: Fantastic Four Vol. 1. New York: Marvel, 2005. ISBN: 0785118586 (Digest)

Marvel Adventures: Spider Man Vol. 1: Sinister Six. |New York: Marvel, 2005. ISBN: 0785117393. (Digest)

Marvel Adventures: Spider Man Vol. 2: Power Struggle. New York: Marvel, 2005. ISBN: 0785119035. (Digest)

Marvel Comics Presents Wolverine Vol. 1. New York: Marvel, 2005. ISBN: 0785118268.

Marvel Comics Presents: Wolverine Vol. 2. New York: Marvel, 2005. ISBN: 0785118837.

Marvel Heroes Big Color & Activity Book with Stickers. New York: Marvel, 2005. ISBN: 0696226804. (Children's book)

Marvel Heroes Jumbo Color & Activity Book. New York: Meredith Books, 2005. ISBN: 0696226596. (Children's book)

Marvel Knights 2099. New York: Marvel, 2005. ISBN: 0785116133.

Marvel Knights 4 Vol. 2: The Stuff of Nightmares. New York: Marvel, 2005. ISBN: 0785114726.

Marvel Knights 4 Vol. 3: Divine Time. New York: Marvel, 2004. ISBN: 0785116788.

Marvel Knights: Spider Man. New York: Marvel, 2005. ISBN: 078511842X. (Hardcover)

Marvel Knights Spider-Man Vol. 2: Venomous. New York: Marvel, 2005. ISBN: 0785116753.

Marvel Knights Spider-Man Vol. 3: The Last Stand. New York: Marvel, 2005. ISBN: 0785116761.

Marvel Knights: Spider Man Vol. 4:Wild Blue Yonder. New York: Marvel, 2005. ISBN: 078511761X.

Marvel Masterworks: Amazing Spider Man Vol. 7. New York: Marvel, 2005. ISBN: 0785116370 (ltd); 078511 6362.

Marvel Masterworks: Avengers Vol. 5. New York: Marvel, 2005. ISBN: ISBN: 0785118489.

Marvel Masterworks: Captain America Vol. 2. New York: Marvel, 2005. ISBN: 0785117865 (ltd) 0785 117857.

Marvel Masterworks: Captain Marvel Vol. 1. New York: Marvel, 2005. ISBN: 0785118217; 0785118225 (ltd).

Marvel Masterworks: Daredevil Vol. 3. New York: Marvel, 2005. ISBN: 0785116966; 0785116974 (ltd).

Marvel Masterworks: Dr. Strange Vol. 2 . New York: Marvel, 2005. ISBN: 0785111808; 0785117407 (ltd).

Marvel Masterworks: Fantastic Four Vol. 8. New York: Marvel, 2005. ISBN: 078511694X; 0785116958 (ltd).

Marvel Masterworks: Fantastic Four Vol. 9. New York: Marvel, 2005. ISBN: 0785118462; 0785118470 (ltd).

Marvel Masterworks: Golden Age All Winners Vol. 1. New York: Marvel, 2005. ISBN: 0785118845; 0785 118853 (ltd).

Marvel Masterworks: Golden Age Captain America Vol. 1. New York: Marvel, 2005. ISBN: 0785116192; 0785116206 (ltd).

Marvel Masterworks: Golden Age Human Torch Vol. 1. New York: Marvel, 2005. ISBN: 0785116230; 0785 116249 (ltd).

Marvel Masterworks: Golden Age Sub-Mariner Vol. 1. New York: Marvel, 2005. ISBN: 0785116176.

Marvel Masterworks: Iron Man Vol. 2. New York: Marvel, 2005. ISBN: 0785117717; 0785117725. (Ltd).

Marvel Masterworks: Mighty Thor Vol. 4. New York: Marvel, 2005. ISBN: 0785118802.

Marvel Masterworks: Uncanny X-Men Vol. 5. New York: Marvel, 2005. ISBN: 0785116982; 078511788 1 (ltd). *Marvel Nemesis: The Imperfects*. New York: Marvel, 2005.ISBN: 0785117784. (Digest).

Marvel 1602. New York: Marvel, 2005. ISBN: 0785110739. (Paperback)

Marvel Team-Up Vol. 1: The Golden Child. New York: Marvel, 2005. ISBN: 0785115951.

Marvel Team-Up Vol. 2: Master of the Ring. New York: Marvel, 2005. ISBN: 078511596X.

Marvel Visionaries: Chris Claremont. New York: Marvel, 2005. ISBN: 078511887X. (Hardcover)

Marvel Visionaries: Steve Ditko. New York: Marvel, 2005. ISBN: 0785117830. (Hardcover)

Marvel Visionaries: Stan Lee. New York: Marvel, 2005. ISBN: 0785116931. (Hardcover)

Marvel Visionaries: John Romita Jr. New York: Marvel, 2005. ISBN: 0785119647.

Marvel Visionaries: John Romita Sr. New York: Marvel, 2005. ISBN: 0785117806. (Hardcover)

Marvel Weddings. New York: Marvel, 2005. ISBN: 0785116869.

Marvels. New York: Marvel, 2005. ISBN: 0785100490. (Reprint)

Mary Jane. New York: Marvel, 2005. ISBN: 0785113088. (Paperback novel)

Mary Jane Vol. 2: Homecoming. New York: Marvel, 2005. ISBN: 0785117792. (Digest).

Maximum Fantastic Four. New York: Marvel, 2005. ISBN: 078511792X. (Hardcover)

Mystique Vol. 4: Quiet. New York: Marvel, 2004. ISBN: 0785114750.

Mega Morphs. New York: Marvel, 2005. ISBN: 0785 118683 (Digest)

New Avengers Vol. 1: Breakout HC. New York: Marvel, 2005. ISBN: 0785118144. (trd) 0785114793 (pbk).

New Avengers Vol. 1: Caterpillar File. New York: Marvel, 2005. ISBN: 0785114793.

New Captain America Vol. 1: Out of Time. New York: Marvel, 2005. ISBN: 0785116516.

New Invaders: To End All Wars. New York: Marvel, 2005. ISBN: 0785114491.

New Invaders Vol. 2. New York: Marvel, 2005. ISBN: 0785117415. (Never Published)

New Mutants Vol. 1: Back to School. New York: Marvel, 2005. ISBN: 0785112421.

New Thunderbolts Vol. 1: One Step Forward. New York: Marvel, 2005. ISBN: 078511565X.

New Thunderbolts Vol. 2: Modern Marvels. New York: Marvel, 2005. ISBN: 0785117946.

New X-Men Academy X Vol. 2: Haunted New York: Marvel, 2005. ISBN: 078511615X.

New X-Men: Academy X Vol. 3: X-Posed. New York: Marvel, 2005. ISBN: 0785117911.

New X-Men: Hellions. New York: Marvel, 2005. ISBN: 0785117466.

Nightcrawler: The Devil Inside. New York: Marvel, 2005. ISBN: 0785114289.

NYX Vol. 1: Wannabe. New York: Marvel, 2005. ISBN: 078511243X.

NYX: X-23. New York: Marvel, 2005. ISBN: 078511 825X.

Omega: The Unknown Classic. New York: Marvel, 2005. ISBN: 0785120092.

Ororo: Before the Storm. New York: Marvel, 2005. ISBN: 0785118195.

Physics of Superheroes. New York: Gotham, 2005. ISBN: 1592401465.

Power Pack: Pack Attack. New York: Marvel, 2005. ISBN: 0785117369. (Digest)

Powerless. New York: Marvel, 2005. ISBN: 0785115110.

Powers Vol. 1. New York: Marvel, 2005. ISBN: 0785118055. (Hardcover)

Powers Vol. 8: Legends. New York: Marvel, 2005. ISBN: 0785117423 (Icon series)

Pulse Vol. 2: Secret War. New York: Marvel, 2005. ISBN: 0785114785.

Punisher Max Vol. 1. New York: Marvel, 2005. ISBN: 0785118403 (Hardcover)

Punisher Max Vol. 3: Mother Russia. New York: Marvel, 2005. ISBN: 0785116036. (Max series)

Punisher Max Vol. 4: Up Is Down and Black Is White. New York: Marvel, 2005. ISBN: 0785117318.

Punisher: River of Blood. New York: Marvel. 2005. ISBN: 0785115420. (Reprint)

Quest (Marvel Heroes). New York: Marvel, 2005. ISBN: 0785112987.

Rogue: Forget-Me-Not. New York: Marvel, 2005. ISBN: 0785117342.

Rogue: Going Rogue. New York: Marvel, 2005. ISBN: 0785113363.

Runaways Vol. 1. New York: Marvel, 2005. ISBN: 0785118764. (Hardcover)

Runaways Vol. 3: The Good Die Young. New York: Marvel, 2005. ISBN: 0785116842. (Digest)

Runaways Vol. 4: True Believers. New York: Marvel, 2005. ISBN: 0785117059. (Digest)

Sabretooth: Open Season. New York: Marvel, 2005. ISBN: 0785115072.

Science of Supervillains. New York: Wiley, 2005. ISBN: 0471482056. (Hardcover)

Scorpion: Poison Tomorrow. New York: Marvel, 2005. ISBN: 0785117121. (Digest)

The Sea Monster (Fantastic Four). New York: Meredith Books, 2005. ISBN: 0696225093. (Children's book)

Secret War. New York: Marvel, 2005. ISBN: 07851183 73.

Secret Wars. New York: Marvel, 2005. ISBN: 0785118 73X. (Reprint)

The Sentry. New York: Marvel, 2005. ISBN: 0078512 1242. (Reprint)

Shanna—The She-Devil. New York: Marvel, 2005. ISBN: 0785119728. (Hardcover)

She-Hulk Vol. 2: Superhuman Law. New York: Marvel. 2005. ISBN: 0785115706.

Six from Sirius. Dynamic Forces, 2005. ISBN: 1933305045 (trd); 1933305037. (pbk) (Epic reprint)

Spectacular Spider-Man Vol. 5: Sins Remembered. New York: Marvel, 2005. ISBN: 0785116281.

Spectacular Spiderman Vol. 6: The Final Curtain. New York: Marvel, 2005. ISBN: 0785119507.

Spellbinders: Signs and Wonders. New York: Marvel, 2005. ISBN: 0785117563. (Digest)

Spider-Girl Vol. 3: Avenging Allies. New York: Marvel. 2005. ISBN: 0785116583. (Digest)

Spider-Girl Vol. 4: Turning Point. New York: Marvel, 2005. ISBN: 0785118713.

Spider Man. New York: Marvel, 2005. ISBN: 141559 466X. (Hardcover)

Spider-Man Big Color & Activity Book with Stickers. New York: Meredith Books, 2005. ISBN: 069622 6790. (Children's book)

Spider Man: Black Cat: Evil that Men Do. New York: Marvel, 2005. ISBN: 078511095X.

Spider Man Breakout. New York: Marvel, 2005. ISBN: 0785118071.

Spider-Man/Doctor Octopus: Year One. New York: Marvel, 2005. ISBN: 0785115323.

Spiderman: Down These Mean Streets. New York: Pocket Star, 2005. ISBN: 1416509682. (Novel)

Spider-Man Giant Color & Activity Book. New York: Meredith Books, 2005. ISBN: 0696225174. (Children's book)

Spider Man: A Great Day. New York: Meredith Books, 2005. ISBN: 0696225158. (Children's book)

Spider Man/Human Torch: I'm with Stupid. New York: Marvel, 2005. ISBN: 0785117237. (Digest)

Spider-Man: India. New York: Marvel, 2005. ISBN: 0785116400.

Spider Man: Jumbo Color and Activity Book. New York: Marvel, 2005. ISBN: 0696225131.

Spider-Man: Spidey Strikes Back Vol. 1. New York: Marvel, 2005. ISBN: 078511632X. (Digest)

Spider Man Team-Up Vol. 1: Little Help from My Friends. New York: Marvel, 2005. ISBN: 0785116117. (Digest)

Spider-Man Team-Up Vol. 2: Amazing Friends. New York: Marvel, 2005. ISBN: 078511758X. (Digest)

Spider Man vs. The Black Cat Vol. 1. New York: Marvel, 2005. ISBN: 0785115595.

Squadron Supreme. New York: Marvel, 2005. ISBN: 078510576X. (Reprint)

Stan Lee: Comic Book Writer and Publisher. New York: Ferguson Publishing, 2005. ISBN: 0816058318.

Stoker's Dracula. New York: Marvel, 2005.

Stormbreaker: Saga of Beta Ray Bill. New York: Marvel, 2005. ISBN: 0785117202.

Strange: Beginnings and Endings. New York: Marvel, 2005. ISBN: 0785115773.

Super Spider (Spider Man). New York: Meredith Books, 2005. ISBN: 0696225166.

Superheroes and Philosophy: Truth, Justice, and the Socratic Way. Chicago: Open Court Publishing, 2005. ISBN: 0812695739.

Supreme Power: High Command: Vol. 1. New York: Marvel, 2005. ISBN: 078511369X. (Hardcover)

Tales to Astonish: Jack Kirby, Stan Lee and the American Comic Book Revolution. New York: Bloomsbury, 2005. ISBN: 158234566X. (Paperback)

Thing: Freakshow. New York: Marvel, 2005. ISBN: 0785119116.

Thor, Son of Asgard Vol. 2: Worthy. New York: Marvel, 2005. ISBN: 0785115722. (Digest)

Toxin: The Devil You Know. New York: Marvel, 2005. ISBN: 0785118047.

Transformers: Aspects of Evil. London: Titan, 2005. ISBN: 1845760557. (Reprints material originally published by Marvel)

Transformers: Dark Star. London Titan, 2005. ISBN: 1840239603. (Reprints material originally published by Marvel)

Transformers: Fallen Star. London: Titan, 2005. ISBN: 1845760603. (Reprints originally published by Marvel)

Transformers: The Last Stand. London: Titan, 2005. ISBN: 1845760093 (trd); 1845760085 (pbk) (Reprints material originally published by Marvel)

Transformers: Way of the Warrior. London: Titan, 2005. ISBN: 184576059X. (Reprints material originally published by Marvel)

Ultimate Adventures: One Tin Soldier. New York: Marvel, 2005. ISBN: 0785110437.

Ultimate Elektra Vol. 1: Devil's Due. New York: Marvel, 2005. ISBN: 0785115048.

Ultimate Fantastic Four Vol. 1. New York: Marvel, 2005. ISBN: 0785114580. (Hardcover)

Ultimate Fantastic Four Vol. 3: N-Zone. New York: Marvel, 2005. ISBN: 0785114955.

Ultimate Fantastic Four Vol. 4: Inhuman. New York: Marvel, 2005. ISBN: 0785116672.

Ultimate Galactus Vol. 1: Nightmare. New York: Marvel, 2005. ISBN: 0785114971.

Ultimate Galactus Vol. 2: Secret. New York: Marvel, 2005. ISBN: 0785116605.

Ultimate Spider-Man Vol. 2: Learning Curve. New York: Marvel, 2005. ISBN: 0785108203. (Reprint)

Ultimate Spider-Man Vol. 6. New York: Marvel, 2005. ISBN: 0785118411. (Hardcover)

Ultimate Spider-Man Vol. 9: Ultimate Six. New York: Marvel, 2005. ISBN: 0785113126 (Reprint)

Ultimate Spider-Man Vol. 12: Superstars. New York: Marvel, 2005. ISBN: 078511629X.

Ultimate Spider-Man Vol. 13: Hobgoblin. New York: Marvel, 2005. ISBN: 0785116478.

Ultimate Spider-Man Vol. 14: Warriors. New York: Marvel, 2005. ISBN: 078511680X.

Ultimate X-Men Vol. 3: World Tour. New York: Marvel, 2005. ISBN: 0785109617. (Reprint)

Ultimate X-Men Vol. 4. New York: Marvel, 2004. ISBN: 0785112510. (Hardcover)

Ultimate X-Men Vol. 10: Cry Wolf. New York: Marvel, 2005. ISBN: 078511405X.

Ultimate X-Men Vol. 11: The Most Dangerous Game. New York: Marvel, 2005. ISBN: 0785116591.

Ultimate X-Men Vol. 12: Hard Lessons. New York: Marvel, 2005. ISBN: 0785118012.

The Ultimates 2 Vol. 1: Gods And Monsters. New York: Marvel, 2005. ISBN: 0785110933.

Uncanny X-Men: The New Age Vol. 2: The Cruelest Cut. New York: Marvel, 2005. ISBN: 0785116451.

Uncanny X-Men: The New Age Vol. 3: On Ice. New York: Marvel, 2005. ISBN: 0785116494.

Vision: Yesterday and Tomorrow. New York: Marvel, 2005. ISBN: 0785119124.

What If: Classic Vol. 2. New York: Marvel, 2005. ISBN: 0785118438.

What If...?: Why Not Vol. 1. New York: Marvel, 2005. ISBN: 0785115935.

Wolverine/Black Cat Vol. 1. New York: Marvel, 2005. ISBN: 0785118500.

Wolverine Classic Vol. 1. New York: Marvel, 2005. ISBN: 0785117970.

Wolverine Classic Vol. 2. New York: Marvel, 2005. 0785118772.

Wolverine: Enemy of the State Vol. 1. Marvel: New York. ISBN: 0785118152 (Hardcover); 0785114920 (Paperback).

Wolverine: Enemy of the State Vol. 2. New York: Marvel, 2005. ISBN: 0785119264. (Hardcover)

Wolverine/Nick Fury: Scorpio. New York: Marvel, 2005. ISBN: 0785114912. (Reprint)

Wolverine Soultaker. New York: Marvel, 2005. ISBN: 0785115056.

Wolverine Vol. 5. New York: Marvel, 2005. ISBN: 0785116273.

Wolverine Weapon X. New York: Pocket Star, 2005. ISBN: 141652164X. (Paperback)

X-Factor Visionaries: Peter David Vol. 1. New York: Marvel, 2005. ISBN: 0785118721.

X-Force & Cable Vol. 1: The Legend Returns. New York: Marvel, 2005. ISBN: 0785114297.

X-Force: Shatterstar. New York: Marvel, 2005. ISBN: 0785116338.

X-Men Big Color & Activity Book with Stickers. New York: Meredith Books, 2005. ISBN: 0696226782. (Children's book)

X-Men: Bizarre Love Triangle. New York: Marvel, 2005. ISBN: 0785116656.

X-Men: The Complete Age of Apocalypse Epic, Book 1. New York: Marvel, 2005. ISBN: 0785117148.

X-Men: The Complete Age of Apocalypse Epic Book 2. New York: Marvel, 2005. ISBN: 0785118748.

X-Men: Dark Mirror. New York: Pocket Star, 2005. ISBN: 141651063X. (Novel)

X-Men: Day of Atom. New York: Marvel, 2005. ISBN: 078511534X.

X-Men: The End, Book One: Dreamers And Demons. New York: Marvel, 2005. ISBN: 0785116907.

X-Men The End, Book Two: Heroes and Martyrs. New York: Marvel, 2005. ISBN: 0785116915.

X-Men: Eve of Destruction. New York: Marvel, 2005. ISBN: 0785115528.

X-Men/Fantastic Four. New York: Marvel, 2005. ISBN: 078511520X. (Hardcover)

X-Men: Golgotha. New York: Marvel, 2005. ISBN: 0785116508.

X-Men Jumbo Color & Activity Book. New York: Meredith Books, 2005. ISBN: 0696226553. (Children's book)

X-Men: The New Age of Apocalypse. New York: Marvel, 2005. ISBN: 0785115838.

X-Men: Phoenix—Endsong. New York: Marvel, 2005. ISBN: 0785116419. (trd) 0785119248. (Paperback)

X-Men: Reload Vol. 2: Heroes and Villains. New York: Marvel, 2005. ISBN: 078511646X.

X-Men Vignettes Vol. 2. New York: Marvel, 2005. ISBN: 0785117288.

X-23 Vol. 1. New York: Marvel, 2005. ISBN: 0785115021.

X-23: Innocence Lost. New York: Marvel, 2005. ISBN: 078511825X. (Hardcover)

Young Avengers: Sidekicks Vol. 1. New York: Marvel, 2005. (Hardcover)

Appendix 2:
Selected Marvel-Related
Game Books

This is a selected list of Marvel-related game books. There just was not enough time to track down and annotate all of these items, but I hope that this list will give the reader an idea what has been published

Bennie, Scott, et al. *Gamer's Handbook of the Marvel Universe*. Lake Geneva, WI: 1989. ISBN: 0880387 661.

Bogen, Tim, et al. *Hulk: Official Strategy Guide*. Indianapolis, IN: Brady Games, 2003. ISBN: 07440 02796.

Cook, Dave, et al. *Lone Wolves: Marvel Super Heroes*. Lake Geneva, WI: TSR, 1984. ISBN: 0880381310.

Cook, David, et al. *Flames of Doom: Marvel Superheroes*. Lake Geneva, WI: TSR, 1987. ISBN: 0880 384824.

Costello, Matthew, et al. *Daredevil: Guilt by Association*. Lake Geneva, WA: TSR, 1988. ISBN: 0880385332.

Dakan, Richard, et al. *Fantastic Four Roster Book*. Renton, WA: TSR, 1999. ISBN: 0786913207.

Dakan, Richard, Mike Selinker, Teeuwynn Woodruff, et al. *Fantastic Four: Fantastic Voyages*. Renton, WA: TSR, 1999. ISBN: 0786913304.

David, Peter, John Statema, Mark Nelson, et al. *The Amazing Spider Man: As the World Burns*. Lake Geneva, WI: TSR/Puffin, 1989. ISBN: 01403293 07; 0880384387.

Davis, Scott, et al. *Webs: The Spider Man Dossier*. Lake Geneva: WI: TSR, 1993. ISBN: 1560764058.

Denning, Tory, et al. *Cosmos Cubed: Marvel Super Heroes*. Lake Geneva, WI: TSR, 1988. ISBN: 08803 85472.

Denning, Troy, et al. *Ringnarok and Roll: Marvel Super Heroes*. Lake Geneva, WI: TSR, 1988. ISBN: 0880385685.

Eastland, Kim, et al. *Fault Line: Marvel Super Heroes*. Lake Geneva, WI: TSR, 1985. ISBN: 08803822 79.

_____. *Last Resort: Marvel Super Heroes*. Lake Geneva, WI: TSR, 1985. ISBN: 0880382252.

_____. *Pit of the Viper: Marvel Super Heroes*. Lake Geneva, WI: TSR, 1985. ISBN: 0394545761.

_____. *Realms of Magic: Marvel Super Heroes*. Lake Geneva, WI: TSR, 1986. ISBN: 039455423X.

_____. *X-Men: Children of the Atom*. Lake Geneva, WI: TSR, 1986. ISBN: 0880382929.

Epperson, Jerry, James M. Ward, Bart Sears, et al. *Night of the Wolverine*. Lake Geneva, WI: TSR, 1989. ISBN: 0880383011; 0140329277.

Epperson, Jerry, et al. *Weapon's Locker: Marvel Super Heroes*. Lake Geneva, WI, 1985. ISBN: 08803822 95.

Farkas, Bart, et al. *Blade Official Strategy Guide*. Indianapolis, IN: Brady Games, 2000. ISBN: 074400 0513.

_____. *Blade II Official Strategy Guide*. Indianapolis, IN: Brady Games, 2002. ISBN: 0744001919.

Grau, Matt, Harold Johnson, Mike Selinker, et al. *A Guide to Marvel Earth*. Renton, WA: TSR, 1998. ISBN: 0786912308.

Grubb, Jeff, et al. *Amazing Spider Man: City in Darkness*. Lake Geneva, WI: TSR, 1986. ISBN: 088038 2996.

_____. *Breeder Bombs: Marvel Super Heroes*. Lake Geneva, WI: TSR, 1984. ISBN: 0880381256.

_____. *Cat's Paw: Marvel Super Heroes*. Lake Geneva, WI: TSR, 1985. ISBN: 0880381329.

_____. *Concrete Jungle: Official Character Roster*. Lake Geneva, WI: TSR, 1985. ISBN: 0880382260.

_____. *Judges Screen: Marvel Super Heroes*. Lake Geneva, WI, 1984. ISBN: 0880381264.

_____. *Murderworld: Marvel Super Heroes*. Lake Geneva, WI: TSR, 1984. ISBN: 0880381299.

_____. *Project Wideawake: Marvel Super Heroes*. Lake Geneva, WI: TSR, 1985. ISBN: 0880381930.

_____. *Secret Wars: Marvel Super Heroes*. Lake Geneva, WI: TSR, 1984. ISBN: 0880381841.

_____. *Uncanny X-Men: Marvel Super Heroes*. Lake Geneva, WI: TSR, 1990. ISBN: 0880388889.

Guaraldo, Richard, et al. *Computer Fun, Book One: Marvel Super Heroes*. New York: D.I. Fine, 1984. ISBN: 0917657055.

_____. *Computer Fun, Book Two: Marvel Super Heroes*. New York: D.I. Fine, 1984. ISBN: 0917657063.

Henson, Dale, et al. *X-Terminate: X-Men*. Lake Geneva, WI: TSR, 1991. ISBN: 1560760664.

Herring, Anthony, et al. *After Midnight: Marvel Super Heroes*. Lake Geneva, WI: TSR, 1990. ISBN: 0880388323.

_____. *Night Moves: Marvel Super Heroes*. Lake Geneva, WI: TSR, 1990. ISBN: 0880388749.

_____. *Stygian Knight: Marvel Super Heroes*. Lake Geneva, WI: TSR, 1991. ISBN: 1560761032.

_____. *Warlord of Baluur*. Lake Geneva, WI: TSR, 1991. ISBN: 1560761008.

_____. *X-Force: Mutant Update*. Lake Geneva, WI: TSR, 1992. ISBN: 1560764031.

Hill, Simon, et al. *X-Men: Children of the Atom*. Rocklin, CA: Prima, 1998. ISBN: 0761507841.

_____. *X-Men vs. Street Fighter: Prima's Official Strategy Guide*. Rocklin, CA: Prima, 1998. ISBN: 0761517766.

Kenson, Steven, et al. *Avengers: Masters of Evil*. Renton, WA: TSR, 1998. ISBN: 0786912324.

Kramer, Greg, et al. *Spider Man 2: Enter Electro Official Strategy Guide*. Indianapolis, IN: Brady Games, 2001. ISBN: 0744000904.

Kunkel, Bill, et al. *Maximum Carnage: Official Game Secrets*. Rocklin, CA: Prima, 1994. ISBN: 1559586788.

Lummis, Michael, Brady Games, et al. *X2 Wolverine's Revenge Official Strategy Guide*. Indianapolis, IN: Brady Games, 2003. ISBN: 0744002508.

Marcus, Philip, et al. *Spider Man: Official Strategy Guide*. Indianapolis, IN: Brady Games, 2002. ISBN: 0744001609; 1566869994.

_____. *X-Men: Reign of Apocalypse/Spider-Man: Mysterio's Menace Official Strategy Guide*. Indianopolis: Brady Games, 2002. ISBN: 0744001072.

Mineau Diane, et al. *Marvel Comics Super Heroes Giant Game Board Book*. Montreal: Tormont, 1994. ISBN: 2894295634.

_____. *Marvel Comics Super Heroes Game Book: 6 Electronic Games*. Montreal: Tormont, 1994. ISBN: 2764115555.

Moore, Roger, et al. *Games of What If*. Lake Geneva, WI: TSR, 1987. ISBN: 0880382287.

Mortika, Chris, et al. *Gamer's Handbook of the Marvel Universe: Module 1*. Lake Geneva, WI: TSR, 1988. ISBN: 0880385405.

Nesmith, Bruce, et al. *Avengers Assembled*. Lake Geneva, WI: TSR, 1984. ISBN: 0880381280.

_____. *Thunder over Jotunheim: Marvel Super Heroes*. Lake Geneva, WI: TSR, 1985. ISBN: 0880381981.

_____. *Time Traps: Marvel Super Heroes*. Lake Geneva, WI: TSR, 1984. ISBN: 0880381272.

_____. *X-Men: Mutating Mutants*. Lake Geneva, WI: TSR, 1990. ISBN: 0880388412.

Novak, Kate, et al. *Captain America: Rocket's Red Glare*. Lake Geneva, WI: TSR, 1986. ISBN: 0880383003.

_____. *Captain America: Rocket's Red Glare*. New York: Puffin, 1987. ISBN: 0140324615.

_____. *Uncanny X-Men: An X-Cellent Death*. Lake Geneva, WI: TSR, 1987. ISBN: 0880384379.

Olmedahl, Bill, Michele Carter, Mike Selinker, et al. *Marvel Super Heroes Adventure Game*. Renton, WA: TSR, 1998. ISBN: 0786912278.

Pratte, Eric Lionel. *Marvel vs. Capcom 2: New Age of Heroes: Prima Official Strategy Guide*. Roseville, CA: Prima Games, 2000. ISBN: 0761531300.

Puhl, Adam, et al. *X-Men: Mutant Academy 2 Official Strategy Guide*. Indianapolis, IN: Brady Games, 2001. ISBN: 0744001064.

Quick, Jeff, et al. *The Avengers Roster Book*. Renton, WA: TSR, 1998. ISBN: 0786912316.

Richards, Reed, J. Jonah Jameson, Wizards of the Coast, et al. *The Reed Richards Guide to Everything*. Renton, WA: TSR, 1999. ISBN: 0786913401.

Sollers, Edward, David Cook, et al. *Avengers Coast-to-Coast*. Lake Geneva, WI: TSR, 1986. ISBN: 0880382937.

Spector, Caroline, Warren Spector, et al. *Reap the Whirlwind: Marvel Super Heroes*. Lake Geneva, WI: TSR, 1987. ISBN: 0880384816.

Spector, Warren, et al. *The Thing, One Thing after Another*. Lake Geneva, WI: TSR, 1987. ISBN: 0880384360.

Swan, Rick, et al. *Spore of Arthros: Fantastic Four*. Lake Geneva, WI, 1991. ISBN: 1560761016.

TSR eds. *Gamer's Handbook of the Marvel Universe*. Lake Geneva, WI: TSR, 1988. ISBN: 0880385766; 0880386010; 1560764074; 0880388668; 0880386177; 156076600X.

_____. *Night Life: Marvel Universe*. Lake Geneva, WI: TSR, 1990. ISBN: 0880388935.

_____. *Marvel Super Dice Clash*. Renton, WA: TSR, 1998. ISBN: 0786907010.

_____. *Marvel Super Heroes: Advanced*. Lake Geneva, WI: TSR, 1986. ISBN: 0394554221.

_____. *Marvel Super Heroes: Deluxe City Campaign*

Set. Lake Geneva, WI: TSR, 1989. ISBN: 0880387 505.

Varney, Allen, et al. *Doctor Strange: Through Six Dimensions.* Lake Geneva, WI: TSR, 1987. ISBN: 0880384352.

Varney, Allen, Bart Sears, Mike Nelson, et al. *Dr. Strange: Through Six Dimensions: Marvel Super Heroes.* Lake Geneva, WI: TSR/Puffin, 1987. ISBN: 0140326030.

Walsh, Doug. *Spider-Man 2: The Gamer's Official Strategy Guide.* Indianapolis, IN: Bradygames, 2004. ISBN: 0744003938.

Ward, James M., et al. *Fantastic Four/Dr. Doom: Doomsday Device.* Lake Geneva, WI: TSR. 1986. ISBN: 0880383054.

_____. *The King Takes a Dare: Daredevil vs. Kingpin.* Lake Geneva, WI: TSR, 1987.

_____. *X-Men Battle for New York City.* Renton, WA: TSR, 1998. ISBN: 0786906731.

Warner, Rita, Brenda Jackson, Ronald L. McDonald, *X-Men: Crazy Game.* New York: Price-Stern Sloan, 1997. ISBN: 0843179864.

Watson, Christine. *Guide to X-Men 2: Clone Wars.* Indianapolis, IN: 1995. ISBN: 1566862949.

Williams, Eric, Adam Puhl, John Edwards, et al. *X-Men: Next Dimension Official Strategy Guide.* Indi-

anapolis, IN: Brady Games, 2002. ISBN: 07440 01765.

Winter, Steve, et al. *Nightmares of Future Past: Marvel Super Heroes.* Lake Geneva, WI, 1987. ISBN: 0880384026.

Winninger, Ray, et al. *All This and World War II: Marvel Super Heroes.* Lake Geneva, WI: 1989. ISBN: 0880387181.

_____. *The Left Hand of Eternity Resource Book: Marvel Super Heroes.* Lake Geneva, WI: TSR, 1988. ISBN: 0880385839.

_____. *The Weird Weird West: Marvel Super Heroes.* Lake Geneva, WI: TSR, 1989. ISBN: 0880387416.

_____. *Revenge of Kang: Marvel Super Heroes.* Lake Geneva, WI: TSR, 1990. ISBN: 0880387777.

Wizards of the Coast, et al. *Fantastic Four Roster Book.* Renton, WA: TSR, 1999. ISBN: 0786911320.

_____. *Gamer's Handbook of Marvel Universe.* Lake Geneva, WI: TSR, 1988–1993. ISBN: 08803854 05; 0880385766; 0880386010; 0880387661; 08803 88668; 1560761024; 1560764074; 0880386177; 0880386010; 156076600X.

_____. *X-Men Roster Book.* Renton, WA: TSR, 1998. ISBN: 0786912286.

_____. *X-Men: Who Goes There.* Renton, WA: TSR, 1998. ISBN: 0786912294.

Appendix 3:
Unpublished Books

This list contains information about Marvel and Marvel-related books that are listed in places and have ISBNs, but I could find no evidence that they were actually published. Please note that some of these may have been published, in some form, by the time this book is published, or sometime in the future. Dates given here represent those that appear in places where the books are listed.

Aladdin. New York: Marvel, 1995. ISBN: 0785101055.

Amazing Spider-Man Hardcover. New York: Marvel Ltd. ISBN: 5552544684.

Annotated Death of Gwen Stacy. New York: Marvel, 1997. ISBN: 0785102604.

Ant-Man. New York: Marvel, 2004. ISBN: 0785113 290. (Max)

Avengers Hardcover. New York: Marvel Ltd. ISBN: 5550314878; 555254143X.

Barbie. New York: Marvel, 1992. ISBN: 0871358786.

Beauty and the Beast. New York: Marvel, 1995. ISBN: 0785101020.

Best of Barbie. New York: Marvel, 1997. ISBN: 07851 01896.

Best of Marvel 1997. New York: Marvel, 1997. ISBN: 0785105824.

Blade Hardcover. New York: Marvel Ltd. ISBN: 5552 541324.

Cable Hardcover. New York: Marvel Ltd. ISBN: 5552 547241.

The Call: Call of Duty. New York: Marvel, 2003. ISBN: 0785111522.

Call of Duty: Brotherhood Hardcover. New York: Marvel Ltd. ISBN: 5552444930.

Call of Duty: Precinct Hardcover. New York: Marvel Ltd. ISBN: 5552444922.

Call of Duty: Wagon Hardcover. New York: Marvel Ltd. ISBN: 5552541561.

Captain America. New York: Marvel, 1991. ISBN: 0871356538.

Captain America Hardcover. New York: Marvel Ltd. ISBN: 5552544765.

Captain America: Truth. New York: Marvel 2004. 0785110682.

Captain America: What Price Glory. New York: Marvel, 2003. ISBN: 0785112278.

Captain Marvel Hardcover. New York: Marvel Ltd. ISBN: 5552543599.

Daredevil Hardcover. New York: Marvel Ltd. ISBN: 5552547152.

Deadpool Hardcover. New York: Marvel Ltd. ISBN: 5552541421.

Eden's Trail. New York: Marvel 2002. ISBN: 0785111 077.

Elektra Hardcover. New York: Marvel Ltd. ISBN: 5552541367.

Exiles Hardcover. New York. Marvel Ltd. ISBN: 5552541383.

Fantastic Four Hardcover. New York: Marvel Ltd. ISBN: 555254465X.

Fantastic Four 1234 Hardcover. New York: Marvel Ltd. ISBN: 5552541391.

Flintstone Kids and the Wrestling Day Disaster. New York: Marvel, 1987. ISBN: 0871352494.

Flintstone Kids in the Bedrock Rock and Roll Talent Show. New York: Marvel, 1987. ISBN: 0871352516.

Fury Hardcover. New York: Marvel Ltd. ISBN: 5552 541359.

Gambit Stolen Soles. New York: Marvel, 2002. ISBN: 0743452453.

Gambit Upstarts Uprising. New York: Bullseye Publishing, 1995. 067987660X.

Howard the Duck Hardcover. New York: Marvel Ltd. ISBN: 5552541308.

Hulk: NightAmerica. New York: Marvel, 2004. ISBN: 0785110275.

Iceman Hardcover. New York: Marvel Ltd. ISBN: 5552543750.

Incredible Hulk Hardcover. New York: Marvel Ltd. ISBN: 5552544714.

Inhumans: Lunar. New York: Marvel, 2004. ISBN: 0785113037.

Iron Man Hardcover. New York: Marvel Ltd. ISBN: 5552541456.

Killraven. New York: Marvel, 2003. ISBN: 0785110836.

Little Mermaid. New York: Marvel, 1995. ISBN: 078 5101012.

Marvel, 2003. ISBN: 078511050X. (Box set for retailers?)

Marvel Assortment I: Best of Spider-Man/Ultimate Spider-Man/Wolverine-Origin/Daredevil-Yellow.

Marvel Knights Universe Hardcover. New York: Marvel Ltd. ISBN: 5552543548.

Marvel Must Haves Hardcover. New York: Marvel Ltd. ISBN: 5550314983; 5552544676.

Marvel Universe: Banner Hardcover. New York: Marvel Ltd. ISBN: 5552543653.

Marvel Universe: Role-Playing Game: Guide to Wolverine. New York: Marvel, 2004. ISBN: 0785113533.

Marvel Universe Role-playing Game: Guide to Spider-Man's NYC. New York: Marvel 2004.

Marville Hardcover. New York: Marvel Ltd. ISBN: 5552541251.

Meet the Flinstone Kids. New York: Marvel, 1987. ISBN: 0871352508.

Megalomaniacal Spider-Man Hardcover. New York: Marvel Ltd. ISBN: 5552541294.

Mystique Hardcover. New York: Marvel Ltd. ISBN: 5550315041.

Nadesico, tome 1. New York: Marvel, 2001. ISBN: 2845380372. (May have been published outside United States)

Namor Hardcover. New York: Marvel Ltd. ISBN: 5550315017.

Namor: Sea and Sand (Marvel Heroes). New York: Marvel, 2004. ISBN: 0785112413.

New Mutants (X-Men). New York: Marvel, 2004. ISBN: 0785112421. (Hardcover)

New X-Men Hardcover. New York: Marvel Ltd. ISBN: 5552545494.

Nightcrawler Hardcover. New York: Marvel Ltd. ISBN: 5552544986.

Peter Parker: Spider-Man Hardcover. New York: Marvel Ltd. ISBN: 5552390555; 5552547314.

Punisher Hardcover. New York: Marvel Ltd. ISBN: 5552545133.

Rap Dictionary. New York: Marvel, 1991. ISBN: 0871357542.

Robot City. New York: Marvel, 1996. ISBN: 0871358840.

The Silver Surfer. New York: Marvel, 2001. ISBN: 0785101179.

Soldier X. New York: Marvel, 2003. ISBN: 0785110135.

Spider-Girl Hardcover. New York: Marvel, 2003. ISBN: 5552543580.

Spider-Man and Power Pack. New York: Marvel, 1984. ISBN: 9998670101.

Spider-Man: Get Kraven. New York: Marvel, 2004. ISBN: 0785110127.

Spider-Man's Tangled Web Hardcover. New York: Marvel Ltd. ISBN: 5552545044.

Thor Special Hardcover. New York: Marvel Ltd. ISBN: 5552541235.

Ultimate Adventures Hardcover. New York: Marvel Ltd. ISBN: 5552541243.

Ultimate Adventures: One Tin Soldier (Marvel Heroes). New York: Marvel, 2004. ISBN: 0785110437.

Ultimate Spider-Man Issue 1 Special Hardcover. New York: Marvel Ltd. ISBN: 5552541286; 5552541413.

Ultimate X-Men Hardcover. New York: Marvel Ltd. ISBN: 5552541405.

Ultimates Hardcover. New York: Marvel Ltd. ISBN: 5552541332.

Uncanny X-Men Hardcover. New York: Marvel Ltd. ISBN: 5552544668.

War Machine Hardcover. New York: Marvel Ltd. ISBN: 5552541340.

Weapon X: Defection. New York: Marvel, 2004. ISBN: 0785114076.

Weapon X Hardcover. New York: Marvel Ltd. ISBN: 555254126X.

Wolverine Hardcover. New York: Marvel Ltd. ISBN: 5552544986.

Wolverine Snikt Hardcover. New York: Marvel Ltd. ISBN: 5550314991.

X-Factor. New York: Marvel, 2003. ISBN: 07851101 6X.

X-Force Hardcover. New York: Marvel Ltd. ISBN: 5552545508.

X-Men: Beware the Blob. Texas: Premier, 1997. ISBN: 187933240X.

X-Men Evolution Hardcover. New York: Marvel Ltd. ISBN: 5552545087.

X-Men Icons: Cyclops. New York: Marvel, 2004. ISBN: 0785108718.

X-Men Icons: Iceman. New York: Marvel, 2002. ISBN: 0785108890.

X-Men Icons: Rogue. New York: Marvel, 2002. ISBN: 0785108769.

X-Men Mangaverse Special Hardcover. New York: Marvel Ltd. ISBN: 5552541316.

X-Men: Storm. New York: Bullseye Books, 1994. ISBN: 9994696378.

X-Statix Hardcover. New York: Marvel Ltd. ISBN: 5552541278.

X-Treme X-Men Hardcover. New York: Marvel Ltd. ISBN: 5552545184.

Title Index

Artist and Author Index

Subject Index